German Big Business
and the Rise of Hitler

**INSTRUMENT IN THE HAND OF GOD?
PUPPET IN THE HAND OF THYSSEN!**

"The Führer regards himself as God's instrument in the completion of his mission." (Kube, Prussian State Councillor, Governor of Brandenburg, National Socialist leader in the Prussian State Parliament)

The great industrialist Fritz Thyssen, owner of a fortune of 125 million marks, leader of one of the largest German trusts, has been named economic dictator of Germany's most important industrial region, Rhineland-Westphalia.

Photomontage by John Heartfield from the Communist *Arbeiter–Illustrierte Zeitung.* Courtesy International Institute for Social History, Amsterdam.

GERMAN BIG BUSINESS
AND
THE RISE OF HITLER

HENRY ASHBY TURNER, JR.

New York   Oxford
OXFORD UNIVERSITY PRESS

Oxford University Press

Oxford   New York   Toronto
Delhi   Bombay   Calcutta   Madras   Karachi
Petaling Jaya   Singapore   Hong Kong   Tokyo
Nairobi   Dar es Salaam   Cape Town
Melbourne   Auckland

and associated companies in:
Beirut   Berlin   Ibadan   Nicosia

Library of Congress Cataloging in Publication Data
Turner, Henry Ashby.
German big business and the rise of Hitler.
Bibliography: p.   Includes index.
1. Industry and state—Germany—History.
2. Big business—Germany—History.
3. Germany—Politics and government—1918–1933.
4. Nationalsozialistische Deutsche Arbeiter—Partei—History.
5. National socialism—History. I. Title.
HD3616.G35T87   1985   943.085   84-5645
ISBN 0-19-503492-9
ISBN 0-19-504235-2 (pbk.)

2 4 6 8 10 9 7 5 3 1
Printed in the United States of America

To
William Alexander Jenks
and
James Graham Leyburn

Exemplars

Acknowledgments

So many institutions and individuals have contributed to this undertaking as to preclude an expression of gratitude to each in this limited space. But despite the risk of an oversight, I do want to acknowledge some of those who have rendered especially valuable help. The research that has culminated in the volume was made possible by grants from the following institutions: The German Fulbright Commission, the German Marshall Fund of the United States, the Guggenheim Foundation, the Historische Kommission zu Berlin, the Lehrman Institute, the National Endowment for the Humanities, the Rockefeller Foundation, and the Yale Center for International and Area Studies. The Lehrman Institute seminars, at which draft chapters of the book were discussed by panels of scholars, proved extremely helpful, and I want to thank the participants, the moderator, Charles S. Maier, and the executive director of the institute, Nicholas X. Rizopoulos. The Institut für Wirtschafts- und Sozialgeschichte of the Free University of Berlin several times provided me with hospitality, helpful criticism, and practical assistance, and I want to acknowledge my gratitude to its director, Wolfram Fischer, and his colleagues.

I am especially indebted to the archivist of the Gutehoffnungshütte, Bodo Herzog, for opening to me that treasure trove of high-quality documentation and for helping me to gain access to other company archives. Four fellow pioneers in those archives—Gerald D. Feldman, Larry Eugene Jones, Ulrich Nocken, and Reinhard Neebe—generously shared information with me. Further help in locating and obtaining access to documentation came from Fritz Klein, Hans Mommsen, Werner Jochmann, Max Koch, John Taylor, and Robert Wolfe. My colleague

Hans W. Gatzke proved an unfailing source of sound advice. My students Peter Hayes and William L. Patch, Jr., provided many a stimulating suggestion. So did Tim Mason and David Schoenbaum. William Sheridan Allen and Richard F. Hamilton followed the development of the book closely and offered invaluable guidance at countless junctures. Hans-Ulrich Wehler gave the penultimate version a close critical reading and spared me quite a few blunders. Finally, I owe more than I can express to my colleague Peter Gay, who saw me through times of discouragement and gave generously of his time and talents in closely scrutinizing my drafts; in the process he has improved, at least somewhat, my usage of the language that is his second but my first.

Contents

IV CAPITALISTS, NAZIS, AND THE POLITICS OF DEEPENING DEPRESSION

V POLITICS AND ECONOMICS IN THE POWER VACUUM

VI BIG BUSINESS AND THE TRIUMPH OF NAZISM

CONCLUSIONS

Introduction

1. *The Issues and the Sources*

Did big business play a significant part in Adolf Hitler's rise to power? Did German capitalists undermine the Weimar Republic? Did they finance the Nazi Party? Did they use their influence to help secure Hitler's appointment as chancellor? Beginning in the early 1930s and continuing down to the present, such charges have been repeatedly made. They form the core of one of the earliest and most persistent explanations for the origins of the Third Reich. That explanation accords a decisive role to big business and classifies Hitler's regime as a manifestation of capitalism. That view has proved too doctrinaire and reductionist for most historians, who prefer analyses that take a larger range of factors into consideration. Yet because of the surface plausibility of the charges leveled against big business and the ceaseless repetition of those charges, even mainline historians have, with few exceptions, felt obliged to include big business support among the factors contributing to the triumph of Nazism. If the charges against big business are valid, however, it scarcely suffices—as has been the widespread practice—to allude to hostility toward the Weimar Republic on the part of the business community, to mention the names of a few purported capitalist patrons of Nazism, and to cite some incidents that suggest endorsement of Hitler's quest for power by big business. If the capitalists of Germany in fact sabotaged the Republic, if they in fact bankrolled the massive party machinery with which Hitler rode to power, and if they in fact made effective use of influence in high places on behalf of his installation in the chancellorship, then mainstream historical interpretations of the Third Reich's origins would have to be radically revised. Until the role of big business is clarified, a major question mark will thus continue to hang over efforts to identify the causes of one of history's most reprehensible regimes.

This question mark persists, at least in considerable part, because of a deficiency of research. Legions of historians have painstakingly analyzed the weaknesses of the Weimar Republic and minutely documented developments at the national, regional, and local levels that contributed to the growth and spread of Nazism. Analyses of Germany's cultural and intellectual traditions and social structure have provided explanations for Nazism's appeals. Other studies have closely scrutinized the roles played by the military, by the political rivals and collaborators of the Nazis, and by numerous other components of German society. The Nazi Party itself has become the focus of an extensive body of detailed scholarship. But in contrast to the abundance of investigation into such topics, research into the political role played by big business has attained only very modest proportions. Publications on that subject have, moreover, been marred by grave qualitative defects. Some that long passed as important contributions have proven so unfounded and unreliable as to be virtually useless.[1] Others are too hobbled by ideological constraints to merit serious consideration.[2] Still others violate the rules of historical scholarship so flagrantly as to render them worthless.[3] In recent years scrupulous and thoroughly researched studies have begun to appear, but these have thus far dealt only with partial aspects of the question.[4]

The aim of this book is to provide a comprehensive examination of the questions raised above. It spans the period from the inception of the Nazi Party through the first months of the Third Reich. It begins with an analysis of the place of big business in the Weimar Republic and its role in republican politics. There follows an examination of the early years of the Nazi Party and the attitudes of its leaders—especially Adolf Hitler—toward economic questions. Most of the book is then devoted to scrutiny of the documented contacts between the Nazis and the men who presided over the business community. This study represents the first attempt to view those contacts from both sides and within the full economic and political context so to assess the motives of both Nazis and big businessmen, as well as their perceptions of each other. The book's ultimate goal is to provide answers to the above questions which are grounded in all the available evidence.

One reason for the paucity of research on this topic lies in the assumption, widespread for many years, that insufficient evidence would preclude any comprehensive inquiry. At the outset of the research for this book, well-intentioned colleagues cautioned that documentation would pose problems. That proved to be the case, but not in the sense they had in mind. Instead of a dearth of evidence, its daunting abundance quickly became a major difficulty. The voluminous documentation collected for, and generated by, the trials of major industrialists on war crimes charges at Nuremberg after World War II turned out to have been assessed only in very cursory fashion. Even more important, the archives of major German corporations yielded up large amounts of hitherto unexamined, high-quality documentation from the period in question. Fortunately, most of the executives who presided over those corporations in the 1920s and early 1930s had not yet become attuned to that deadly enemy of the historian, the telephone. They preferred to exchange letters with each other and with a wide variety of other people, including many active in political life. And they had excellent staffs that preserved the letters and other communications they received, as well as carbon copies of their communications to others, and much additional relevant documentation. In orderly German fashion, those materials found their way into well-organized company archives that, with remarkably few exceptions, were sucessfully shielded from the ravages of World War II. The decision, on the part of the latter-day successors to those executives, to open some of the major corporate archives of Germany to historical research made this book possible and has raised the level of scholarly discourse on its subject by a quantum leap.

One historian has charged, with reference to some preliminary studies of mine on certain aspects of the subject, that the contents of the German corporate archives cannot be relied upon.[5] Any incriminating evidence, he has argued, might well, for all anyone knew, have been removed before historians were given access. A number of considerations undercut the validity of that charge, however. It is, first of all, very difficult to expunge completely any important items from a substantial body of correspondence. If something of significance to the correspondents is involved, some trace of it almost invariably eventually appears elsewhere in their exchanges. Only wholesale destruction of documents can obliterate such evidence. But such obliteration is difficult, if not impossible, to achieve in large-scale organizations which have to maintain complex systems of internal communication in order to function effectively. This is demonstrated by the experience of IG Farben. During the final months of World War II Farben's management ordered the destruction of many categories of documents at the firm's Frankfurt headquarters, including the minutes of the meetings of its chief executive bodies.[6] Nevertheless, despite the burning of an estimated fifteen tons of documentation, it has proved possible to reconstitute, to a very large degree, the records of those executive bodies as well as of the firm's operations since copies of the minutes of important meetings and other vital documents had been sent, at the time of their inception, to Farben's executive offices in other parts of Germany, where they have survived. As a consequence, sufficient documentation escaped destruction to provide the evidentiary basis for the trial and conviction of Farben executives on war crimes charges at Nuremberg and for searching scholarly studies of the firm's policies and operations.[7] There is no evidence of attempts to destroy deliberately the other corporate records used here.

Nor are there grounds to suspect a "cleansing" of those records designed to remove damaging documents. Surely, if such efforts had been undertaken they would have concentrated on the period after the Nazi takeover rather than on that dealt with in the present study. Yet in the cases of two of the major collections drawn upon here, Flick and Krupp, abundant incriminating evidence on the period 1933-1945 survived to serve as the basis for war crimes convictions. Only those who have actually done research in one of the major corporate archives of Germany can fully appreciate the magnitude of the obstacles that stood in the way of any temptations to remove evidence. Short of total destruction of their contents, the volume and complexity of the collections would have necessitated the allocation, over a considerable period of time, of much skilled and completely reliable personnel to the task of reading and evaluating thousands of documents. From all indications no such allocation was made for the corporate archives used here. Those archives represent a priceless mine of contemporaneous documentation of the highest quality for the subject of this book, as well as for many other subjects. Their contents provide nothing less than unique opportunities for examining the behavior of large, modern corporations and their executives, as no comparable degree of access is possible to the records of such corporations in other major industrial countries for so recent a period.

A few observations also seem appropriate with regard to the use made here of testimony given during, or in preparation for, the Nuremberg war crimes trials. Accounts of past events rendered under such circumstances clearly do not represent the optimal form of historical evidence. But the historian must take into consideration all the evidence, and so much information on the subject of this book came to light at Nuremberg that no choice remains except to scrutinize and assess it with due caution. The need for caution becomes, however, less great in a number of instances in which Nuremberg witnesses (many of whom were not themselves under indictment) were questioned about the same matters repeatedly—often after considerable lapses of time—and nevertheless gave essentially consistent accounts. In other instances the accounts of two or more witnesses can be checked against each other or against surviving documentation from the period in question. I have sought to maximize such tests of reliability by examining all the relevant Nuremberg testimony, including the seldom used pre-trial interrogations. I have also sought to indicate to the reader those points at which I draw upon Nuremberg testimony, pointing out (sometimes in the notes) the nature of that evidence and any aspects of it that seem germane to assessing its reliability. The critical reader will wish to take that information into consideration.

The task of citing the evidence used in this volume is complicated by the unsettled state of a relatively recent body of documentation. Some of the documents which I used in one repository have now been moved to another. Others are accessible in microfilm collections as well as in archival form. Some, such as certain Nuremberg documents, appear in two or more collections under various designations. Still others have been published. As a rule, I have cited the repositories or collections where I myself located the documents used here, indicating, where known, the present location of those which have been moved. Only in the case of impeccable scholarly editions have I relied on published versions of materials I originally used in archival form.

This book has been long in the making. It was preceded by a succession of articles (listed in the bibliography) in which readers can find fuller treatments of some of the more technical and detailed aspects of the topic. One purpose of those preliminary studies was to test the validity of my initial interpretations by giving other scholars an opportunity to challenge them. As the published exchanges to which those studies gave rise attest, that proved a fruitful approach, and its results are reflected in these pages. A further purpose of those preliminary studies was to encourage other scholars to bring forward additional relevant evidence. That, too, has been realized. It now seems clear that enough evidence has been brought to light to justify the summing up that this book represents.

2. Big Business in the Weimar Context

The concept of big business exists in both English and German, where, to be sure, it takes a variety of forms, such as *Grossindustrie, Grossunternehmen, Grosswirtschaft,* or, in the period covered by this study, simply *die Wirtschaft*. Yet, despite its frequent use, that concept is rarely defined with any precision.[1] In this volume it will denote large-scale private enterprises owned and operated by Germans in the fields of commerce, finance, industry, and insurance. Since railways and most bus lines, as well as city transport systems, had long since been taken over by government, and since air travel still amounted to only a minor factor, transportation falls outside this definition. So do utilities such as those providing electrical power and water, as they were either operated municipally or by large public-private enterprises in which various government entities usually enjoyed a dominant position. In addition, an appreciable portion of industrial enterprise rested in public hands during the Weimar Republic, not because of any far-reaching socialization but rather because the national and state governments had inherited a large number of factories and mines from the political entities that had comprised the Empire that collapsed in 1918.[2] Because such publicly owned or dominated enterprises did not form part of the private sector and could not operate as free agents in the political sphere, they are not included in the definition of big business applied in this study.

A basic problem in any definition of big business lies in how to determine size. Writers who have attempted to use the term systematically have employed a number of criteria for the purpose of measurement, including the number of employees, the annual turnover, capitalization, and total assets. For this study the most appropriate yardstick is *Nominalkapital,* or the book value of issued stock. Virtually all of the largest firms in Weimar Germany operated as joint-stock corporations *(Aktiengesellschaften),* and an abundance of readily accessible statistical data permits a quite precise delimitation of size in line with that criterion. As a somewhat arbitrary cutoff point, the bottom level of *Nominalkapital* qualifying a firm for inclusion in Weimar big business will be set here at twenty million post-stabilization marks. This appears justifiable statistically since the number of firms increases rapidly while their size diminishes appreciably below that level. Also, the application of that cutoff point produces an assemblage of enterprises that encompasses all those usually considered part of big business by contemporaries and scholars alike.[3]

Although this is not a study in economic history, a glance at some characteristics of the firms that comprised Weimar big business may be helpful for readers not acquainted with its distinctive features. To begin with its quantifiable aspects, big business in the first German Republic was marked by a very high degree of capital concentration. The 158 *Aktiengesellschaften* operating in 1927 with *Nominalkapital* of twenty million marks or more comprised only 1.32 percent of all joint-stock corporations, but together they accounted for 46.67 percent of the total *Nominalkapital* of joint-stock firms, which in turn comprised virtually all of large-scale economic enterprise.[4] These figures are somewhat misleading since they include corporations owned or dominated by government, by municipalities, and by foreign enterprises. But, even allowing for that, the degree of capital concentration remains striking, as does the sheer size of the great private corporations of Weimar Germany.[5] The most gigantic clustered in the young chemical and electrical equipment industries, in the older industries of coal, iron, steel, and in banking. At the top of the 1927 list of giants towered the chemical concern IG Farben, with a *Nominalkapital* of 1.1 billion marks. At its formation in 1925 Farben became the largest corporation in Europe, surpassed worldwide only by three American corporate titans, General Motors, U.S. Steel, and Standard Oil of New Jersey. The extent of Farben's domination of the German chemical industry becomes evident when one notes that the next largest firm in that branch rested on only slightly over a tenth as much *Nominalkapital.* By 1930, according to one educated estimate, Farben produced 100 percent of Germany's synthetic dyes, between 60 percent and 85 percent of its nitrogen, 40 percent of its pharmaceuticals, and 30 percent of its rayon.[6] Two other great enterprises bestrode the rapidly growing field of electrical equipment: the Siemens combine, with *Nominalkapital* amounting to 217.5 million marks in 1927, and AEG (Allgemeine Elektricitäts-Gesellschaft), with 186.25 million marks. Together with their subsidiaries, they accounted by 1930 for 60 percent of production in their branch of industry.[7] Dominating the iron and steel industry stood the United Steel Works (Vereinigte Stahlwerke). Formed in 1926 by a merger of three major concerns and commanding *Nominalkapital* of 800 million marks, it immediately became the second largest steel firm in the world behind U.S. Steel. The other major iron and steel producers, Mannesmann, Krupp, Klöckner, Gutehoffnungshütte, Hoesch, and Mitteldeutsche Stahl, registered *Nominalkapital* ranging from approximately 160.3 million marks for the first to 50 million marks for the last. Together with United Steel, they accounted for more than 80 percent of German iron and steel production by the late 1920s.[8] In finance, five great banks operating nationwide—Deutsche Bank, Disconto-Gesellschaft, Dresdner Bank, Commerz- und Privatbank, and Darmstädter und Nationalbank—loomed far above all competitors, with *Nominalkapital* of between 150 million marks for the first and 60 million marks for the last.

A widespread characteristic of German big business during the Weimar period that is not immediately evident from statistical data on major corporations was the high degree of vertical intergration in industry. By the 1920s a great many major industrial corporations themselves produced many of the raw materials and components needed for their end products as well as much of the energy they used. Thus IG Farben, United Steel, as well as most of the other major iron and steel producers, ranked among the major bituminous coal mining firms of the country. In fact, many of the great iron and steel firms remained that only in name, long since having become diversified "mixed enterprises" because of their heavy involvement in mining. Large, independent coal-mining firms had, as a consequence, dwindled to a relatively small number by 1927. IG Farben and most of the major iron and steel firms had by then also become vertically integrated in the other direction, making not only chemicals, iron, and steel but also finished products that they themselves marketed directly or through subsidiaries. Farben produced photographic film and pharmaceuticals, while Krupp and other iron and steel producers turned out vehicles and machines in addition to pig iron and bars or sheets of steel. Some major firms had diversified to the point of becoming proto-conglomerates. The Gutehoffnungshütte, originally an iron and steel corporation, had by the middle of the 1920s acquired control of a host of diversified firms in widely scattered parts of Germany that produced copper, industrial machines, ships, trucks, wire, and operated a bookbindery and a hotel.[9] Such proto-conglomerates, or *Konzerne,* as contemporaries referred to them, defy the attempt—which one frequently encounters in writings about the subject of this book—to consign all major firms and their executives of the Weimar period to simplistically hermetic categories, such as "heavy industry" (coal, iron, and steel), more appropriate to an earlier stage of economic development.

Another striking characteristic of Weimar big business lay in the extremely uneven geographical distribution of industry. Large-scale industrial enterprises operated in only a very few areas of the country, as revealed by statistics the 1925 census provided on the horsepower of machines used for productive purposes.[10] Most of the sixteen smaller federal states and the fourteen provinces of Prussia (which were more comparable to those states than was Prussia as a whole, with its 61.2 percent of the population) registered a share of national horsepower that lay below or only slightly above the percentage of the population that lived within their boundaries. In some instances the statistics reflect a striking degree of industrial backwardness. Bavaria, with 11.8 percent of the population, accounted for only 7.3 percent of national horsepower; East Prussia, with 3.6 percent, for only 1.1 percent. At the other extreme lay the two Prussian provinces of Rhineland and Westphalia. Together they comprised 19.4 percent of the national population but accounted for 40.6 percent of the country's horsepower. That region served as the center of operations for "western industry," as it was generally known at the time. It encompassed the highly developed Ruhr Valley, but also extended beyond that to the northern Rhenish industrial complex. It was in this Rhenish-Westphalian area that most of the great corporations maintained their headquarters and operated the bulk of their plants, making it the industrial heartland of German industry.[11]

Only Berlin could come close to challenging Rhineland-Westphalia as a geographical focus of big business. Although the capital city showed up poorly in terms of the ratio of horsepower to population, it, too, served as a base for large-scale enterprise. The electrical equipment and machine-building industries, which required less energy than did mining or iron and steel production, were heavily represented there. In addition, major mining and manufacturing firms operating in the central Prussian provinces and Silesia frequently maintained their headquarters in the capital. Berlin also dominated the field of large-scale finance. All five of the giant national banks centered their operations there, and the capital's stock market had by the republican period eclipsed those of other financial centers such as Cologne, Frankfurt am Main, and Hamburg. Big business did not, of course, remain wholly restricted to Berlin and Rhineland-Westphalia. The major shipping firms clustered in the port cities of Hamburg and Bremen; Stuttgart had become the focus of some of the major automotive industries; and the region around Hanover had begun to develop some large-scale enterprises. But in terms of sheer preponderance, big business in Weimar Germany centered on Rhineland-Westphalia and Berlin.

Well before the Weimar period, a multiplicity of organizational ties had come to link the component firms of German big business together, leading to its characterization as "organized capitalism."[12] Certainly, by the 1920s Germany's large industrial and commercial corporations did not function, in line with the classical model of a capitalist economy, as completely autonomous units in a freely competitive market. Republican Germany inherited from the Empire one of the world's most pervasive collections of cartels designed to "stabilize" and otherwise regulate markets by means of agreements setting prices and limiting production levels.[13] Such cartels, some of which had dissolved after the war but later recoalesced in the mid-1920s, numbered in excess of fifteen hundred in industry alone by 1925.[14] In numerous branches the large corporations played a leading role in the cartels by virtue of their size, and the cartels in turn bound those corporations together in many ways. Another aspect of the "organized" character of Weimar big business lay in its highly developed structure of well-financed and professionally staffed trade associations, or *Verbände*.[15] A tight weave of branch and regional associations crisscrossed the entire country, bringing together at the national level producers of similar goods and linking at the regional level producers of various goods who operated within the same geographical area.

In industry two separate associational structures existed side by side, one to deal with labor-management issues and one to deal with broader issues of economic policy, especially those involving government. These culminated nationally in the so-called industrial *Spitzenverbände*, or peak-associations: the Vereinigung der Deutschen Arbeitgeberverbände (union of employers) and the Reichsverband der Deutschen Industrie (national industrial league—referred to in this study as the industrial Reichsverband). A network of chambers of commerce and industry linked those two branches together and maintained a national organization, too, the Deutscher Industrie- und Handelstag. Other branches of large-scale enterprise, such as banking, wholesale commerce, and insurance, had separate peak-associations of their own, which, like those of industry, provided members with information and lobbied on behalf of their interests. Furthermore, a plethora of special-purpose business associations provided still additional links between the components of big business. In this study, these trade associations—or at least the major ones—will frequently provide evidence of the attitudes and actions of German big business in the political sphere. Their executive officials, who had by the 1920s won recognition as quasi-professionals (*Syndikus*, singular; *Syndizi*, plural), often served as executive agents of the various components of big business.

The internal managerial structure of German corporations of the Weimar period also displayed some distinctive characteristics.[16] At the top stood the *Aufsichtsrat,* or supervisory board, a largely honorific body elected by the stockholders. It met at most a few times a year and nominally exercised surveillance over the actual executive body, the managing board or *Vorstand* (sometimes designated as *Direktion),* which it appointed. In most instances, only the chairman of the supervisory board concerned himself closely with the operations of the corporation. Day-to-day decisions, and in most cases even major decisions, rested with the managing board, composed of directors. Its composition varied from firm to firm. In some, the managing board operated on a collegial principle, with authority dispersed among several directors. Other firms concentrated authority in the hands of the chairman, who reigned in near-monarchical fashion as *Generaldirektor,* the most prestigious and awe-inspiring title in German corporate circles. Neither the *Vorstand* nor the *Aufsichtsrat* usually had cause to fear a challenge from the stockholders. Most of the stock was owned by other corporations or was routinely voted in large blocks by banks holding proxies for the actual owners, so that opposition to corporate policy rarely occurred.[17] Stockholders' assemblies amounted, as one contemporary observed, to *Jasagemaschinen* (yes-saying machines), which regularly ratified decisions, voted proposed dividends, and "elected" the members of the *Aufsichtsrat,* who in turn installed or confirmed the directors who made up the *Vorstand.*[18] The democratization of the German state after World War I had not been accompanied by a parallel development in the corporate sphere.

A final word is needed here about the manner in which the terms "big business" and "business community" (used here interchangeably) will be employed in this study. Particularly where political affairs are concerned, these terms will usually denote not the entirety of big business as it has been defined here but rather those individuals, firms, and trade associations which became active politically, if only to the extent of expressing views on political issues or on economic issues of political importance. That sort of political involvement varied widely among the components of big business in the broader, economic sense of that term. The executives of some of the biggest corporations, such as the Mannesmann steel firm and the Daimler-Benz automotive works, conspicuously abstained from any political activities and even from an active role in the major national trade associations. On the other hand, Ernst von Borsig, one of the heirs to a venerable Berlin locomotive and machine-building firm that by the 1920s ranked in size near the bottom of the assemblage of firms designated here as big businsss, played an active political role and participated prominently in the formation of the policies of the major industrial associations, at least until his firm went bankrupt in 1931. Neither size of firm nor the branch of the economy in which it operated appear to have determined which executives would become involved in larger issues outside the direct purview of their managerial roles. That seems to have been a decision that normally rested with the individual executive, although the consistent abstention by executives of firms like Mannesmann and Daimler-Benz suggests the possibility in some cases of a corporate prohibition on outside activities, at least of a political sort. As will become apparent in these pages, only a relatively limited portion of big business, in the purely economic sense, actively involved itself in such activities.

German Big Business
and the Rise of Hitler

I
Big Business During the Decade of Weimar Democracy

1. German Capitalism Survives a Revolution

To all appearances, big business formed an integral part of the privileged order of the German Empire felled by revolution in November 1918. The creation of the new state in 1871 had swept away the last obstacles to an integrated national economy. The Empire's adoption of liberal economic legislation spurred rapid industrialization under private auspices. The imperial government's shift to a protectionist trade policy in response to the recession of the 1870s sheltered the emerging industry of Germany from foreign competition. Government toleration of cartels designed to "stabilize" markets by limiting production and suppressing price competition allowed established businesses to protect their advantages. When the spread of a mass anti-capitalist workers' movement posed a threat to big business, the government shielded it, first by means of anti-socialist legislation, later by less conspicuous repressive measures designed to hobble the Social Democratic Party (SPD) and its trade union affiliates.[1] These and many other favors from the state made big business seem very much a pampered child of imperial Germany.

However, the Empire was not always experienced as a halcyon era by businessmen. Most would have preferred even stronger state repression of the Social Democratic Party to the policy of limited toleration that permitted it to participate in parliamentary politics and grow into the largest political force in the country by the end of the Empire. The mounting price of Bismarck's attempt to mollify the wage earners of Germany with the most elaborate system of state insurance programs in the world also offended many. So did the growth and pretensions of the bureaucracy. Many looked with particular apprehension on repeated bureaucratic attempts to restore to state ownership some of the holdings in a basic industry such as coal that had been turned over to private enterprise only a few decades earlier.[2] Even as German capitalists sought the aid of the government in combating the Social Democrats, they suspected officials of harboring ambitions for a form of state socialism nearly as unacceptable from their point of view as that proposed by the SPD. They could take no comfort either in the public advocacy of state intervention in the economy on behalf of social justice that earned some of the country's most eminent economists, holders of professorships at government-maintained universities, the reputation of "socialists of the lectern."[3] Some academic economists even challenged the whole thrust of industrialization and urged the government to initiate policies designed to check its further development.[4]

Germany's capitalists found it difficult to present a united front during the Empire since conflicts of interest set them against each other on numerous issues. Trade policy in particular gave rise to acrimonious divisions. The branches of business that relied heavily on exports for their profits strenuously opposed protectionist tariffs on the grounds that these provoked retaliation against sales of their goods abroad. The burgeoning iron and steel industry, by contrast, sought to reserve the rapidly expanding German market for itself by joining with the grain-growing agrarians of eastern Prussia, in the so-called alliance of iron and rye, to press for tariffs shielding the products of both groups from foreign competition. Cartels provided the cause for still further divisions, as businessmen opposed to restraint of the open marketplace clashed with those who regarded such combinations as an essential means of containing the destructive effects of all-out competition. Throughout the lifetime of the Empire, various components of big business clashed with each other.[5] During the final decade and a half of the peacetime Empire, the mounting threat posed by the swelling ranks of the Social Democratic Party and a sustained period of prosperity served to mute somewhat these often acrimonious conflicts of interest. Those years bestowed on the imperial period, in the memory of Germany's big businessmen, the somewhat misleading image of a stable, harmonious era in which the fortunes of big business and the nation as a whole seemed synonymous.

The capitalists of Germany paid a price for the favors they received from the imperial order. As the sociologist Ralf Dahrendorf has observed, in a certain sense the Empire "developed into an industrial, but not into a capitalist society," that is, a pre-capitalist elite still held sway in the Empire and especially in the predominant state, Prussia.[6] Despite their growing wealth, even the most powerful men of business had to defer to the aristocrats, military men, and bureaucrats who occupied the top ranks of society and the political power structure. As the economic importance of businessmen increased, they gradually gained admission to at least the periphery of the inner circles of the Empire. Many came to affect the haughty manner and imperious views of their social superiors, often outdoing the latter in ostentatious display. Their ranks provided many examples of the "feudalization" of the upper middle class so characteristic of imperial Germany. This shaped their attitude toward employees, which reflected the hierarchical structure of both state and society, giving rise to a *Herr-im-Hause* (lord-of-the-household) outlook. According to the assumptions underlying that amalgam of authoritarianism and paternalism, the employer, even in a huge, impersonal industrial enterprise, functioned as master of all, to whom employees owed respect and obedience, receiving in return a livelihood and benevolent treatment. In some cases, genuine paternalism in the form of company housing and welfare programs mitigated this overbearing attitude; but while examples of such solicitude received wide publicity, only a few firms went very far in that direction. Despite their aristocratic pretensions, few big businessmen of imperial Germany displayed a greater sense of responsibility toward those they employed than did their counterparts in other countries.

The imperial period left its mark on the mentality of the men of German big business in still other ways.[7] Whereas their counterparts in most other capitalist countries still generally held to the tenets of classical liberalism and viewed any extensive intervention by the state in economic affairs with suspicion, they applied a sharply bifurcated double standard. Accustomed to government assistance of numerous sorts, they had no quarrel with state involvement in the economy so long as it benefited their enterprises. By contrast they denounced governmental economic measures in the interest of wage earners, who constituted the bulk of the population, as demagogic politicization of the economy. Similarly, they viewed it as their right to combine in restraint of trade by forming cartels and expected the government to acquiesce to such combinations, whereas most of their number denied any legitimacy to trade union demands for collective bargaining and to use of the strike. Most capitalists in other countries at the time held basically similar views on worker efforts to organize and act collectively, but a special vehemence marked the prevailing outlook on that subject among Germany's entrepreneurs. They saw labor-management relations as much more than merely an economic matter; for them, these amounted to nothing less than part of the struggle to defend, against a challenge from below, the precarious system of privilege on which the Empire, and ultimately their whole society, rested. Like the other favored groups in imperial Germany, they paid for their advantages with insecurity. Recognizing that the regime whose policies enabled them to prosper had failed to win the allegiance of urban wage earners, most feared that any shift of strength toward the workers and their organizations might undermine the whole imperial order, which they saw as the only effective obstacle to working-class radicalism. Nor did they see themselves threatened solely from the left. The unusually strong persistence in Germany of nostalgic and reactionary forms of anti-capitalist and anti-industrial agitation further heightened their sense of insecurity.[8] The defensiveness and sense of jeopardy displayed by Germany's capitalists during the Weimar Republic did not come into being with the revolution of November 1918; those attitudes had to a considerable extent already taken shape during the basically conservative and authoritarian German Empire.

As part of the imperial elite, big business bore a share of responsibility for the revolution. During the final decades of the Empire, some of its leading spokesmen joined with others from the privileged and propertied orders to advocate a variety of schemes for the expansion of Germany's economic and political influence in the world. They thus contributed to a climate that encouraged the rulers of the Empire to embark on the reckless foreign adventures that offended one great power after another and eventually plunged Germany into a general European war aligned only with the moribund Hapsburg and Ottoman empires.[9] The business community had no voice in determining the specific policies that took Germany into war in the summer of 1914. As an expert on that period has observed:

> It cannot be said . . . that particular economic pressure groups had any direct influence on the decisions taken by the German government on the eve of the First World War, or that special attention was given to particular economic problems by the men in power at that very moment. As far as we can trace any influence of men from business circles in June and July 1914, they were working against rather than in favor of going to war. . . .[10]

Once the conflict had begun, however, most of the business community responded enthusiastically to the war effort. Some of its leading figures, moreover, soon grew impatient at the government's hesitancy to commit itself openly to a policy of territorial expansionism. In an effort to force the government's hand, they joined with other groups in agitating for sweeping annexationist war policies.[11] After participating in the successful campaign to bring down Chancellor Theobald von Bethmann Hollweg in 1917, these pro-expansionist spokesmen of big business eagerly endorsed the military dictatorship headed by Hindenburg and Ludendorff, whose policies effectively eliminated the last possibility of a compromise peace. Significant segments of German big business thereby contributed directly to the ruinous wartime policies that culminated in the crisis of 1918 and the collapse of the imperial order. Big business contributed indirectly as well. The refusal of most employers, particularly in large-scale industry, to abandon their traditional *Herr-im-Hause* stance in labor-management relations led them to resist stubbornly their workers' mounting demands for recognition of trade unions and for collective bargaining. This resistance in turn strengthened the Social

Democratic movement's militant left wing, whose adherents were to play such a crucial role in precipitating the revolution.

Despite the close identification of big business with the privileged groups of the Empire and its implication in the disastrous wartime policies of the imperial government, German capitalism managed to survive virtually unscathed when socialists assumed power in November 1918. This remarkable turn of events is usually explained by the inability, or the unwillingness, of badly divided factions of German socialism to effect fundamental economic or social changes after the unexpected collapse of the imperial system; the capitalists have generally been viewed as the lucky beneficiaries of the socialists' failure to make use of the power thrust on them. But big business by no means remained a passive bystander during the autumn of 1918. Instead, its spokesmen assumed an active role in ensuring the survival of capitalism in Germany. Well before there were any overt signs of revolution, prominent members of the business community had covertly laid the basis for an alliance with the leaders of organized labor that would place formidable obstacles in the way of any attempt to socialize the German economy.

Ironically, the imperial government itself had brought big business and labor together.[12] Under increasingly heavy pressure from the army to secure the trade unions' cooperation in assigning workers to industries vital for the military effort, the government in 1916 forced employers to grant de facto recognition to the unions and sit with their officials on boards set up to deal with labor problems. At first, most of big business went along with this arrangement only under protest, but in the course of collaborating with the union leaders on behalf of the war effort, a bond of understanding developed between the two. That bond grew largely out of a common enmity toward the government's economic policies during the war. The labor leaders shared the alarm of big business at the vast and intricate web of state controls (*Zwangswirtschaft*) imposed on economic activity by the swollen wartime bureaucracy. Heartened by the progress they had made during the war toward legal recognition and collective bargaining, the trade unionists did not want to see their role reduced or usurped by government officials. They were thus quite ready to collaborate with big business in an effort to resist bureaucratic encroachments on labor-management relations and to prevent the perpetuation of wartime restrictions in the postwar period. Negotiations between the two sides began in 1917 and continued sporadically and tentatively until the autumn of 1918, when the collapse of the military and the prospect of a long period of demobilization under bureaucratic auspices quickened the pace of the talks. The revolution of November 9 failed to disrupt this rapprochement, which culminated on November 15 in the signing of a formal accord.

Since the two chief signatories were Hugo Stinnes, then the most prominent figure among the industrial magnates of the Ruhr, and Carl

Legien, head of the socialist, or "free," trade union movement, that pact became known as the Stinnes-Legien Agreement. It was endorsed as well by the country's major industrial employer organizations and by the smaller Christian and liberal trade union organizations. By the terms of the accord, industry agreed to recognize the unions as agents of the labor force, accept full collective bargaining on an industry-wide basis, introduce the eight-hour workday, and withdraw financial support from "yellow," or company, unions. To implement these terms and to regulate future relations between labor and management on a basis of social partnership, participating organizations agreed to establish a nationwide network of working communities (*Arbeitsgemeinschaften*) for all major branches of industrial production, in which labor and management would have equal representation. The accord of November 15 also provided a capstone for this structure in the form of a national body of similar composition in which spokesmen of both sides from all branches of industry would be brought together. Established in 1919, this body came to be known as the "central working community" (Zentralarbeitsgemeinschaft or ZAG). It was testimony to the influence wielded by the signatories of the Stinnes-Legien Agreement that their accord received immediate endorsement from the ruling revolutionary Council of People's Commissars, which promptly published its text in the official government bulletin, thus giving it legal status.

While its specific provisions seemed to make labor the chief beneficiary, the circumstances under which the Stinnes-Legien Agreement came into being unquestionably gave the advantage to big business. Since a revolutionary government had assumed power only six days earlier, management conceded nothing it could reasonably have hoped to retain under the new political circumstances. Merely by abandoning lost positions, the leaders of industry escaped unscathed from the first wave of revolution. By appeasing the socialist trade union leaders, the Stinnes-Legien Agreement served to reduce pressure for immediate socialization of large-scale industry within the Majority Social Democratic Party, where those unions wielded much weight. This, along with the reluctance of that party's leaders to act on such a fundamental issue without a parliamentary mandate and their preoccupation with the problems of peacemaking, military demobilization, a critical food shortage, and a "bolshevik" threat from the far left, sufficed to frustrate demands by the Independent Socialists, coalition partners of the majority party, for immediate socialization of at least certain key industries. In retrospect it seems clear that the only opportunity for swift and thoroughgoing socialization occurred during the period between the November revolution and the election of the National Assembly in mid-January 1919, when socialists held exclusive power in Germany. But German industrial leaders helped to thwart such a move, adding to the divisions among the socialists by introducing into their camp—along with the trade union leaders—a Trojan horse, the Stinnes-Legien Agreement.

Although the Stinnes-Legien Agreement has attracted far less attention, it served much the same function as the accord produced by the Ebert-Groener telephone conversation of November 9, 1918. That understanding, between the head of the new revolutionary government and the First Quartermaster General of the army, allowed the officer corps to remain intact and retain control over the military in return for a pledge to defend the new republican government—at least against threats from the extreme left. The Stinnes-Legien accord produced much the same results for German industry. Like the officer corps, the leaders of big industry had coolly and soberly assessed the new situation. They had concluded that their old alliance of "iron and rye" with the Junker aristocrats would henceforth be far less effective because of the Junkers' diminished political influence. The middle classes were too fragmented to represent a potent ally. Only a strategy of at least temporary alliance with management's chief adversary, the trade unions, held out the promise of seeing private industry through a critical period of imminent change.

The Stinnes-Legien Agreement and the Ebert-Groener understanding enabled key components of the old imperial order to arrive at a modus vivendi with the new order and ensure their own survival by making relatively minor concessions. Both revealed the extent of the Empire's bankruptcy, as two of its privileged groups abandoned the imperial cause without resistance. Even more important, both erected—at the very birth of the new German Republic—formidable barriers to fundamental change. The industrialists who entered into the Stinnes-Legien Agreement claimed to have acted in the best interests of their country. Whether or not that was the case, it cannot be denied that at a moment of grave peril the leaders of German industry acted, like the generals of the army, with boldness and discernment in defense of their own interests.

After effecting their accommodations with the new republican order, big business and the officer corps collaborated to ward off bids for power by the extreme political left that began with armed uprisings in Berlin during December 1918 and January 1919. The military responded to entreaties for protection from the beleaguered Majority Socialist government by replacing the demoralized and disintegrating wartime army with mercenary units, the *Freikorps*. Since state funds were in short supply, industrialists and bankers, particularly in Berlin and the Ruhr, where the extremists were most active, contributed heavily to finance the new mercenary units, as well as to disseminate "anti-Bolshevik" propaganda.[13] The *Freikorps* successfully carried out the tasks assigned them, repeatedly suppressing leftist uprisings throughout

1919 and 1920. But under the command of former regular army officers, those units frequently acted with a brutality and bloodthirstiness that contributed to the poisonous political and social hostilities that would so heavily handicap Germany's first attempt at democracy. Until their disbandment in the summer of 1920 the *Freikorps* also served as training schools for a generation of young, reactionary political hoodlums who would later assassinate prominent republican leaders, serve as foot soldiers in the Munich Beerhall Putsch of 1923, and man the political armies that eventually turned the streets of Germany into battlefields. The big businessmen who helped finance the *Freikorps* thus incurred a share of responsibility—along with the Majority Socialists who called these units into being—for swelling the ranks of the violence-prone young men who would bedevil the democratic processes of the Republic throughout its brief existence.

Neither the suppression of leftist extremism by the *Freikorps* nor the Stinnes-Legien Agreement sufficed to guarantee the preservation of capitalism in Germany. Big business still had to weather a prolonged debate on socialization in the National Assembly elected in January 1919 and in the first republican Reichstag chosen in June 1920.[14] Later, Paul Silverberg, a prominent executive in the coal industry, boasted that big business had killed socialization by constantly suggesting new ways to achieve it.[15] Although Silverberg exaggerated, the parliamentary spokesmen of big business in fact repeatedly made what they characterized as constructive proposals during the debate over socialization, instead of adopting a wholly negative stance. Understandably anxious to stave off nationalization of their firms, they offered a variety of schemes for according the public and the workers a share in the ownership and profits of basic industries while reserving ultimate control for private management. Those proposals further muddied the increasingly murky national debate on socialization. Sabotage by big business proved unnecessary, however, as neither the socialist politicians nor boards of experts appointed by the Republic could agree on the form socialization should take or what sectors of the economy it should encompass. Also, as parliamentary tests of strength repeatedly revealed, no majority in favor of thoroughgoing socialization existed in either the National Assembly or the first republican Reichstag. Only two ineffectual "socialization" laws were enacted. They subjected the coal and potash industries to supervision by boards representing the government, the public, and the workers in those industries but left ownership in private hands.

Big business not only escaped any appreciable socialization but found itself in some respects in an even stronger position than it had occupied during the Empire. Developments of the war years left large-scale industry with a greater share of markets than before.[16] This came about in part as a consequence of the preference of military procurement offices for dealing with a few big firms rather than distributing lucrative war matériel contracts across the full range of producers. In addition, larger firms could more readily provide funding and personnel for the quasi-official wartime boards that allocated resources and manpower. Given the resulting composition of those boards, the needs of large firms generally met with favorable responses. Part of the large profits realized from those contracts financed plant expansion and replacement of outdated machinery, so that much of big business entered the Republic greatly strengthened. The status of the men of big business also improved markedly as a result of the lost war and the revolution. Because of the damage done to the prestige and influence of the military and the aristocracy, German capitalists no longer had to rest content with a secondary place. They could, and in many cases did, now regard themselves as the paramount socio-economic elite. And in a number of objective respects, they were. As owners or managers of great concentrations of capital and as experts in managerial skills in a country inescapably dependent on industrial production for its well-being, they occupied a key position, to say the least. The course of events in 1918–19 linked the fortunes of the young Republic inextricably to theirs. In the absence of any significant socialization, the Republic could flourish only to the extent that German capitalists did; only if the business community prospered could the masses, in whose name the revolution had been made, better their material lot. Paradoxically, a revolution made by socialists had enhanced both the prestige and importance of big business while perpetuating labor's dependence on it.

The consequences of this quickly became evident. Faced with the necessity of reabsorbing millions of former servicemen into civilian life and reviving industrial exports to pay for desperately needed foodstuffs, the leaders of republican Germany saw no choice except to rely on the existing economic order by fostering private enterprise. So, while the republican government extended little or no help to returning veterans, who had sacrificed years of their lives, it speedily compensated industrial firms that had lost mines and factories in territories Germany was forced to cede to neighboring countries by the terms of the Versailles settlement and subsequent plebiscites.[17] Companies holding unfilled military contracts at the time of the armistice obtained generous cash settlements from the government.[18] Big business also received a voice in the determination of national demobilization policies that regulated wide areas of economic activity or freed them from controls.[19] This arrangement, too, repeatedly redounded to the advantage of big business, frequently at public expense.

Despite these favorable results, Germany's big businessmen—with rare exceptions—regretted the replacement of the Empire with a republic. Their attitude did not spring from political principle or from sentiment; die-hard monarchists were rare in their ranks. To men who thought primarily in terms of smokestacks and slagheaps, entry ledgers and profit margins, the fate of crowned heads mattered little. The monarchy had, like an ill-managed enterprise, failed and gone into receivership. To lament its demise was futile. Those formerly associated with the bankrupt had to avoid being driven to the wall themselves. Yet if Germany's men of big business did not mourn for the Hohenzollerns and the lesser dynasties deposed in 1918, most felt an enormous sense of insecurity after the demise of the military-bureaucratic state and the authoritarian system it had enforced. Like other unreconstructed elements, they generally withheld from the events of November 1918 recognition as a true revolution. Instead, they habitually referred to it, in the anti-republican terms of the time, as "the collapse." They thus joined those who confounded the democratization of their country with the military debacle brought on by the policies of the imperial authorities. Weimar and Versailles, democracy and defeat, would remain linked in the minds of most German capitalists throughout the lifetime of the Republic.

Some major businessmen did, to be sure, seek to find a positive side to the change of regimes. Opportunism, rather than political conviction, shaped their outlook, however. The chemical executive Carl Duisberg, soon to become one of the architects of IG Farben, had become frustrated by the inefficiencies of the imperial regime even before the revolution and welcomed the advent of a parliamentary, democratic government. But his correspondence reveals that he expected a republic, even a "red" one, to give rise to a "more commercial-technical spirit" that would prove more congenial to business than the "largely formalistic, even if strictly logical way of thinking and doing things brought into our administration by the jurists" of the Empire.[20] A more sober assessment came from Robert Bosch, the elderly Stuttgart pioneer in the manufacture of spark plugs and other electrical accessories. A man of relatively progressive outlook, he shared the widespread view that there had been only one alternative in 1918 to a parliamentary, democratic republic: Bolshevism. In 1919 Bosch tried to explain to a fellow industrialist unwilling to accept the results of the revolution how the Republic must, viewed in that perspective, appear as a distinctly lesser evil: "If your house catches fire, you have to use even dung-water if you don't have any fresh water."[21] A great many German capitalists acquiesced in the new regime because they, too, believed they had been rescued from a Bolshevik conflagration by a dousing of democratic "dung-water." The lingering after-effects might be distasteful, but frightening thoughts of what might have happened helped to quiet misgivings about the course of events.

This sort of acquiescence rarely produced any firm allegiance to the Republic, and most German capitalists remained full of reservations about the political turn taken by their country. Like millions of other

Germans, they viewed the new state as a product of usurpation that bore the shameful taint of the "stab in the back" allegedly inflicted on the German army in 1918 by traitors at home. The Republic remained for them, as for so many of their countrymen, a polity lacking in legitimacy and, probably, in permanence. While unwilling to conspire at overthrowing the Republic, mainly for fear of triggering a new, still more radical leftist revolutionary upheaval, most big businessmen felt no obligation to support the new regime during its shaky early years against threats from the right. The Kapp Putsch of March 1920, in which a reactionary cabal and part of the officer corps of the army used *Freikorps* units to seize control of Berlin, forcefully demonstrated this.[22] Much of the business community privately deplored the putsch, not on grounds of political principle but rather because of concern that the resulting turmoil would interrupt a promising upturn in economic activity. As long as the attempted overthrow of the republican government seemed to have a chance of success, the leading men of big business nevertheless maintained a posture they characterized as "neutrality," which amounted to according the new government parity with the old. Only when the failure of the venture became evident did they distance themselves from the putschists. Later, their spokesmen sought to justify this temporizing behavior by likening it to their response to the revolution of November 1918. They thus showed themselves incapable of recognizing the important distinction between, on the one hand, a conspiratorial attempt by remnants of the old privileged elite to overthrow a parliamentary republic established by a democratically elected National Assembly and on the other, a popular uprising against the only partially reformed and thoroughly discredited Empire.

While the leaders of the Republic labored to cope with the often seemingly overwhelming difficulties that beset the new state during its early years, some elements of German big business remained hopeful that the new system of government would prove unworkable and have to be abandoned in favor of one less democratic. This sentiment gained open expression during the crisis-ridden autumn of 1923, when parliamentary disputes over economic issues threatened to deprive the national government of a workable majority in the Reichstag. As the crisis approached its zenith in early October, the executive board of the national organization of iron and steel manufacturers briefly abandoned its practice of abstaining from political stands to proclaim publicly: "The parliamentary system of government has failed to work. Only men of strong will with clear goals who are supported by the trust of the people can help us to surmount the current emergency."[23] At about the same time this statement appeared, Germany's most prominent capitalist, Hugo Stinnes, toyed with the idea of replacing the republican government with a directorate of three strongmen.[24] The Republic of course survived, so that the prophecy of the iron and steel men and Stinnes' project proved premature. But those responses to the first great crisis of the new state revealed lingering hopes in influential big business circles for a drastic curtailment, if not elimination, of the powers of the democratically elected parliaments of republican Germany.

The election of Field Marshal Paul von Hindenburg as president of the Republic in 1925 once again aroused such hopes. In December of that year, in the midst of an economic slump, a deputation of industrialists made use of an audience with the president to plead for intercession on his part on behalf of the business community. As a means to reduce government expenditures and thus taxes, they proposed circumscribing the authority of the Reichstag by according the finance minister a veto over all government outlays. One member of the deputation, the prominent Ruhr industrialist Paul Reusch, broached the possibility of a resort to the president's sweeping emergency powers under Article 48 of the constitution to ensure sound economic practices by the government.[25] But despite a sympathetic response, Hindenburg showed no inclination then or during the rest of the decade to flex the full powers of the presidency in order to shape economic or fiscal policy.

The attitude of big businessmen during the republican period had much in common with that of the officer corps of the army. Both focused their political allegiance not on the Republic but on such "higher" notions as *Vaterland* or *Reich*. Both drew a distinction between what they viewed as the permanence of "the state" and the transitoriness of a particular constitution, including that adopted by the Weimar National Assembly. Each regarded itself as the rightful, if self-appointed, guardian of a vital aspect of Germany's national life. The generals saw themselves as the custodians of their country's proud military heritage; the leaders of big business considered themselves to be the stewards of something also of lasting value to the nation, though of less venerable origin: *die Wirtschaft*. Although that literally means "the economy," in their usage it connoted not the national economy as a whole but rather its large-scale commercial, financial, manufacturing, and mining enterprises. Just as the officers at the head of the Republic's military establishment, the Reichswehr, regarded themselves as the army and claimed the right to speak for it, so the major figures in the business community habitually referred to themselves as *die Wirtschaft* and presented themselves as its spokesmen. While quite willing to broaden the base of their constituency by allowing proprietors of small and medium-size enterprises to identify themselves with *die Wirtschaft*, the leaders of big business arrogated to themselves the privilege of determining its interests and representing them before the German people and the holders of political office. Although repeatedly emphasizing their weighty responsibility for *die Wirtschaft*, they rarely showed any sense of being responsible to anyone for the execution of that stewardship. Throughout the Weimar Republic, the attitudes of big business—like those of the military—revealed the shortage of social and political integration that posed such a handicap to Germany's first experiment with democracy.

Germany's big businessmen also entered the republican era with an essentially unaltered conception of their economic role. While they no longer openly asserted the *Herr-im-Hause* standpoint, their attitudes toward the firms they headed remained basically proprietary and paternalistic. They continued to profess the sanctity of private property and the superiority of private enterprise. They viewed themselves as men somehow called to a special responsibility. In the words of Carl Duisberg, one of the founders of the IG Farben chemical trust formed in 1925 and chairman of the industrial Reichsverband from 1925 to 1931, *die Wirtschaft* bore the weighty responsibility to "provide for the material necessities of the nation in a clearheaded and objective manner."[26] As Germany's entrepreneurs saw it, they alone possessed the capacity for the enlightened and disinterested execution of this task, since selfishness and shortsightedness disqualified all other groups. This opinion received forceful expression from Ernst Brandi, director of a large portion of the coal-mining operations of the giant United Steel Works formed in 1926:

> The workers, supported by the completely unjustified but legally sanctioned power of the unions, pursue in a one-sided, egotistical and even ruthless fashion their interest in higher wages as well as less and easier work. They have succeeded to a very large degree in securing their demands, to the detriment of the branches of the economy involved, to the detriment of the whole nation. . . .
>
> By comparison, the employer represents the general interest of his whole branch of the economy and as a result safeguards the economic basis of the whole nation. This activity of the employer is therefore not an egotistical one, but rather one of general value, which is exactly the opposite of the ruinous activity of the workers and their organizations.[27]

Brandi's words, to which most entrepreneurs in the Republic would have assented, convey the extent to which German big business clung to naive and self-serving notions about its role. They reflect, as well, a myth that had played no small part in the political history of the Empire: that a carefully selected and highly trained cadre of able men could transcend all self-interest and group pressure to govern in an objective and unbiased (*sachlich*) manner. Discredited, at least temporarily, in the political sphere by war, defeat, and revolution, that myth persisted in big business' perception of its own role in Weimar Germany. It served to veil what amounted to a claim to privileged status by one set of participants in the pluralistic scramble for advantage among socio-economic groups

Stuttgart. 3. Dezember 1928   **Preis 60 Pfennig**   33. Jahrgang Nr. 36

SIMPLICISSIMUS

Herausgabe: München   BEGRÜNDET VON ALBERT LANGEN UND TH. TH. HEINE   Postversand: Stuttgart

„Alle Räder stehen still — wenn Mein starker Arm es will!"

A caricaturist's depiction of the German industrialist of the Weimar era (the features closely resemble those of Paul Reusch). The caption is a variation on a verse by the radical poet of the 1848 revolution, George Herwegh:

> All gears to turn shall cease—
> If such my mighty arm decrees.

Courtesy Yale University Library.

Members of the presidium of the industrial Reichsverband standing before the executive office building of IG Farben in Leverkusen, September 19, 1929. In the front row, left to right are; Philipp Rosenthal, the porcelain manufacturer; Carl Duisberg, of IG Farben; and Ernst von Borsig, head of the Borsig locomotive firm of Berlin. In the second row, third from the left, is Paul Reusch, of the Gutehoffnungshütte conglomerate; next to him, with white beard, stands Robert Bosch, the Stuttgart pioneer in the field of automotive electrical equipment; second from the right, with hand in jacket pocket, is Wilhelm Cuno, of the Hamburg-America shipping line and former Reich Chancellor. In the third row, second from the right, with close-cropped hair, is Albert Vögler, of United Steel; behind him and to the right, with bow tie, stands Paul Silverberg, the coal magnate. *Courtesy Bayer Archiv, Leverkusen.*

in the Republic. It underlay a widespread reluctance to accord to German workers full equality in the determination of the country's economic and social policies. This belief in the special and disinterested role of the men who controlled *die Wirtschaft* also revealed a residue of authoritarian political ideology that would rise to the surface again whenever the new state faltered in the face of economic difficulties.

The Social Democrats who proclaimed the Republic and dominated its cabinets repeatedly experienced chagrin at finding themselves compelled to collaborate with big businessmen who still harbored such attitudes. But the failure of the country's socialists to effect any thoroughgoing changes in the economic structure left them no choice except to shore up the existing capitalist order, thus adding to the profits and economic influence of big business. They could seek consolation in their party's position that the capitalist Weimar Republic represented only a way station in the inevitable progress toward the socialist Republic of the future. But neither they nor any other significant republican political force succeeded in formulating a set of policies for effecting such a transition. In fact, no one ever mounted a determined effort to resolve the central paradox of the Weimar Republic, a state called into being and governed during its formative phase by socialists, who nonetheless fostered capitalism and relied on it for the material well-being of the nation.

2. *Money Versus Votes*

From the standpoint of big business, the political institutions of the Republic represented a potentially grave threat. In the Empire, as a consequence of constitutional barriers to parliamentary authority, the elected representatives of the people had exercised only limited influence on government policy. In most federal states discriminatory electoral laws had limited representation for those with little property. At the national level, despite universal and nominally equal manhood suffrage in Reichstag elections, the failure to reapportion constituencies after 1871 had resulted in increasing underrepresentation of the urban population in an era of rapid migration from countryside to city. That had limited the political impact of the swelling tide of workers' votes in industrial cities. The advent of the democratic, parliamentary Republic swept away these obstacles to full popular sovereignty and equitable representation. For the first time, matters of vital concern to big business became subject to the will of the equitably elected representatives of the people at large. Without a mass following to defend their interests at the polls, Germany's big businessmen felt vulnerable. The knowledge that a parliamentary majority could at any time threaten their economic role considerably dampened their relief at escaping socialization; and so did the knowledge that the Weimar constitution explicitly authorized future challenges to their position by empowering the government to nationalize any private enterprise deemed suitable for socialization and by guaranteeing employees parity with employers in the determination of wages, working conditions, and the "overall economic development of productive forces." Such provisions negated, in the eyes of Germany's businessmen, the equally explicit constitutional guarantees of private property and fair compensation in the event of state confiscation.

For the business community the most disturbing aspect of the new republican order lay in the extent to which it threatened to subjugate economics to politics, and democratic politics at that. Germany's capitalists partook of nineteenth-century liberal economic doctrines sufficiently to regard politics as a sphere of activity quite different and essentially separate from that of economics.[1] The latter appeared to them more central, more basic, more determinative than politics, and like the Marxists they accorded economics primacy—if for different reasons—over politics. They, too, saw economics as an objective matter, governed by immutable, discernible laws, while politics, by contrast, seemed vulnerable to dangerous passions and given to unpredictability, particularly where the unpropertied masses enjoyed full political rights. To assign ultimate responsibility for the nation's economic policies to a popularly elected parliament appeared to most big businessmen a grave folly, if not a violation of the most basic principles of human society. Virtually all agreed it could lead to no good for *die Wirtschaft* and for the men who bore the responsibility of caring for its needs.

During the first years of the Republic the leaders of German industry responded to the perils they saw in the new polity by seeking to de-politicize questions of economic policy. They found support in that endeavor among their new allies in organized labor. Many trade union leaders shared with industrialists the belief that practical men accustomed to dealing with the realities of economic life could better determine sound economic policies than parliamentarians and bureaucrats, who often lacked first-hand knowledge of the everyday world and were subject to pressures extraneous to the economic matters at issue. Hence, at the outset of the republican period, both large-scale industry and the trade unions favored removing broad areas of economic decision making from state control and assigning those matters to quasi-official bodies in which labor and management enjoyed equal representation.[2] This arrangement appealed to the capitalists since it offered a means of offsetting the otherwise insuperable numerical superiority of the workers. If economic policy could be brought under the influence of bodies in which management enjoyed equal representation with labor, Germany's politically active industrial leaders would find it easier to defend their interests than if such matters were left to the free play of forces in the democratically elected parliaments of the Republic.

For a time, this strategy of de-politicization appeared to succeed. It received institutional form in the Zentralarbeitsgemeinschaft (ZAG), the national capstone to the structure of labor-management boards established under the auspices of the Stinnes-Legien Agreement. During 1919, with the state apparatus still debilitated as a result of the revolution and overtaxed by the problems of demobilization and peacemaking, the ZAG arrogated to itself a variety of quasi-official functions. With its industrial and union spokesmen cooperating frequently by virtue of a shared commitment to restoring peacetime productivity, the ZAG managed to exert a strong, often decisive influence on the shaping of postwar German economic policy. It played an important role in dismantling the wartime web of economic controls, a step that greatly facilitated the efforts of big business to free itself from government constraints.[3] The ZAG also proved useful in quashing leftist threats to restoration of the business-as-usual conditions desired by Germany's capitalists. When leftist political groups pressed, in 1919, for a shorter workday in the mines, despite an acute coal shortage, the union spokesmen in the ZAG backed management's resistance to this step. They also joined with management by throwing the ZAG's weight against proposals to bestow extensive powers on the workers' councils that had sprung up in the wake of the revolution and which posed a threat not only to management's authority but to the unions' role as agents for the workers as well. From the standpoint of big business, the ZAG proved resoundingly successful in the early phases of the Republic in insulating the economic sphere from the new pressures of mass politics released by the revolution.

Reemergent stresses between management and labor soon undercut the effectiveness of the ZAG. The refusal in March 1920 of the industrial leadership to denounce the Kapp Putsch and endorse the unions' general strike appeal soured relations considerably. But ultimately the experiment in class collaboration succumbed to a host of pressures, especially those exerted by the chronic postwar inflation. Management could cope with inflation simply by raising prices at its discretion. Because of its strengthened bargaining rights, organized labor initially did not fare badly. But in the phase of hyper-inflation, wages—which were paid only at set intervals—lagged increasingly behind prices.[4] Despite pleas by labor representatives in the ZAG for wage increases to keep pace with prices, most industrial firms preferred to exploit the favorable situation and maximize profits. As a result, the ZAG's labor support eroded as various unions withdrew from participation. The authority of the ZAG also dwindled as a consequence of assumption of many of its advisory functions by the provisional economic council (vorläufiger Reichswirtschaftsrat, or RWR), a consultative chamber established by the Weimar constitution and made up of labor, management, and public-interest delegates. In 1923, with the ZAG already severely weakened by union defections and encroachments of the RWR, it received a fatal blow when the coal industrialists took advantage of the Franco-Belgian occupation of the Ruhr to force a suspension of the eight-hour workday that formed one of the cornerstones of the Stinnes-Legien Agreement, which had given rise to the ZAG. The organization lingered on for some years but ceased to wield any meaningful authority. With its incapacitation, the strategy of de-politicization also came to an end.

Well before the disintegration of the ZAG, the limitations of that strategy had become evident. Once the Reich bureaucracy recovered from the shock of revolution and underwent personnel changes making it acceptable to the new regime, it began reasserting its control over economic policy. With the convening of the first republican Reichstag in the summer of 1920, matters of vital concern to big business, such as taxes, increasingly became the subject of parliamentary legislative battles and of struggles within the political parties and coalition cabinets. The leaders of big business had prepared for this development, having decided early on to supplement the strategy of de-politicization by plunging into the partisan politics of the new Republic. During the Empire, they had felt little need for personal political involvement since businessmen usually found it more convenient to bypass the parties and deal directly with government officials, who were, for the most part, well disposed toward their interests and whom the quasi-authoritarian constitutional order shielded from popular and parliamentary pressures. During the final decades of the Empire, overt participation by prominent businessmen in partisan politics had declined markedly, although some sought to defend their interests by exerting behind-the-scenes influence on the parties of the right.[5] The advent of the democratic Republic brought a sharp reversal of that trend, however, as some of Germany's most prominent businessmen abandoned their accustomed nonpartisan stance to assume an active and open role in the so-called *bürgerlich*, or bourgeois, parties.[6]

Most big businessmen who entered politics affiliated themselves with the major rightist party, the German National People's Party (DNVP), or—in even greater numbers—the more moderate and liberal German People's Party (DVP). Smaller numbers joined the Catholic Center Party and the left-liberal German Democratic Party (DDP), both of which collaborated with the Majority Social Democrats in the "Weimar coalition" that governed the Republic during much of its early existence. Factors that differed from person to person determined the choice of parties: religion, traditional loyalties, regional political configurations, and personal ties. But regardless of formal party affiliation, politically active big businessmen felt a tie to each other that transcended partisan divisions since politics remained for them a mere matter of interests and convenience. Most carried little ideological baggage aside from a commitment to private property and private enterprise. They shared an abhorrence of socialism in all forms and a strong aversion to government regulation of economic activity as well as to expanded state welfare measures that necessitated increased taxes. But apart from sharing in the generally

nationalistic outlook toward the rest of the world and the bitter rejection
of the Versailles territorial settlement then so widespread in Germany,
they seldom displayed interest in non-economic issues. When they made
a rare effort to articulate their political philosophies, they most often
employed the words "national" and "liberal." In the German usage of
the day, a "national" outlook amounted to a self-proclaimed dedication
to disinterested pursuit of the nation's interest that all too often masked
a nostalgic allegiance to the status quo of 1914. The meaning of the word
"liberal" has frequently been problematical in Germany, but in business
circles of the republican period that term carried especially sweeping
connotations. One industrialist gave expression to this when he explained his position to an acquaintance after the demise of the Republic:
"As you well know, I have always been liberal, in the sense of Kant and
Frederick the Great."[7]

Some members of the business community not only joined political
parties but also secured election as parliamentary deputies. The Republic's system of proportional representation facilitated this by enabling
candidates to gain election on a party list of nominees without having to
campaign actively. The new system took effect with the elections for the
first republican Reichstag in 1920, which produced a chamber studded
with prominent figures from the ranks of big business, including Hugo
Stinnes; his general director, Albert Vögler; Kurt Sorge, a Krupp director and chairman of the industrial Reichsverband; former Krupp managing director, Alfred Hugenberg; and Carl Friedrich von Siemens of
the Berlin electrical equipment dynasty. But as most of these men devoted their attention primarily to their day-to-day business affairs and in
some cases also sat in the ZAG or RWR, they could not spare much time
for parliamentary responsibilities. They attended plenary sessions of the
Reichstag only infrequently and took little part in the work of its standing committees. Because of their demanding business activities, as well as
an aversion to assuming political responsibility at a time when intractable
circumstances made unpopular measures unavoidable, most declined
ministerial posts, thus costing their parties opportunities for increased
influence at the cabinet level.[8] Their parliamentary colleagues soon
came to regard them with misgiving since they frequently failed to attend important roll calls, yet served as vulnerable targets for leftists seeking to portray the bourgeois parties as lackeys to the great capitalists.[9]
Since their parliamentary duties proved a tedious burden, most of the
major big business figures had decided before the 1924 elections to withdraw from the Reichstag. Thereafter, the parliamentary representation
of big business devolved upon men not actively involved in management
at all or upon secondary management figures.

In none of the bourgeois parties did big business hold a wholly commanding position, and in the often heated competition with other interest groups for favorable places on the parties' lists of candidates,

big business suffered from a severe handicap. Unlike most of those groups—the trade unions, the organizations of artisans, white-collar workers, retail merchants, government officials, and farmers—it lacked a mass constituency of its own. In bargaining for advantageous candidacies, the spokesmen of big business could not promise to the parties the prime commodity of electoral politics: large blocs of reliable votes. To compensate for this deficiency, big business drew on another commodity needed by the parties, one it possessed in relative abundance: money. From the standpoint of Germany's big businessmen, elective politics in the Weimar Republic quickly became a matter of offsetting the numbers behind other interest groups with the financial resources of big business—a matter of pitting money against votes.

In using money to protect their political interests, big businessmen employed a variety of stratagems.[10] Some of their spokesmen received coveted "safe" places on the bourgeois parties' lists of nominees when business interests interceded on their behalf with the national leadership of those parties by holding out the prospect of financial aid. In other instances, big business interests concentrated their resources at the local or regional level to secure the nomination and election of their candidates by essentially the same method. A more direct solution involved simply buying the services of parliamentarians: A deputy or prospective deputy received a place on a company's payroll in a sinecure with the tacit understanding that he would serve as a parliamentary agent. A decorous way to achieve the same goal entailed giving an influential politician a seat on a company's supervisory board, a post that entailed few duties and little responsibility but carried with it a lucrative honorarium. In still other instances the initiative came from the side of the parties. Hoping to obtain subsidies from big business interests, party leaders sought out persons from the business community and bestowed on them places on their candidate lists that assured election, thereby demonstrating the party's concern for the welfare of big business. On the whole, the bourgeois parties welcomed business participation, since it usually brought financial support.

The case of IG Farben, the giant chemical corporation formed in 1925, illustrates the possibilities for using business money to gain parliamentary representation.[11] In the late 1920s Farben's supervisory board included three Reichstag deputies, one each in the DDP, the Center, and the DVP. In addition, one of the firm's directors, Wilhelm Kalle, served as DVP deputy both in the Reichstag and the Prussian Landtag. A special secret committee, presided over by Kalle and known as the Kalle-Kreis or the Kränzchen, managed Farben's political money. Acting with far-reaching discretionary powers, it bestowed each year a total of about 300,000 marks on the DDP, the Center, and the DVP, with the largest amount normally going to the DVP. During national or Prussian election campaigns the firm distributed additional payments of roughly the same magnitude to the same parties. These were considerable sums at a time when the annual budget of the national headquarters of a major party such as the DNVP came to only about half a million marks and when a bourgeois party could mount an election campaign in some of the thirty-five electoral districts of the Republic for as little as 20,000 to 30,000 marks.[12]

Farben by no means stood alone in contributing to more than one party. Few big businessmen felt a strong loyalty to any of the Weimar parties, with the possible exception of some devout Catholics who clung to the Center Party on grounds of religious identification.[13] For most, party politics amounted to little more than a bothersome sphere of activity that required at least a minimal amount of attention and the allocation of some funds. They regarded their contributions as investments for the purpose of maintaining barriers to socialism and assuring access to those in power for their firms. They would have preferred a single united bourgeois party and looked with envy to the United States, where a simpler party system seemed to make it easier for their American counterparts to influence the shape of national policy.[14] In the absence of such a united party, others joined Farben in spreading their political money across the political spectrum in hopes of thereby strengthening the bourgeois elements in Germany's politics and ensuring that they would have friends in power regardless of which parties governed at any particular time.

The absence of any centralized direction or even coordination of efforts on the part of big businessmen to pit money against votes greatly hampered the effectiveness of those efforts. Contrary to widespread belief, the national or peak-associations of big business—the so-called *Spitzenverbände*—which might have served as levers for pressure on the politicians, played no part in either the collection or disbursement of political money.[15] The leaders of the industrial Reichsverband, which rested on a precarious merger of groups whose economic interests frequently conflicted, scrupulously refrained from partisan political activity in order to avoid additional internal dissension; so, for similar reasons, did the leadership of the Vereinigung der Deutschen Arbeitgeberverbände, the national association of employers' organizations charged with defense of industry's interests in labor-management questions. More specialized national trade associations, representing particular branches of big business, similarly abstained from direct involvement in party politics. All of these national associations engaged in political activities, of course, as their officials assiduously cultivated key figures in the bureaucracy and lobbied vigorously in the parliaments of Germany on behalf of big business. But they played no direct part in the delicate process of transforming money into influence.

Lacking any nationwide system for managing their political money, big businessmen pooled their financial resources for political purposes in a variety of ways. In some parts of the country, the smaller and frequently more homogeneous regional industrial associations collected money from member firms and disbursed it to political parties. From all indications, however, much more appreciable sums came from regional pooling arrangements established specifically for political purposes outside the framework of the existing trade associations. The Kuratorium für den Wiederaufbau des Deutschen Wirtschaftslebens of Berlin, created in 1919, managed the political funds of industrial firms in and around the capital as well as those of the large Berlin banks that served all of Germany.[16] It sought to bring as many active businessmen as possible into politics and to influence the policies of the parties. To those ends it disbursed sizeable sums to all the major bourgeois parties during national election campaigns. The largest share went, at the outset, to the DDP, later to the DVP, with the Center Party and the DNVP also receiving sizeable allotments. In 1928 the resources of the Kuratorium suffered a major diminution when the major Berlin banks, preferring to manage their political contributions themselves, withdrew their support. Later, the depression reduced the organization to insignificance by drastically curtailing the willingness of the remaining participants to contribute. Other regional organizations similar to the Kuratorium, about which less is known, operated in many parts of the country.[17]

The coal, iron, and steel firms of the Ruhr also sought to combine their political money to increase its impact. In the early years of the Republic, they made use of an autonomous organization established late in the Empire for just that purpose: the Kommission zur Sammlung, Verwaltung und Verwendung des Industriellen Wahlfonds.[18] Its funds, like those of the Kuratorium, derived from assessments levied on participating firms. At the time of the 1919 and 1920 elections, the Kommission disbursed considerable sums to the bourgeois parties, earmarked in many cases for candidates regarded as especially valuable from the standpoint of industry. But with the depreciation of its financial reserves during the inflation, it faltered. In 1924, after stabilization of the mark, the Kommission gave way to a less formal arrangement whereby the coal industrialists on the one hand and those of iron and steel on the other established separate funds which were disbursed in coordinated fashion.

Administration of these two funds fell initially to Alfred Hugenberg, who had long played an important behind-the-scenes role in the Kommission.[19] A former civil servant who sat as a DNVP deputy in the national parliament throughout the Republic, after serving as managing director of Krupp from 1909 to 1918, Hugenberg was at the time—and still is—often mistakenly portrayed as an agent of industry. By shrewdly investing the large amounts of industrial money placed at his disposal during the war to mobilize public opinion in favor of annexationist aims, he made himself financially independent of his backers in the postwar period and became a political force in his own right. Although he continued to command a following in industrial circles of the Ruhr, particularly among the coal operators, he alienated many of the most influential men of the iron and steel industry during the late 1920s. They resented his growing arrogance and deplored his ideological adherence to the rigid line of the ultranationalist Pan-German League. On occasion his beliefs led him to slight the immediate economic interests of big business, as with the Dawes Plan, which he opposed despite German industry's desperate need for the American credit which only approval of the Dawes Plan would make available. These differences came to a head in 1927, when Hugenberg sought to use the political money of industry to gain control of the DNVP by denying its chairman, Count Kuno von Westarp, a voice in the allocation of that party's share of those funds. Some of the leading Ruhr iron and steel industrialists, who had long mistrusted Hugenberg because, among other reasons, of his closer ties with the coal operators, regarded this move as a high-handed misappropriation of their money and a threat to the unity of a party they regarded as a bulwark of conservatism. Supplying Westarp generously with funds raised by a special levy on the iron and steel firms, they circumvented Hugenberg and took over administration of their own political money.[20] Hugenberg, who captured the leadership of the DNVP in 1928, continued to command the allegiance and financial backing of influential industrialists and to represent the political hopes of extreme right-wing elements in the business community, at least until the final phase of the republican period. Then, as will be discussed below, his followers in big business circles dwindled, becoming alienated by his obdurately negative policies, which deprived him of any voice in government, as well as by his support for agrarian interests in their increasingly acrimonious clashes with industry over trade policy.

Collaboration of the Ruhr iron and steel industrialists with the coal operators resumed early in 1928 when the most influential of Hugenberg's industrial critics, Paul Reusch of the Gutehoffnungshütte combine, took the lead in forming a secret organization of twelve top industrialists, the Ruhrlade.[21] This group, drawn from the coal and iron industries of the Ruhr and Rhenish regions, met once a month, formally attired for an evening of sociability and deliberation about matters of common interest. In March 1928 they agreed to use their new organization to administer the political contributions of the great Ruhr industrial firms during the campaign for the May Reichstag elections of that year. The men of the Ruhrlade themselves took over the task of assessing and collecting the contributions of the iron and steel industry. Assessment and collection of the levy for the coal industry remained in the hands of the coal operators. The Ruhrlade, however, arrogated to itself authority over the expenditure of both levies and continued that practice in following years. On the basis of available evidence, the annual sum at its disposal amounted, in the period 1928–30, to at least 1.2 million marks, and possibly to as much as 1.5 million marks. This gave its members control over the largest political fund of big business, and probably of any special interest group, in Germany. At the time of the 1928 elections, the Ruhrlade contributed at least 200,000 marks to the national headquarters of the DNVP, which amounted to nearly half the money that party received from large donors. A similar amount probably went to the DVP, with a lesser sum going to the Center Party. The Ruhrlade also supported individual candidates it regarded as especially friendly to industry. After the elections of 1928, it subsidized the DNVP and DVP to the extent of 5,000 marks a month each, and it gave 3,000 marks every month to the conservative Catholic Bavarian People's Party.

These efforts by big business to use its money to gain influence over the non-socialist parties and to secure representation for its interests in the parliaments of the Republic yielded disappointing results.[22] Despite the often formidable financial resources the capitalists and their agents could bring to bear, the politicians showed themselves disconcertingly resistant to manipulation through material rewards and punishments. This proved particularly true with regard to the crucial allotment of those coveted top places on the parties' lists of parliamentary candidates that virtually guaranteed election under the Republic's proportional system of representation. While the leaders of the bourgeois parties displayed a willingness to assign a few such nominations to spokesmen of big business, they stubbornly resisted pressure to expand their number appreciably. The political agents of big business repeatedly retaliated by threatening to withhold financial contributions unless the parties met their demands. That tactic produced little in the way of results, however. From the politicians' point of view, big business amounted to merely one clamorous pressure group among many, and far from the most potent in a political sense. While it could threaten to withhold money, its competitors from less wealthy pressure groups could confront party leaders with a more dire prospect: loss of the blocs of voters over which they exercised influence. Moreover, the politicians knew from experience that the threats of big business almost invariably proved empty, since the capitalists had no real alternative. Their prime political concern lay with maintaining the non-socialist parties as a bulwark against the parties of the left; to withhold customary contributions at election time would only subvert that aim. Politicians could thus defy big business with impunity. After blustering and delaying, its spokesmen virtually always made donations as usual in the end, fearing that failure to do so would only strengthen the enemies of capitalism at the polls. Only the tumultuous upheavals of 1932 would eventually lead some politically active capitalists to withhold their usual contributions.

Because of these limitations big business remained weakly represented in the Reichstag. Its spokesmen amounted to small minorities even in the bourgeois parties. In the chamber as a whole, the proportion of in dustrial spokesmen fluctuated between 4 and 7 percent prior to 1930, when massive Nazi gains reduced the level still further.[23] Considerably stronger representation went to spokesmen of interest groups comprising large numbers of voters. Despite the continuing shrinkage of agriculture, agrarian spokesmen commanded a steady 14 percent of the seats in the parliaments of the 1920s.[24] Educated estimates of the number of deputies identified with civil service interests ran as high as a quarter of the chamber, counting all those, such as retired military officers and also clergymen, dependent on government pay or pensions.[25] Another large and potent block of deputies comprised spokesmen and members of the three trade union movements—socialist, Christian, and liberal. Because of the union membership of most SPD deputies, the union bloc carried far more weight than the number of out-and-out union officials in the chamber would suggest.[26]

Big businessmen also suffered many disappointments in their efforts to influence politics indirectly through control of the press.[27] Taking advantage of the setbacks which war and inflation had dealt to the independent entrepreneurs who previously owned most of the German press, big business interests gained control over many of the important newspapers of Germany during the early 1920s. Hugenberg, employing the funds entrusted to him by his wartime industrial backers, put together a media empire that encompassed a nationwide press service, scores of provincial newspapers, several large newspapers in Berlin, and, eventually, the country's biggest film studio. However, Hugenberg soon began to use the media he controlled for political purposes that, as already noted, sometimes clashed with the interests of the business community. During the inflation Hugo Stinnes, purportedly the richest industrialist in Germany, acquired a string of newspapers, including the *Deutsche Allgemeine Zeitung (DAZ)*, one of the major dailies in the capital. After the collapse of Stinnes' financial empire following his death in 1924, the government covertly subsidized the *DAZ* to prevent its acquisition by Hugenberg or by left-liberal critics of the government. In 1927, when public disclosures made continuation of this arrangement impossible, the *DAZ* secretly passed, through the intermediacy of Foreign Minister Gustav Stresemann, into the possession of a consortium of big business interests that included Ruhr industrialists, the major shipping firms of Hamburg and Bremen, and the large banks of Berlin. When the *DAZ* began to incur deficits with the onset of the depression, it received heavy subsidies from the Ruhrlade, as did a major conservative paper of the Ruhr, the *Rheinisch-Westfälische Zeitung* of Essen. The chief figure of the Ruhrlade, Paul Reusch, also exercised control, through the financial holdings of his firm, over three major newspapers, the *Münchner Neueste Nachrichten* in Munich, the *Schwäbischer Merkur* of Stuttgart, and the *Fränkischer Kurier* of Nuremberg. In 1929 IG Farben secretly invested heavily in a prestigious left-liberal daily that commanded a national readership, the *Frankfurter Zeitung,* thus bringing yet another major newspaper at least partially into the orbit of big business.

From the standpoint of the big businessmen involved, these efforts to shape public opinion by exercising ownership rights over newspapers yielded meager results. It proved difficult even to control the content of the papers in which they had invested. Much of the difficulty lay in the very nature of newspaper operations. The necessity for rapid, on-the-spot decision making under the pressure of inexorable deadlines effectively precluded sustained day-to-day dictation of news and editorial content by financial backers themselves heavily engaged in the demanding tasks of managing large business concerns and associational organizations. Big businessmen thus usually found themselves forced to depend on intermediaries in their dealings with the newspapers in which they had invested. The case of Hugenberg, who exploited his role as an intermediary to dictate, for his own political ends, the editorial policies of the papers he had acquired, illustrates the perils of such an arrangement. So do the experiences of Stinnes, Reusch, and the consortium that owned the *DAZ,* all of whom had to rely heavily on the editors of the papers over which they enjoyed financial control. To a striking extent, those editors could make use of their control over day-to-day operations to maintain an appreciable degree of independence from their papers' financial backers.[28] Another limitation of the effectiveness of big business' efforts to use the press lay in the paradox that overt or conspicuous control of the newspapers in question only diminished their effectiveness by discrediting them as capitalist mouthpieces in the eyes of much of the reading public they were intended to influence. This consideration dictated IG Farben's circumspect handling of the *Frankfurter Zeitung,* which left that paper's staff free from direct interventions in editorial policy. Big businessmen involved directly with the press occasionally sought to overcome these obstacles by issuing policy guidelines, planting editorials of their own devising, or securing the dismissal of an offending journalist.[29] They doubtless succeeded in disseminating a great deal of propaganda simply by keeping the papers they subsidized afloat. But these members of the business community who became involved with the press remained, almost without exception, dissatisfied with the results of their often extremely expensive ventures into journalism.

Efforts by big business interests to disseminate their viewpoints through the public relations agencies created by various industrial organizations during the 1920s proved similarly disappointing.[30] In general, only newspapers and magazines already well disposed to the business community drew on publications and handouts from these agencies. The major liberal newspapers, whose high-quality coverage of economic affairs gained them a wide readership in influential political and business circles, showed themselves impervious to such heavy-handed attempts at influence. Moreover, to the frustration of Germany's big businessmen, the prestigious and influential liberal press consistently assumed a critical stance toward the country's large-scale enterprises, trusts, and cartels. Even the *Frankfurter Zeitung,* despite Farben's holdings of its shares, steadfastly denounced the perils of large concentrations of capital—although avoiding explicit denunciations of Farben itself—and defended the principle of a pluralistic economy of many entrepreneurial co-equals.[31] Not surprisingly, most big businessmen regarded the press as a predominantly hostile force throughout the Republic.

Another disillusioning aspect of big business' involvement in politics lay in the unwillingness of politicians to stay bought. Hugenberg provided the most conspicuous and painful example. His doctrinaire intransigence and his frequent disregard for the immediate material interests of the business community progressively alienated those who had originally propelled him into politics. By the end of the republican era, increasing numbers of his former backers in industry were seeking—in vain—to remove him from the leadership of the DNVP.[32] Gustav Stresemann provided a less dramatic example of the same phenomenon.[33] He had entered politics during the Empire as a spokesman for finishing and consumer-goods industries. After the revolution he solicited support from the leaders of the business community for his new party, the DVP, assuring them it would defend their interests. Yet he, too, proved a disappointment since he vigorously resisted efforts to turn the DVP into a mere tool of big business. He pursued what most business leaders regarded as a foolhardy and perilous policy of collaboration with the Social Democrats, playing a leading role in bringing them into the cabinet in 1923 and again in 1928. Not until Stresemann's last years, when he became preoccupied with his duties as foreign minister and suffered from declining health, did he neglect his loosely organized party's affairs sufficiently to allow big business interests to increase the number of its deputies beholden to them. But until his death in 1929 he managed, if with mounting difficulty, to hold the party behind his policy of conciliation with the left.

Stresemann's party colleague and successor as foreign minister, Julius Curtius, provides another example of the unreliability of politicians from the viewpoint of big business. A lawyer with numerous industrial clients as well as close family links to one of Germany's largest mining, iron-producing, and manufacturing combines, the Gutehoffnungshütte, Curtius was elected a DVP deputy with big-business support. When he became economics minister in 1925, he was initially regarded as the business community's man in the cabinet, but he eventually attracted the ire of many of his former backers by making decisions based on his perception of the general welfare, as when he vetoed proposed increases in the price of coal.[34] By the time Curtius left the Economics Ministry in 1929 to succeed Stresemann at the Foreign Ministry, he had come to be viewed with suspicion and dislike in most big business quarters. A similar fate befell his short-term successor as economics minister, Paul Mold-enhauer, another DVP parliamentarian, whom IG Farben had recruited through election to its supervisory board.[35] Moved to the post of finance minister late in 1929, just as the first effects of the depression became felt, Moldenhauer quickly roused the ire of the business community through his attempts to devise a politically viable fiscal policy. In the spring of 1930, hostility on the part of industrial elements within his own party contributed to his decision to resign.

Contemporary observers, as well as most historians, have tended to attribute great effectiveness to the financial resources German big business brought to bear on politics during the Weimar Republic. The businessmen themselves saw things in a very different light. They became, in fact, fully aware of the multiple and formidable obstacles they encountered in attempting to transform their economic potency into political influence. While they readily agreed with those observers who saw the contest between money and votes as an uneven one, from their viewpoint the advantage lay not with superior financial resources but with superior numbers.

3. Assets

Although frequently frustrated in their attempts to influence electoral processes, to mold public opinion, and to manipulate politicians, Germany's capitalists did not see their worst fears about the new democratic Republic realized. After the abortive efforts of the post-revolutionary period, the issue of socialization receded. Instead of the economic decline many had predicted, a startling recovery took place during the second half of the decade. Once the hyper-inflation and the severe deflationary policies of stabilization had been surmounted, the economy regained lost ground at an astonishing pace. Despite territorial losses that substantially reduced the country's supply of numerous key natural resources and diminished its industrial capacity, and despite the overall contraction of economic activity in Europe, the industrial output and foreign trade of the Republic had outstripped those of the considerably larger Empire by the late 1920s. Although the rate of growth lagged well behind that of the pre-war era and unemployment remained high, an appreciable degree of prosperity nevertheless returned to Germany, bestowing sizeable profits on most of its capitalists. In addition, the men of big business found in the course of the 1920s that under the Republic they possessed quite a few notable assets, some of which they owed, at least in part, to developments since 1918.

Even the despised Versailles peace settlement, which so offended the nationalistic sensibilities of Germany's big businessmen, did not lack beneficial side-effects for them. The reparations issue proved especially important in that regard. By conjuring up the specter of a confiscation of physical assets by the victors, that issue added to the obstacles to socialization since it was widely assumed that the country's former enemies would respect the principle of private property more than that of public ownership.[1] The practicalities of reparation payments also quickly restored the influence of the business community in the now republican governmental circles of Berlin. Faced with a myriad of technical economic and financial problems, many international in scope, the leaders of the new state began early to rely on the expertise of prominent bankers and industrialists in devising responses to the victors' demands. Far from becoming outsiders facing a hostile official environment, some of the country's most prominent capitalists found their guidance in matters with far-reaching ramifications eagerly sought by the leaders of the new state.[2] The reparations issue strengthened the hand of the business community in domestic politics as well, giving to its economic interests a weight far in excess of the number of its parliamentary supporters. As republican officials soon discovered, the victorious powers preferred reparations arrangements that enjoyed at least the acquiescence of the industrial and banking circles that controlled the major sources of capital in Germany. Since the victors demonstrated a much less accommodating attitude about reparations schedules and modalities of payment in the absence of such acquiescence, even leftward-oriented cabinets found themselves forced to make important concessions to the political spokesmen of big business interests during the early years of the Republic in order to demonstrate that those interests stood behind at least the fiscal aspects of government policy. This need to placate foreign opinion with an eye to the reparations issue contributed significantly to the inability of the early republican governments to enact legislation that would have made large-scale enterprises shoulder a realistic share of taxes when the postwar inflation rendered the existing revenue system ineffective.[3] In the autumn of 1923 the collapse of German passive resistance to the Franco-Belgian occupation of the Ruhr after the Reich's default on reparations enabled the country's industrial leadership to undercut one of labor's principal revolutionary gains. Exploiting the need for increased production in order to meet the victors' demands for reparations, the industrialists brought the Berlin authorities to relax the prohibition against a workday of more than eight hours.[4] Big business did not exact all it had hoped to from the reparations issue, having failed to secure the return of the state railways to private ownership, for example. But Germany's capitalists, even as they denounced as exorbitant and unworkable the "tribute" extracted from their country by its former enemies, exploited the problems the reparations issue created within Germany to enhance their own position in the new postwar order.

The chronic inflation of the Republic's first half-decade also offered advantages to much of the business community, especially large-scale industry.[5] The depreciation of the currency not only drastically cut the real value of the taxes paid by firms but also gave them an opportunity to reduce the effective costs of their payrolls, which underwent upward adjustment at less frequent intervals, and thus more slowly, than did prices. In addition, the runaway inflation sharply diminished the indebtedness of those business enterprises whose managements chose to pay off old debts in greatly devalued paper currency. German industry in particular increased its assets dramatically at the expense of its creditors, including the banks that had traditionally controlled great quantities of investment capital. Extensive new investments took place at what amounted to public expense, as the national bank, the Reichsbank, permitted firms to borrow, at interest rates far below the currency's rate of depreciation, the money it frantically printed to keep pace with a spiraling demand for credit. Alert industrialists promptly plowed those loans into capital goods that retained value, then repaid the loans with depreciated paper marks, which the Reichsbank accepted at face value. The decline of the mark's value in relation to foreign currencies spurred this industrial expansion by increasing demand abroad for German exports, which sold at prices well below those of competitors. While big business did not, as some critics charged, control or determine the course of the great inflation, many of the country's big enterprises took abundant advantage of the hapless government policies that allowed the currency to lose value. Part of the business community helped to fuel the inflation, profited from it, evaded a meaningful share of taxation, and emerged with holdings enlarged at the expense of social groups less able to take advantage of the opportunities offered by rapid currency depreciation.

Following stabilization of the currency in late 1923, the non-socialist cabinets that reordered the economy adopted policies highly favorable to the business community.[6] Most vestiges of wartime *Zwangswirtschaft* disappeared. The government permitted employers to require longer hours of work in ever more industries. New tax laws gave favorable treatment to corporations and limited income taxes on the wealthy while increasing the excise levies that weighed most heavily upon the mass of consumers. Past business tax debts were scaled down or written off. The industries of the Ruhr received generous compensation from the state treasury in new, hard marks for the reparations deliveries in kind they had made after the collapse of passive resistance. The government effectively obstructed efforts on the part of aggrieved creditors to require prompt and equitable restitution from debtors, including the many industrial firms that had profited when inflation wiped out financial obligations set in fixed amounts of depreciating paper marks.[7]

Republican foreign policy proved, during the years of stabilization, to offer advantages for the business community. The Dawes Plan, which in 1924 provided for a regularization of reparations payments along lines laid down by an international committee of experts, produced a large infusion of foreign credit, especially from the United States. That development helped shield Germany's capitalists from the full impact of the deflationary monetary policies of the post-inflation period. With the help of credit from abroad much of industry embarked on what became known as the rationalization movement.[8] Production in many branches became concentrated in large units utilizing assembly lines and the management techniques pioneered by the American Frederick W. Taylor; sophisticated labor-saving machines automated and accelerated production; and the need for labor diminished. Trade policy benefited the business community, too. When, by the terms of the Versailles Treaty, Germany regained control over its tariffs in 1925, a rightward-oriented cabinet presided over adoption of a schedule of import duties that went far toward providing the protection demanded by an alliance of industrial and agrarian interests.[9] During the rest of the decade the government sought to placate protectionist interests even as it negotiated agreements with other European countries designed to reduce barriers to trade so as to increase German exports. By taking advantage of the business community's continuing need for loans and investments from western European countries and the United States, the Foreign Ministry under Stresemann managed to dampen opposition from that quarter to the policy of meeting reparations obligations and conciliating Germany's former enemies in the West, especially Britain and France. As the architect of German foreign policy throughout the period of stabilization, Stresemann sought to exploit Germany's robust economy to offset the military and political advantages of the victorious powers. As a result, the Foreign Ministry worked hand in hand with big business interests— particularly those in the key iron and steel industries—in an effort to coordinate public and private economic policy in such fashion as to yield the greatest foreign policy gains in the direction of a revision of the Versailles settlement. When the interests of business groups came into conflict with government policy, the latter prevailed, sometimes to the considerable chagrin of the businessmen involved. But at a time when Germany possessed no military force with which to back its aims in the international sphere, Stresemann and the other officials of the Foreign Ministry looked upon big business as a vital asset. The leaders of the business community could, on the whole, expect solicitous responses to their wishes from the side of the Wilhelmstrasse.[10]

Throughout most of the republican period, Germany's capitalists could also count upon support from the Economics Ministry.[11] After 1922 it remained, with only one brief interruption, in the hands of a succession of non-socialist ministers well disposed to the interests of the business community. Spokesmen of big business could count on a sympathetic hearing from its officials, who enforced most regulatory laws and drafted much national economic legislation. The requests of business interests did not always meet with approval, as those officials upheld the traditions of the proud, professional German civil service and showed themselves quite capable of rejecting entreaties from even the most imposing of petitioners. Still, a number of biases predisposed the men who ran the Economics Ministry to look favorably on big business. A product of the war, that ministry continued to bear the marks of its formative years, during which the imperial government chose, in the name of efficiency, to deal predominantly with large firms and the associational organizations they dominated. Its officials tended as well to prefer the seeming rationality of business "self-regulation" to the less orderly workings of a free-wheeling competitive marketplace. In considerable measure because of this orientation of its personnel and its domination by pro-big business ministers, the ministry undercut the Republic's one major piece of cartel-regulating legislation, enacted in 1923 while the Social Democrats participated in the cabinet. Under the benign scrutiny of the Economics Ministry, which had responsibility for enforcing the 1923 law, cartels continued to flourish in much of industry, limiting production and setting prices.[12] With the blessing of the ministry, huge trusts dominating key industries horizontally sprouted alongside the more loosely organized cartels, the most conspicuous being the IG Farben chemical combine formed in 1925 and the United Steel Works brought into being a year later by an amalgamation of some of the largest iron and steel firms in the country. Encouraged by both the Foreign and Economics ministries, German steel producers also played a prominent part in forming, in 1926, the international steel cartel, which regulated production and prices throughout western Europe. The acquiescence of the republican government to these combinations in restraint of trade permitted some of Germany's most prominent capitalists, despite their affirmations of the virtues of capitalism, to indulge—as during the Empire—a persistent aversion to competition as well as a penchant for controlling production and setting prices in an effort to ensure for themselves risk-free, guaranteed-profit markets.[13]

The leaders of big business could legitimately claim a share of credit for the striking improvement in their position during the 1920s. In terms of organization, Germany's industrialists enjoyed far greater cohesion than they had during the Empire. Wartime economic mobilization and curtailment of foreign trade mitigated differences of interest that had formerly produced repeated open clashes between domestically oriented basic industries and export-oriented manufacturers. Previously organized nationally into rival associations, these two groups cooperated closely during the war and the revolutionary period. In 1919 they joined, along with the young chemical industries, in a single industrial association, the Reichsverband der Deutschen Industrie.[14] Concerned primarily with national economic policies, the Reichsverband assumed a place alongside the nationwide league of industrial employer organizations, the Vereinigung der Deutschen Arbeitgeberverbände, created shortly before the war, and the venerable national organization of local chambers of industry and commerce, the Deutscher Industrie- und Handelstag.[15] Of these *Spitzenverbände,* or peak-associations, the most politically active, the Reichsverband, was dominated by big business interests. Well financed, elaborately organized, and led by prominent industrialists, it took up the task of heading the lobby for *die Wirtschaft.* Its officers enjoyed access to the highest officials of the Republic, including chancellors and presidents, and could present their arguments directly to them. Its professional staff bombarded cabinet members, ministerial officials, and parliamentarians with barrages of statistics and position papers designed to back up those arguments. The able and well-connected officials of the Reichsverband helped to mold the industrial spokesmen in the Reichstag, who sat scattered among the bourgeois parties, into a small but cohesive bloc that sometimes proved very effective at trading votes with other interest groups to build or block majorities on issues of importance to industry.[16] The Reichsverband itself served as a national forum where disparate industrial interest groups could seek to reconcile differences.

A general diminution of strife within the industrial camp facilitated these efforts at reconciliation on the part of the Reichsverband. In part, that development reflected a heightened solidarity among men who shared a sense of being on the defensive in a hazardous new political environment. To some extent it reflected as well the spread of large-scale, mixed enterprises with involvements sufficiently complex as to blur some of the lines that had sometimes divided industry into warring camps during the Empire, particularly on trade policy. But a major factor in the lessening of conflict within the industrial camp lay in the success of interindustrial diplomacy at arranging compromise settlements among branches of production with divergent interests. The most important of these settlements came about in the middle of the decade, when the major iron and steel producers reached the first of a series of secret accords, known as the AVI Agreements, with the principal users of iron and steel in manufacturing.[17] Those accords removed the objections of the chief domestic processors of those vital commodities to the higher prices that would result from protectionist tariffs, since the producers guaranteed them sizeable rebates on those portions of their iron and steel purchases they put into exported products. This enabled the manufacturers to compete in the world market by charging lower prices for the goods they sold abroad than for those they sold in the protected German market. As a result, they abandoned their traditional opposition to protective tariffs, at least until the depression upset these arrangements. In such ways, German industry closed ranks in response to the loss of the sheltered and privileged position it had enjoyed during the Empire.

The remarkable improvement in the fortunes of the business community during the 1920s owed more than a little to the disarray in the ranks of its chief adversaries, the country's socialists. War and revolution had left them irreconcilably divided politically by schisms that eventually hardened into fratricidal strife between the Social Democratic and Communist parties. During Weimar, big business no longer had to face a formidably united, steadily growing socialist movement of the kind that had seemed to menace the capitalist order before the war. In the larger of the socialist parties, the SPD, moderate revisionist, reformist elements held sway after the secession of its radical Marxist wing and the failure of attempts at socialization. They looked toward a gradual transformation of the capitalist system rather than its overthrow. A residual Marxist determinism led much of the intellectual leadership of the SPD and the closely affiliated socialist trade union movement to view positively the overall course of capitalist development in Germany. With optimistic fatalism men like Rudolf Hilferding, the ranking theoretician of the Weimar SPD, concluded that the "organized capitalism" they saw taking shape would lead inexorably toward an even more organized socialism if the capitalists were permitted to continue reshaping the economic order.[18] Even cartels and other price-fixing, production-regulating combinations seemed to represent positive portents of a rapidly decaying capitalist individualism and evidence of an emergent collectivistic trend.[19] Viewing themselves more as eventual heirs of the capitalist system than as it conquerors, the Social Democrats, under the leadership of men of Hilferding's outlook, offered little resistance, even while their party sat in the government of the Republic, to the domination of overall national economic policy—*Wirtschaftspolitik*—by non-socialist political forces well disposed toward the business community.

4. Liabilities

Despite their overall good fortune the capitalists of Germany found that the republican order not only left them with notable assets but also imposed certain distressful liabilities on them. The most onerous of these, from their point of view, came to be known collectively as *Sozialpolitik*.[1] In the context of the Weimar Republic that term stood for an array of welfare-state measures designed to improve the lot of wage earners. Building on the foundations laid by Bismarck, the republican regime expanded Germany's already elaborate system of social insurance, capping it in 1927 with a comprehensive national unemployment insurance program. Further measures regulated the hours and conditions of work, governed labor-management relations, and protected the interests of wage earners in still other ways. This expansion of *Sozialpolitik* enjoyed broad political support not only from the left but also from the middle and even the right of the political spectrum. As Count Kuno von West-arp, leader of the rightist DNVP, explained in 1927 to a disgruntled capitalist who had complained about his party's backing for an additional piece of legislation for *Sozialpolitik*, the matter boiled down to elementary political arithmetic: Three-quarters of the voters were wage earners.[2]

One aspect of Weimar *Sozialpolitik* came to attract the particular ire of the business community: the state system for binding arbitration of labor-management disputes.[3] Beginning in 1923, unresolved contract negotiations went before joint labor-management boards, each presided over by a government official who cast the deciding vote in the event of a deadlock. On the request of either of the two sides, the government arbitrator's verdict became legally binding for both. Even in the absence of such a request, he could impose a settlement. Coupled with the system of industrywide contracts instituted during the early years of the Republic at labor's insistence, the new system vested government arbitrators with enormous authority in the field of labor-management relations. Initially, management acquiesced in the new system, which provided a convenient means of compelling employees to work longer than eight hours, in line with the government's concessions to management following the collapse of passive resistance to the Ruhr occupation in 1923. After the stabilization of the mark, however, labor-management disputes centered increasingly on wages, as the trade unions sought, with growing success, to improve the remuneration of labor in a time of reviving prosperity. As judgment after judgment resulted in wage increases, the business community came to view the Labor Ministry, which administered the arbitration system, as hostile and biased. A mounting chorus of protest charged that Germany's capitalists were being forced to pay excessive wages that had little or nothing to do with the market forces that should determine the value of labor in a sound economy and still did so in countries with whose industries German producers had to compete.[4] *Zwangswirtschaft,* the coercive and—in the eyes of the business community—stultifying system of economic regulations imposed by the state during and immediately after the war, seemed to have survived at a crucial nexus in the productive process: the relationship between employer and employee.

Despite the objections of the business community, the Republic's *Sozialpolitik* continued to expand throughout the 1920s, so that by the end of the decade Germany had outstripped all comparable European countries in terms of the proportion of productivity allocated by the national government to social and welfare purposes.[5] At other levels of government a similar pattern prevailed as federal states and municipalities spent heavily on new public facilities and expanded their entrepreneurial activities in such fields as utilities to an extent that seemed a kind of "cold socialization" to much of the business community.[6] Defenders of *Sozialpolitik* contended that the country could well afford the taxes required to support this long overdue redistribution of its wealth among those whose toil ultimately created it. Real wages in Germany, they pointed out, lagged behind those in such competing industrialized countries as Britain, Sweden, and the United States. Trade union leaders argued that, by increasing mass purchasing power, *Sozialpolitik* would set off renewed industrial expansion in response to rising domestic demand.[7] But in the virtually unanimous opinion of the country's capitalists, the burgeoning *Sozialpolitik* of the Republic amounted to a burdensome, even crippling, intrusion of state power into economic affairs that contravened all sound principles and imperiled the country's recovery.[8] They attributed the country's continuing economic problems to ever accelerating increases in taxation and other levies for social and welfare purposes, which they contrasted with the much lower prewar levels. Citing the shortage of capital that kept German interest rates significantly higher than those in any other major country, they charged that heavy levies for *Sozialpolitik* impeded the capital formation needed to fuel the sort of large-scale investment that had made possible the sustained economic growth of the prewar era. Because of wartime capital losses and the burden of reparations, they argued, Germany simply could not afford a great increase in public expenditures for nonproductive purposes. Instead, as much capital as possible must be left in the private sector in order to spur investment. Wages pushed to artificial heights by the state arbitration system had, they contended, hampered investment by withholding capital from those in a position to put it to productive uses. They blamed the persistent unemployment of even the Republic's most prosperous years on the arbitration system, arguing that when some workers received wages higher than productivity warranted, others must lose their jobs since the money available for payrolls no longer sufficed for all. Pointing to Germany's prevailingly negative balance of trade, they warned that inflated wages handicapped efforts to export German goods by forcing up their prices while at the same time stimulating non-essential imports by increasing mass purchasing power at home. The economy had become neither capitalist nor socialist, big business critics charged, but instead a bastard construct they and the business press referred to variously as state socialism, pensioners' state, or trade union state.[9]

This indictment of Weimar *Sozialpolitik* could be, and was, challenged on many counts.[10] As so often in the case with disputes about economic matters, the data employed did not always meet the highest standards of accuracy or objectivity. For example, the business critics of the state arbitration system habitually exaggerated the magnitude of pay increases by comparing republican wage rates with those of the Empire on a nominal basis rather than in terms of purchasing power. They also omitted mention of the trend toward the welfare state even under the imperial government. Nor did they allow for the possibility that the labor-displacing effects of the postwar industrial rationalization movement might have contributed significantly to the disconcerting unemployment that marked even the relatively prosperous years of the late 1920s. The business indictment of the interventionist welfare state was not free of inconsistencies, either. Some of the same prominent capitalists who joined in the chorus of complaints about government assistance to work-ers showed no hesitancy about requesting state aid when their own en-terprises encountered difficulties.[11]

Despite all this, the business critics of Weimar *Sozialpolitik* cannot be dismissed altogether as hypocritical and biased. The costs of welfare state measures did in fact increase rapidly, a development that unavoid-ably led to a higher level of taxation and to significantly increased social levies on employers. During the second half of the decade, wages shot up dramatically as a result of state arbitration rulings in favor of labor. The criticism of republican *Sozialpolitik* from the side of the business community unquestionably raised legitimate questions about the effects on prices and capital formation of a rapid expansion of the welfare state and of state intervention in labor-management relations. Most of the professional economists of the day sided with the critics of *Sozialpolitik*.[12] A half-century later the research of a respected economic historian has led him, too, to conclude that republican *Sozialpolitik* went too far, too fast, outstripping productivity and acting as a brake on growth.[13] These complex questions seem bound to remain the subject of controversy for some time to come. But regardless of who was, or is, right, the important point here is that it became an article of faith among German men of big business that state intervention in socio-economic matters had during the republican era exceeded all sound limits. *Sozialpolitik,* they firmly be-lieved, lay at the root of many, if not most, of the nation's economic difficulties.

This negative assessment of republican *Sozialpolitik* prevailed among the executives of the great firms located in Weimar Germany's industrial heartland, the Ruhr. Those firms had developed during the nineteenth century mainly through their production of heavy industrial products, especially coal, iron, and steel. By the 1920s, however, diversification and vertical expansion had involved many of the Ruhr firms so deeply in the manufacture of finished products as to make anachronistic the desig-nation "heavy industry" generally applied to those firms at the time and ever since. To be sure, the Ruhr firms still owed their prominence in considerable measure to their output of coal, iron, and steel, but the heightened demand for these basic industrial commodities as a conse-quence of war and reparations served to conceal the slackening need for them in the maturing domestic economy of Germany. The Treaty of

Versailles had further heightened the prominence of the Ruhr by severing from the Reich some of its other major industrial regions. During
the Republic, industrial production centered to an unprecedented extent in the Ruhr, with the result that the executives of its great firms
loomed larger than ever before within the business community. These
executives rarely possessed a socially progressive outlook. Their enterprises still required large labor forces, despite increasing rationalization
and mechanization, so that wages and the terms of work bulked large in
their operations. These issues had given rise to a long history of labor-
management strife that stretched back into the imperial period and had
shaped the outlook of the Ruhr executives of the Weimar period. Their
adversarial attitude toward labor became further heightened during the
early years of the Republic, when the region became the focal point of
violent civil conflict. In response to the Kapp Putsch of 1920, armed
leftist bands had seized control of extensive portions of the Ruhr until
Freikorps units suppressed them in bloody and protracted street fighting.

Surrounded by an often sullen, sometimes openly hostile army of
manual laborers, the Ruhr magnates looked back nostalgically to the
days of the Empire, when they had ruled their industrial domains according to the *Herr-im-Hause* principle. They also looked back longingly
to the double-digit profits they had achieved before the war. By contrast,
they found the postwar profitability of their firms lagging behind those
of other industries, and they had no doubt what was to blame; they
blamed, of course, the actions of the republican governments.[14] The so-
called coal socialization law remained a particular source of resentment.
It left in private hands ownership of the mines that yielded that vital
extractive product of the Ruhr, but it restricted management's authority
by subjecting certain aspects of the coal industry's operations—most important, prices—to government regulation. *Sozialpolitik,* too, had reduced the decision-making freedom of the Ruhr industrialists. They
particularly deplored the legal restrictions placed on the length of the
workday, which made more costly their practice of operating blast furnaces and mines around the clock. They denounced as "political wages"
the labor contracts imposed by the state arbitration system. These wages,
they maintained, coupled with the added taxes and other levies for welfare-state purposes, had driven up production costs and hence the prices
of their products. Potential purchasers, themselves handicapped by the
shortage of investment capital attributable in large measure to the excesses of republican *Sozialpolitik,* had to curtail their orders. Their troubles, the men of the Ruhr complained, arose from misguided laws
enacted by politicians seeking the favor of the uninformed masses without any regard for the dictates of economic rationality. Critics of Ruhr
industry, however, had another explanation for these troubles. They
charged that the management of the big firms there had miscalculated
the demand for iron and steel and overexpanded their plants during the

postwar period. This had saddled their companies with burdensome excess capacity and debilitatingly high interest payments on large amounts of borrowed—as opposed to invested—capital. The industries of the Ruhr had not fallen victim to Weimar's *Sozialpolitik*, their critics charged, but had instead imposed their problems on themselves through faulty investment and financial decisions.[15]

The Ruhr industrialists remained impervious to such countercriticism, convinced as always that the sources of their problems lay with others. Grouped together in a small, compact area and linked by personal and organizational ties, they formed a distinctive clan within the business community, unified as much by common experiences, regional solidarity, and shared prejudices as by specific economic interests. Among other things, a strong aversion to organized labor and the SPD bound them together. They also mistrusted virtually everyone outside their *Revier*, or "preserve," as they referred to the Ruhr. This mistrust applied especially to the republican government in Berlin, but also to businessmen elsewhere and in other branches of production. The executives of the Ruhr accepted high offices in the industrial Reichsverband, but by the middle of the decade their leaders had begun to find that broad-based national organization too cautious, too conciliatory toward labor, and too friendly toward export interests for their tastes. To give greater weight to their own hard-line views, they developed a set of interlaced regional associations that enabled them to mount a lobby of their own even while maintaining the facade of industrial solidarity by remaining within the Reichsverband. The largest and most active of these regional associations was the venerable Verein zur Wahrung der Gemeinsamen Wirtschaftlichen Interessen in Rheinland und Westfalen, the so-called Langnamverein, or "long-name" association. Linked closely to the regional branch of the iron and steel producers' trade association, the Langnamverein became the chief forum and lobbying instrument of Ruhr industry, providing it with an institutionalized form of privileged access to the politicians and cabinet members of the Republic. During the latter part of the 1920s its hard-line voice increasingly became heard alongside that of the Reichsverband as the men of the Ruhr sought to marshal stronger resistance to those aspects of the republican era, especially its *Sozialpolitik*, which they deplored.[16]

In 1928 the Ruhr iron and steel industrialists resorted to direct action by defying an arbitration ruling.[17] When a government arbitrator, acting at the request of labor, declared binding a finding, rejected by management, which raised wages in those industries, the Ruhr industrialists refused to recognize that ruling on technical grounds and then summarily shut down their plants, locking out nearly a quarter-million workers. That act of defiance demonstrated the vulnerability of the republican government, which proved unable to enforce compliance with the arbitration ruling. But the iron and steel men saw their triumph become a Pyrrhic one when most of the rest of industry, including the Reichsverband, refrained from endorsing their action, which affected the livelihood of close to a million men, women, and children. So strong was the public reaction that two-thirds of even the normally pro-business DVP deputies voted with a Reichstag majority in favor of providing government aid for the victims of the lockout. In the end, the embittered iron and steel industrialists had to back down and accept a modified arbitration ruling, having been deprived of a decisive victory over the "trade union state" by what they saw as the subservience of politicians to the masses and the pusillanimity of most of their fellow businessmen.

In 1929 the Ruhr industrialists again broke step with the rest of industry by opposing the Young Plan, the new reparations settlement that would reduce Germany's annual payments but spread them over the coming fifty-nine years.[18] Despite reservations about Germany's ability to pay, the leaders of the Reichsverband tacitly assented to the plan. In their eyes its drawbacks were outweighed by the lower taxes and the continued flow of foreign credit they expected from it, as well as by the promised withdrawal of the last occupation troops from the Rhineland five years ahead of schedule. The Ruhr industrialists objected, however, to permitting political considerations to override what they saw as an unacceptable financial commitment on Germany's part and serious technical flaws in the mechanisms of the new plan. Balking at the government's obvious effort to yoke industry to the plan, they brought the Langnamverein to eschew any responsibility for its implementation. Their opposition certainly helped to fuel the nationalistic reaction against the new reparations settlement. But only a handful of Ruhr industrialists went so far as to endorse the unsuccessful effort, led by Alfred Hugenberg, to block the Young Plan by means of a plebiscite backed by an array of rightist groups that included Adolf Hitler's small party. When Albert Vögler of United Steel resigned from the German delegation rather than approve the plan, Ludwig Kastl, executive director of the industrial Reichsverband, took his place and affixed his signature to the final version.[19]

Although the contentious attitudes of the Ruhr industrialists did not typify the outlook of the business community as a whole, a new militancy became evident at the end of the decade even within the leadership ranks of the traditionally reserved Reichsverband.[20] A major factor in this was the rapidly growing deficit in the budget of the Reich government as a result of the recession that became noticeable early in 1929. The business community placed primary blame for the recession and the deficit on republican *Sozialpolitik*. The decline in economic activity, and hence in tax revenues, seemed to the men of big business the direct result of a capital shortage produced by exorbitant welfare levies and inflated "political wages." On the expenditure side of the deficit, business spokesmen pointed to the mounting outlays for welfare-state purposes, particularly for the national unemployment insurance system established in 1927. The regular income of that system, derived from levies imposed on employers and employed workers, quickly proved inadequate to cope with the sustained high unemployment of the late 1920s, so that the system became dependent on large subsidies from the national treasury. For a time the Young Plan seemed to offer hope of a way out by lowering the government's annual reparations payments. A widespread belief prevailed at first that the new plan would not only allow the government to cover its deficit but also permit tax reductions that would stimulate the economy by encouraging business investment. But as the international negotiations necessary to implement the plan dragged on beyond the end of 1929, the ever growing deficit rendered such hopes illusory. The leaders of the Reichsverband responded to this turn of events in December with a barrage of angry speeches and a manifesto bearing the alarming title "Rise or Ruin?"[21] No longer could one expect the Young Plan to solve the Reich's fiscal problems, they warned. Instead, Germany could hope to meet even its new, reduced reparations obligations only if it effected sweeping changes in its domestic policies to free as much capital as possible for investment in the private sector. To that end the Reichsverband set forth a long list of demands. Expenditures for welfare-state purposes must be cut; the bureaucracy must be pared down; state interference in labor-management disputes must be limited to cases that affected the most basic needs of the population; direct taxes, such as the graduated income tax and corporate taxes, must be reduced; indirect taxes on mass consumption items must be increased; a general overhaul of public finance at all levels must be undertaken to achieve the greatest possible economy in government. The time had come, the Reichsverband proclaimed, for an end for compromises with socialism. In effect, its leaders had proclaimed something less abstract: an end to their acquiescence in the tacit socio-economic compromise that had come to lubricate the parliamentary system of Weimar democracy through appeasement of labor by means of *Sozialpolitik* and management by means of *Wirtschaftspolitik*.

This growing dissatisfaction with government policies gave rise at the end of the decade to renewed criticism of the political institutions of the Republic. Well into the 1920s some prominent businessmen continued to express a longing to return to the "non-partisan" state of the imperial period.[22] But so long as the Republic seemed to accept capitalism, most reconciled themselves to living with parliamentary democracy.[23] The nearly half a decade of non-socialist rule that began with the SPD's departure from the cabinet in late 1923 made that accommodation easier. It became more difficult when, following impressive SPD gains in the spring Reichstag election of 1928, a Social Democrat, Hermann Müller, assumed the chancellorship of a great coalition cabinet that encompassed Stresemann's pro-business DVP on the right. Despite abundant evidence that the SPD had become a cautiously reformist representative for organized labor's interests, German capitalists seized on the remnants of Marxist rhetoric in its programs and pronouncements as proof that the "Reds" had not abandoned their aim of overthrowing capitalism. Particularly ominous seemed the espousal in 1928 by the socialist trade unions of a long-term program aimed at achieving "economic democracy." One tenet of that program called for an ever-increasing voice for workers in decision making at the company level.[24] Since that could come about only at the expense of the authority of management, "economic democracy" appeared to Germany's business leaders nothing other than socialization in new garb.[25] The strong presence of the SPD in the new government also posed a formidable obstacle to the curtailment, or even containment, of republican *Sozialpolitik*. Roughly coincidentally with the formation of the new cabinet, attacks on the parliamentary system began to appear with increasing frequency in the business press and in the statements of business spokesmen.[26] Yet, while the opinion was often ventured that too much authority lay in the hands of the popularly elected parliament and the parties that dominated it, no consensus prevailed about how to remedy that situation. One formula discussed in the business press called for the establishment, alongside the Reichstag, of a corporatist chamber with veto power over socioeconomic legislation. Composed of representatives of labor, management, and consumer interests from all sectors of the economy, such a chamber would, its proponents argued, act as a check on the wage-earning masses and foster greater realism about economic constraints. But corporatism struck many leaders of big business as a stultifyingly rigid system that might well benefit the more numerous small producers at the expense of the larger ones. Corporatist schemes thus found little in the way of a following in the business community. Except for the steel industrialist Fritz Thyssen, whose views were shaped by Catholic social thought, the proponents of corporatism were professors, journalists, and associational officials.[27] In any event, creation of a corporatist chamber would, like other schemes proposed as checks on the Reichstag— such as enlargement of the authority of the president or the finance minister—have necessitated the two-thirds majority in the national parliament required for constitutional alterations.[28] Given the composition of the Reichstag elected in 1928, which saw a resurgence of the SPD, such a majority lay far beyond the realm of feasibility.

It would be misleading to leave the impression that a tide of concerted opposition to the Republic swept through the business community at the end of the 1920s. The available evidence does not permit any such conclusion. One finds instead a complex pattern of attitudes, ranging from negative to positive. In September 1929 the influential liberal daily, *Frankfurter Zeitung*, detected a division in political outlook among the country's industrialists.[29] On the one hand, particularly in the Ruhr, mounting dissatisfaction with republican institutions seemed unmistakable. On the other hand, the Frankfurt paper found that elsewhere a widespread readiness for positive cooperation within the framework of the new state prevailed in the industrial circles. The paper saw as a challenge to disgruntled circles in the Ruhr the September meeting of the industrial Reichsverband in Düsseldorf, the seat of the Ruhr's principal association, the Langnamverein, rather than, as had been customary, in Berlin. At that meeting, which has attracted far less attention from historians than the one that produced the "Rise or Ruin?" manifesto three months later, the chairman of Germany's largest association of industrialists, Carl Duisberg of IG Farben, took an outspoken position with regard to the Republic. "The Reichsverband of German industry," he proclaimed at the plenum session in Düsseldorf, "cannot adopt a stand of opposition to, or aloofness from, the new state as it is today but must instead take its stand in that state and with that state." The very fact that Duisberg felt compelled to make such a statement reveals, of course, that allegiance to the Republic was far from self-evident in industrial circles. But after quoting Duisberg's words, the *Frankfurter Zeitung* drew, on the eve of the Great Depression, an optimistic conclusion about where the industrialists of Germany stood politically after a decade of democracy: "By far the larger part of industry has long since aligned itself with this positive outlook."

II
The Early Party, Businessmen, and Nazi Economics

1. Patrons of the Fledgling Movement

Early in January 1919, two weeks before the election of a National Assembly to draft the newly proclaimed Republic's constitution, the organization destined to replace the republican order was born in a back room of a Munich tavern. Initially named the German Workers's Party, Nazism began its tumultuous course as the creation of a collection of social misfits: skilled workers who could not accept the internationalism or the proletarian self-image of the socialist movement, marginal petty tradesmen, unsuccessful professional men, and embittered ex-servicemen without fixed occupations. Throughout its first year the tiny fledgling party remained only one of a score of similar *völkisch,* or racist, splinter groups that rejected both the new Republic and the old imperial system. It would very likely have fallen victim to the factionalism and organizational weakness that destroyed the rest of those organizations had not the Munich branch of German army intelligence ordered one of its agents, ex-corporal Adolf Hitler, to gather information on the party at a public meeting it held in September 1919. Impressed by what he heard, Hitler joined. By making use of his remarkable demagogic talents, he soon became the driving force in the young organization. In February 1920 he announced to a rally in a Munich beer hall the party's assumption of the name National Socialist German Workers' Party (Nationalsozialistische Deutsche Arbeiterpartei, or NSDAP). On that same occasion he proclaimed the twenty-five-point program that was to remain the party's official doctrine until its apocalyptic demise a quarter of a century later.[1]

The program adopted in February 1920 revealed much about the new movement.[2] Its opening sections left no doubt about the party's vehement rejection of the Versailles Treaty and commitment to uniting all Germans in Europe in a great Reich that would reign over a colonial empire. Next came a set of anti-Semitic planks that called for withdrawal of citizenship rights from the Jews of Germany, an end to Jewish immigration, and the expulsion of Jews if difficulties arose in feeding and providing work for the population. Then followed a set of demands that had a socialistic ring, including abolition of "incomes unearned by work" as well as the "thralldom of interest payments" for borrowed money, confiscation of all war profits, state takeover of "all (hitherto) already incorporated (trusts) firms," and "profit-sharing in the great industries." Further planks in the program called for an expansion of welfare-state measures to aid the disadvantaged, as well as corporatist vocational chambers to execute the law. The program stopped considerably short of espousing a socialist solution to Germany's economic and social problems, however. Particularly informative in this respect was a commitment to maintenance of a "healthy middle class." As steps toward that goal, the Nazis proposed to "communalize" department stores and rent them to small traders at low rates and also to direct state purchasing to small merchants. As this revealed, Nazism's anti-capitalism focused from the very outset on large-scale enterprises and spared smaller, old-fashioned businesses.

Despite the hostility of the 1920 program toward big business, rumors circulated during the early years of the decade, as the Nazis expanded their activities to other parts of southern Germany, to the effect that the NSDAP depended on financial aid from the country's great capitalists.[3] The plausibility of those rumors derived in part from the Nazis' unremitting bellicosity toward "Marxists," a term they used interchangeably with Bolsheviks and applied indiscriminately to moderate, reformist Social Democrats and to revolutionary Communists. Opposition to Marxism early on assumed a central place in Nazi propaganda. Party spokesmen placed the blame for the Empire's defeat in the war and the outbreak of the revolution on Marxist agitators and conspirators. They branded Marxists as traitors bent on subjugating the hard-working, honest but unsuspecting German nation—as they had already done in the case of the Russians—to an international conspiracy controlled by Jews who wrought their will as adeptly through socialist agitation as through stock-market manipulation. Because of the emphasis the Nazis placed on their anti-Marxism, the suspicion arose in some quarters that the growing size of the NSDAP could be attributed to subsidies from those who had the most to lose in the event of a Marxist revolution, Germany's big businessmen.

Hitler himself lent added plausibility to those suspicions by consorting with capitalists as early as 1922. These initial contacts were an apparently unforeseen by-product of efforts on his part to establish a branch of his Bavarian movement in Berlin. Among his ardent early followers in the capital was Emil Gansser, an eccentric chemist and would-be inventor who had worked at the Siemens electrical equipment firm until 1919. Gansser played an active role in the National Club of 1919, whose membership consisted mainly of army officers and senior civil servants but also included some businessmen. He arranged for Hitler to address the club on May 29, 1922, personally issuing the invitations.[4] According to the later recollections of some of those present, Hitler skillfully tailored his version of Nazism's goals for his conservative audience. He omitted any mention of his party's hostility toward big business or its programmatic commitment to socialistic measures. Instead, he emphasized the need to rescue Germany from the clutches of Russian Bolshevism and French vindictiveness. His party, he promised, would play a key role in the struggle for national emancipation. He portrayed the anti-Marxism of the traditional parties as ineffective, since those parties could not strike at the beachhead international Marxism had already established in Germany by virtue of its support among the country's workers. Only the NSDAP, he informed his listeners, offered the sort of economic, political, and social renewal necessary to turn the workers against their Marxist seducers. Only his party enjoyed complete freedom from the three other international forces that threatened Germany: Jews, Freemasons, and political Catholicism. Nazism stood ready to oppose terror with terror, to halt the inflation and moral decay that sapped Germany's strength, and to reverse the disastrous policy of attempting to fulfill the terms of the shameful Versailles Treaty, dictated to Germany by its victorious foreign foes.

Hitler's appearance before the National Club must have seemed a great success. His listeners rewarded him generously with applause, and he received an invitation to return, which he did, delivering a second talk the following month.[5] His Berlin speeches also brought him into touch with the industrialists of Bavaria, with whom he had previously had no contact. Among those who had heard him speak before the National Club was Hermann Aust, an elderly executive of a malt-coffee firm from Munich, who happened to be in the capital on a visit. Impressed by what Hitler had said, Aust arranged for him to meet informally with some members of the League of Bavarian Industrialists at the organization's Munich headquarters. That encounter led to a somewhat expanded meeting in the rooms of an exclusive Munich men's club, the Herrenklub, and then to a talk by Hitler before a larger audience of businessmen in the hall of the Merchants' Guild.[6] No record exists of what Hitler told his listeners in Munich on these occasions, but in all likelihood they heard much the same interpretation of Nazism's goals as had his Berlin audiences. When reports of these appearances by Hitler reached the press, the suspicions of journalists and other concerned observers that the self-appointed Marxist-slayer of Bavaria enjoyed the financial backing of at least part of German big business seemed confirmed.[7]

These suspicions did not wholly lack foundation, at least for a time. Hitler apparently made a very favorable impression upon some of those businessmen who in 1922 heard him deliver the version of Nazism he had tailored for conservative audiences. According to later testimony by Aust, some of those who had attended the talk at the Munich Merchants' Guild afterwards pressed money on him with the request that he pass it along to the Nazi leader. To be sure, Aust insisted that only modest sums had been involved.[8] Nor would anyone expect the industrialists of Bavaria to be the source of large amounts of political money since that part of Germany had remained relatively underdeveloped. And Hitler himself later complained that a tight-fisted petite bourgeoisie predominated in Munich.[9]

Berlin was a different story. The capital had taken the lead in numerous branches of manufacturing during the nineteenth century and still commanded this position in several of these in the early twentieth century. Hitler's efforts there in 1922 won him for a time the backing of one of Germany's more prominent industrialists, Ernst von Borsig. Although the Borsig family's venerable Berlin firm, which manufactured locomotives, boilers, and other heavy industrial equipment, had long since ceased to count among the largest in Germany, Ernst von Borsig continued to play a leading role in the nation's business community. A charter member of the governing presidium of the Reichsverband, he would in 1923 be elected chairman of the Vereinigung der Deutschen Arbeitgeberverbände, which defended the interests of industrial employers at the national level in labor-management matters. He had also served since 1919 as chairman of the north German branch of the principal organization of the steel industry, the Verein Deutscher Eisen- und Stahlindustrieller. In addition, Borsig had played a major part in the labor-management Zentralarbeitsgemeinschaft set up under the terms of the Stinnes-Legien Agreement of November 1918, serving as the first management co-chairman. In that capacity, Borsig appeared to identify himself with a moderate and conciliatory approach toward trade unions and workers in general. But his true political sentiments, which he concealed both because of his role in the ZAG and out of concern for his firm's heavy dependence on contracts from the republican government, lay with the far right. Like many big businessmen, he contributed money to both the DVP and the DNVP, but he also covertly channeled funds to such extreme rightist organizations as Eduard Stadtler's Anti-Bolshevik League, the Pan-German League, the Stahlhelm veterans' legion, various *Freikorps* units, and the "Black Reichswehr" (troop units covertly maintained by the army in excess of the limitations imposed by the Versailles Treaty).[10]

Borsig encountered Hitler when his private secretary, who had at his request attended Hitler's first talk at the National Club, persuaded him to attend the second.[11] What he heard left him greatly impressed, he later explained. He believed he had found in Hitler "a man who could, through his movement, make a contribution toward bridging the cleft between the social classes by reviving the national sentiment of the working class."[12] Through his secretary, Borsig arranged a private meeting with the Nazi leader in the course of which he asked how he might assist Hitler's efforts to extend his movement to Berlin. Not surprisingly, the answer involved money. In addition to contributing on his own, Borsig set out to raise funds among other Berlin industrialists to help Hitler establish a branch headquarters of the NSDAP in the capital. In this undertaking he had the assistance of Karl Burhenne, who administered workers' benefits for the Siemens electrical equipment firm, which had until the revolution championed the "yellow," or company, trade union movement.[13] An acquaintance of Emil Gansser, Burhenne also received a personal visit from Hitler. He, too, came away from that talk believing that National Socialism held out the promise of luring workers away from the Marxist parties. As a result, he joined Borsig in attempting to raise funds to help Hitler open a Berlin branch of the NSDAP. Neither joined the party, however.

During the Third Reich, when it would have been in their interest to claim the contrary, both Borsig's secretary and Burhenne conceded that these efforts to raise money for the Nazi cause during 1922 had produced disappointing results. This seems confirmed by the failure of Hitler's attempt to establish a branch office of the NSDAP in Berlin at that time. Burhenne explained his and Borsig's lack of success in terms of the hyper-inflation of that time and the distracting effects of the French occupation of the Ruhr, which, however, did not begin until January 1923.[14] According to Borsig's secretary, the industrialist managed to convince only a handful of the die-hard nationalists among his most intimate business associates to contribute funds to the NSDAP. The secretary attributed the undertaking's failure to the dominance in Berlin business circles of "non-Aryan" elements.[15] While Jews may have held more prominent business posts in Berlin than elsewhere, only a gross distortion could portray their influence as so pervasive as to preclude political activities displeasing to them on the part of non-Jewish businessmen in the capital. Why most Berlin businessmen refused to support the NSDAP in 1922 remains uncertain, but very possibly they may have gained an adverse impression of Hitler's movement even at that early date. Even Borsig may have soon revised his initially favorable opinion of the NSDAP since his efforts on behalf of that party seem to have been of only brief duration.[16] By the time Hitler returned to Berlin in the spring of 1923, Nazism's stock in the capital had fallen sharply. He was reduced to riding back and forth across Berlin in the back of a paneled delivery truck piloted by the eccentric Gansser, who drove him from one prospective donor to another. A companion who waited in the truck during the stops came away with the impression that these exertions produced meager results.[17] Not until 1925 did a branch of the NSDAP come into being in Berlin, and when it did, it sprang from humble origins, without aid from the capitalists of the capital city.[18]

Attitudes in business circles elsewhere toward the NSDAP may help to explain the resistance encountered by Borsig and Burhenne in Berlin. As early as 1921 Paul Reusch, a leading Ruhr industrialist, had formed a decidedly negative assessment of the new party. The Nazis began soliciting funds from Reusch that spring, knowing that his firm controlled one of the major manufacturing enterprises in Bavaria, the Maschinenfabrik Augsburg-Nürnberg. Reusch responded by indicating an unwillingness to become involved in Bavarian politics.[19] But when the manager of his firm's Bavarian subsidiary sent him a pamphlet that included excerpts from the NSDAP's program, he angrily informed the Nazi spokesman who had asked him for funds that he could not comprehend how anyone could support a movement which, "along with a great deal of other nonsense in its program demands the nationalization of all incorporated business enterprises." He had notified his Bavarian manager, Reusch tersely informed his Nazi correspondent, "that we have no reason to support our own gravediggers."[20] A similar outspokenly negative verdict was rendered on Nazism in an editorial published in the organ of the association of Württemberg industrialists in late 1922. No educated and politically aware person could accord sympathy, the editorial stated, to a movement that displayed such poverty of political ideas, such economic quackery, and such crude behavior. Industry, in particular, could not countenance an appeal to resolve political differences by a resort to force, since that would only add to industry's already enormous difficulties.[21]

In spite of such negative responses, Hitler and other Nazi spokesmen continued to seek financial aid from businessmen down to the abortive beer hall putsch of 1923.[22] But even those businessmen in the industrial North who were ideologically attuned to National Socialism did not always take the small, struggling southern German movement seriously. Such was the case with Ludwig Roselius, heir to a firm in Bremen that had become wealthy by processing and marketing a highly successful brand of low-caffein coffee, Kaffee Hag. Roselius enjoyed close ties to *völkisch* circles and took an active part in promoting "genuine German" art and architecture.[23] In 1933, by which time he had become an enthusiastic adherent of Nazism, he recounted in a memoir volume a visit he had received from Hitler eleven years earlier. Hitler had left no doubt about the purpose of his visit: "I am building a party," Roselius reported his announcing. "Do you want to help me?" To Roselius's chagrin in

1933, he admitted having replied negatively. He had explained to his visitor, he wrote, that he could accomplish more on his own than in a party. But Roselius's account suggests strongly that in 1922 he had taken Hitler for a mere dreamer.[24] How many other men of commerce and industry reacted similarly remains unknown, but, aside from Borsig, there is no solid evidence of any notable businessman having aided the NSDAP prior to 1923. This was certainly not from want of effort on the part of Hitler and other Nazis, who showed little compunction about soliciting funds from the very capitalists they castigated in their speeches and threatened with their radical program of 1920. In what was to become a familiar pattern, when confronted with allegations of receiving financial aid from business sources, Hitler heatedly denied everything, branding such reports as "filthy lies."[25] Obviously, he recognized early that the establishment of a link between his movement and big business would cost him valuable support among his anti-capitalist followers.

A fresh wave of rumors about alleged big business subsidies for the NSDAP swept through the leftist press during the summer and autumn of 1923. At that time the Weimar Republic underwent one of its most severe crises, as runaway inflation, foreign occupation of Germany's industrial heartland in the Ruhr, separatist movements in the Rhineland, and defiance of federal authority by the Bavarian government threatened to set an early end to the Republic. Extremism, and along with it the Nazi party, flourished. In some quarters, the suspicion again grew that the Nazis must owe their obviously expanding resources in considerable measure to the country's capitalists. Not surprisingly under the circumstances, fingers began to point accusingly at the greatest German capitalist of all, Hugo Stinnes.[26] Having begun his business career by expanding the family shipping firm in the Ruhr, Stinnes had moved into coal and steel before the war and had then exploited the great inflation to acquire a huge conglomerate of widely disparate enterprises. By 1923 he commanded vast amounts of capital. Yet despite Stinnes's inclination toward an authoritarian solution to the political crisis of 1923, no evidence has ever been produced to implicate him or his subordinates in aiding the NSDAP or Hitler.[27] Indeed, Hitler's denunciations of Stinnes, in speeches and in print, for having spread the preposterous notion that Germany's problems could best be solved by economic rather than political measures, render the rumors of support by Stinnes for the NSDAP implausible.[28]

Although leftist allegations about aid from Stinnes have proved groundless, the Nazis probably benefited in 1923 from the largesse of another Ruhr industrialist, Fritz Thyssen. The restless and frustrated fifty-year-old heir of an octogenarian titan of the steel industry who refused to relinquish control of the family firm to his son, the younger Thyssen channeled his energies increasingly into politics in the early 1920s.[29] He had become an implacable foe of the Republic at the very outset as a consequence of being seized, along with his father and other Ruhr industrialists, in December 1918 by worker vigilantes and transported under guard to Berlin, where he and the others were imprisoned briefly under harsh conditions until charges that they had collaborated with the French were dropped. Staunch Catholics and hitherto loyal supporters of the Center Party, the Thyssens moved to the right, shifting their allegiances to the DNVP. When the French occupied the Ruhr in early 1923, Fritz Thyssen defied the occupation authorities, who responded by arresting him, convicting him before a court-martial, and fining him heavily. Returning home as something of a popular hero, he lent support to a terrorist paramilitary organization in the Ruhr until the German army quashed it. Then, in October 1923, he traveled to Munich to aid the rebellion against the Republic taking shape there. At that time, according to an often cited passage in Thyssen's memoirs, he donated the appreciable sum of 100,000 gold marks to the NSDAP. That passage is of dubious authenticity, however, since Thyssen's memoirs were ghostwritten.[30] In the light of all the available evidence, it seems unlikely that Thyssen gave any such sum to the Nazis. Another passage in the same paragraph of his purported memoirs explicitly states that Thyssen made his contribution not to Hitler but to General Erich Ludendorff, then by far the most prominent figure in rightist anti-republican circles in Munich, "to use it as best he could." In the interviews with his ghostwriter prior to preparation of the memoirs as well as in responses to interrogations after World War II, Thyssen consistently held to that version, maintaining that he had given his money to Ludendorff rather than to the still comparatively obscure Hitler.[31] The general in all likelihood allocated some of Thyssen's contribution to the Nazis, but he stood at the head of a sizeable coalition of rightist groups and could hardly have afforded to favor one to the exclusion of the others.

If, as clearly seems the case, the money that reached the NSDAP during its early years from prominent capitalists such as Fritz Thyssen and Ernst von Borsig did not suffice to meet the material needs of a growing party that by the fall 1923 could lay claim to more than 55,000 members, where did Hitler and his followers get their money? No precise answer to that question will ever be possible since whatever records the party kept were destroyed at its dissolution following the attempted Munich putsch.[32] But a variety of evidence provides a reasonable basis for reconstructing the sources of the party's funds. Virtually all those who have looked into the matter agree, for example, that in its early years the NSDAP received aid, in the form of both money and equipment, from the Bavarian component of the Republic's army.[33] Other funds probably came from the Pan-German League, which, although in its declining phase, still commanded a sizeable following, although not in big business circles.[34] Some of Hitler's well-to-do early followers also provided funding for the young party. Among them one finds a motley assortment of persons that included obscure noblemen, White Russian émigrés, Swiss sympathizers, and a wealthy widow from Finland.[35]

In the very early stages of the party's development, when modest sums of money could mean the difference between survival and extinction, the party repeatedly received aid from some of Hitler's close associates. One of these, the elderly racist poet and publicist Dietrich Eckart, a luminary in reactionary Munich literary and artistic circles, provided both funds of his own and contacts with other benefactors.[36] During the period of hyperinflation, money also came from Ernst Franz Sedgewick ("Putzi") Hanfstaengl, the quasi-bohemian offspring of a German-American family of art dealers, who had studied at Harvard and operated the family gallery in New York throughout the war, thanks to highly placed Harvard acquaintances. In 1921 Hanfstaengl returned to Munich, where he fell under Hitler's sway and made available to the Nazis some of his dollar resources, the purchasing power of which was enormously increased by the precipitous decline in the value of the mark. According to Hanfstaengl's memoirs, his contributions to the party were not always wholly voluntary.[37] On one occasion, he recounted, he came to the rescue of the *Völkischer Beobachter* at the height of the great inflation by extending to the party newspaper a loan in American dollars which he never succeeded in getting repaid.[38] A further source of coveted foreign currency during the inflation was another of Hitler's early associates, Kurt Ludecke, a footloose young man who had accumulated some foreign assets by buying and selling various commodities during travels throughout Europe and North America.[39] Because of the extraordinarily favorable exchange rates during the inflationary period, Ludecke could convert those relatively modest assets into large amounts of German currency. This enabled him, among other things, personally to recruit, outfit, and feed a Nazi storm trooper unit.[40] In addition, Ludecke traveled to Italy in the summer of 1923 and to the United States the following winter in vain efforts to obtain financial aid for the NSDAP from Mussolini and Henry Ford.[41]

A number of businessmen also figured among the early and loyal patrons of the party, but those known to have aided the NSDAP significantly did not stand, by any stretch of the imagination, in the forefront of Germany's highly industrialized and cartelized capitalism. They came instead from much humbler backgrounds. Scrutiny of their livelihoods reveals a collection of obscure Munich tradesmen, artisans, and retail merchants; a wealthy farmer who had married into a brewer's family in a northern Bavarian village; the proprietor of a family firm that processed and purveyed cooking oils and spices in Augsburg and the surrounding region; the operator of an underwear manufactory in a provincial Swabian town; and one of the owners of a family firm that processed inexpensive brands of ersatz coffee in Ludwigsburg, not far from Stuttgart.[42] Not all of these minor business patrons simply gave money to the

NSDAP. Some extended credit when the party's own resources ran out, which could prove vitally important, as in the case of the printers who produced Nazi newspapers, propaganda tracts, and posters.[43] Others donated from their merchandise, including furniture for party offices and other badly needed supplies. Still others loaned the NSDAP automobiles and trucks to transport its uniformed legions to rallies.[44] Some of the aid from these small businessmen amounted to something short of pure donations. The heir to the Ludwigsburg coffee processing works, for example, provided Hitler with 60,000 badly needed Swiss francs in 1923—when hyperinflation had rendered the mark all but worthless—but only against the security of jewelry and art works given to the Nazi leader by female admirers.[45]

These female admirers have occasioned considerable confusion about the sort of people who aided the NSDAP financially during its early years. In many accounts, Edwin Bechstein and Hugo Bruckmann receive prominent mention as businessmen who stepped forward to subsidize the Nazis at that time. In actuality, both men came into Hitler's orbit only by virtue of their wives' social lives. The two women, Helene Bechstein and Elsa Bruckmann, were in the early 1920s well into middle age. Comfortably fixed materially and hungry for entrée to the world of arts and letters, they presided when in Munich over competing salons frequented by intellectuals and aesthetes drawn from the Bavarian capital's reactionary high society. Jealous of each other on many counts, they shared a devotion to the operas of Richard Wagner that entitles them to the status of archetypical wealthy Wagnerians. When they discovered, through mutual acquaintances, an intense young Austrian who could expound as eloquently about the master of Bayreuth as about the Versailles Treaty, the Bolshevik Revolution, and countless other political topics, both women became fascinated by him.[46] Hitler began receiving invitations to their salons, where they took pleasure in displaying him as an exotic conquest from the menacing lower orders of society. From all accounts, the habitués of their circles found it titillating to attend a gathering where a fellow guest among other things, would upon arriving hang on the coatrack, alongside his coat and hat, a whip and holster belt complete with pistol.[47] The jealous competition of the two women for Hitler's attentions sometimes assumed comic dimensions, as when Frau Bruckmann indignantly denounced reports that Frau Bechstein had given Hitler the whip he carried, claiming that she herself had presented it to him, quite unaware that Hitler had received whips from both his patronesses, allowing each to believe that he possessed only hers.[48]

Because their wives made Hitler a frequent guest, Edwin Bechstein and Hugo Bruckmann came into contact with Hitler and soon became sympathizers with his cause. Both undoubtedly extended him material assistance, but neither was in a position to dispense large sums of money for political purposes. Both were men of personal wealth, in large measure inherited, who lived in the style of the nineteenth-century haute bourgeoisie. But their financial resources shrank to insignificance when compared to those generated by the giant enterprises of modern German industry, commerce, and finance. Bechstein, along with several brothers, had inherited a well-established Berlin piano factory that placed the family name on quality instruments exported around the world. But despite its renown, the Bechstein firm remained a very small operation by the standards of twentieth-century German industry, dependent as it was on skilled handicraft labor. Not until 1923 did the owners convert it from a purely family enterprise into a joint stock company, and three years after that its capitalization stood at only three million marks.[49] Bechstein's circumstances thus set limits to his political largesse. In 1924 Frau Bechstein testified that her husband had repeatedly helped Hitler deal with the financial difficulties of the *Völkischer Beobachter*.[50] But according to Hanfstaengl's memoirs, he and Hitler discovered that Bechstein did not disburse money with abandon when Hitler dwelt at length on the financial plight of his movement during an evening they spent at the Bechsteins'.[51] This obvious appeal for funds drew a blunt reply from his host: The Bechstein firm had its own problems, and no money was available at that time, although circumstances might perhaps become different later on. Hanfstaengl reports that he himself then ventured the observation that the party could survive for several months on the money that could be obtained at a pawnshop merely for the jewelry Frau Bechstein wore that evening. That suggestion may have led Frau Bechstein to bestow on Hitler the valuable art objects she told of giving him when she was interrogated in the wake of his failed putsch of 1923.[52] She visited him during his imprisonment, and the Bechsteins remained loyal to him after his release in 1924. At that time Edwin Bechstein helped to re-launch Hitler's political career by countersigning a bank loan of 45,000 marks to him, most of which Bechstein eventually had to make good on since Hitler repaid only a part of that sum.[53]

Like Edwin Bechstein, Hugo Bruckmann commanded only limited financial resources. One of several heirs to a Munich publishing house, he had in 1917 struck out on his own, establishing an independent publishing venture that he operated until 1930, when the depression apparently forced him to liquidate it and rejoin the family firm.[54] The Bruckmann family publishing house registered a capitalization of only 2.8 million marks in the prosperous year of 1926, and Hugo Bruckmann's independent venture was, from all indications, considerably smaller than that.[55] How much direct material aid Bruckmann extended to Hitler remains uncertain, but one acquaintance later reported that in the late 1920s Bruckmann helped Hitler acquire a lease on a luxurious apartment in a fashionable district of Munich, which lent the Nazi leader an aura of respectability, by guaranteeing the landlord that he would make good on any default by Hitler on rental payments.[56] If that story is true, Bruck-mann's material involvement was minimal, but Hitler benefited signi-ficantly from it. As with Bechstein, Bruckmann's aid went to Hitler personally rather than to the NSDAP; both sought to further a protégé of their wives as much as a political cause.

Despite their limited material resources, the Bechsteins and the Bruckmanns could bestow on Hitler gifts less tangible than money but nevertheless of indispensable value for an aspiring politician of obscure and socially limited background. As a guest in their salons and at their dinner tables, he mastered the basic canons of polite appearance and demeanor sufficiently to enable him later to move with confidence in the uppermost reaches of society and politics.[57] At the urging of Frau Bech-stein and Frau Bruckmann he abandoned the tattered suit of clothes made from an old army uniform that he habitually wore during the early phase of his political career. They introduced him to fashionably tailored blue pinstripe suits, tuxedos, and patent leather shoes. At their tables he learned how to deal with exotic dishes such as artichokes, which until then had mystified him. In addition to initiating him to these ar-cana of the upper classes, the Bechsteins and Bruckmanns opened a whole new stratum of society to their plebeian protégé, who had pre-viously moved almost exclusively in the circles that frequented Munich's coffeehouses and beer halls. At their salons he met professors, writers, established artists, and noblemen.[58] At Frau Bruckmann's he enlisted for his cause the future Nazi youth leader Baldur von Schirach, who in turn won over to Nazism another young aristocrat, Prince Friedrich Christian of Schaumburg-Lippe. The presence of such men in the party unquestionably lent respectability to the NSDAP in the eyes of some con-servative Germans. The Bechsteins first introduced Hitler to the Wag-ner family in Bayreuth, thereby giving him entrée to the network of contacts among the Wagnerians of Germany, which likewise enhanced his stature as a plausible political leader.[59] Within a year his introduction to the Wagner family brought him a valuable endorsement from the bard of Valhalla's son-in-law, Houston Stewart Chamberlain, the aging prophet of Germanic racist doctrine.[60] At Frau Bruckmann's home Hitler was to gain his first opportunity to speak at length with a major industrialist from the Ruhr.[61] At a crucial juncture in January 1933 the Bechsteins' social connections would enable him to meet secretly at their Berlin residence with a key figure in the military establishment in his successful effort to gain its acquiescence to his appointment as chan-cellor.[62]

Hugo Bruckmann also helped Hitler and his movement to gain re-spectability by playing a leading role in a Nazi front organization de-signed to make inroads into conservative artistic and intellectual circles, the Kampfbund für Deutsche Kultur, founded in 1927 purportedly to combat alien influences on Germany's cultural life. Eschewing any formal ties with the NSDAP, which it could do by virtue of Bruckmann's not belonging to the party, the Kampfbund recruited members from the cultural elite and repeatedly espoused Nazi positions in the heated artistic and literary controversies that raged during the late Weimar period. By the end of the decade the Kampfbund was holding public meetings in the main auditorium of the University of Munich at which such well-known academicians as Professor Othmar Spann of Vienna, a proponent of corporatism as an alternative to capitalist democracy, spoke to large audiences.[63] Although Bruckmann served as an officer of the Kampfbund, he made clear his inability to remedy its chronic financial difficulties.[64] Still, his conspicuous role in the organization doubtless lent it respectability and led others to join and thus come under the sway of Nazism.

Far more important than whatever direct or indirect material assistance Hitler received from his wealthy Wagnerian patrons, or from well-to-do persons to whom they introduced him, was the respectability their social sponsorship bestowed on him. They made him *gesellschaftsfähig*, acceptable to polite society. This played an invaluable role in transforming him from an outlandish, awkward, and gauche figure from the lower strata of society into a man eligible for admission to the upper reaches of politics and, ultimately, for high state office. The fascination Adolf Hitler exerted on his two ardent female admirers, Helene Bechstein and Elsa Bruckmann, brought him an advancement in his quest for power of a sort difficult, if not impossible, to achieve with mere money.

Overall, large monetary contributions from patrons seem to have played a minimal role in the growth of Nazism during its early years. Contrary to the assumptions of many journalists, the NSDAP did not depend as heavily on large-scale subsidies as did the traditional non-socialist parties of the Republic. Early on, the Nazis adopted the Social Democrats' practice of enforcing the regular collection of dues from their members. Even though that system was at first less efficiently managed than in later years, it yielded a steady source of income that was divided between local units and the party's headquarters, at least until inflation made the value of even huge amounts of currency problematical.[65] During the hyper-inflation of the spring of 1923, the party reported that a fund-raising campaign to mark Hitler's birthday had yielded eleven million marks.[66] The party raised still more money by frequently having its adherents subscribe to interest-free loans, which in time of inflation amounted to gifts to the party.[67] Many members also aided their party by donating long hours of volunteer labor, providing services and equipment for which the traditional parties had to pay cash or go into debt.[68] Very early in their party's development, the Nazis began using mass rallies as a means of raising funds, charging for admission and then passing cups and hats after their orators, especially Hitler, had whipped up the passions of their listeners. The readiness of people of modest means to donate what were for them sizeable sums of money bordered, in the opinion of one observing police agent, "on the unbelievable."[69] Another reported seeing money collected "by the bushel" after a Nazi rally.[70] Clearly, Hitler and his associates brought a message for which many humble people were willing to pay, even at considerable material sacrifice for themselves. Far from depending on subventions from Germany's capitalists, Nazism was in its early years a genuinely populistic movement that took root and grew into a full-fledged political movement because of the fanatical devotion of its rank-and-file followers.

2. The Cacophony of Nazi Economic Policies

By 1924 the NSDAP had grown into a full-blown political party of national significance. In the May Reichstag elections of that year, a slate composed of its candidates and those of a northern German *völkisch* organization tallied nearly two million votes and captured thirty-two seats. More than half of those votes melted away in a second national election held that December, so that the Nazi-*völkisch* bloc retained only fourteen seats in the chamber. In 1928 the Nazis, who had in the interval bested or absorbed their *völkisch* rivals, won only twelve Reichstag seats in an election held at the height of the Republic's brief period of stability and prosperity. But even during Nazism's lean years, its presence in the national legislature made its economic policies a matter of interest for those concerned with such questions. Anyone who attempted to establish where the NSDAP stood on the vital issues of Germany's economic life faced a daunting task, however. Despite the NSDAP's authoritarian structure, it spoke on economic affairs with a multitude of voices. And far from attaining anything approaching unison, those voices proclaimed a dissonant array of positions on even some of the most basic issues of economic policy.

Early on, prominent figures in the party sought to cast light on its principles and aims by publishing their interpretations of the twenty-five-point program of 1920 and by elaborating further on the party's position on important issues, including economic policy. The first of these commentaries, a forty-five-page pamphlet that appeared in late 1922 or early 1923, came from the pen of Alfred Rosenberg, would-be ideologue of National Socialism and editor of the party newspaper, *Völkischer Beobachter*. Promising in its title to reveal the "nature, fundamental principles, and goals" of the NSDAP, Rosenberg's pamphlet conveyed the impression of being party endorsed. The author adorned it with a dedication to Hitler and explained in his foreword that he had written the pamphlet to counter false reports about National Socialism until a forthcoming publication by the party leader appeared.[1]

Readers of Rosenberg's commentary may well have concluded that one such false report involved a firm commitment on the part of the NSDAP to the word "socialist" in its name. Rosenberg avoided using that word except in the neutralizing compound *Nationalsozialismus*. He stripped the second part of that compound of any economic specificity, defining it by means of a ponderous circumlocution as "the recognition that merely extending social charity to those who help create and build a state does not suffice, but rather that the state has the duty to exercise a supervisory function over all those things that each of its members needs."[2] Rosenberg then proceeded to circumscribe that supervisory function by sharply qualifying the most anti-capitalist tenet of the NSDAP's 1920 program, Point 13, which called, in garbled language, for a state takeover of "all (hitherto) already incorporated (trusts) firms." That plank should not be construed, Rosenberg explained, to mean a commitment to "full socialization," a pernicious doctrine that spelled death to all "creative entrepreneurship." Point 13 merely indicated National Socialism's determination to "fight" and "break" those forces that obstructed free and creative enterprise by establishing monopolies. Foremost among those forces bulked the "world trusts" controlled by a powerful network of international bankers and stockbrokers, ultimately masterminded by a worldwide conspiracy of Jews.[3] Nazi trust-busting, as expounded by Rosenberg, tended to become virtually synonymous with anti-Semitism. For him, economic problems reduced easily to questions of "race."

Hard-working, honest German industrialists had little to fear from Rosenberg's brand of National Socialism. The Nazis in no sense opposed "inventive, productive entrepreneurship" or Germany's "national industry," he reassured his readers.[4] Not even the growth of large firms disturbed Rosenberg. National Socialism, he explained, refused to regard enterprises as evil simply because of their size since in many instances large firms could provide the people with needed goods at the lowest cost. What mattered was not the size of a firm but rather whether it was being employed in the interests of the nation. If German businessmen met that criterion, Rosenberg had no objections to their making millions in profits; only if they did not measure up to that rather vague standard would they have to contend with the wrath of a Nazi state.[5]

While much of Rosenberg's commentary might allay the concerns of the business community about Nazi economic policy, other passages in that publication could only heighten those concerns. Throughout his pamphlet Rosenberg displayed an implacable hostility toward bankers and stockbrokers, to whom he attributed virtually all economic ills. Whereas he softened the 1920 program so far as it concerned other kinds of businessmen, he went far beyond that program with regard to those two groups. A Nazi government, he announced, would immediately transfer to state ownership Germany's banks and stock exchanges.[6] Rosenberg did not altogether spare the rest of big business, however. His pamphlet included an endorsement of the 1920 program's commitment to profit sharing in large enterprises.[7] Even more ominously, except for his rejection of "full socialization," Rosenberg nowhere set limits to the authority of a Nazi state to intervene in the private sector to ensure that German businesses and businessmen served what the NSDAP regarded as the national interest.

Within a year of the publication of Rosenberg's pamphlet, a second commentary on the programmatic aims of Nazism appeared in the form of a two-hundred-page book by Gottfried Feder.[8] A Bavarian construction engineer, Feder had, after a moderately successful professional career, found his way to the Deutsche Arbeiterpartei before Hitler. Through earlier published tracts, he had gained a deserved reputation as a radical fanatic on monetary and credit questions. One of his slogans, "Breaking the Thralldom of Interest Payments," occupied a prominent place in the NSDAP's program of 1920. His commentary, which appeared at the time of the abortive beer hall putsch of November 1923, gave the appearance of being even more official than Rosenberg's. It was the first book issued by the party's own publishing house, the Eher Verlag, and it opened with a statement by Hitler in which he described it as the "catechism" of the NSDAP's programmatic declarations. In a conventional party, Feder's book would have signaled a fundamental policy departure, for it omitted the twenty-five-point program of 1920, which Feder dismissed as "the old program."[9] In its place, Feder set forth a thirty-nine-point program of his own devising which eliminated some tenets of the original program, altered others, and added totally new planks.[10] The NSDAP was not a conventional party, however. Despite the official trappings of his 1923 book, the twenty-five points of 1920 continued as the official program of the party. Indeed, when Feder himself published, in 1927, a second, different gloss on the party's aims, he included both the original twenty-five points and his own thirty-nine points of 1923, without any explanation of the relationship between those two frequently divergent programs.[11]

Although Feder's 1923 commentary contained radical commitments, such as his pledge that a Nazi government would at once take over the Reichsbank and other banks of issue, he shared Rosenberg's aversion to the word "socialism." He tempered his anti-capitalist strictures by invoking a distinction long popular in radical rightist circles. The same capital, Feder explained, became something very different when it was employed productively on the one hand or exploitatively on the other. If they remained true to their heritage, Germans used capital productively, to meet the needs of their fellow countrymen, not to register profits. Jews, by contrast, always used capital exploitatively, as a means to accumulate further wealth and transform it into power.[12] Like Rosenberg,

Feder attributed most of Germany's economic ills to foreign forces he variously labeled as "loan capitalism," "stock-market capitalism," or "world usury capitalism," behind all of which he saw Jews. His commentary accorded the highest priority to protecting and preserving the *Mittelstand* of "self-employed persons, especially in medium and small enterprises."[13] To the wage earners of Germany he promised no fundamental reform of the capitalist system. Instead, he held out the prospect of a gradual amelioration of the workers' material lot through expanded welfare-state measures and enhanced opportunities for achieving economic independence by means of the easy, interest-free credit he proposed as part of his plan for monetary reform. By according the state absolute control over monetary policy, Feder called for an enormous expansion of its power. Like Rosenberg, he set virtually no limits to the state's authority to intervene in the private sector of the economy, aside from eschewing a thoroughgoing program of nationalization.

Whereas Feder summed up his attitude toward economic matters in 1923 in the scarcely radical phrase "to each his own," he eventually proved considerably less accommodating toward big business than Rosenberg.[14] In contrast to Rosenberg's ready acceptance of large firms as long as their management remained German, one of the thirty-nine points of Feder's 1923 program pledged the NSDAP to combat "giant enterprises."[15] At the time, he undercut that pledge with major qualifications: It did not, for instance, apply to branches of production, such as heavy industry, where the dictates of efficiency required large-scale organization.[16] Nor did it apply to large enterprises that had remained in the hands of "creators" who operated them in the public interest. Such was the case, Feder specified, with three major iron and steel firms, Krupp, Mannesmann, and Thyssen.[17] A close reading of Feder's 1923 commentary revealed that a large firm would incur the wrath of the Nazis only if it became a "syndicate," which Feder defined in characteristically apodictic fashion as an enterprise that ignored the general welfare by engaging in such practices as price fixing.[18] But even with regard to transgressions of that sort, Feder's 1923 commentary left considerable doubt about the NSDAP's will to adopt any radical countermeasures since one of his thirty-nine points added an important commitment missing from the party's original program: "National Socialism accords fundamental recognition to private property and places it under protection of the state."[19] His 1927 commentary displayed, however, a more anti-capitalist outlook. There he stated that large, bureaucratized, and anonymous firms that sought to stifle competition and pursued profit for profit's sake made themselves "ripe for socialization."[20] A Nazi state, he promised, would use its authority to lower prices held artificially high by such firms.[21] At the end of his 1927 commentary he set forth, in bold type, a statement hardly reassuring to the business community: "National Socialism is a world-view that stands in sharpest opposition to the

present-day world of capitalism and its satellites."[22] By 1930 the version
of his thirty-nine-point program that appeared in reprintings of his
1927 commentary had been altered to call for—as did point 13 of the
NSDAP's official program—a state takeover of incorporated enterprises.[23] Such words did not escape notice. In 1930, the conservative
financial newspaper *Berliner Börsen-Zeitung* identified him with what its
editors viewed as "Marxist tendencies" in the NSDAP.[24]

To link Nazis with Marxism involved a fundamental misapprehension, of course, but by the latter half of the 1920s changes within the
NSDAP led many observers to take more seriously the words "socialist"
and "workers" in the party's name. Those changes resulted in large measure from Nazism's penetration, beginning in 1924, of parts of Germany
far more urban and industrialized than Bavaria and the other southern
German regions where the party had originally taken root. This geographical extension of the party produced the so-called Nazi left wing.[25]
Its proponents came for the most part from the ranks of those Nazi
organizers who labored to win a following in the Rhineland, the Ruhr,
Westphalia, Saxony, and Berlin. They judged it essential to compete
there with the established working-class parties for the allegiance and
votes of the millions of industrial wage earners who made up the largest
component of the population in those parts of Germany. Whereas the
NSDAP had previously placed primary emphasis on "national" issues
such as Versailles and the purported subservience of the republican regime to treasonous, internationalist influences, these left-wing Nazis
stressed "social" issues, asserting the NSDAP's claim to the status of a
workers' party and emphasizing the socialistic components of its program. Some left-wingers referred to themselves as *nationale Sozialisten,* a
formulation that elevated the second word to the status of the substan-
tive and reduced the first to a mere adjective.[26] Although cynical opportunism may have motivated some left-wing Nazis, others sincerely
wanted far-reaching changes in the economic system. Their ardor
sprang, however, not from a vision of an emancipated proletariat conquering the new industrial order and displacing the bourgeoisie but
rather from petit bourgeois resentment toward the rich and powerful, as
well as from a nostalgic and often romantic vision of the pre-industrial
past. They challenged only the large-scale, impersonal, international,
and industrial capitalism of the twentieth century, not private enterprise
as such. Their projects for the "socialization" of even large enterprises
stopped far short of outright state takeovers. They proposed instead
elaborate formulas to disperse varying degrees of ownership among employees on the one hand and federal, state, and municipal governments
on the other, with large portions of investment capital to remain in private hands.[27] They wanted a kind of compromise with socialism that
would result in a wider dispersal of the ownership of capital rather than
thoroughgoing state control of the economy. They sought a greater de-

gree of economic and social equality, but they wanted to achieve that goal through a process of upward leveling, that is, the absorption of members of the working class into the middle class, not through a decisive triumph of the proletariat over the bourgeoisie.

Since these limitations on the radicalism of the Nazi left wing seldom gained public expression, observers outside the NSDAP usually heard from that quarter only a barrage of anti-capitalistic rhetoric that sounded disturbingly similar to that employed by the Social Democrats and Communists. In 1927, for example, the most prominent spokesman for the left wing, Gregor Strasser, published in a party periodical a statement that seemed to leave no doubt about where the Nazis stood on economic questions: "We socialists are enemies, deadly enemies of the present capitalist system with its exploitation of the economically weak, with its injustice to wage earning . . . and we are resolved under all circumstances to destroy this system."[28] Two years later Strasser proclaimed that the Nazis must always "represent the most radical demands of the workers."[29] Also in 1929 a Nazi periodical published by Strasser and his circle resorted to even more radical language in proclaiming that "the path to German freedom leads through the conquest of the bourgeoisie by the German proletariat."[30] In each issue, that periodical printed a column headed "Capital against Labor."[31] Joseph Goebbels, a Nazi agitator in the industrial Rhineland and then gauleiter of Berlin beginning in 1926, employed similarly radical anti-capitalist rhetoric. "We are socialists . . . ," he wrote in 1925, adding, "the day is not far off when we shall disclose all. . . . Then they will be appalled by the radicalism of our demands."[32] Three years later, in *Der Angriff*, the weekly Nazi newspaper he launched as gauleiter of Berlin, Goebbels gave expression to the theory of human alienation through capitalism in words that might well have attracted the envy of a Marxist agitator: "The worker in the capitalist state is—that is his greatest misfortune—no longer a lively human being, no longer a creator, no longer a shaper of things. He has become a machine. A number, a gear in a factory devoid of understanding or comprehension."[33]

Such pronouncements in sectarian Nazi publications might pass unnoticed by the leaders of big business and their agents, but the behavior of the NSDAP's delegation in the Reichstag less easily escaped their attention. Developments in the national legislature received routine coverage in major newspapers, and the parliamentary spokesmen of big business kept their patrons informed about the activities of the Nazi deputies.[34] These activities perplexed most contemporary observers. On issues of foreign policy, defense, and law enforcement, the Nazis seemed part of the extreme right, but on socio-economic issues the NSDAP frequently adopted positions virtually indistinguishable from those of the extreme left. The Nazis's location in the chamber seemed to underline this indeterminateness. From 1924 to 1928 the deputies of the NSDAP sat toward the back, between the DVP and the DNVP, and from 1928 until 1930 they perched ambiguously at the rear of the chamber, amidst a cluster of small parties. They did not adopt their final position to the right of all the other parties until after the election of 1930, by which time the Reichstag had lost control of vital national legislation and ceased even to meet regularly. In the years when the parliament represented the focus of power in the Republic, Nazism thus seemed an enigmatic phenomenon that defied placement on the customary political spectrum.

The socio-economic radicalism of Nazi parliamentarians found expression in a variety of ways. Their own relatively few legislative initiatives in that sphere displayed a provocative extremism. These initiatives included the repeated introduction of bills embodying some of Gottfried Feder's pet schemes, such as state-enforced reduction of interest rates, interest-free state credit, and the nationalization of all banks.[35] The Nazi deputies also laid before the chamber several times bills calling for the confiscation of "the fortunes of the princes of bank and stock market" as well as of all profits derived from the war, the inflation, and—later—the depression.[36] None of these bills stood any chance of securing a majority and so could be dismissed as demogogic publicity stunts, even if their thrust could scarcely fail to occasion concern in propertied circles. Less easily dismissed was the Nazis' inclination to vote with the traditional parties of the left on legislative issues that would determine the course of national economic policy. On one perennial issue, taxation, the Nazis repeatedly voted against increases in indirect taxes, rejecting such increases, like the parties of the left, on the grounds that such levies unfairly added to the burden on the mass of wage earners and weighed less heavily on the rich.[37] Similarly, the Nazi deputies generally supported proposals by the parties of the left for increases in the levels of expenditures for state welfare and social programs. They also joined with the left in rejecting demands by the parties of the right that a means test be required of applicants for state welfare aid.[38] In 1925, when the Reichstag dealt with the question of tariffs for the first time in the Republic, the Nazis voted with the Democrats, Social Democrats, and Communists to reject the protective schedule of duties carried by the majority, which favored producer interests over those of consumers.[39]

In addition to this general tendency to side with the left on socio-economic issues, the Nazi parliamentarians on a number of occasions were the only party to endorse extreme anti-capitalist proposals made by the Communists. They did this even though the NSDAP otherwise branded the Communists as traitors to the cause of Germany's workers and tools of a Jewish conspiracy that extended from the stock exchanges to the Kremlin. On one such occasion in 1927, the Nazi delegation announced its support of a Communist bill that would, if adopted, have struck a heavy blow at the major iron and steel firms of the Ruhr by requiring them to refund hundreds of millions of marks they had received from the government as compensation for deliveries of coal and other reparations in kind they had made after passive resistance to the Franco-Belgian occupation had collapsed in 1923.[40] Later in 1927 the Nazis again joined with the Communists, voting against the national unemployment insurance law adopted by virtually all the other parties. On slightly different grounds, the Nazi deputies concurred with the Communists' contention that the new law's provisions slighted the workers.[41] The Nazis alone supported repeated Communist proposals to raise sharply the level of tax-exempt wages for low-income groups, reduce the tax rates for those groups, and impose heavier taxation on the wealthy.[42] At the time of the lockout in the iron and steel industry in the Ruhr in 1928, only the NSDAP delegation voted for a Communist bill to compensate the idled workers at a rate much higher than that endorsed by the majority parties and to make the industrial firms involved bear the full cost of that compensation.[43] On an issue of the utmost sensitivity for German industry—the length of the workday—the Nazis in the Reichstag repeatedly sided with the Communists and Social Democrats in calling for restoration of the eight-hour day and opposing such compromises as that effected in 1927, which permitted employers to require work in excess of eight hours.[44]

On these occasions, as well as others, the rhetoric of the Nazi deputies rivaled that of the Communists for vehement anti-capitalism. In explaining the Nazis' vote against the 1925 tariff, their spokesman branded it as the product of pressures exerted by "great syndicates" and "powerful lobbies" and predicted it would lead to the "plundering" of consumers.[45] During the debate on the Ruhr lockout, the spokesman for the Nazi delegation protested against the flow of "gigantic profits" into the pockets of "coupon clippers" and "those who do nothing but sit on supervisory boards." German industry had allied itself with finance capital, he complained, thereby adopting a position "hostile to that of the *Volk* in an absolute sense." He added a warning that must have sounded ominous to economically privileged groups: "This lofty chamber will again become representative of the *Volk* only when battalions of workers march in here and set things straight."[46] Early in 1929 another Nazi deputy used the floor of the Reichstag to attack the SPD in words virtually indistinguishable from those employed by the Communists against the Social Democrats. The SPD, he announced, had become a timorous party of self-serving trade union officials. It had betrayed the workers by not effecting far-reaching changes in 1918–19 and was now again selling them out by collaborating in the great coalition with the "party of heavy industry" (DVP) and the "party of bank and stock-market capital" (DDP). In contrast to the dishonest and morally bankrupt SPD, which had abandoned the principles of such socialist leaders as Ignaz Auer and August Bebel, the NSDAP stood unflinchingly for the interests of the workers of Germany, the Nazi spokesman proclaimed from the floor of the national legislature.[47] Such an attack on the SPD could scarcely have heartened Germany's capitalists, despite their own hostility toward the Social Democrats.

Although a radical tone prevailed in the NSDAP's Reichstag delegation on economic issues, the Nazi left wing did not gain official endorsement for its brand of National Socialism. Its chief spokesman, Gregor Strasser, made such an attempt in early 1926, when he circulated among Nazi organizers in northwest Germany the draft of a new party program which included in its economic section the left wing's proposal for dispersing the ownership of large firms. Nothing came of Strasser's draft, however, since Hitler made clear to a meeting of party officials at Bamberg in February 1926 his unwillingness to consider any revision of the party program.[48] Four months later Hitler sought to stifle any further discussion of the NSDAP's program by having the rubber-stamp General Membership Assembly of the party reaffirm the "unalterable" status of the twenty-five points of 1920.[49]

Hitler did not throttle the left-wing elements altogether. Even after the party began, toward the end of the decade, to broaden its appeals to encompass economically conservative farmers and middle-class voters, the left wing continued to compete vigorously with the leftist parties for worker support. Hitler even acquiesced when left-wing organizers circumvented his ban on Nazi trade unions by founding party factory cells. These cells conducted Nazi agitation and ran candidates in the elections for the factory councils established by the Weimar constitution as a means of providing representative forums for the expression of workers' viewpoints and grievances. Since Social Democratic and Communist workers had usually dominated those councils, the left-wing Nazis' new factory cells provided them with a means of challenging the pre-eminence of the traditional workers' parties at the workplace. By the fall of 1929 the factory-cell movement had grown into a full-fledged organ of the party, the National Socialist Factory Cell Organization (NSBO), and had won Hitler's recognition.[50] Hitler also raised no objections to the anti-capitalist rhetoric that pervaded a number of widely circulated quasi-official periodicals published by the two Strasser brothers. Otto Strasser's quarrel with Hitler and his exit from the party in July 1930, after charging that Hitler had betrayed the socialists in the NSDAP, had little or no effect on the Nazi left wing. Only a handful of insignificant figures followed the younger Strasser out of the party and joined him in a vain effort to establish an organization to rival the NSDAP.[51] After Otto's departure his brother Gregor, who had denounced his accusations against Hitler and broken with him, continued to uphold the anti-capitalist line of the left wing. So did Goebbels, the leaders of the NSBO, much of the Reichstag delegation, and numerous lesser party spokesmen. Right down to Hitler's installation in the chancellorship, in fact, left-wing elements persisted in their radical agitation.

Because of the many divergent interpretations of the NSDAP's position on economic matters, Hitler came under mounting pressure from within the party in the late 1920s to clarify Nazi policy on that score. After staving off numerous such requests, he finally agreed on the eve of the party congress of 1929 to authorize the preparation of a "catechism" which would set forth Nazi economic doctrine and distinguish it from both liberal capitalism and Marxism. As the author, he designated Hans Buchner, economic editor of the *Völkischer Beobachter*.[52] Buchner produced a pamphlet on Nazi economic theory which appeared in 1930 under the imprint of the party publishing house in the "National Socialist Library" series, for which Feder served as general editor.[53] In contrast to the aversion of Rosenberg and Feder for even the word "socialism," Buchner proclaimed "state socialism" as the goal of Nazi economic policy.[54] Yet a reading of his pretentiously phrased and often abstruse pamphlet reveals no traces of what is usually thought of as socialism. Instead, he committed National Socialism to a thoroughgoing corporatist economic order, holding up Mussolini's Italy as a model.[55] The twenty-five points of 1920 and Feder's thirty-nine points of 1923 both had included provisions for corporatist, or occupational, chambers, but neither accorded those chambers as central a role as did Buchner. A Nazi state, he announced, would organize all productive units into estates (*Stände*) corresponding to the branches of the economy. In pyramidal fashion, local estates would send representatives to regional chambers and these would do likewise to national bodies. At each level, spokesmen of both labor and management would comprise these chambers. Working together, they would resolve their problems and achieve a self-administered economy. Buchner's version of corporatism held out no immediate threat to the existing distribution of wealth. National Socialism, he proclaimed, accorded "fundamental recognition" to private property.[56] Insofar as his brand of corporatism would produce changes in the economy, these would come about only gradually and with the consent of the representatives of management. Any businessmen who took the trouble to look at Buchner's scheme would have been pleased to find that he not only rejected class conflict but also ruled out the use of the strike in labor-management disputes. But although his corporatist scheme held out the promise of a self-administered economy, it provided no formulas for overcoming the differences between labor and management. In the final analysis Buchner, like Rosenberg and Feder, accorded potentially unlimited authority over all aspects of the private sector of the economy to the Nazi state of the future.

Although Buchner's pamphlet went through five printings before the Nazis came to power and was echoed in his columns for the party's national newspaper, it did not resolve the confusion about National Socialist economic policy. About the time it first appeared in print, a member of the party's Reichstag delegation took the floor to respond to charges from the left that the Nazis were the German counterparts of Mussolini's movement and no more friendly toward labor than the repressive Italian regime. "We are not fascists," he angrily announced. "We are socialists."[57] Moreover, despite Hitler's describing Buchner's pamphlet in advance as a "catechism," the party leader continued to insist on the "unalterable" nature of the twenty-five-point program of 1920, from which Buchner's views departed in numerous respects. Alongside Buchner's publication, the earlier commentaries on the party's policies by Rosenberg and Feder circulated in new editions. In some instances, these new editions incorporated small but not always insignificant changes into their economic sections.[58] In the early 1930s, both Rosenberg and Feder further muddied the already murky programmatic waters of Nazism by publishing new commentaries that departed in certain respects from their own earlier writings.[59] In addition, still other Nazis issued idiosyncratic commentaries on the party's economic program.[60] Throughout the whole *"Kampfzeit,"* the views of left-wing Nazis on economic matters continued to find expression in the quasi-official publications controlled by Gregor Strasser and in such local organs as Goebbels's Berlin newspaper, *Der Angriff.* On the increasingly rare occasions when the Reichstag met after 1930, the statements of Nazi deputies contributed little toward a clarification of the NSDAP's position. Anyone seeking to establish the economic policies of National Socialism on the basis of the public programmatic statements of Nazi spokesmen themselves faced a dizzying profusion of crosscurrents, right down to Hitler's installation as chancellor in January 1933.

How such diverse and sometimes incompatible positions could exist side by side in the highest echelons of a single political party has perplexed many observers, then and since. The explanation is, however, simple: The NSDAP was no ordinary political party. It was, of course, not a democratic organization, so that its programs and policies arose neither from majority decisions nor from a consensus among its members or even among its leaders. And except for its racism, the NSDAP was not fundamentally a doctrinal party; that is, its other policies, including those dealing with economic issues, did not derive from a single, coherent body of theory. Instead, the Nazi Party was at bottom a charismatic movement whose cohesion resulted from the loyalty of its members, whatever their views on particular issues, to one man: Adolf Hitler. He welded into a viable political organization the disparate northern and southern components of Nazism he found tenuously linked on his release from prison at the end of 1924. He held the party together and determined its course thereafter, often in times of adversity and demoralization. Any attempt to understand Nazi economic policies, or the absence thereof, must therefore turn on an analysis of Hitler's own attitude toward such matters.

3. Hitler's Economics

With Hitler, it is misleading to speak of economic thought in the usual sense. Although his acquisition of dictatorial authority over one of the most advanced industrial nations of the world eventually forced him to grapple with concrete economic problems for more than a decade, often with remarkable success, he never attained even a basic grasp of the formal discipline of economics. From the testimony of those who served him, as well as from his own writings and recorded utterances, it is obvious that he knew virtually nothing about micro-economics and had no more grasp of macro-economics than could be gained by reading newspapers. Once in power he repeatedly showed himself incapable of accepting even the simplest fact of economics, the scarcity of goods.[1]

A major reason for Hitler's ignorance of economics undoubtedly lay in the nature of his education. Not having completed secondary school, he became of necessity an autodidact whose acquaintance with most fields of knowledge derived principally from an unsystematic reading of popularized, pseudo-scholarly publications. He managed on his own to accumulate a considerable, if highly opinionated and distorted, smattering of anthropology, history, and social and political theory. Quite obviously, however, his reading circumvented the more technical and, for the layman, less readily accessible field of economics. Another factor in Hitler's ignorance of formal economics may be that its rationality and utilitarianism, its acceptance of constraints and limitations, made it uncongenial to his overweening cast of mind. Once he entered political life, however, Hitler could no longer simply ignore economic matters altogether. What emerged, in his speeches and writings, may best be described as a loose cluster of sometimes contradictory socio-economic attitudes.

In an early speech Hitler gave succinct expression to the role he was to assign to economics in human affairs throughout his political career: "The economy is something of secondary importance."[2] In *Mein Kampf* he denounced what he regarded as a dangerously widespread and potentially ruinous misperception of the relationship between economics and politics:

> . . . The state has, however, nothing whatsoever to do with a particular economic outlook or line of development.
>
> It is not a combination of contractual parties to economic transactions in a specifically delimited living space for the purpose of accomplishing economic tasks, but rather a community of physically and spiritually alike creatures for the purpose of facilitating the perpetuation of their species as well as the attainment of the goal of their existence, as pre-

scribed by providence. This and nothing else is the purpose and meaning of a state. The economy is in that context merely one among many
resources that are requisite for the achievement of that goal. It is, however, never the source or the purpose of a state, unless the latter rests
upon a foundation that is false because from the very outset it is in
defiance of nature.[3]

To some extent this disdain doubtless reflected the would-be artist's
aversion for material pursuits as well as the autodidact's uneasiness
about—and hence hostility toward—something significant beyond the
compass of his mind. But Hitler's view of humanity and society played a
part, too. As has long been recognized, his thought contained nothing
original; it consisted instead of an amalgam of nineteenth-century
pseudo-scientific theories that together formed one of the most pernicious social and political creeds of all time. A basic element of that creed
was racism, which—in the form of virulent anti-Semitism—Hitler was to
pursue to the point of the most appalling campaign of premeditated
genocide in history. But more central to his view of economic affairs was
another key element of his creed: Social Darwinism. By the time he entered politics he had accepted uncritically the collectivistic Austrian variant of that doctrine. Instead of seeing life primarily in terms of a
competition for advantage and advancement among individuals, as did
most English and American Social Darwinists, Hitler believed that for
humans the crucial Darwinian struggle took place among nations. That
conflict entailed for him more than merely advantage and advancement;
it ultimately condemned some nations to extinction and destined others
for glory and greatness. Hitler viewed this "struggle for existence"
(*Lebenskampf*) among peoples in an optimistic light. It alone ensured that
among mankind, as among other forms of life, the fittest would survive
while the weak and defective perished. It alone made possible continued
evolutionary progress by according to the strongest and ablest nations
control over mankind's destiny.

The outcome of the struggle among nations must, Hitler believed,
always ultimately be determined by war, or as he frequently put it, by the
"sword" or the "risking of blood" (*Bluteinsatz*). To the state, the wielder
of weapons, he therefore accorded an absolute primacy over the economy. The economy must always remain, he insisted, the "maidservant"
of the state, never its mistress, since no nation could ever survive
through reliance solely on economic endeavor nor could war ever be
replaced by peaceful economic domination. A preoccupation with
peaceful economic pursuits seemed to Hitler thus not merely misguided;
it was harmful, potentially even suicidal. "World history teaches us," he
said in a speech in 1922, "that no people has become great through its
economy but that a people can very well perish thereby."[4] He saw as the
qualities necessary to construct and maintain a state "always the heroic
virtues and never the egoism of the tradesman, since the preservation of

the existence of a species requires the individual's readiness for self-sacrifice." As proof that such "heroic virtues" had nothing to do with economic matters, Hitler offered a stark maxim: "People will not die for business but only for ideals."[5] A peaceful policy based on economic considerations could, to his mind, only lead to a "dissolute pacifism" that would leave those afflicted by it defenseless against anyone stronger and prepared to make use of "the more authentic forces of political power."[6]

The cast of mind which led to success in economic pursuits was, in Hitler's judgment, fundamentally incompatible with the attributes necessary for political achievements. Only in the rarest of instances, he wrote in *Mein Kampf*, did a state's periods of political strength coincide with economic prosperity. Prussia's history demonstrated conclusively that "the creation of a state is made possible not by material attributes but solely by ideal virtues."[7] A strong state could provide the basis for economic development, but the reverse never held true. Indeed, Hitler insisted that in German history triumphs of political power had repeatedly been undone by materialistic preoccupations fostered by the prosperity generated by those very triumphs. This had happened under Bismarck's successors, whose reliance on peaceful economic development had resulted in what Hitler scornfully referred to as the nation's "subjugation to economics."[8] He attributed the loss of the war ultimately to the displacement of ideals by materialistic—that is, economic—concerns.[9]

Hitler's proclivity for simplification enabled him to relegate huge areas of economic activity to the periphery of reality. Just as he reduced international affairs to a Darwinian struggle to the death among nations, so he reduced that struggle essentially to the level of biology. He saw mankind motivated, like all other species, at bottom by two elemental drives: the need for nourishment and the desire for procreation. When sound and vital, a people would invariably increase in number. But instead of drawing the usual pessimistic Malthusian conclusion from this assumption, Hitler regarded population increase in a wholly optimistic light; indeed, it represented for him the most reliable index of a nation's health. He recognized that unchecked indulgence of the desire for procreation would lead to a shortage of food; he accepted that unquestioningly as an inexorable law of nature. In his eyes, however, the resultant deprivation had positive value. For hunger drove hardy, vital nations to engage in what he described as "natural imperialism," that is, to stamp out weaker, thus inferior, peoples and thereby carry forward the process of human evolution. This quest for more food could only be realized through the acquisition of additional arable land by conquest, or, as Hitler sometimes euphemistically phrased the same formula, through the "adjustment from time to time of the amount of land to the increased population."[10] In his contradiction-ridden thought, this "struggle for existence" had, despite its material basis, nothing to do with the "materialism" he roundly and regularly denounced. Indeed, he warned against allowing excessive idealism to distract a people from the elemental task of conquering more land.[11]

Hitler's foreign-policy aims bore the imprint of these Social Darwinist assumptions. Early in his political career, he began to view Germany's population growth, which he assumed had long since outstripped the country's food-producing capacity, as the central factor in its relations with the rest of the world. In 1920 he adopted the position to which he would hold until the end of his life. The only remedy for this purported imbalance lay, he proclaimed, in obtaining additional "land and soil." For a time Hitler thought in terms of overseas colonies suitable for large numbers of German settlers. But by 1924, at the latest, he had opted for the conquest of "living space" (*Lebensraum*) to the east, mainly in Russia, where millions of Germans would be resettled on the land.[12]

The cold-bloodedness with which Hitler proclaimed his aggressive intentions toward Russia and the "border states" of eastern Europe in *Mein Kampf* and then later sought to achieve his goals through war has distracted attention from a revealing aspect of his foreign policy, namely, its agrarian basis. In his writings on the subject, he justified the conquest of *Lebensraum* exclusively in terms of the need for soil to guarantee Germany's agricultural self-sufficiency. Only a nation that possessed within its own borders land enough to produce all the food it consumed could survive in the Darwinian jungle, a world "where one creature lives off another" and where "there can be no other way to deal with an enemy than to kill him."[13] The only indications that Hitler took any note, prior to acquiring power, of other economic resources to the east, such as fuels and industrial raw materials, appear in reports by contemporaries of conversations with him. And strikingly, even in conversation, where broader considerations were bound to be touched on, Hitler consistently accorded a subordinate role to the non-agrarian potentialities of his dream of *Lebensraum* in the east.[14] His conception of economic autarky remained narrowly and archaically agrarian, assigning at most a secondary status to the vast and immensely valuable industrial resources which the realization of his grandiose scheme for conquest would have placed at Germany's disposal. During the years when he strove to gain control over one of the world's most advanced industrial nations, Adolf Hitler accorded primacy, in his plans for the future, to the agrarian aspects of economic life.

Hitler's agrarian bias echoed the views of those critics of German industrialism who, in the great controversy at the end of the nineteenth century, opposed increased reliance on commerce and manufacturing through freer trade and argued that the country must retain a balance between its industrial and agricultural sectors.[15] He deplored the setbacks suffered by that school of thought. He traced to the inroads made by the advocates of industrialism and free trade much that had gone wrong since then, including Germany's estrangement from England in the years before 1914. Throughout the 1920s he repeated in his writings and speeches the viewpoints of the turn-of-the-century critics of industrialism. When speaking of Germany's industrialization he usually employed such adjectives as "harmful," "excessive," or "unbridled," and he referred frequently to the country's "over-industrialization."[16] Like so many other critics of industrialism, he also harbored a profound distaste for the huge urban concentrations of population to which that process had given rise. He looked on the great industrial cities of Germany with loathing as "abscesses on the body of the *Volk,* in which all evil vices, bad habits and sicknesses seem to converge."[17]

Hitler's negative outlook toward industry and cities carried over into his attitude toward the practitioners of big business. In referring to Germany's capitalists in *Mein Kampf,* he repeatedly made use of pejorative clichés, referring to "dividend-hungry businessmen," their "greed and ruthlessness," and their "short-sighted narrow-mindedness."[18] Early in his political career he had made two big businessmen into targets of his ire: Ruhr magnate Hugo Stinnes and Wilhelm Cuno, the managing director of the Hamburg-America shipping line who had served as Reich chancellor in 1922–23 at the time of the Ruhr occupation, the unsuccessful passive resistance to it, and the final, runaway phase of hyperinflation. As already noted, Hitler repeatedly pilloried Stinnes publicly for spreading the "nonsensical notion" that "the economy as such could by itself raise Germany up again."[19] Cuno, to whom he referred as "a merchant dabbling in politics," became the butt of his ridicule. The shipping executive, he maintained, had committed the folly of approaching problems of state as though these were business transactions, which had inevitably resulted in disastrous failure.[20] Such rhetoric might be dismissed as a demagogue's exploitation of widespread hostility toward the conspicuous rich had not Hitler displayed much the same scorn and mistrust for the practitioners of big business even in private conversations where tactical considerations of that sort played no role. According to one participant, for example, he told a small group of Nazi leaders in 1932, "I won't let those captains of industry put anything over on me. Captains! I'd like to know the bridge on which they've ever manned the helm. They're shallow people who can't see beyond their petty affairs."[21] The passage of nine years, during eight of which he had ruled as dictator, did nothing to improve his opinions. Speaking in private to his entourage in October 1941, he referred to big businessmen (*die Wirtschaft*) as "rogues" and "cold-blooded money-grubbers" who ceaselessly bemoaned their plight. He had never met an industrialist who, on catching sight of him, had not put on a woebegone expression in hopes of obtaining something.[22]

Hitler did not draw from his aversion to industrialism and his scorn for its practitioners the sort of radical conclusion that some left-wing

Nazis did. Again, Social Darwinism determined his outlook. But he went beyond the collectivistic variant of that doctrine prevalent in central Europe. While convinced that the primary struggle for survival occurred among nations, he accorded a place to struggle among individuals as well. In his world of pervasive strife, individuals battled with each other for advantage within nations just as nations battled with one another in the international arena.[23] This involved him in at least two contradictions. First of all, this insistence on conflict within the nation could not logically be brought into accord with his promise to forge the German nation into a unified, even monolithic, folk-community. Secondly, despite his strictures regarding the harmful effects of a preoccupation with materialistic concerns, he assumed that struggle among individuals within a nation took a mainly economic form. That assumption provided the basis for another, namely, that economic competition—or, as he sometimes characterized it, the "play of free forces"—was essential for a nation's health.[24] Only through competition could the "aristocratic principle of nature" assert itself in the life of a nation, thus ensuring that the fittest persons, the "superior individuals" (*Persönlichkeiten*), as he put it, would prevail.[25] For Hitler, the cardinal error of Marxism lay in denying this elemental law of nature and stifling economic competition to promote the welfare of the masses; the result of such a misguided policy would be to doom to inferior leadership—and thus a subordinate status—those nations that fell victim to it. Similarly, Hitler condemned the assault of Marxism on private property. He regarded the intense commitment that arose from the individual's risking the loss of his own personal resources in order to achieve gain as the only possible basis for the kind of economic competition he held essential to a nation's health and to progress.[26]

At that time and since, observers have repeatedly alleged that Hitler abandoned the socialistic tenets of the NSDAP during his pursuit of power in order to placate big-business patrons. Yet an examination of his writings and utterances reveals that Hitler had nothing to abandon; he had never been a socialist, in the sense of favoring state ownership of the means of production.[27] His commitment to economic competition and private property derived not from expediency but rather from his fanatically held Social Darwinist beliefs about the nature of mankind and human society. So did his refusal to accept the legitimacy of class struggle, which had no place in his essentially biological view of the world in which the fundamental divisions in humanity ran along lines of race, never of class. Hitler was an anti-socialist out of conviction, not out of opportunism.

His words and behavior betrayed his attitude in a number of ways. He early on became obviously uncomfortable with the NSDAP's official twenty-five-point program of 1920. Although he had a part in preparing that program, he apparently did not write a great deal of the basic draft;

nor did he at that time command sufficient influence to dictate its content.[28] Subsequently, even while proclaiming the correctness of the program as a whole, he consistently refrained from citing its terms in detailed fashion. He conspicuously omitted its text from *Mein Kampf*, where he alluded to it disparagingly as "the so-called program of the movement."[29] Since the political and racist tenets of the twenty-five points coincided closely with Hitler's repeatedly expressed views, his unwillingness to spell out the terms of the NSDAP's official program in public resulted in all probability from objections to its radical, if sometimes vague, economic promises. Hitler also felt ill at ease with the prominent place in his party's name occupied by the word "socialist," a legacy from the NSDAP's early days, like the 1920 program. "Socialism! That is an unfortunate word altogether," he reportedly exclaimed in a discussion with a group of Nazi leaders in early 1929.[30] On another occasion he lost his temper in a revealing fashion, according to one of those present: "Socialism! What does socialism really mean? If people have something to eat and their pleasures, then they have their socialism."[31] Despite this cynical outlook, Hitler was too shrewd a demagogue not to recognize the advantages that could be derived from allowing those persons who wished to see him and his movement as socialistic, or at least anti-capitalistic, to continue doing so. His public utterances were therefore sprinkled with affirmations of the NSDAP's "socialism." He could not, however, go much beyond rhetorical invocations of that term without coming into conflict with his own personal commitment to competition and private property. Accordingly, he usually portrayed socialism as an ethical creed that entailed no specific economic system. In a speech of 1922 he even ascribed to socialism an exclusivist racial basis, describing it as a "noble conception that sprang only from the Aryan heart and came to spiritual fruition only in Aryan brains."[32] Much of the popular appeal of the NSDAP derived, as has long been recognized, from the Nazis' contention that they had succeeded in reconciling two great ideas, long considered antithetical, which had deeply divided Germany: nationalism and socialism. In his writings and utterances, Hitler almost invariably linked these two ideas and accompanied them with the claim that he had found a way to synthesize the two. Examination reveals, however, that instead of synthesizing the two he actually subsumed socialism under nationalism. In the speech of 1922 quoted above, he proclaimed:

> Every truly national principle is in the final analysis social, that is: whoever is prepared to devote himself so completely to his *Volk* that he recognizes no higher idea than the welfare of his *Volk*, whoever understands our great anthem "Deutschland, Deutschland über Alles" to mean that nothing in this world is more important to him than this Germany, *Volk* and land, land and *Volk*, he is a socialist.[33]

A year later, he pointed to what he regarded as two model "socialist" institutions worthy of emulation by National Socialists, the German army and civil service.[34]

While Hitler was no socialist, neither was he a proponent of liberal capitalism. He viewed private property and economic competition as the prerequisites for a healthy society, but the principle of laissez-faire had no place in his thought. As he envisioned and later put into practice in the Third Reich, private ownership of the means of production must always remain contingent on conformity with the purposes of the state. To ensure that this was the case, the one-party state must enjoy unlimited authority to intervene in the economy—as in all other spheres of life. Political control, in short, would know no limits in a Nazi state. And that control would be so pervasively applied that the aspirations of the socialists would pale by comparison. Early in the Third Reich Hitler explained his outlook to a confidant:

> The party is all-embracing. It regulates life in its whole breadth and depth. . . . There is no license any more, no private sphere where the individual belongs to himself. That is socialism, not such trivial matters as the possibility of privately owning the means of production. Such things mean nothing if I subject people to a kind of discipline they can't escape. Let them own as much land or as many factories as they want. The decisive consideration is that the state, working through the party, disposes over them whether they are property owners or laborers. Understand this: all that means nothing any more. Our socialism goes deeper. It doesn't alter superficial forms but instead orders the relationship of the individual to the state, to the folk-community. . . . What need have we to socialize banks and factories? We socialize human beings.[35]

Hitler wanted not to socialize German big business but rather to conscript it.[36] He wanted, that is, to press it into service in his grandiose scheme to conquer the *Lebensraum* that would provide the foundation for a new, vastly expanded, and reinvigorated Reich.

Despite the remarks quoted here, Hitler never reconciled himself to leaving unaltered the "superficial forms" that prevailed in Germany's economic life during his rise to power. His unease with the inherited order of things arose from a contradiction between his commitment to a Social Darwinist formula in the economic sphere and his views on contemporary German society. On the one hand, he upheld private property and economic competition as essential to a salubrious environment of struggle within the nation. On the other hand, he harbored a deep contempt for the propertied elite of his own time, which had arisen largely—if not solely—by exploiting that "play of free forces" in the economic marketplace which Hitler extolled as the key to social well-being. The pages of *Mein Kampf* abound with sneering, deprecatory remarks about Germany's *Bürgertum*, or bourgeoisie. Hitler portrayed the *Bürgertum* of his day as a self-indulgent, indolent, cowardly, base, and degenerate social group, "worthless for any lofty task of humanity."[37] His attitude betrayed resentments accumulated during his years of deprivation and social marginality in Vienna and Munich prior to the war and possibly also psychic scars that reached even further back in his life. But whatever the reasons, Hitler made it clear in *Mein Kampf* that National Socialism would not preserve the advantages of the privileged; instead, Nazism would clear the way for the rise of a new master elite of character and talent.[38] Here, however, Hitler faced a dilemma. For how could one displace the propertied elite without replacing, or at least drastically modifying, the existing economic system, whose central features Hitler regarded as essential to the rise of the fittest participants in the economic life of the nation?

Throughout his political career, Hitler wrestled with this dilemma without ever finding a way to resolve it. In *Mein Kampf*, to be sure, he claimed to have discovered very early a formula that explained how the wrong people had gotten to the top in Germany. In one of his rare acknowledgments of intellectual indebtedness, Hitler wrote that he owed this discovery to Gottfried Feder, who had cast new light on the subject in a talk to one of the first Nazi meetings Hitler had attended in 1919. Feder had attributed Germany's economic ills to laxness and lack of vigilance on the part of previous German governments toward alien elements. As a consequence, "international finance and stock-market capital" had encroached on the country's basically sound "national business community" (*nationale Wirtschaft*). Whereas the latter invested capital for productive, socially beneficial ends, the former manipulated capital for non-productive, speculative purposes in order to accumulate enormous profits without honest work, all at the expense of honest, hard-working Germans.[39] In line with Feder's distinction, Hitler directed his public criticisms of Germany's economic system primarily at "international finance and stock-market capital," which he, like Feder, identified as a basically Jewish phenomenon. Frequently, he used another of Feder's formulas, distinguishing between productive German "industrial capital" and exploitative international or Jewish "loan capital."[40]

But even in *Mein Kampf* Hitler betrayed an awareness that excluding "alien" influences from German life would not suffice to do away with the social inequities that irked him. He deplored the concentration of capital in huge joint-stock companies, decrying their ruinous effects on the old individualistic *Mittelstand* of shopkeepers and small, independent manufacturers. He lamented the impersonality of large-scale enterprises and the ease with which the idle rich increased their fortunes without personal exertion. He expressed dismay at the growing anonymity of economic activity and the virtual disappearance of opportunities for advancement by venturesome and diligent individuals in an economy dominated by large corporations. He complained that property had become too unequally distributed and spoke of the desirability of spreading ownership more widely. So, too, he further declared, must income differentials between white-collar and blue-collar workers not be allowed to grow too great.[41]

While Hitler was far from being a defender of the existing social order, neither was he an altruistic social reformer. In *Mein Kampf* he assigned a purely instrumental function to the socio-economic changes he broached there. He specified that the "nationalization of the masses"—their conversion to nationalistic values—represented an indispensable prerequisite for Germany's re-attainment of its "external freedom." And he made clear that the "national education of the great masses" could come about only "via a process of social uplift" of a material sort that would create the preconditions necessary to permit everyone to "share in the cultural riches of the nation." That, he warned, would require "economic concessions" from employers, but the rewards would prove so great that they would far overshadow this price. The attainment of ethnic and cultural (*völkisch*) solidarity within Germany would open the way both to a restoration of national power in the world and to a lasting economic revival. But, most important for him, that solidarity would prepare Germany to do battle with adversaries in the international sphere, another example of to what extent Social Darwinism shaped Hitler's social attitudes.[42]

In his thinking about how to address these problems, Hitler proved receptive (like so many others who found early twentieth-century industrial capitalism repellent but could not accept socialism as an alternative) to the notion of a "third way," a wholly new economic system neither capitalist nor socialist. In *Mein Kampf* and in some of his speeches he seemed to commit the NSDAP to a corporatist economy that would seek to eliminate class conflict and social injustice by uniting employers and employees in common organizations encompassing each branch of the economy.[43] For a time, the example of Fascist Italy encouraged Hitler in that direction, and he repeatedly spoke admiringly of Mussolini's economic policies.[44] But when the elaborate corporatist structures of the Italian regime proved a mere facade that provided no corrective for social problems and no remedy for the Great Depression, Hitler turned elsewhere. According to Joseph Goebbels's diary, Hitler spoke in private as early as 1926 of establishing a mix of individualism and collectivism that would involve nationalizing mineral and other resources under the soil as well as trusts, transport, and finishing industries while leaving all other production in private hands.[45] At the beginning of 1931 he established an Economic Policy Section in the Munich Reichsleitung of the party to prepare plans for a coming Nazi regime.[46] During the months when he launched the final drive for political power that would take him to the Reich Chancellery in January 1933, he attached sufficient importance to the efforts of that new organization to participate in a series of lengthy seminars organized by its head, Otto Wagener. During those sessions Wagener and other self-proclaimed Nazi economic experts presented their schemes for a new economic order that would effect a synthesis of liberal capitalism and state socialism. Some of their proposals entailed far-reaching changes in the existing patterns of ownership and management; but so long as these schemes preserved the principles of private property and economic competition, Hitler raised no fundamental objections. According to Wagener's memoirs, Hitler responded enthusiastically to an elaborate proposal of his that would have shifted much of the capital of industry from the current shareholders to the employees of each business firm by means of a gradual transfer process designed to reward diligent and thrifty persons and penalize those who sought to live on unearned income derived from investments. Nothing came of the projects generated by the Economic Policy Section, however. By the fall of 1932 Hitler had become dissatisfied with Wagener, who relinquished his post in the Reichsleitung, clearing the way for the neutralization of his organization.[47]

As he approached power, Hitler increasingly spoke of economics as a question simply of willpower and force. During the last phase of his quest for the chancellorship, he explained to a confidant:

> Inflation is lack of discipline. . . . I'll see to it that prices remain stable. That's what I have my storm troopers for. Woe to those who raise their prices. We don't need legislation to deal with them. We'll do that with the party alone. You'll see: once our storm troopers visit a shop to set things right—nothing similar will happen a second time.

Hitler then added "I have the gift of simplification, and that makes things happen. Difficulties are merely imaginary!" Referring specifically to economics, Hitler explained, "All that's no secret science, as the professors think, but rather a matter of common sense and willpower."[48] Managing a complex economy did, of course, prove more complicated than this. Hitler had to rely heavily on technocrats such as Hjalmar Schacht, the former head of the Reichsbank during the Republic, and Albert Speer, the architect who became a remarkably effective minister of armaments during World War II. But he used them, as he used the German economy, for his purposes rather than adjusting his purposes to economic constraints. This would prove a major factor in his ultimate failure. It demonstrated, however, that Hitler had meant what he said when he proclaimed that economics must play the role of maidservant to politics.

During Hitler's rise to power few, if any, of his thoughts about formulas for reshaping the economy reached the public or even went beyond a small circle of confidants. Apparently he sensed early on that fundamental economic questions posed an explosive, potentially divisive threat to a party with as heterogeneous a following as the NSDAP's. He therefore sought, with remarkable success, to avert discussion of such questions, either in public or in the larger forums of the party. The twenty-five-point program of 1920, with its specific—if, in some cases, muddled—commitments on certain sensitive economic issues, posed a particular problem for him. From all indications, he soon became disillusioned with the economic planks of his party's program but had no clear notion of what to put in their place. He first responded to this problem simply by distancing himself from the 1920 program, as in his disparaging remarks about it in *Mein Kampf*. Eventually he arrived at an ingenious solution for dealing with this potentially divisive and constraining set of promises: By having the "unalterable" nature of the program reaffirmed in 1926, he in effect ruled out any open discussion, even inside the party, of its worrisome economic tenets. Whenever proposals of that sort arose, he could then invoke the program's unalterable status to suppress all proposed revisions and thus any consideration of basic economic issues.

Hitler adopted similarly evasive tactics whenever the NSDAP confronted a major issue that threatened to raise fundamental questions about its economic policies and thus divide its ranks and alienate potential followers. The plebiscite calling for expropriation of the German princes, which the Communists and Social Democrats sponsored in 1926, posed a particular challenge since the Nazi left-wingers wanted to support it while others in the party held, along with the middle-class parties, that it posed a threat to the very institution of private property. Endorsement of the plebiscite would have aligned the NSDAP with the left on an issue that commanded nationwide attention and aroused extremely strong feelings. Adeptly, Hitler avoided a split among his followers by muddying the issue. The NSDAP held no brief for the princes, he explained, since most of them were hostile to it, but as Germans they deserved to have their property protected from the Jewish system of exploitation that dominated the Republic.[49] Hitler also resisted agitation for the formation of Nazi trade unions, a move that would have entailed a commitment to one side in the conflict between labor and management that divided so much of the country. But in rejecting Nazi unions he avoided the basic issues involved and instead invoked a variety of practical obstacles to put off those who wanted the party to compete for representation of the workers in the collective-bargaining arena. The party would take up the matter at a later, more favorable time, he repeatedly assured those who wanted Nazi unions; but he never permitted the issue to come before a party congress, despite sustained pressure from left-wing Nazis.[50] During the seminars arranged by Otto Wagener of the Economic Policy Section, Hitler repeatedly admonished the participants to complete secrecy, according to Wagener's later account of those meetings. News of the sort of reforms they were considering, Hitler warned, would deliver dangerous weapons into the hands of those who sought to discredit the NSDAP before the public. They must therefore "conceal the glowing torch behind locked doors."[51]

In view of his obvious sensitivity to the potential danger of economic issues for the NSDAP, it seems astonishing at first sight that Hitler displayed virtually complete indifference to the cacophonous chorus of viewpoints on those issues publicly expressed by others in the party. Although he enjoyed sovereign control of the party from the summer of 1921 on, he made no effort to restrain the NSDAP's Reichstag deputies from employing radical rhetoric on economic issues or to curb the often strident anti-capitalism of the left-wing Nazi press. Nor did he display any displeasure at the frequently idiosyncratic and sometimes conflicting versions of Nazi economic policy set forth in the publications of Rosenberg, Feder, and Buchner, despite their wide circulation and seemingly official nature.[52] Hitler took, in fact, no public notice of what other Nazis said or wrote about economic issues or how the party's parliamentary representatives voted, so long as neither the 1920 program nor his own personal authority were challenged. Whether this resulted from the audacious cunning that characterizes so much of Hitler's political career or from his general reluctance to commit himself publicly on economic questions remains uncertain. But whatever the explanation, Hitler's posture proved a shrewd solution. By permitting other Nazis to adopt a variety of positions on economic matters and by keeping the party's official position and his own utterances ambiguous, he allowed persons drawn to the NSDAP to seize on those Nazi viewpoints that pleased them and discount any of a contradictory sort. The party thus enjoyed the advantages of seeming, if not all things to all men, at least many things to many interest groups. In private, or in closed gatherings before particular kinds of audiences, Hitler himself enjoyed the advantage of being able to dissociate himself from statements by other Nazis or even to dismiss as unauthorized departures from party policy any that particularly disturbed his listeners of the moment. As a perceptive observer noted in the left-liberal *Frankfurter Zeitung*, "The strength of the National Socialists lies to a considerable extent in not saying exactly what they want."[53]

4. An Abortive Courtship of Ruhr Industry— Nazism in Disrepute

On June 20, 1926, the *Rheinisch-Westfälische Zeitung*, a conservative newspaper published in Essen, reported that two days earlier Adolf Hitler had spoken in that city for an hour and a half before a closed gathering of "invited business leaders of the district" at the behest of a "circle of west German businessmen." That report proved notable on several counts. First of all, it marked the success of a ruse, for the initiative behind Hitler's appearance in Essen actually lay with the Nazis. The local party organization had rented the hall, issued invitations that served as tickets of admission, and obtained advance police permission for a closed meeting of ticketholders, thereby evading the Prussian state's ban on public speeches by Hitler.[1] But, most important, the newspaper article recorded the beginning of an eighteen-month courtship by Hitler of business circles in the Rhenish-Westphalian region known to outsiders as the Ruhr and to insiders as *das Revier*. During that period Hitler addressed under similar circumstances three more audiences in Essen and another in the Rhenish resort town of Königswinter.[2] These appearances and the response of the west German industrial elite to them reveal much about the state of relations between that elite and the NSDAP. Hitler's first courtship of the Ruhr, and its aftermath, also established certain patterns in his approach to the business community—and in the attitudes of big business toward National Socialism—that would persist into later years.

Although sometimes sketchy, the press reports on Hitler's four Essen speeches included sufficient information to reveal not only what he sought to convey to his listeners but also what he chose to conceal from them.[3] Most notably, he obviously did not want to share with his audiences his drastic plans for transforming Germany. Having apparently learned that big businessmen regarded anti-Semitism as a distasteful, plebeian phenomenon, he omitted from his Essen talks the tirades against Jews he usually wove into virtually all his political and economic arguments. No one attending Hitler's Essen speeches could have known from what he said that they were listening to a murderously fanatical anti-Semite bent on extirpating all Jews from German society. The Nazi leader also hedged on another of his central goals, the acquisition of *Lebensraum* by means of a war of conquest against Russia. Although he had already set forth in the first volume of *Mein Kampf*, published in mid-1925, his belief that only such a foreign policy could enable Germany to survive, he did not confide to his Essen listeners the full extent of his bellicose and expansionist aims. In several of his speeches there, he referred to Germany's need for more arable land in order to ensure an adequate food supply for its population; but he made no mention of conquering soil from Russia. Indeed, in his final appearance, in late 1927, he explicitly ruled out a resort to conquest. To his audiences he must have seemed merely another territorial revisionist bent on regaining for Germany by unspecified means lands lost at Versailles. Nor did he denigrate, as he had in *Mein Kampf*, an economic policy of promoting exports. Presumably well aware of industry's heavy reliance on sales abroad, he gave his listeners no reason to assume that he had any objection to the promotion of foreign trade.

In the first of his Essen speeches, entitled "German Economic and Social Policy," Hitler withheld even more from his listeners. He made no mention of the radical economic planks in the NSDAP's official program, or of the monetary and credit schemes Gottfried Feder had proposed in official party publications, or of the Nazi left wing's anticapitalist agitation for working-class support. Nor did he betray his own objections to Germany's "over-industrialization," his scorn for the country's *Bürgertum*, or his misgivings about an economic system that had allowed such an element of society to prosper at the expense of others and had produced what he regarded as an unhealthy distribution of property and opportunity. Nor did Hitler reveal his conviction that the state should enjoy a primacy over the economy so absolute that it must command unlimited authority for intervention in the private sector. Instead, he merely assured his listeners—truthfully—of his convictions about the superiority of private property and private enterprise. By way of underlining that conviction, he left no doubt about his opposition to the pending Social Democratic–Communist referendum proposing expropriation of the German princes, which the business community viewed with alarm as a threat to the sanctity of property rights. Anyone who knew nothing about Hitler except what he said in Essen on the evening of June 18, 1926, could only have concluded that he had no quarrels with the existing social and economic order.

As in Hitler's first Essen appearance, the content of his other three speeches before closed audiences there reflected their titles. On December 3, 1926, he spoke about "New Paths to Power"; on April 27, 1927, about "Leader and Mass"; and on December 5, 1927, about "Germany's Foreign Policy: Our Final Downfall or Our Future." But Hitler seldom, if ever, adhered to a single topic in any of his thousands of speeches, which customarily abounded with lengthy digressions. Such was the case with his Essen talks, which varied in duration between an hour and a half and two and three-quarter hours. Nevertheless, a common set of refrains that constituted the message Hitler wanted to convey to his listeners ran through all four speeches. He had conveyed much of that same message to the Berlin National Club in 1922 and had presented a fully elaborated version to the equally conservative and establishmentarian National Club of Hamburg in February 1926.[4] Half a decade after his Essen appearances, in his much-publicized speech to the Düsseldorf Industry Club, he delivered essentially the same message. The central points Hitler made on those occasions, and probably in other, unrecorded utterances to similar types of listeners, coincided to a considerable extent with the deeply held views he expressed in *Mein Kampf* and elsewhere. His listeners in Essen heard what amounted to a carefully edited version of his view of the world and received a very limited glimpse of his plans for their country's future. They heard nothing about the specific issues of economic policy that preoccupied most of the business community. Instead, Hitler held out to them the prospect of sweeping away the nation's economic problems by means of a bold political stroke.

The underlying message that Hitler wove into his Essen speeches of 1926 and 1927 consisted of an arraignment of Germany's recent past, an idiosyncratic and reductionist diagnosis of the causes of what he por-

trayed as a precipitous and continuing national decline, and—finally—
an arrestingly simple prescription for reversing that decline. He traced
the root cause for the country's decline to an assumption he claimed had
prevailed since the late imperial period, namely, that a strong economy
would suffice to maintain and protect Germany's place in the world.
Germany's leaders, he charged, had ignored the central fact of world
politics: that only political power—manifested ultimately in weapons—
could ensure a nation's security and material prosperity. Invoking the
doctrine of the absolute primacy of politics so central to his own thought,
Hitler explained that although the economy served as an indispensable
handmaiden of the state by providing sustenance for the population and
weaponry for the military, it could never take precedence over the state.
A strong state could make possible prosperity, but material productivity
would never alone suffice to make a nation strong. Germany's fate in the
war and at the Versailles Conference had demonstrated the folly of assuming the contrary. So, too, had postwar efforts to remedy the country's ills by economic means. Until the Germans recognized that only a
revival of their country's political power could reverse its slide into impotence and humiliation, no improvement could occur. In his first Essen
speech Hitler could point to skyrocketing unemployment resulting from
the severe recession of 1925–26 as proof of the futility of republican
efforts at recovery. In his later talks there he dismissed receding joblessness and other signs of returning prosperity as superficial fluctuations
that only temporarily masked the country's fundamental debility. Germany remained, he insisted, a shackled colony of its victorious former
foes, who controlled and exploited its economy for their own en-
richment.

Having set forth this lugubrious diagnosis, Hitler went on to present a
simple cure. He ridiculed as hopelessly irrelevant the efforts of republican statesmen to arrive at remedies by means of new economic policies at
home and treaties abroad with the implacably hostile and rapacious
Entente powers. So long as the German people remained divided politically, he believed, no policies and no treaties could remedy their fundamental weakness. Only when a united national will again pervaded the
nation could it burst its chains and return to power and respectability.
But two obstacles stood in the way of such a restoration of national will:
Marxism and democracy. Marxism had driven a wedge into the populace, dividing it into two roughly equal parts that stood opposed to each
other, one still loyal to sound national values and the other infected with
a subversive internationalist creed that turned its adherents against their
own nation. Democracy, a malignant fruit of the collapse of 1918, had
spread the divisiveness fostered by Marxism into the very core of the
state, rendering the governments of the Republic ineffectual. Marxism,
in turn, exploited the new political order to extend democratization into
economics, destroying all legitimate authority in that sphere of national

life, too. Working in tandem, Marxism and democracy had in less than a decade reduced Germany to virtual impotence at home as well as in the international sphere. Only by extirpating both could the nation rise again.

His party alone possessed the means to carry through this extirpation, Hitler repeatedly assured his Essen listeners. The bourgeois parties could never win back millions of workers so infected with Marxist doctrine that they could no longer even comprehend bourgeois ways of thinking. Only a totally new idea could free Marxism's adherents, and his movement, Hitler announced, possessed just such an idea since it had successfully wedded nationalism and socialism. He and his comrades had discovered that, when properly understood, socialism and nationalism formed two complementary components of an integral whole. Nationalism obligated the individual to serve the nation as a whole, while socialism obligated the whole nation to serve its constituent individuals. Armed with that potent new idea, he and his party had set out on a mission to break the hold of Marxism on half the population and thereby restore the united will necessary for a national resurgence. As in *Mein Kampf*, Hitler served notice that winning back the workers would also require concessions of a material sort from employers. But, he contended, those concessions shrank in significance when compared to the incalculable benefits of bringing the workers back to the national camp. As proof that workers could be wooed away from Marxism, Hitler pointed to the example of Fascist Italy. Mussolini's regime had achieved the "miracle," he claimed, of transforming a demoralized people into a proud, united nation once again. Like Fascism, National Socialism would banish internationalism in favor of nationalism, majority rule in favor of government by strong-willed men, and pacifism in favor of resistance to foreign oppression. In concert with its natural allies, Italy and England, a Germany united and revivified by National Socialism would then break the stranglehold on its national life enjoyed since 1918 by its archenemy, France. Thus would the Reich rise again to its rightful place in the world.

From all accounts, Hitler's Essen audiences proved highly receptive to his speeches, which he sprinkled with ingratiating remarks about the superior qualities of Germans in that part of the country. He would hardly have returned three times to address such groups had his remarks not been well received. The reports of journalists writing for conservative newspapers in the Ruhr unanimously agreed on the favorable response of his listeners. Those journalists noted that his words had won him warm applause and even shouts of agreement. His audiences also grew steadily in size, filling larger and better-known halls. The first numbered only some forty persons, but estimates on the subsequent gatherings ran into the hundreds, ranging up to a high of from 600 to 800 at the last Essen speech.[5]

Those Nazis who organized the Essen gatherings sought to convey the impression that Hitler's audiences included the managerial elite of the Ruhr, and the reporters from the conservative press parroted that version. But, in fact, the Nazis failed to attract the leading industrialists of the Ruhr to Hitler's speeches of 1926 and 1927. In none of the surviving, often voluminous, private papers left behind by some of the Ruhr's most prominent executives of that time does one find any indication that they, others of their circle, or even any of their subordinates, attended. The only mention of Hitler's Essen appearances in the surviving correspondence of the leading Ruhr industrialists occurred when one of the newspaper accounts of the final speech there came to the attention of Paul Reusch, the Ruhr magnate most active in politics. He had it clipped and enclosed with a message to another politically engaged industrialist, Albert Vögler, managing director of the giant United Steel Works. After noting that Vögler had perhaps also read of Hitler's activities and mentioning a desire to discuss Nazism with Vögler when an opportunity arose, Reusch gave vent to his own reaction to Hitler's courtship of the Ruhr: "Hitler will bring us little joy in the *Revier*."[6]

If not the managerial elite of the Ruhr, who did comprise the increasingly sizeable audiences that greeted Hitler's Essen speeches so enthusiastically? Unless lists of those the Nazis invited turn up belatedly, no one will ever know with any certainty; but in all likelihood the businessmen in attendance came predominantly from the numerous small and medium-sized industrial enterprises of the Ruhr. The obscure man named Arnold who organized Hitler's first Essen appearance provides a case in point. An active party member, he held a managerial position at the Henrichshütte, a medium-sized iron-smelting company in Hattingen, a town near Essen. When United Steel swallowed up the company in 1930 and sharply reduced its personnel, Arnold lost his job, whereupon he became an embittered Nazi critic of large-scale enterprise.[7] The Ruhr abounded in businessmen like Arnold. Although most escaped his fate, they too were excluded from the inner circles of the powerful organizations of large-scale industry, and their firms also had to depend on the giant cartels and trusts for the iron and steel they processed and the coal on which they relied for energy. Such men frequently found themselves at odds with big business. Moving in milieus less exalted than those of the barons of industry and finance, they presumably also felt less uncomfortable about exposing themselves to the plebeian ambience that characterized the NSDAP in the Ruhr in the 1920s. Furthermore, to the Nazis they seemed imposing figures from the world of business.[8]

Hitler's Essen audiences by no means consisted entirely of businessmen. Some of the press reports and two letters written by Hitler's private secretary, Rudolf Hess, to another Nazi reveal the presence of some very different sorts of people as well. One press account referred to "intellectual circles," and Hess to "scientists," for examples.[9] Since the Ruhr had neither a university nor any major research institutes, this meant in all likelihood that technical personnel from some industrial firms and teachers from local secondary schools had attended. The conservative *Rheinisch-Westfälische Zeitung* also noted after Hitler's appearance in April 1927 the presence of numerous politically active persons of the immediate region, including a large contingent from the Stahlhelm veterans' organization.[10] The NSDAP's own organ, the *Völkischer Beobachter*, reported following his last Essen speech that at Hitler's own express wish, "party members from all walks of life" had been in attendance.[11] That report may have amounted in part to a tactical gesture designed to shield the party leader from charges of consorting with capitalists behind closed doors. But in view of the active role played by the local Nazis in arranging the Essen gatherings, it seems probable that they accounted for a considerable part of the hundreds who attended Hitler's last two Essen speeches.

Still another group swelled those audiences as well. As Hess confided in his correspondence, the Nazis went to great lengths to entice "the ladies" to attend. Perhaps reflecting Hitler's experiences with wealthy Wagnerian women in Munich, Hess explained that "once they have been won over, they are often more important than the men and exert an influence upon their husbands that is not to be underestimated."[12] Efforts in that direction apparently met with success, since one of the reporters covering Hitler's fourth Essen appearance noted a remarkably large number of women in attendance.[13]

Although Hitler's Essen appearances failed to attract the then current leaders of Ruhr industry, they did pave the way for one notable conversion to Nazism. In April 1927 Hitler's audience included "the Bismarck of coal," Emil Kirdorf, a living monument at eighty years of age to the exuberant early decades of the Ruhr's emergence as Germany's industrial powerhouse.[14] One of the founders during the 1870s of a major coal-mining firm, the Gelsenkirchener Bergwerks AG, Kirdorf served as its managing director throughout the Empire, expanding its holdings into iron and steel. He also played a leading part in forming the bituminous-coal cartel, the Rheinisch-Westfälisches Kohlensyndikat, during the 1890s. An implacable foe of trade unionism and state social welfare measures, he came to personify the reactionary *Herr-im-Hause* industrial executive during the latter stages of the Empire. His unyielding adherence to his principles eventually led him to break with Christianity in favor of a Teutonic cult because of the churches' attitudes toward labor. He also spurned a decoration from Wilhelm II, whom he never forgave for permitting Bismarck's anti-socialist laws to lapse. Fiercely nationalistic, Kirdorf belonged to virtually all the so-called patriotic leagues that agitated during the Empire for a stronger military and a more aggressive foreign policy around the globe. He also dabbled in imperial politics, according behind-the-scenes financial support, along with other Ruhr industrialists, to right-wing political figures as well as to newspapers that followed a conservative, nationalistic editorial policy. During the war Kirdorf figured prominently in the annexationist camp that pressed for the imposition of draconian territorial claims on Germany's foes after the anticipated victory. The Reich's defeat and the revolution of 1918–19 came as crushing blows for him. He regarded the revolution as an act of treason and the Republic as its misbegotten and illegitimate offspring. In the early years of the Republic, he gravitated to the party of the far right, the DNVP, but by the latter half of the 1920s he had become disillusioned by that party's participation in the republican government, its acquiescence to Foreign Minister Gustav Stresemann's conciliatory policies toward Germany's former enemies, and its support for expansion of the republican welfare state. When he heard Hitler for the first time in Essen Kirdorf was in an embittered and restless state of mind politically. What he heard so favorably impressed him that he rose from his seat at the end of the speech and stepped forward to shake the speaker's hand.

This exposure did not suffice to make a Nazi out of Emil Kirdorf. Hitler seems not to have immediately recognized the aged industrialist, and too great a social gulf separated the local NSDAP from a man of Kirdorf's stature to permit a follow-up at that level. Only through the efforts of a socially acceptable intermediary did Kirdorf eventually come together with Hitler. That role of go-between was played by Elsa Bruckmann, Hitler's longtime admirer and patroness in Munich society circles. Having learned that Kirdorf was vacationing in Austria in the summer of 1927, she wrote him that she had taken it upon herself to bring Hitler into contact with prominent industrialists. A mutual acquaintance, Prince Karl zu Loewenstein, had especially recommended him to her, Frau Bruckmann informed Kirdorf. In view of the fact the prince had presided over the meetings of the Berlin Nationalklub at which Hitler had spoken in 1922, and in view of Frau Bruckmann's indulgence of her protégé, it seems not inconceivable that promptings from the Nazi leader gave rise to her invocation of a mutual acquaintanceship with the prince to entice Kirdorf to meet with Hitler in Munich on his way back from Austria. But regardless of who set the train of events in motion, Kirdorf accepted Frau Bruckmann's invitation. On July 4th he met for four and a half hours with Hitler at the Bruckmann residence. Once again, Kirdorf succumbed to Hitler's rhetoric. The aged industrialist had long been convinced that the key to a restoration of national health lay in inoculating the workers of Germany against Marxism and inculcating them with national values. The version of Nazism's mission that Hitler employed in his courtship of the Ruhr thus found willing ears. Only two aspects of Nazism disturbed Kirdorf: its complacency toward what he perceived as the menace of Catholicism and its anti-Semitism. Hitler allayed his concern on the first count by observing that they could not do battle simultaneously against both Marxism and Catholicism. Anti-Semitism posed a more difficult problem since it so conspicuously pervaded Nazism's public pronouncements, as Kirdorf well knew, and since he himself did not subscribe to its tenets and counted Jews of conservative, patriotic outlook among his close friends and associates. Kirdorf managed, however, to surmount his reservations about that side of Nazism, too. As he explained to a longtime Jewish friend, he had become convinced that Nazi anti-Semitism amounted to a mere tactical weapon for winning over the broad masses. Once that task had been accomplished, the unsavory attacks of the National Socialists on Jews would cease, he confidently predicted.

His reservations overcome, Kirdorf joined the NSDAP. Although no evidence has ever come to light to prove that he marked his entry into the party with a financial contribution, in all likelihood he did. Improbable, however, is a tale told by Albert Speer, Hitler's armaments minister and confidant during World War II. According to Speer, Hitler confided to him many years afterwards that the NSDAP had been close to bankruptcy when Frau Bruckmann brought him together with Kirdorf, who promptly paid off virtually all the party's outstanding debts.[15] That story seems implausible on several counts. First, there are no indications that the NSDAP experienced any greater financial problems in the summer of 1927 than it did throughout the latter half of the decade.[16] Second, Kirdorf was an unlikely source of large amounts of money in 1927. His business fortunes had declined precipitously in the wake of the peace treaty, which had stripped his firm of its extensive iron ore holdings as a result of the cession of Lorraine to France. Unable to cope effectively with the postwar inflation, Kirdorf had to assent to the merger of his firm with Hugo Stinnes's industrial empire and then, after Stinnes's death in 1924, to its absorption into the United Steel Works. With each of these rearrangements, the elderly industrialist's role became more peripheral, and he gradually withdrew into retirement. By 1926–27 he remained an honorary officer of organizations such as the coal cartel, but he no longer commanded large amounts of corporate money nor had a decisive say in the deployment of associational funds. Any contribution Kirdorf made on becoming a Nazi would therefore in all probability have had to come out of his own pocket. Since he deservedly had a reputation as a frugal, self-made man who dug into his own pocket neither often nor generously, a contribution on his part does not seem likely to have been enormous.[17]

More important than whatever funds Kirdorf may have donated on becoming a member of the NSDAP in the summer of 1927 were his efforts to proselytize in Ruhr industrial circles on behalf of the party. At his urging, Hitler wrote out a summary version of what he had said during their four-and-a-half-hour meeting at Frau Bruckmann's. Kirdorf then had that document handsomely printed as a twenty-two-page

pamphlet by Hugo Bruckmann's Munich publishing house under the
title *Der Weg zum Wiederaufstieg,* or *The Road to Resurgence,* with Hitler
designated as author.[18] Although it bore all the appearances of a published work, the pamphlet received only limited, private circulation, and
a notation on its cover left no doubt about its provenance: "Presented by
Emil Kirdorf." If any question existed about the purpose of the pamphlet, a sentence in the letter which Hitler had sent to Kirdorf along with
the text and which appeared as its preamble left little room for speculation: "I shall do my best in the darkness of these days to clear the way for
this will [to pursue internal and external resurgence] and shall be happy
if you, esteemed Privy Councillor, wish to help spread these ideas in
your circles." Emil Kirdorf, the "Bismarck of coal," had volunteered to
serve as a Nazi recruiter.

In *The Road to Resurgence* Hitler once more tailored his words, as he
had in his Essen speeches, to fit an audience of businessmen. He down-
played his anti-Semitism, condemning only once the "international Jew"
in a context that made it possible for his readers to think his remark did
not apply to patriotic Jewish Germans. Concealing his commitment to a
foreign policy aimed primarily at the conquest of *Lebensraum,* he led his
readers to assume that he believed a traditional, export-oriented economic policy should accompany a pursuit of additional arable land
through restoration of territory lost at Versailles. Making no mention of
the radical economic planks of the NSDAP's twenty-five-points program
of 1920, he alluded once in cryptic fashion merely to the "so-to-speak
scaffold-like program" of the party. As in his Essen speeches, he gave no
hint of his own dissatisfaction with many aspects of the social and economic orders to which capitalism had given rise in Germany. Instead, he
presented himself as a defender of private enterprise and individual
initiative, which he portrayed as imperatives dictated by a Darwinian
world. His diagnosis of Germany's ills echoed what had been said in
his speeches. Marxism and democracy, internationalism and pacifism
threatened to sap the people's will and make impossible a restoration of
the nation's inner strength and resolve, which alone could preserve it
from predatory foreign enemies. Again Hitler contended that the remedy for economic ills lay in the political sphere rather than the other way
around. In the international marketplace, he warned, "the decisive factor . . . has never yet rested in the relative skill and know-how of the
various competitors, but rather in the might of the sword they could
wield to tip the scales for their business and hence their lives." As in his
Essen speeches, he contended that only his movement could restore potency to Germany's sword. Only the NSDAP, thanks to its successful synthesis of nationalism and socialism, could draw the workers back into the
national fold. Again he specified that concessions, amounting only to
"the fulfillment of rightful social demands," would be required for that
task. But such concessions must, he wrote, be viewed against the "im-

mense gain to be derived from an intimate, all-embracing national community and the power it engenders."

As Hitler apparently recognized, the improving business conditions of 1927 detracted from the plausibility of his contention that the economic climate had steadily deteriorated ever since establishment of the Republic. He therefore devoted considerable space in his pamphlet to a discussion of unemployment, the balance of trade, foreign loans, and bankruptcies. He clearly wanted not only to cast doubt on the soundness of the current boom but also to demonstrate his command of economics to his readers; for their edification he even included what he must have regarded as a recondite footnote. But any business executive who read *The Road to Resurgence* would have had little difficulty in recognizing that the author's acquaintance with economics did not exceed what he could have garnered from a perusal of the daily press. Indeed, Hitler provided more than one example of his muddled notions about elementary economic matters.[19]

The question remains as to who read *The Road to Resurgence*. No record has survived of how many copies Kirdorf had printed or to whom he sent them. At the time and for more than forty years thereafter, it remained a secret document. In subsequent years only Kirdorf himself ever referred in public to its existence. Except for the survival of one sole copy, the pamphlet could have disappeared with barely a trace. The fact that the surviving copy belongs to the library of a major Ruhr industrial firm indicates, however, that Kirdorf distributed it to prominent industrialists in the *Revier*.[20] But if the pamphlet received distribution under such venerable auspices, why did it gain so little attention? The most probable answer is that those who got copies were busy men who could not know at the time that the author would soon become an important— eventually the most important—politician in the country. If any of the leading executives of the Ruhr bothered to grapple with Hitler's prose long enough to read what he had written, it must have seemed quite remote from their preoccupations in 1927. They would have found no mention of trade unions, nor of binding state arbitration of labor-management disputes. They would have found no stand by Hitler on the question of legislative regulation of the length of the industrial workday, or on any other concrete manifestations of government intervention in economic affairs. Instead, they would have found what must have seemed a farfetched panacea for all of Germany's ills, offered by the leader of an insignificant political party who had recently served time in prison after leading a near-farcical attempt to overthrow the national government in the distant capital of Bavaria, where his movement still found its principal following. Under the circumstances, many, if not most, of those who received copies of Hitler's *The Road to Resurgence* may well have decided that it did not merit even a quarter-hour of their time.

The near-total disappearance of copies of the pamphlet suggests strongly that most of the recipients consigned it to their wastebaskets.

These same handicaps may have thwarted Kirdorf's further efforts to win support for Hitler and his movement. In his privately printed memoirs, written years later, Kirdorf recalled that in addition to distributing *The Road to Resurgence,* he succeeded in bringing Hitler together at his home in October 1927 with fourteen of his close friends from industry, whose names he did not disclose.[21] Like the Essen speeches, that meeting went unrecorded in the surviving correspondence of prominent Ruhr executives. This suggests that the leaders of the Ruhr did not attend the meeting at Kirdorf's home, in all likelihood for the same reasons Hitler's pamphlet attracted so little attention. Kirdorf himself conceded in his memoirs that some of those he invited to meet the Nazi leader declined to come. Just who did attend remains unknown, but given the likely age of the close friends of a man of eighty, it seems probable that a good many of those who met Hitler at Kirdorf's home in 1927 had, like Kirdorf, already withdrawn into retirement. Those who did meet Hitler, and listened to him explain his ideas and aims for three hours at Kirdorf's in October 1927, apparently did not all succumb as easily as had their host. In his memoirs Kirdorf specified that they had raised objections to the NSDAP's anti-Semitism and to its socialistic orientation. So far as is known, the gathering resulted in no further conversions to Nazism.

As Kirdorf's memoirs reveal, Nazi socialistic rhetoric remained a barrier between the NSDAP and the business community, despite Hitler's efforts to counter it with reassuring words of his own. The day after the October 1927 gathering at Kirdorf's home, Paul Reusch wrote to Albert Vögler, enclosing a copy of Gottfried Feder's newly published second commentary on the program of the NSDAP. Although Feder scarcely stood on the far left of the party, his views placed him well outside Reusch's range of acceptability. In alerting Vögler to Feder's new publication, Reusch confined himself to the laconic observation, "Comment superfluous!"[22] Reusch later had additional copies of Feder's commentary distributed to other industrial leaders, instructing his secretary to underline what he described as "the most remarkable passages."[23] Thanks in part to the wide distribution achieved by Feder's publication, knowledge of the socialistic planks of the Nazi program spread throughout the business community. Two years after its publication, a Nazi organizer in Hamburg reported finding that prominent business leaders there recoiled from National Socialism, finding it more "social" than "national" and fearing that it might endanger private property if it ever got power. One retired Hamburg banker, a longtime friend of Emil Kirdorf, delivered a particularly stinging rebuke. An "abyss" separated him, he informed the Nazi organizer, from a party whose press and parliamentarians called for the expropriation of Germany's banks.[24] Rudolf

Hess encountered similar hostility when he attempted to solicit contributions for the NSDAP in Hamburg business circles at the end of the decade. The party's stock stood so low in the Hanseatic trading city that the local Nazis could find only five or six businessmen willing even to listen to what Hitler's secretary had to say. When they arrived at the appointed hour, Hess handed them a series of pictures depicting scenes of mass revolutionary tumult in which red flags occupied prominent places. He then showed them pictures of uniformed formations of SA and SS men, marching in tightly disciplined formations. When his tiny audience grew visibly impatient at passing these pictures about, Hess announced that they were seeing, on the one hand, a "force of destruction" that threatened their factories and warehouses and, on the other, a "force of order" filled with fanatical determination to extirpate the "spirit of insurrection." When Hess failed to respond in an informative manner to concrete queries about the policies of the NSDAP, his increasingly skeptical listeners sought to provoke him—unsuccessfully, according to a witness's later account—with such sarcastic questions as, "Surely, you don't mean to tell us, Herr Hess, that your NSDAP wishes to serve as a kind of security-guard service for large-scale property?" That hardly seemed plausible, they taunted Hess, in view of abundant indications to the effect that rank-and-file Nazis regarded themselves as "thoroughly revolutionary and anti-capitalist." After less than forty minutes the meeting ended, with Hess leaving empty-handed.[25]

The socialistic agitation of the Nazi left wing soon proved too much even for Emil Kirdorf.[26] In August 1928, little more than a year after he joined the NSDAP, Kirdorf angrily submitted his resignation to the party's Munich headquarters. During the year he belonged to the party Kirdorf managed to put up with the anti-capitalism that pervaded the pronouncements of the Nazi left wing. But in the summer of 1928 an article in a Nazi publication in the Ruhr struck a sensitive nerve by attacking the bituminous-coal cartel which he had taken a leading part in founding and which he still regarded as one of his cardinal achievements. In his letter of resignation Kirdorf charged that the article "takes up the same methods of combat employed by the homelandless trade unions in their incitement of workers against entrepreneurs." He therefore felt compelled to break with Nazism, Kirdorf announced, in spite of his sympathy and friendship for Adolf Hitler. After leaving the NSDAP he quietly rejoined the DNVP. The election of his old friend Alfred Hugenberg as its chairman in October 1928 strengthened Kirdorf's recommitment to his old party. Hitler repeatedly sought to lure him back into the Nazi fold, sending him effusive New Year's greetings at the beginning of 1929 and bringing him to the party congress as an honored guest in August of that year. But although he continued to express his admiration for Hitler, Kirdorf left no doubt that he found parts of the Nazis' program an insurmountable barrier. Not until years later, under the vastly different conditions following the Nazis' acquisition of power, did he reconsider and, thanks to the personal intercession of Hitler, re-enter the NSDAP as the proud bearer of his old, prestigiously low membership number. Hitler ordered that his membership records be rewritten to conceal his apostasy, and until his death in 1938 at the age of ninety-one, the regime celebrated him as an *alter Kämpfer*, one of those early followers of the Führer who had never broken faith in the difficult years before the party's successes.

Kirdorf's brief involvement aside, Nazism's stock remained at low ebb in the business community throughout the late 1920s. Despite the reassurances Hitler sought to broadcast, businessmen found nothing attractive in a splinter party awash with anti-capitalist slogans and socialistic programmatic commitments, tainted with illegality, and given to unsavory street rowdiness. The experience of those Bavarian businessmen who had been hauled before an investigating committee after the abortive beer hall putsch because of rumors linking them to the NSDAP must have served as a further deterrent to involvement with Nazism. As Kirdorf's memoirs reveal, many in the business community also found Nazi anti-Semitism repellent. This distaste for something associated in the minds of most business leaders with the lower orders of society could lead to unpleasant consequences for Nazis dependent on big business for a livelihood. Robert Ley, gauleiter in the Rhineland and later head of the Labor Front in the Third Reich, discovered this in 1927. A chemist employed at a laboratory of the giant IG Farben combine, Ley offended his employers when he launched anti-Semitic attacks in the local Nazi press against a prominent Hamburg banker, Max Warburg, who sat on Farben's supervisory board. When Farben gave Ley a choice between ceasing to speak out politically and getting fired, he refused to back down and so lost his job.[27] Still another indication of the low repute of Nazism in big business circles during the latter half of the decade is provided by an item in a 1927 issue of the house organ of Stuttgart's largest industrial firm, the Bosch spark plug company. That item consisted of the text of a letter of solicitation addressed by the Württemberg state headquarters of the NSDAP to "non-Jewish circles in industry and commerce," including the Bosch firm. Despite assurances in the letter of the NSDAP's commitment to protect "rightfully acquired property" and combat leftist terrorism, Robert Bosch, the patriarch of the firm, ordered it published under a headline that succinctly conveyed his opinion of Nazism: "A Letter That Was Not Answered."[28] A year later, the *Deutsche Allgemeine Zeitung* of Berlin, a newspaper owned by a consortium of big business interests, dismissed the NSDAP as an insignificant Bavarian movement with an "Italian salad" of a program. Hitler had, the paper observed, discredited himself through his actions of 1923 and the barbarous excesses of his followers.[29]

Considerable evidence indicates that Germany's businessmen believed during the latter half of the 1920s that even the appearance of a link to Nazism could hurt their firms. In 1926 the Bechstein piano firm, which depended on a sophisticated, cosmopolitan clientele, summarily expelled Edwin Bechstein when reports of his fraternization with Hitler surfaced in the press. The firm publicly announced that he had resigned from its supervisory board, sold his holdings in the firm, and severed all connections with it. Without specifically mentioning his offense, the Bechstein firm issued assurances that it maintained "complete neutrality with regard to politics."[30] Similarly, when the press carried rumors during 1927 to the effect that Ernst von Borsig was subsidizing Hitler, that industrialist, whose firm relied heavily on contracts from the republican government, felt compelled to distance himself from Nazism. In a press release, Borsig admitted encountering Hitler twice in Berlin prior to the attempted putsch but denied any contact since then. At the time Hitler had favorably impressed him, Borsig stated, but he explained that National Socialism had then not yet taken on the political character it later assumed. Without specifying whether he was referring to the past as well as the present, Borsig denied the allegations about his giving money to Hitler.[31] The experiences of some lesser figures from the ranks of business suggest that Borsig had good grounds for feeling uneasy about the reports linking him with Nazism. A minor executive in the Ruhr who became an active Nazi in 1926 soon found his political affiliation such a business liability that he officially resigned from the party less than half a year later, after assuring the local gauleiter that he would continue to work for the NSDAP covertly.[32] Hitler himself had become aware by the end of the decade of the handicap that membership in his party could present for businessmen. When Emil Kirdorf's stepson, who operated a family-owned tile factory in Bonn, expressed to him a desire to join the NSDAP in 1929, Hitler advised him that he could serve the party's interests more effectively, and without peril to his business, if he refrained from officially joining.[33]

Despite repeated press rumors about capitalists purportedly providing the Nazis with enormous sums of money, Hitler's first courtship of the Ruhr industrial circles as well as subsequent Nazi efforts to win over members of the business community failed to bridge the wide gap that separated the NSDAP from big business in the second half of the 1920s. Hitler seems to have recognized that his efforts were in vain, and abandoned his cultivation of industrialists, at least for the time being. The press accounts of his appearances behind closed doors before audiences of businessmen had occasioned some consternation among rank-and-file Nazis, giving rise to denials by the *Völkischer Beobachter* that he said anything different to the industrialists of the Ruhr than he did to the rallies of party members he also addressed on his visits there.[34] He himself again felt compelled to rebut allegations by political foes that he accepted subsidies from capitalists.[35] Under these circumstances, the abandonment of his cultivation of the Ruhr industrialists probably came easy to Hitler. He had no qualms, however, about addressing similar but less conspicuous audiences elsewhere. In March 1928 he spoke in Heidelberg before another specially invited audience consisting largely of businessmen.[36] He also continued to adopt positions conducive to an eventual rapprochement with the business community. Prior to the national election of 1928, for example, he in effect amended the NSDAP's twenty-five-point program of 1920. Responding to the exploitation by other parties of the NSDAP's programmatic pledge to enact a law empowering the government to effect agrarian reform by confiscating land without compensation, Hitler appended a footnote to that item in the program which qualified it drastically and, in addition, officially committed his party for the first time to the principle of private property.[37] During the campaign for the 1928 elections the party avoided economic issues and emphasized national ones, directing its fire at Germany's foreign adversaries and those at home whom the Nazis found guilty of insufficiently defending the national interest.[38] In the summer of 1929 Hitler publicly disavowed those left-wing Nazis who wanted to seek coalitions with the SPD and KPD in state governments, thereby revealing that he favored collaboration with the parties of the right.[39] As if to underline his position on that score, that same summer he had the NSDAP join with the DNVP, rightist splinter parties, and the Stahlhelm veterans' organization in support of the referendum against the Young Plan, which revised arrangements for Germany's reparations payments. But despite these signs of movement toward the right, suspicion and mistrust toward National Socialism prevailed in big business circles, which could not put out of mind the radical rhetoric of numerous Nazi spokesmen. The predominant attitude in those circles found expression in a set of guidelines on editorial policy that Paul Reusch put into effect in late 1929 for the newspapers controlled by his firm. In those guidelines the NSDAP appeared, together with the Communists, the Social Democrats, and the trade unions, as one of the bearers of Marxism, its pernicious "idea of class conflict" and its "utopian goals in the sphere of economic policy."[40]

As one of Hitler's associates later observed, his first sustained effort to cultivate the managerial elite of Germany's industrial heartland met with disappointingly little success.[41] He had displayed great adroitness at tailoring a version of National Socialism cut closely to the preferences of big business. By concealing many of his party's programmatic commitments on economic matters, as well as his own aspirations for alterations in the existing order, he had presented National Socialism as a movement without any fundamental objections to capitalism. His party's aim, as he portrayed it to businessmen, was to purge Germany of Marxism and restore it to power and greatness in the world. Yet despite all his efforts, these blandishments had failed to allay the mistrust of Nazism in the upper echelons of the Ruhr. This response demonstrated that Hitler's strategy of cultivating ambiguity with regard to his party's position on economic matters had its limitations. Whereas the Nazis could get away with making conflicting promises to such groups as farmers, shopkeepers, and urban wage earners, it proved less easy to gull the great capitalists of the country. They commanded too many means of gathering information to hear only what Hitler chose to tell them, and what they had heard from other elements of the NSDAP repelled them. Regardless of what the leader of the party might say, they knew that other Nazis spoke a very different language, one they found incompatible with their economic views. So long as Hitler refused to rein in his party's radicals, a formidable obstacle separated him from the business leaders he had hoped to reach in 1926 and 1927. His courtship of the Ruhr did not, however, remain wholly without positive results from his point of view. He had begun to construct for himself the reputation of a moderate Nazi on economic issues which he would later seek to cultivate. Also, his insistence, at a time when the Weimar Republic seemed to succeed in restoring a modicum of stability and prosperity, on the faulty bases of that recovery may well have led some of those business executives who learned of the message he brought to the Ruhr to take him somewhat more seriously once the Great Depression swept away the accomplishments of the republican regime in the economic sphere.

III
Parliamentary Democracy Ends and Nazism Breaks Through

1. The Great Coalition Gives Way to Presidential Rule

The year 1930 brought major transformations in Germany's political life. The Republic's decade of democracy ended as parliamentary government ceased to function. Never again would a cabinet rest on an affirmative democratic majority in the Reichstag. Instead, the national government began to rely on the sweeping emergency powers accorded the president by the Weimar constitution. The erosion of republican institutions that would end in the bloodless transfer of power to a tyrant had begun. A national election that gravely weakened the moderate parties and propelled the Nazis into national prominence lent added impetus to this process of erosion. These developments began with the collapse in March 1930 of the great coalition cabinet that had held office under Social Democratic Chancellor Hermann Müller since 1928. The issues that split the coalition were of vital concern to big business, and its role in the cabinet's breakup has long given rise to controversy. So have the ensuing events, which gave birth to a "presidential" system of rule.

The dissension that tore apart the great coalition arose over questions which seemed novel at the time but which have since become familiar dilemmas of twentieth-century capitalistic welfare states. At stake was whether, in a time of economic contraction, social programs should be maintained, regardless of the cost, in order to help those most affected by the hard times or whether those programs should be curtailed in order to permit the private capital accumulation needed to spur investment and renewed growth. When the German economy went into decline at the end of the 1920s, even before the onset of the worldwide depression, the Social Democrats and their trade union allies vigorously opposed all efforts to scale down the achievements of republican *Sozial-*

politik. With especial vehemence they defended the 1927 unemployment insurance program, on which debate came increasingly to focus in late 1929 when the swelling ranks of the jobless exhausted the program's regular sources of income, turning it into a drain on the national budget and a major factor in the rapidly burgeoning deficit in the Reich budget. For the SPD, the social legislation of the Republic represented the principal tangible gain from the revolution for Germany's wage earners. The Social Democrats therefore balked at demands raised by their coalition partners for curtailment of *Sozialpolitik* in favor of a more stimulative *Wirtschaftspolitik*. Led by the DVP, the "wing party" on the right, nonsocialists in the coalition insisted on a reduction of taxes and government spending in order to remedy the capital shortage to which the business community and most economists attributed the downturn in the German economy. A shared commitment to the Young Plan for a downward revision of reparations payments held the coalition together until March 1930. At that point, final passage of the laws necessary to implement the new reparations plan removed the foreign-policy constraints that had produced a sequence of stopgap solutions to the increasingly grave fiscal problems of the government. While agreement prevailed in the coalition that the deficit of the unemployment insurance fund must be brought under control, deep differences emerged over how to achieve that goal. The Social Democrats insisted on maintaining unemployment benefits at the levels set in 1927. They proposed to meet the costs by increasing the levies on employers and employed workers that provided the regular income of the fund, by extending government subsidies to it, and by imposing new taxes to cover the national deficit. The bourgeois parties resisted these proposals as simply more of the fiscal irresponsibility and excessive welfare taxation to which they in large measure attributed the slump in economic activity. From the side of the bourgeois parties came proposals for reductions in the level and number of unemployment benefits, a tightening of the program to eliminate waste and abuse, and a general lowering of taxes on capital. During March 1930 repeated attempts were made to resolve these differences through compromise. But late in the month, with the two sides separated by only relatively minor differences, negotiations broke down and the coalition came to an end.[1]

Some historians have placed heavy, even decisive, responsibility on Germany's industrial leadership for the collapse of the great coalition, but such indictments appear exaggerated in the light of the evidence. Certain Ruhr industrialists clearly had become convinced that the time had come for a break with the SPD.[2] But the political spokesmen of industry, not all of whom shared that conviction, lacked the parliamentary strength to block legislation, much less threaten a cabinet's survival, on their own. Even within the DVP, which was known as the party of big business, they remained in the minority.[3] To the extent that they managed to influence the course of events in March 1930, they could do so

only because they had allies. These they found among middle-class interest groups that had become aroused when the Müller cabinet realized
in the face of a runaway deficit that more than mere adjustments in the
unemployment insurance program would be needed to restore fiscal
equilibrium. Whereas the public had been led to expect that the Young
Plan would make possible a reduction in taxes, the cabinet now hastily
proposed in early 1930 a variety of special taxes which threatened the
material interests of numerous groups. Projected changes in the income
tax law struck the usual sensitive nerves; a plan for a special tax on
persons with fixed incomes stirred resentment among civil servants; projected increases in the excise tax on beer encountered stubborn opposition from the Bavarian People's Party. During the great coalition's final
month these bread-and-butter issues became inextricably entangled with
that of *Sozialpolitik* since each proposed formula consisted of a complex
bundle of taxes and reform measures for the unemployment insurance
program. This situation enabled the right-wingers in the DVP, including
opposition spokesmen for Ruhr industry, to mobilize their own party as
well as elements of the other non-socialist coalition parties and block
approval of a succession of such proposals.[4]

But while industrial interests contributed importantly to the escalation
of differences over fiscal policies into a cabinet crisis, they did not bring
down the Müller government. For as the crisis approached its climax,
most of the parliamentarians who had joined with the DVP's right wing
dropped their opposition to a resolution of the disputed issues by the
great coalition. In late March a compromise formula put forward by
Centrist leader Heinrich Brüning appeased sufficient interest groups to
win the approval of a sizeable majority of the DVP deputies, leaving that
party's right wing an isolated minority. With the exception of the Bavarian People's Party, whose votes were not crucial, the other bourgeois
parties also approved the Brüning compromise. It failed, however, when
the SPD rejected it, thereby bringing down the cabinet. It has been argued that the Brüning plan leaned so far in the direction of the bourgeois parties as to make it impossible for the Social Democrats to accept
it. At the time, however, much of the leadership of the SPD, including
most of its cabinet ministers, did not believe this. They vigorously advocated adoption of the compromise. It has also been contended that the
DVP's support for the compromise amounted to a mere tactical move,
designed to shift the onus for the cabinet's fall to the SPD. That view
presupposes foreknowledge on the part of the DVP that the Social Democrats would reject the compromise. Yet the support of the SPD leadership for the plan made its prospects seem good at the time, and DVP
Finance Minister Moldenhauer, who favored the compromise, detected
no deviousness in the behavior of his own party.[5] The DVP's right wing,
which presumably would have supported a tactically motivated approval
of the Brüning compromise, simply lost out when the DVP deputies had

to face the question of whether to accept the compromise or break up the coalition. Confronted with the same choices, a majority of the SPD deputies bowed to strong pressure from the socialist trade unions and voted to reject the Brüning compromise. By their act they toppled the last Weimar cabinet headed by a chancellor from the ranks of the SPD and plunged Germany into an uncertain future. From all indications, many in their ranks gave in to a growing urge to flee from governmental responsibility at a time when remaining in power would have entailed assuming responsibility for decisions unpopular among the party's followers. Although some historians have exhibited great reluctance to place the blame for bringing down the Müller cabinet on the SPD, those Social Democratic leaders who opposed their delegation's rejection of the final compromise did not hesitate to do so. The SPD deputies' action, wrote Rudolf Hilferding, amounted to "committing suicide for fear of death."[6]

While at least part of the business community bore a sizeable share of responsibility for the crisis that ended in the breakup of the great coalition, no evidence supports the contention that big business launched in the spring of 1930 an offensive aimed at destroying the democratic institutions of the Republic.[7] That charge rests on hindsight. At the time few contemporaries, including the leaders of the business community, saw a major constitutional turning point at hand. One cabinet had fallen; another would replace it, as always. Somehow, the problem of parliamentary backing would be worked out, even in the absence of a majority coalition, since minority cabinets had shown themselves quite viable in earlier years. A general expectation prevailed that the next cabinet would be located somewhat to the right of the old one, and would be headed by someone situated on the political spectrum somewhere between former chancellor Müller and DNVP leader Alfred Hugenberg.[8] No consensus existed in the business community about who would make the best chancellor. Until only a short time before the fall of the great coalition, considerable sentiment had existed for returning to the chancellorship Hans Luther, who had filled that post in a non-party capacity from 1925 to 1927.[9] But Luther's acceptance in mid-March of the presidency of the Reichsbank, following Hjalmar Schacht's resignation in protest against the Young Plan's implementation, made his retention of that economically important new post seem essential, both to him and to his big business supporters, at least for the time being.[10] The business community thus faced the aftermath of the great coalition's collapse with no candidate for the chancellorship, no agreement about the most desirable makeup of the next cabinet, and—as it turned out—no access to the locus of decision making, the presidency. It was, in short, exceedingly ill equipped to launch a political offensive of any kind.

The assault on the democratic institutions of the Republic that began in the spring of 1930 came not from big business but rather from another, but much more politically potent, remnant of the imperial era: the military.[11] As Germany's capitalists looked on passively, and unconsulted, the generals stepped in and set in motion a reshaping of the political institutions of the country. Taking advantage of their privileged access to Hindenburg, Defense Minister Wilhelm Groener and his aide, General Kurt von Schleicher, helped to turn the president against the great coalition. As the crisis of the Müller cabinet deepened, its ministers, including those from the SPD, gave serious consideration to settling the troublesome fiscal issues facing them by making use of the emergency powers accorded the president by Article 48 of the constitution, an idea also then current in rightist political circles, which had, however, a government of different composition in mind.[12] Initially, the president indicated a willingness to place his emergency powers at the disposal of the cabinet.[13] But at the height of the political crisis of March 1930 Hindenburg, at least in part under the influence of his military confidants, struck the Müller cabinet a heavy blow by letting it be known that he would not use Article 48 on its behalf.[14] Well in advance of the cabinet's fall, the military leadership had chosen Müller's successor. He was, of course, Heinrich Brüning, leader of the Catholic Center Party's Reichstag delegation, former Christian trade union official, and—not least important—erstwhile commander of a machine gun unit in the war. In the final months of the great coalition, Groener and Schleicher saw to it that a special relationship developed between Hindenburg and Brüning. In the Centrist leader, they believed—rightly, as it turned out—they had found a politician willing to reduce the dependence of the executive on the democratically elected parliament. At the very outset of his chancellorship Brüning unmistakably indicated the direction he planned to take. Pledging to keep his cabinet above the parties, he announced his readiness to resort, if necessary, to "all available constitutional means," which observers correctly interpreted to mean that the new chancellor had assurances from the president about access to Article 48.[15]

Although the business community had no voice in the installation of Brüning in the chancellorship, it soon warmed to the new cabinet. Despite the chancellor's trade union career, he came from a solidly middle-class background, and his proposals for dealing with the economic crisis closely paralleled those of the business community. Immediately upon assuming office, Brüning announced his commitment to fiscal austerity. He promised to curtail government expenditures and grant tax relief in order to bring about economic recovery. His cabinet also held out the prospect of a general reform of financial policies at all levels of government so as to eliminate waste and reduce the tax burden—a step for which big business had long clamored. Moreover, Brüning's cabinet quickly demonstrated that it dealt in more than promises. Less than two weeks after taking office it secured adoption, by a right-center Reichstag majority, of a series of measures designed to reduce the budget deficit by just the formula demanded by the industrial Reichsverband and other big business associations: increases in the excise taxes that weighed heavily on low-income groups, and reductions in the direct taxes that hit businesses and the holders of capital.[16] These measures so encouraged the business community that it uncomplainingly accepted an increase in the levy for unemployment insurance, despite having resisted that step to the point of provoking the fatal crisis of the great coalition. In June came another heartening development from the standpoint of big business. To the consternation of the trade unions, Brüning's labor minister bestowed binding authority, at management's request, on an arbitration board's recommendation for a reduction of wages in the iron and steel industries of the Ruhr.[17] After years of settlements favoring labor, the Republic's system of binding arbitration yielded a cut, rather than an increase, in a wage dispute. Even while upholding its objections to binding arbitration in principle, the business community welcomed the minister's action.[18] The new chancellor also agreed with the contention of Germany's capitalists that wage cuts must precede the price reductions needed to set off an upward economic swing.

The most momentous political innovation of the Brüning cabinet came with its routine reliance on presidential emergency powers to enact fiscal legislation. The business community displayed no principled objections to employment of Article 48, which had frequently been used—only temporarily, to be sure—by earlier republican cabinets. But when the issue arose in the spring of 1930, influential figures in big business circles viewed apprehensively, for practical reasons, the prospect of such a circumvention of the parliament by the executive. Their concern arose from the fear that even the appearance of a constitutional conflict might undermine confidence in Germany abroad and trigger a withdrawal of the foreign capital on which the economy so heavily depended. In early March the industrial Reichsverband had encouraged the Müller cabinet to resolve its fiscal problems by means of a parliamentary enabling act, a method of bestowing exceptional authority on the cabinet without raising constitutional issues. That proposal proved, however, impracticable because the deepening divisions among the parties of the great coalition ruled out authorization of such a measure by the Reichstag.[19] When Brüning began his chancellorship with a threat to invoke Article 48, the executive director of the principal association of bankers at once warned that any measures of an anti-parliamentary nature must be avoided because of the possible reaction of American creditors.[20] Later, during the summer, when Brüning made good on his threat by enacting the first fiscal measures by means of Article 48, even Paul Reusch, the politically active Ruhr industrialist not known as a defender of parliamentary democracy, feared that conflict between the executive and the legislature could shake Germany's credit rating in the world.[21]

If big business could have shaped political developments during the spring and summer of 1930, Brüning would have had no chance to call on the president for use of Article 48. That is, had those business spokesmen who sought to influence the course of events succeeded, Brüning and his cabinet would have enjoyed the backing of a parliamentary majority, thereby obviating the need for exceptional powers. Anxious to avoid a period of governmental instability and convinced of the need to cooperate with the SPD, moderate elements in the business community worked in the spring of 1930 toward a restoration of labormanagement collaboration along the lines of the ZAG established by the Stinnes-Legien Agreement, which had lapsed at the time of the inflation.[22] Under the leadership of Hans von Raumer, executive director of the association of electro-technical industries and one of the architects of the ZAG, spokesmen of the industrial Reichsverband and the national association of employers began negotiating with officials of the socialist trade unions in May. The two sides aimed at a compromise formula based on mutual material sacrifices that would enable the Brüning cabinet to balance the budget and spur recovery by lowering both prices and wages. If they could reach agreement, they expected that the two chief political exponents of industry and management, the DVP and the SPD, would fall in behind the new Brüning cabinet and give it a reliable parliamentary majority by reestablishing the great coalition on at least a de facto basis. For much of industry, the increasingly extreme demands of agricultural interests for higher import duties on foodstuffs, which would provoke retaliation abroad against German manufacturing exports, made attractive the prospect of renewed cooperation with organized labor, which was committed to low food costs and promotion of exports. Despite resistance by some hard-line industrialists against concessions to the unions, the industrial spokesmen came close to hammering out an agreement with the trade unionists. The negotiations finally collapsed at the end of June when the labor spokesmen withdrew, having concluded that their position had become too unfavorable as a consequence of the arbitration ruling in the iron and steel industry by Brüning's labor minister and other developments. The Reichsverband insisted, nevertheless, that prospects were good for a revival of labormanagement collaboration and held the door open for renewed negotiations.

While some big business spokesmen sought a parliamentary basis for the Brüning cabinet on the left, others looked rightward to the DNVP. If the votes of that conservative party's Reichstag deputies could be brought behind the new cabinet and combined with those of the middle and right-of-center parties that had already rallied to the chancellor, a narrow majority would become feasible. Even though Brüning had pledged to keep his cabinet free of formal ties to any party, he had indicated from the outset that he would welcome support from the DNVP.

With that in mind, industrial spokesmen in the DNVP joined with its agrarian wing, which also looked with hope to the new government, in pressing the party to fall into line behind Brüning. Their efforts foundered, however, on the obdurate resistance of the party's national chairman, Alfred Hugenberg.[23] Although he permitted the DNVP Reichstag delegation to join in providing Brüning with a majority in the first vote of confidence on his cabinet, Hugenberg had no intention of allowing his party to contribute to an even partial resuscitation of the parliamentary system. Motivated by a reactionary outlook colored by his close association with the Pan-German League, he sought nothing short of destruction of the whole republican political system and the eventual ascendancy of a bloc that would encompass all rightist groups under his leadership. When Brüning made clear his unwillingness to renounce Germany's reparations obligations under the Young Plan and proposed his package of new taxes designed to close the budget deficit in April, Hugenberg denounced the new cabinet as another faint-hearted, temporizing, make-shift administration and ordered his party into the opposition. However, joining with deputies who spoke for other interest groups that also placed their hopes in Brüning, the spokesmen of big business in the DNVP Reichstag delegation defied the party leader throughout the spring and early summer by repeatedly voting for government-sponsored measures.

In the ensuing test of strength Hugenberg prevailed, but at the cost of weakening his party's ties to the business community. Bringing to bear his press empire and his control over the party's organizational apparatus, he held the majority of the DNVP deputies in opposition to Brüning, thus blocking enactment of the chancellor's fiscal program when it came before the Reichstag in July. But he again failed to keep most of the industrial spokesmen in the DNVP delegation from breaking ranks and siding with the cabinet. It was in response to this defeat that Brüning first invoked Article 48 to enact his cabinet's fiscal measures. The cabinet's measures were at once revoked when a Reichstag majority, which included the crucial votes of the bulk of the DNVP delegation, overrode this use of presidential emergency powers by a narrow margin. Once more most of the industrial spokesmen in the DNVP defied Hugenberg and took the cabinet's side. That brought their relations with the party leader to the breaking point, and during July they joined with other opponents of Hugenberg's policies in seceding from his party.[24] Never again would the DNVP be as closely linked to the business community as during the first decade of the Republic. It had become an ideological party, dominated by an obsessive leader ruthlessly bent on capturing control of the state by means of a block of nationalistic, rightist forces. For Hugenberg, the pursuit of immediate economic goals by Germany's business leaders seemed parochial and petty in comparison to his own far-reaching aims. He would in the future side with them at times, and he retained a hard core of followers, especially in the Ruhr, but he defiantly resisted efforts on their part to harness him and his party for their purposes.

Brüning's defeat in the Reichstag precipitated his first steps to curtail the authority of the parliament. The chancellor responded to his setback by obtaining a presidential order dissolving the Reichstag and scheduling a national election for the end of September. He then invoked Article 48 again to enact an even more sweeping set of fiscal measures than those revoked by the chamber. Brüning thereby launched Germany on the course of rule by presidential emergency powers that would eventually eviscerate the Republic's parliamentary system. But despite widespread reservations about the parliamentary system in big business circles, the actual developments that resulted in Brüning's move in that direction in July 1930 had come about in spite of, rather than because of, activity on the part of political spokesmen for the business community. Those spokesmen had, to the end, sought to provide the chancellor with parliamentary majorities. Content with the substance of his policies, they saw no need for a radical shift in the method of governing that might precipitate a constitutional crisis and alarm the foreign creditors on whose capital the German economy so heavily depended. The decision to embark on that fateful course lay with Brüning and with President Hindenburg and his small coterie of advisers, which included no spokesmen for big business.[25]

Once it became clear that Brüning's confrontation with the Reichstag had not, as feared, set off a withdrawal of foreign credit, the business community readily accepted his latitudinarian use of Article 48. In fact, some of its spokesmen encouraged his cabinet to make immediate and sweeping use of presidential emergency authority while the Reichstag was out of session during the election campaign, in order to set the country on what they saw as a new and sounder economic course.[26] But even those who urged that course initially saw Brüning's use of Article 48 as merely the same kind of temporary expedient resorted to by previous republican governments. They, like most other observers, expected the parliament to reassert its authority after the election. They merely hoped the chancellor would, in the interval before the Reichstag reconvened, exploit to the fullest the opportunity presented by its dissolution in order to present the new chamber with a series of faits accomplis. Brüning needed no encouragement from big business on that score. Well before its spokesmen made their views known, he and his aides had already begun drafting the next set of sweeping "emergency" measures.[27]

As the campaign for the September Reichstag elections got under way, political activists in the camp of big business sought to buttress the Brüning cabinet's parliamentary position. Much of their support went to a new organization, the pro-Brüning Conservative People's Party (Konser-

vative Volkspartei, or KVP).[28] Formed in July by defectors from the
DNVP, including virtually all the significant industrial spokesmen in that
party's old Reichstag delegation, the KVP labored under great handicaps. It suffered from acute organizational weakness since Hugenberg
had retained control over the apparatus of the DNVP, from its local
units to its national headquarters as well as the party press. The KVP
failed as well to gain the allegiance of the DNVP agrarians who had also
broken with Hugenberg over his opposition to Brüning. Bent on sharp
increases in agricultural tariffs, the agrarians shied away from an alliance with a party oriented toward industry, which opposed higher foodstuff duties for fear they would result in retaliation abroad against
German manufacturing exports. Rejecting an offer of Ruhr industrial
subsidization if they would join the KVP, the former DNVP agrarians
entered the Christian National Farmers' and Rural People's Party, a
splinter group that had in 1928 gained a small representation in the
Reichstag. Some industrialists harbored misgivings about the KVP because of the presence among its leadership of former DNVP members
active in the country's largest union of white-collar employees, which
collaborated with blue-collar unions on many issues.[29] But the new party
nevertheless became the beneficiary of extensive aid from big business
interests. Recognizing that money alone would not suffice, big business
even assigned some of its own personnel to the KVP in hopes of offsetting the thinness of its ranks and its organizational frailty. Both IG
Farben and the Ruhr iron and steel industry dipped into their junior
managerial ranks and associational staffs to provide the new party with
campaign aides and even candidates.[30] The KVP carried with it into the
1930 election campaign the hopes of much of the business community,
as well as some handsome financial contributions.[31]

The established parties that normally enjoyed the backing of big business also received subsidies for the election campaign. But in contrast to
previous practice, the large, collective political subsidies of big business
did not flow in routine fashion.[32] Instead, the politically active leaders of
big business attempted to use their money to reverse what they regarded
as an alarming fragmentation of the right-of-center sector of the political spectrum. By 1930 the fission and proliferation of parties that was to
plague the Republic's politics during its final years had perceptibly accelerated, spurred on by the defections from the DNVP. In hopes of avert-
ing internecine strife that might lead to disillusionment and abstention
by middle-class voters or wasted votes in the case of ballots cast for hopelessly small splinter parties, the principal big business groups active in
politics lent encouragement to the efforts of some politicians of the middle and moderate right to effect a consolidation of parties. At the outset
of the campaign, spokesmen of the Ruhrlade, which disbursed the political funds of Ruhr coal and steel, and the large Berlin banks jointly
informed the leaders of the bourgeois parties other than the Catholic

Center and the DNVP that they would not make their usual financial contributions until those parties surmounted their differences and worked together. Optimally, big business would have preferred to see the parties in question merge into one large bourgeois unity party. When it became evident that such a sweeping solution would not be possible, the political agents of big business insisted that the six component parties of the badly splintered non-Catholic middle portion of the political spectrum agree at least to a common campaign appeal and a joint list of candidates at the national level. Under the Republic's complex proportional electoral system such a joint list would have maximized the representation of those groups in the next Reichstag.

In an effort to force the politicians into line, the political agents of big business mounted a vigorous and sustained lobbying campaign, alternating threats with enticements.[33] Warning that no financial contributions would be available unless significant progress toward cooperation among the parties was achieved, they held out the prospect of handsome subsidies even after the election. But their efforts proved fruitless. The rivalries among the parties, their policy differences, and the reluctance of most of the party leaders to surrender their prerogatives erected insuperable obstacles. Not even a unity list at the national level could be achieved. Conceding their impotence, the men of the Ruhrlade gave in. Rather than risk seeing the parties of the middle lose votes, they backed down and handed over the usual contributions. Anxious to strengthen all bourgeois forces, the Ruhrlade even surmounted the hostility of some of its members toward Hugenberg and authorized subsidies for the DNVP. However, they sought—in vain—to exercise a moderating influence on Hugenberg by insisting that he maintain no relations with the Nazis and end the attacks of his press organs on the new Conservative People's Party and the other defectors from the DNVP, so as to keep open the possibility of collaboration in the new Reichstag.[34]

As their actions in the campaign of 1930 showed, the politically engaged big businessmen of Germany approached the election still willing to work within the parliamentary framework of republican politics. Most preferred, to be sure, a turn to the right, but they rejected the sort of intransigence practiced by Hugenberg. Some of those who supported the move for a consolidation of the middle and right-of-center parties did so because they saw that as the best way to create a bourgeois counterpoise that they hoped would be strong enough to exclude the SPD from influence on the government. But the direction of their efforts clearly indicated their assumption that the Reichstag would continue to be the decisive locus of power. Its composition still seemed of enormous importance to them, despite Brüning's recourse to Article 48. Moreover, had their efforts been successful, the position of the parliament would have been buttressed significantly, even if that was not the primary intent of all of the businessmen involved. That part of the moderate sector of the political spectrum they sought to strengthen formed one of the traditional components of Reichstag majorities. If it had gained in the election, as the activists in the capitalist camp had hoped, it could have provided a parliamentary base for the Brüning cabinet. That would have obviated the need for what was to become Brüning's permanent reliance on Article 48 and reduced his dependence on President Hindenburg and the cabal of reactionaries who surrounded the aged field marshall. A revitalization of that part of the political spectrum in 1930 might, in fact, have arrested Germany's fateful drift toward authoritarianism. But the futility of the efforts of the spokesmen of big business to halt the splintering of the party system and build up a strong right-of-center bloc only demonstrated again the extremely limited political efficacy of money in the complex politics of the Weimar Republic.

The outcome of the balloting on September 14, 1930, reinforced the feelings of impotence experienced by politically active big businessmen during the campaign. The new Conservative People's Party, on which they had lavished so much attention, money, and personnel, proved a fiasco. It tallied less than 1 percent of the vote and emerged with only four seats in the new Reichstag. Hugenberg's once-powerful but now truncated DNVP lost nearly half of its seats, salvaging only 41, none of which was occupied by a big business spokesman. The business community still enjoyed representation in the liberal parties, the DVP and the State Party (formerly the DDP), but these suffered heavy losses at the polls. Just as those who pressed for consolidation had feared, splinter and minor special-interest parties had drained away large blocs of votes, leaving the DVP with only 30 seats, and the State Party with a mere 20. The only victors were the extremists. On the left the Communists increased their Reichstag representation from 54 to 77 seats, in part at the expense of the SPD, which declined from 154 to 143. The real triumph, however, belonged to the Nazis. They scored the most spectacular gains ever made in a single election by any German party since the first national elections of 1871, emerging with 107 seats, 95 more than they had held in the old chamber, and the votes of nearly six and a half million Germans. The obscure, inscrutable fanatics of the 1920s had suddenly become a major force in national politics.

2. The Wherewithal of the Nazi Breakthrough

Although the magnitude of the NSDAP's breakthrough surprised everyone, including the Nazis themselves, the party's massive, elaborate, and sustained election campaign had alerted political observers that something unusual was under way. Many of those who sought an explanation jumped to the conclusion that only big business could foot the bill for the expenses of such a campaign. Well before the balloting, a consensus to that effect emerged along a spectrum that extended from leftist journalists to liberal editors, the conservative minister president of Bavaria, and the American chargé d'affaires in Berlin.[1] For many observers the Nazi triumph in September 1930 amounted to an expression of the political power of Germany's capitalists. A columnist for the fashionable leftist weekly *Die Weltbühne* summarized a widely held view when he wrote just after the election, "National Socialism is in the pay of industrialists who seek to split the proletariat into warring factions according to the principle of 'divide and rule.'"[2] The Communist Party organ *Die Rote Fahne* branded the Nazis as "the hired agents of finance capitalism . . . the last card of the German bourgeoisie."[3]

The few scraps of information offered by way of substantiating these allegations prove less than convincing on close examination. Not surprisingly, in view of the publicity generated by his presence at the Nazi party congress in August 1929, Emil Kirdorf figured prominently in reports of capitalist aid to the NSDAP. In a public statement issued in late August, however, Kirdorf vigorously denied supporting the Nazis in any way during the 1930 campaign.[4] He had joined the NSDAP in 1927 because of differences with the leadership of the DNVP at the time, Kirdorf announced, but had resigned a year later, despite his friendship and esteem for Hitler, because of the stance adopted by the latter's representatives in the *Revier*. He supported only Hugenberg's DNVP in the 1930 campaign, Kirdorf concluded. No evidence contradicted his statement. Hugenberg himself was the other individual most often accused of channeling big business money to Hitler, but he did not deign to respond to such charges, which were in any event scarcely plausible. The parliamentary spokesmen of big business in his DNVP had seceded at the outset of the election campaign in protest against his opposition to the Brüning cabinet, so that he commanded far less financial support from that quarter than previously. Faced with the task of paying for the campaign of his own diminished party, Hugenberg would have contravened his own most elementary political interests if he had shared whatever big business money came his way with a rival such as Hitler, whose party was clearly intent on enticing voters away from the DNVP. For Hitler, subsidization by Hugenberg would have entailed potentially grave political risks since acceptance of funds from such a source would have made the Nazi leader dangerously vulnerable to blackmail or exposure before his followers as a hireling of moneyed interests. Hugenberg may have helped the Nazis enhance their respectability when he accepted them as participants in the campaign against the Young Plan in 1929, but the NSDAP tapped no major source of subsidies by joining in that campaign, whose fund-raising efforts proved disappointing, in part because of the opposition of most of the business community.[5] Nor are there any grounds for the oft-repeated allegation that Hugenberg served as a conduit for big business subsidization of the NSDAP thereafter. Indeed, no evidence has ever been found to support any of the allegations about subsidization of the Nazis by the business community that appeared widely in the German press during and after the election campaign of 1930. These charges, which marked the inception of what soon became a widespread version of the relationship between Nazism and big business, seem in retrospect noteworthy only insofar as they reveal a widespread predisposition to assume that Germany's capitalists must somehow be in a league with the NSDAP.

Actually, the politically active figures in the camp of big business held National Socialism in low repute at the time of the 1930 election campaign, and for good reasons. Right down to the dissolution of the Reichstag in July, Nazi parliamentarians had continued to align themselves with the left on socio-economic issues. After joining the Social Democrats and Communists in excoriating the iron and steel industry during the lengthy lockout in the Ruhr during late 1928, the Nazi Reichstag deputies again sided with them in defending workers' unemployment insurance benefits during the prolonged controversy over that issue in the winter of 1929–30.[6] Under Brüning the Nazi deputies voted with the Social Democrats, the Communists, and the Hugenberg wing of the DNVP against government fiscal proposals favored by the business community. During the election campaign the catch phrase used by Otto Strasser in announcing his break with Hitler in early July—"The Socialists leave the NSDAP"—seemed not in the least borne out by the pronouncements of the party's spokesmen.[7] By making extensive use of a slogan calling for creation of a "workers' and soldiers' state," they employed words likely to evoke in business circles disturbing memories of the revolution of 1918–19 or conjure up frightening images of Bolshevik Russia.[8] In the official party newspaper Gottfried Feder laid out his radical monetary and credit theories while strenuously flaying the capitalist system. Great concentrations of economic and financial power, he proclaimed, posed an even greater threat to honestly acquired private property than did the "Marxist rabble."[9] Joseph Goebbels, writing in a special election edition of his Berlin newspaper, denied charges that the NSDAP favored the abolition of private property, but he did so in a fashion hardly likely to still concern about Nazi radicalism in big business circles. The NSDAP planned, Goebbels explained, to expropriate only banks and the giant trusts and concerns, which had long since ceased to be private enterprises.[10] All across the country attacks on capitalists, capitalism, and high finance abounded in the party's election propaganda.[11] To be sure, Nazi agitators also kept up their verbal assaults on "Marxists" and "Marxism," and the NSDAP continued its attempts to woo workers away from the traditional leftist parties. The Nazis' efforts to gain wage earners' votes provided scant comfort for big business, however, since their attack on the SPD included accusations to the effect that the Social Democrats had not done enough to further the material interests of the workers while in power.[12] By way of indicating what the NSDAP would do with power, the party press proposed an array of new welfare measures, including generous aid for the growing army of unemployed.[13] Since such measures would unavoidably have necessitated tax increases, their endorsement by propagandists of the NSDAP could only reinforce the overwhelmingly negative assessment of Nazism in the business community.

This negative assessment found expression in an analysis of "The National Socialist Economic Program" that appeared on the eve of the election campaign in the organ of the industrial employers' association.[14] The author took note of the Nazis' relegation of economics to a secondary place behind politics, but he warned that statements by prominent party leaders revealed they actually sought nothing less than a fundamental transformation of the existing economic order. Citing Feder's proposals for monetary and credit policies, he concluded that Nazism in power would lead to inflation and stifle incentives to invest. Citing a demand by Gregor Strasser for worker participation in management decisions, he concluded that the NSDAP favored the kind of economic democracy advocated by socialist trade unionists. He found National Socialism laden with "utopian demands" and pervaded with an "aggressive hostility toward the business community." To drive home the latter point he quoted Goebbels, who had recently described businessmen as lackeys of an economic system that "seems to us immoral and intolerable, so that we hate it out of the depths of our hearts, struggle against it, and one day shall radically eliminate it." Dismissing the Nazis' praise of individualism as mere political rhetoric, the author concluded that the goal of the NSDAP was state socialism. Whatever its spokesmen might claim, he wrote, Nazism belonged to the conspiratorial, demagogic, and terroristic strand of contemporary socialism.

During the election campaign the industrial Reichsverband also addressed itself, if in veiled terms, to the problems posed by National Socialism. Stung by Communist charges that it had collected political funds from member firms and channeled these to the Nazis through Hugenberg, the organization issued a public denial early in August.[15] When that failed to still rumors of industrial aid for the NSDAP, the Reichsverband issued a second statement in which it took the unusual step of recommending a line of political action to its members.[16] Germany needed, this statement proclaimed, a government with a broad basis of support that would be willing to effect reforms and able to get things done. To achieve that, Germany's industrialists should vote and "take an active part in the preparation for the election." They should support, however, only those parties that upheld the constitution, unambiguously endorsed private enterprise and private property, and rejected all "collectivistic experiments." It was not difficult to identify the implied target of these admonitions. Little danger existed that members of the Reichsverband would consider aiding the Communists or Social Democrats, and of the remaining parties only the NSDAP's position on economic issues could be characterized as ambiguous or experimental.

The prominent industrialists who belonged to the secretive and elitist Ruhrlade shared this mistrust of National Socialism at the time of the 1930 campaign. Their political agent in Berlin expressed the prevailing attitude in their circle when in late August he pointed to the danger that the parties of the middle would, unless they joined together, suffer decimation at the polls, possibly clearing the way for an absolute majority consisting of Communists, Social Democrats, and Nazis that would preclude a bourgeois government.[17] A month earlier that agent recorded a decision by the men of the Ruhrlade to extend financial aid to the DNVP, but only on condition that Hugenberg maintain no ties to the NSDAP.[18] This mistrust of Nazism received further expression when an engineer who belonged to the NSDAP attempted during the campaign to smuggle Nazi leaflets into copies of a company newsletter he was charged with printing and distributing to the employees at a plant owned by the conglomerate headed by the founder of the Ruhrlade, Paul Reusch. Despite his pleas that those leaflets represented weapons in the struggle to win the workers away from the "reds," management officials ordered the engineer to desist from violating the company's policy of political neutrality with regard to its work force. His stupid employers, the indignant Nazi wrote to the party propaganda office in Munich, regarded National Socialists as nothing more than "rowdies and fanatics."[19]

If the mistrust of big business ruled out subsidies from that quarter for the Nazis in 1930, there remains the question of how they financed their impressive campaign of 1930 as well as their expanding organization. An abundance of evidence indicates that the Prussian political police came close to the mark when they agreed with the party's own answer to that question: The Nazis raised most of the money themselves.[20] The police also noticed that the NSDAP required less money than did the bourgeois parties with which it competed for votes. Like the Social Democrats and Communists, the National Socialists had built a "party of mobilization" that demanded not only financial sacrifices but also personal engagement from its members; and the fanatic dedication of many of the party's followers produced a willing response to those demands.[21] This enabled the Nazis to reduce their costs by relying heavily on volunteer labor and contributions in kind. Whereas the bourgeois parties had to pay to have posters pasted up and campaign literature distributed, Nazi storm troopers and other party activists performed these tasks without charge. Drawing on this same volunteer manpower, the Nazis magnified their political impact by mounting the uniformed parades through the streets of Germany that became their hallmark. Party activists made up the cheering claques at Nazi rallies as well as the heckling sections and "adjournment squads" (*Sprengtruppen*) that disrupted or broke up meetings of other parties. Members with artistic talents contributed their services by designing posters or providing music at rallies. Those who owned automobiles or trucks placed these at the disposal of the party in the evening or on weekends, when campaigning became especially intense. Some of those who were printers provided leaflets free of cost. Because of the extraordinary level of commitment among the party's members, noted by all contemporary observers, these volunteer efforts represented a major asset to the NSDAP, magnifying the effectiveness of the funds at its disposal.[22]

Numerous contemporaries regarded the NSDAP's impressively large storm-trooper auxiliary, the SA, as proof of the Nazis' dependence on outside subsidies. How else, they asked, could so many men be fitted out in uniforms and, in some cases, provided with food and shelter?[23] The answer, now confirmed by an abundance of documentation, is that, just as the Nazis claimed, they financed the SA almost exclusively with their own resources and by their own efforts.[24] The regular income of the SA derived from a share of the NSDAP dues paid by its own members (all of the dues in the case of those who did not join the party) plus the yield of a surcharge levied on the dues of all party members except SA men. In addition, local and regional party organizations paid subsidies to SA units in their purview. SA units supplemented these sources of income by conducting solicitation campaigns among party members, a practice that occasioned friction with the political leadership, which complained that unauthorized fund raising by the SA interfered with the party's own efforts of that sort. The SA leadership expected individual storm troopers to fit themselves out with uniforms, boots, and other equipment at their own expense, but patrons from among better-off Nazis stepped in to cover the costs of such items for those who could not afford them. Indigent storm troopers also benefited from charitable efforts on their behalf financed and staffed by volunteers from party organizations, especially those for women. The SA soup kitchens and hostels that spread throughout much of Germany as the depression worsened did not depend, as often assumed, on large financial subsidies but were instead made possible by countless small donations, many in kind, on the part of devoted party members.

The SA augmented its financial resources through a variety of inventive entrepreneurial ventures. As early as 1927 the leaders of the storm troopers recognized that alert manufacturers and merchants had begun to derive profit from the needs of their men for brown shirts, caps, swastika armbands, and other accoutrements indispensable to the well-equipped storm trooper, such as brass knuckles, daggers, and first-aid kits. In an effort to capture those profits for their own organization, the SA leaders established a service that sold officially certified paraphernalia, using the proceeds to finance the SA. By 1930 this undertaking had grown into a nationwide quartermaster agency (Reichszeugmeisterei) that offered mail-order delivery and managed more than a dozen retail outlets throughout the country.[25] The SA further added to its revenues by entering into commodity franchise agreements whereby it lent its endorsement to mass-consumption products in return for a share of the profits derived from their sales. Beginning in 1929 the Nazis thus promoted razor blades under the suggestively dynamic brand name of "Stürmer" and, later on, a margarine under the incongruous label of "Kampf."[26] Ironically for a party headed by a notorious non-smoker, cigarettes proved the most lucrative market for such Nazi-endorsed products. Under an agreement with a Dresden cigarette manufacturer, the SA had during 1929 extended official recognition to a cigarette labeled "Sturm."[27] In February 1930 the commandant of the SA ordered its members to smoke nothing else and to "show a little energy" in order to dissuade the owners of taverns frequented by party members from stocking competing brands.[28] Those who bought packages of "Sturm" obtained coupons they could apply toward the purchase of SA equipment from the quartermaster agency. By way of providing additional incentive for purchases, each local SA unit received a rebate based on the number of sales in its area.[29] Before long tobacco shops, taverns, and kiosks where cigarettes were sold became battlegrounds, as SA men physically impressed on consumers the superiority of "Sturm" over competing brands such as the Stahlhelm's "Ostfront" or products named "Kameradschaft," "Staffel," and "Kommando," which rival Nazi organizations sponsored in return for a similar share of the profits.[30] In the superheated atmosphere of the late Weimar Republic, even the choice of a package of cigarettes became a partisan political act full of potential perils. For the NSDAP, however, the tobacco trade proved a valuable source of income.

Even Nazi propaganda served as a source of income. Local organizations purchased officially approved pamphlets and leaflets from the national headquarters and then sold them at marked-up prices to members and others. Hitler's *Mein Kampf*, sales of which increased rapidly when it was re-issued in an inexpensive one-volume edition in May 1930, bolstered not only his personal income but also that of the Eher Verlag, the party publishing house.[31] It printed and distributed most Nazi propaganda publications, including the National Socialist Library, a series of pamphlets edited by Gottfried Feder, which numbered nineteen by the time of the 1930 campaign. The Eher Verlag also published the official newspaper, *Völkischer Beobachter*, which had from all indications attained a firm financial footing well before the 1930 campaign. The finances of other Nazi newspapers, which were left to the party's regional and local organizations or to individual party leaders, varied widely. Some papers had chronic money problems while others, such as Goebbels's Berlin organ, *Der Angriff*, yielded profits for the local organization.[32] Of greater importance than such cash yield, however, was the Nazi newspapers' indirect augmentation of party resources. By providing places on their payrolls for propagandists who doubled as speakers and agitators during election campaigns, the papers swelled the ranks of the party's full-time, salaried activists. Among the parties of the Weimar Republic, only the Social Democrats and the Communists made similar broad-gauged use of the press.

The Nazi press served another vital function by promoting what the Prussian political police rightly saw as a major source of the party's income: its public rallies. By 1930 the Nazis had come close to perfecting the fine art of separating people from their money while subjecting them to torrents of propagandistic rhetoric. By that time the typical Nazi rally combined elements of a religious revival meeting, a carnival, and a military review. Especially in small backwater cities and towns, this formula added entertainment value to the political appeals of Nazism. Rallies in such a setting were normally preceded by a parade of brown-shirted SA troopers through the streets to the hall or tent in which the meeting was to be held, where a band concert entertained the audience as it awaited the arrival of the speakers.[33] As an added enticement the Nazis frequently included in their rallies various forms of entertainment, such as plays, movies, and songs.[34] Whereas the traditional non-socialist parties usually opened their public meetings to all comers free of charge, and the Social Democrats levied at most a small entrance fee to cover their expenses, the Nazis charged substantial amounts for admission to their rallies. At rallies where party notables spoke, the standard admission charge in 1930, with reductions for storm troopers and the jobless, came to 1 mark.[35] At a time when a typical postal employee earned less than 90 pfennigs an hour, when a senior insurance clerk could support a family in Berlin on less than 250 marks a month, and when a serviceable men's suit of clothes cost 25 marks, and a pair of socks 95 pfennigs, that amounted to a sizeable expenditure for persons of modest means.[36] According to the calculations of two journalists, three rallies in the Berlin Sportpalast at which Hitler and other prominent Nazis spoke during the 1930 campaign attracted a total of 38,000 persons who paid as much as 2 marks each for admission. The journalists reckoned that the Nazis cleared at least 30,000 marks from those three events alone.[37] The political police estimated that a single rally at which Hitler spoke in Essen during the 1930 campaign drew about 10,000 persons and yielded a profit of 12,000 marks. The traditional parties in the same region, the police observed, needed only 20,000 to 30,000 marks to mount an entire election campaign.[38] All estimates of the NSDAP's income from its rallies unavoidably fell short since outside observers could have no knowledge of the money collected during and after the rallies by uniformed SA men who passed the hat among those present for "war chest contributions" (*Kampfschatzspenden*).[39]

Virtually all contemporary observers expressed amazement at the large number of rallies held by the Nazis. Beginning in the late 1920s, they had departed from normal political practice by scheduling frequent rallies even when no election was pending; in effect, the Nazis launched a permanent campaign. Even before the dissolution of the Reichstag in 1930, the Prussian political police estimated that the NSDAP had held an average of 100 rallies a day throughout Germany. During the campaign the Nazis boasted they would mount no fewer than 34,000 such meetings within six weeks, a figure the political police did not find implausible.[40] At the time, outsiders did not know of the calculated system of incentives that spurred on this unprecedented barrage of rallies. The speaking honoraria that Nazi leaders—except for Hitler, who refrained from charging for his appearances—received for performing at such gatherings represented an important supplement to the income of most. By keeping the ceiling of the honoraria low during election campaigns, the party forced its luminaries to speak frequently to realize significant gains, giving them a material interest in holding more rallies.[41] Moreover, the Nazis assembled what amounted to an auxiliary army of semi-professional agitators by recruiting unemployed and underemployed young men of ambition and talent as itinerant speakers for small rallies in out-of-the-way places. In 1929 the party established a correspondence school to provide ideological indoctrination and coaching in political rhetoric for aspiring Nazi orators.[42] Once they had obtained certification from regional party officials, graduates of that school moved from town to town, receiving free meals and lodging from party members and collecting a minimal speaker's fee, sometimes as little as seven marks, for each rally they could prevail on local party units to allow them to hold.[43] The local units of the party also had a strong incentive for scheduling as many rallies as possible since the bulk of the yield went into their treasuries. Given a mounting receptivity among the public, these incentives became something of a self-perpetuating and accelerating force, multiplying the number of rallies and the funds they yielded. The Prussian police reckoned if the Nazis merely held to their pre-campaign pace of 100 rallies a day, an average attendance of 500 persons at each rally would, even if one assumed a profit after expenses of only ten pfennig per head, produce an annual income of 1.75 million marks.[44]

Rallies brought in money, but the staple of the Nazi Party's income derived from the dues and other contributions of members.[45] When the party was reconstituted following Hitler's release from prison in late 1924, a colorless but shrewd bureaucrat, Franz Xaver Schwarz, took over as treasurer and placed its internal finances on such a solid basis that Hitler no longer needed to seek subsidies from persons of wealth. Schwarz copied the Social Democrats' practice of issuing each member a party booklet resembling a passport. These contained a blank for each

month onto which official stamps were pasted when the member paid his
dues. Only when a stamp covered the blank for each elapsed month did
a member enjoy good standing. A person officially became a member
only after his or her application had been forwarded by the local unit to
the regional (Gau) organization and from there to the treasurer's office
in Munich for registry in a master membership file. This kept the treasurer informed about the number of dues-paying members in each unit
of the party. That knowledge amounted to power, as it enabled the national headquarters to hold the regional organizations responsible for
the portion of membership dues owed to it, which amounted to 40 percent in the summer of 1930. Another 35 percent went to the regional
headquarters, with the local units retaining 25 percent. To ensure regular collection of dues and a smooth upward flow of funds from the local
units to the regional organizations, and from there to the national headquarters, the party treasurer had at his command some very effective
sanctions. He could withhold membership booklets and dues stamps,
obtainable only from the treasurer's office in Munich, from a delinquent
unit, effectively crippling its efforts to recruit and retain members. Or
he could deny such units the services of the party's most prestigious orators, a major handicap to local fund-raising efforts.[46] Local units thus
felt strong pressure from above to collect dues promptly and forward
the requisite shares to the higher organs of the party. They in turn
subjected delinquent members to sanctions ranging from persuasion
through ostracism by exclusion from meetings and even public rallies to
outright expulsion.[47]

These arrangements allowed the NSDAP to become the only party
(with the possible exception of the secretive Communists) to join the SPD
in establishing an effective and reliable system for collecting dues from
members.[48] However, whereas Social Democrats paid a flat rate—usually twenty pfennigs a week for men, ten for women—the Nazis frequently extracted more than the required amount from their members.
The minimum rate for ordinary members was, by the summer of 1930,
one mark a month, with certain categories of party activists, such as SA
and SS men, having to pay only eighty pfennigs. But when regional organizations found during the late 1920s that they could demand more
than the minimum, the national headquarters condoned that practice
once an agreement had been reached assuring it a share of the additional income. At the beginning of September 1930, in the midst of the
election campaign, Hitler effected changes in the dues system designed
to extract still more money from members. The SA surcharge was doubled, from ten to twenty pfennigs a month. In addition, the party instituted a graduated scale of dues by issuing stamps of six different colors,
in denominations up to five marks, with which well-off members could
adorn their membership booklets each month. A seventh stamp, bearing
no denomination, became available for those able and ready to pay dues

in excess of five marks a month, the amount being entered in ink by the local party treasurer.

The party supplemented income from dues in a number of inventive ways. When an insurance plan designed to cover the medical costs of SA men injured in the line of duty proved attractive to other members as well, Hitler decreed participation in the plan obligatory for all members in early 1930.[49] By the time of the election, the fund built up by the premiums—thirty pfennigs a month per member—provided the SA with a handsome surplus beyond what it needed to care for its disabled members.[50] Additional funds were raised by levies on the membership from time to time for a "war chest" (*Kampfschatz*) to finance an election campaign, bolster the SA, or otherwise further the Nazi cause materially.[51] With permission of the party treasurer, local units could add to their income by imposing special levies on members. Nazis willing to pledge themselves to making extraordinary financial sacrifices could join "circles" (*Opferringe*) established to encourage and recognize such commitment.[52] Nor did the Nazis refuse to accept money from non-members. They recognized by the late 1920s that many persons sympathized with the party but could not bring themselves to join it, either because they felt unready for such political commitment or because they feared that open affiliation with the NSDAP would prove damaging, costing them their jobs, clients, or customers. To accommodate such sympathizers, the Nazis made it easy for them to contribute money unobtrusively. Less apprehensive non-members could pay contributions into postal accounts established by the Nazis, knowing that the party would receive a record of their benefactions.[53]

Although the NSDAP seems to have experienced recurrent financial difficulties throughout the 1920s despite these stratagems for raising money at the grass roots, there are abundant indications that its financial fortunes improved sharply in 1930. This improvement correlates closely with a rapid growth in membership, which more than doubled during that year.[54] By swelling the ranks of those who paid dues and contributed to levies, this influx of new members presumably made it easier for local and regional organizations to meet their financial obligations without dipping into the substantial share of locally raised funds owed to the national headquarters, as had so often happened earlier. In May Party Treasurer Franz Xaver Schwarz proclaimed that almost all the regional organizations had submitted to the national headquarters its share of membership dues, marking a noteworthy improvement over past performances.[55] The party's increased prosperity found expression in the rapid expansion of the paid staff of the national headquarters during 1930.[56] Partly in response to that expansion, the party entered into a major financial commitment late in the spring when it contracted to purchase a large, ornate villa in a fashionable section of Munich—the future Brown House—to accommodate the staff of the national headquarters,

which had hitherto operated out of rented rooms in an unprepossessing
building on a nondescript street.[57] In order to raise money toward the
purchase price and extensive remodeling, the party asked the members
to contribute at least two marks each, rewarding those who complied
with a special certificate.[58] Clearly, National Socialism had ceased to
be a hand-to-mouth undertaking well in advance of the 1930 election
campaign.

If documentary proof is required that this rising tide of Nazi money
sprang from internal sources, the surviving records of the party's finances provide it. These records do not amount, however, to a complete or
comprehensive record. The relevant files of the treasurer's office in
Munich appear to have been almost completely destroyed at the end of
World War II, leaving no clues about either the magnitude or the
sources of the national headquarters' income during the early 1930s.
With one exception, the financial records of the regional organizations
seem also to have been destroyed. That exception is the Rhenish Gau,
from whose Cologne office a Prussian police agent regularly purloined
copies of reports on financial matters.[59] These eventually found their
way into the safekeeping of government archivists and so survived both
the Third Reich and the war. Prepared periodically by the Gau treasurer, the reports recorded the amounts of money received by the regional headquarters from its subordinate units and the sums forwarded
by the Cologne office to Munich between August 1930 and February
1932. They reveal a party organization phenomenally successful at raising money. In one month, August 1930, at the height of the election
campaign, the local units of the region delivered to the Gau treasurer
money collected in the form of dues, registration fees, and other levies
on the membership amounting to approximately eighteen marks for
each member. Since the local organizations were allowed to retain a
quarter of the dues and part of other collections as well, the total yield
per member was actually still higher. The sum passed to the Gau that
was attributed to "donations"—and possibly came in part from non-
members—represented less than 14 percent of the total. Of the money
received by the Gau treasurer, over 30 percent went to the national
headquarters in Munich. During the more normal quarter year of September through November, only the first two weeks of which fell within
the election campaign, the local units continued to send money to the
Gau at a rate of between six and seven marks per member each month,
over half of which the Cologne office forwarded to Munich.

If all the roughly 200,000 members of the NSDAP at the time of the
1930 election contributed as freely as did those of the Rhenish Gau in
August, the party would have raised from its own ranks in just one
month more than the just under three million marks the Social Democrats reported spending on their entire national election campaign.[60] It
is, however, problematic to expect accurate results from extrapolations

based on the finances of only one of more than thirty regional organizations. The Rhenish Gau may conceivably have been atypical, although government tax statistics reveal no significant deviation of that region from the national economic norm.[61] Nevertheless, that Gau remains the sole component of the party for which reliable financial data on the early 1930s has survived, so that the implications of its success in soliciting money from party members cannot be ignored. It will perhaps put the matter in perspective to assume for a moment that Nazi officials throughout the country were only three-quarters as successful, on a per capita basis, in attracting their followers' money as were those of the Rhenish Gau during September, October, and November of 1930. If that had been the case, the NSDAP extracted funds from its own ranks at a rate that would have produced an annual national yield of about twelve million marks, roughly the same as that achieved in 1930 by the SPD, whose members outnumbered those of the NSDAP by about four to one at that time.[62] Even if Nazi organizations elsewhere met with only half the success of those in the Rhenish Gau, the party commanded impressive regular sources of income. These calculations, it should be noted, understate the party's full income since the documents of the Rhenish Gau do not record the appreciable revenues which local units derived from rallies.

Those contemporary observers who immediately concluded from the Nazis' massive election campaign of 1930 that they must be heavily subsidized made the mistake of viewing the NSDAP as just another upstart party depending on financial handouts. It was instead a remarkable political innovation, an organization that combined charismatic leadership with meticulous bureaucratic administration, a party of mobilization that applied socialist organization and financial techniques to a considerably more affluent following than that of the SPD. The NSDAP had in these respects little in common with the non-socialist parties of the Republic. Those parties had proved incapable either of enrolling more than a small fraction of their voters as members or of collecting dues regularly from those who considered themselves members. Consequently they derived only very limited regular income from their memberships, so that they depended heavily on subsidies from organized interest groups outside their organizations, especially during election campaigns. Even with those subsidies, the budgets of those parties remained modest. One of the largest, the DNVP, budgeted its national headquarters at only about half a million marks in 1931.[63] When the Nazi Party burst onto the German political stage as a major national force, it had become, by contrast, an unprecedented money-generating contrivance. Whereas the traditional non-socialist parties drained their coffers to cover campaign expenses, the NSDAP prospered financially from the 1930 election, which it adeptly exploited for fund-raising purposes. Its leaders could truthfully boast in 1930 that the appreciable wherewithal that underlay the party's triumph at the polls had come in the form of contributions from the pockets of members and sympathizers, not as subsidies from big business.[64]

3. A "Long Guessing Game" Begins

The outcome of the Reichstag election of 1930 immediately had a damaging impact on the already ailing German economy. Prices on the stock exchange plunged by an average of 10 percent; German loan issues declined in value sharply on international money markets; a flight of foreign capital that took over 700 million marks out of the country within six weeks shook the great banks of Berlin and placed a heavy drain on the foreign exchange holdings of the Reichsbank, forcing it to raise its discount rate sharply.[1] Investors at home and abroad had taken alarm at the Nazis' spectacular gains. Nor did Hitler help matters. Ten days after the election he added to the panic in financial circles abroad when, at the trial of three young lieutenants accused of organizing Nazi cells within the army, he conjured up images of bloody civil strife by pledging that heads would roll in revenge for November 1918 once the NSDAP came to power.[2] In the columns of the business and financial press gloom prevailed. Pointing to the losses of the middle parties to the Nazis, one prominent economic journalist concluded that the election had dashed the hopes, harbored in some quarters, that the NSDAP would weaken the leftist parties and the trade unions. Instead, the Nazis had accelerated the spread of anti-capitalism in Germany, drawing middle-class elements, young people, and members of the intelligentsia away from parties with a bourgeois orientation. Nazism now threatened Germany, the journalist concluded, with a new kind of socialism, petit bourgeois in outlook, hostile toward both organized labor and anonymous concentrations of capitalist power.[3] Another economic journalist subjected the NSDAP's economic policies to devastating critical scrutiny, reminding his readers of the Nazis' opportunistic shifts on issues pertaining to the economy and warning about the inflationistic effects of the monetary schemes proposed by Gottfried Feder.[4] An editorial in a business weekly published in the Ruhr characterized the election results as a victory of anti-capitalists and pointed out that for the first time more than half the German electorate had cast ballots for parties opposed to the private enterprise system: the SPD, the KPD—and the NSDAP.[5] The yearly report of the Hansa-Bund, a pro-free-trade, anti-cartel organization with a sizeable following in banking, commercial, and manufacturing circles, bemoaned the gains of the NSDAP, which it branded as a "vigorous enemy of the individualist and capitalist order for which we stand."[6] On the day after the election Erich von Gilsa, a DVP deputy with close ties to industry who had lost his seat in the election, warned the Ruhr industrialist Paul Reusch against Nazism, which he accused of nothing less than "pure Marxism." The election might well mark, he lamented, "the irreversible beginning of the socialist Republic of Germany." [7]

Big business responded initially to the election results and the shock these produced in financial circles by rallying behind the Brüning cabinet. Just how to bolster the cabinet politically in view of the composition of the new Reichstag quickly became a source of disagreement, however. Although Brüning had indicated from the outset of his chancellorship a determination to remain free of ties to the political parties, his cabinet, like previous non-party governments, had to muster at least ad hoc parliamentary majorities, either to enact its legislative proposals or to prevent the Reichstag from overriding its use of Article 48. There remained the problem of where those majorities should be sought, which in the new Reichstag reduced to the question of left or right. The leadership of the industrial Reichsverband, backed by a broad spectrum of support, especially in manufacturing circles, urged the chancellor to broaden his cabinet's support to the left by including the Social Democrats in a firm parliamentary bloc supporting the government.[8] Such a move, which would calm the international financial community by stilling speculation about the dangers of civil strife in Germany, also enjoyed support in banking circles.[9] Before the board of directors of the Reichsverband, its managing director, Ludwig Kastl, observed prophetically on September 19 that democracy had one last chance. The industrial organization's highest body, its presidium, had decided, Kastl announced, that it would be folly not to seek to resolve the crisis within the constitution rather than blunder toward a possible catastrophe. The presidium had therefore resolved to take advantage of democracy's last chance by pressing for a renewal of the great coalition.[10] The managing director of the national organization of iron and steel producers, Jakob Wilhelm Reichert, usually found on the right politically, also saw a great coalition as the only possible solution, at least until the Nazis revised their "half socialist and half fog-shrouded party program." [11]

Although Brüning quickly let the officials of the Reichsverband know that he contemplated no formal revival of the great coalition, his cabinet encouraged them in their efforts to bring the SPD behind the government. Responding to an initiative by his labor minister, spokesmen of the chief national industrial associations renewed their attempt of the spring to reach a compromise agreement on economic and social policy with the socialist trade unions that would resolve many of the sensitive issues that separated the labor movement and the SPD from the bourgeois center of the political spectrum. After a promising beginning, however, those negotiations again foundered on opposition within the union movement.[12] In the absence of such an agreement, the SPD proved unwilling to throw its votes in the Reichstag behind the Brüning cabinet's austerity policies, which imposed increasing sacrifices on German wage earners. The Social Democrats nevertheless decided to avert an open

clash between the cabinet and the parliament. Rather than face another
election and additional lost votes, the SPD extended to the cabinet its
toleration, withholding its support from no-confidence motions and refusing to support resolutions to invalidate the measures Brüning and his
ministers put into effect with the presidential powers of Article 48. The
SPD thus became a component of the semi-parliamentary system of rule
on which the Brüning cabinet came to rely.

Some industrialists dissented from the decision of the Reichsverband
to attempt to broaden the Brüning cabinet's base to the left. Particularly
among the Ruhr industrialists there was strong opposition to any revival
of cooperation with the SPD. From their point of view the sort of compromises necessitated by such cooperation had caused the severity of the
economic crisis and would make impossible the decisive measures necessary to restore fiscal stability and bring about a recovery of the economy.
Instead of a return to compromises with the left, they believed the country needed a government dominated by bourgeois forces that would
reassure foreign creditors and staunch the flow of capital out of Germany.[13] On the eve of the opening session of the new Reichstag in
mid-October, the men of the Ruhrlade resolved to seek a merger of the
splintered right-of-center parties. Once that had been accomplished,
they anticipated negotiations with the Catholic parties, the Center and
the Bavarian People's parties, in order to prepare the way for possible
contact with the NSDAP. As their eventual goal they envisioned a rightist bloc of about 300 deputies, aligned behind the Brüning cabinet.[14]
Brüning himself aimed at the same arrangement. Like any number of
moderate conservative politicians, the chancellor believed that bringing
the Nazis into the cabinet would sober them by forcing them to assume
responsibility for unpopular measures in difficult times and also make it
impossible for them to go on garnering votes by virtue of being free to
criticize everything from a posture of irresponsible opposition.[15]

These hopes of a rightist bloc quickly faded. As the opening of the
new Reichstag in mid-October approached, Hugenberg made clear his
continuing unwillingness to merge the DNVP with other parties or to
throw the votes of its deputies behind the Brüning cabinet. Despite
personal pleas for support of the cabinet by some of Germany's most
prominent capitalists during the autumn, he held to his course of uncompromising opposition.[16] The Nazis likewise showed no signs of alter-
ing their oppositional stance. At the first session of the new Reichstag
they joined with the DNVP, the Communists, and some splinter parties
in sponsoring a no-confidence motion which a majority, bolstered by the
votes of the SPD, succeeded in tabling.[17] Showing no signs that their
election gains had produced the moderating effects expected by many
conservatives, the Nazis seemed intent on demonstrating that they
would not abandon the radical stands on socio-economic issues that had
become their parliamentary hallmark. On the eve of the new legislative

session, Goebbels published still another interpretation of the NSDAP's economic program in the party's Berlin organ, *Der Angriff*. Reaffirming the binding nature of the twenty-five-point program of 1920, he emphasized its commitment to "the socialization of large incorporated enterprises, concerns, and trusts" as well as to profit sharing for workers. Furthermore, every aspect of economic life would be reassessed by a Nazi government, Goebbels announced.[18]

When the new Reichstag convened, the NSDAP's greatly enlarged Reichstag delegation acted quickly to show where it stood on economic issues. At the earliest possible moment it introduced a flood of demagogic bills of the sort its predecessors had specialized in during the 1920s. If enacted, their proposals would have radically altered the country's *Wirtschaftspolitik*. The Nazis proposed to nationalize all large banks; to ban trading in stocks and bonds; to outlaw impersonal transfers of stock by requiring registration of ownership with a state agency; to limit interest rates to 5 percent, with 1 percent of interest payments counting toward amortization; and to confiscate the property of "princes of banking and the stock exchange" as well as all profits derived from the war, the revolution, or the inflation.[19] So as to leave no doubt about the party's position, the *Völkischer Beobachter* trumpeted these proposals on its front page.[20] They had an immediately chilling effect on the business community, and especially on those of its members who had hoped that it would be possible to work with the Nazis. In the face of the NSDAP's barrage of radical Reichstag bills, businessmen who had harbored such hopes suddenly began to suffer from cold feet.[21] So did two business-oriented conservative newspapers that had after the election looked with favor on the idea of according the Nazis a share of governmental responsibility. The Nazis had now made unmistakably clear, the *Deutsche Bergwerks-Zeitung* of Düsseldorf warned, that they represented a threat to private property and differed little from the Communists.[22] The *Deutsche Allgemeine Zeitung* of Berlin, owned by a consortium of Ruhr industrialists, bankers, and shipping firms, observed that even as the Social Democrats distanced themselves from Marxism, the Nazis seemed intent on assuming that heritage.[23]

The business community also found extremely disturbing the NSDAP's support for a major strike during the fall of 1930.[24] Two days after the new Reichstag convened, more than 126,000 metalworkers in Berlin laid down their tools in protest against an arbitration board's ruling that they had to accept substantial pay cuts. The Social Democrats and Communists at once embraced the worker's cause. So did the Nazis. The local leader, Goebbels, ordered Nazi workers to stand picket and warned his followers that participation in strikebreaking activities would result in expulsion from the party. When the Communists introduced a resolution in the Reichstag demanding revocation of the arbitration ruling, the Nazis voted with the KPD and SPD to secure its passage.[25] Nazi councilmen in at least one other city joined with leftists there in appropriating funds to aid the Berlin strikers.[26] Throughout the strike the Nazi press urged the strikers to persist in their cause, which it sought to portray as a revolt against the reparations burden placed on Germany by the Young Plan. But big business could not derive much solace from the NSDAP's tactics in that regard since the Nazi press castigated industry for acceding repeatedly to reparations, to which the Nazis attributed the hardships of the workers.[27] Nor could capitalists find anything reassuring in reports to the effect that Goebbels had announced that strikes such as that of the Berlin metalworkers would not only be permitted during the coming "Third Reich" but that the state would then favor the workers, not—as in the present dispute—the employers.[28]

To be sure, Hitler, after approving Nazi participation, ended by equivocating about the metalworker strike. After the workers had agreed to return to work if the dispute went to arbitration again, he wrote about the issues raised by the strike in an article for the *Völkischer Beobachter*.[29] Avoiding any specific mention of the Berlin dispute, he addressed himself to a wave of strikes then taking place, assigning to them two causes. On the one hand, many workers suffered from atrocious conditions, for which he blamed the mistakes of the bourgeois parties. On the other hand, the "November criminals" were inciting strikes in order to distract attention from the fact that economic hardship resulted from their policy of paying reparations. National Socialism recognized the right of workers to make justified wage demands, Hitler stated. But he set strict limits to what qualified as justified: Demands for better wages must endanger neither the social health of the nation nor its independent national economy (here he used the ambiguous term *die Wirtschaft*, which could also mean the business community). Under existing conditions, he observed, it seemed at first sight that reason counseled against a resort to strikes for better wages since the whole economy stood on the verge of collapse. On the other hand, that objection lost much of its validity if one recognized that *die Wirtschaft* managed to pay to foreigners more than two billion marks a year in reparations. As long as the business community continued to cover financially the crimes of republican foreign policy there could be no justification for wage reductions or the maintenance of inadequate wages, Hitler wrote. Nevertheless, he warned that under existing conditions any strike could only come to a bad end. The "November provocateurs" saw this and urged the workers to strike in order to distract them from the true source of their plight. These provocateurs wanted to create chaos so that the workers would see in Bolshevism their only hope. National Socialism's task lay, he concluded, in protecting the German workers against both the madness of the business community in paying reparations and against the intrigues of the "November provocateurs." This included, Hitler added, pointing out to workers what was impossible and would only result in their own ruin rather than their salvation. While according at least a lukewarm retroactive legitimation to the Berlin strike, he seemed to end by warning other workers against striking, thus dissociating the NSDAP from the latest work stoppages.

In his ambiguous article Hitler again gave evidence of his unwillingness to allow his party to become committed to either management or labor. He also adopted a position calculated to allow him to appear as a moderate on socio-economic issues within the NSDAP. These maneuvers did not escape the critical scrutiny of the prestigious *Frankfurter Zeitung,* which commanded a wide readership in business circles. In a careful exegesis one of its reporters pointed out the calculated duplicity of Hitler's words. He also subjected Hitler's command of economics to ridicule. In an aside in his article the Nazi leader had contended that paying two billion marks in reparations a year actually amounted to subtracting the equivalent of ten to twelve billion marks from the German economy, since two billion marks in circulation would in the course of the year generate many times that amount in wages and salaries. Here Hitler invoked what has since become known as the multiplier effect but was then a new and controversial concept largely limited to professional economic circles. That earned him a scornful rebuke from the reporter of the *Frankfurter Zeitung* with which virtually all the businessmen of the day would have agreed: "We refrain here from all criticism since we need to demonstrate to no one the simple fact that one coin can never simultaneously rest in several purses."[30]

In addition to his equivocating stand on the issue of strikes, Hitler conveyed his own version of Nazism's aims directly to prominent members of the business community during the fall of 1930. At the end of September he met in Hamburg with former chancellor Wilhelm Cuno, then head of the Hamburg-America shipping line. Earlier in the year a group of admirers that included Paul Reusch had raised Cuno's hopes for a political comeback. They thought it not unlikely that Hindenburg might not finish out his seven-year term as president, and they wanted in any case to prepare for the regularly scheduled presidential election of 1932 by drumming up support for Cuno.[31] In hopes of bringing the NSDAP behind a Cuno presidential candidacy, former Admiral Magnus von Levetzow, one of the chief instigators of that project, arranged for the former chancellor to meet with Hitler in Cuno's Berlin hotel on September 29.[32] As usual, Hitler dominated the conversation. He set forth his foreign-policy goals in terms of a unilateral German cessation of reparations payments and the reacquisition of the Polish corridor by means of an Anglo-German-Italian alliance against Bolshevism and France. He also left no doubt about his resolve to destroy the "corrupt" democratic, parliamentary system and punish the "November criminals" with death if they were found guilty of treason. With regard to the economy, Hitler expressed to Cuno much more modest goals. His movement intended to break, he explained, with the existing economic system, which fostered egotism and greed rather than the general welfare. National Socialism would encourage individual initiative, entrepreneurial zeal, and love of work. It would promote private capital but intervene uncompromisingly against wealth gained at the expense of the general public by fraudulent means. Obviously aware of the distaste Nazi anti-Semitism aroused in big business circles, Hitler took pains to relieve Cuno's mind about that side of National Socialism. His party would proceed against the "Jewish predominance in the state," not against Jewish persons as such. There would be no violent persecution of Jews in a Nazi-ruled Germany, Hitler assured Cuno. According to Levetzow, who was present during the latter part of Cuno's interview with Hitler, the former chancellor came away very favorably impressed with the Nazi leader. One factor in the cordiality of the meeting, Levetzow confided to a friend, had been Hitler's apologetic dissociation of himself from his scornful comments about Cuno in *Mein Kampf,* which a Nazi publication had reprinted only a short time before.

In hopes of harnessing the NSDAP to his own political ambitions, Cuno arranged for Hitler to address the conservative Hamburg National Club. Formed after the revolution of 1918 by well-do-do conservatives, the club comprised roughly 500 aristocrats, former military officers, rightist politicians, retired senior civil servants and diplomats, judges, lawyers, shippers, merchants, and other businessmen. Hitler had spoken there once before, in January 1926.[33] At that time, when he had still been relatively unknown, a general curiosity had prevailed among the club's members. By the time Cuno arranged for him to address the club again, he and his movement had become much better known. As a result, significant protest arose among the membership after the club's executive board announced that Hitler would speak on December 1, 1930.[34] Nevertheless, Hitler's speech went off as scheduled, lasting more than two hours.[35] As so often before such audiences, Hitler sought to educate his listeners about the causes of human events. In particular, he sought to disabuse them of the notion that economic problems could be solved by economic solutions. Politics, not economics, he gave them to understand, determined which nations prospered and which perished; and in the end politics came down to the resort to force. In a world where other nations were busily making themselves self-sufficient, he warned, a reliance on trade would be fatal. Germany needed more land to support its population. Other, less worthy peoples had more land than they needed. In such a case, he informed his audience, the right of the stronger applied. But Germany would be in no position to invoke that right so long as it remained crippled by the class conflict that divided its people against each other. His movement's paramount goal was therefore to heal that internal division in the *Volk* by instilling the nation's workers once again with nationalist ideals. Only National Socialism could accomplish that task, he announced, since it alone possessed the kind of idealism so totally lacking in the older parties. Socialism meant to him merely subordinating the interests of everyone to the general interest of the whole German *Volk*, not a radical change in the economic system. It meant preserving the healthy German worker, but also a national, independent *Wirtschaft*. Here Hitler again adeptly exploited the double meaning of *die Wirtschaft* to awaken among his listeners the impression that he intended to guarantee the independence of the business community vis-à-vis the state. By way of reinforcing that impression, he approvingly alluded to the example of Fascist Italy. He also drew applause from those members of the club present by intimating that the NSDAP intended to cut the number of bureaucrats on the government payroll and reduce taxes. Otherwise, Hitler avoided any mention whatsoever of where he or his party stood with regard to the pressing economic problems of Germany. He also omitted the anti-Semitic themes that usually abounded in his speeches. At the close of his harangue he drew fervent applause from his listeners, according to an eyewitness.[36] After his speech Hitler withdrew to a smaller room in the Atlantik Hotel, where about fifty of his audience heard him elaborate still further. A DNVP politician noted with relief that in these later remarks the Nazi leader made no mention of a resort to force and explicitly committed himself to pursue his aims through legal methods.[37]

Later in the fall, probably toward the end of November, Hitler presented his views to a sizeable group of Ruhr industrialists at the home of Emil Kirdorf, near Mülheim.[38] It is unclear from which side the initiative for this gathering came, but it seems not unlikely that Kirdorf took that step. Despite his objections to the anti-capitalist elements in the NSDAP, the apostate Kirdorf made no secret of his continuing admiration for Hitler as an individual, although he had himself returned his political allegiance to Hugenberg's DNVP. By bringing the Nazi leader together with a group of industrialists, he may have hoped to influence Hitler's attitude toward economic questions by exposing him to men of "sound" views. Or he may have hoped that some of those men would, after meeting Hitler, enter the NSDAP and attempt to give it an economic orientation favorable to private enterprise. There is evidence that he encouraged at least one young coal executive to join the party.[39] As to who attended the gathering at Kirdorf's home in the fall of 1930 or what Hitler said on that occasion, little is known. The only descriptions of what Hitler told those in attendance come from Ernst Poensgen, one of the senior executives of the United Steel Works and a nationally respected, generally sober-minded man who remained aloof from Nazism before and throughout the Third Reich.[40] He recalled that Hitler had made a lengthy presentation of his political views, so that it seems likely that those present heard the same sort of reassurances Hitler had given Cuno. Poensgen also recalled that Hitler had attacked the Brüning gov-

ernment and urged his listeners to repudiate the chancellor. According
to Poensgen, that had provoked him to reply that the industrialists stood
behind the Brüning cabinet since it pursued the same goals as they did,
even if not with the speed they thought necessary. After World War II
Poensgen, then in exile in Switzerland, claimed to have expressed his
reaction at the time in the words, "The man left me completely cold." He
also doubted whether Hitler's appearance at Kirdorf's home had won
him a single new adherent.

Hermann Göring went even further than Hitler in attempting to allay
fears of Nazi socio-economic radicalism. In late September he led former Admiral Levetzow, one of the reactionary promoters of Cuno's prospective presidential candidacy for 1932, to believe that the National
Socialists would be willing, in the meantime, to reinstall Cuno in the
chancellorship if the NSDAP gained entry to the national government.[41]
A month later, at the end of October, Göring sought to reassure Levetzow and Georg von Holten, another of Cuno's supporters, about the
NSDAP's economic policies. They, like many on the right, viewed with
alarm the barrage of demagogic bills which the Nazi delegation had laid
before the Reichstag that month. They found particularly disturbing the
bill that called for expropriation of the "princes of banking and the stock
exchange." They also regarded as ominous the NSDAP's support for the
metalworkers' strike. When pressed on these matters by Cuno's promoters, Göring supplied an unlikely explanation for the offending Reichstag bill. It had been a mistake, he explained. The Nazis had intended
merely to introduce a bill reducing the per diem of Reichstag deputies.
Since the NSDAP had proposed that economy measure earlier, in the
1920s, the Nazi deputies requested that the old bill be placed on the
agenda again. But in their haste to save money for German taxpayers
they had neglected to notice that the earlier bill contained other clauses,
including the one calling for expropriation. Those other clauses, Göring
further explained, had been drawn up by the totally different, much
smaller NSDAP delegation in the previous Reichstag. Those clauses in
no way reflected the views of the new Nazi delegation elected in September. He left no doubt about his own distaste for them. However, he
confidentially informed Levetzow that the party leadership had decreed
that in future no bills were to be introduced without its approval. Identifying himself as part of that leadership, Göring assured Cuno's friends
that there would in the future be no more Nazi parliamentary blunders
such as those of October. As for the metalworkers' strike, Göring gave
Cuno's promoters an equally farfetched explanation. The NSDAP, he
flatly stated, fundamentally opposed strikes of any kind, whether of an
economic or political nature. His party could not stand by, on the other
hand, and see certain occupational groups victimized by the sacrifices
imposed by the Brüning government's policy of continuing to extract
"tribute" from the German people in order to pay reparations. The

Nazis would demand material sacrifices when they got power, Göring added, but of all, not just some, Germans. They would demand those sacrifices, just as had Prussia during the Napoleonic era, in order to smite foreign foes, not to aid them, as was the case with the hardships imposed by Brüning. In supporting the metalworkers' strike, Göring summed up, the NSDAP had only been opposing the fulfillment policy of Brüning. He expressed disapproval, however, of the Berlin party's initiative in supporting the strike. Such matters should be decided by the national party, he insisted, intimating that the NSDAP's stand would have been different if the leadership, including himself, had been consulted. Göring's virtuoso performance worked brilliantly. Admiral Levetzow found his words "very reassuring," even "wise." In all likelihood Göring presented the same or similar mendacious explanations for radical stands by the NSDAP when he delivered the scheduled speeches on the NSDAP's economic program in Berlin, Munich, Dortmund, and Krefeld which he had mentioned to Levetzow and Holten in late October.

However reassuring the words of Göring and Hitler may have seemed during the autumn of 1930, the Nazis' performance during and after the brief session of the Reichstag in December could only have made those reassurances seem of dubious value. Joining with the Communists and Hugenberg's DNVP, the Nazi deputies sponsored at the outset an unsuccessful motion to rescind the legislative decrees on fiscal matters issued by the Brüning cabinet under Article 48. Then, as their spokesman in the debate on the budget for 1931, which the Brüning cabinet had implemented by decree, they chose Gottfried Feder. Because of his identification with the NSDAP's twenty-five-point program, his crusade against the "thralldom of interest payments," and his proposal for printing fiat currency, Feder had long since won a reputation in big business circles as an anti-capitalist eccentric with strong inflationary inclinations. Since 1929 hopeful rumors had circulated in those circles to the effect that his influence had gone into eclipse.[42] But during the election campaign he had come to the fore again. In an article published in the *Völkischer Beobachter* in late August he attacked "the existing capitalist form of economy."[43] The choice of Feder as the Nazi spokesman on the key issue of the budget could only seem an ominous sign to the business community. Even though he went out of his way during his Reichstag speech to disclaim "socialistic tendencies" on the part of the NSDAP and affirm its respect for private property, he undid much of the mollifying effect those words might have had on the business community by reiterating the NSDAP's commitment to tax away bank and stock-market profits as well as all profits from the war.[44] After the legislative session he soon resumed advocating publicly his pet scheme for the nationalization of all banks and investment houses.[45]

During the December session the rest of the Nazi Reichstag deputies served notice that they, too, had not altered their ways. As the session drew to a close, they alone joined the KPD in voting for unsuccessful Communist bills that would have rescinded the Brüning cabinet's cuts in unemployment and health insurance coverage and extended state-subsidized health insurance to the unemployed.[46] If enacted, those measures would have necessitated large increases in taxes, something to which the business community remained adamantly opposed. On the last day of the session the Nazis voted for a Communist proposal to provide aid for the needy during the coming winter at government expense.[47] After the chamber adjourned the NSDAP announced with great fanfare in the *Völkischer Beobachter* its sponsorship of a bill calling for heavy taxes on stock dividends and on fees for service on boards of corporations, proposing that the yield be used to subsidize meat and other necessities for Germany's jobless workers.[48] In an article in the same issue of the party organ, its economic editor, Hans Buchner, elaborated on the Nazi concept of private property in a fashion scarcely comforting to the country's capitalists. Denying charges in the bourgeois press that the NSDAP was hostile toward the private ownership of property, he proclaimed the party's support of that principle. He qualified this significantly, however, by adding that National Socialism would not countenance the kind of selfish, exploitative use of private property that lay at the basis of the capitalist economic system. A Nazi government would, Buchner explained, attach duties to the privilege of private ownership of property in the interest of the general welfare. To achieve this goal it would place limits on both the amount of property that could be so held and on the uses to which that property could be put. In that undertaking, Buchner warned, National Socialism would not be deterred by those who found their material circumstances altered to their disadvantage.[49]

As a consequence of these and other developments, great uncertainty and ambivalence marked assessments of Nazism in the business community at the turn of 1930–31. The *Deutsche Allgemeine Zeitung* of Berlin, which was controlled financially by a consortium of big business interests, addressed the riddle posed by Nazism in an editorial in mid-December. The new party's ideology consisted, the editorial explained, of a melange of anti-pacifist nationalism, "wild" anti-Semitism, and a "problematic socialism." Because of the latter, the Nazis had to make concessions to "vulgar anti-capitalist propaganda," as revealed by the recent speech on a mining disaster by their Reichstag spokesman, which "could have just as well been made by a Communist." The editorial branded Gottfried Feder's economic program as "unclear and utopian," but reported that the leadership of the party was attempting to clarify its economic goals and had indicated a readiness to accept the help of economically knowledgeable persons. The editorial characterized Hitler, however, as "more orator than statesman." It predicted that the struggle between the anti-capitalistic and the nationalistic elements in the party would become increasingly fierce. Even while expressing the hope that National Socialism might be "canalized" and led into the "right river-bed," the editorialist concluded that the outcome of the struggle within the party remained "completely uncertain."[50]

Among prominent men of big business similar doubts and ambivalence about National Socialism prevailed at the turn of the year. The Ruhr industrialist Paul Reusch saw the NSDAP as a "not undesirable phenomenon" so far as foreign policy was concerned, presumably because he believed its growth would serve as a warning to the victorious powers of the radicalizing effects on Germany of their continued insistence on reparations, and would also exert pressure on the Berlin government to seek an end to those payments. But in domestic politics Reusch regarded the activities of the Nazis as "extremely disturbing" because of their positions on economic matters.[51] Walter Rademacher, a leading figure in the Saxon coal industry, who had served as a DNVP Reichstag deputy until he broke with Hugenberg before the 1930 election, found the contradictions in Nazism's positions on basic economic issues alarming. Whereas all Nazi theorists accorded recognition to private property, individual initiative, and private profit, he noted that they qualified that recognition with the proviso that the pursuits of private businessmen were acceptable only so long as they served the general welfare. And the authority to determine what served that general interest, Rademacher observed, seemed to rest wholly with the state in Nazi blueprints for their Third Reich. If the state could contravene the rights of businessmen at any time simply by declaring that they had used their property improperly, Rademacher concluded, nothing would remain of private enterprise or the businessman's control over his property.[52] Hans von Raumer, the shrewd business manager of the organization of electro-technical manufacturers, voiced similar concerns. The growth of the NSDAP represented in his judgment a shift to the right politically, but to the left economically. But how far to the left on economics the Nazis might go remained unclear to Raumer because of the vagueness and contradictory aspects of the party's pronouncements and actions.[53]

As the year 1931 opened, industrialists and bankers among the membership of the conservative National Club of Düsseldorf sought enlightenment on Nazi economic policies from the chairman of the party's Reichstag delegation, Wilhelm Frick, by inviting him as a guest speaker.[54] A lawyer and former civil servant, Frick became the first Nazi to hold a ministerial post at the time of the party's entry into the Thuringian cabinet in January 1930, and he was widely regarded as the most respectable and responsible figure in the party's leadership cadre. Frick's talk seems to have gone unrecorded, but a journalist in the employ of the iron and steel industry who had attended with high hopes came away extremely disappointed. Frick had completely missed his chance, the journalist wrote to a colleague who was, like himself, favorably inclined toward Nazism.[55] A clue to his disappointment might be found in Frick's response, after another talk elsewhere in the Rhineland a week later, to a request from a businessman to explain the economic policy of National Socialism. He was happy, Frick replied, to report that the NSDAP had no economic program. The Nazis rejected the crassly materialistic outlook that prompted such a question. Their concern lay with making German policy, not economic policy. Such mundane matters could be handled on a case-by-case basis once they had attained power, he assured his questioner. Frick's remarkable statement earned him the following headline in a newspaper widely read in business circles, the *Frankfurter Zeitung:* "Happy to have no economic program, says State Minister Frick."[56]

While some big businessmen sought to learn from leaders like Hitler and Frick where the NSDAP stood on economic issues, others attempted to find out what Nazis said among themselves about such matters. The Ruhr industrialist Paul Reusch adopted that approach and did not like what he discovered. Early in 1931 Reusch obtained a copy of a Nazi directive setting forth guidelines for factory workers who had taken up the party's cause and become its functionaries at their places of work. Those guidelines emphasized that Nazi workers should remain within the existing trade unions, join in strikes for better wages and working conditions, and give their full support to all strikes. Although the NSDAP made use of the factory council system set up by the Weimar Constitution, that system fell far short of the party's goals, the directive explained. Those goals would be realized only when the National Socialist state accorded the workers a share of property, participation in management, and profit sharing.

> As socialists [the directive proclaimed] we have the duty to exploit the existing arrangements for everything that can possibly be gained from them. The National Socialist functionary has the obligation to serve not merely in a passive, consultative role; that is, he should not merely give advice if someone comes to him, but should instead seize the initiative as an activist in these matters.

Reusch found this directive so informative that he sent copies to other prominent industrialists after having marked the passages he found most noteworthy. In his covering letter Reusch merely stated, "Any comment on these guidelines is superfluous."[57]

At about the same time that Reusch took alarm at what he discovered being said within the NSDAP, a well-placed covert Nazi sought to reassure Germany's capitalists about the party by identifying it with Italian Fascism. He was Hans Reupke, a lawyer on the staff of the division of the industrial Reichsverband that dealt with legal problems arising from foreign trade. Reupke, whose membership in the NSDAP since the summer of 1930 was not generally known, became an enthusiast for Fascism during a trip to Italy to do research on that country's commercial law.[58] In 1930 he published a book on the economic policies of Mussolini's regime.[59] As discussions of Fascist Italy in the German business press of the early 1930s reveal, opinions differed sharply on its economic institutions and policies. Some viewed Fascist corporatism as a collectivistic and interventionist system that imperiled individual economic initiative and private enterprise, while others looked favorably on the Fascist regime.[60] In his book on the subject, Reupke gave the economic system of Fascism very high marks. Private enterprise and the individual entrepreneur enjoyed full protection from the regime in Italy, he asserted. Fascist corporatism represented nothing more than a non-doctrinaire experiment with new ways of structuring a capitalist economy. Reupke also proclaimed that Mussolini's government had succeeded in keeping *Sozialpolitik* within the limits imposed by productivity as well as in holding down state expenditures to a level that encouraged private investment. His book won him a private commendation from Hitler and a favorable review in the newsletter of the industrial Reichsverband, which announced that members could purchase copies at reduced prices.[61] One of those who read the book was Albert Vögler of United Steel, who responded with enthusiasm and recommended that the presidium of the Reichsverband call on Reupke to present his principal conclusions at one of its sessions.[62]

In February 1931 Reupke followed his publication on Fascism with a short volume on the economic orientation of National Socialism in which he again made no disclosure of his membership in the NSDAP.[63] He warned against what he characterized as the widespread error of mistaking the economic provisions of the twenty-five-point program of 1920 or the demagogic Reichstag bills sponsored by Nazis as evidence of hostility on the part of the NSDAP toward capitalism. Focusing on such ephemeral details distracted attention from essential matters, he cautioned. Too often overlooked were the NSDAP's respect for private property, its commitment to individual initiative and the leadership principle, and its rejection of collectivism and a state-directed and planned economy. What others took for anti-capitalism in Nazism Reupke dismissed as mere anti-materialism of a healthy sort. He assured his readers that once in power National Socialism would, as a dynamic movement, feel no more bound by doctrines or programmatic pledges than had Mussolini and his followers. The Nazis could also be counted on to follow the example of the Fascists by breaking the Marxists' hold on the minds of the workers and thereby restoring national unity. National Socialism would give the economy a different shape, Reupke predicted, one that would accord greater attention to the general welfare. But he added that it would put an end to the handout social welfare policies of the Republic, including its wasteful, demoralizing unemployment insurance program. In the new Nazi economy there would be no need for such humiliating doles since there would be employment for all, as he alleged was the case in Fascist Italy. Germany's businessmen would, he predicted, have no more difficulty in a Nazi-ruled Germany than their counterparts had in Mussolini's Italy.

Reupke's book got a mixed reception in the business press. In contrast to its favorable review of his study of Italian Fascism, the newsletter of his employer, the Reichsverband, made no mention of the new book. A newsletter for executives accused him of attempting to dismiss as bagatelles the anti-capitalist tendencies of the Nazis, who had yet to learn that capitalism and socialism could not be reconciled.[64] A business weekly in the Ruhr saw in Reupke's book an attempt to strengthen circles in the NSDAP favorable to capitalism and to commend to them the course taken by Italian Fascism. But it observed that, although Reupke had persuasively argued that Nazism need not be anti-capitalist, young firebrands in the party rivaled the Marxists in their hostility to capitalism. With regard to the economy, the weekly concluded that the situation within the NSDAP remained—in contrast to Reupke's rosy picture—still very much in flux.[65] Some Ruhr industrialists were nevertheless sufficiently interested in Reupke to have him speak at a gathering of iron and steel executives.[66]

Unfortunately for those who saw in Reupke's publication a hopeful sign of change within the NSDAP, the book met with a sharply divided response among Nazis. The national edition of the *Völkischer Beobachter* initially accorded it a brief, favorable review.[67] A few days later, however, the Berlin edition of the same paper carried a long article denouncing it as "the totally miscarried private venture of an unauthorized individual" who "unpardonably commingled National Socialist ideas with those of Fascism." Furthermore, the article stated, this work of a "rightist-deviant" writer had immediately been placed on the party index wherever it had reached the rank and file.[68] Reupke's version of Nazism's relationship to Italian Fascism received another public rebuke at the hands of the gauleiter of East Prussia, Erich Koch. In an issue of the radical organ of the NSDAP's factory cell organization, *Arbeitertum*, Koch roundly denounced the "muddled scribblings of a certain Dr. Reupke." "We are no Fascists!" Koch wrote. "We are Socialists!" Lest any doubt arise about what that meant, he went on to explain the implications of that distinction for economic policy: "While Fascism in Italy endorses and upholds the capitalistic economic system both theoretically and politically, we National Socialists are conscious socialists for whom the downfall of capitalism is both a demand of our program and a necessity of our policies."[69] Soon after copies of the issue of *Arbeitertum* containing Koch's article began to appear in factories, his words came to the attention of the executive director of the organization of Ruhr coal operators, the Bergbauverein, one of whose responsibilities was to inform his employers about such political developments.[70]

During the spring of 1931 some leaders of the business community caught sight of other Nazi pronouncements on economic matters that revealed outlooks very different from those of Reupke. Such was the case with an unpublished draft for a pamphlet that Otto Wagener, the recently appointed head of the Economic Policy Section of the NSDAP's Reichsleitung, had written at the time of the 1930 election under the title "Economic Tasks of National Socialism."[71] The following spring it had come to the attention of the circle around Paul Reusch, the most politically active and influential of the Ruhr industrialists.[72] The reaction of Reusch and the other industrialists with whom he shared Wagener's draft pamphlet has gone unrecorded, but it could scarcely have been positive. To be sure, Wagener did not challenge the principle of private property and even proposed that the entrepreneur's position be enhanced by placing him at the head of a *Werksgemeinschaft*, or factory community, in which trade unions would lose their role as labor's bargaining agents and be reduced to guild-like self-help associations. The main thrust of Wagener's proposals was, however, less reassuring from the point of view of men like Reusch, for Wagener accorded to the Nazi state of the future a role in the economy far more pervasive and commanding than hitherto experienced, even during the high-water period of *Zwangswirtschaft*, or coercive economic policies, during and after the war. The Nazi state would take over all banking and trading in stocks; it would have the authority to assume control of unproductive enterprises and expropriate their owners "with suitable restitution"; it would supervise trusts closely or, if need be, nationalize them. The Nazi state would regulate not only wages but also profits. In that regard Wagener specified a ceiling of 8 percent for corporate dividends; any profits beyond that would belong to the state. Toward big business Wagener displayed a pronounced animus. The Nazi state, he announced, would put an end to the anonymous trading in stocks that bred speculation and profiteering. Under a Nazi government, shares in corporate enterprises would have to be registered in the owners' names with a special state agency that would supervise their transfer from one owner to another. The stock market would vanish, along with its spurious quotations and fluctuations. The Nazi state would also curb the lucrative honoraria with which big businessmen rewarded each other for service on supervisory boards and management boards; like wages and profits, such honoraria would come under state regulation.

Wagener's draft pamphlet also displayed a paternalistic concern for the interests of workers and a tendency to side with labor and against management in matters currently under dispute. Industrial executives must have found particularly disturbing Wagener's rejection of the contention that the ten-hour workday permitted greater productivity than did the eight-hour day. Nor could industrialists have viewed with equanimity Wagener's dismissal of wage cuts as a means of dealing with the depression or his express denunciation of current efforts by "heavy industry" to reduce the pay of its workers. Equally unacceptable to men like Reusch were Wagener's plans for combating the depression by means of a special state credit institute that would issue loans to small entrepreneurs at artificially low interest. His vagueness about the financing of such state loans, coupled with his invocation of Feder's slogan for "breaking the thralldom of interest payments," could only have awakened the fears of currency manipulation and a renewed inflation that still haunted the German business community. Wagener's call for high protectionist tariffs, especially on agricultural products, and an overall national policy of economic autarky must have roused concern about retaliation abroad against the German industrial exports on which even iron and steel producers depended precariously for markets in 1931. The corporatist organization which Wagener proposed to impose on the economy carried with it the danger, from the standpoint of big business, that such a system of "self-administration" would place large enterprises at the mercy of the far more numerous small ones. Wagener's crude Nazi anti-Semitism, which branded the profit principle as a Jewish abomination and found an international Jewish conspiracy behind both the stock market and the Marxist political parties, could only have occasioned distaste in Reusch and the other members of the Ruhrlade, including the "non-Aryan" Paul Silverberg, with whom Reusch shared the draft pamphlet.[73]

In an effort to get more information about Wagener's draft pamphlet, Reusch passed it along to his political adviser and agent in Berlin, Martin Blank.[74] Blank, in turn, made inquiries about the document with a man who was assuming a growing importance in the relations between big business and the Nazis, August Heinrichsbauer. A free-lance writer on economic affairs based in Essen, Heinrichsbauer produced a weekly newsletter subsidized by Ruhr industrialists.[75] Following the NSDAP's successes in the election of 1930 Heinrichsbauer developed contacts within the party and began to serve as a conduit of information about the NSDAP, particularly for the politically active industrialists of the Ruhrlade and the organization of Ruhr coal operators, the Bergbauverein.[76] In response to Blank's inquiry about Wagener's draft, Heinrichsbauer dismissed it as a "purely private work" without any official party status whatsoever.[77] In reporting this to Reusch, Blank enclosed a critique of Wagener's views by an academic economist that has since become separated from his letter in Reusch's papers. Blank further informed Reusch that since Wagener had written his draft another attempt had been made to issue a "National Socialist economic manifesto," a copy of which he also appended to his letter. The provenance and content of that document remain unknown since the copy Blank enclosed has also become separated from the letter. It may or may not have been a draft document circulated within the party in March 1931 by Konstantin Hierl, who, as head of Division II of the *Reichsorganisationsleitung,* the NSDAP's national executive body, was Wagener's immediate superior.[78]

He had learned from Heinrichsbauer, Blank reported to Reusch, that this "manifesto" had been withdrawn from circulation because of the criticism it had encountered, especially that of Heinrichsbauer himself, who had written letters about it to Wagener and Gregor Strasser after consulting with a number of friends, including Blank.[79] That Heinrichsbauer would claim credit for quashing a Nazi economic manifesto hostile to big business does not surprise in view of his dependence for a livelihood on the leading circles of Ruhr industry. It is unlikely, however, that any intercession on his part was necessary to prevent publication of such a manifesto.[80] As is demonstrated by the preparation of at least one lengthy counter-draft directed against Wagener's views from the left wing of the NSDAP, any such effort at a clarification of party's nebulous economic position would immediately have set off an acrimonious debate within its ranks, endangering the internal cohesion of National Socialism and costing it the support of many members and even more voters.[81] No one knew this better than Adolf Hitler. Because of his steadfast opposition to any commitment of the party to a specific set of economic measures, any precise attribution of specific economic policies to the NSDAP had no chance of publication as an official Nazi document. When Wagener again attempted in 1932 to spell out the NSDAP's position on economic questions, he got his thoughts into print and between covers only to see his pamphlet suppressed, with Hitler's acquiescence, by his foes within the party hierarchy.[82] For men like Reusch and the other members of the Ruhrlade who read Wagener's draft pamphlet in 1931, what must have seemed most important was not that it had gone unpublished. What must have interested—and concerned—them above all would surely have been the state-interventionist and anti-big business attitudes revealed in the draft written by the man Hitler had appointed head of his party's Economic Policy Section at the beginning of 1931.

Throughout the spring and into the summer of 1931 the men of big business continued to search for signs of what they took for National Socialism's position with regard to the economy. Some took heart during the early spring when Hitler suppressed a rebellion by dissident stormtrooper elements in Berlin.[83] The leader of that rebellion, Walter Stennes, had the reputation of a radical on economic issues, so Hitler's expulsion of him from the party seemed a hopeful sign from a business standpoint, as did the suppression of undisciplined, violence-prone elements.[84] At least one prominent figure from big business, Hermann Bücher of the AEG electrical equipment firm, had, however, channeled funds to Stennes, possibly because the latter's archenemy, Berlin gau leiter Joseph Goebbels, seemed a more dangerous Nazi radical.[85] For some observers Hitler's reaffirmation, at the time of the Stennes rebellion, of his oft-repeated pledge to seek power only through legal means seemed to reinforce the view that he represented a force for moderation within the NSDAP.[86] There remained, however, the NSDAP's troubling ambiguity or silence on most of the issues of pressing importance to big business, such as binding state arbitration, industry-wide labor contracts, unemployment insurance, prohibitive tariffs on agricultural imports, and the basic question of the relationship of the private sector and the state—in short, virtually the whole range of issues pertaining to both *Wirtschaftspolitik* and *Sozialpolitik*. To the extent that any consensus existed about National Socialism in business circles by mid-1931, the movement appeared torn between a potentially reasonable, yet wavering, leadership headed by Hitler and socialistic, even communistic, elements.[87] The trouble was, as a writer for the bi-weekly business newsletter, *Deutsche Führerbriefe*, observed in mid-June, that Hitler had not extended his "legality principle" from the political sphere to that of economics.[88] Germany's capitalists were forced, as a consequence, to continue what Jakob Wilhelm Reichert, manager of the national association of iron and steel industrialists, would in 1933 look back on with bemusement as a "long guessing game."[89]

4. Capitalist Fellow Travelers and Subsidized Nazis

While most big businessmen pondered National Socialism with puzzlement and skepticism in the wake of its spectacular election success of September 1930, contacts began to develop between the NSDAP and the capitalist camp. These came about informally, usually arising from social relationships, as individuals came into contact with each other through mutual acquaintances. Only a few outright conversions of important businessmen to the cause of National Socialism resulted prior to the Third Reich. As early as the winter of 1930–31, however, the Nazis began to benefit from the influence and, in some cases, the financial resources of well-connected fellow travelers and other benefactors from big business circles. For a variety of motives, these members of the capitalist camp chose to view Nazism in an optimistic light.

The earliest recorded big business initiative toward establishing such contact with the Nazis after their election triumph came from Emil Georg von Stauss, a director of the Deutsche Bank und Disconto-Gesellschaft, one of the largest of German banks. Regarded by some as a ruthless parvenu whose allegedly dubious Württemberg patent of nobility occasioned ridicule in some Prussian circles, Stauss had established himself in Berlin during the late Empire by exploiting the social opportunities opened to him by his marriage to the daughter of Admiral

Georg von Müller, for many years chief of the last Kaiser's Naval Cabinet.[1] During the Republic Stauss joined Stresemann's DVP and contributed generously to it financially.[2] In 1930 he entered the Reichstag as one of the DVP's diminished delegation. He quickly began to ingratiate himself with the much larger Nazi delegation. As the opening of the new session approached he reportedly arranged a meeting with President Hindenburg for Hitler and Göring at their request but so as to leave the impression that the initiative had come from the president.[3] The day before the new Reichstag convened, Stauss lunched with members of the new Nazi delegation and helped to arrange for Nazi support of the unsuccessful attempt by the new leader of the DVP, Ernst Scholz, to unseat the longtime Social Democratic president of the Reichstag.[4] The Nazi delegation's proposal a few days later of bills calling for nationalization of all large banks and confiscation of the property of "bank and stock-market princes" apparently disconcerted Stauss at least temporarily and made him the butt of ridicule in the liberal press.[5] But that and other manifestations of Nazi economic radicalism did not deter him from his efforts to maintain contact with the National Socialists. At the end of October he assured an acquaintance that, despite obvious difficulties, it would be possible to work with the NSDAP in the Reichstag.[6]

The Nazi with whom Stauss found he had most in common was Hermann Göring, deputy chairman of the greatly enlarged National Socialist Reichstag delegation. The son of a governor of the German colony of Southwest Africa, Göring became an ace pilot in the war and served as the last commandant of the famed Richthofen Fighter Squadron. For his feats in air battles he received Germany's highest decoration for valor, the *Pour le Mérite* medal. Educated for an officer's career, he had developed aristocratic pretensions that were reinforced by his marriage after the war to a woman from a Swedish noble family. Since he moved easily in fashionable and affluent circles, Göring could, unlike most prominent Nazis, deal with a man like Stauss on a footing of social equality. His cynicism about the "socialism" of Nazism presumably added to their compatibility. Göring was thus in an excellent position to serve as an intermediary between the banker and Hitler. During the spring or summer of 1931 he arranged for the two to talk at length in the course of a cruise along the rivers outside Berlin on Stauss's motorboat. Another of the guests on that occasion, Otto Wagener, later recalled that Hitler's presentation of his political views during the voyage so impressed Stauss that he offered to break with the party he represented in the Reichstag and join the NSDAP at once. But, according to that same account, Göring dissuaded Stauss from taking such a step by arguing that the banker would be more valuable to the Nazis if he remained in the DVP and used his influence there in the interests of the NSDAP.[7] While this story remains uncorroborated, Stauss did continue as a DVP deputy and financial contributor right down to the Nazi takeover in 1933, even though

Wagener later counted him among the advisers to his Economic Policy Section of the NSDAP.[8] Stauss's friendly relations with Nazis soon became so widely known that Jewish customers of the bank he served as a director reportedly protested or even withdrew as clients.[9] His reputation also suffered as a consequence of his part in the banking crisis of the summer of 1931.[10] In 1932, at the relatively young age of fifty-five, he resigned his directorship and withdrew to the less active and conspicuous role of a member of the bank's supervisory board.[11] Although Stauss never became a Nazi Party member, he later received a seat in the hand-picked Reichstag of the Third Reich, becoming a guest of the Nazi delegation and vice-president of the chamber.

Not long after he himself had established contact with the Nazis, Stauss put them in touch with a man who would eventually become one of their most helpful fellow travelers: Hjalmar Schacht. A Freemason and one of the founders of the staunchly republican German Democratic Party, Schacht must have seemed an unlikely candidate for that role. This was especially so in view of repeated Nazi denunciations of him because of his role as president of the Reichsbank from 1923 until his resignation in March 1930.[12] Nazi agitators had also pilloried him on numerous occasions as a key figure in the international Masonic conspiracy purportedly bent on taking over Germany.[13] In 1929 Gottfried Feder dealt with Schacht so abusively in a speech that he instituted slander proceedings, dropping the action only when Feder took refuge behind his parliamentary immunity.[14] But following Schacht's resignation from the Reichsbank in protest against certain modalities of the implementation of the Young Plan, he moved rapidly to the right. From his self-imposed exile at his country estate Schacht made repeated forays into the political arena, delivering speeches in which he denounced the efforts of the Brüning cabinet to fulfill the terms of the Young Plan, which he himself had helped to negotiate. Following the Nazi election gains in September 1930, Schacht began to view the NSDAP in a more positive light. In December he publicly expressed admiration for the vitality of the NSDAP and proclaimed the impossibility of governing very long in opposition to the will of the nearly six and a half million Germans who had cast their ballots for the Nazis.[15] When his old banking acquaintance Stauss invited him to dine with Hermann Göring in mid-December, he readily accepted. Schacht seems to have got along well with Göring, who arranged for him to have dinner on January 5, 1931, at his home so that he could meet an even more prominent Nazi, Adolf Hitler.[16]

That meeting, too, proved successful. Schacht, as he later repeatedly confirmed, came away with a favorable impression of Hitler's energy, convinced he had found a man with whom one could cooperate.[17] Hitler, for his part, seems to have marked Schacht as a prestigious expert who might prove valuable when he needed such men to run the government. Neither side publicized this meeting of minds, and Nazi propagandists continued to attack Schacht well into 1931.[18] Yet by mid-year rumors began to circulate to the effect that he had joined the NSDAP. As Schacht never became a party member, he could truthfully deny those reports.[19] His favorable attitude toward Hitler became known in business circles, however, long before he began actively to promote the Nazi leader's cause in 1932. This certainly represented an asset for Hitler, for although Schacht had at the time no active role as a businessman, most of the leaders of German big business held him in high regard.

Still another significant figure from the capitalist camp, Fritz Thyssen, dined at Göring's along with Schacht and Hitler on January 5, 1931. By the time his octogenarian father died in 1926, most of the Thyssen family's holdings had been absorbed by the United Steel Works. As chairman of that enterprise's supervisory board, Thyssen held a largely honorific post that left him free to play a prominent part in the international steel cartel and to dabble in politics. His political course took him rightward within the DNVP. Whereas most of the big businessmen in the DNVP became dissatisfied with Hugenberg's hard-line and obstinate negativism, Thyssen remained loyal to the party chairman. In 1929 he actively supported Hugenberg's sponsorship of the referendum against the Young Plan, from which most of big business held aloof.[20] At a public meeting of the national committee for the referendum, Thyssen again encountered Hitler, whom he had met briefly in Munich in the fall of 1923.[21] No sustained contact resulted, but the Nazis' gains in the election of September 1930 aroused in Thyssen hopes for a rightist resurgence. An enthusiast for corporatist ideas, he found especially appealing the commitment in the NSDAP's program to the creation of corporatist chambers as part of a restructuring of the state.[22] When Brüning attended a meeting of the industrial Reichsverband in November 1930, Thyssen expressed the hope that the chancellor would manage to bring the Nazis behind his government.[23] He similarly urged Hugenberg and other DNVP leaders to seek ties with the NSDAP.[24] Thyssen's own relations with the Nazis became closer soon thereafter when an acquaintance, Wilhelm Tengelmann, a junior coal executive who had joined the NSDAP at the urging of Kirdorf in October 1930, introduced him to Göring.[25] Thyssen at once developed a liking for the former flying ace, whom he found both impressive and reasonable. Göring, in turn, saw to it that Thyssen soon sat listening to Hitler across his dinner table.[26] Thyssen, like Schacht, seems to have responded favorably to this personal cultivation. Although he remained a member of the DNVP for another year and officially joined the NSDAP only after the "seizure of power" in 1933, Thyssen made no secret of his sympathy for Hitler and his movement even before he openly committed himself to the Nazi cause in 1932.[27]

Others from the capitalist camp who became Nazi fellow travelers after the NSDAP's stunning electoral gains of 1930 enjoyed none of the prominence of Stauss, Schacht, and Thyssen but proved in some cases even more valuable to the Nazi cause. The journalist August Heinrichs-bauer provides a case in point. Because of his connections in Ruhr indus-trial circles, it was an event of some significance when he met Gregor Strasser through a mutual acquaintance in the fall of 1930.[28] Heinrichs-bauer, a militant foe of socialism and a hard-liner on labor-management relations, found he had much in common with Strasser, despite the lat-ter's links to the Nazi left wing and his occasionally strident anti-capitalist rhetoric. Friendly relations developed between the two, and Heinrichs-bauer began to report favorably on Strasser to his industrialist patrons. Emphasizing Strasser's endorsement of private property and entrepre-neurial initiative while downplaying his hostility toward big business, Heinrichsbauer contrasted Strasser with Goebbels and depicted him as a man of moderate views on economic issues.[29]

Through Heinrichsbauer, Strasser met still another journalist, Wal-ther Funk, who became an active Nazi after a brief period as a fellow traveler.[30] As economic editor of a conservative Berlin financial news-paper, the *Berliner Börsen-Zeitung*, Funk had attracted considerable at-tention in rightist circles by virtue of his hostility toward the SPD and the trade unions, his attacks on parliamentary democracy, and his militant opposition to the Young Plan.[31] When Strasser found Funk well dis-posed to National Socialism, he introduced the journalist to Hitler.[32] The Nazi leader quickly assuaged Funk's major misgiving about the NSDAP by informing him that the programmatic writings of Feder and other Nazi economic theorists need not be regarded as binding on the party in the future.[33] According to Funk's postwar testimony, after his contacts with the Nazis became known, businessmen of his acquaintance, particularly among the coal and steel industrialists of the Ruhr, ap-proached him and urged him to join the NSDAP.[34] They were worried about that party's attitude toward economic affairs, he explained, and wished to see someone in the party's leadership whose judgment on such matters they trusted. Whatever the circumstances, Funk resigned his ed-itorial job at the end of 1930 and went to work for the new Economic Policy Section of the NSDAP. In June 1931 he officially became a mem-ber of the party.[35] Once or twice a year, Funk stated at Nuremberg, he met with the industrialists who had urged him to join the NSDAP and shared with them his impressions of the economic orientation of the party.[36]

Still another Nazi fellow traveler came from the ranks of journalism, Theodor Reismann-Grone, editor of the conservative Essen daily, *Rhein-isch-Westfälische Zeitung*.[37] One of the founders in the 1890s of the right-wing, nationalistic Pan-German League and long a supporter of anti-republican tendencies, Reismann-Grone had given favorable coverage in his paper to the Nazis' 1930 election campaign.[38] Later, in 1933, he would become the first Nazi mayor of Essen.[39] When the Nazis decided they needed a newspaper in Essen, they sought his advice through Otto Wagener, the former manager of a small manufacturing firm who had become chief of staff of the SA in the fall of 1929 and was preparing a year later to set up the party's Economic Policy Section. Although Wagener harbored what he took for socialist aspirations, his upper-middle-class background as a former army officer and businessman made it easy for him to establish rapport with men like Reismann-Grone. According to Wagener's later account, Reismann-Grone extended his help despite recognizing the potential competition for his own enterprise that a Nazi paper would represent. Through his intermediacy, a printing shop was found and arrangements made to publish what became the *National-Zeitung* of Essen.[40] Moreover, Reismann-Grone's son-in-law, Otto Dietrich, later Hitler's press spokesman, gave up his job as the Munich correspondent of a major Leipzig paper to become one of the editors of the new paper.[41] When Wagener encountered financial problems in launching the *National-Zeitung*, he turned to Hans von Loewenstein, executive director of the Bergbauverein, the association of Ruhr coal operators.[42] Wagener does not explain in his memoirs how he gained entrée to Loewenstein, but it seems likely that Reismann-Grone again played a role. Reismann-Grone had served earlier as general secretary of the Bergbauverein and still enjoyed good relations with that organization, which had rescued his paper from financial difficulties in 1929 by purchasing a sizeable block of its stock.[43] According to Wagener, Loewenstein gave no aid but referred him in turn to Ludwig Grauert, managing director of the employers' association of the iron and steel industry in the Ruhr, generally known as Arbeitnordwest, located in Düsseldorf. As both Wagener and Grauert recalled independently after the war, Grauert arranged for a loan from the association to the *National-Zeitung*, which Wagener recalled as 50,000 marks, Grauert as 100,000. Grauert testified that he obtained approval for the loan from the association's chairman, Ernst Poensgen of United Steel, by arguing that it represented an opportunity to dampen the anti-capitalist agitation of the NSDAP by putting one of the party's newspapers into debt to an important business organization.[44] With the help of the loan, which Grauert later remembered the Nazis never repaid, the *National-Zeitung* commenced publication in mid-December 1930, soon gaining a reputation as a comparatively genteel Nazi organ.[45]

Ludwig Grauert himself soon became a Nazi fellow traveler. The demise of the short-lived Conservative People's Party, for which he had stood unsuccessfully as a Reichstag candidate in 1930, had left him politically homeless. Moreover, like Fritz Thyssen, he found corporatism attractive and read his hopes in that direction into National Socialism.[46] So, after the election Grauert accepted an invitation from his acquaintance Heinrichsbauer to meet Gregor Strasser.[47] Further indication of interest on his part came in January 1931, when the Düsseldorf National Club, whose executive board Grauert headed, invited Wilhelm Frick to give what turned out to be his disappointing speech to that organization.[48] Grauert had been acquainted with another prominent Nazi, Hermann Göring, since the war, when they served in the same airforce squadron. He did not become a Nazi, however, until 1933, when he was appointed state secretary in the Prussian interior ministry by Göring.[49]

Grauert was by no means the only fellow traveler to channel funds to the Nazis in the aftermath of the 1930 election. Some money came via Stauss. Although the banker continued to support the DVP financially, Otto Wagener reports in his memoirs that Stauss told him in 1931 he had placed a sizeable sum of money at the disposal of Göring and stood ready to supply more as the need arose.[50] Also, at the launching of the Essen *National-Zeitung*, its credit rating received a boost, according to Wagener, when Stauss's bank held out the prospect that the fledgling paper could count on a loan if it needed additional funds.[51] Wagener further recalled that when the *National-Zeitung* later faced financial ruin because of a ban imposed on it for several weeks by the Prussian authorities, Stauss responded to his appeal for help by providing the funds necessary to ensure the paper's survival.[52]

Fritz Thyssen also became a source of subsidies.[53] In post-war testimony corroborated by some of his former office employees, Thyssen explained he had concentrated his generosity on Hermann Göring, whom he regarded as a bulwark against the economic radicalism of the Nazi left wing. In hopes of bolstering Göring's position in the party, Thyssen turned over to him sums of money later estimated at about 150,000 marks by the de-nazification court that tried the industrialist in 1946. According to an account confirmed by a number of independent sources, Rudolf Hess approached Thyssen on the advice of Kirdorf, probably in early 1931, with a request for aid in raising money to help cover the costs of the elaborate reconstruction and decoration of the new party headquarters in Munich, the Brown House. Thyssen responded by countersigning a loan from a Dutch bank to the NSDAP in an amount he later variously estimated at sums ranging from 200,000 to 400,000 marks. Thyssen claimed he entered into this arrangement under the assumption that the Nazis regarded the loan as a normal commercial obligation, but according to his postwar testimony, corroborated by that of Party Treasurer Schwarz, the party repaid only about half of the debt, so that Thyssen had to make good on the rest.

Although Göring boasted that he had laid sole claim to Ruhr industrial money, funds from sources there reached other Nazis, too.[54] Some flowed through the hands of the journalist Heinrichsbauer. In postwar accounts he consistently told of passing along money to Gregor Strasser and Walther Funk for a group of Ruhr industrialists, beginning in the spring or summer of 1931.[55] Heinrichsbauer apparently also conveyed money to a close associate of Strasser's, former army lieutenant Paul Schulz, recently paroled from the prison sentence resulting from his part in a rightist political murder.[56] Strasser, Heinrichsbauer recalled, received about 10,000 marks a month, Funk between 2,000 and 3,000. In most of his statements Heinrichsbauer gave the Ruhr coal industry as the source of these funds. When pressed many years later to identify the individual involved, he named two coal executives of the United Steel Works, Ernst Brandi (who also served as chairman of the coal operators' association, the Bergbauverein) and Herbert Kauert, as well as Ernst Tengelmann, chairman of the board of directors of a major independent coal-mining firm, the Essener Steinkohlenbergwerke AG, until its absorption into the Gelsenkirchener Bergwerks AG, a subsidiary of United Steel, in 1930. But Heinrichsbauer's backers seem not to have been limited to the coal industry. He also named two prominent Ruhr executives whose primary activities lay in iron and steel production, Fritz Springorum, of the Hoesch firm, and Albert Vögler, general director of United Steel.[57] The involvement of the iron and steel men seems borne out by documents originating with the Ruhrlade which record payments of 2,500 marks to Funk during the summer of 1931 and 15,800 marks to Strasser between mid-October 1931 and mid-January 1932.[58] The disparate business affiliations of the men named by Heinrichsbauer suggest that the funds he relayed to Funk, Strasser, and Schulz came from a loose, informal collection of individuals rather than from an organizational source. At least in the cases of Strasser and Schulz, that money also seems not to have been paid out in regularly scheduled, flat sums but rather to have taken the form of subsidies earmarked for particular purposes such as travel expenses.[59]

As a familiar figure in big business circles because of his journalistic career, Funk was in a position to raise funds on his own. An episode recorded in the memoirs of Otto Wagener attests to Funk's excellent connections with prominent businessmen.[60] Wagener relates that Hitler became concerned in February 1931 that the reactionary clique around President Hindenburg might attempt a coup d'état by using the army, thereby setting off a civil war with the Social Democrats and Communists. Such a turn of events, Hitler feared, might tear the NSDAP apart by setting its left and right wings against each other. To deter the "reactionaries," Hitler proposed to gain access to weapons for the Nazi SA, the only force in Germany large enough to challenge the army. Wagener reports that when he suggested they seek financial support for this undertaking from the business community by exploiting Funk's contacts, Hitler at once consented. Wagener recounts that he then reached Funk in Berlin by telephone from Munich and, as agreed with Hitler, informed him only that the party leader wanted to obtain pledges of financial aid for the purpose of arming the SA in case of a civil war launched by the left. Funk consented to help by arranging meetings between Hitler and businessmen of his acquaintance in Berlin. He insisted, however, that if Hitler were to have any hope of success, he must stay at the large and fashionable Kaiserhof Hotel across the street from the Reich Chancellery in Berlin, instead of at the modest hotel near the railway terminus from southern Germany he had previously frequented. Hitler agreed and, according to Wagener, on arriving in Berlin on February 3, 1931, found that Funk had engaged for him and his entourage a luxurious suite of rooms at the Kaiserhof, which would serve as his headquarters while in Berlin until his appointment as chancellor.

The afternoon of their arrival at the Kaiserhof, Wagener's account continues, Funk brought two prominent executives of one of Germany's largest insurance firms, the Allianz und Stuttgarter Verein Versicherungs-AG, to meet Hitler. These were Kurt Schmitt, the firm's director and later minister of economics in the Third Reich, and August von Finck, a partner in the Munich banking house of Merck, Finck & Co. and chairman of the insurance firm's supervisory board. After Hitler had subjected these two to a lecture in which he conjured up the specter of unemployed masses rising in a leftist revolt, Funk retired with the guests into the next room. When Funk returned alone five minutes later, Wagener reports, he announced that the two callers had pledged five million marks to the SA in the event of a civil war. Wagener notes that Hitler's astonishment at the magnitude of this sum left him briefly speechless—a truly extraordinary condition for the Nazi leader. But Funk had only begun. During the following days Funk paraded a succession of prominent Berlin businessmen through Hitler's hotel suite, where they received the same treatment. Of those who came Wagener names only three, all executives in the potash industry based in Berlin, August Diehn, Günther Quandt, and August Rosterg. When the procession ended, the total amount pledged came, according to Wagener, to twenty-five million marks.[61] The accuracy of that figure, recalled fifteen years later by Wagener, is of no material importance since the civil war on which delivery of the funds was contingent never occurred, so that the businessmen involved were not called on to make good on their pledges. Still, this episode at the Kaiserhof Hotel in February 1931 illustrates the extent of Funk's contacts in the business world and Hitler's effectiveness in dealing personally with businessmen. It also reveals a readiness early in 1931 on the part of some prominent figures of German big business to view Nazi storm troopers as a potential shield in the event of a leftist uprising.

After Funk became a full-fledged Nazi instead of merely a fellow traveler, he began to deal in cash rather than in the sort of conditional commitments he extracted from the men whom he exposed to Hitler's spell at the Kaiserhof Hotel. To support his Berlin office he sold subscriptions to the fortnightly Nazi economic newsletter whose editorship he took over in mid-1931. In Nuremberg after the war he estimated that about sixty industrialists had paid well for that publication, which he supplemented with a non-ideological bulletin of his own about political and economic developments.[62] As already mentioned, he began receiving subsidies at about that time from Ruhr industrial circles. He subsequently asked other businessmen as well for subsidies, leading those he approached to believe that he would use any money he obtained to press his outlook on economic matters within the NSDAP through his publishing and editorial activities. How much he obtained in this fashion remains uncertain, but his success in at least several instances is convincingly documented.[63] Funk also disclosed at Nuremberg that in 1932 he had solicited contributions from business sources several times at the request of Rudolf Hess, the deputy leader of the party. Funk's estimates of the amount of money he raised on these occasions varied wildly. On one occasion he maintained that he had obtained only minimal results; on another he stated that his efforts yielded about 500,000 marks.[64] His performance at the Kaiserhof Hotel, as recorded by Wagener, certainly makes the latter figure appear more plausible. Yet it would be erroneous to assume that Funk functioned mainly, or even extensively, as a Nazi fund raiser. In most of his contacts with businessmen he assumed the pose of an expert seeking to steer the party's economic policies onto sound ground, not that of a party functionary whose role lay in extracting money from the business community to further the Nazi cause. Maintaining that distinction was essential since assumption of the latter role would have detracted from his success in the former, the credibility of which required that Funk preserve a degree of detachment from the political leadership of the NSDAP. In order to succeed, that is, he had to appear to most of the business community to be a kind of capitalist agent within the NSDAP rather than just another Nazi party functionary. This may explain why he held no official position in the party until late 1932, when Hitler accorded him—as will be seen—very ambiguous status at best. Judging from the surviving fragmentary records, Funk seems to have limited his requests for larger donations to Nazi fellow travelers or business officials he knew were friendly to the party. When he approached other businessmen his practice was, by contrast, to ask only for limited subsidies which he justified in terms of his efforts at economic enlightenment within the NSDAP, not in terms of support for that party's drive for power.

Good grounds exist for believing that Funk used for his own personal purposes a significant portion of the subsidies he obtained from big business sources. Despite having exchanged a well-paid editorial position with a major newspaper for a much less prestigious and remunerative post in the NSDAP, he managed to avoid any decline in his style of living. Indeed, Funk's financial circumstances may even have improved after he began working for the Nazis. His nominal superior in the party,

Otto Wagener, records in his memoirs an eventful tour of Munich's nightlife with an increasingly inebriated Funk in 1931. According to Wagener, Funk persuaded the orchestra at the fashionable restaurant in which they dined to accompany him in a song he wished to sing by presenting the bandmaster with a 100-mark note. The clientele's response to that performance resulted in a request from the management to leave the premises. In a nightclub Funk then insisted on visiting, Wagener reports that his companion ordered champagne and, after sampling it, disappeared into the ladies' room. He emerged at once with the uniformed female attendant in tow and led her on a spin around the dance floor before ostentatiously thrusting a 100-mark note into her hand. Funk was thereupon forcibly ejected from the nightclub, shouting to its indignant habitués as he departed, "That's National Socialism!" Wagener recalled tracing Funk to still another nightclub with the help of the doorman, who had hailed "the fine cavalier" a taxi and received a 50-mark note for that effort.[65] Whether such use of the industrial money entrusted to Funk aided the Nazi cause seems debatable.

Göring unquestionably made personal use of the money placed at his disposal by his patrons in the business community. Indeed, as Fritz Thyssen later explained, he gave subsidies to Göring expressly to enable that swashbuckling foe of Nazi radicalism to live in a style that would reflect the importance Thyssen thought the former flying ace merited in the leadership ranks of the NSDAP.[66] From all indications Göring did not disappoint Thyssen in this regard. During 1931 he took over the adjacent apartments in the building where he lived in Berlin, knocked out the walls, and had constructed a suite of spacious rooms, which he furnished and appointed opulently. There, attired in expensive clothes and presiding over a fine kitchen and a well-stocked wine cellar, Göring and his aristocratic wife entertained on an extravagant scale, cutting just the kind of swath in Berlin society Thyssen seems to have had in mind. This certainly magnified his already imposing figure in some influential circles. Whether other businessmen who gave to Göring expected him to use their money in this fashion is not known. But from all appearances he had no qualms about applying for his personal purposes money that came into his hands because of his political activities. Göring also seems to have used some of the money Thyssen and others gave him to enhance his stature and influence within the NSDAP in a very direct fashion. According to Otto Wagener, Göring told him at the time that he shared with Hitler part of the subsidies he received from Thyssen and others.[67]

Hitler's finances have long remained a source of speculation. He handled his money matters with great secretiveness at the time, and only fragmentary evidence about them has survived. It is clear that he kept his financial affairs sharply separated from those of the NSDAP. He drew no salary as party leader and accepted no money from the central party treasury. The party treasurer knew nothing of his finances, and Hitler knew little or nothing about the details of the NSDAP's finances.[68] That arrangement, about which Hitler boasted publicly, enabled him to enhance the reputation for selfless asceticism which he so assiduously cultivated. But that arrangement also had a practical side since he was quite obviously an unscrupulous tax evader who sought by all possible means to minimize the amount of income he reported on his yearly returns.[69] As Party Treasurer Schwarz explained to Otto Wagener at the time, Hitler feared that the republican tax officials would pry into the account books of the party and so did not want his name to appear there.[70] Hitler left the management of his own money to his private secretary, Rudolf Hess.[71] When Hess approached Fritz Thyssen about countersigning the note for a loan to cover refurbishment of the Brown House and asked Walther Funk to seek business contributions in 1932, he acted on behalf of Hitler.[72] There is no credible evidence of Hitler's soliciting funds directly from business sources in the 1930s. That would have detracted from his increasingly larger-than-life image by bringing him down to one of the most mundane levels of human affairs in front of influential persons of the sort he now preferred to overawe rather than cajole. In contrast to the upstart politician of the early 1920s, who had not scrupled to ask for money from wealthy persons, the would-be Führer of the 1930s left such matters to others.

If Hess did in fact approach Thyssen and Funk on Hitler's behalf, that would suggest that his expenditures sometimes exceeded the money at his disposal, but he seems as a rule not to have depended on big business subsidies. Even before the NSDAP drew widespread attention to itself through its election triumph of 1930, Hitler had prospered personally. He moved to a large apartment in a fashionable section of Munich in 1929 and owned an expensive Mercedes-Benz automobile.[73] He also began accumulating an entourage of secretaries, adjutants, chauffeurs, and bodyguards, for whom he provided on his many trips about Germany. The discrepancy between his life-style and the income he reported, which derived solely from royalties from *Mein Kampf* and other publications, aroused the suspicions of the tax officials, but they never subjected his income tax returns to a searching audit, preferring instead to extract as much revenue from him as they could by disallowing many of the deductions he claimed.[74] An audit would almost certainly have turned up evidence of a great deal of unreported income. From the early days of his political career, Hitler had grown accustomed to accepting money from wealthy patrons such as the Bechsteins and Bruckmanns. As he became a celebrity of sorts, representing an extreme point of view that aroused passionate allegiance in certain sorts of people, he no longer had to solicit aid personally, as he had in the first years of National Socialism. He needed merely to let eager supporters know where they should send donations. The presence on the letterhead of his stationery of the number of his personal postal checking account in Munich suggests how he went about accomplishing this.[75] After the Nazis' startling gains at the polls in September 1930, Hitler's income leapt upward, since *Mein Kampf* became a best-seller. Whereas in 1929 he reported receiving royalties of 15,448 marks, for 1930 he reported 45,472 marks from the same source.[76] As a measure of that sum's worth, Funk stated at Nuremberg that he had received a yearly salary of 36,000 marks as an editor of a major financial daily in Berlin.[77]

Hitler had still additional sources of income aside from donations from his devoted followers and the royalties from *Mein Kampf*. Whereas he refused to accept a salary or any other payment from the NSDAP as such, he had no scruples about taking money from component units of Nazism. Thus he let himself be paid for the frequent articles he contributed to the party organ, the *Völkischer Beobachter*.[78] Its sales, like those of *Mein Kampf*, skyrocketed in 1930, so that Hitler's fees presumably rose at that time as well.[79] Baldur von Schirach recalled in his memoirs Hitler's having received 800 marks for a single article in the early 1930s.[80] Hitler took pride in pointing out publicly that he, unlike other Nazis, accepted no honoraria for the countless speeches he delivered on behalf of the party during its drive toward power. But, according to Schirach, these speaking appearances nevertheless served as a source of income for him. Although Hitler refused honoraria, Schirach recalled in his memoirs that the party leader received expense money for each of his speeches for the party. Schirach also recalled that the amount paid by the party organization that invited Hitler to speak did not represent reimbursement for the actual expenses incurred by the party leader and his often sizeable entourage. Instead, the payments varied according to the profit produced by the admission charges and the solicitations during the rallies at which Hitler unleashed his oratorical talents. His traveling adjutant and "Reisemarschall," Julius Schaub, bargained about these arrangements with the local Nazi chieftains, Schirach wrote, while Hitler remained aloof from such mundane aspects of his appearances on behalf of the party.[81] Since these payments came in the guise of reimbursements for expenses, they represented a covert form of internal party subsidization that provided Hitler with an additional source of tax-exempt income. In view of the large number of speeches he delivered between 1930 and 1933, he very likely pocketed significant amounts of money in that fashion.

As Nazism forced itself increasingly on the attention of the world, Hitler found that he could exploit his newly won international notoriety to augment his income still further. He discovered that foreign correspondents in Berlin, under heavy pressure from their editors for first-hand accounts of Germany's fierce new demagogue, would pay for the privilege of interviewing him and pay even more for articles written by him exclusively for their publications. Reminiscing in 1942, Hitler claimed that these interviews and articles had brought him $2,000 to $3,000 each, which at the exchange rate prevailing in the early 1930s amounted to between 8,400 and 12,600 marks. His foreign press chief, Ernst Hanfstaengl, had done the bargaining on these occasions, he reported. Once Hanfstaengl had come to him, he recounted, with an offer from a British paper of 1,000 pounds, or about 21,000 marks, for an article, only to be turned away because Hitler had not been interested in the kind of article requested.[82] Hitler quite possibly exaggerated the amounts of money involved as he regaled his dinner guests of 1942 with these tales of the *Kampfzeit*, but his story of payments from the foreign press is corroborated by the memoirs of Otto Dietrich (later Reich press chief), Schirach, Hanfstaengl, and a former British correspondent in Berlin, Sefton Delmer.[83] Hanfstaengl claimed that Hitler shared with him 30 percent of the money received for articles and interviews he arranged.[84] In seeking to cover Hitler some foreign newspapers inadvertently became part of the story of his rise by covertly augmenting his material resources.

Hitler did not need enormous sums of money in the early 1930s. The party took care of itself, thanks to the orderly upward flow of its regular income, which growing membership rolls swelled. The staff of the Reichsleitung at the Brown House received party salaries, so that they did not require any assistance from Hitler. So, in all likelihood, did the members of his personal entourage, such as his secretary, Rudolf Hess, "Reisemarschall" Schaub, and the "Chauffeureska," as Hanfstaengl dubbed Hitler's drivers and bodyguards. Hitler thus had to cover out of his own pocket only his rather austere personal needs, plus the rent and maintenance of his Munich apartment, the upkeep of the vacation house he had bought near Berchtesgaden in 1928, fuel and repairs for his automobile, and the travel expenses he and his entourage incurred, which were at least in part offset by the "expense money" he received in connection with his party speeches. During his reminiscences at the dinner table in 1942 he told his captive audience that during the *Kampfzeit* a week's stay for him and his entourage at the Kaiserhof Hotel, meals included, had cost about 10,000 marks a week.[85] Here he exaggerated grossly, very possibly because he knew little of such financial details, having left them to Hess. Whatever the explanation for the discrepancy, receipted bills for his stays at the Kaiserhof tell a quite different tale. At the depth of the depression, prices even at that luxury hotel had dropped sharply. As an itemized receipted bill for one of Hitler's stays there in early 1932 shows, a room could be had for only 6 marks a night.[86] Another bill reveals that late in 1931 Hitler and an entourage occupying seven rooms paid only 650.86 marks for a stay of three days, meals and services included.[87] Luxury came cheaply in the Germany of 1931 and 1932.

Since Hitler lived a life of affluence and ease, moving about in luxurious chauffeur-driven cars and staying in the best hotels, the leftist and liberal press not surprisingly abounded with allegations to the effect that only capitalist money could make possible such a style of living. The Nazi press indignantly denied such reports, as did other party leaders. Hitler himself rarely responded to these taunts in the hostile press. When he did, it was with his customary brazenness. In response to a report in the liberal *Berliner Tageblatt* in August 1931 to the effect that he would soon break with SA chief Ernst Röhm because of pressure from his capitalist patrons, he denied, in the *Völkischer Beobachter*, any intention of dismissing Röhm and urgently requested information about where he could locate some capitalist patrons. "I constantly seek capitalist patrons," he concluded, "but have hitherto unfortunately discovered that they are to be found exclusively in the camp of the parties aligned with the *Berliner Tageblatt*."[88] Later, in the latter part of 1932, when the fortunes of National Socialism went into a precipitous decline, Hitler apparently did seek financial aid from big business by having Hess ask Funk to solicit contributions. But until that time the Nazi leader had no need to resort to the expedient he dismissed with such heavy-handed irony in this mocking statement of the summer of 1931.

In the cases of those big business patrons who extended subsidies to Nazis in the wake of the party's electoral gains of 1930, a pattern emerges. With few exceptions, their support did not reflect a conversion to National Socialism. Most did not sever their previous political ties but continued to contribute to, or be active in, other parties. They subsidized Nazis at least in part in hopes of assuring themselves friends in power if the phenomenal growth of the NSDAP should sweep it into government. In this respect their support merely amounted to adding additional coverage to the political insurance policies many had carried since the establishment of the Republic. In the case of the NSDAP, however, big businessmen gave not to the party as such but rather to particular Nazis, ones they considered "reasonable" or "moderate" on economic issues. In his memoirs Otto Wagener recalled having heard this in the early 1930s from the Nazi gauleiter in the Ruhr, Josef Terboven. Businessmen were only concerned, Terboven explained, about ensuring that the NSDAP did not impinge on their economic interests. They therefore gave no money to the party but instead subsidized individual Nazis, such as Göring, Terboven told Wagener.[89] In increasing the material resources of men like Göring, Funk, and Strasser, their capitalist patrons hoped to influence the economic policies of the party by strengthening the position within the party of Nazis they regarded as opposed to its socially and economically radical elements. Efforts to solicit funds from the same sources for more general party purposes in 1930 and 1931 met, so far as is known, with no success. According to Heinrichsbauer, the group of Ruhr industrialists who subsidized Strasser and Funk through him responded negatively in the summer of 1931 to a request he relayed to them from Hitler for additional money to cover the costs of outfitting the Brown House.[90] They also turned down, Heinrichsbauer recalled, a request for funds to underwrite establishment of a party indoctrination center.[91] On the other hand, Heinrichsbauer reported that they readily provided Strasser with a subsidy for a week-long series of lectures for Nazi labor organizers by August Winnig, a renegade Social Democrat turned rightist journalist who advocated working-class nationalism and class reconciliation.[92] Such a project held out the prospect of steering National Socialism in a direction congenial to capitalism, whereas redecorating the party's headquarters or setting up an indoctrination center did not. The same was the case with the loan for the Essen *National-Zeitung* arranged by Grauert and the aid extended to that "respectable" Nazi daily by Stauss. The capitalist patrons who channeled funds to Nazis through such ambitious fellow travelers as Heinrichsbauer and Grauert sought, that is, not only to use their money to protect themselves against an uncertain furture but also to manipulate and reshape the NSDAP.

The attention bestowed on individual Nazis by fellow travelers and others from the capitalist camp in the wake of the NSDAP's election gains of 1930 probably helped to make the party seem more respectable in those circles and certainly prepared the way for later contacts. But the money that passed hands boosted the material fortunes of National Socialism only very marginally, especially since most of it went not to the party but to individual Nazis, some of whom used at least part of it for personal rather than strictly political purposes. The sums involved shrink in significance when compared to the party's enormous and rapidly growing regular income from the dues and special levies paid by members, from its rallies, and from its other numerous methods of fund raising. The main thrust of the party's phenomenally successful efforts to recruit additional members and spread its message among potential voters continued to be fueled financially by the money that surged up through the Nazi organization from the grass roots of that mass movement. The NSDAP had not approached fellow-traveling benefactors from the capitalist camp with hat in hand; the latter had sought out particular Nazis and pressed money on them after the NSDAP had—without the help of big business—already become a potent force in German politics.

IV

Capitalists, Nazis, and the Politics of Deepening Depression

1. Disillusionment with Brüning—The "Harzburg Front"—
Capitalists in Fear of the Ruler

During 1931 Germany plunged ever deeper into an economic abyss. Of all the European countries, it suffered most acutely from the worldwide depression. Deteriorating conditions surpassed the worst expectations of even the most pessimistic businessmen. Overall industrial production plummeted to a level about a third below that of 1928. Unemployment had already passed the four million mark as the year began and surged well beyond five million before its end. Over a quarter of the labor force fell victim to joblessness. Tax revenues declined precipitously along with economic activity; the national government's deficit grew apace. The outflow of foreign capital accelerated, at times reaching hemorrhage proportions. Exports dropped off drastically as a wave of protectionism shut German goods out of their accustomed markets abroad. In September the devaluation of the English pound dealt another blow to German exports by lowering the prices of competing goods from that country. Orders dried up and inventories accumulated as much of industry drifted listlessly on a sea of red ink. Growing armies of sullen, laid-off workers loitered in the streets, where quasi-military political gangs fought with one another and the police, heightening the growing sense of disorder and dissolution.

These developments gave rise to a broad consensus among big businessmen about the causes of Germany's plight.[1] The depression had resulted, they firmly believed, from a shortage of investment capital and not, as trade unionists and Social Democrats insisted, from insufficient consumer purchasing power. When industry, deprived of adequate supplies of new capital, began to contract rather than expand, the unemployment rolls swelled, consumer demand fell off, and the downward spiral began. The source of this capital shortage lay, in the judgment of the leaders of big business, not in the sphere of economics but rather in that of politics. Reparations on the one hand and an excess of *Sozialpolitik* on the other had, they believed, deprived the economy of an adequate supply of capital. Reparations had transferred German capital abroad and inhibited the formation of additional domestic investment capital by contributing to the high interest rates needed to attract from abroad the loans with which the Reich so largely met its obligations to the victorious powers. Excessive *Sozialpolitik* had diverted large amounts of capital to unproductve purposes and discouraged investment by imposing burdens on business that raised production costs to a point where the profit margin became too narrow to stimulate new entrepreneurial ventures. The remedy for these problems seemed obvious to the business community: a return to sound *Wirtschaftspolitik*. Its spokesmen insisted there could be no real recovery unless the capitalist system was allowed to function fully once again. In the summer of 1931 a group of prominent industrialists summed up their position in a letter to Brüning: "We must remove the chains from business and free it to conduct its affairs according to the eternally valid laws of economics, so that it can unleash its might."[2]

Widespread agreement also prevailed in the business community about the specific measures required for recovery.[3] In numerous communications its spokesmen instructed Brüning and his ministers on that score. Above all, the cabinet must do everything in its power to facilitate and encourage new investment. It must speedily bring to an end, or at least suspend, reparations payments. Accelerating withdrawals of foreign loans made such a step seem ever more urgent, for with Germany no longer able to meet its reparations obligations, as it had during the 1920s, with borrowed capital, its own dwindling capital reserves became gravely imperiled. The cabinet must, in addition, take measures to lower the cost of production so as to make investment attractive by widening the profit margin of business. To that end it must make good on its promises of further tax cuts. It must deliver, too, on its pledges to reform state finances and reduce the size and cost of the bureaucracy. It must also cut the levies imposed on business for welfare state programs. To make that possible it must lower expenditures on those programs, especially national unemployment insurance, by reducing the size and number of benefits. The cabinet must allow wages to move downward freely in line with the severely depressed economy so as to lower the cost of production and restore the profit margin. To accomplish this the cabinet must loosen restrictions, imposed during the Republic, that made it impossible to revise the terms of existing long-term wage contracts before their expiration, despite a drastic deterioration in business conditions. The cabinet must furthermore put an end to governmental interference in labor-management relations by limiting binding state arbitration to disputes directly threatening the national interest. By 1931 the Brüning cabinet was making extensive use of the arbitration system to impose one round of wage cuts after another. But labor-intensive industries complained that those cuts amounted to less than untrammeled bargaining would have yielded in a period of massive unemployment. Overall, the business community's prescription for countering the depression called for a sweeping rollback of a decade of republican *Sozialpolitik*. Its spokesmen were convinced that the depression had vindicated their dire predictions of the late 1920s, and they hoped to see the country emerge from the crisis with an economy permanently liberated from many of the governmental restraints placed on it in the wake of the "collapse" of 1918. They therefore looked initially with optimism to the Brüning cabinet. Its proudly professed independence from political parties and its use of presidential emergency powers held out the prospect of rational government free of the parliamentary pressures which much of the business community believed had accorded an undue influence to what they saw as the opportunistic and shortsighted political spokesmen of organized labor. Such a cabinet, big business hoped, would restore the rightful primacy of "the eternally valid laws of economics."

During the first half of 1931 disillusionment with the Brüning cabinet nevertheless spread in the business community. The chancellor sought, with some success, to counter this by cultivating the leaders of big business.[4] He made himself personally accessible to their spokesmen with unprecedented frequency and appeared repeatedly before their organizations to explain his policies. On those occasions he left the impression that he basically shared their views about what needed doing. Nor did Brüning dissemble in that respect. Despite his career in the Christian trade union movement, he remained basically a laissez-faire liberal in economic matters. He believed that the government could best contribute to recovery by means of a deflationary policy that reduced taxes and government spending to the lowest possible level so as to allow the business cycle to move as swiftly as possible into the phase of renewed expansion that had invariably followed all previous depressions. Like the leaders of big business, Brüning deplored the growth of governmental interventionism that had produced a form of economy he, too, characterized as neither capitalist nor socialist. As did they, he wanted Germany to emerge from the crisis with a stripped-down, austere economy that would give it the advantage in the world marketplace.[5] And he wanted to put an end to reparations once and for all. With such views Brüning could usually mollify the leaders of big business on the many occasions when he came face to face with them, but his failure to act decisively in line with his reassurances gave rise to mounting disaffection. Despite his agreement about the urgent need to end reparations, he resisted all pressure for a unilateral German suspension of payments. Although he cut the pay of civil servants, he made no move toward the thoroughgoing overhaul of the bureaucracy or the reform of state finances he had encouraged businessmen to expect. He also took no steps to cut back significantly the programs that comprised the *Sozialpolitik* of the Republic. Instead, his cabinet increased the levies for unemployment insurance and imposed new "crisis taxes" to cover the deficits occasioned by welfare state commitments. The cabinet preserved the state arbitration system of the Republic and even increased its authority to impose wage settlements. Likewise, Brüning ignored all appeals to permit a downward revision of existing industrial wage contracts before their expiration. On the other hand, his cabinet intervened through the use of presidential emergency powers to force reductions in the prices fixed by cartels. In the same fashion the cabinet gained authorization in mid-1931 to lower the industrial workweek from forty-eight to forty hours, a step advocated by the trade unions as a way to reduce unemployment by spreading available jobs among more workers. Although the chancellor held back from using that authorization, his obtaining it caused unease in some industrial circles. Despite Brüning's talk of the desirability of freeing business from government interference, it seemed to some that his policies actually tended toward the worst kind of *Zwangswirtschaft*—economics by coercion—and reflected an alarming deference to organized labor.

Those of Brüning's policies that created mounting unease in some business circles did not, for the most part, result from free choice on his part.[6] His idea of how to achieve economic recovery departed from those of the business community in only one major regard. Whereas big business believed that wages must fall earlier and more rapidly than prices in order to widen the profit margin and stimulate new investment, the chancellor sought to drive down prices along with wages so as to boost exports and entice hoarded domestic purchasing power into the marketplace. Most of the other divergences of his policies from those advocated by the business community proved necessary because of the strategy he adopted in an effort to terminate reparations payments once and for all. Convinced that any unilateral renunciation of those obligations by Germany would provoke a withdrawal of foreign capital so massive as to cripple the economy, Brüning sought to end reparations in a slower and more arduous fashion. He set out to demonstrate to the victorious powers Germany's inability to make further payments despite a policy of drastic fiscal austerity that cut domestic spending to an unprecedented extent and shrank the German economy to a degree that diminished its capacity to provide a market for the exports of those powers. To carry through this strategy, Brüning had to maintain the confidence and goodwill of the Western democracies, including the United States, in order to secure their consent to a termination of both reparations and the inter-allied war debts that had become inextricably entangled with them, as well as to prevent a calamitous wholesale withdrawal of the loans from those countries that propped up the precarious German economy. This dependence on official and public opinion in those countries made it essential to avoid any development that would call into question the political stability of the Reich. Because of the obdurate opposition of Hugenberg's DNVP, Brüning thus had no choice but to rely on the toleration of the SPD in order to avert a clash with a hostile parliamentary majority that could easily escalate into a governmental, or even constitutional, crisis. As the price for that toleration, the chancellor had to make extensive concessions to the Social Democrats and their trade union allies in the area of *Sozialpolitik*. Sustained pressure for such concessions also came from the Christian trade union wing of Brüning's own party, whose loyalty he could not afford to lose.

The chancellor sought to placate the increasingly discontented business community by holding out the prospect of more palatable policies. Without disclosing any details of his strategy he repeatedly intimated to spokesmen of big business during the first half of 1931 that he intended to reconstruct his cabinet along lines more to their liking. Recurrent rumors, originating with the chancellor himself or with his close associates in the capital, held out the prospect of a revamping of the cabinet to include one or more prominent businessmen.[7] But, at the same time, Brüning invariably resisted all importunities to bring his policies uncompromisingly in line with the wishes of the business community, always citing immediate exigencies, such as the problem of reparations, with which he had first to deal before moving in that direction.[8] Unsurprisingly, this awakened skepticism and mistrust in some businessmen, who began to fear that despite his conciliatory words Brüning might be nothing more than just another republican political trimmer of the familiar stripe, willing to continue the ruinous practice of mixing for the sake of political opportunism what they saw as two irreconcilable systems, capitalism and socialism.

The spread of disillusionment with the Brüning cabinet in industrial circles proceeded unevenly, giving rise to dissension in those circles during the first half of 1931. The Ruhr industrialists, most of whose firms were suffering alarming setbacks because of their dependence on the rapidly dwindling demand for producer goods, lost patience with the cabinet earliest. Through the regional Langnamverein, whose leadership they dominated, they issued ever more strident appeals for a decisive shift of government policy in the direction long advocated by big business.[9] To their disappointment, the national organization of industry, the Reichsverband, continued to follow a conciliatory line toward the cabinet. In its councils spokesmen of manufacturing industries less direly affected by the crisis remained willing to rely on Brüning. That was particularly true of the chairman of the Reichsverband, Carl Duisberg, one of the chief executives of the IG Farben chemical corporation, which enjoyed a pioneer status in numerous fields of that young industry that ensured it a sizeable share of one of the few still robust world markets and enabled it to register profits throughout the depression. Duisberg considered Brüning the most able chancellor since Bismarck and saw him as a bulwark against the insistent demands of agrarian interests for tariffs on foodstuffs so prohibitively high as to ensure ruinous retaliation abroad against German industrial exports.[10] The professional staff of the Reichsverband, headed by Ludwig Kastl, a former civil servant who had come to enjoy Brüning's trust, shared Duisberg's confidence about the chancellor's abilities and good intentions toward the business community. This outlook placed the leadership at loggerheads with the increasingly impatient and skeptical industrialists of the Ruhr and imposed severe strains on the capacity of the Reichsverband to preserve the national organizational unity of industry achieved in 1919. Spokesmen of Ruhr industry denounced the leadership of the Reichsverband in private as too soft on the left and the trade unions, too governmental in its readiness to cooperate with whatever cabinet held office, and too concerned with the interests of exporting industries as opposed to those which produced mainly for the home market. Some of the more militant Ruhr industrialists, such as Ernst Brandi of the Bergbauverein, the chief organization of the coal industry, and Fritz Thyssen of the United Steel Works, threatened a withdrawal from the national organization. Others, like Paul Reusch, opposed such a breach and urged instead that the industries of the Ruhr seek greater influence within the Reichsverband.[11] Their counsel prevailed. During the spring the inner circle of industrial executives who dominated the Reichsverband worked out a compromise solution. Seizing the opportunity for change without the appearance of disruption provided by Duisberg's long-announced intention to relinquish the chairmanship on his seventieth birthday in September, the oligarchs of the Reichsverband designated as his successor Gustav Krupp von Bohlen und Halbach.[12] A major Ruhr figure who had not sided with the militant critics of either Brüning or the previous leadership of the Reichsverband, Krupp could mollify all industrial interests. As a concession to moderates, Kastl and the rest of the organization's permanent staff remained unaffected by the change in chairmen.

During the late spring and summer of 1931 the bank crisis that rocked the financial system of Germany forced Brüning's industrial critics to put into abeyance their campaign of protest against his failure to meet the demands of big business.[13] In the wake of the ill-fated project for an Austro-German customs union, massive withdrawals of French capital from the Creditanstalt of Vienna led to the collapse of that financial institution. Its ties to major Berlin banks set off in turn a run on their holdings that threatened their solvency and raised the prospect of a collapse of the entire financial system of the Reich. Another massive withdrawal of foreign capital ensued, and the stock market plunged alarmingly. This crisis had the immediate political effect of making Brüning appear indispensable from the standpoint of the business community. With the cabinet struggling to restore the country's badly shaken confidence in the banking system, Germany's capitalists had no interest in awakening the impression that the chancellor's position might be insecure. Also, the respect that Brüning commanded in foreign capitals made it seem essential to strengthen him in the delicate negotiations regarding the international ramifications of the financial crisis. When the DVP threatened in June to join the opposition to the Brüning cabinet, influential elements of the business community therefore intervened to force that party back behind the chancellor.[14] Soon thereafter Brüning's gradualist strategy for ending reparations achieved its first major success, as President Herbert Hoover of the United States initiated a one-year moratorium on both reparations and interallied war debt payments. The chancellor's fortunes received still another boost when his cabinet succeeded in halting the run on the banks and in restoring stability to the country's financial system.

The forbearance occasioned in big business circles by these successes on Brüning's part did not last long. Once the financial crisis had subsided, industrialists from the Ruhr again began voicing discontent with the cabinet. The summer had brought no relief to their hard-pressed firms. Gigantic heaps of coal had built up at the pitheads of the *Revier*, unsold and with no customers in sight. Accumulating backlogs of iron ore, which the Ruhr steelmakers had obligated themselves to buy at pre-depression prices under a long-term contract with Swedish mining companies, awaited smelting at blast furnaces that operated at only a fraction of their capacity. A total inventory estimated at 400 million marks weighed down the heavy industry of the Ruhr, saddling it with staggering interest payments.[15] More and more workers had to be laid off each month. Viewed from the Ruhr, the Brüning cabinet's success in bringing the run on the banks under control seemed of only transitory significance. Businessmen everywhere found alarming the degree of governmental intervention to which the cabinet had resorted during the banking crisis when it imposed stringent controls on foreign exchange, restricted the right to transfer capital abroad, and in effect nationalized several large banks.[16] And, quite aside from these concerns, the industrialists of the Ruhr chafed under the cabinet's failure to take decisive action along the lines laid out by industry's numerous appeals over the previous year and a half.

In addition to these objections to the cabinet's policies, some of Germany's leading industrialists rankled at the unresponsiveness of Brüning and his ministers to their increasingly desperate entreaties for aid. They did not, as often assumed, place high hope on armament contracts. With the disarmament restrictions of the Versailles Treaty still in effect, any large-scale production of war matériel remained a remote possibility which held out no prospect of the kind of immediate markets sought by industry. Clandestine rearmament projects had during the 1920s proved disappointingly unrewarding and too risky for large firms intent on adhering to legality and concerned about the reaction of customers abroad.[17] Rearmament lacked allure particularly for the Ruhr industrialists since the Reichswehr had decided against assigning extensive weapons production to firms in militarily exposed regions like their *Revier*, preferring to rely on small companies in more secure interior areas like Saxony and Thuringia.[18] Germany's industrialists presumably also knew that for the country's military experts the first step toward rearmament would consist of inducting and training more soldiers rather than of investments in military hardware.[19] Since that would necessitate additional government expenditures of little or no benefit for the most stricken of industries, such as iron and steel, rearmament promised no relief from the immediate problems of *die Wirtschaft*. The industrialists of the Ruhr had more mundane aspirations. They pled, with only very limited success, for an extensive program to renew the tracks and rolling stock of the national railway system that would quickly generate orders for iron and steel.[20] They sought in vain to have the cabinet intervene with the Swedish government to abrogate their long-term contract for iron ore deliveries.[21] They also achieved disappointing results with their requests for additional governmental guarantees for credits to the Soviet Union that would make possible an expansion of the "Russian orders" for goods made with German steel, which anti-Bolshevik industrialists eagerly sought as other markets contracted.[22] Brüning, however, proved reluctant to involve the Reich further in such commercial dealings with the Soviet Union, fearing repercussions for German foreign policy from the Western powers, whose support he needed in his effort to put a final end to reparations.[23] The president of the Reichsbank, Hans Luther, proved no more accommodating to the pleas from industry for aid. Still haunted by his experiences during the great inflation, he adhered to a tight-money policy that held interest rates high and ruled out credits for new governmental expenditures of the kind sought by industry. As a consequence, Luther lost favor among the Ruhr executives who had only a year earlier regarded him as their candidate if Brüning should fall.[24] With Luther thus under a shadow, the business community found itself without a candidate for political leadership as Germany plunged deeper into its growing crisis.

As the financial crisis of the summer subsided, the unresponsiveness of the cabinet to the appeals of big business for a decisive change of course reduced Brüning's standing in those circles to a new low during the early autumn of 1931. Max Schlenker, manager of the Langnamverein and the associations of iron and steel industrialists in the Ruhr, returned from a trip to Berlin in September with the impression that the attitude of the Reich Chancellory had become worse than ever from the standpoint of industry.[25] At the Reichsverband Ludwig Kastl struggled to rein in Ruhr industrialists like Paul Reusch, who pointed with mounting alarm to the approaching collapse of numerous major enterprises and demanded "the sharpest possible" opposition to the cabinet. Reusch had concluded that, despite all of Brüning's reassurances of an approaching reorientation of his cabinet, none would come. The chancellor, Reusch wrote to Kastl, simply lacked the courage to take the essential step and break, once and for all, with the Social Democrats. The only hope, Reusch held, lay in drawing a sharp line between right and left and bringing the bourgeois parties to cooperate as closely as possible against the SPD and the trade unions. But he no longer believed Brüning capable of bringing about such a realignment.[26] At the end of September, the Reichsverband adopted a harder line toward the cabinet. Joining with nine other major business associations, it sponsored a manifesto that sharply criticized the cabinet's inactivity and reiterated the long-standing demands of the business community with renewed urgency.[27] Early in October the *Deutsche Allgemeine Zeitung* of Berlin, which was owned by a consortium of big business interests, expressed the hope that Brüning would return to the sound principles he had enunciated at the outset of his chancellorship. He could achieve that, the paper asserted editorially, by revamping his cabinet to include men who commanded general respect and by governing without regard for the parties, including the SPD, whose policy of toleration had entrapped the chancellor and forced him to limit his government to halfway measures.[28] According to widely circulating rumors, the DVP, under pressure from its business wing, stood resolved to throw its votes to the opposition when the Reichstag convened in mid-October after a six-month self-imposed recess.[29]

Brüning's cabinet reshuffle in October 1931 failed to placate his increasingly numerous critics in the business community. Although motivated primarily by a desire to get rid of some ministers who had become discredited and to satisfy President Hindenburg's desire for more nonparty ministers, Brüning also attempted to include some prominent industrialists in his realigned cabinet.[30] He broached that possibility in consultations with coal executive Paul Silverberg, to whom he offered the Ministry of Transport, with Hermann Schmitz, the financial director of IG Farben, and with Albert Vögler, general director of United Steel. They in turn sought a commitment from him for a fundamental shift in governmental policies affecting the economy. When Brüning proved evasive on that point, the industrialists declined to participate in the cabinet.[31] The chancellor did manage to secure Professor Hermann Warmbold, who sat on the managing board (*Vorstand*) of IG Farben, as his new economics minister. But Warmbold, an agronomist and expert on chemical fertilizers who had served briefly during the early 1920s as Prussian agricultural minister, did not belong to the inner circles of either Farben or the business community. His appointment represented less a reconciliation between the cabinet and big business than an effort to find a minister who could mediate between industry and agriculture, two groups that increasingly came into conflict over trade policy.[32] Warmbold's inclusion in the cabinet made little impression on Brüning's business critics. Egged on by industrial spokesmen in its ranks, the DVP defected to the opposition when the chancellor presented his new cabinet to the reconvened Reichstag in mid-October. That narrowed the cabinet's parliamentary support dangerously, making it more dependent than ever on toleration by the SPD. Brüning nevertheless retained the backing of the decisive political figure, President Hindenburg. Although Hindenburg had hoped, according to Brüning, to see representation granted to *die Wirtschaft* in a reshuffled cabinet, the president resisted a behind-the-scenes effort by former chancellor Wilhelm Cuno aimed at bringing him to impose an out-and-out pro-big-business policy line on Brüning.[33] Accepting the new version of the cabinet, the president again placed his emergency powers at Brüning's disposal. Armed with that authority, the chancellor secured the adjournment of the Reichstag until late February only four days after the October session opened.

On October 11, just prior to the beginning of the Reichstag session, a well-publicized meeting of rightist organizations took place in the town of Bad Harzburg. In an oratorical marathon, Hugenberg, Hitler, and other self-styled spokesmen of the "national opposition" vied with one another in indicting the Brüning cabinet and the Weimar coalition government of Prussia for all of Germany's misfortunes. Claiming to speak for the majority of Germans, the orators of Bad Harzburg appealed to the president to install them in power and schedule new elections so that the political will of the populace could find expression. They pledged themselves to renounce both Germany's reparations obligations and the disarmament provisions of the Versailles Treaty as soon as they attained power. All of this astonished no one, echoing as it did the line taken when most of the same groups had banded together behind two unsuccessful plebiscites, the one aimed at disavowing the Young Plan in 1929 and a second designed to force dissolution of the Prussian parliament and new elections in that state earlier in 1931. The only real surprise at the Bad Harzburg gathering came when Hjalmar Schacht, whose participation had not been announced in advance, mounted the rostrum and joined the other speakers in roundly attacking the economic policies of the Brüning cabinet. In the course of his remarks the former president of the Reichsbank impugned the veracity of that institution under his successor, Hans Luther, and expressed doubts about Germany's capacity to meet its foreign debt obligations. In closing with the observation that Germany's economic ills could ultimately be cured not by specific policies but only by means of firm national unity, Schacht seemed to align himself with the "national opposition."[34]

Because of Schacht's speech, which occasioned something of a sensation, as well as the alleged presence in Bad Harzburg of persons identified with industry, the leftist press at once portrayed big business as a partner in the "Harzburg Front" proclaimed by the political leaders at the meeting.[35] Although that interpretation has enjoyed wide currency ever since, it does not accord with the facts. Schacht's appearance on the podium and his inflammatory remarks represented an independent venture on his part; nothing indicates that he even gave his friends in the business community advance notice of his plans. His words surprised some of the most prominent figures in big business as much as they did anyone else. There is a simple explanation for this: By October 1931 the former Reichsbank president had become a political adventurer, thirsting for a return to power. From that time on he cannot be regarded as a spokesman or agent of big business. When it suited his political purposes, Schacht readily made use of his connections to the business community; but he unhesitatingly ignored its interests when they stood in the way of his ambitions. He thus had no qualms about casting doubt at Bad Harzburg on both the Reichsbank's trustworthiness and Germany's capacity to meet its debts, despite the possibly damaging effects on big business of such insinuations by an internationally known financial expert at a time when German bankers and industrialists lived in dread of a further loss of confidence by foreign creditors. Only with considerable effort and some dissimulation did Schacht manage afterwards to mollify the alarm his Bad Harzburg speech had occasioned among his industrial admirers in the Ruhr.[36]

Contrary to virtually all historical accounts of the Bad Harzburg meeting, no significant number of industrialists or other men of big business attended. Those accounts all derive ultimately from a single, quite dubious source: a list of those in attendance which was published by Hugenberg's wire service, the Telegraphen-Union, and widely printed in newspapers throughout Germany.[37] As is not surprising under the circumstances, the Telegraphen-Union list awakens the impression of a broadly based gathering, attended by important men from numerous walks of life. Some twenty-five (in some versions twenty-six) of these, it proclaimed, came from the ranks of die Wirtschaft. Curiously, those newspapers that relied on the eyewitness accounts of their own reporters rather than the Telegraphen-Union list recorded no such concentration of big businessmen.[38] Close scrutiny of that list reveals why: It consisted mainly of padding. Only one of the many names belonged to a businessman of nationally recognized stature, Ernst Brandi, head of one of United Steel Works' coal-mining divisions and chairman of the organization of Ruhr coal operators, the Bergbauverein. Another, Ernst Middendorf, held what might seem an exalted position as general director of

Germany's major petroleum supplier, Deutsche Erdöl-AG which, with capital in excess of 100 million marks, ranked among the country's largest firms. But Middendorf did not belong to the industrial elite and played no part in the councils of the Reichsverband, presumably because his firm was largely a commercial enterprise dealing heavily in imported oil and gasoline. Some of the other names included by the Telegraphen-Union were so obscure as to occasion misspellings in newspapers that made use of the list;[39] some continue to defy identification today.[40] Most of the rest came, at best, from the *zweite Garnitur,* the second-string, of *die Wirtschaft;* that is, they either occupied secondary positions in large firms or, more commonly, top positions in obscure small or medium-size enterprises.[41] Nearly a quarter of those listed were not businessmen at all but rather *Syndizi,* staff officials of industrial associations or cartels.[42] Such men served as convenient observers for their employers since their presence at political gatherings in no way bound the organizations for which they worked; they also had no authority to commit those organizations. Some of those present owed whatever national prominence they enjoyed more to their political activities than to their economic importance.[43] Still others took part in the gathering as members of the right-wing veterans' organization, the Stahlhelm.[44] The Stahlhelm enjoyed considerable prestige in big business circles, which had subsidized its efforts to unseat the SPD-led Weimar coalition in Prussia by means of a referendum earlier in 1931.[45] But big business in no sense controlled the Stahlhelm, which helped to organize the Bad Harzburg meeting and mobilized its followers so as to match the Nazis' expected show of strength.[46] Some prominent Ruhr industrialists who did not belong to the Stahlhelm reportedly received invitations from that organization but did not attend.[47]

By adding still more names to the list disseminated by the Telegraphen-Union and mistakenly identifying some of those on that list, numerous historians who have written about the Bad Harzburg gathering have fallen prey to Hugenberg's propaganda machine.[48] The myth of an impressive showing by big business in general and industry in particular has become entrenched in virtually all historical works on the period.[49] Yet well-informed contemporaries recognized that *die Wirtschaft* had been conspicuous at Bad Harzburg only by virtue of its absence. A reporter for the *Berliner Tageblatt* pointedly commented on this in his dispatch on the event.[50] Paul Reusch, who did not attend, learned about it from one of his political informants, Erich von Gilsa, who was active on the right wing of the DVP and had attended in his capacity as a Stahlhelm activist. Not a single one of "the real leaders of industry" had been present, Gilsa reported to Reusch afterwards.[51] Obviously angered, Schacht chided Reusch a few days after the gathering, "Too bad industry was absent at Harzburg." Industry would sacrifice its integrity, Schacht warned, if it continued to collaborate with the existing "system" and failed to summon up the courage to stand for its convictions.[52] Many participants had noticed the absence of business leaders, Gilsa reported to Reusch. Several, he related, had taunted him with the charge that his industrialist friends had stayed away because they were afraid of Brüning and unwilling to risk the loss of government contracts.[53]

The taunts hurled at Erich von Gilsa at Bad Harzburg contained more than a mere grain of truth. The businessmen of Germany had reason to avoid involvement in political actions that would offend those in power at a time when *die Wirtschaft* found itself becoming—actually or potentially—dependent to a growing extent on the state. As a consequence of an economic crisis that deepened relentlessly and without prospect of recovery, they looked with mounting desperation to the state for aid. They accepted with eagerness the orders for new rails and rolling stock for the state railways that the Brüning cabinet finally approved during the fall of 1931, and they hungered for more such orders. They grasped at the orders from the Soviet Union that depended on governmental credit guarantees or acceptance of Soviet notes by the Reichsbank, and they hoped for additional orders from that quarter, too. In the summer of 1931 the business community had looked on in horror as some of the greatest banks of the country survived only through drastic government intercession that amounted to nationalization of those financial institutions. No one could be sure that his own firm might not need similar state aid to avoid the abyss of bankruptcy. Under such circumstances it seemed imprudent to challenge politically the holders of power in an open and direct fashion. Criticism of particular policies or behind-the-scenes pressure on the DVP to bring that party to threaten to withhold its parliamentary support unless the cabinet adopted measures requested by the business community lay within the realm of the permissible. But participation in an openly oppositional political demonstration such as that at Bad Harzburg was another matter. Lest any doubt arise about that, the Brüning cabinet took measures to drive home that point. In advance of the gathering spokesmen of the cabinet let it be known in industrial circles in no uncertain terms that any executive thinking of taking part should realize that such a step would not be without effect on the chancellor's future decisions.[54] After the Bad Harzburg gathering Gilsa, filled with enthusiasm for what he had witnessed and confident that the "national opposition" would soon triumph, warned Reusch that industry must not hang back until too late. Expressing a commitment to the "Harzburg Front" only after it had attained power, he strongly implied, would prove a handicap in dealing with a new government of that complexion.[55] Reusch remained cautious, however. Brüning might just muster a majority when his new cabinet went before the Reichstag in mid-October, he reminded the impatient Gilsa.[56] When the chancellor succeeded in doing just that, Reusch and the other leaders of Ruhr industry kept to themselves their mounting restiveness with his cabinet. Far more pressing to them than political maneuvering were the contracts for railway equipment and the credit backing for orders from the Soviet Union, for which they desperately needed the existing government's help. The resulting fear of losing favor with the ruler, Hjalmar Schacht later explained to Adolf Hitler, had, in combination with the NSDAP's unclear economic program, kept Germany's businessmen from considering it as a viable political alternative.[57]

2. Ruhr Coal: Canards and Calculations

In accounts of Hitler's rise to power one repeatedly encounters a story of his successfully touring Germany in order to win over the key business leaders of the country during the second half of 1931.[1] All such accounts have a common source, a volume of memoirs by the press chief of the NSDAP, Otto Dietrich, which the party publishing house issued in a mass printing beginning in 1934. According to Dietrich's memoirs:

> In the summer of 1931 the Führer suddenly decided to cultivate systematically the authoritative leaders of *die Wirtschaft* who stood at the center of resistance as well as the parties they supported so as to break them, stone for stone, out of the structure of the regime. . . . During the following months the Führer crisscrossed the whole of Germany in his Mercedes compressor. He turned up everywhere for confidential conferences with leading figures. They were arranged everywhere, whether in the capital of the Reich or in the provinces, in the Kaiserhof Hotel or in an isolated woodland glade in God's free nature. Confidentiality had to be preserved in order not to provide the press with material for agitation. The desired effect did not go unattained.[2]

Through sheer repetition, but possibly because of its literary panache, Dietrich's account has become generally accepted as a reliable source of information. Yet as a master practitioner of the Nazi "big lie" propaganda technique, the Otto Dietrich of 1934 scarcely seems a likely candidate for trustworthiness. His book proves, under examination, a sycophantic codification of the myths the NSDAP generated about Hitler's feats on his way to the Reich Chancellory. Dietrich's portrayal of Hitler's pursuing and breaking down the resistance of Germany's business leaders so closely conformed to the official party line, according to which the Führer obtained power by winning the confidence of Germans from all walks of life, as to merit the greatest skepticism. Moreover, in his less quotable post-war memoirs, written without the aid of the Nazi propaganda apparatus, a much subdued Dietrich made no mention of any such successful pursuit of business leaders on Hitler's part. Instead, he recalled: "The authoritative men of *die Wirtschaft* and the associational officials of industry displayed a cool political reserve and awaited developments. Hitler 'the drummer' had to rely in his propagandistic endeavors on the financial sacrifices of his party comrades, on membership dues and entrance fees for rallies."[3] Curiously, these words of Dietrich have gone unmentioned in the numerous studies that accept his propagandistic tract of 1934 as the truth.

If the numerous meetings Dietrich alluded to in 1934 had in fact taken place, it is difficult to explain why these left no traces in the rich and extensive private papers of the leading industrial figures of the Ruhr. Those men were by 1931 quite curious about Hitler, yet their correspondence, which reveals contacts of some of their number with the Nazi leader during 1930 and 1932, records none for 1931. Letters found in the files of three major Ruhr industrial figures do reveal, to be sure, that in September 1931 Hitler had let it be known a week in advance through intermediaries such as Funk and Heinrichsbauer that he stood ready to discuss the political situation with twelve or fifteen spokesmen of heavy industry at a *Bierabend* scheduled in his honor at the Berlin apartment of Prince Viktor zu Wied, a retired diplomat whom Göring had befriended through his Swedish wife's family. All three of those whose replies are preserved—Paul Reusch, Gustav Krupp von Bohlen und Halbach, and Hans von Loewenstein, executive director of the Ruhr coal industry's principal association, the Bergbauverein— declined.[4] Their curiosity about Hitler obviously did not suffice to merit disrupting their schedules and traveling to Berlin in order to sip beer in the presence of Germany's most notorious teetotaler. Other industrialists may conceivably have attended the gathering at Prince Wied's, but if they did the absence of any reference to the occasion in subsequent correspondence suggests they learned nothing they considered of sufficient importance to share with those who had declined to go. In any event, such a casual invitation through intermediaries hardly constituted hot pursuit of Germany's industrial elite on the part of Adolf Hitler.

The background of another oft-repeated tale about purported secret doings of big businessmen with Hitler that took shape in 1931 provides some sobering insights into the origins of the sort of journalistic accounts that form the basis for so many of the allegations of aid from that quarter to the NSDAP. It began with an article published in mid-January in a left-liberal, pacifist newspaper, the *General-Anzeiger* of Dortmund, a major Ruhr coal center.[5] Hitler had visited Essen at least three times in recent months, the article reported, to negotiate with Hans von Loewenstein of the Bergbauverein. These negotiations had taken place for the most part at opulent dinners to which Hitler sat down with the "princes of coal." He had moved about Essen in a car loaned to him by his hosts and spent his nights there at one of their residences. In the course of their consultations Hitler had assured the coal executives of his willingness to be flexible about the length of the workday, despite the NSDAP's public pledge to uphold republican laws establishing eight hours as the standard. In return the coal executives had made two sizeable financial contributions, each in six figures, to the Nazi Party. They had also underwritten a bank loan of 90,000 marks to the Nazi newspaper in Essen, the *National-Zeitung*.

Repeated in numerous leftist newspapers, this story quickly began to develop elaborations and embellishments. By the spring of 1931 reports of additional half-million-mark contributions to the NSDAP by the Bergbauverein—often supplying considerable detail about the purported secret sessions at which those grants were approved—became commonplace in the Social Democratic press, despite flat denials by the officials of that coal operators' organization.[6] In October Rudolf Breitscheid, a widely respected Social Democratic leader, confidently proclaimed from the rostrum of the Reichstag that the coal industry had imposed a levy of fifty pfennigs on each ton of coal the miners brought out of the ground in order to raise funds for the coffers of Hugenberg's DNVP and Hitler's NSDAP.[7] Spokesmen of the industry countered by pointing out that a levy of such magnitude would yield around fifty million marks a year, a sum those two parties might find difficult to use up; the same spokesmen also cited an official government inquiry to the effect that the total overhead cost per ton of coal amounted to only forty-two pfennigs.[8] Subsequent repetitions of the story reduced the size of the alleged political levy on coal to the more plausible figure of five pfennigs a ton, apparently by the simple expedient of striking off a zero. By November the Social Democratic press began to portray the Nazis as the sole beneficiaries of coal funds, with the levy attributed not to the Bergbauverein but to the bituminous-coal cartel, the Rheinisch-Westfälisches Kohlensyndikat.[9] At some point the story acquired still another twist when responsibility for the cartel's decision to support the NSDAP was assigned to eighty-four-year-old ex-Nazi Emil Kirdorf, who by 1931 had been retired from an active role in the coal industry for five years.[10]

Republican Prussia's political police, who served a Social Democratic interior minister, took a lively interest as early as January 1931 in the reported secret meetings in Essen between Hitler and the coal executives of the Ruhr. The day before the *General-Anzeiger* story appeared the two journalists responsible for it contacted a police agent in Essen and gave him essentially the same account, but with additional details.[11] The journalists specified that the two contributions to the NSDAP had amounted to 700,000 and 400,000 marks. They claimed that Hitler had spent the night at Loewenstein's house as early as August 15, 1930, after addressing a Nazi rally in Essen. Their information, they explained, came from an Essen industrialist privy to the doings they reported on but whose identity they could not yet disclose. A week after the *General-Anzeiger* printed its story, the police found it potentially significant that the Nazi *National-Zeitung* had denied only the charge that the coal operators had underwritten a loan for it. The paper had passed over in silence, the police noted, the allegations about meetings between Hitler and the operators as well as about contributions from the latter to the NSDAP.[12] The official investigation continued for six months, until July 1931, when the police abandoned in frustration their efforts to verify the *General-Anzeiger* story. The journalists' source, the provincial governor explained in his final report to the Prussian interior minister, had refused to make an official statement, and the police had been unable to find any corroborating evidence. The governor added that the Essen police insisted that the source did in fact have close relations with the industrialists in question and was holding to his story.[13] The governor might also have noted, but did not, how curious it seemed that not one of the other 650,000 inhabitants of Essen had noticed any repeated comings and goings by Germany's most controversial and least inconspicuous politician.

If the Prussian police had known more about the political behavior of the coal operators, they would have assessed the tale of the *General-Anzeiger* reporters with greater skepticism. They would then have recognized the unlikelihood, on at least three counts, of the claim that contributions totaling 1.1-million marks had flowed to the Nazis in late 1930 and early 1931 from that quarter. First, the coal executives had since 1928 pooled their principal political funds with those of the iron and steel producers, with the Ruhrlade disbursing both. A unilateral contribution of the dimensions alleged by the two Dortmund journalists would have amounted to such an abrupt break with established practice as to be unlikely. Second, the reported magnitude of the contributions would have amounted to an unprecedently large grant to a single party; the collective subsidies which the coal executives combined with the iron and steel producers to bestow on all the bourgeois parties they supported in national election campaigns normally totaled only between 1.2 million and 1.5 million marks. Third, it seems questionable whether the coal executives would have been willing to make contributions on such a scale at a time of vanishing profits when they had so recently depleted their political funds for the national election campaign of 1930. The police would have had still additional grounds for skepticism about the story told them by the journalists from Dortmund if they had been better informed about the past relations between the Ruhr industrialists and the Nazis. They would then have known of the indifference, if not coolness, toward the NSDAP that pervaded industrial circles prior to the Reichstag election of September 1930. Knowing that, they would have found highly dubious the claim that a man such as Hans von Loewenstein had invited Adolf Hitler to be an overnight guest at his house following a rabble-rousing speech to a Nazi mass rally in Essen in the early stages of the campaign for that election. If they had possessed fuller information, the police would also have been skeptical about the trustworthiness of the *General-Anzeiger* as a source of facts on relations between industrialists and Nazis. Ever since April 1930 that Dortmund paper had repeatedly described, without benefit of evidence, ill-intentioned Ruhr industrialists lurking behind the NSDAP, bankrolling that party.[14]

Breitscheid's story of a levy on each ton of coal for the NSDAP and DNVP bears up no better under close scrutiny. That tale's origins probably lay in a one-time levy of seven pfennigs per ton of coal mined in 1929 that the executive committee of the Bergbauverein had imposed on member firms in February 1930. In their notification to the firms, Loewenstein and the chairman of the Bergbauverein, Ernst Brandi, explained that the levy was required to meet a variety of needs during the 1930s. The yield would go toward scientific research, technical training institutes, and scholarship aid for students of mining; toward the promotion of sports; toward support of causes in the national interest, such as strengthening the isolated province of East Prussia and promoting ties with Germans abroad, as well as to cover a special assessment levied by the industrial Reichsverband.[15]

Such levies to cover the variegated activities of business associations like the Bergbauverein had long been common practice, but the hefty size of the impost of 1930, coming as it did at a time of onsetting depression and declining demand for coal, provoked protest from smaller firms not represented in the association's executive committee. The general director of one such company complained that if his firm met the new levy in addition to the regular annual dues payments owed the Bergbauverein and the Zechenverband, the latter's labor-relations affiliate, it would have to pay out a sum equal to half the amount of the firm's managerial salaries.[16] In responses to the aggrieved executive, Brandi and Loewenstein informed him that the decision to impose the levy had been made on a representative basis by the fourteen large firms that accounted for upwards of 82 percent of the yearly total of coal mined in the Ruhr; considerations of confidentiality precluded submitting such decisions to the full membership. They made clear that the small firm in question would have to pay up, consoling the executive with the thought that it was a one-time expenditure.[17] The indignation occasioned by such treatment of small firms by an organization dominated by their giant neighbors was presumably not invariably confined to such letters of protest to the Bergbauverein. It seems not unlikely that some of those executives who resented being shut out of a decision-making process that inflicted financial hardship on their firms might have departed from the rigid confidentiality in which the coal industry usually wrapped its collective activities. One angry reference to the seven-pfennig levy in the presence of an indiscreet or disaffected office employee could have sufficed to open the leak to the trade unions or the Social Democratic press that apparently provided the core of the tale Breitscheid took to the

Reichstag in one version and which then underwent innumerable subsequent transformations.

Whatever the origins of the seven-pfennig coal levy of 1930 and the rumors about it, there remains the question as to whether the men of the Bergbauverein might not indeed have used at least some of its yield to aid the DNVP or the NSDAP. The money involved amounted to a considerable sum, even if part of the approximately seven million marks the levy would have yielded if all member firms paid at the specified rate went to the Reichsverband. A number of constraints, however, militated against its use for political contributions. According to time-honored practice, funds raised by such general levies of large industry-wide business associations were not employed for partisan purposes since the disparate political preferences of the members ruled out the possibility of any agreement on the proper allocation among parties and candidates. In providing their share of the money distributed to the parties by the Ruhrlade since 1928, the coal executives had drawn on a fund fed by special informal levies explicitly designated as political.[18] Any use for partisan purposes of official Bergbauverein funds would have risked bitter dissension and seriously weakened, if not destroyed, that association, a development its officers and permanent staff would hardly have so lightly chanced. A second deterrent arose from the membership in the Bergbauverein and Zechenverband of mines owned by the Prussian state government.[19] The executives of those mines answered to the government of Prussia, which in 1931 was still ruled by a Weimar coalition government headed by one of Germany's most vigorous Social Democratic politicians, Otto Braun. To allocate money raised in part from the mines of republican Prussia to the political archenemies of the Social Democrats would have been akin to striking a match in a poorly ventilated, coaldust-laden mine shaft. Even after the Braun cabinet was deposed in July 1932, when the right-wing Papen government took over administration of the state, the chief Prussian mining officials asked Brandi for an explanation when reports of lavish financial aid to the Nazis from the Bergbauverein and the Zechenverband received prominent display in the Dortmund *General-Anzeiger* in August 1932. In replying, Brandi flatly denied that any funds belonging to either of the coal organizations had been used to support the NSDAP.[20] Whatever Brandi's standards of veracity, such a categorically negative response would have been folly if the facts did not bear it out, for the Prussian cabinet could have demanded an audit of the associations' financial accounts. Contributions to the NSDAP from the bituminous-coal cartel were even less likely than from the Bergbauverein. In 1919 the cartel had undergone conversion to a semi-public body whose supervisory board included not only officials of the Prussian state government but also representatives of the miners' unions.[21]

As with Hitler's purported pilgrimages to the "princes of coal" in Essen, one would expect to find traces of any large-scale subsidization of the Nazis by the coal associations during 1931 in the voluminous surviving correspondence of the leading industrialists of the Ruhr. Yet none has ever come to light. To be sure, Loewenstein did touch on the matter once in a letter to Brandi in June of that year, when he alluded to a newspaper clipping on the subject enclosed in a letter to him from Hugenberg, Brandi's predecessor as chairman. Hugenberg's letter indicates that the clipping—which was not preserved—contained one of the frequent Social Democratic allegations of contributions to the NSDAP by the Bergbauverein. He had no doubt, Hugenberg informed Loewenstein, that the charges were groundless; Loewenstein would not allow any such thing.[22] Nor does the letter with which Loewenstein forwarded Hugenberg's letter and the newspaper clipping to Brandi exhibit the tone one would expect in a communication of one conspirator with another.[23] Instead, the executive director of the Bergbauverein seemed to regard the press allegations, which by that time had been appearing for months, as a troublesome but familiar annoyance. Moreover, he expressed alarm at Hugenberg's growing pessimism and proposed that he and Brandi find ways to help the DNVP financially. Loewenstein warned that if the DVP, to which Brandi belonged, foundered and went under in the state parliamentary elections of the coming fall, as many were predicting, industry would be able to rely only on Hugenberg's party. These hardly seem the words a large-scale covert financial backer of Nazism would address to a co-conspirator.

The implausibility of the canards of the day about massive coal subsidies to the NSDAP does not mean that no Ruhr coal funds went to the Nazis in 1931, for, as already noted, Walther Funk and Gregor Strasser then began receiving regular subsidies from a group that included prominent coal executives. In assuming a receptivity to Nazism on the part of the coal industrialists, the inventors and embellishers of the tales of huge donations to the NSDAP were probably moved in part by the knowledge that the coal men of the Ruhr represented, as a group, the most recalcitrant component of large-scale German industry, both socially and politically. During the Empire, coal had been an embattled industry. The coal operators had resisted unionization and collective bargaining more stubbornly than their counterparts in the less labor-intensive iron and steel industry, giving rise to some of the most violent and protracted strikes of the late imperial era.[24] Moreover, as late as the first decade of the twentieth century the coal industry had to fight off a determined drive by officials of the royal Prussian bureaucracy to reimpose, at least partially, the system of state ownership and operation of mining that had predominated until the mid-nineteenth century.[25] Then, in the wake of the revolution of 1918–19, coal—along with potash—became the target of the few so-called socialization laws adopted by the new republican government. Under the terms of the coal law the industry became subject to a host of special controls, including a veto by the Reich minister of economics over any price increases.[26]Although most of those controls proved neither as effective nor as onerous as expected, the repeated government vetoes on price increases embittered the coal executives. Even before the depression struck their industry with particularly devastating force, they had as a group developed greater hostility to the republican order and its *Sozialpolitik* than had their counterparts in other branches of industry.[27] That they should look at least with interest on an avowedly anti-Marxist movement pledged to destroy that system does not seem surprising.

The men who directed the Bergbauverein and the Zechenverband, which shared the same headquarters and the same officers, fully qualify for the label "reactionary." Ernst Brandi, the chairman since 1927, headed in his business capacity one of the four regional mining units of United Steel.[28] He bore the esteemed title of Bergassessor a.D., which indicated that prior to his career in private business he had survived the rigorous theoretical examinations and the demanding practical apprenticeship required for employment in the tradition-laden state mining regulatory system of Prussia.[29] Certainly in part as a result of being thus steeped in the ethos of the old Prussian bureaucracy, Brandi had managed to preserve throughout the republican years an undiluted patriarchal attitude toward workers and an unrelenting hostility toward trade unions. He firmly believed that management sought to further the economic welfare of the whole nation, whereas organized labor shortsightedly and ruthlessly pursued its aims in total disregard for the effects on the rest of society. Brandi succinctly expressed his scorn for everything smacking of democracy in an angry letter on discovering that a special economic advisory council established by President Hindenburg in October 1931 would include a spokesmen of organized labor as well as management:

> We will only become ever more deeply mired in misfortune with these democratic methods, i.e., methods according to whose principles everyone gets a say and so-called parity prevails. Nothing will really improve until a "real man" ["Kerl"] finally comes along who relentlessly carries through what is recognized as right.

Brandi, who had been among the leaders in the drive to force Brüning to bring his cabinet's policies into line with the policy demands of industry, announced to his correspondent that he had abandoned all hope for the chancellor.[30] Longing for a revival of the *Sammlungspolitik* that had sought to unite all anti-socialist forces during the Empire,[31] Brandi manifested his opposition to Brüning, as already noted, by attending the Bad Harzburg meeting twelve days before writing this letter.

The background of the executive director of the two Ruhr coal associations, Hans von Loewenstein, resembled that of Brandi except for its coloration by a venerable patent of nobility. A graduate of the Royal Prussian Mining Academy at Clausthal-Zellerfeld and, like Brandi, a former Bergassessor, Loewenstein had served as a full-time functionary of the coal organizations since 1906.[32] He harbored a heartfelt and scarcely concealed scorn for the Republic; after the rightist putsch of March 1920 had failed to overthrow the new state, he publicly expressed admiration for its leader, Wolfgang Kapp.[33] An advocate of an elitist form of corporatism, Loewenstein also became an admirer of Mussolini during the 1920s.[34] By 1931 he corresponded with Nazis like Hans Reupke and Prince Friedrich Christian of Schaumburg-Lippe, who wanted to pattern the economic policies of the NSDAP after those of Italian Fascism.[35] He attended the Harzburg meeting in his capacity as an ardent supporter of the Stahlhelm, and afterwards wrote an acquaintance that he had felt exalted by the "national excitement" the gathering generated.[36] He apparently met Hitler there and soon thereafter sent him a book on the German resistance to the French occupation of the Ruhr.[37]

Although historians have habitually subsumed the coal operators under the catch-all label "heavy industry," those men actually thought of themselves as quite distinct from the iron and steel executives who dominated the great "mixed" firms that had swallowed up much of the Ruhr's mining operations by the 1920s. While their associations, the Bergbauverein and Zechenverband, were becoming increasingly anachronistic by any realistic measure, the coal men clung jealously to their separate identity. Ernst Brandi provides a case in point. Although an executive of United Steel, he maintained his allegiance to coal, proudly wielding the title Bergassessor a.D. and playing a leading role in the coal associations. For him and others like him, attainment of the coveted title of Bergassessor carried with it a lifetime membership in an exclusive fraternity inaccessible to even the most powerful iron and steel executives. They displayed a clannishness not unlike that of the coal miners, perhaps because of their participation in the extraordinary subterranean society of mining during their apprenticeships in the Prussian mine inspectorate. They therefore smarted at the subordination of mining to iron and steel production and manufacturing in the great "mixed" firms that had come to dominate the Ruhr. They resented what they regarded as insufficient resistance on the part of executives of those firms to encroachments on their industry by the Republic. They believed that their industry, which was losing, according to a government inquiry of June 1931, thirty-two pfennigs per ton of mined coal, bore an undue share of the depression's ravages.[38] They chafed at the administration of the political funds they raised by the Ruhrlade, in which they felt underrepresented.[39] They regarded themselves as underrepresented as well in the industrial Reichsverband and insufficiently served by its leadership. These resentments came to a head in the winter of 1930–31, when the Bergbauverein, led by Brandi, touched off an acrimonious feud in the Ruhr by threatening to have its members leave the Reichsverband. Only when Paul Reusch threatened in turn to have the "mixed" firms of the Ruhr cancel the memberships of their coal subsidiaries in the Bergbauverein did the coal men back down.[40]

In view of the resentful, embattled outlook of the Ruhr coal operators and the political and social attitudes of men like Brandi and Loewenstein, it does not surprise that some of the earliest industrial subsidies for Walther Funk and Gregor Strasser came from circles close to the Bergbauverein. Traces also remain of support by Brandi for a local Nazi notable, Essen Gauleiter Josef Terboven. In the summer of 1934, when the Bergbauverein became embroiled with Terboven, by that time a powerful personage in the Third Reich, Brandi appealed for help to Herbert Kauert, chief of the sales division of United Steel's coal operations and a nephew of Emil Kirdorf. Brandi asked Kauert, who was on friendly terms with Terboven, to remind the gauleiter of the support he had received from Brandi, through the intermediacy of Kauert, before the Nazis came to power.[41] According to Heinrichsbauer, that support took the form of regular subsidies to Terboven, beginning in the spring of 1931, of the same sort that went to Walther Funk and Gregor Strasser from Ruhr coal circles. Heinrichsbauer also specified that the money used for these subsidies had not come from the regular funds of the Bergbauverein and surmised that it had been raised by means of a special levy outside the framework of that association.[42] If Brandi and the other coal men had, as the leftist press charged, supplied the NSDAP with hundreds of thousands of marks, Brandi would certainly have been able to marshal a far stronger case regarding his past benefactions when he needed ammunition to protect himself in 1934. But not even the allegation of the Dortmund *General-Anzeiger* about a loan of 90,000 marks for the Essen *National-Zeitung* holds up in the light of the available evidence. In seeking funds for the new Nazi paper, Otto Wagener met with no success when he broached that subject with Loewenstein. The latter did, however, refer Wagener to Nazi fellow traveler Ludwig Grauert, of Arbeitnordwest, the Ruhr iron and steel industry's employers' association, who—as already mentioned—arranged for a loan.[43] Later the Bergbauverein, along with the organizations of the iron and steel men, included the *National-Zeitung* among the newspapers in which it bought space for announcements, but that hardly amounted to large-scale subsidization.[44]

Judging from their attitudes and actions prior to the Nazi takeover in 1933, such coal men as Brandi and Loewenstein adopted, despite their own strong reactionary bent, a cautious approach toward the NSDAP, in all probability because Nazi socio-economic radicalism made them wary. They retained their ties to the traditional right and placed their hopes for political leadership in it.[45] Contrary to the allegations of the leftist press, they made no six- or seven-figure contributions to the NSDAP in order to propel it into power. Instead, they, like others in the business community, distributed relatively modest subsidies to particular Nazis. Presumably they, too, wanted to assure themselves of friends in power should Germany's most dynamic new political movement capture control of the state. They seem also to have hoped, as did others, that by aiding Nazis like Funk and Strasser they might counter the disturbing radical elements within the NSDAP by strengthening the position of party spokesmen widely viewed in the business community as moderate and reasonable so far as economic questions were concerned. The leaders of Ruhr coal appear, in short, to have acted on the basis of calculation rather than commitment in dealing with Nazism before 1933.

3. The Proliferating Forks of Nazism's Tongue

In the course of 1931 those in the business community who sought to discern the NSDAP's position on social and economic issues of vital concern to them found that task becoming no easier. Instead, the enigma of Nazi economic policy seemed to deepen as still more voices joined the dissonant chorus of those claiming to speak for the movement, which continued to grow and spread rapidly all across Germany.

Those in the business community who in 1931 approved subsidies for individual Nazis or particular party organizations they hoped might serve their interests did so despite a mounting wave of radical agitation directed at workers from the side of the NSDAP. Much of that agitation emanated from the NSBO, the factory cell organization, which gained the status of a nationwide organ of the party at the beginning of 1929. Its mission lay in cultivating worker support by organizing Nazi cells in factories and gaining representation for these on the factory councils elected by workers under a provision of the Weimar constitution.[1] In March the NSBO began publishing a fortnightly organ, *Arbeitertum*, an elaborate yet inexpensive magazine addressed to industrial workers and recommended to all Nazis by the *Völkischer Beobachter*.[2] It poured forth a steady stream of Nazi anti-capitalist slogans, calling for an end to the "liberal-capitalist economic system," for "state socialist nationalization of basic industries," and for removal and prosecution of the "hyenas of the economy." *Arbeitertum* also denounced as "parasites of the working class" the "yellow," or company, unions that many employers still hoped to see restored to a leading role. Loyal Nazi workers, *Arbeitertum* proclaimed, gave up their jobs rather than joining a company union. Through the pages of *Arbeitertum* the NSBO made known its endorsement of the worker's right to strike and proclaimed that any Nazis caught strikebreaking would be expelled from the party. During 1931 the NSBO actively participated in four highly publicized strikes, raising funds from its membership throughout the country to help support the idled workers. In some places NSBO officials even called and led strikes. In September Goebbels, as gauleiter of Berlin, launched with much fanfare and publicity a campaign to win over the industrial workers of the capital to the NSBO and the party, using the slogan "Into the Factories" (Hib-Aktion). In the Gau daily, Der Angriff, he instructed Nazi agitators to place primary emphasis on "our revolutionary socialist purposes." Throughout Germany the functionaries of the NSBO and their worker followers distributed a flood of inflammatory pamphlets and handbills at factories and mines.

One NSBO "combat sheet" published in the Ruhr directed some of its most radical fulminations specifically at the coal executives of that region. In an issue of November 1931 it responded vociferously to an announcement by the Zechenverband to the effect that it did not intend to renew the existing contract with the coal miners' union when that agreement expired at the end of the year.[3] As the industry made no secret of its intention to press for another large wage cut, the Nazi publication announced that this stand bared "the grizzly mug of capital." The plans of the Ruhr coal industrialists meant that "an entire industrial province is to be condemned to hunger unless heavy industry's demands for wage cuts are given in to. . . ." Those plans meant, furthermore, that the German people would have to suffer from the cold during the coming winter. In order for coal from the Ruhr to undercut English competition on the international market once again, the German coal industrialists had decided to reduce still further the "hunger wage" they paid their miners. That, the Nazi publication proclaimed, revealed the "essence of the capitalism that is praised to the skies in those quarters that profit from it." The coal operators could have derived scant consolation from the Nazi publication's indictment of the socialist and Christian trade unions for inadequate defense of the coal miners' interests against their exploitative employers. Nor could they have found very reassuring the proclamation at the end of the publication: "German workerdom (Arbeitertum) under the leadership of the worker Adolf Hitler will one day imbue the economy with a very different ethos. The economy does not exist for profits but rather for the sustinence of the German people. Common interest before self-interest!" From the point of view of the business community, such diatribes differed little from those of the extreme political left.

While such anti-capitalist Nazi tracts circulated at the local level, upper-echelon party spokesmen provided a quite different version of National Socialism for business audiences.[4] In mid-October Walther Funk addressed the exclusive Berlin Herrenklub, which counted numerous important personages from the business community among its members.[5] A few weeks later in Essen more than 300 persons from the technical and managerial ranks of the coal industry responded to invitations from the local Nazi organization and paid two marks each to hear a speech by Gottfried Feder timed to coincide with a major conference on coal-mining technology sponsored by the Bergbauverein.[6] During the second week of November the party staged a special "conference" on economic policy in Düsseldorf.[7] It consisted of two speeches appended to a meeting of the local Gau organization of the NSDAP. On that occasion, according to the Prussian police, 200 persons, many from the business community, heard Feder speak, while 800 attended a simultaneous talk by Otto Wagener, head of the party's Economic Policy Section. Gregor Strasser, who had been scheduled to deliver a talk at the Düsseldorf conference but dropped out at the last minute, spoke in early December to about thirty coal executives after dining with them in a private room at an Essen hotel.[8]

Examination of the probable motives behind this barrage of speaking appearances by some of the prominent figures of the NSDAP provides some interesting insights into Nazi attitudes toward big business and strategies for dealing with it. From all indications, the purpose of the appearances by Funk, Feder, Strasser, and Wagener was not fundraising; aside from the usual admission fee charged by the local Nazis who engaged the halls used for the party-sponsored occasions in Düsseldorf and Essen, no collections were made on the spot, and there is no trace of any follow-up solicitations. Nor do the speeches seem to have been aimed at recruitment of members, as there are no indications of any systematic efforts in that direction. If the talks had no ulterior aims of these sorts, their purpose would seem to lie in their content. And, judging from the sketchy surviving reports, the speeches were clearly designed to counter the fears in big business circles about socialistic economic intentions on the part of National Socialism. That raises an interesting question: Why should allaying the fears of a small social group for which no prominent Nazi had high regard—with the possible exception of Walther Funk (whose importance in the party as of 1931 is debatable)—merit such efforts on the part of speakers under heavy demand in more obviously active sectors of the political battlefront? Clearly, the Nazis believed something more important than money or new members could be gained by cultivating big businessmen.

An observation of Hitler's from the early 1930s, which Otto Wagener recalled in his memoirs, offers a revealing clue to the party leader's thinking on this subject. Wagener, who fancied himself a social radical, reported provoking the observation by urging Hitler to speak out openly in favor of what Wagener saw as the NSDAP's commitment to bring about far-reaching economic changes by effecting a synthesis of private enterprise and socialism. Hitler explained that his reticence arose out of concern about the adverse political effects of the business community's reaction to public advocacy of such changes. Wagener recalled having countered that the party should not hold back out of consideration for

big businessmen, who were natural enemies of National Socialism, incapable of comprehending its goals. In response, according to Wagener,
Hitler warned him that he underestimated the political power of the
men of big business; he had the feeling, Hitler said, that the NSDAP
would not be able to attain power if they opposed it. Wagener's plans
must remain secret, Hitler continued, until the Nazis had achieved
power and brought at least two-thirds of the people solidly behind
them.[9] These revealing remarks, which are consistent with Hitler's own
behavior toward big businessmen, strongly suggest that he held to the
assumption, usually associated with the left, that control over the means
of production gave rise to great political potency. Hitler's reasoning, as
recorded by Wagener, further suggests that he believed big business had
merely to be neutralized, not won over, to enable Nazism to triumph. He
thus felt no need to try to turn Germany's capitalists into party members.
As for money, the NSDAP's own financial capabilities made it unnecessary to rely on them as donors. A shrewd political tactician like Hitler
would certainly also have recognized that if the Nazis could neutralize
the objections of big business to their party, they could weaken their
political opponents and rivals by lessening business support for them.
Similarly, if big businessmen were subjected to enough of Nazism's propagandistic assaults on the Weimar "system," their remaining confidence
in the existing order might diminish to an extent that would make them
receptive to the idea of a thoroughgoing break with the immediate political past. If thoughts along these lines did in fact shape Hitler's strategy,
his lieutenants' cultivation of big business circles during the fall of 1931
without any attendant efforts either to extract money or enlist converts
becomes less difficult to comprehend.

Unfortunately, from the Nazi point of view, the oratorical efforts of
these party spokesmen who sought to reassure the big businessmen in
their audiences hardly amounted to a rousing success. For *Vorwärts,* the
SPD daily, the fact that some businessmen had gone to hear what a Nazi
speaker had to say sufficed to prove that they contributed money to the
NSDAP. That paper branded Nazism as "one big yellow movement, paid
by sharp business practitioners to combat workers' organizations."[10]
Eyewitness accounts, however, reveal a much less positive response on
the part of the businessmen who heard Funk, Feder, Wagener, and
Strasser in the autumn of 1931. The evidence is fullest on Funk's speech
to the Berlin Herrenklub on October 16, which bore the promising title
"National Socialism and the Economy." It became the subject of a
lengthy report prepared by Jakob Wilhelm Reichert, the business manager of the iron and steel manufacturers' association, for the leading
industrialists in that organization, who, like their counterparts in other
branches of production, seldom attended speeches by politicians.[11]
Funk, Reichert reported, expressed a commitment to the preservation
of private property and a sharp opposition to Marxism. He also indi-

cated receptivity to a break with the existing system of industry-wide labor contracts. He emphasized the NSDAP's intention to create jobs for the unemployed but, Reichert pointed out, without providing any satisfactory explanation of how this could be done at state expense without unleashing inflation and undermining the currency. Funk spoke as well of the need for some state direction of foreign trade, from which he quickly backed away when Reichert, reacting to what he took to be a whiff of Nazism's loudly proclaimed autarkic commitment to reduce, or even eliminate, Germany's economic dependence on foreign countries, raised objections during the discussion that followed the speech. Even more alarming, Reichert reported, Funk had suggested a complete halt to all German payments of foreign debts, both for reparations and for ordinary commercial credit. That proposal must have called to mind similar proclamations issued publicly by other Nazi spokesmen, including Hermann Göring. It provoked a warning to Funk from Reichert that any such step would provoke massive retaliation against German commercial interests on the part of other countries and risk a breakdown of the foreign credit and trade without which Germany's economy could not function. In his report Reichert found just as disturbing as these foolhardy schemes set forth by Funk the latter's failure to suggest any solutions to the problems uppermost in the minds of big business at that time: the runaway growth in the Reich's budget deficit generated by the unemployment insurance program or the burdens imposed on industry by social welfare levies, wages set by binding state arbitration, and the limits, set by state regulation, on hours of work. Funk's performance, Reichert concluded, had proved a disappointment. And since Funk enjoyed a reputation as the Nazi most sympathetic to big business, that disappointment must have bulked all the greater. One of those disturbed by Funk's speech was Fritz Springorum, the general director of Hoesch Steel and treasurer of the Ruhrlade. He had not attended the speech but wrote to Funk criticizing it after he learned of it through Reichert's report. Funk, hard-pressed to explain away his remarks, resorted in his evasive answer to Springorum to the not very reassuring contention that no one could say precisely what a party's specific policies would be without knowing the economic circumstances at the moment it took power.[12]

Surviving reports on Feder's speeches in Essen and Düsseldorf and Strasser's talk in Essen on December 7 provide only sketchy impressions of their remarks. Even though Strasser was widely regarded as standing on the left of the NSDAP, his personal appearances made a favorable impression on many businessmen. This can perhaps be explained by his ability, as the former proprietor of an apothecary shop, to speak, in at least a rudimentary fashion, the language of profits and losses, interest rates and overhead costs, something few other prominent party officials could do from personal experience. On the occasion of his Essen appearance, one of his audience recalled years later, he assured his listeners that the Nazis did not intend to socialize the economy since state direction would suffice for their purposes.[13] Feder usually gave basically the same speech before such audiences, emphasizing his commitment to the principle of private property and then attempting to explain to his listeners why that principle would not be imperiled by granting to the state unlimited authority to employ any measures it deemed necessary, even expropriation, when private property was used contrary to the interests of the *Volk*. Feder also found it difficult to avoid his favorite projects, the abolition of credit interest and the creation of work for the unemployed by printing new money, schemes that seldom failed to provoke objections, even derision, among big businessmen. The Prussian police reported, on the basis of what they described as a reliable source, that Feder's Essen speech "met with agreement only among a small part of his audience."[14]

One observer who attended the Nazi economic conference of November in Düsseldorf made no mention of Feder's speech when he reported on that event anonymously in a newsletter that circulated among businessmen. He found much more noteworthy the remarks of Otto Wagener. After delivering a barrage of "cheap demagoguery," he recounted, Wagener went on to reveal "an astounding economic dilettantism." He endorsed autarky as a national economic policy and recommended two currencies, one for domestic use, one for transactions with the outside world. He also invoked Feder's notorious slogan, calling for the "breaking of the thralldom of interest payments." In place of credit based on interest, the head of the Economic Policy Section of the NSDAP proposed that creditors become part-owners in any enterprise to which they advanced funds, gaining if it made profits, losing if it did not. As for the problems of reparations, he assured his listeners that Germany could easily render France powerless to collect further "tribute" by allying with England and Italy. Wagener had left an impression, the report continued, of "great shallowness, flaccidity, and primitiveness." He lacked even originality since most of his notions could be found elsewhere. "If Wagener embodies the economic policy elite of National Socialism," concluded the observer at the Düsseldorf conference, "not very much can be expected from the movement's involvement in that sphere."[15]

However limited their success, Feder, Funk, Strasser, and Wagener all attempted, to varying degrees, during the autumn of 1931 what Hitler had sought to accomplish ever since writing his confidential pamphlet for industrialists at the behest of Emil Kirdorf in 1927. That is, they tried to assure their listeners that National Socialism should not be confused with socialism of the traditional sort. Whatever Nazi labor agitators and journalists might say, their message ran, Nazism did not aim at an abolition of private property or a thoroughgoing socialization of the economy. The "socialism" of National Socialism, they intimated broadly, served merely as window dressing designed to entice Germany's workers away from their "Marxist" seducers.[16] The difficulty with all such reassurances, even for those in business circles ready to lend credence to them, lay in the fact that they indicated at best what Nazism was not. They failed to reveal what it was or what it would do if it came into power. Nor did Funk, Feder, Strasser, and Wagener provide any clear idea of the economic policy of a Nazi government, except insofar as general inferences could be drawn from their remarks on various subjects. Businessmen who studied their words in an effort to discern a pattern could scarcely have been reassured by their advocacy of the abolition of interest; economic autarky or trade restriction; repudiation of foreign debts; potentially inflationary currency schemes and projects to create work for the unemployed; or by their explanation that Nazism merely sought unlimited governmental authority to "direct" the economy. Even if the men of big business assigned credibility to those forks of the Nazi tongue that spoke to the business community in conciliatory fashion, the messages that emanated therefrom were neither clear nor comforting.

In view of the bewildering variety of impressions reaching the business community from the NSDAP during 1931, it is not surprising that the guessing game about the party's economic orientation continued, even intensified, as the Nazis swept from one triumph to another in the state and local elections of that year. Curiosity mounted steadily about a phenomenon both baffling and daily more difficult to ignore; scraps of information, often mere rumors, became the subject of grave scrutiny in the executive suites of German big business. In the judgment of some the key question was: Which Nazis controlled the party, those who made radical noises about the economy or those who seemed moderate on that front? In the resulting speculations Hitler naturally figured prominently. Most observers from big business were inclined to classify him as a moderate. In part this seems to have resulted from his well-publicized advocacy of adherence to political legality and his suppression of the socially radical SA units aligned with the would-be rebel Stennes in the abortive Berlin SA mutiny of the spring. But Hitler's reputation as a moderate also derived from his silence on most economic matters and the oracular ambiguity of his few utterances on that subject, such as his statement about the Berlin metalworkers' strike of 1930.

Some associated with the business community dissented from this optimistic assessment of Hitler in the summer of 1931. Among these was Erich von Gilsa, the political informant of Paul Reusch, who would, as already noted, leave the October Bad Harzburg rally enthused at the prospect of a "national opposition" government that would include the Nazis. In August Gilsa saw things quite differently when he relayed to Reusch the report of a "leading rightist politician" (whom he left unnamed) on a private meeting with Hitler. The politician had come away, Gilsa related, feeling that he had talked to a "possessed person" who had an enormous supply of willful energy which could, however, erupt in unforeseen directions. The politician had been, moreover, wholly frustrated in his attempts to pin Hitler down about what the NSDAP planned to do if it were, as Hitler demanded, admitted to the government. Hitler had replied to his questions, the politician had told Gilsa, by setting forth "all sorts of wide-ranging historical-philosophical views, lots about the soul of the *Volk,* imponderables, race questions, and the like." Hitler had not, however, mentioned "a single practical and concrete measure that he wanted to put through." As a consequence Gilsa's informant had told him that Nazi participation in the government would be impossible in the foreseeable future. Gilsa himself characterized Hitler as "erratic" and expressed grave doubts about his ability to govern. He concluded his report to Reusch by observing that a close reading of *Mein Kampf* could lead to the conclusion that Hitler intended to leave the details of political action to his associates in the NSDAP and would content himself with setting the party's overall goals. But there was no guarantee of this, he warned.[17] A few days after receiving Gilsa's report, Reusch got another from his Berlin agent, Martin Blank, that cast doubt on the wisdom of placing hopes in the men around Hitler. Blank reported that leading circles of the Stahlhelm viewed Hitler with the greatest skepticism, an assessment in which he himself concurred. Furthermore, in a conversation the previous evening, two prominent participants from the NSDAP had spoken out critically and concernedly about conditions in the Brown House, the national headquarters of their party. The only high Nazi who commanded any respect seemed to be Gregor Strasser, Blank wrote to Reusch, whereas all the other occupants of the Brown House appeared for various reasons unreliable or incompetent.[18]

While the great majority of big businessmen and the professional experts they relied on in political matters seem to have withheld final judgment on National Socialism during 1931, some voices within the business community ceaselessly portrayed Nazism as a deadly enemy of private enterprise. Such was the case with the Hansa-Bund, the national organization of liberal-oriented commercial, financial, and industrial interests. In its 1931 handbook on public affairs, the article on National Socialism cautioned its members against being misled by the anti-Marxism of that party. The Nazis rejected only the materialism of Marxism, the Bund explained; they shared Marxism's fundamental hostility to capitalism and its commitment to socialism, which in their case sprang from romantic, rather than materialistic, notions. And socialism remained socialism, with just as fatal consequences for the owners of capital, regardless of its ideological origins. Gregor Strasser had left no doubt that he and his comrades were mortal foes of the capitalist economic system. Gottfried Feder accorded recognition in principle to private property, but he branded the income derived from property as unearned and, since it was allegedly gained at the expense of those who labored, as immoral.

The goal of such men, the Hansa-Bund warned, was socialism, call it what they might, and with them there could be no compromise. "We must therefore see to it," the article concluded, "that Germany's *Bürgertum* does not conclude, as has sometimes been the case hitherto: Excellent! These are the shock troops who will safeguard the ideological and material foundations of our existence!" [19]

Another assessment of Nazism came from those who might be called optimists, who regarded the NSDAP as a passing phenomenon. One of the most notable of these was Carl Friedrich von Siemens, head of his dynasty's huge electro-technical manufacturing firm. Speaking in New York in late October to an audience of American financiers—and thus, with an eye to bolstering Germany's sagging credit rating, probably prone to painting a rosy picture—Siemens dismissed Hitler and his followers as idealistic opponents of socialism with childish notions of their own about economics. Nazism was essentially a protest movement, Siemens explained. Many Germans had given it their votes only because of their frustration with the parliamentary and socialistic excesses of postwar governments. Most of those who sympathized with the movement could not really commit themselves to it beyond casting a protest ballot because of its ruthless opportunism, its demagogy, and its "play on lower instincts"—apparently a euphemism for anti-Semitism. Like that of the Communists, Siemens contended, the burgeoning strength of the NSDAP at the polls represented merely a feverish symptom of economic distress. It would subside and disappear from the political scene, along with communism, once economic recovery set in. [20]

More numerous than either outright pessimists or optimists were those who can best be characterized as would-be realists. They viewed Nazism as a kind of elemental force, unlike anything ever seen in German politics, which they could not explain or understand. That outlook prevailed at a revealing meeting of staff officials of regional industrial associations in Berlin at the end of October. The participating *Syndizi,* some of whom had been at Bad Harzburg, were obviously still very much under the influence of that gathering and the massive SA rally in Braunschweig, a week later, where Hitler had reviewed the marching columns of more than 100,000 of his uniformed followers in the largest Nazi paramilitary demonstration to that time. All those present quickly agreed that National Socialism still seemed to be gathering momentum. Moreover, they gave general assent to a proposal by Martin Blank, Paul Reusch's Berlin representative, that the business community strive to influence the development of Nazism by providing it "not with money but with men and ideas." Max Schlenker, business manager of the key associational complex of the Ruhr iron and steel producers, urged that industry find a way to implant its spirit in National Socialism and suggested that reliable men with a sound understanding of economic necessities might even be ordered to join the Nazi ranks. The goal, Schlenker contended, must be to find a way to make use of Nazism in what remained for the business community the alpha and omega of politics, the struggle against "Marxism" and its allies. He and the others who spoke at the meeting regarded Nazism with a mixture of fascination and unease. On the one hand, it represented, as an enemy of their enemy, a potential ally; on the other hand, the chronic ambiguities and cacophonies of Nazi utterances about the economic sphere remained a source of nagging concern. General agreement emerged that in order to bring the NSDAP onto a sound economic course, it must be stabilized by bourgeois ballast. The prime task at hand was therefore to find ways to strengthen the bourgeois political forces of the country so that they could deal with Nazism from a position of strength. But those present at the meeting also agreed that if there were any hope of mobilizing a bourgeois bloc sufficiently potent to brake and steer National Socialism, it did not lie in wasting more money on the traditional parties, which had become too discredited in the eyes of the public. Ways must therefore be found to use the political influence and money of the business community to unite the "nationally" oriented bourgeois elements, either above or outside the old parties.[21]

Not surprisingly, the political agents of big business who had gathered in Berlin at the end of October 1931 looked with great interest toward the "national opposition" that seemed to have coalesced at Bad Harzburg two weeks earlier. For although Nazism, regardless of which fork of its tongue one listened to, could not qualify for the accolade *"bürgerlich,"* or bourgeois, the Nazis were as undeniably "national" as was Germany's *Bürgertum.* A "national opposition" thus seemed to offer a meeting ground. It also offered several prospective advantages from the big business point of view. Whereas the country's *Bürgertum* embodied economic reliability, it was cut off from the working masses who weighed so heavily in an age of participatory politics.[22] The Nazis, while a doubtful factor on economic issues, clearly commanded a mass following that extended, most of big business was convinced, into the industrial working force. What more optimal arrangement therefore than to yoke the dynamic and unpredictable NSDAP to bourgeois forces that could be counted on to defend the economic interests of big business, thereby directing all of Nazism's aggressiveness against the "Marxists"? As Gilsa, who had again become skeptical about Nazism, put it during December in a memorandum to Reusch, which later somehow fell into the hands of the press: "If Hitler and his economic staff are actually firmly resolved to leave the core of the private enterprise system unmolested, it will be easier for them to reorient their people if they can point, as they educate their followers, to a strong private enterprise group in the national front."[23]

Those political agents of big business who left the Berlin meeting at the end of October with such a strategy in mind must have found the developments of late 1931 highly disconcerting. Within a month of the Bad Harzburg gathering the heralded "national opposition" began to show signs of fragility, as the Nazis and the Stahlhelmers quarreled publicly and vituperatively with each other about alleged affronts to each other's honor, while the NSDAP and the DNVP resumed the mutual recriminations that normally marked their relationship in the absence of an immediately common cause.[24] By early 1932 even President Hindenburg found inescapable the conclusion that "the 'Harzburg Front' is only a fiction, or, more accurately, de facto never came into being."[25] In Hesse, where the Nazis scored a resounding electoral triumph in November by capturing nearly 40 percent of the seats in a state parliament in which they hitherto had had no representation, their new deputies promptly proposed a massive increase in aid to the unemployed, which would have raised state expenditures by almost 30 percent.[26] Furthermore, despite denials from both sides, rumors persistently circulated throughout the fall to the effect that the Catholic Center Party was negotiating with the Nazis with the aim of forming coalition governments dominated by these two parties, both at the state and national levels.[27] In big business circles such a constellation conjured up the frightening prospect of Catholic union leaders joining with left-wing Nazis to win over the workers of Germany by making concessions at the expense of the business community.[28] As 1931 drew to a close, there seemed to be no way to predict the next move of the rapidly expanding, enigmatic political prodigy which spoke with a tongue with ever-proliferating forks.

4. Nazis and Lesser Businessmen

It would be misleading to create the impression that the Nazis made no business converts during 1931. From all indications, increasing numbers of businessmen all across Germany became party members or sympathizers that year. Those who did so, however, came not from the ranks of big business. They came instead from the middle reaches of industry, commerce, and finance. They headed in some cases quite sizeable enterprises, employing hundreds of workers and involving capital that sometimes ran as high as millions of marks. But most such firms fell far short of the big business threshold of twenty million marks of nominal capital applied here. These smaller firms outnumbered many times over the ones which comprised big business, as defined earlier in this volume, and their owners and executives were far more numerous than those of the largest firms. Collectively they controlled vast amounts of capital. At the end of 1929 nearly half of the aggregate capital of the most widespread form of incorporation, the *Aktiengesellschaften*, rested with firms capitalized at levels below twenty million marks.[1] Yet despite their numbers and the amount of capital they commanded, executives of such firms found themselves, to their frequent resentment, with little or no voice in the national associations of *die Wirtschaft,* in particular the industrial Reichsverband, whose councils were dominated by spokesmen of large-scale enterprises.[2]

The middle reaches of German business had provided the NSDAP with some of its leadership cadre even before the depression struck. From the ranks of the small manufacturers came Martin Mutschmann, the Nazi gauleiter of Saxony from 1925 until the demise of the Third Reich twenty years later. Incongruously for a Nazi tough who distinguished himself as much through the use of his fists as through any other qualities, Mutschmann presided in private life over three lace factories in the small city of Plauen in the backward Vogtland district of Saxony.[3] In northern Baden Wilhelm Keppler, later one of Hitler's economic advisers and holder of a number of high positions in the Third Reich, played a prominent role in developing a potent local party organization after joining in 1927. Keppler worked in the town of Eberbach for a chemical company, owned by an uncle, that produced photographic gelatin under an agreement with the American firm of Eastman Kodak. In March 1928 Keppler reportedly sent out 800 invitations to a talk by Hitler in the Heidelberg municipal hall. A police report described the 670 who attended as "almost exclusively industrialists." In view of the small-scale manufacturing that predominated in northern Baden, it seems likely that those present came, like Keppler himself, from the ranks of Germany's lesser businessmen.[4] In Munich the party won an active supporter and advocate within business circles in Albert Pietzsch, the proprietor of a small but prosperous suburban chemical plant that produced a hydrogen peroxide hair bleach. In the Third Reich Pietzsch headed the Nazis' Reich Economic Council.[5] In August 1929 Otto Wagener abandoned a business career to become chief of staff of the Nazi SA and, later, head of the party's Economic Policy Section. Formerly director of a Karlsruhe firm that manufactured sewing machines and bicycles, he gave up a partnership in a wholesale company that dealt in plywood and veneers to cast his fortunes with the NSDAP.[6] Wagener shared with Mutschmann, Keppler, and Pietzsch a fierce hostility not only toward the "Marxist" parties but also toward trade unions. All four boasted that they had kept the plants they directed free of organizers and strikes. That sort of anti-union militancy survived much more strongly in the middle reaches of German industry than in big business circles, where employers had been forced to come to terms with organized labor or see their enterprises paralyzed. This animus toward trade unionism pervaded the pages of the weekly publication that catered to the informational needs of the middle range of entrepreneurs, *Die Deutsche Arbeitgeber-Zeitung.* It adopted a much harder line in that respect than the organ of the association of large industrial employers, *Der Ar-*

beitgeber, and became the first entrepreneurial publication to accord favorable attention in its columns to the NSDAP.[7]

The political importance of the middle range of business bulked particularly large in the state politics of the Republic's federal system, as the Nazis' experience in gaining their first foothold in government demonstrated. The NSDAP crossed that significant frontier in January 1930, when Wilhelm Frick became Thuringian minister for the interior and education in a coalition cabinet installed with the votes of four bourgeois parties and the NSDAP.[8] The negotiations preceding the formation of the Thuringian cabinet proved arduous, as the six DVP deputies in the newly elected Landtag, whose votes were needed to make a majority, came under great pressure not to support the installation of the NSDAP in the government. Spokesmen of the DVP elsewhere in the country warned in the name of German liberalism against allying in a coalition with an anti-parliamentary party such as the NSDAP, and local business interests in the DVP balked at that step because of socialistic pronouncements in the Nazi press. Eager to obtain for his party its first ministerial appointment, with the attendant gain in national respectability, Hitler himself intervened. Accompanied by Rudolf Hess, Otto Wagener, and Frick, he traveled to the state capital, Weimar, and met with a selected group of about twenty prominent persons drawn from the bourgeois parties, the state bureaucracy, and the Thuringian business community invited to tea by Gauleiter Fritz Sauckel in a private dining room at the well-known Hotel zum Elephanten.[9] That evening Hitler addressed a much larger audience of the elite of Thuringia's *Bürgertum* at another Weimar hotel, an occasion also arranged by the local Nazis. According to a pro-DNVP newspaper in Weimar, he carried off something of a tour de force by not once mentioning the words "National Socialist" in his two-hour speech. Nor did Hitler deal with economic questions, aside from asserting that Germany needed to reduce its reliance on foreign trade and increase its arable soil in order to become less dependent on other countries. Most of his talk seems to have been devoted to denunciations of parliamentary democracy and Germany's Marxist subverters, who were, he warned his listeners, leading the country toward civil war. The audience responded, according to the Weimar newspaper account, with enthusiastic applause.[10] Two weeks later, after protracted negotiations, the proposed coalition cabinet, including Frick, gained office when the DVP deputies cast their votes with those of the other bourgeois parties and the NSDAP.

A few days after Frick's installation as minister in Thuringia, Hitler boasted in a letter to a loyal follower that he had turned the tide in Thuringia by bringing the business community there to exert pressure on the DVP in support of the NSDAP's admission to the state government.[11] In view of the DVP deputies' abandonment of their initial resistance to that arrangement, this seems a not implausible boast. Some documentation from Thuringian industrial circles lends additional credence to Hitler's claim. In a report to member firms in March 1930, the manager of a Thuringian business association—who had joined the NSDAP in January—described having intervened in the political process to bring about a "suitable" cabinet formation and thus help resolve the parliamentary crisis.[12] The organization in question was the Labor Relations League of the Thuringian Cement Industry. The league's principal members, the dozen firms producing cement and related construction materials, bulked fairly large in the industrial landscape of Thuringia, a region politically fragmented until 1920, sparsely endowed with mineral resources, unblessed by economically strategic rivers, and bypassed by the development of modern big business. A territory of small towns, Thuringia lacked a city with as many as 100,000 inhabitants. Its industries, specializing mainly in glass products, porcelain, toys, and precision instruments, still reflected their origins in the first half of the nineteenth century or even earlier. Its factories had remained small by twentieth-century standards and, with the exception of the optical-instrument industry of Jena, were often outmoded. Virtually all lagged far behind their larger, more innovative competitors in other parts of the country.[13]

The executives of the member firms of the Thuringian Cement League felt strong hostility toward the great capitalists of Germany. Having observed the bourgeois parties backed by big business repeatedly join the Social Democrats in adopting costly welfare-state measures in the Reichstag, they took seriously charges to the effect that the capitalist magnates in Berlin had secretly allied with the SPD in a plot to make the country's small entrepreneurs shoulder an ever heavier tax burden.[14] Such businessmen probably found very attractive the Thuringian Nazis' pledges to reduce government spending sharply by lowering the salaries of ministers and other state officials, thereby clearing the way for tax cuts, if the NSDAP were admitted to the cabinet.[15] From all indications, the cement producers also proved receptive to assurances from their organization's manager that the NSDAP's official program need not be taken seriously. Despite public statements by some of its spokesmen, he told them, the party neither favored socialization nor opposed the sort of price fixing the cement producers had long practiced by means of a cartel.[16]

A request for legislative help sent to the party's Thuringian headquarters in early 1932 by the owner of a fever thermometer factory employing 600 workers in the town of Roda suggests that the attitudes of the cement producers did not represent an aberration in the context of that state's business community. That manufacturer had joined the NSDAP in the spring of 1931, apparently in large part because of wrathful indignation about the ruinous effects on his business of a "Marxist" law enacted during the Republic that subjected fever thermometers to accuracy tests. He ended his plea for help by reminding the leaders of the National Socialist German Workers' Party in Thuringia that in his region the Nazis were to be found among the small manufacturers, not among the workers.[17] By the autumn of 1931 relations between the Nazis and the manufacturers of Thuringia had already developed to the point that the statewide industrial association extended a formal invitation to the six Nazi deputies in the Landtag to attend a meeting of its members in Weimar.[18]

Not all Germany's small and middle-range manufacturers shared the cramped attitudes of those who ran outmoded factories in remote Thuringian towns, but virtually all suffered acutely under the impact of the depression. The economic crisis threatened them much more profoundly than it did the men of big business. Large enterprises resembled the proverbial well-to-do profligate debtor for whom, when illness struck, creditors would hire the best medical experts they could find, not being able to afford his demise. Numerous buffers, backed by sizeable reserves of capital, protected large firms from the businessmen's ultimate nightmare: insolvency and a plea of bankruptcy. The national government itself represented the buffer of last recourse. The Brüning cabinet demonstrated the unwillingness of the Reich authorities to allow big enterprises to suffer the consequences of insolvency when several of the large nationwide banks had to halt payments in the summer of 1931 and when the Borsig Locomotive Works, one of Berlin's largest industrial employers, could not meet its creditors' demands during the autumn.[19] In those and other cases the government, unwilling to face the predictable economic, social, and—ultimately—political consequences of permitting the collapse of large enterprises that had failed by the going rules of capitalism, attempted to refloat them with public funds. In other instances the government fended off bankruptcies by guaranteeing commercial credits, or even extending loans itself, to imperiled large firms. Such enterprises, though not necessarily their executives, had clearly come to enjoy a kind of economic immortality simply by virtue of their size.[20] Their failure would set off chain reactions of bankruptcies on the part of others who had lent them funds or depended on them for business. Cessation of their operations would thrust on the state unemployment fund not only their own employees but also those of the firms that supplied them with raw materials or distributed their products. The cost of such far-reaching consequences in terms of further reduction of business activity, exacerbation of the already chronic decline in tax revenues, and additional unemployment with all its attendant expenses and risks simply seemed unacceptable to any government of rational men. For smaller enterprises, however, such deterrents against ultimate calamity rarely applied. Their jeopardy seldom sufficed to unite their creditors behind an agreement to suspend demands for repayment of debts until they weathered the crisis. Nor did a danger of insolvency on their part attract the attention and awaken the protective impulses of government. They were too numerous, too inconspicuous, and the consequences of their failures were too limited to make them eligible for the kind of buffers that shielded big business. For these smaller enterprises, failure and extinction remained frighteningly real possibilities as the Great Depression relentlessly throttled business activity to an extent no one had imagined possible. The really desperate businessmen of Germany held forth in the middle and lower ranges of industry, commerce, and finance, not in the charmed circle of big business.

A Rhenish manufacturer recalled in his memoirs what it felt like to experience the depression from such a vulnerable position.[21] A young man at the time, he struggled to help save two family factories founded in the city of Krefeld in the nineteenth century to produce specialized industrial machinery. At the outset of the depression the factories had employed some 650 workers and operated profitably. But the crisis struck them hard. Each week consisted of a struggle with ever more insistent creditors and indignant bankers who threatened foreclosure on overdue debts. The management frantically shifted funds from one account to another, borrowing money at ever higher interest to meet obligations it could no longer stave off. The family had to post more and more of its possessions as collateral. It had to lay off workers, some with considerable seniority, in increasing numbers, so that the work force dwindled to little more than half its size prior to the depression. Overshadowing every day's disheartening efforts was the fear of failure and bankruptcy, which amounted to personal disgrace for a family rooted in its community and proud of a long tradition of honesty, prudence, and solvency. For businessmen in such a plight, the liberal Hansa-Bund observed in its annual report for 1931, politics could be reduced easily to a formulation coined by the famous eighteenth-century German aphorist Georg Lichtenberg: "I really can't say whether things will be better if they are changed; what I can say is that things must be changed if they are going to improve." And, according to the Hansa-Bund, that outlook was leading many German businessmen where it led the young manufacturer from Krefeld: into the Nazi Party.[22]

For such men Nazism's calculated ambiguity about basic questions of economy policy probably seemed less disconcerting than it did to big businessmen. Trapped, from their point of view, between politically determined wages on the one hand and supply prices set by the cartels and trusts of big business on the other, small and medium manufacturers were in any event less likely than the giants of industry to take alarm at the pledge in the NSDAP's program to nationalize business trusts. Because of their incessant struggles with bankers during the depression, they were more likely to view hospitably Nazi schemes for a nationalized system of credit and a "breaking of the thralldom of interest payments."

Desperate for any development that would generate orders for their products, they were less likely to feel concern about the possible inflationary effects of Nazi calls for make-work projects or currency-printing schemes to set the unemployed to work. Those not directly dependent on export markets must have found less threatening than did most of big business Nazi talk of repudiating foreign debts, reducing or controlling foreign trade, or even attaining economic autarky. Indeed, for many desperate small and middle-range producers, such talk probably held out the welcome prospect of relief from foreign competitors. Men who daily lived with the fear of losing their livelihoods and everything they owned were also less inclined to examine carefully all the implications of the assurances from one fork of Nazism's tongue to the effect that in a National Socialist Germany there would be no socialism in the "Marxist" sense, but merely unlimited government interventionist authority to direct and discipline business enterprises in the interest of the "community of the *Volk.*" Finally, Nazism's anti-Semitism represented less of a deterrent to such entrepreneurs since the fastidiousness and urbanity that made anti-Semitism socially unacceptable among big businessmen were less in evidence in their circles.[23]

For these reasons the lesser businessmen of Germany seem more likely to have shown susceptibility to Nazism than the executives of the great firms that comprised big business. This would seem borne out by the attention the Nazis lavished during 1931 on business audiences in provincial manufacturing centers where such businessmen predominated. In May, for example, Gottfried Feder addressed a group of Augsburg businessmen invited by the local Nazi leadership—typically—to a private room at the most elegant hotel in town. According to a report of the Social Democratic daily *Vorwärts*, he assured his listeners that the NSDAP planned no socialization save in a few areas of transportation and distribution. Honestly acquired property, he emphasized, would remain in private possession. Nazism aimed at ending the class conflict artificially stirred up by socialists. Employers and employees must be brought into a closer relationship, and the socialist unions that had come between them must disappear. The Nazis would take care of that. They would also put the unemployed to work through a compulsory labor service. In addition, they would break "the thralldom of interest payments" and severely curtail the importation of foreign goods. Where more refined methods did not work in the latter regard, direct action would. Nazi storm troopers had, Feder informed his provincial audience, already begun to express disapproval at the purchase of foreign automobiles by hauling their owners out of the alien upholstery and physically giving them a taste of patriotic German anger.[24]

In October Feder addressed a similar audience of about 150 Aachen businessmen invited in the same fashion to a restaurant engaged for the occasion by the local Nazis. The Prussian police agent who observed the gathering noted that many of those present had long been members of the DVP. The agent did not record what Feder said, but his remarks presumably paralleled those he made in Augsburg, with adjustments for local interests.[25] In November Otto Wagener addressed an invited gathering of businessmen in Halle, a manufacturing center in the Prussian province of Saxony. He advocated economic autarky, lower taxes, and reduced interest rates. To free businessmen from dependence on financiers, he proposed measures that would facilitate the self-financing of investment. Finally, Wagener sketched for his listeners a scheme of corporatist organization for the whole economy that would grant far-reaching administrative and regulatory authority to the various branches of production and greatly enhance the influence of small- and medium-size producers.[26]

Sustained Nazi attention to the businessmen of certain provincial cities indicates the likelihood of particular success in those places. One such was Düren, a venerable Rhenish manufacturing town located halfway between Cologne and Aachen which produced a variety of textiles and specialty consumer goods. It had pioneered in the introduction of industrial techniques into Germany in the eighteenth century, but had by the 1930s long since passed its heyday as a manufacturing center. Moreover, the town's small, often antiquated factories specialized in fine, high-quality, even luxury consumer goods—carpets, specialty fabrics, glasswares, fine papers, and the like—whose markets were among the first to dry up when the depression produced a sharp contraction in expendable income.[27] In late March 1931, as the Prussian political police later learned through one of those present, Hermann Göring visited Düren and addressed a group of local industrialists in a private dining room at a fashionable restaurant. The police did not report on what Göring said, but it seems to have been well received since he was invited to return.[28] He did so in mid-June, according to the police, speaking to a larger group that included several members of two Düren families, the Schoellers and the Schülls, known as "millionaire dynasties" as early as the 1820s, as well as some latecomers to that status, such as the director of the Dürener Bank.[29] At least one of those present soon became an active Nazi: a member of the Peill family, which operated a factory that produced components for highly regarded modern lamps designed at the Bauhaus. Peill styled himself as an industrialist and also a Rittergutsbesitzer—owner of a "knight's estate"—because of his extensive landholdings outside Düren, where he resided and operated a sugarbeet processing plant.[30] Like those of the Schoellers and the Schülls, Peill's economic fortunes undoubtedly suffered setbacks because of the depression, but he remained a man of considerable wealth, backed by capital patiently accumulated over generations. He and the others who gathered to listen to Hermann Göring during his visits to the private dining room at the Harmonie Restaurant in Düren were thus in a position to see to it that their visitor—who seldom concealed from favorably disposed persons of wealth his difficulty in finding the material means required for his lofty political mission—left their town with greater purchasing power than when he arrived.

Repeated contacts also took place in 1931 between Nazi spokesmen and local manufacturers in another provincial industrial city, Solingen, situated between Cologne and the Ruhr. Considerably more populous than Düren, it ranked as a center of the Kleineisenindustrie, small ironware industry, of the region called Berg and Mark because of the names of the two minor principalities between which that part of Germany had been divided before Prussia acquired both. Ironworking enjoyed a venerable tradition there, having thrived since the sixteenth century and even earlier in some places.[31] The quality of the iron and steel wares produced in the region—especially knives, other cutlery items, needles, razors, scissors, and small tools—continued to set the standard for Germany into the twentieth century. Firms in Berg and Mark typically remained small and their proprietors continued as stubborn defenders of tradition. When large-scale industry struck its truce with organized labor at the time of the Stinnes-Legien Agreement of 1918, most of the ironware manufacturers of Berg and Mark defiantly dissociated themselves from that pact, refusing to recognize unions as bargaining agents of their workers.[32] During the Empire the relationship between the ironware manufacturers of Berg and Mark and the large firms to the north in the Ruhr, on which they depended for their supplies of iron and steel, had grown increasingly antagonistic.[33] The producers strove with mounting success to hold their prices well above the world market level by means of protective tariffs and cartel-administered prices. The ironware manufacturers, much of whose market lay in other countries, struggled to keep their prices internationally competitive. This antagonism persisted into the Republic, and relations between the two groups remained fractious throughout the first half of the 1920s. Then, beginning in 1924, the AVI Agreements reconciled the two sides by providing the ironware manufacturers with rebates on the iron and steel they purchased to produce goods for export. The AVI Agreements preserved peace between the two sides until the depression, when the world price for iron and steel plummeted so sharply that the gap between the domestic prices of the Ruhr iron and steel producers, which were propped up by their cartels, and prices for the same commodities on the world market widened immensely. Early in 1931 the producers rebelled against continuing such large rebates and served notice that they would withdraw from the agreement as of the end of May 1931. That threat, which was eventually averted by a compromise, came as a profound shock to the small ironware manufacturers of Berg and Mark, who now had to choose between buying all the iron and steel they needed at artificially high German domestic prices or finding replacements abroad, which involved paying the stiff German tariff. Either way they ended up at a disadvantage when they sought to sell their own finished products abroad at world prices. Encroachment on their shrinking markets by the finishing subsidiaries of the iron-and-steel-producing firms compounded their woes. This represented an especially vexatious development since the ironware makers, like other independent users of iron and steel, suspected the producers of supplying their manufacturing subsidiaries with those key commodities at prices far below the cartel-dictated level, thus enabling those subsidiaries to undercut their independent competitors. Repeated appeals on the part of the ironware industry to the Brüning cabinet, asking that the producers' cartels be dissolved, yielded no results, however. As a consequence, anger and resentment against both the republican government and big business mounted in the ranks of the ironware manufacturers of Berg and Mark throughout Brüning's chancellorship.

Shortly after the 1930 election a major textile executive who played a prominent role in the industrial Reichsverband reported to that body's main committee having discovered while in Berg that a considerable number of small and not-so-small manufacturers there had voted Nazi.[34] Apparently recognizing fertile ground, the NSDAP assiduously cultivated the increasingly disgruntled ironware manufacturers. In January 1931 the Prussian political police, the *General-Anzeiger* of Dortmund, and an SPD daily in Cologne all reported that industrialists from Solingen as well as from the neighboring city of Remscheid and from the surrounding area had responded to an invitation from the Nazi leadership of Solingen to come to a closed meeting at a local restaurant.[35] Attendance, which the *General-Anzeiger* estimated at between 300 and 400, proved so unexpectedly strong that extra rooms in the restaurant had to be taken over to accommodate the turnout. The guest speakers were Karl Florian, gauleiter of the region, and Josef Klein. Leader of the NSDAP in the town of Uerdingen near Krefeld, Klein worked as a personnel official at the nearby branch plant of IG Farben in Dormagen, where his duties involved supervision of such facilities as the employees' cafeteria as well as all contacts between the plant's workers and its management.[36] In addressing the announced theme of the gathering, "Tasks for the German Economy," Florian blamed the plight of German businessmen in the depression on the "Marxist policies" of the Republic. The gauleiter assured his audience that the NSDAP stood ready to assume responsibility for the government and could be counted on to protect the interests of German business. Klein attributed the depression to hypertrophied welfare levies and excessive wages imposed on employers by the republican governments. According to the Cologne SPD newspaper, *Sozialistische Republik,* he advocated putting an end to unemployment insurance. Both he and Florian reportedly touched liberally upon the "bolshevik peril" and strongly urged their listeners to join the

NSDAP. Klein, one of those Nazis particularly enamored of corporatist schemes for according a degree of administrative authority to the various branches of production and granting small-scale industry greater influence, may well have played on those themes, too.[37] If so, his message would seem to have been favorably received, for later in the year the Solingen party organization staged another closed gathering at the same restaurant, inviting as the chief speaker one of the most articulate Nazi advocates of corporatism in that part of the country, Paul Karrenbrock. That meeting, according to a police report, drew about 200 businessmen from Solingen and the surrounding area.[38]

Since the reports on these gatherings in Solingen, unlike those for Düren, supply no names of those businessmen who attended, and since there are no studies of the development of the NSDAP in Berg and Mark, the degree of success achieved by the Nazi courtship of the ironware manufacturers of that region cannot be established with any degree of precision. A recent study that deals primarily with the ironware industry reveals, however, that the Nazis made considerable headway among small and middle-range industrialists there. Left politically homeless by the indifference displayed toward their increasingly alarming plight by the Brüning cabinet and the traditional parties, many of their number gravitated toward National Socialism.[39] Concern about losing customers through open identification with such a controversial party presumably kept most from openly joining the party. But once the Nazis' acquisition of power in January 1933 removed that constraint, large numbers of the ironware manufacturers of Berg and Mark suddenly revealed themselves as Nazis and proclaimed that the party's triumph represented their victory, too. The historian best acquainted with its industries has observed that "a veritable orgy of celebration" spread throughout the region.[40]

Not all the ironware manufacturers in Berg and Mark concealed their commitment to the NSDAP, as Paul Pleiger, a small industrialist of the region, demonstrated. A self-made man, Pleiger had attended a technical school at night while completing his apprenticeship as a machinist, then worked for several years in the machine-construction shop of one of the larger coal-mining firms of the Ruhr. In 1925 he established a factory of his own to produce machines, pumps, and fittings for the mining industry.[41] By the 1930s he had acquired a reputation for hostility toward both the government of the Republic and the large industrial concerns of the Ruhr, especially the iron and steel producers.[42] In March 1932 he joined the NSDAP and became an activist, serving as Ortsgruppenleiter, or town leader, in Sprockhoevel, where his factory was located. After the Nazis took power, Pleiger became the Gauwirtschaftsberater, or economic policy adviser, for the regional party organization in South Westphalia. He later joined the staff of the Nazi Four-Year Plan and eventually became head of the largest economic enterprise in Nazi Germany, the Hermann Göring Works, which, among other attainments, successfully challenged the Ruhr iron and steel firms' domination in production of those commodities.[43]

Elsewhere in Germany men from the middle and lower ranges of business also suddenly emerged in 1933 as Nazi activists, indicating success by the NSDAP in recruiting followers or sympathizers among such businessmen prior to Hitler's acquisition of power. Hans Kehrl, who soon after the Nazi takeover became president of the Chamber of Industry and Commerce in the Lower Lusatian region of Prussia and also economic policy adviser to the Kurmark Gau of the party, provides an example.[44] A member of the third generation of cloth manufacturers with a sizeable factory in the city of Cottbus, Kehrl spent several of his youthful years traveling and studying manufacturing and management techniques in the United States during the 1920s. In his memoirs he reports reading both Karl Marx and Frederick W. Taylor while in the United States, finding the former repellent, the latter enormously exciting. After completing a correspondence course on "scientific management" with the Taylorite Alexander Hamilton Institute of Boston, he returned to work at his family's factory, which produced specialty cloths, primarily for coats. There he chafed at the resistance he encountered to the "progressive" ideas he had brought back with him from the United States. When the depression struck and deepened, his experiences closely paralleled those of the young machinery manufacturer in Krefeld described above. By mid-1932 the Kehrl family factory normally operated with no more than two weeks' worth of orders on hand at any time, despite his repeated trips to Berlin in an effort to drum up new business. It laid off workers and went to a reduced workweek. Kehrl lost all confidence in the government and the bourgeois parties, including the DVP, to which he—like other members of his family—had belonged during the Republic. The cabinets in Berlin and the leaders of the traditional parties seemed to him devoid of plans for combating the economic crisis and generally lacking in the will to act. The NSDAP, by contrast, appeared to him an energetic force that at least denied the inevitability of an ever-worsening depression and gave every indication of being resolved to seek decisive remedies. At the beginning of 1932, Kehrl reports, he covertly made his sympathies for the party known to the local Nazis and began making financial contributions. But he joined the party officially only after the Nazi takeover a year later, in all probability because the largest customer for the products of the Kehrl factory was a mail-order house owned by a Jewish family. Once he revealed himself as a Nazi, Kehrl rose rapidly, becoming a key figure in the Nazi economic bureaucracy, first in the Four-Year Plan, then in the Economics Ministry, and finally in Albert Speer's wartime Ministry for War Matériel.

The political peregrinations of Pleiger and Kehrl have become known as a consequence only of their later prominence, but from all indications many scores of obscure businessmen from the middle and lower reaches of the industrial economy gravitated to Nazism for similar reasons in the years just prior to 1933. Some, like Pleiger, joined the party before it came to power and gained honors and offices soon after the takeover. Another who similarly attained a certain prominence in the Third Reich was Werner Daitz, a chemist, inventor, merchant, and independent entrepreneur who presided over several small but profitable specialized manufacturing companies in Lübeck and was involved with numerous others, there and elsewhere. He, too, joined the party in 1931.[45] Others refrained from joining but openly displayed sympathy for the NSDAP. Walther Dyckerhoff, head of a large family cement plant in the Rhineland that had suffered calamitous setbacks because of the depression as early as 1930, signed a petition in July 1931 urging Hindenburg to assign the Nazis the leading place in a new cabinet.[46] But overt political actions by such lesser businessmen remained the exception. Most, like Kehrl, avoided open announcement of their commitment to Nazism lest it cost them or their enterprises customers at a time when they desperately welcomed every sale, even to a Social Democrat or a Jew. Presumably out of concern for possible lost business, Ludwig Roselius, the coffee merchant of Bremen who had turned Hitler away empty-handed when first approached in 1922, concealed his conversion to National Socialism a decade later. Roselius extended much warmer hospitality to Hitler in the early 1930s when the Nazi leader returned to Bremen as a successful politician. According to Otto Wagener, Roselius even agreed to serve as an unofficial adviser to Wagener's Economic Policy Section.[47] In Breslau the proprietor of a 200-year-old family banking house, Kurt von Eichborn, secretly aided the party there and permitted one of his sons, an ardent Nazi activist, to hold clandestine party gatherings in his home.[48]

To the extent that Nazism achieved a breakthrough with businessmen in 1931, Hitler's purported personal cultivation of business leaders had nothing to do with it, nor did that breakthrough involve the men of big business. Instead, the NSDAP penetrated the ranks of lesser businessmen, most of whom stood at the helm of small and medium-sized businesses—often still operated by the original families—that belonged to an older, more traditional component of the economy.[49] The extent of that breakthrough remains to be established, for the cases cited here scarcely suffice to prove that most of Germany's lesser businessmen went over to the Nazis in large numbers. There were, after all, tens of thousands of such entrepreneurs. But it is clear that, with few exceptions, it was men such as these, rather than the executives of the new, large-scale enterprises that comprised *die Wirtschaft*, who made ready converts to Nazism.

V

Politics and Economics
in the Power Vacuum

1. Hitler's Industry Club Speech
and Its Aftermath

As 1931 drew to a close, disillusionment with the Brüning cabinet continued to mount in business circles. Although the chancellor sought to restore a basically laissez-faire economic order, his efforts to deal with the effects of the depression and hasten recovery led him to increasingly extensive state interventions in the economic sphere. In the eyes of a growing number of businessmen, the similarities to the coercive state-controlled economy of the war and the immediate postwar period became more and more disturbing. Brüning's fourth and last major economic decree, issued in December 1931, offended even some of his most loyal supporters in big business. For the first time the cabinet invoked the emergency powers of the president to force a reduction by 10 percent of all prices set by cartels or similar arrangements. The decree also lowered interest rates on mortgages and other long-term loans by 25 percent. That step struck much of the business community as not merely another unwarranted intrusion of state power into the private economic sector, but seemed nothing less than a staggering blow to the sanctity of contracts, the very foundation of the capitalist system. The cabinet's decision not to abolish the state arbitration system added to the dismay of big business. Even though that system operated at the time solely to lower wages, most of the leaders of industry believed they could achieve still greater pay reductions in untrammeled bargaining with employees fearful of losing their jobs in time of mass unemployment. Most unpardonable of all, none of the Brüning cabinet's measures seemed to have any effect on the dizzying downward spiral of the depression-ridden economy. The domestic market for industrial goods continued to shrink, and demand for exports declined sharply after the devaluation of the English pound in the fall of 1931 gave that country's goods a price edge over those of Germany. Firm after firm curtailed production, went into the red, and ceased paying dividends. The stock market plummeted. Unemployment spread relentlessly, topping six million early in 1932 and leaving over 30 percent of the work force without livelihoods. Despite a tight regimen of austerity, state expenditures rose because of the cost of aiding the growing army of jobless, which outstripped revenues and necessitated increased taxes. As the new year opened, confidence in the economy and in the government's ability to remedy its ills had sunk to an alarming nadir.

In this dismal atmosphere the Industry Club of Düsseldorf announced to its members that the leader of the country's largest and most rapidly growing opposition party, Adolf Hitler, had accepted an invitation to address the club on January 26, 1932.[1] That invitation resulted from an unusual chain of events.[2] Late in 1931 the club had departed from its long-standing practice of excluding politicians from its roster of guest speakers by inviting a Social Democrat, Max Cohen-Reuss, to speak. Some members took offense at Cohen-Reuss's appearance, and Fritz Thyssen, who sat on the club's executive committee, demanded equal time for a spokesman of the NSDAP. Thyssen initially had in mind Gregor Strasser, who was already fairly well known in the Ruhr, but when Thyssen encountered Hitler in Berlin and told him of his plans, the Nazi leader indicated that he preferred to speak himself. Thyssen relayed this message, and the executive committee of the club acceded. No record exists of Hitler's explaining his motives for wanting to address the Industry Club. He may simply have wished to keep Strasser from assuming too prominent a role. It seems more likely, however, that his willingness to speak to such an audience arose from the same concern about his party's negative image in business circles that led him to hold an unprecedented press conference for foreign reporters in early December 1931.[3] In his well-publicized remarks on that occasion, Hitler went out of his way to allay concern in business circles about the effect on Germany's shaky international credit rating of assertions by other Nazis that a government led by the NSDAP would repudiate all foreign indebtedness. Whereas a Nazi regime would refuse to recognize Germany's reparations obligations, Hitler assured the reporters, it would not interfere with private debts to creditors abroad. Remarks made by Ernst Hanfstaengl, Hitler's foreign press secretary, to an American diplomat shortly before the Industry Club speech also suggest concern on the part of the Nazi leader about the business community's perception of the NSDAP. The party must quickly become acceptable for a role in government, Hanfstaengl had explained, and a prime task therefore lay

Hitler speaking to the Industry Club, January 26, 1932, at the Düsseldorf Park Hotel. *Courtesy U.S. National Archives.*

Steel industrialiust Fritz Thyssen addressing his remarks to the Düsseldorf Industry Club after Hitler's speech. Hermann Göring is seated between Thyssen and Hitler. *Courtesy U.S. National Archives.*

Views of the audience at Hitler's Industry Club speech. *Courtesy U.S. National Archives.*

in gaining acceptance among the country's economic elite, even at the cost of losing some support among workers.[4]

A poorly kept secret, Hitler's approaching appearance before the Industry Club occasioned considerable stir.[5] Demand among members of the club for tickets became so unprecedentedly strong that its officers suspended the members' usual privilege of bringing guests. To accommodate the expected turnout, the club reserved the grand ballroom of Düsseldorf's Park Hotel, where the members usually heard invited speakers in a smaller room. To reach the hotel on the evening of the speech, the members had to run something of a gauntlet through a turbulent mob. Alerted by the Social Democratic and Communist press, a hostile crowd had gathered in front of the hotel during the late afternoon, chanting anti-Nazi and anti-capitalist slogans, distributing leaflets, and scuffling with the police and pro-Nazi demonstrators. To prevent damage by hurled objects, the hotel's management ordered the shutters lowered on its first and second floors, giving the building the appearance of a beleaguered fortress. While the police struggled to maintain order at the front of the hotel, Hitler arrived by car, virtually unnoticed, at a side entrance shortly before the scheduled beginning of his speech, set for six in the evening. Inside he joined Hermann Göring and Fritz Thyssen on a speaker's podium improvised on the ballroom's bandstand. The audience far exceeded the expectations of the club's officers. Approximately 650 members, more than two-thirds of the total membership, attended. They filled all the available chairs, and some had to stand. Latecomers could not get into the crowded ballroom at all and had to hear the evening's proceedings from a loudspeaker in an adjacent room.

After a brief introduction by the DNVP mayor of Düsseldorf, Hitler launched into a two-and-a-half-hour oration.[6] As in his earlier talks to comparable audiences, and as in the pamphlet he had written for Emil Kirdorf in 1927, he withheld from his listeners much about the NSDAP and his own aims. He did not utter the word "Jew" once, made no reference to his party's twenty-five-point program, and veiled his commitment to the conquest of *Lebensraum* from Russia. Much of his speech amounted to a didactic lecture on the determinants of human affairs, supported with examples drawn from history and interpreted to support his views. With little in the way of specific references to the Germany of 1932 or its problems, he set forth his belief in the primacy of politics over economics and, within the political sphere, of the primacy of a people's spiritual outlook. Germans could not blame other nations for their plight, he warned, nor could they hope to find remedies in the realm of foreign affairs. They must instead look to themselves, to the condition and attitudes of their own nation.

When he turned to Germany's immediate plight, Hitler refrained from pillorying the economic policies of the Empire, as he had during the 1920s. Instead, he launched into a discussion of the depression.

Knowingly, if not always knowledgeably, he spoke of worldwide over-production, heightened international competition for markets, mounting unemployment, and spreading protectionism. He provided no coherent explanation for the economic crisis, however. He finally characterized it as merely another of those struggles for economic survival that occurred from time to time, rather like massive epidemics, when relations between peoples "broke down," spreading "sickness" through their economies. In the face of a development of such magnitude, the Brüning cabinet's tinkering with the economy amounted to futile efforts to cure a malady by treating its symptoms. The ultimate cause of Germany's plight, Hitler told his listeners, did not lie in the sphere of economics at all, but rather in that of politics. Only when Germany again became mighty as a nation could it compete successfully in the international power struggle that always had and always would determine the economic winners and losers in history. Only a strong state guaranteed a strong economy.

Having shifted his focus from economics to politics, Hitler went on to present his familiar formula for Germany's salvation. Until the nation again achieved the unity of will it had shown in Bismarck's time, it would remain weak and vulnerable. To achieve that unity, the alien, subversive Marxism that had divided Germans into patriotic and internationalist camps must be extirpated. Only a potent new faith could achieve that task, and National Socialism alone possessed such a faith. Once Germany's strength had been restored through unity of will, it would solve its economic problems, whether it chose to increase its exports, to concentrate on the development of the home market, or to solve the "problem of space" (*Raumfrage*) by acquiring new *Lebensraum*. As so often before similar audiences, Hitler had begun by addressing economic issues and ended by proposing a political panacea.

While Hitler said nothing about what concrete economic measures a Nazi-led government would adopt, he did seek to allay some of the misgivings he must have known many of his listeners at the Industry Club harbored about his movement's intentions. He went to considerable pains to explain, in Social Darwinist terms, his approval of private property and the unequal distribution of economic rewards. These could no longer be regarded as self-evident principles, he warned, but must be ethically justified. That presented no difficulties, however, if one believed—as he left no doubt he did—that the accomplishments of individuals varied. Equalizing rewards or subjecting property to the will of all amounted to according the incompetent and indolent a voice equal to that of the most able and accomplished individuals, which could only lead to socially disastrous results. Because the abilities and attainments of people varied, private property and unequal rewards on the basis of individual merit remained indispensable principles for a healthy economy, Hitler explained. Leaping abruptly from that point to the political sphere, he derided the Weimar Republic, charging that democracy rested on the diametrically opposed principle that all people were the same and that politics required no special abilities. Such a dichotomy between the underlying principles of the political and economic systems of a nation could not last, he warned. Only by extirpating the destructive principle of democracy and according full recognition to individual accomplishment could the German *Volk* attain the rule of the most able in all spheres of life and so realize its enormous potential. In the new Germany, he assured his listeners, individual responsibility, authority, and obedience, not the weight of numbers, would determine the shape of society and the course of events, in the economic sphere as in all others.

As he approached the end of his long address, Hitler interposed a disingenuous disclaimer. He had not come before them, he told the men assembled at the Park Hotel, to seek their votes or any favors for the NSDAP. He then proceeded, however, to invoke a specter calculated to evoke sympathy for his movement: bolshevism. Without the bravery and self-sacrifice of hundreds of thousands of idealistic uniformed Nazis, the streets of Germany would not be safe for any *Bürger*, he boasted. Without the blood his storm troopers had spilled, the perverse new religion sweeping into Europe from Asia would already have triumphed and reduced Germany to a lower level of existence. Proudly, he quoted Trotsky to the effect that Nazism represented the only real barrier to bolshevism. He portrayed the NSDAP as the mightiest popular political movement in German history. Despite his own humble origins, he had built it against the opposition of public opinion, the press, the government—and the business community *(die Wirtschaft)*. The NSDAP's triumph, which he again pledged would come about only by legal means, would transform the downtrodden country they saw about them. Looking to that day, he concluded by invoking the prospect of a regenerated, powerful Germany under Nazi leadership, merciless toward foes at home and elsewhere but ready to live in friendship and peace with all who shared that readiness.

After the acting chairman of the Industry Club, Karl Haniel, had briefly thanked Hitler for his speech, Fritz Thyssen read some prepared remarks. According to eyewitness accounts he identified himself fully with Hitler's statements. Obviously determined to leave no doubt about his allegiance, Thyssen ended his remarks by directing an incongruous salutation to Hitler: "Heil, Herr Hitler!" Ernst Poensgen later recalled that Albert Vögler—like both Thyssen and Poensgen an official of the United Steel Works and member of the Ruhrlade—then rose in an attempt to direct a question to Hitler and initiate a discussion. But Thyssen ignored Vögler and abruptly closed the session.[7] Hitler, who had declined an invitation from the club to remain for the supper that customarily followed appearances by guest speakers, retired for a short time to a hotel room, where he met briefly with the mayor of Düsseldorf before departing. Göring remained for the club's supper, which about 500 members attended.[8]

The response to Hitler's speech by those in attendance at the Park Hotel on January 26, 1932, immediately became a matter of controversy and has remained such ever since. Since the club permitted no journalists to attend, newspaper reports about the speech conveyed only second-hand impressions or hearsay and varied widely in their assessments of the audience's reaction. Leftist papers portrayed Hitler's listeners as responding with unanimous enthusiasm to his words.[9] The Catholic *Kölnische Volkszeitung*, on the other hand, characterized the audience as "cool"; the liberal *Vossische Zeitung* of Berlin described the listeners as "conspicuously reserved"; another liberal daily, the *Berliner Tageblatt*, detected a divided response, with prominent businessmen particularly dubious about Hitler's views.[10] Even among eyewitnesses no agreement prevailed about how those in attendance had responded. An official of the Prussian political police, who had gained entry by virtue of the club's request for police protection, reported that Hitler's words had made a deep impression on his listeners, who had rewarded him with heavy applause. Hitler could be sure of the loyalty of those in attendance, the police official concluded.[11] Another eyewitness, the mayor of the Ruhr industrial city of Duisburg-Hamborn, contested the police observer's impression of general assent on the part of the audience at the Park Hotel. He had observed that the applause for Hitler came in response to remarks in which the Nazi leader endorsed general national goals shared by countless Germans, rather than distinctively Nazi views.[12] The earliest systematic investigator of Nazism, the extremely resourceful and scrupulous journalist Konrad Heiden, who later wrote the first serious biography of Hitler, cited eyewitnesses to the effect that only about a third of the assemblage gave their assent to Thyssen's "Heil, Herr Hitler," and that the response to the speech by the majority had been lukewarm or even negative.[13]

Attempts to draw significance from the amount or the motivation of the applause elicited by Hitler's words have a limited value for determining the impact of his speech on the important capitalists in attendance. Contrary to an impression widespread both at the time and since, the membership of the Industry Club of Düsseldorf did not consist solely of the industrial elite of Germany.[14] The club was a large facility that served as a convenient meeting place for nearly 1,000 members from throughout Germany who in one way or another were connected with industry. They included not only leading executives of the largest industrial firms but also their less eminent subordinates as well as executives of medium-sized and even small enterprises, sales representatives, trade association officials, and business lawyers. In tone, the club fell considerably short of the capitalistic grandeur its name suggests. It provided its members with facilities at the Park Hotel for dining, card playing, and bowling as well as with a reading room. During the summer an annual club excursion took place to a picturesque spot in the countryside. Each fall the members partook of a traditional goose dinner to commemorate St. Martin's day. Major industrial figures, such as the men of the Ruhrlade, did not take part in these activities, nor did they have time to make use of the club's leisure facilities. Like virtually everyone of any stature in industrial circles, they retained memberships, however, and occasionally attended talks by guest speakers.[15]

By 1932 the Industry Club was feeling the pinch of the depression.[16] Out of regard for the plight of financially hard-pressed members, its board of officers lowered the dues from 200 marks a year to 150 for the year 1931, and then to 100 marks for 1932. At the then current exchange rate, this amounted to less than twenty-four American dollars. The Park Hotel, in which the club held a financial interest, survived only by reducing service to the barest acceptable level. Premises in several other buildings owned by the club and rented to supplement its income had become vacant by 1932, arousing concern among the club's board of officers about its solvency. The members, they complained in their report for 1932, did not help matters by dining less and less frequently at the Park Hotel and ordering, when they did frequent the dining room, only the least expensive dishes. Realities at the Düsseldorf Industry Club in 1932 clearly fell far short of the aura of exclusivity and opulence usually attributed to that institution.

Since the official club roster of those who attended Hitler's speech did not survive, only spotty information exists about the composition of that evening's audience. The presence of Ernst Poensgen, Fritz Thyssen, and Albert Vögler of United Steel and Karl Haniel of the Gutehoffnungshütte is well documented. Ernst Brandi of the Bergbauverein reportedly attended.[17] Police observers recognized some other persons as well.[18] But the police commented pointedly on the conspicuous absence of some of the best-known figures in industrial circles, such as Carl Duisberg of IG Farben; Gustav Krupp von Bohlen und Halbach, chairman of the industrial Reichsverband; Paul Reusch, chief of the Gutehoffnungshütte; and Fritz Springorum of the Hoesch Steel Works.[19] Paul Silverberg, the prominent coal executive, also apparently did not attend.[20] On the other hand, the police were struck by the presence of a sizeable contingent of small ironware manufacturers from the region of Berg and Mark, into whose ranks, as already noted, Nazism had made deep inroads. Most of the large audience went unrecognized by the police and other observers, however. Some idea as to why is provided by the identity of one such unfamiliar face. It belonged to the young Krefeld manufacturer whose memoirs describing his family's struggle to keep their two small factories during the depression were cited in the last chapter. He attended because his father, who, like many other lesser businessmen, belonged to the club, had given him his member's ticket.

According to that young man's later account, he had already become a Nazi sympathizer before he entered the Park Hotel. Years later he still vividly recalled Hitler's express endorsement of the principle of private property. And his memoirs leave no doubt that he joined enthusiastically in the applause for the Nazi leader's words.[21]

Considering the size and diverse composition of the audience that listened to Hitler's speech, the response of its various components assumes greater importance than the frequency, volume, or timing of the applause. On that score, two well-informed eyewitnesses independently reported that the applause came mainly from the young and the obscure, whereas the important senior industrial leaders remained reserved. Gustav Brecht, an executive of the country's largest lignite-mining firm, conveyed that verdict to an acquaintance soon after attending the speech.[22] The mayor of Hamborn told the Prussian police that the major figures from industry had felt disappointed that Hitler had spoken only in general terms, and mainly about politics.[23] They had come to learn about his position on the specific economic questions of the day, the mayor noted, but insofar as the Nazi leader had touched on those matters, his remarks had been so unclear and noncommittal that they could gain no understanding of where he stood. The chief of the Prussian administration in Düsseldorf detected the same disappointment in those of Hitler's listeners whom he later queried about the speech.[24] They seemed impressed by the rhetorical brilliance of the speech and its nationalistic idealism but had found in it no significant content, particularly on the vital point of National Socialism's intentions for the economy. Years later, under interrogation at Nuremberg, Ludwig Grauert, the managing director of the iron and steel employers' association of the Ruhr who had become a Nazi fellow traveler well before the Industry Club speech, recalled having pointed out to an elderly manufacturer afterwards that Hitler had said nothing whatever about any measures that might help him to find purchasers for his firm's products.[25]

Those who had come to hear Hitler's speech in hopes of learning where he stood on economic issues certainly had good cause for disappointment. He had, to be sure, gone out of his way to identify himself with the principles of private property and unequal distribution of economic rewards, so that no one who took him at his word could mistake him for a socialist in the conventional sense of that word. But he had said such things for years, as the well-informed members of his audience must have known. They undoubtedly hoped to learn where he stood on more specific matters of urgent concern to them, such as monetary and trade policies, about which other Nazi spokesmen were making such alarming statements. They must also have hoped to find out where Hitler stood on unemployment insurance, state regulation of prices, wages, interest rates, and hours of work. They surely wanted to know his position on binding state arbitration of labor-management disputes, industry-wide contracts, and the collective bargaining prerogatives of the trade unions. Most urgently, the many executives responsible for firms struggling to survive the effects of the depression must have gone to the gathering at the Park Hotel hoping to learn how the leader of the country's most rapidly growing political party proposed to deal with the economic crisis if he came to power. But since Hitler adhered to his strategy of calculated ambiguity with regard to questions of economic policy, none of his listeners came away from his talk any better informed about his position on these matters of pressing concern to the business community.[26]

It does not follow that Hitler's speech evoked wholly negative reactions from all the seasoned, prominent businessmen in the audience at the Park Hotel. Exactly how his performance affected them can never be fully established because of the dearth of evidence. The limited documentation does, however, include a report on one prominent industrial executive who reacted otherwise. The man in question was an executive of the Krupp firm, who attended when Gustav Krupp von Bohlen declined to alter his plans to be in Berlin on the day of Hitler's appearance.[27] Testifying at Nuremberg after the war, Krupp's brother-in-law, Tilo von Wilmowsky, identified this executive as Arthur Klotzbach, a member of the three-man Krupp managerial board who supervised the firm's coal-mining operations and who also belonged to the Ruhrlade, the secret organization of twelve prominent industrialists.[28] Contemporary documentation and a book later commissioned by the Krupp firm make it seem more likely, however, that the man in attendance for Krupp was actually Friedrich Janssen, a more junior executive who shared responsibility with another man for a branch of Krupp charged with overseeing its holdings in other firms.[29] Whoever the Krupp executive was, Wilmowsky characterized him as a sober, skeptical businessman. Nevertheless, Wilmowsky testified, he had come away from Hitler's speech impressed. Whether this meant that he had come away impressed with the substance of what Hitler had said or with the Nazi leader's personality and oratorical performance remains unclear from Wilmowsky's account. But Wilmowsky's recollection of the skeptical Krupp's response on hearing his company's executive describe his experience implies the latter rather more than the former: "Yes, that's all just a lot of empty phrases; there's not much behind them."[30] Still, this case reveals that even seasoned executives in major business firms were not necessarily immune to the charismatic, almost hypnotic effect that direct exposure to Hitler's oratory had, if sometimes only temporarily, on so many Germans.

In numerous accounts of Hitler's Industry Club appearance in historical works, one finds a greatly simplified version of what took place: Hitler came, spoke, and conquered. As those versions reveal, many historians have, as in the case of the Nazi leader's purported campaign to cultivate big business support in the summer of 1931, fallen prey to the propagandistic artistry of the Nazis. That is, those versions of the Industry Club appearance ultimately derive from the same source as did that of the Nazis: Otto Dietrich's 1934 party-line "memoir" of Hitler's rise. That volume provides a vivid account of the gathering in Düsseldorf:

> January 27, 1932, will always be a memorable day in the history of the NSDAP. On that day the Führer achieved a breakthrough with the captains of western German industry. . . .
>
> I can still see the prominent men at that gathering. We arrived from Godesberg and drove into the courtyard of the hotel amidst the howlings of the Marxists. The room was overflowing. The elite of *die Wirtschaft* of western Germany crammed into the rows of chairs. Familiar and unfamiliar faces. . . .
>
> Joyful expectation on the part of those already won over. Cool reserve in the superior expressions on the faces of a large majority who—perhaps flattered that Hitler had come to them—had been attracted by curiosity and inquisitiveness. . . . They had no thought of conversion but came with a critical attitude, intent on confirming their own, infallible opinions.
>
> The Führer, greeted with the greatest of reserve, speaks from a slightly raised ballustrade that juts into the room, resting his hands lightly on the cast iron railing in front of him. I sit, in the midst of listeners, behind him, take notes, observe the effect of his speech of more than two hours. The Führer develops the relationship between economics and politics in a world-historical perspective, their interplay, the consequences in Germany. Why it has come to this pass in Germany and the only way to make it otherwise.
>
> The impression on this circle of sober listeners is astounding. After only an hour cool reserve gives way to passionate interest. The Führer speaks about the unprecedentedly heroic struggle of his political soldiers, poor and hatefully persecuted, but sacrificing everything, even life, to their *Volk.* . . .
>
> The faces begin to flush, the eyes hang upon the lips of the Führer, one senses that the hearts grow warm. They follow intently, they lose themselves in the words. At first the hands move hesitantly, then salvos of applause roar forth. As Adolf Hitler ceases to speak, he has won a battle.[31]

This compelling description by a man who, after all, was an eyewitness has made a profound impact on the historical record of Hitler's rise to power. Accepted unquestioningly, right down to the erroneous date, in two seminal studies upon which a host of subsequent authors have since relied, it has given rise to one of the many tenacious legends surrounding the relations between big business and the Nazis.[32] Especially revealing, in the eyes of most authors who have relied upon Dietrich's 1934 publication, is a sentence that follows the account of the Industry Club appearance: "The effect on the businessmen, so far as they deserved that name, was profound and became evident in the ensuing difficult months of struggle."[33] This has generally been taken as testimony by Dietrich to the effect that big business subsidized Hitler heavily as a consequence of his speech of January 26, 1932. If one consults Dietrich's more prosaic memoirs of 1955, one finds a very different story, however. There, in a style so different as to suggest that he relied heavily in 1934 on his large and talented staff for the preparation of his first memoir, one finds these recollections:

> Not until 1932, after Göring had established close relations with the Stahlhelm leader [sic] Fritz Thyssen and the latter had openly spoken out for Hitler in the industrial gathering at Düsseldorf did the ice break and numerous sympathetic attitudes come to expression. On that occasion a collection was attempted at the door which produced some well-meaning but insignificant sums. Beyond that, one could not speak of any support worthy of mention, much less of a financing of Hitler's political struggle by die Wirtschaft or "heavy industry," although some more or less notable contributions may have reached local party organizations at their rallies from individually sympathetic businessmen of their regions. Hitler's great propaganda tours of 1932 financed themselves exclusively through the entrance fees for giant rallies, at which seats in the front rows often went for fantastic prices.[34]

Despite this very different account by the Otto Dietrich of 1955, his propagandistic tract of 1934 has repeatedly served as a seminal source on the Industry Club speech and its aftermath, often in conjunction with an equally embellished account in the ghostwritten "memoirs" of Fritz Thyssen.[35]

From all indications, neither Hitler nor any other Nazis mounted any sustained follow-up campaign either to extract financial support from those who had been present at his Industry Club speech or otherwise to enlist them for their purposes. There is, in fact, evidence of only one brief and apparently ill-fated effort in that direction. It occurred the day after the speech, when Thyssen invited his fellow United Steel executives Ernst Poensgen and Albert Vögler to meet at his home in the Ruhr with Hitler, Göring, and Ernst Röhm, chief of the Nazi storm troopers. On that occasion, Poensgen later recalled, Göring took him aside and asked whether Ludwig Grauert, who was Poensgen's subordinate in the iron and steel employers' association of the Ruhr, might be available for appointment as Reich minister of labor. Grauert, Göring explained, felt attracted by some of Hitler's social and corporatist ideas.[36] Since Grauert, who had played a prominent part in the great Ruhr lockout of 1928, ranked among the most militant anti-trade-union figures in the service of industry, Göring's inquiry would seem a heavy-handed attempt on his part to indicate that big business could expect a hard line toward labor from a government headed by the Nazis. Whether Göring acted on his own or in concurrence with Hitler remains unclear. But he employed the wrong approach with Poensgen, who—in contrast to Thyssen—regarded corporatist schemes with great misgiving and did not in the least share Grauert's growing enthusiasm for the ideas of Othmar Spann, the influential Austrian theorist of corporatism. From all reports Poensgen remained, despite his exposure to Hitler and Göring, skeptical and cool toward Nazism right down to the creation of the Third Reich, and even afterwards.[37] As for Vögler, an acquaintance of his reported hearing soon after the gathering at Thyssen's house on January 27 that Hitler had again avoided discussing economic issues on that occasion, leaving his much smaller audience there frustrated once more in their efforts to pin down the Nazi leader on matters of vital interest to them.[38]

Hitler's failure to follow up vigorously on the entrée he had gained to the business community through his Industry Club speech tends to substantiate the hypothesis that he sought merely to neutralize big business, not to bring its leaders actively behind the NSDAP or to exploit its financial resources for his party. However, even if he had wanted to, he would have paid a costly price for cultivating further contacts with the business community, since the political left quickly turned his Düsseldorf appearance into a damaging propaganda weapon against the NSDAP. The Communist press in particular vigorously exploited the event. The KPD party organ, *Die Rote Fahne,* depicted Hitler's performance at the Park Hotel as a hireling's obsequious accounting to his masters behind locked doors; fabricated texts attributed to him ingratiating answers to fictitious questions purportedly posed by members of the audience; cartoons and articles portrayed him devouring afterwards an expensive seven-course banquet with flowing wine, surrounded by overstuffed capitalists.[39]

The Nazi press initially sought to play down the event. The day after the speech, party newspapers, quoting the Nazi press office in Munich, printed a brief, laconic announcement to the effect that Hitler had achieved a great success for the ideas of National Socialism by addressing a large group of industrialists in Düsseldorf.[40] The response of wage earners among the party's rank and file to the propaganda of the left clearly disturbed the leadership, however. The Nazi daily in Cologne revealed this concern when it sought to counter the leftist charges with an article headlined "Hitler Recruits for Socialism." It proclaimed that the party leader had sought to dismantle class barriers by sharpening the social conscience of his audience at the Industry Club.[41] Hitler himself refrained from accepting an invitation to address another business audience in Hannover, which was extended to him soon after his Düsseldorf speech.[42] When the left nevertheless kept up its barrage of allegations, the leadership of the NSDAP felt compelled to respond. In mid-February the party's national organ denied reports by "slanderers" that Hitler had in his speech declared war on the trade unions before partaking of a lavish banquet with the members of the Industry Club. Actually, the *Völkischer Beobachter* maintained, Hitler had declared war on materialism and admonished his listeners to become sensitive to the plight of their less fortunate "racial comrades."[43]

Despite this and other Nazi attempts to lay the matter to rest, the left's version of the Industry Club speech continued to dog Hitler and his party long after the event. When Chancellor Brüning made use of it during the spring election campaigns, the Nazis became sufficiently concerned to indulge in one of their rare exercises in truthfulness. In an effort to counter the many allegations about what Hitler had told his Düsseldorf audience, the *Völkischer Beobachter* devoted four of its pages in mid-April to extensive verbatim excerpts from the speech.[44] As the paper further announced, the full text had been printed as a pamphlet by the party publishing house and could be purchased for only twenty pfennigs. A foreword to that pamphlet made clear that the text was being published at considerable expense solely to refute charges by Brüning and others that Hitler had told his Industry Club audience something different from what he said in his other speeches.[45] From all indications, the aftermath of the Industry Club speech proved highly embarrassing for the NSDAP.

As if in response to unrest among the NSDAP's wage-earning followers, the radical fork of the Nazi tongue spoke out with intensified anti-capitalist rhetoric in the wake of Hitler's Düsseldorf appearance. The Nazi Factory Cell Organization (NSBO) issued a pamphlet protesting the exploitation of workers by the "liberal capitalist system" and calling for its destruction and the establishment of a "supply economy" in place of the existing "profit economy."[46] In another pamphlet a member of the Economic Policy Section vehemently denounced "the great trusts" and "private monopolies," proclaiming that these must be broken up or taken over by the state.[47] These publications immediately attracted the notice of the business press. Commenting on the NSBO pamphlet, the pro-business *Deutsche Bergwerks-Zeitung* of Düsseldorf concluded that its meaning would not be altered if, wherever "National Socialism" appeared, the word "socialism" were substituted. In explaining their "German socialism," the paper noted that some Nazis laid great stress on the principle of individual accomplishment. Yet the party's idea of a "supply economy" seemed to have little to do with accomplishment. It amounted instead to nothing less than socialistic economic planning. In assuming that the economy could be set right only by such means, the Nazis differed in no way from the Social Democrats, who also held out the vision of a future perfect order. Germany's workers must beware of all such false economic prophets, the *Deutsche Bergwerks-Zeitung* warned.[48]

A document published in the official parliamentary bulletin of the NSDAP only a week after Hitler's appearance at the Industry Club also attracted concerned attention in business circles. Apparently a response to the spurious questions and answers concocted by the Communist press, it consisted of unusually straightforward responses to ten questions about specific matters of economic policy.[49] Although the original text did not attribute the answers to Hitler himself, non-Nazi publications assumed he was their source when they reprinted the questions and answers. As a consequence Hitler appeared to have endorsed some unusually forthright and—from the standpoint of the business community—highly disturbing stances. These included endorsement of the eight-hour day, the inviolability of union-wide collective bargaining contracts, and the right of workers to strike so long as the existing immoral capitalist system prevailed. The Hitler movement did not oppose trade unions, another response announced; it basically favored unions, objecting only to labor leaders who fostered class conflict and promoted fulfillment of the Versailles Treaty. Still another response proclaimed Nazism's opposition to both the efforts of the capitalist system to reduce the wages of workers and measures by the Brüning government aimed at curtailing such workers' benefits as social insurance and pensions. Other responses called for an expansion of *Sozialpolitik* through stricter state safety regulations in factories, additional housing for workers, and expanded state protection for working youths. These pronouncements received prominent display in conservative and liberal publications.[50] They also circulated among some of the leading industrialists of Germany, who studied them with concern.[51]

Proclaimed by an official Nazi publication, and widely attributed in the press to Hitler himself, these ten pronouncements went far toward negating whatever reassurances the business community might have derived from Hitler's remarks before the Industry Club. In his Düsseldorf speech he had sounded like a friend of the businessman; now his party sounded almost indistinguishable from a trade union. Only a few weeks after Hitler's appearance at the Industry Club, those businessmen who sought to comprehend the economic position of Germany's most dynamic and rapidly expanding political party could be forgiven for once more perceiving it as a bewildering, enigmatic collection of contradictions.

2. Big Business Approaches the Political Maelstrom in Disarray

During the half year following Hitler's appearance at the Industry Club, the swirling political currents of Germany began to converge into the maelstrom soon to engulf the entire country. In March and April the electorate went through two rounds of balloting before re-electing Hindenburg as president of the Reich. In the latter part of April the voters of Bavaria, Prussia, and several smaller states chose new parliaments in which the Nazis enjoyed greatly strengthened positions. At the end of May Brüning had to resign as chancellor, and Hindenburg replaced him with the obscure Franz von Papen. At Papen's request, the president dissolved the Reichstag early in June and scheduled an election for July 31. The outcome of the balloting made the NSDAP the strongest party in the national legislature. These developments repeatedly confronted the politically active big businessmen of Germany with perplexing problems. In responding, they no longer displayed the degree of consensus that had marked their political behavior in the past. They now found themselves frequently at odds and cross-purposes. Many felt greater constraints than before on their financial involvement in politics, either because of economic stringencies or disillusionment arising from past failures to influence political developments. Others balked at granting their customary subsidies when the bourgeois parties ignored their renewed demands for a merger that would end their disunity. With big business divided and increasingly hesitant about its political role, General Schleicher had to intervene and seek out subsidies for the DVP and the DNVP at the time of the Reichstag election of July 1932. As the German political crisis approached its climax, the politically active elements of big business displayed less cohesion and commitment to political involvement than ever before in the republican period.

The presidential election of 1932 posed a dilemma for much of the business community, just as it did for other Germans on the right. The familiar political spectrum became confused when the incumbent Hindenburg, behind whom big business had rallied along with the rest of the right in 1925, stood for re-election with the backing of the Brüning cabinet and the moderate parties of the Republic, including the SPD. His challengers in the first round of balloting were Hitler, the Communist Ernst Thälmann, and Theodor Duesterberg, the candidate of the DNVP and the rightist veterans' organization, the Stahlhelm. From the outset most observers expected Hindenburg to win, as he eventually did with 53 percent of the vote in the April runoff after falling four-tenths of a percentage point short of the requisite majority in the March balloting. Hitler ran second both times, first tallying 30.1 percent and then 36.8 percent. After gaining only 6.8 percent of the vote in the first round, Duesterberg withdrew. The campaign involved more than election of a president; it became something of a plebiscite on the Brüning cabinet. By thoroughly identifying himself with the president's re-election campaign and assuming a leading role in it, the chancellor made a vote for Hindenburg seem to many Germans an expression of confidence in his cabinet's policies as well. As a result, many on the right found themselves torn between loyalty for the venerable head of state and opposition to a cabinet they had come to view as unacceptable.

This alignment of presidential candidates divided the politically active elements of big business. The Berlin daily, *Deutsche Allgemeine Zeitung*, which belonged to a consortium of business interests, came out squarely for Hindenburg.[1] So did a number of prominent individuals, including the chairman of the industrial Reichsverband, Krupp von Bohlen, and its former chairman, Carl Duisberg of IG Farben.[2] Assuming an active role in the campaign, Duisberg headed on behalf of the president's re-election a national financial committee that raised a sizeable campaign war chest in business circles.[3] But with notable exceptions such as Krupp von Bohlen, Friedrich Flick, and Paul Silverberg, the coal, iron, and steel magnates of the Rhenish-Westphalian *Revier* responded negatively to Duisberg's requests for contributions. Although they occasionally cited financial constraints, their replies to Duisberg and their correspondence with each other leave no doubt that they regarded aid for the Hindenburg campaign as tantamount to support for Brüning and his policy of compromising with the Social Democrats and the trade unions.[4] But despite Fritz Thyssen's public endorsement of Hitler and his distribution to other industrialists of a pamphlet that portrayed Hitler as the heir to the Prussian tradition of stern paternalism, most of the prominent men of Ruhr industry were not attracted to the Nazi leader's candidacy.[5] Paul Reusch, the influential leader of the Ruhrlade, cast his ballot for Duesterberg.[6] While the Stahlhelm leader had no chance of winning, his candidacy provided a means of registering a protest vote on the right. Also, Duesterberg's political strategist, Alfred Hugenberg of the DNVP, held out what proved the vain hope that if a second round of voting became necessary, a bargain might be struck with the Hindenburg camp whereby Duesterberg would withdraw in favor of the president and the latter schedule new Reichstag elections that would produce a cabinet drawn from the right.[7] In the campaign for the runoff, with Hindenburg requiring only a small increment of votes to attain the necessary majority and Duesterberg having freed his supporters to vote for the president, most of the Ruhr industrialists declined Duisberg's renewed request for funds. Viewing the re-election of the president as a foregone conclusion, they preferred to marshal their political funds for use in the campaigns for the state elections of April 24, 1932.[8] Deserted by much of the business community, the hard-pressed Hindenburg forces had to draw clandestinely on state funds to mount a campaign for the second round of presidential balloting that would at least rival the Nazis' all-out exertions on behalf of Hitler.[9]

The Prussian election bulked particularly large from the standpoint of big business. The headquarters and legal home of most large enterprises lay in that state—by far the biggest and most populous of the federal states—as did many of their operations. Prussia's taxes and expenditures, its laws and its judiciary, its police, its regional and local administrators affected the business community in countless ways. With brief exceptions, the state government had been headed throughout the republican period by Social Democrats and backed by the Weimar coalition of Social Democrats, Centrists, and Democrats that had originally shaped the Republic. Under this "red-black" regime Prussia had become, in the eyes of the business community, a major source of excessive taxation, wasteful spending, and creeping state socialism. In the spring of 1932 one of the most impressive and forceful of the SPD's leaders, Otto Braun, stood at the head of the Prussian cabinet. Because of its large bureaucracy, Prussia served as the principal remaining source of the patronage on which the SPD could draw to provide jobs for its top-heavy leadership ranks. The Braun cabinet thus struck many business-men as a particularly irksome vestige of the "Marxist" era from which Germany at last appeared to be emerging.[10] A year earlier an attempt to topple the Prussian government before the expiration of its four-year term by means of a Stahlhelm-sponsored plebiscite had failed despite financial aid from some members of industry.[11] But in the spring of 1932 most of big business looked hopefully to the approaching quadren-nial state election, which virtually all observers agreed would sweep away the Weimar coalition's majority.

Widespread agreement prevailed in Ruhr industrial circles about the most desirable outcome of the Prussian election. Like most observers, the executives of the Ruhr expected the Nazis to score sizeable gains. Most viewed that likelihood in a positive light, hoping that such results would, despite the internecine conflict on the right to which the presi-dential election had given rise, open the way to a coalition of bourgeois political forces and Nazis that would wrest the state government from the "Marxists" and their allies. Such a coalition at the state level would, they expected, saddle the Nazis with responsibility, thereby diminishing their appeal to the electorate but without giving them a voice in national policy making. It would also relegate the economically and socially radi-cal elements of Nazism to the periphery and strengthen the moderates in the NSDAP. In order to enable a coalition of that sort to function as they wished, those businessmen who favored such an outcome decided they must concentrate their financial resources on maximizing the show-ing at the polls of its potential bourgeois component.[12]

Agreement ended there, for dissension quickly arose over how best to strengthen the bourgeois forces. Gustav Krupp von Bohlen and Paul Reusch, among others, strongly believed that the time had come for a merger of the DNVP, the DVP, and the smaller parties to the right of the Catholic Center. Only the creation of such a new party could, they insisted, end the chronic disunity of the traditional right and assure a dominant bourgeois voice in a new Prussian coalition including the Nazis. When it quickly became apparent that Hugenberg would not per-mit the DNVP to enter into such a merger, Krupp and Reusch favored deposing that imperious party leader by promoting rebellion against him within the DNVP's ranks.[13] They met with unyielding opposition, however, from such fellow members of the Ruhrlade as Fritz Spring-orum and Albert Vögler as well as from Ernst Brandi of the Bergbau-verein. These men resisted any attempt to oust Hugenberg, arguing that his removal would offend so many loyal followers that much of the

DNVP would remain outside any new party created by merger. The best hope for consolidating the bourgeois right, these men argued, lay in concentrating financial aid on the DNVP and making that party so strong that the followers of the lesser parties would be drawn away from those faltering organizations and absorbed into an enlarged DNVP that would soon encompass the entire bourgeois right. Hugenberg had his shortcomings, his defenders conceded, but he was at least an established leader. He must stay, they insisted.[14] Because of this disagreement, the Ruhrlade remained paralyzed politically until close to the end of the Prussian campaign. With only ten days left before the election, Reusch and those who had sided with him finally gave in to the insistence of the organization's treasurer, Springorum, that at least nominal contributions must be made in order to retain contact with the parties they had customarily supported. But those contributions fell far short of the sizeable subsidies of earlier years, reflecting both the depressed economic state of Ruhr industry and the disgust of men like Reusch and Krupp with the disunity and ineffectuality of the bourgeois parties.[15]

Those parties also received less money than in former times from other big business sources during the campaign for the Prussian election. Brüning's nearly two years of "non-party" rule by presidential decree had diminished the importance of the parties in the eyes of most businessmen. Because of the abysmal economic conditions, those industrialists still willing to contribute reduced the size of their payments.[16] Other sources of big business political money dwindled to a trickle or dried up altogether. The major banks of Berlin, which had formerly given significant sums in routine fashion to all the bourgeois parties, could disburse little or no political money in the spring of 1932. Some had emerged from the banking crisis of the summer of 1931 under government control while the remainder had at best a precarious hold on their financial independence. Individual bankers could still make personal political contributions, but the size of these fell far short of the former corporate donations of the large banks.[17] The banks themselves could at most extend credit through their branch offices to local or regional units of the bourgeois parties.[18] Still other sources of big business contributions in previous campaigns became unavailable because of a combination of adverse business conditions and disillusionment with politics. One of those moved by such considerations in the spring of 1932 was Carl Friedrich von Siemens, head of the Berlin electrical equipment dynasty. A founder of the Kuratorium established in the capital after the revolution to fund the bourgeois parties and increase the influence of big business within them, Siemens had by 1932 despaired about the possibility of influencing the course of politics through the application of money. Concerned about the worsening circumstances of his family's enterprises and discouraged by the fragmentation of the bourgeois camp, he drew back from further financial involvement in politics. At the time of the first round of presidential balloting Siemens reluctantly responded to Duisberg's appeal with a 40,000-mark donation to the Hindenburg campaign, explaining that only a personal plea by Brüning had overcome his resolve to abstain. As the Prussian election approached, Siemens made known his unwillingness to contribute further, citing the disunity of the bourgeois parties as his reason.[19]

Not all of big business held back from involvement in the Prussian election campaign. IG Farben apparently continued its practice of spreading its political money across the full spectrum of bourgeois parties, and the industrialists of Hanover raised funds for the DNVP and DVP as usual.[20] The chairman of the Bergbauverein, Ernst Brandi, assumed a more active role than ever before. His heightened political zeal undoubtedly resulted in considerable part from renewed trade union demands for socialization of the coal industry.[21] But whatever the cause, Brandi took advantage of the stalemate in the Ruhrlade to wrest from that organization control over the coal operators' political money. He then used those funds to subsidize the campaign of the DNVP for the Prussian election. In contrast to earlier years, none of that money went to the DVP because Brandi had decided the best way to achieve bourgeois unity was to destroy the DVP, leaving its followers with no choice except to fall in behind Hugenberg.[22] In pursuit of that aim, Brandi helped to bring about the defection to the DNVP of a major DVP regional unit in the Ruhr. He received aid in that undertaking from one of Paul Reusch's political advisers, Erich von Gilsa, who made a much-publicized move from the DVP to the DNVP.[23] Adolf Hueck, a director of the United Steel Works who had represented the DVP in the Reichstag, followed the same path, leading the local officials of the DVP in the Ruhr to conclude that the general director of that combine, Albert Vögler, also wished to see the expiration of their party.[24] The DVP proved, however, not so easy to eliminate. Still, the defections incited by its foes in the Ruhr further undermined a party badly shaken by the expulsion or resignation of some of its few remaining nationally prominent figures and weakened by the diminished flow of business contributions. As a consequence, the DVP gave the appearance of a rapidly declining, disintegrating party as the voters of Prussia went to the polls on April 24, 1932.[25]

The balloting in Prussia reduced the DVP to insignificance in the new state parliament, leaving it with only 7 of the 40 seats it had formerly held. Contrary to the expectations of the industrialists who encouraged defections from the DVP to the DNVP, the smaller party's disaffected voters did not flock in large numbers to the DNVP. That party also suffered heavy losses, salvaging only 31 of its 40 seats. Since another component of the right-of-center, the Economics Party, lost all its 21 seats, the bourgeois parties emerged from the elections as no match for the NSDAP, which had gained the support of most of the voters the others lost. By capturing 36.3 percent of the votes and increasing their representation from 6 to 162, the Nazis scored one of their greatest election triumphs. They displaced the SPD, which plummeted from 136 to 94 seats, as the strongest party in the new parliament of Germany's largest state. But because of the losses incurred by the bourgeois parties of the right, the Nazis' seats did not suffice for a coalition majority that would give rise to a *national-bürgerlich* majority government, as some of the executives of Ruhr industry had hoped. The stock market reacted calmly to the election results of the balloting in Prussia and elsewhere. The reporters of the *Frankfurter Zeitung* who covered the markets in Berlin and Frankfurt attributed this to a lack of surprise, the outcome having come close to what had been expected in light of the presidential election results.[26] That is, investors had adjusted in advance instead of being suddenly taken aback, as at the time of the 1930 Reichstag election. Nor did the results produce a political upheaval of the sort that might upset investors. Since the Catholic Center Party declined to desert its long-standing partnership with the Social Democrats in Prussia to join in forming a new right-center majority, the old cabinet headed by Social Democrat Otto Braun, now backed by only a minority of the deputies, remained in office. And despite their gains at the polls in the other states, the Nazis managed to gain entry into the government only in the small state of Anhalt.

Almost all the politically active leaders of big business had wished to strengthen the bourgeois forces in the Prussian election, yet they ended by contributing in numerous ways to the debility of that portion of the political spectrum. All indications are that the parties of the traditional right, including the DNVP, labored under severe financial handicaps in attempting to mount their campaigns. Like most voluntary organizations, they found it increasingly difficult to raise funds in a time of economic depression. By holding back their customary contributions, because of their own disagreements, until shortly before the election and then giving at a reduced level, the men of the Ruhrlade added to those handicaps. So did those, like Siemens, who withdrew from political involvement altogether. The particularly acute financial deprivation of the DVP, along with the partial disintegration of that party deliberately fostered by political activists in Ruhr industry, further sapped the strength of the bourgeois camp. To be sure, additional money and organizational support by politically active industrial executives would hardly have sufficed to reverse altogether the declining political fortunes of the increasingly discredited parties of the traditional right. But more support from big business might have enabled those parties to make at least a somewhat stronger showing in the battle of posters, pamphlets, and rallies that preceded the balloting in Prussia on April 24, 1932.

As the events of the spring of 1932 revealed, the long-standing dependence of Germany's bourgeois parties on financial contributions from big business began to assume the proportions of a deadly liability. Having become accustomed to receiving handsome subsidies regularly and predictably from that quarter during the Republic's years of stability and prosperity, the leaders of the traditional parties of the middle and right found themselves without adequate alternative sources of funds when economic depression and political upheaval greatly reduced the flow of subsidies from big business. Because of the easy availability of those contributions in the past, they had taken no effective steps to broaden their parties' memberships or even to collect regular dues from those who became members.[27] Nor did they engage extensively in other methods of raising money, such as charging for admission to rallies and launching sustained solicitation campaigns using volunteer personnel. Hugenberg's press and film empire, which he used to generate funds for the DNVP, represented something of an exception. But its yield, too, diminished with the onset of depression, so that it proved no substitute for grass-roots fund raising.[28] Altogether, the bourgeois parties were woefully unequipped to adjust to a sudden diminution of big-business subsidies. Those parties had become accustomed to a plentiful downward flow of funds, whereas their new and potent adversary, the NSDAP, had perfected an upward flow from the grass roots that enabled it to outspend them by far. The Nazis could now count among their assets the deepening financial woes of the traditional parties, which were in part caused by the shortsightedness, stubbornness, and lack of political acumen of some leading figures of German big business.

Little more than a month after the unsettling outcome of the Prussian election, German politics received an even greater jolt when Brüning suddenly resigned at the end of May, having lost the confidence of President Hindenburg. That news had hardly reached print when Communists and trade unionists charged that industrial interests had conspired with other reactionary elements to poison the president's mind against the chancellor.[29] During the subsequent half century, however, no evidence substantiating that charge has come to light. In the well-documented record of the immediate events leading to Brüning's fall, big business does not figure directly.[30] Rather, Brüning's resignation came as the culmination of a progressive estrangement between the chancellor and Hindenburg, who had become increasingly disappointed at Brüning's failure to make good on promises to shift the basis of his cabinet to the right. The breach between the two widened when the cabinet imposed a ban on Nazi storm troopers but not on leftist para-military organizations, a step that provoked indignant protests from conservative and military circles close to the president. Particularly damaging was the desertion of Brüning by the man who had much to do with obtaining the chancellorship for him, General Kurt von Schleicher. Convinced that the SA ban would obstruct the army's efforts to mobilize rightist paramilitary organizations as part of its effort to expand Germany's military strength, Schleicher turned against both the chancellor and his defense minister, General Wilhelm Groener. The cabinet aroused still further opposition when it announced a plan to foreclose on hopelessly indebted landed estates in eastern Germany and divide them up in order to turn farms over to settlers as a means of combating mass unemployment. That plan, which called forth accusations of "agrarian Bolshevism" against Brüning from eastern agrarians and others who enjoyed access to Hindenburg, sealed the fate of the cabinet.

This is not to say that Germany's capitalists played no part at all in Brüning's fall. Although they did not participate directly in the chancellor's ouster, a rising chorus of protests from the business community against the economic policies of his cabinet contributed to the general deterioration of Brüning's position. Despite attempts at restraint by the leadership of the industrial Reichsverband, Ruhr industrial circles in particular became increasingly vocal and open in their criticism of the cabinet during the spring of 1932.[31] The coal, iron, and steel industries ranked among the sectors of the economy most heavily damaged by the depression. By 1932 bituminous coal production sank to a level 36.6 percent below that of 1929; the decline in pig iron output for the same period came to 76 percent, that in iron and steel to 65 percent.[32] Although cartelized pricing policies partially shielded these industries from the impact of contracting demand by enabling them to prevent prices from falling rapidly, they experienced their worst slump ever. As their losses mounted ominously, the market value of their stocks sank to hitherto unimagined lows. Not surprisingly, their executives and associational spokesmen became ever more critical of a government that seemed incapable of stemming the decline. The chancellor nevertheless held resolutely to his course of conciliating the SPD and the trade unions and failed to respond to demands for a fundamental revision of his position on economic and social issues along the lines proposed by the business community. Indeed, his cabinet showed what appeared to be a readiness for still further concessions to labor. In mid-April Brüning's labor minister, Adam Stegerwald, also a Catholic Centrist, publicly endorsed trade union demands for a reduction of the industrial workweek from forty-eight to forty hours as a means of spreading available jobs among more workers.[33] That proposal, which would have given rise to a significant labor cost increase in around-the-clock industries by necessitating a changeover from the prevailing two-shift system to a three-shift system, added to the unrest in industrial circles.[34] Stegerwald's proposal seems to have figured as well in the decision of Economics Minister Hermann Warmbold to resign in late April. Although Warmbold, an agronomist, could not accurately be characterized as a spokesman of the business community, and appears to have resigned quite on his own for a complex set of reasons, his having held a post with IG Farben unavoidably made his departure appear as part of a growing big business rejection of Brüning.[35] Warmbold's withdrawal did not suffice to bring down the cabinet, but it hardly strengthened Brüning's position. The same held true of the increasingly unrestrained attacks on his cabinet in the business press.[36] Brüning's estrangement from Hindenburg thus occurred in a context of mounting discontent on the part of the business community that could only weaken the chancellor's position and strengthen that of the men who finally prevailed on the president to drop him.

Even if Brüning's big business critics had wished to intercede with President Hindenburg to turn him against his chancellor, as leftist journalists alleged they did, they were in no position to do so. There existed, of course, the possibility of submitting a memorandum to the president or seeking an audience with him, but both these avenues of approach had been repeatedly used in the past and had yielded disappointing results. When Ruhr industrialist Paul Reusch proposed in September 1931 that industrial spokesmen meet with the president to explain their grievances, Ludwig Kastl, the veteran executive director of the industrial Reichsverband, discouraged the idea. "Experience has shown," he explained to Reusch, "that such presentations to the Reich president do not achieve much." Kastl then went on to express to Reusch his belief that an attempt to enlist Hindenburg in the cause of *die Wirtschaft* would amount to wasted effort.[37] The situation might have been different if the business community had been able to make use of the sort of informal, unofficial channels of influence that played such a crucial role in shaping the president's attitudes in his later years. But the spokesmen of big business had no such avenue of influence at their disposal. Not a single businessman could command the sort of informal access to the presidential ear enjoyed by numerous military men and agrarian spokesmen. That held true even of the aristocratic chairman of the industrial Reichsverband, Gustav Krupp von Bohlen und Halbach. Krupp's background had enabled him to host the newly elected Hindenburg at a large banquet held in his honor in 1925 at the family palace, the Villa Hügel, outside Essen.[38] But Hindenburg remained remote even for a Krupp. A few days after Brüning's fall and his replacement by Franz von Papen, Krupp von Bohlen expressed his displeasure at the turn of political events to a senior staff member of the Reichsverband in a letter written from the Austrian resort to which he had repaired the previous week. Krupp added that he had considered postponing his vacation because of the cabinet crisis but had decided against that. "After all," wrote the best-known industrialist of Germany and head of the paramount association of big business, "it would hardly have been possible for me to intervene in the course of events."[39]

The appointment of the obscure Papen as chancellor came as just as much a surprise to even the best-informed leaders of big business as it did to the rest of Germany.[40] As with the installation of Brüning two years earlier, the military, again in the person of Schleicher, had chosen the new head of government. Papen was not, however, quite as un-known in big business circles as he was in the country at large. Some businessmen knew him socially as a result of his marriage to the daughter of a prominent Saarland manufacturer of earthenware and porcelain products. Others had met him at the exclusive Berlin Herrenklub, which he regularly frequented. Papen's political career as a right-wing Center Party deputy in the Prussian state parliament had brought him to the attention of still other members of the business community, although he was linked mainly with Catholic agrarian interests. So had his position, since 1925, as chairman of the supervisory board of the Catholic newspaper *Germania*. Papen had initially acquired that position with financial aid from aristocratic Catholic agrarians, but when *Germania,* like so many papers, began to incur deficits during the depression, the Ruhrlade extended Papen a monthly subvention of 1,000 marks to offset its losses.[41] Some men of big business thus knew Franz von Papen and were favorably inclined toward him because of his conservative outlook. But none regarded that elegant, yet also shallow and frivolous political dilettante as a serious contender for high office. His appointment as chancellor initially produced considerable unease in business circles, particularly because of the fear among industrialists that he would give into organized agriculture's demands for tariffs on foodstuffs so prohibitively high as to provoke retaliation abroad against German industrial exports. That unease increased when Papen chose to make his first speech as chancellor before a gathering of agrarians and to speak in conciliatory fashion about the plight of agriculture while criticizing the "errors of the capitalist system."[42]

The early actions and proclamations of the Papen cabinet dispelled some of that unease. The non-party composition of the cabinet, underlined by the Center Party's angry expulsion of Papen for accepting the chancellorship without obtaining the consent of its leadership, held out promise of a government free of that dependence on politicians and parliamentary support to which so many big business spokesmen attributed what they saw as the failings of the Brüning cabinet. Also, in announcing Papen's appointment, Hindenburg had called on him to form a "government of national concentration." In the context of the time, those words strongly suggested an intent to bring behind the cabinet the groups that had proclaimed themselves as the "national opposition" at Bad Harzburg the previous autumn. Such an arrangement still held great appeal for political right-wingers within the business community. It would exclude the SPD and the trade unions from any influence on government policy. It also held out the prospect of luring the NSDAP out of its radical oppositional stance and placing it under the tutelage of economically reliable bourgeois elements, thereby undercutting the "socialist" wing of Nazism. Papen certainly seemed determined to win the support of the Nazis. Soon after taking office he met two of their most insistent demands by lifting the ban placed on the SA by the Brüning cabinet and by agreeing to a dissolution of the Reichstag so that a new national election could take place at the end of July. He also exerted pressure on the Center and DNVP delegations in the Prussian state parliament to reach agreement on a coalition government there with the greatly strengthened NSDAP delegation. The "national opposition" of Bad Harzburg seemed in June 1932 well on the way to becoming the kind of "national government" so much of big business longed for.

In other respects, too, the new cabinet heartened political right-wingers in the business community. Papen's interior minister, the reactionary Baron von Gayl, lost no time in making clear the cabinet's intention to revise the Weimar constitution. Since neither he nor the chancellor concealed their dislike of parliamentary democracy, the direction of such a revision seemed clear, even if Gayl refused to elaborate on his intentions. Two weeks after taking office the cabinet issued an emergency decree that went a considerable way toward meeting business criticism of republican *Sozialpolitik*.[43] Abandoning Brüning's plans to cover the growing deficit of the unemployment insurance fund by coupling modest cuts in benefits with government subsidies raised in part by means of a new income tax, the Papen cabinet further reduced the benefits of the jobless. In addition to reintroducing a means test for unemployment insurance, the cabinet cut the rates of aid as much as a quarter to a half of the levels prescribed by the 1927 law that had established unemployment insurance.[44] In place of the proposed income tax, the new cabinet raised the rates of indirect taxes that burdened primarily lower-income groups. Although the cabinet took no steps to rescind the legislative bases of the state system of compulsory arbitration of labor-management disputes that had so long attracted the ire of industry, Papen's labor minister effectively made it a dead letter by simply not using it. The cabinet's most dramatic step came, however, on July 20, when Papen issued a presidential emergency decree deposing the Braun cabinet in Prussia and giving the chancellor authority over the state government. "Marxist" rule in the largest federal state, that rankling remnant of Weimar's decade of parliamentary democracy, at last came to an end at the hands of the new "government of national concentration." As the Reichstag election of July 31 approached, the business leaders of Germany had reason to feel well disposed toward the Papen cabinet even though it had not yet clarified its positions on many of the pressing economic questions that preoccupied them.

During the summer Reichstag campaign the behavior of those components of the business community that had in the past made sizeable political contributions followed much the same pattern as at the time of the Prussian state election. As in the spring, financial strictures, disillusionment with politics, and disagreements about how best to strengthen the bourgeois forces curtailed the flow of funds from big business to the parties it had traditionally underwritten. Siemens again abstained altogether, and the great Berlin banks, still suffering from the aftereffects of the shattering banking crisis of the previous year, proved no more forthcoming than they had been during the Prussian campaign.[45] In general, the incentive to contribute suffered from the increasingly questionable importance of political parties in the face of the new cabinet's expressed resolve to govern without regard to parliamentary opinion. Those who wanted to buttress the position of the new government faced an additional dilemma since none of the parties—not even the DNVP—aligned itself fully with the Papen cabinet, and since the cabinet did not endorse any of the parties. In hopes of strengthening the bourgeois forces in case a national front including the Nazis emerged from the election, Paul Reusch and other prominent figures in the Ruhr, as well as IG Farben executives, revived the project of amalgamating the traditional parties of the right and right-center into a united bourgeois party. As the leader of such a broad new organization Reusch and others had in mind Carl Goerdeler, the DNVP mayor of Leipzig and Reich price commissar since December 1931, who later played a prominent role in the conservative anti-Nazi conspiracies during the Third Reich. But again Hugenberg stymied all efforts at bourgeois unity by refusing to relinquish the chairmanship of the DNVP.[46] His obduracy revived the frictions within the Ruhrlade that had paralyzed it politically for most of the Prussian campaign, as Reusch and those who sided with him declined to authorize any contributions to the DNVP as long as Hugenberg stood at its head.

As the result of still another divisive issue, the Ruhrlade remained completely immobile politically during most of the Reichstag campaign. That issue arose when the press suddenly disclosed in June that the Brüning cabinet had secretly purchased from the financier-industrialist Friedrich Flick a majority of the stock in the Gelsenkirchen mining firm at an inflated price. Because of a complex holding-company arrangement, possession of that block of stock by the Reich carried with it a controlling interest in the country's largest producer of iron and steel, the United Steel Works. When they learned of the Gelsenkirchen transaction, Paul Reusch and Fritz Springorum, the leaders of the Ruhrlade, angrily denounced it as a dangerous step in the direction of state socialism. By consenting to the sale of a controlling interest in United Steel to the Reich, its executives had, they implied, betrayed the cause of private enterprise. Since three of the top executives of United Steel, Ernst Poensgen, Fritz Thyssen, and Albert Vögler belonged to the Ruhrlade, these charges gave rise to considerable tension among its members, with the result that by the summer that group ceased to meet regularly.[47] Capitalizing, as during the spring, on the paralysis of the Ruhrlade, Brandi and Loewenstein of the Bergbauverein again took over disbursement of the coal operators' political money, which the Ruhrlade had formerly allocated. As loyal Hugenberg men, they directed funds toward his DNVP, excluding the DVP in line with Brandi's strategy for unifying the right.[48] They also reportedly diverted some funds to the NSDAP, a matter which will be dealt with below.

The diminished flow of subsidies from big business produced a grave financial crisis within the DVP. Brandi's strategy of starving that party into extinction spread throughout the industrial regions of western Germany, as the national headquarters learned from increasingly despairing party officials there. Repeatedly, firms that had formerly contributed regularly to the DVP made it known to that party's representatives that their money would now go only to the DNVP.[49] The finances of DVP organizations in the Ruhr became increasingly desperate. In the electoral district of Southern Westphalia the party's one full-time paid official had to be let go in the midst of the campaign because no money could be found to pay his salary.[50] Similar conditions developed in areas such as Braunschweig, where the defection of lesser businessmen to Nazism handicapped the party.[51] The DVP's election campaign suffered accordingly. Lacking money to print sufficient leaflets for the Reichstag campaign, the party resorted to distributing pro-Hindenburg literature left over from the presidential election.[52]

As the election day of July 31 approached, the chairman of the foundering DVP, Eduard Dingeldey, desperately appealed for help to General Schleicher, now Papen's minister of defense.[53] Schleicher apparently feared that a collapse of the DVP would drive many of that party's former voters to the NSDAP, thus strengthening the Nazis' hand in the negotiations with the Papen cabinet that would have to take place after the election. In hopes of shoring up the position of the cabinet he had played such a large role in creating, the general intervened in the finances of the campaign. Through the intermediacy of a personal acquaintance, the Cologne iron merchant Otto Wolff, Schleicher asked Albert Vögler for a quarter of a million marks for the purpose of producing an election outcome favorable to the Papen cabinet. Vögler responded by bringing the men of the Ruhrlade to meet Schleicher's request with the political funds of the iron and steel industry that had been frozen because of the continuing paralysis of that dissension-ridden organization.[54] Schleicher promptly gave 200,000 marks of that money to the DVP and 50,000 to the DNVP.[55] Three days later, on July 28, the general responded to renewed appeals for aid from Dingeldey by obtaining another 110,000 marks from Vögler, again via Otto Wolff.[56] As these developments reveal, the big business community's system for financing the bourgeois parties of Weimar faltered badly, for a variety of reasons, at the time of the July Reichstag election of 1932. For the first time, intervention from the side of the government proved necessary to produce anything approaching an adequate flow of funds to parties that had hitherto received regular subsidies from the politically active components of the business community.

The eleventh-hour infusion of funds brokered by Schleicher proved inadequate to rescue the two chief bourgeois parties of the right from damaging losses in the national balloting of July 31. The DVP suffered a devastating defeat, as more than two-thirds of its 1930 electorate deserted the party, leaving it with little more than 1 percent of the vote. Having entered the campaign as a respectable party of 30 Reichstag deputies, the DVP emerged from the election with only 7, too few to qualify even for the privileges of a recognized parliamentary delegation. The DNVP escaped with less severe losses, but its share of the vote fell below 6 percent and its seats declined from 41 to 37. With the exception of the two Catholic parties, the Center and the Bavarian People's Party, which actually increased their strength, the middle portion of the political spectrum shrank dramatically. As in 1930, the Communists scored gains on the left, while the Social Democrats again lost ground. The real victory belonged to the Nazis. They more than doubled both their votes of 1930 and their seats in the Reichstag. With 37.4 percent of the national electorate behind them and 230 of the 608 deputies in the new chamber, the NSDAP emerged as Germany's most powerful political party.

Germany's stock markets remained stable when the results of the July balloting became known. A financial reporter for the liberal *Frankfurter Zeitung* at that city's exchange attributed this to a general feeling of relief that the Nazis' gains had not been even greater. Again, as at the time of the Prussian and other state elections in April, the number of Nazi votes did not come as the sort of surprise that could trigger seismic tremors in the market. The paper's Berlin stock-exchange reporter observed a widespread belief that the outcome of the election would not disturb the continuity of government which the financial community prized above all other political considerations.[57] Investors remained sanguine about the Papen cabinet's ability to retain control of the government, even in face of the spectacular gains of the Nazis. Yet despite these expressions of confidence by the stock market, the election results made it clear that anyone seriously concerned with Germany's future would have to think seriously, if they had not already begun to do so, about the impact on the economy of the now expanded and exultant brown-shirted battalions of Adolf Hitler.

3. *Attempts at Dialogue with the Nazi Hydra*

As the National Socialist electoral juggernaut gathered momentum during 1932, a number of attempts were made to establish communications between the business community and the NSDAP. The party's remarkable successes gave rise to heightened concern among big businessmen about its policies with regard to the economy and led some to seek to exert influence on those policies. At least one prominent big businessman sought to moderate the NSDAP's position on economic issues by removing obstacles to a coalition at the state level between it and conservative bourgeois forces. Others looked for ways to protect the particular interests of their firms. For a time, encouraging signs seemed to indicate a receptivity on the part of some prominent Nazis, most notably Hitler himself, to exchanges of information and views with big business. It even seemed likely that formal channels of communication could be established. But little of consequence resulted from the various efforts undertaken in that direction. Instead, a strong drift on the part of the NSDAP toward a more pronounced radicalism led during the "year of elections" to mounting alarm about that party even among some of those men of big business who had earlier looked with favor on including the Nazis in government.

In their efforts to establish contact with the country's fastest-growing political party, spokesmen of the business community labored under a handicap since few of their number could be found in the ranks of the NSDAP. In fact, the only prominent big businessman to identify himself with the party by 1932 was Fritz Thyssen. But although he considered himself a Nazi at the latest by the fall of 1932, Thyssen failed actually to become officially a "party comrade" until 1933, after Hitler's assumption of power.[1] His uncritical adulation of Hitler and his effusiveness led, in any event, to his frequently not being taken wholly seriously by other businessmen on the subject of politics.[2] The few other big business executives who became Nazis did not rank high enough in the business community or in the party to carry much weight in either. That was the case with Wilhelm and Walter Tengelmann. Sons of a prominent Ruhr coal operator, Ernst Tengelmann, they were in their early thirties and held obscure junior positions in the coal-mining industry when they joined the NSDAP in 1930 and 1931, respectively.[3] Somewhat more senior was another Nazi mining executive, Erich Winnacker, director at age forty-three of one of United Steel's four regional coal operations in the Ruhr. Formerly a right-wing member of the DNVP, Winnacker shifted to the NSDAP in April 1932.[4] His entry into the party seems unlikely to have reflected corporate policy, however, since he defected from the DNVP just as Ernst Brandi, the most prominent and the most politically active of United Steel's coal executives, was seeking by every possible means to strengthen Hugenberg's party in preparation for the upcoming Prussian state election.[5] From all indications, Winnacker did not become a Nazi out of calculation or convenience. He seems to have been the real article, a true believer. Long a fanatic on the subject of Marxism, he not only became a "party comrade" but also joined the local SA stormtrooper unit, donned its uniform, and took part in its activities in his hometown of Hamborn, the scene of violent clashes between Nazis and Communists. Nazism took firm root in Winnacker's household. His wife, who entered the party a month earlier than did he, also become a Nazi activist, founding a branch of the Nazi women's auxiliary, the NS-

Frauenschaft, in Hamborn.[6] There are no signs that Winnacker secured the approval of his superiors at United Steel for his entry into the NSDAP or for his activities on its behalf. He remained, in any event, basically a technician, far removed from the policy-making echelon of the firm. Much the same applies to Wilhelm Rudolf Mann, the sole executive of IG Farben who joined the party before the Nazi takeover. A thirty-eight-year-old decorated veteran of the war and son of one of the founders of Farben, Mann was a sales official of the firm and a deputy member of Farben's large managing board at the time of his entry into the NSDAP in December 1931.[7] At Nuremberg after World War II he explained that he had joined the NSDAP because of his fear of Communism and his growing belief that only National Socialism represented a bulwark against it. In testimony that went unchallenged by that of other Farben officials, he further stated that he had, in his business capacity, made no mention of his party membership and doubted whether even some of his closest associates at Farben knew of it.[8] This would seem borne out by the failure of Farben's leadership to make any use of Mann in its efforts, described below, to establish contact with Hitler and other Nazis. Mann's exertions on behalf of the NSDAP seem to have been limited to a pledge of voluntary monthly dues of fifty marks, a figure he reduced by half in April 1932, citing a decline in his income.[9]

Although the NSDAP remained an unattractive personal option for most big businessmen, some went out of their way to meet the mysterious man who had led it to national importance. One such was Friedrich Flick, the upstart iron and steel magnate whose precarious financial fortunes inclined him to survey the political scene with great care as he began the negotiations with the Reich government that would lead to the controversial Gelsenkirchen transaction. Through the intermediacy of Walther Funk, whose acquaintance Flick's deputy, Otto Steinbrinck, had earlier made, Flick managed in late February 1932 to meet alone with Hitler, then on one of his increasingly frequent visits to the Kaiserhof Hotel in Berlin. According to Flick's testimony at Nuremberg in 1947, Hitler unsuccessfully appealed for his support in the upcoming campaign for the presidential election. But aside from mentioning that Hitler had done all the talking, Flick disclosed nothing more about this meeting.[10] Additional light on what happened came, however, from the testimony of Steinbrinck, who had accompanied Flick to the Kaiserhof. A submarine hero from World War I, Steinbrinck testified that he waited while Flick met with Hitler. Then, as they walked back to their Berlin offices, the former naval officer recalled, Flick told him with bemusement how Hitler had apparently confused him with Steinbrinck. The Nazi leader had explained to him at length, Flick reported, his plans for a German naval flotilla in the Baltic large enough to challenge the Polish navy. Steinbrinck remembered that Flick had come away from the encounter with Hitler puzzled and disappointed.[11] As his generous financial support of Hindenburg's presidential campaign reveals, Flick chose to give tangible expression to that disappointment.[12]

Paul Reusch, the influential Ruhr industrialist and leader of the Ruhrlade, also sought a meeting with Hitler. The mounting strength of the NSDAP filled him with concern since he feared that Nazism's socialist inclinations would become stronger as its mass appeal grew. Reusch especially dreaded the prospect of an alliance between the NSDAP and the Catholic Center Party, fearing that such a combination would impose upon the Reich a leftist government of nationalistic coloration that would bode evil for the business community.[13] By way of blocking such an alignment he sought to encourage coalitions between the Nazis and the bourgeois parties of the right at the state level. Since his firm had extensive operations in Bavaria, Reusch had over the years cultivated good relations with the Catholic and conservative Bavarian People's Party.[14] He hoped to use his influence with the leadership of that party to promote a coalition between it and the NSDAP at the state level in the aftermath of the Landtag elections scheduled in Bavaria for April 1932. That plan held out the advantage of saddling the Nazis with governmental responsibility at a time when unpopular measures were unavoidable, but without giving them access to national policy or the central organs of the Reich. The presidential election endangered Reusch's plan, however, by setting the Bavarian People's Party, which endorsed Hindenburg, against the NSDAP in an acrimonious campaign. After observing with concern the bad feeling generated by the campaigning that preceded the first round of presidential balloting, Reusch sought and obtained a private meeting with Hitler at the Brown House, the Munich headquarters of the NSDAP, six days after the initial voting.

In the course of what developed into a two-hour conversation with Hitler on March 19, Reusch succeeded in bringing up a number of matters in which he was particularly interested.[15] Disturbed about the leftward drift of the responses to ten economic policy questions published by the Nazis' parliamentary bulletin shortly after Hitler's Industry Club speech, Reusch confronted the Nazi leader with an article reprinting their text. He had let Hitler know his opinion about those responses, he informed Krupp's brother-in-law, Wilmowsky, the next day, but without mentioning Hitler's reaction. Reusch also reported afterwards having urged Hitler to rely on first-rate experts in the formulation of his policies regarding economics, as well as financial, foreign, and internal affairs. Hitler had, he recounted, agreed with him when he proposed that qualification for such tasks, rather than membership in the NSDAP, should determine the appointment of men to those posts. Reusch met with no success with his major proposal, however, which called for Hitler to withdraw his presidential candidacy in view of the virtual certainty of Hindenburg's re-election in the second round of balloting. In making that proposal, Reusch obviously hoped to avoid another round of the bruising campaign attacks and counterattacks that had already badly poisoned relations between the Nazis and the Bavarian People's Party. Hitler proved unresponsive to Reusch's plea, leaving no doubt about his determination to continue to bid for the presidency. In hopes of at least dampening the campaign invective, in order to facilitate an eventual coalition between the NSDAP and the Bavarian People's Party, Reusch then secured what he took for Hitler's assent to an agreement.[16] In return for reciprocal assurances from the Nazi leader, he promised that the two major Bavarian newspapers over which his firm exercised financial control, the capital city's *Münchner Neueste Nachrichten* and the *Fränkischer Kurier* of Nuremberg, would desist from any personal attacks on Hitler. As a further earnest of his goodwill, Reusch promptly instructed the editor of the *Fränkischer Kurier*, who with his permission had endorsed Hindenburg before the first round of balloting, to maintain strict neutrality prior to the second round.[17]

Like virtually everyone who attempted to enter into bargains with Adolf Hitler, Reusch ended up decidedly on the short end of the one he believed to have struck on March 19, 1932. Whereas he imposed tight constraints on the papers owned by his firm, the Nazi press continued to indulge in its customary vituperative attacks on everyone who stood between Hitler and power, including Hindenburg and the leaders of the Bavarian People's Party. When confronted with these Nazi violations of his agreement with Hitler, Reusch naively protested to Hitler's deputy, Rudolf Hess. In keeping with their usual tactics, the Nazis countered with charges against his firm's newspapers. As evidence of violation of the agreement by the editors of the *Münchner Neueste Nachrichten*, the Nazis angrily cited that paper's publication of direct quotations from articles in the *Völkischer Beobachter*, including some in which various Nazis had in earlier years praised Hindenburg and sworn their loyalty to him.[18] Reusch nevertheless held to his side of the agreement, forcing his firm's papers to maintain neutrality during the campaigns for the second phase of the presidential balloting and for the Bavarian state election of April 24. Even when the results of the latter election failed to produce a coalition between the NSDAP and the Bavarian People's Party, he refused to abandon hope that such an arrangement could eventually be reached. The editors of the *Münchner Neueste Nachrichten*, who had chafed under Reusch's directives, finally rebelled against them in June. Unable to run the paper himself and unwilling to take on the task of restaffing the entire editorial board, Reusch gave up in frustration and resigned from the paper's administrative board.[19] The venture he had launched with such high hopes at the time of his meeting with Hitler on March 19 thus ended in virtually complete failure from his standpoint. Hitler, by contrast, had managed to muzzle support for Hindenburg and criticism of his own fitness for the presidency in two influential Bavarian dailies without surrendering anything more than empty assurances in return. With one lie he had duped Germany's politically best-informed and most influential industrialist, who had made the mistake of attempting to play the game at which Adolf Hitler excelled: power politics.

The day after his meeting with Hitler, Reusch received a proposal that held out the prospect of sustained big business influence on the economic policy makers of the NSDAP. It came from Hjalmar Schacht, the former Reichsbank president who had aligned himself with the "national opposition" at Bad Harzburg. In his quest for a return to high office, Schacht had begun during 1931 to cultivate Hitler and other top Nazis by offering them advice on the political and economic situation.[20] In March 1932 Schacht wrote to Reusch that the results of the first presidential ballot a week earlier had demonstrated the growing strength of the rightward movement in German politics and the important role of the Nazis in that movement.[21] This raised with renewed urgency, Schacht continued, the problem of the NSDAP's economic policy. Since little hope remained that Hugenberg would be able to dissuade the Nazis from foolishness in that regard, he believed the time had come for the business community to steer the economic outlook of National Socialism in a "reasonable direction." He therefore proposed hiring, for an initial period of two years, a politically experienced man who commanded his confidence. That man would establish contact with Hitler's economic policy organization in order to work through the problems at hand in such fashion as to produce a program for the NSDAP which industry and commerce would find acceptable. Success seemed to him possible, Schacht added, but even in its absence the business community would gain a clearer view of matters. As the cost of such an arrangement, Schacht projected a modest yearly honorarium of 12,000 marks for the man he had in mind, plus 3,000 marks annual expenses for an office. As those figures reveal, he had in mind only a part-time post. Schacht indicated his readiness to bear 10 percent of the cost himself and asked Reusch whether he believed the rest could be raised. Reusch responded enthusiastically in the affirmative to Schacht's proposal.[22] He also interested several other members of the Ruhrlade in Schacht's plans for such an "office," or Arbeitsstelle.[23] Moreover, Schacht soon obtained what he took for encouragement from Hitler for his project.[24]

Despite this promising beginning, Schacht, like Reusch, fell prey to Hitler's duplicity. Unbeknownst to him or to Reusch and the men of the Ruhrlade, the Nazi leader had authorized the establishment of an advisory group of businessmen from the side of the NSDAP at about the same time Schacht launched his undertaking. The man commissioned by Hitler with the formation of that group was Wilhelm Keppler, one of the lesser businessmen attracted to Nazism in the late 1920s and a loyal "party comrade" ever since. After playing a significant part in National Socialism's penetration of his region of northern Baden, Keppler was summoned to Munich in late 1931 by Hitler.[25] According to Keppler's testimony at Nuremberg, Hitler confided to him his dissatisfaction with the NSDAP's economic policies. He attached no sanctity, Hitler explained, to the twenty-five-point program of 1920, which he had declared unalterable in 1926. He also lacked confidence in the advice he received on economic issues from such Nazis as Gregor Strasser, Gottfried Feder, and Otto Wagener.[26] Hitler expressed concern that their talk of socialism would upset businessmen and inhibit the restoration of business confidence essential for recovery when the Nazis came to power. Economic policy should not be subordinated to political considerations, Keppler remembered Hitler's saying, but must instead be shaped solely in line with economic rationality. The state should leave the economy alone as much as possible, intervening only when private initiative proved ineffective. In hopes of guiding Nazi economic policy along such lines, Hitler invited Keppler to accept a post in the Reichsleitung of the party. Keppler declined, explaining that he did not want to subject himself to the authority of the party bureaucracy. He accepted, however, when Hitler asked him to become his personal adviser on economic matters. In early 1932 Keppler sold his business interests and moved to Munich to devote himself full-time to his new responsibilities.

At Hitler's instruction, Keppler began to contact businessmen of his acquaintance without previous ties to the NSDAP and to sound them out on providing the party with economic guidance. His task, Keppler later explained, was to act as emissary to a business community "very skeptical" about National Socialism.[27] At the end of April Keppler met with Hitler to report that the responses to his soundings had been favorable.[28] He proposed formalizing the contacts he had made by establishing a standing body of businessmen-advisers under his leadership. Hitler at once accepted this plan and, noting that Schacht had recently approached him in a similar vein, suggested that Keppler include the former president of the Reichsbank in his advisory group. At another meeting with Hitler, on May 14, Keppler received assurances that he need not concern himself with economic theories generated in the Brown House. Hitler stood ready, Keppler later reported him saying, to suppress publications emanating from Otto Wagener's Economic Policy Section of the NSDAP.[29] Keppler thus had good reason to believe that he and his group would be in charge of shaping the party's economic policies. Sometime also in the middle of May, Hjalmar Schacht, still under the impression that he had staked out for himself the role of emissary between big business and the NSDAP, as well as that of economic adviser to Hitler, received what must have been a most unpleasant surprise when the Nazi Wilhelm Keppler invited him to become a member of an economic advisory group which Keppler, with personal authorization from Hitler, was forming.[30]

During the ensuing month a quiet struggle took place between Keppler and Schacht for preeminence in establishing formal relations between the Nazis and the business community. Schacht at first responded noncommittally to Keppler's invitation to join what soon became known as the Keppler circle.[31] Then, late in May, he in effect declined that invitation in a letter to Keppler. He had decided, Schacht announced, to press on with his plans to establish an independent "office," but he stood ready to cooperate with Keppler, an arrangement he reported Hitler had found satisfactory.[32] In the meantime Keppler had begun undermining Schacht's position. Since Keppler's pilgrimage to the business community had led him to two of the men who had pledged money for Schacht's project, the potash industrialist August Rosterg and Cologne banker Kurt von Schröder, he sought to convince them that Schacht's project would be inadequate. Keppler argued that Schacht had chosen his associates not for their brains but for their pocketbooks. The interests of the business community would be better served, he contended, by a broader-based group of the sort he was assembling, one that would extend beyond industry and banking into agriculture and even to consumer cooperatives.[33]

Keppler quickly won out over Schacht. He had help in this from Hitler, who in a letter written in late May informed Schacht that he expected him to work together with Keppler and his associates.[34] Hitler also began letting it be known throughout the party that he had commissioned Keppler with establishing contact with the business community and gaining its advice on economic questions.[35] Schacht tried, even after receiving Hitler's letter, to remain independent of Keppler's undertaking, proposing merely to maintain communication with it.[36] But in early June Schacht capitulated, agreeing to become a member of the Keppler circle.[37] He kept alive the preparations for his own Arbeitsstelle, but a subtle change took place in its stated mission. Whereas Schacht had originally held out the prospect of exerting influence on Nazi economic policy, he now informed Reusch that the Schacht Arbeitsstelle would maintain contact with two men commissioned by Adolf Hitler, Keppler and his assistant. The Arbeitsstelle would seek, he explained, to make sure that the views on economic policy it generated would remain in harmony with the positions of the NSDAP.[38] In pursuit of his own ambitions, Schacht was plainly prepared to convert what he had projected as an instrument for influencing Nazi economic policy into an adjunct of the Nazi-led Keppler circle. But the latter group went its own way, so that Schacht's Arbeitsstelle failed to play even that role. The financial journalist he hired to man his Arbeitsstelle, Carl Krämer, languished in isolation in his small Berlin quarters, turning out an occasional recondite position paper on a technical economic problem for the edification of the subscribers who had underwritten his honorarium and expenses.[39] By December 1932 one prominent subscriber, Krupp von Bohlen, wondered why Schacht should send him a paper on state import monopolies via an office in Berlin presided over by someone named Krämer.[40] Because of the victory scored by the Nazi Keppler over Schacht, the latter's "office" remained essentially stillborn, along with the hopes he had aroused in the business community of shaping the economic policy of the NSDAP.

There remained the Nazi-inspired Keppler circle. Its composition reflected the shape of German big business even less than did the backers of Schacht's project. At its inception in June 1932 it consisted of an odd assortment of men whose selection reveals no plan and little freedom of choice. Aside from Schacht, whom Hitler had specified to Keppler, the membership of the circle seems to have been shaped by Keppler's success in exploiting his own personal and business ties, plus those of some of the men he enlisted. Keppler labored under a handicap in that undertaking since he himself did not carry much weight. His role in the management of two small chemical factories operated by relatives of his in a provincial town in southwestern Germany had won him no recognition in big business circles. Initially, a man like Schacht could not take him seriously and assumed that one of the somewhat better-known members of the circle must actually be in charge.[41] But in his business career Keppler had formed some acquaintanceships which he now exploited. He had met the banker Kurt von Schröder a year or so earlier, for example, in the course of unsuccessful efforts to borrow money for a business venture, which took him first to a partner in a small private banking house in Hamburg and, through him, to Schröder.[42] The same Hamburg banker introduced Keppler in the spring of 1932 to Emil Helfferich, younger brother of the late imperial treasury secretary and DNVP politician Karl Helfferich. Having recently returned from many years as a plantation manager in the Dutch East Indies, Helfferich had no firm commitments and eagerly responded to Keppler's invitation to join his circle.[43] Helfferich then served as intermediary between Keppler and two Hamburg merchants who promptly joined the circle, Karl Vincent Krogmann, who became the Nazi mayor of Hamburg in 1933, and Franz Heinrich Witthoeft.[44] Helfferich also won for the group Friedrich Reinhart, a director of the Commerz- und Privatbank of Berlin, who had known his older brother.[45] Keppler himself recruited an executive of the Siemens electrical equipment firm, Rudolf Bingel, whom he had apparently come to know during Bingel's long employment at a small Siemens branch plant located in Baden, near the town where Keppler worked.[46] By means of other contacts that remain unclear, Keppler enlisted Count Gottfried von Bismarck as a spokesman of agriculture, as well as the two most notable industrial members of the original circle, the potash executive August Rosterg and Ewald Hecker, president of the chamber of industry and commerce of Hanover and chairman of the managing board of the Ilseder Hütte, a medium-size iron and steel firm in Lower Saxony. Keppler further augmented the group by adding his cousin, Emil Meyer, a lawyer who served as an expert on consumer cooperatives for the Dresdner Bank in Berlin.[47] His efforts to recruit spokesmen from the front ranks of industry failed. For a time the potash executive Rosterg held out the prospect that Reusch, whom he informed about the group, would join, but the leader of the Ruhrlade did not.[48] In mid-June Schröder informed Keppler that Albert Vögler, with whom he sat on the supervisory board of an industrial firm, had joined, but there is no trace of Vögler's ever having attended any of the circle's conferences.[49] Ruhr industry, as well as the chemical and textile industries, thus remained without representation in the Keppler circle as it was originally constituted in the spring of 1932.

The circle recruited by Keppler did not amount to an imposing array of big business talent. Only two members, Rosterg and Schacht, enjoyed widespread recognition in the business establishment. But even they stood outside the inner circles of big business. Schacht had made his name as a government official and had played no active role in business after resigning as president of the Reichsbank. Rosterg ranked among the most important men in potash mining and processing, but that industry's dispersed operations and strong ties to agriculture made it something of an anomaly that did not fit into any of the major regional or sectoral organizations of German industry. Rosterg, who had his headquarters in the provincial city of Kassel, had become widely known mainly through his writings on economic affairs, which he published in such business organs as the *Deutsche Bergwerks-Zeitung*.[50] The only other industrialists in the circle, Hecker and Bingel, belonged, respectively, to the second and third echelons of big business. Hecker, a former professional officer in the imperial army, owed his position to his marriage into the Meyer family that had controlled the Ilseder Hütte since the 1860s and continued to dominate it even after Hecker's nominal advancement to the head of its management in 1929. His election as president of the Hanover chamber of commerce and industry in 1931 reflected only regional recognition, as the predominantly small-scale industry around Hanover remained outside the Berlin-Ruhr-Rhineland axis that dominated the big business establishment.[51] Bingel, a fifty-year-old engineer who managed several of the Siemens firm's branches, had no standing among the prominent figures of big business.[52] None of the three members of the circle from Hamburg, Emil Helfferich and the merchants Krogmann and Witthoeft, qualified as big businessmen.[53] Helfferich could, however, trade on the name of his more famous and important older brother, whom many in big business circles still revered.[54] Of the bankers in the circle, not counting Schacht, Keppler's cousin Emil Meyer was an obscure financial expert, while Friedrich Reinhart had gained some attention in business circles because of his participation in public debate.[55] Reinhart also sat on the boards of numerous small industrial and mining firms in central Germany, Saxony, and Silesia, but not in the Ruhr or Rhineland.[56] The third banker in the circle, Kurt von Schröder, receives prominent mention in most accounts of Hitler's rise to power. Schröder was to become well known, however, only *because* of having joined the Keppler circle. As a measure of his obscurity, one looks in vain for his name in an authoritative directory of 13,000 business and financial executives that appeared in 1929. At the time of his entry into the circle he ranked no better than as one of several partners in a medium-sized, regional, private banking house specializing in just the sort of international financial transactions against which the Nazis railed.[57] Not even a well-informed businessman such as Paul Reusch could be expected to know who he was.[58]

The Keppler circle got off to a rousing start. On June 20, 1932, its members assembled for the first time at the Hotel Kaiserhof in Berlin, where they met Adolf Hitler himself.[59] Three of the members of the circle present at the Kaiserhof later gave substantially the same account of what Hitler said to the group.[60] After thanking them for agreeing to join, he explained his conception of their group's role. The NSDAP, he announced, would soon be assuming power in Germany. When it did he would need the help of men who understood the economy. He understood politics, Hitler said, but not economics. The group's task would therefore lie in providing him with guidance in economic matters while he took care of political matters, with which Keppler and his circle need not concern themselves. Nor need they concern themselves with previous economic policy pronouncements of the NSDAP. The economy must serve the *Volk*, rather than the other way around, but otherwise the group should base its recommendations solely on economic necessities and considerations of effectiveness, particularly in dealing with the pressing problem of unemployment. "I am not doctrinaire," Emil Helfferich later recalled Hitler's having said.[61] Keppler remembered the party leader's telling the group that he intended to abolish the trade unions and all other parties when he assumed power.[62] But the others who gave firsthand accounts of the gathering at the Kaiserhof after the war recalled no such remarks. Schröder, under interrogation at Nuremberg, explicitly denied having heard Hitler speak about suppressing either trade unions or other parties.[63] Nor does it seem likely that Hitler took any such stand, for if he had, it would have amounted to news so sensational that it would scarcely have remained limited to the variegated group of non-Nazis who comprised the Keppler circle; it would instead have quickly swept through the business community. When at length Hitler had finished speaking, Schacht—who after the war denied ever having had anything whatever to do with the circle—closed the meeting with a reply to the Nazi leader which Helfferich later characterized as a "eulogy."[64]

From all accounts Hitler's talk captivated all those present. To their surprise, the rabble-rousing demagogue appeared moderate, understanding, even modest. Keppler later recalled general skepticism about Hitler's ability to impose on the NSDAP, or a government including it, the views about relations between economics and politics he had expressed to them.[65] Nevertheless, testimony of those present leaves no doubt that the group clearly came away excited at having been received in such a manner by the leader of Germany's most dynamic political movement. So far as they could determine, Hitler had in effect asked them—non-Nazis with the exception of Keppler—to prepare economic policies for the eventuality of his capturing power. Through Keppler, whom they had been led to regard as Hitler's chief economic adviser, they now enjoyed direct access to one of the most powerful men in Germany. They eagerly grasped, as Schröder later recalled, at an opportunity to counter the "wild ideas" of Nazi economic theorists like Gottfried Feder.[66] By way of launching their undertaking, the members of the Study Committee for Economic Questions—as the group briefly called itself—divided into three subcommittees for finance, industry, and overall economic policy.[67]

Despite this enthusiastic launching, the Keppler circle soon lost its impetus. Merely assembling the members for meetings proved a chronic problem. Except for Schacht and Helfferich, all of the original group held responsible positions that kept them on tight schedules and made it inconvenient for them to travel from northern Germany to meet with Keppler in Munich. The same was true of a new member added during the summer or early autumn, Otto Steinbrinck, the submarine hero and assistant to the iron and steel industrialist Friedrich Flick.[68] Keppler eased the logistics problem somewhat by moving to Berlin in mid-September, but scheduling meetings still remained a problem.[69] The group also suffered from a lack of staff since it was not an official part of the NSDAP.[70] After formation of the circle, Keppler continued to operate as a personal adviser to Hitler and had to rely solely on the assistance of a nephew, Fritz Kranefuss.[71] As he had in Munich, Keppler maintained no office but operated out of his home following his move to Berlin.[72]

Even more serious difficulties arose when the circle began to address concrete economic issues. As Keppler later recalled, much disagreement developed, for as the members soon established, they no more saw eye to eye on many issues than did Germany's politicians.[73] Divisions began to develop almost at once on such matters as trade policy, monetary policy, and countercyclical, deficit spending. Not surprisingly, those members of the circle active in export-oriented industry and foreign commerce opposed agrarian demands for restrictions on the import of foodstuffs.[74] Those who favored Keppler's pet scheme for devaluing the mark met with resistance from the banker Reinhart.[75] Schacht, who rarely if ever attended the group's meetings, dragged his feet on deficit-spending pump-priming projects, complaining that too much money was already in circulation.[76] Reinhart objected to government make-work projects. The state might just as well, he reportedly said, set some laborers to work for a week tearing up all the paving stones of the Leipzigerplatz, a major Berlin intersection, and then, when they had finished, set the same men to work for another week replacing all the pavingstones they had just removed.[77] Besides these differences, the group found itself divided even on the fundamental question of how best to carry out its mission. Some, led by Helfferich and Krogmann, pressed for the drafting of a new and comprehensive economic program for the NSDAP, whereas others, Keppler and Schacht most strongly, opposed any such effort to commit the party to particular policies.[78] By the fall these differences had effectively immobilized the Keppler circle. Some of its members continued to meet sporadically, but those gatherings produced, according to the memory of one participant, little more than "pure palaver, completely superficial conversation."[79] Whatever went on at its sessions, no blueprints for the economic policies of a Nazi Third Reich emerged.[80] Nor did the group exercise any influence over Nazi economic policy. It went unconsulted about the major programmatic publications of the summer and fall. Keppler, as had Reusch and Schacht, fell victim to Hitler's deceit. As the political struggle intensified during the summer and fall of 1932, the party leader seems to have lost all interest in the circle. Contrary to his assurances to Keppler in May, Hitler took no systematic measures to muzzle the other would-be economic spokesmen of the NSDAP, so that the cacophony of the party on that range of issues continued unabated. By the late summer of 1932 at least one member of the circle had begun to wonder—advisedly, as it turned out—whether Wilhelm Keppler really enjoyed the influence with Hitler that he claimed to have.[81] For its part, the industrial Reichsverband, which was seeking all possible information about National Socialism, apparently remained unaware of the circle's endeavors.[82]

The activities of the Keppler circle not only made no impact on the NSDAP but also had no discernible effect on the thinking of big business about National Socialism during the summer of 1932. The politically active prominent members of the business community seem to have remained ignorant of Hitler's talk before the group and of its members' early, heady optimism. No news of those developments reached even Paul Reusch, the big businessman with the most extensive contacts and most elaborate apparatus for gathering political information. This is not surprising in view of the remoteness of most of the circle's members from the centers of influence in big business. Schacht, the one member who enjoyed easy, direct access to men like Reusch, seems to have chosen to keep what he knew of the circle's activities to himself. In all likelihood he still remained hopeful of becoming the business community's ambassador to the NSDAP and so had no interest in publicizing the endeavors of the group formed by Keppler. Eventually the Keppler circle, or at least some of its members, would play a vital role in Hitler's rise to power. That role lay in the sphere of practical politics, however, not in that of economic policy, and it arose from a fortuitous chain of personal acquaintanceships, not from any intrinsic importance in the business community of the members involved. Still later, after the establishment of the dictatorship, Heinrich Himmler appropriated the circle as a sort of personal entourage of well-to-do persons.[83] In return for his attentions, the members in 1935 or 1936 launched into an activity quite alien to the circle's genteel deliberations under Keppler's leadership: fundraising.[84] During the latter part of 1932 the limited scope of its membership, its internal stalemates, and the indifference of the Nazi leadership toward it marked the breakdown of another attempt to establish formal communications between the business community and the NSDAP.

In the absence of any regularized channels of communication with the Nazis, most big businessmen remained uneasy about the NSDAP's economic policies as that party's strength mounted during the spring and summer of 1932. That unease became especially acute in one branch of the country's largest chemical concern, IG Farben. The fall of Chancellor Heinrich Brüning came as an unwelcome development for Farben. The firm had enjoyed good relations with Brüning's cabinet, and its chief executives had counted among the chancellor's most enthusiastic backers in the business community.[85] Untroubled by conflicts with organized labor, Farben had no objections to Brüning's reliance on the SPD for parliamentary toleration of his government. Since the firm had managed to continue making profits and declaring sizeable dividends despite the depression by dint of exporting approximately half of its production, its leadership welcomed the Brüning cabinet's resistance to demands by agrarian interests for protectionist tariffs on food imports at a level that would predictably provoke retaliation abroad against German industrial exports.[86] At the same time, Farben prevailed on the Brüning cabinet to extend tariff protection to a product in which one of its branches had made an enormous investment: synthetic gasoline.[87] In the mid-1920s predictions of an imminent exhaustion of world petroleum reserves and the availability of new technology had led Farben to launch a major project to extract gasoline from coal by adapting a hydrogenation process originally developed to produce synthetic nitrogen during World War I. That adaptation proved more difficult, more time-consuming, and far more costly than expected. Soon after the new process began yielding results, the onset of the depression and the discovery of vast new petroleum reserves threw its commercial feasibility into doubt by driving the world price of petroleum far below the cost of Farben's synthetic product. The Brüning cabinet responded by raising the German tariff on imported gasoline to a level that made it barely feasible, if still not profitable, for Farben to market its synthetic product. But by the spring of 1932 the firm faced a fundamental decision since the synthetic-gasoline project was approaching the point of no return. With more than ten million marks invested in the project, its proponents, led by one of Farben's founders, the chairman of its managing board, Carl Bosch, argued that the firm had no choice except to press on as the cost of wholly dismantling the installations built to produce synthetic gasoline would exceed that of continuing operations, even at a loss. Others, among them another of the founders of Farben, Carl Duisberg, whose interest focused primarily on its export-oriented dye and pharmaceutical operations, inclined toward writing off the synthetic-fuel project as a bad investment. In the midst of this internal struggle within Farben the calculations of the proponents of the synthetic-gasoline project were upset by the fall of Brüning and his replacement by Franz von Papen, whose cabinet held out the prospect of bringing the NSDAP into the government.

The possibility of the Nazis' imminent entry into the government greatly disturbed the leadership of Farben since the firm had long been under fire from the NSDAP. In his 1927 commentary on the Nazi program, only two years after the chemical trust's formation, Gottfried Feder had singled it out, alone among all the giant corporations of Germany, for an attack as a prime example of selfish profiteering by stockholders at the expense of the general welfare.[88] A year later the Völkischer Beobachter pilloried Farben as a tool of "money-mighty Jews" when the firm dismissed Nazi Robert Ley from his job as a chemist because of his political activities.[89] Thereafter anti-Semitic attacks on Farben became a staple of Nazi propaganda.[90] In 1931 Farben came under especially heavy fire in the Nazi press, which characterized the firm as the creation of Jewish and international financial interests while denouncing its monopolization of markets and its payment of handsome dividends at a time when it was laying off employees.[91]

In an effort to win sympathy for its synthetic-gasoline project, Farben provided tours of its major hydrogenation plant at Leuna in central Germany during early October 1931. Invitations went to journalists and all sizeable parties in the Reichstag other than the Communists, including both the SPD and the NSDAP, each of which were urged to send a deputation for a separate inspection of the plant.[92] With the legislature scheduled to reconvene in mid-October after an adjournment of six and a half months, the firm's management obviously hoped to head off parliamentary efforts to rescind Brüning's use of presidential emergency power during the spring to increase the gasoline tariff sharply. At the Leuna plant Farben officials gave the visiting journalists and politicians a firsthand look at the synthetic-gasoline process as well as a presentation of the firm's arguments for the project's desirability in terms of Germany's national interest. The Nazi response proved heartening. After the luncheon the firm customarily provided for such invited delegations, Otto Wagener, head of the Economic Policy Section of the Nazi Party's Reichsleitung, announced that supplying the German market with German gasoline accorded fully with the aims of National Socialism.[93] In the following months, however, the Nazi press gave Farben's executives cause to question the authoritativeness of Wagener's reassurances, as the synthetic-gasoline project again came under fire in party papers during early 1932.[94] To be sure, on one occasion in the spring of 1932 the *Völkischer Beobachter* accorded favorable coverage to that project, as a promotional slide lecture by a Farben engineer in a Munich motion picture theater received acclaim in the paper.[95] Yet only a short time before, Farben had again come under attack in the party organ, which revived accusations of its subservience to exploitative "international financial lords" and questioned whether the synthetic-gasoline project and the support accorded it by the government were justified.[96] Other Nazi publications had also continued to denounce state aid for the project.[97]

In hopes of clarifying the Nazis' position on synthetic gasoline once and for all, Carl Bosch decided on a direct approach to Hitler. Presumably to minimize the damage if the venture turned out badly, he avoided involving any of the top executives of Farben. Instead, he accepted a proposal for establishing contact with the Nazi leader put forward by Heinrich Gattineau, a young public relations man with Farben.[98] Gattineau commanded a line of communication to the highest quarters of the NSDAP through his former professor, Karl Haushofer, the proponent of geopolitics at the University of Munich, who maintained cordial relations with another former student, Hitler's deputy, Rudolf Hess. In 1931 Gattineau had written Haushofer, asking him to intercede with Hitler against Nazi press attacks on Farben.[99] When Gattineau succeeded in arranging through Haushofer to meet with Hitler in the spring of 1932, Bosch commissioned another young Farben official, Heinrich Bütefisch, technical director of the firm's largest synthetic-gasoline plant, to accompany Gattineau to Munich and explain the details of the hydrogenation process.[100] On a prearranged day in June 1932 a car picked up Gattineau and Bütefisch at their Munich hotel and took them to Hitler's private apartment.[101] As Bütefisch later recalled, Hitler arrived late and weary from an election campaign trip. According to both Bütefisch and Gattineau, he nevertheless warmed at once to the subject of their visit, lecturing them at length on his plans for the motorization of Germany and for the construction of new highways. The production of synthetic gasoline fit ideally into his plans, he informed them. He then interrogated Bütefisch at length on the technical aspects of Farben's process, granting his visitors two and a half hours of his time instead of the half hour originally foreseen. When they at last found an opportunity to ask whether he would have Nazi press attacks on Farben's hydrogenation project halted and continue the protective tariff on petroleum if the NSDAP came to power, Hitler replied in the affirmative. That concluded the interview. Later, at Nuremberg, Bütefisch insisted that neither politics nor the financial needs of the NSDAP were mentioned.[102] When informed by him of the visit with Hitler, Bosch responded, Bütefisch recalled at Nuremberg, "Then the man is more reasonable than I had thought."[103] Soon thereafter Farben decided to press on with the further development of the synthetic-gasoline project.[104]

The mission of Bütefisch and Gattineau proved at most a qualified success. While Nazi journalists henceforth refrained from attacks on Farben's synthetic-gasoline project, the party press continued to denounce the firm itself as a beachhead of international finance capitalism in Germany.[105] The hostility revealed in such articles gave Farben's leadership good reason to remain wary of National Socialism. Nor did Hitler's positive response to the synthetic-gasoline project give Farben a stake in a Nazi victory in the struggle for power. Similar support could be obtained from other quarters, as the Papen government soon demonstrated by committing itself to continue the gasoline tariff at the level set by Brüning's cabinet. The Nazi leader's pledge, backed up by a cessation of press attacks on the coal hydrogenation project, meant at most that the branch of Farben committed to that undertaking need not fear extinction if the Nazis came to power. Still unresolved for Farben were fears about the eventual consequences of the NSDAP's seeming commitment to economic autarky. Only by selling more than half of its output abroad could the firm remain in the black, covering its losses at home with profits from exports. Most of Farben's executives, including Carl Bosch, placed their hopes for recovery from the depression on a revival of world trade and therefore looked with alarm at Nazi slogans calling for a throttling of German imports.[106]

Despite all efforts at dialogue from the side of the business community, Nazi advocacy not only of autarky but also of other radical socioeconomic policies increased during the summer and spring of the "year of elections." Beginning with Hitler's campaign for the presidency, which pitted him against Hindenburg, the NSDAP directed its verbal barrage increasingly against what its spokesmen characterized as the forces of reaction. By the time of the campaign for the July Reichstag election, with Papen's "cabinet of barons" in power, the Nazis sought to portray themselves as socialist advocates of the downtrodden as they directed a considerable part of their efforts to wresting votes away from the Social Democrats and the Communists. Hitler himself joined in the chorus of Nazi radicalism, proclaiming, "I am a socialist because it seems to me to make no sense to tend and use a machine with care yet to allow the noblest representative of work, the *Volk*, to languish."[107] Goebbels's propaganda machine urged party speakers to denounce the "capitalist system of exploitation," defining capitalism as the right to profit at the expense of others.[108] The party propaganda office further instructed these speakers to defend the *Sozialpolitik* of the Republic against attempts to reduce social insurance benefits, to uphold industry-wide collective bargaining contracts and the role of trade unions (except for activities on behalf of internationalist causes and class conflict), and to advocate profit sharing for workers, nationalization of the banking system and of mammoth concerns, as well as strict controls on imports so as to enable Germany to achieve economic self-sufficiency.[109] As a manifest of their concern for the common man, Nazi parliamentarians introduced bills that called for sharp increases in income tax levies on the wealthy and reduction or elimination of taxes on low incomes.[110] Other Nazis concentrated their attacks specifically on big business, characterizing its practice of driving smaller enterprises to the wall as *Konzernbolschewismus*.[111] Gregor Strasser proclaimed that an "anti-capitalist longing" had gripped 95 percent of the population, and promised measures to loosen the hold of exploitative capitalists on the German people.[112] During the summer Reichstag campaign, without any consultation with Keppler's circle, Strasser released in a mass printing a pamphlet that set forth a bold program to combat the depression. This *Wirtschaftliches Sofortprogramm,* or "Immediate Economic Program," promised decisive moves toward autarky and large-scale creation of jobs for the unemployed under government auspices, with that undertaking to be financed by deficit spending and higher taxes on the rich.[113]

As so often in the past, other forks of the Nazi tongue sought to reassure the business community about the NSDAP's intentions for the economy. Hermann Göring, predictably a foe of Nazi socio-economic radicalism, addressed 100 to 150 members of the Dortmund Industry Club sometime during the first half of the year.[114] In April, just prior to the Bavarian state elections, Hitler, in an appearance before the Munich Herrenklub, an exclusive men's club whose membership encompassed much of the local business elite, delivered a talk which one of those present reported could have, with only minor modifications, been made by a member of any non-Marxist party.[115] Walther Funk sought to allay the mounting concern of the business community about the direction taken by the NSDAP by publishing articles and delivering speeches to business audiences. He explained the disturbingly radical statements of other Nazis as mere products of agitational exigencies.[116] Lesser party spokesmen, too, made use of appearances before business audiences invited by local party organizations to suggest that Nazi pronouncements about economic matters need not be taken too tragically since in practice everything would work out in reasonable fashion.[117]

This sort of Nazi cajolery had by 1932 begun to take on a shopworn quality for at least some in the business community. In the face of persistent radical pronouncements from the side of the NSDAP, repetitions of the by then well-known reassurances of "moderate" Nazis aroused skepticism. One of those who expressed this was Tilo von Wilmowsky, Krupp von Bohlen's brother-in-law and confidant. By March he had become sufficiently alarmed about Nazism to employ his influence in Saxon agricultural circles in an effort to drum up opposition to endorsement of Hitler's presidential candidacy by the chief national agrarian association, the Reichslandbund.[118] In a letter written to Paul Reusch in June, just after Wilmowsky had heard Walther Funk give a talk before an association of businessmen in central Germany, he characterized as "the same old picture" the Nazi spokesman's contention that the goals of the NSDAP coincided completely with those of the business community. The trouble was, Wilmowsky exasperatedly observed, that Nazism departed in practice ever more drastically from the aims Funk imputed to it. The hopes and expectations the Nazis were raising among the masses would be difficult to restrain, Wilmowsky feared. He indicated his willingness to make use of Funk's offer to serve as intermediary between the NSDAP and the business community, but he obviously did so without much optimism.[119] Another business leader who took note of what the Nazis were saying to the broad population was Clemens Lammers, a legal adviser to IG Farben and member of its supervisory board who represented the Center Party in the Reichstag from 1924 until 1929 and held a number of high posts in the industrial Reichsverband. In a speech to the main committee of the Reichsverband on June 24, which was soon thereafter published as a pamphlet, Lammers warned against Nazism, denouncing as economically unsound the policies of autarky, economic planning, and corporatism advocated by certain spokesmen of that party. Some businessmen had reported, he noted, that the foremost figures of National Socialism had repeatedly expressed their readiness to accept the cooperation of prominent businessmen in order to ensure that knowledgeable leadership of the German economy would continue. Those who believed such blandishments, Lammers cautioned, ran a grave danger. One had only to listen to what the Nazis were saying to the masses. If one did that, one heard the same message over and over again: The leaders of the NSDAP proposed to take complete control and to tolerate no one around them who did not meet their own standards.[120] Erich von Gilsa, Paul Reusch's political adviser, who had enthusiastically greeted Nazi participation in the short-lived "national opposition," proclaimed at Bad Harzburg in October 1931, once again became extremely skeptical, if not downright negative, about National Socialism as a consequence of his exposure to party orators during the Reichstag campaign of July 1932. On the basis of what he heard, Gilsa labeled Nazism in a report to Reusch as a "grave peril" to the business community.[121] Reusch himself was appalled at what he found in the Nazi "Immediate Economic Program" distributed for the Reichstag campaign under Strasser's auspices. He urged Schacht to enlighten "the gen-

tlemen in Munich" about the "great nonsense" it contained.[122] Schacht
for his part defended the NSDAP in an exchange of letters with Gilsa,
denying that it had ever endorsed socialization of the means of production.[123] In a letter to Reusch, Gilsa characterized Schacht's use of the
word "socialism" as a "juggling act" and warned the industrialist not to
be misled by such casuistry.[124]

Some observers in the business community began in 1932 to show concern about aspects of National Socialism other than the economic policies that had hitherto preoccupied those businessmen who sought to
discern that party's intentions. One such increasingly disturbing feature
of the NSDAP was its vicious anti-Semitism. The leading men of German
big business remained averse to that form of prejudice, which they regarded as benighted and plebeian. Early in 1932 the widely respected
Jewish state secretary in the Reich Finance Ministry, Hans Schäffer, who
served as a close confidant and adviser to Brüning, recorded in his diary
a conversation with United Steel's Albert Vögler, who reported to him
recently having dressed down both Hitler and Göring about their attitude toward Jews.[125] In July, at the height of the Nazis' frenzied campaign for that month's Reichstag election, Paul Reusch applauded the
acceptance of an advertisement from a Jewish firm by the Nuremberg
newspaper controlled by his company. He further urged the paper's
managing director to protest in print against Nazi anti-Semitic agitation.[126] Another feature of National Socialism that caused mounting
concern in business circles was its dictatorial aspirations. During the
presidential election campaign an editorial writer for the business-
oriented *Deutsche Bergwerks-Zeitung* of Düsseldorf noted that if one listened to what the Nazis were saying, it became unmistakably clear that
they intended not to ally with the other participants in the "Harzburg
Front" but rather to subjugate them. The Nazis must learn that Germany would not accept the loss of freedom that Fascism had brought to
Italy, the editorialist stated. What it needed was the sort of mixture of
freedom and authority that had prevailed in the Empire, not the dictatorial straitjacket the Nazis intended to impose on the country.[127] In
June Oskar Funcke, a prominent manufacturer of machine tools in
Westphalia who had long played a leading role in that industry's organizations, spoke out against Nazism and in defense of liberalism. In a
newspaper statement he denounced the NSDAP as "a new league for
human willfulness and servility."[128] In his June Reichsverband speech,
which was published soon thereafter, Clemens Lammers warned that
the Nazis would eventually resort to brutal repression to impose their
will. He asked his listeners to take notice of how heavily existing dictatorial regimes elsewhere relied on political and secret police to rule
their populations.[129]

As the German political caldron approached the boiling point during
the spring and summer of 1932, at least a few voices such as these within

the business community began to warn against focusing solely on the economic policies of the new mass political movement that daily proclaimed total power as its ultimate goal. Although those business executives who gave public expression to their alarm in that regard remained exceptions, National Socialism's political radicalism was becoming a source of concern among an increasing number. During the summer of 1932 that concern converged with a heightened awareness of the still widely divergent Nazi pronouncements on economic issues to drive the stock of the NSDAP in the business community sharply downward.

4. Insurance Premiums and Protection Money for Potential Rulers

During the spring and early summer of 1932 more money than ever before flowed from the business community to various Nazis. This did not happen because increasing numbers of big businessmen had undergone conversion to National Socialism. Despite the efforts of Hitler and other Nazi spokesmen to allay misgivings about their movement, all but a very few figures in big business remained aloof from it. When in February United Steel's Albert Vögler challenged Hans Schäffer, the Jewish state secretary in the Reich Finance Ministry, to name one major business executive aside from Fritz Thyssen who had thrown his lot in with what Schäffer had angrily referred to as Germany's "gang of white guards," the well-informed Schäffer could think of none.[1] Nor had the situation changed by the time of the July Reichstag election. Virtually all the contributions that flowed to the Nazis from big business sources during the first half of 1932 thus sprang from motivations other than conviction. Nor did most result from a desire to see the Nazis succeed. The NSDAP seemed in any case to fare very well in that regard without appreciable help from big business. Advancing from one election triumph to another down to the summer of 1932, the party rapidly expanded its ranks with a swelling stream of new recruits that daily gave added credence to its claim to the title of mass movement. Financially, too, National Socialism continued to flourish, extracting from its members and followers at the grass roots an abundant upward flow of money sustained by the expansion of the movement.[2] The party fairly exuded prosperity. During the campaign for the July Reichstag election, the national headquarters unveiled with great fanfare a new fifty-meter-long, two-story annex to the Brown House made necessary by its expanding officialdom.[3] So successful had the Nazis become that thoughtful observers, including a good many in the business community, had to consider the possibility of their becoming rulers in the near future. Few thought the Nazis stood much chance of attaining total power, but the likelihood seemed increasingly great that they might gain a strong place in the government and perhaps even capture control of the chancellorship. In the light of that possibility, some business executives who found themselves particularly insecure or vulnerable politically began to regard the Nazis with the fear such men customarily feel toward rulers or even potential rulers. They began, as a consequence, to include the Nazis among the recipients of the political "insurance premiums" with which they sought to buy security against shifts in Germany's internal distribution of power.[4] Others responded opportunistically to the prospect of the NSDAP's attainment of a share of power. This took various forms, but one of the most common was the familiar practice of bestowing subsidies on individual Nazis, particularly those regarded as likely to influence their party's economic policy. Still other big business money went in increasing amounts to the Nazi press during 1932 as a result of the commercial opportunities offered by its mass readership. Whatever the causes, the spring and summer of 1932 were to register the high-water mark for the flow of big business money to National Socialism.

The case of Friedrich Flick provides a well-documented example of how the Nazis could exploit a financially insecure and politically unscrupulous entrepreneur. By 1932 Flick's speculative iron and steel holdings had sunk to a level so precarious that he had to resort to desperate means to avert disaster. Only his success in bringing the Brüning cabinet to buy his stock in the Gelsenkirchen mining firm for nearly 100 million marks at more than four times the market value in the spring of 1932 enabled him to survive financially. The "Gelsenkirchen deal" aroused widespread indignation when it became known in June of that year, however. Flick found himself under fire not only from the political left but also from the business press and even from some of the major iron and steel executives of the Ruhr, who denounced the transaction as a first step toward socialization of their industry.[5] Fearing a reversal of the sale, Flick set out, as his assistant Otto Steinbrinck later explained, to apply money toward the maintenance of a businesslike bourgeois government that would, as the Papen cabinet eventually did, leave the "Gelsenkirchen deal" undisturbed.[6] Flick already had considerable political experience. As a member of the DVP he had in 1924 taken part in an unsuccessful insurrection against its leader Gustav Stresemann's policy of collaborating with the Social Democrats.[7]

Flick did not limit his attentions to one party, however. By the early 1930s he and his agents were using money to cultivate ties with all the major bourgeois parties and, despite his earlier objections to Stresemann's collaboration with the SPD, with that party as well.[8] When in 1932 his financial situation became alarming and his dependence on government protection crucial, Flick resorted to lavish political expenditures. At the time of the presidential election he contributed to the Brüning-led campaign for Hindenburg at least 450,000 marks and possibly more than twice that much.[9] During the July Reichstag campaign he bestowed generous contributions on the major bourgeois parties. As documents from his files reveal, he responded with alacrity to General Schleicher's appeal in July for funds to help the financially hard-pressed traditional parties of the right in the final stages of the campaign, donating 120,000 marks of the money the general raised on that occasion.[10] Other documents show that during the campaign for the November Reichstag election, Flick placed 100,000 marks at the disposal of Chancellor Franz von Papen.[11] Flick also claimed at Nuremberg to have continued subsidizing Brüning's efforts in the Center Party long after the ex-chancellor's fall. Also at Nuremberg, Flick placed the total amount he had given during 1932 to non-Nazis variously at 800,000 and 1.45 million marks, contending in the latter instance that he had twice given to the Hindenburg campaign.[12] Surviving records and the testimony of his aides make the former figure seem more likely but the latter not implausible.

In sending 20,000 marks to the DNVP in July, Flick explained to Hugenberg that he was contributing in order to enable Germany's *Bürgertum* to close ranks against National Socialism and in order to prevent that movement from becoming overwhelming.[13] Flick had good reason for apprehension about the NSDAP. That party's program pledged it, after all, to nationalize trusts, and Nazi journalists and orators had long reserved a special measure of invective for stock-market speculators. Flick's own inconclusive attempt to establish contact with Hitler in February had, as already mentioned, produced no encouraging signs that he could expect an exception in his case. To be sure, Hermann Göring made no difficulties when, in his capacity as a Reichstag deputy, he came to Flick's Berlin offices to inspect the firm's records of the Gelsenkirchen sale to the Reich.[14] Presumably Göring found nothing incriminating in Flick's records since whatever irregularities the Gelsenkirchen transaction had involved lay on the side of the Reich and not of Flick. This would seem borne out by the failure of an SPD deputy, who also inspected Flick's records, to cause any problems, despite his party's condemnation of the deal.[15] Other Nazis found the mere absence of evidence against Flick no deterrent. Not long after the transaction became known, an article in a party publication vigorously denounced the deal.[16] A National Socialist government, it announced, would have responded by immediately socializing the whole complex involved, including Flick's Charlottenhütte, the Gelsenkirchener Bergwerks AG, and United Steel. The most the stockholders could have expected would have been compensation, in the form of long-term state bonds, for the prevailing market value of the stock, which came, the article estimated, to about 14 percent of its face value. As for Flick, the article continued, it remained an open question whether he should not have his property confiscated without compensation and go before a high court on charges of having damaged the interests of the *Volk*. Such statements could hardly have contributed to Flick's peace of mind, coming as they did from the political party that seemed likely soon to become Germany's largest.

Under these circumstances Flick leaped at an opportunity to establish ongoing contact with the NSDAP that presented itself during the early summer of 1932. It arose when Wilhelm Keppler and his nephew Fritz Kranefuss arrived at Flick's Berlin office, having been referred there by Albert Vögler, on whom they had just called at his office on the floor above Flick's.[17] The two Nazis were received by Flick's private secretary, Otto Steinbrinck, who testified at Nuremberg that he had suspected that Vögler had phoned ahead and announced the arrival of Keppler and Kranefuss to Flick, who sat in an inner office of his suite. Aside from appearing at the door to shake hands with the visitors, Flick left them to Steinbrinck, the latter testified. They explained the plans for Keppler's circle of businessmen and indicated that Schacht had urged them to recruit more members. With Flick's approval, Steinbrinck agreed to join the circle. At Nuremberg Steinbrinck set forth the motives for that move. It fit in, he explained, with Flick's overall defensive political strategy and, in addition, provided an opportunity to find out "which way the wind was blowing" inside the NSDAP, a party that seemed likely to play a role in government soon.[18] Later in the summer Steinbrinck, who joined the Keppler circle too late for the meeting with Hitler on June 20, journeyed to Munich for his first exposure to one of its gatherings.[19] The proceedings, he testified at Nuremberg, did not impress him. He recalled with bemusement that he, of all people, had been assigned the task of drafting a law to prevent the formation of *Konzerne,* just the sort of large-scale financial amalgamation of several different firms that had enabled his employer to aggrandize himself, as well as another law for the purpose of prohibiting the kind of package sales of stocks that had become the speculative Flick's hallmark. The Keppler circle had set a goat to guard the garden, Steinbrinck observed in 1947. He recalled participating thereafter in only some loosely organized gatherings attended by a few members of the group in Berlin, at least one of which took place in a restaurant.[20] Under interrogation at Nuremberg, Keppler remembered that Steinbrinck once invited him to his home during the winter of 1932–33 to meet Flick, who appeared anxious to talk about the Gelsenkirchen transaction. He let Flick know that he disapproved of the deal, Keppler testified, and Flick promised never to undertake anything of the sort again.[21] There the matter seems to have ended, undoubtedly to the great relief of Flick.

By the time Flick finally managed to plead his case to Keppler, the man he took for Adolf Hitler's chief adviser on economic matters, his defensive strategy had become quite costly as far as the NSDAP was concerned. Because of the hostility toward big business expressed in publications of the party's storm-trooper organization, the SA, Steinbrinck set out to cover Flick in that direction.[22] With more than 400,000 men in uniform, and great numbers of these increasingly visible in the streets of Germany, the SA represented the most forcible manifestation of Nazism's burgeoning strength, so that its leaders bulked large in most outsiders' perceptions of National Socialism. Through an agent hired to observe and report for Flick on radical right-wing organizations, Steinbrinck had come into contact with one of these, Count Wolf Heinrich von Helldorf, commander of the Berlin SA since the spring of 1931.[23] As Steinbrinck related at Nuremberg, Helldorf appeared one day at his office and announced that his SA men needed new boots for an upcoming torchlight parade.[24] Using his discretionary authority to expend up to 2,000 or 3,000 marks on his own, Steinbrinck gave Helldorf a "contribution." Helldorf returned repeatedly, always with pressing new needs, and eventually relieved Flick's till of a total, Steinbrinck later estimated, of about 15,000 marks.[25]

As Steinbrinck quickly discovered, giving money to Nazis was rather like shedding blood while swimming in the presence of sharks. In Saxony the SA leader there, Manfred von Killinger, approached Flick's local office and also obtained funds, Steinbrinck later remembered.[26] During the autumn Reichstag election campaign of 1932 Walther Funk presented himself to Steinbrinck and received 20,000 or 30,000 of Flick's marks.[27] Steinbrinck also later recalled being approached by Rhenish Gauleiter Robert Ley and Count Hans Reischach, managing director of the *Westdeutscher Beobachter,* the Cologne Nazi daily published by Ley.[28] Ley and Reischach thus presumably received some of the money which, according to Steinbrinck, Flick's agents doled out to Nazi newspaper and magazine editors—as well as to those of other political orientations—in hopes of currying favor with them.[29] Steinbrinck also testified at Nuremberg that in the latter part of 1932 he and Flick heard from Hjalmar Schacht that the SS also needed money.[30] Shortly thereafter, Steinbrinck added, its leader, Heinrich Himmler, joined the procession of Nazi solicitors to the door of Flick's office in Berlin. In an effort to contain this proliferation of solicitations from various units of the NSDAP, Flick and Steinbrinck, with the help of Wilhelm Keppler's nephew and assistant, Fritz Kranefuss, reached an agreement late in 1932 with Himmler whereby they would in the future give donations for the NSDAP only to the SS.[31] Prior to the Nazi takeover about 15,000 marks went to Himmler's organization in this fashion, Steinbrinck testified at Nuremberg.[32] In all, Steinbrinck estimated that a maximum of 40,000 marks of Flick's money reached various Nazis in the form of small disbursements prior to Hitler's installation as chancellor.[33] Flick himself estimated the total figure at 50,000.[34] Since no documentary records of his contributions to the Nazis survived, the precise figure will presumably never be known. From the separate testimonies of Flick and Steinbrinck, it would appear that each underestimated the total involved, possibly because the ad hoc fashion in which the money seems to have been disbursed may have left them with no precise knowledge of how much was involved.[35] The important point remains that Flick gave to the Nazis only a relatively small portion of the large sums he distributed across the political spectrum for political purposes in 1932. And what he did contribute to them he gave not because he wanted them to get power but because he wanted to insure himself and his shaky business ventures against that eventuality.

Flick's case had something of a parallel in that of Otto Wolff, although the evidence is scantier in the case of Wolff, who died in 1940 and whose papers have never been found. Of obscure origins, Wolff became a prospering scrap-iron dealer in Cologne early in the century, while still in his twenties.[36] With the help of a partner who served during the war as a procurement officer in the Imperial Admiralty, Wolff obtained numerous sizeable government contacts and expanded his operations rapidly. When his partner successfully survived the transition from Empire to Republic and gained an influential position in the German Armistice Commission, Wolff's good fortune continued into the post-war period. By the early 1920s he had not only become a major iron wholesaler but had also reputedly cornered the German market for tin plate. By adroitly adjusting to the hyperinflation of the early 1920s he extended his holdings into copper mining, shipping, machine manufacturing, and steel production. When one of the steel firms in which he held a controlling interest was absorbed into United Steel at its formation in 1926, he became a member of the supervisory board of that combine. Although never one of its executives, he secured for his enterprises control over United Steel's exports to Russia, the Balkans, and Turkey.[37]

Like Flick, with whom he collaborated for certain purposes, Wolff remained, despite his prosperity, an outsider in the eyes of the industrial elite of Germany. For men like Krupp von Bohlen, Reusch, and even Fritz Thyssen, he appeared an upstart speculator, and a potentially dangerous and unpredictable one at that, who had intruded himself into Ruhr industry and might expand his holdings still further. For his part, Wolff had little in common with such narrow-gauge specialists, being a man of lively mind and wide-ranging intellectual interests. He felt a particular attraction for the French Enlightenment and the revolutionary and Napoleonic eras, collecting a large library on those periods and exchanging early editions of Voltaire's writings with a Berlin banker who shared his enthusiasm for such stirring chapters of history.[38] With the help of a professional historian he set out to write a biography of Gabriel Julien Ouvrard, the French financial speculator who had, by clever transactions, made a fortune during the French Revolution and become, successively, financier to the Directory, Napoleon, King Charles IV of Spain, and Talleyrand. Wolff's labors on Ouvrard came to fruition in 1932, when the book was published. A half century later it remains a respected study of a remarkable historical figure and has appeared in an English translation.[39]

Perhaps in emulation of the daring Frenchman who had so fascinated him and whose business career he seemingly took as a pattern for his own rise, Wolff began dabbling in politics during the early 1920s. He proved especially effective at cultivating rising politicians. By providing subsidies for a liberal newspaper that Gustav Stresemann launched and by seeking to bring other businessmen to back it as well, he gained access to the man who would soon become chancellor and then, as foreign minister, the linchpin of republican politics for six years.[40] Wolff later successfully gained the attention of Heinrich Brüning, becoming something of a confidant to that ordinarily aloof chancellor and enjoying ready access to his office.[41] At the time of the 1932 presidential election Wolff contributed generously to the campaign waged on Hindenburg's behalf by Brüning and helped to persuade others, such as Flick, to do so.[42] With the advent of Franz von Papen, Wolff's political activities intensified since he had become very friendly with Papen's patron, General Kurt von Schleicher.[43] As their relationship grew closer during 1932, Wolff seemed to aspire to play Ouvrard to Schleicher's Napoleon. The two met frequently, and Wolff generously supplied the general with information and advice. When Schleicher set out to raise money from big business to help the DVP and DNVP in the campaign for the July Reichstag election, Wolff lent his assistance.[44] In the fall of 1932 Wolff held a meeting of industrialists at his Berlin home to raise funds in support of the Papen cabinet at the time of the campaign for the November Reichstag election.[45]

Wolff shared more than merely his outsider status with Flick. Like that upstart speculator, he found himself in financial difficulties in early 1932.[46] Apparently having learned from Flick about the Brüning cabinet's preparations for the Gelsenkirchen stock purchase that rescued Flick from ruin, Wolff pled with Brüning for help in covering his own enormous and pressing indebtedness.[47] His pleas met with delays and excuses on the chancellor's part, but Wolff's well-known close ties to the Brüning cabinet, and later to those of Papen and Schleicher, may well have helped him to stave off his creditors.[48] He remained vulnerable to the Nazis, however. Their press took delight in vilifying him as a war profiteer par excellence now bent on additional tainted gains by means of his friendship with Schleicher.[49] In Düsseldorf the Nazis resorted to wall posters directed against Wolff, reportedly moving him to have his lawyer lodge a complaint with the Brown House in Munich.[50] From all appearances at the time, Wolff reciprocated the Nazis' hostility.[51] Regarded as an enemy of National Socialism by many, he counseled against Schleicher's plan to "tame" the Nazis by saddling them with governmental responsibility yet denying them power. If Hitler ever got control of the chancellorship, Wolff warned in August 1932, not even Schleicher would be safe.[52] In September Wolff took part in a plan to have the Prussian state parliament dissolved if the NSDAP's deputies should join with the Catholic Center Party's delegation to oppose the Papen cabinet.[53]

In the light of such an anti-Nazi record, it seems astounding that, according to East German historians, Wolff variously reported during the Third Reich having contributed either 160,800 or 180,000 marks to the NSDAP in 1932.[54] Rumors in circulation at the time held that Wolff gave money to Nazi Robert Ley, then a member of Gregor Strasser's staff.[55] At Nuremberg Walther Funk repeated that allegation but provided no particulars nor any indication of how he had come by such knowledge.[56] Since Wolff operated jointly with Flick the public relations office in Düsseldorf through which some of Flick's political money apparently reached Ley or his Cologne newspaper, such rumors may have arisen from an understandable confusion about who was behind those contributions.[57] Conceivably, of course, Wolff might have played a double game, supporting Brüning, Hindenburg, Papen and especially Schleicher against the Nazi onslaught while covering himself against the eventuality of a National Socialist victory by secretly channeling contributions to that movement as well. More plausible, however, is a version that rests on the memoirs of Günther Gereke, one of Schleicher's confidants who became the commisar for work-creation and eastern resettlement in the general's cabinet.[58] According to this account, Wolff gave his money not to the NSDAP as such but rather to Gregor Strasser; he did so, moreover, not on his own initiative but at the request of Schleicher. By bringing Wolff to support Strasser financially, so this story stemming from Gereke goes, Schleicher hoped to offset the influence of Ruhr industry on Hitler and to make Strasser less dependent on the party leader. Of these versions, Gereke's seems the more plausible. As is well known, Schleicher did in fact seek to bring Strasser to accept a ministerial post, hoping thereby to undercut Hitler's demand for the chancellorship as the price of Nazi entry into the government.[59] If the version attributed to Gereke should prove true, the story of Otto Wolff's contributions to the Nazis becomes another of the many tangled skeins in the web of plots woven by that most mysterious figure of late Weimar politics, Kurt von Schleicher. Such contributions by Wolff would in that case have little or no bearing on the response of the business community to Nazism.

Although no business difficulties as dire as those that dogged Flick and Wolff afflicted IG Farben, it, too, suffered from political insecurity in 1932. The giant chemical corporation's problems arose not from the consequences of speculative overextension but rather, as already noted, from its dependence on high import duties on gasoline to shield from foreign competition its enormously expensive synthetic-gasoline project.

Farben's anxieties in that regard, along with concern about a party that had repeatedly singled out the firm for attacks, made its representatives vulnerable to appeals for funds from the side of the NSDAP, which seemed very likely to assume an important place in the government in the near future as the summer Reichstag election approached. Without authorization, so far as is known, from the senior executives of the firm, some of Farben's junior executives began in 1932 disbursing modest sums to Walther Funk out of discretionary funds at their disposal. Their actions probably reflected more than corporate interest since they could scarcely have overlooked the likelihood that by cultivating favor with leading figures in Germany's most dynamic political movement they stood to enhance their own prospects within the firm.

One such young Farben official was Max Ilgner.[60] A descendant of a family of Prussian officers, Ilgner joined a *Freikorps* unit after the revolution had frustrated his own plans for a military career. Then, after university study devoted to business administration and short-term employment with several firms, he went to work for one of the chemical firms soon to be incorporated into IG Farben at its formation in 1925. Within Farben, Ilgner advanced rapidly for a young man still only in his twenties, thanks presumably to the role of his uncle, Hermann Schmitz, as the firm's principal financial director. By 1932, at age thirty-three, Ilgner headed Farben's Berlin office. From that position he set about making himself indispensable, becoming something of an economic-policy man-about-town in the capital. Among other activities, he took part in the deliberations of the loose grouping of men who, beginning in 1931, formed around Professor Ernst Wagemann, head of the Reich Statistical Office and also of the Institut für Konjunkturforschung, an economic research organization financed by business interests, including Farben. Wagemann and his circle developed plans for countercyclical monetary policies designed to spur economic recovery.[61] Also active in the Wagemann circle was another Farben man, the influential former under state secretary in the Reich Economics Ministry Wichard von Moellendorf, who had worked closely during the war with assassinated Foreign Minister Walther Rathenau and who enjoyed cordial relations with leading Social Democrats. The extended circle encompassed a number of other prominent Berlin business figures, among them some Jewish members, including Farben's legal adviser, Julius Flechtheim.

Not surprisingly, the Wagemann circle became increasingly concerned about the position of the NSDAP with regard to measures against the depression as that party gathered strength in successive elections. But the bewildering cacophony of contradictory pronouncements emanating from persons claiming to speak for National Socialism left the members of the circle just as baffled as it did so many other observers. By way of clarifying that party's stand, and more particularly its response to the plans of the circle, the other members asked Ilgner and Moellendorff, the former testified after the war, to meet with Walther Funk. Through the intermediacy of Wagemann, two such meetings took place during the first half of 1932, Ilgner recalled at Nuremberg, at least one in the restaurant of Farben's Berlin headquarters on Unter den Linden, the principal ceremonial boulevard of the capital. According to Ilgner, Funk at one point also arranged for Hermann Schmitz, Ilgner's uncle, to meet with Hitler.[62] Ilgner later reported in 1946 having found Funk a "liberal man, favorably disposed towards business."[63] As for the plans of the Wagemann circle Funk expressed the view that these seemed reasonable.[64] At his second meeting with Ilgner and Moellendorff, Funk informed them that Hitler had personally expressed his approval of the Wagemann circle's plans.[65] Nevertheless, the second session did not go as well as the first, Ilgner remembered, ending on a discordant note as the result of disagreements between Funk and Moellendorff. That put an end to his meetings with Funk, Ilgner testified after the war.[66]

The cessation of Ilgner's personal contact with Funk did not, however, prevent the young Farben official from subsidizing that Nazi financially. That subsidization resulted from Funk's appeal to Ilgner, at their first meeting, for money to support the office Funk ran out of his home in the Schlachtensee suburb of Berlin. In response to that appeal, Ilgner testified at Nuremberg, he arranged for monthly payments to Funk from the Farben funds at his disposal, in the range of 300 to 500 marks.[67] According to Ilgner, he discovered later in the year that Heinrich Gattineau, the young public relations man who had called on Hitler with Heinrich Bütefisch about the synthetic-gasoline project, was making similar payments to Funk.[68] Gattineau supplied no information at Nuremberg about how he came into contact with Funk, but he did confirm that he had made such payments, which he described as "small monthly subsidies."[69]

Money may also have gone to the NSDAP from the central political fund of IG Farben in the spring or early summer of 1932. Gattineau mentioned at that time to Ilgner having learned that for the first time the Nazis had been included in the contributions distributed to political parties by the Kalle circle, or Kränzchen, the political committee of senior Farben executives headed by Wilhelm Kalle of Farben's board of directors. According to Ilgner's recollection after the war, Gattineau told him that the NSDAP had received 10 to 15 percent of the total of 200,000 to 300,000 marks paid out by the Kränzchen.[70] At Nuremberg Gattineau repeated the same story, setting the allocation for the Nazis at 10 percent.[71] There are grounds, however, to question the reliability of his version. It remains unclear, most basically, how a junior official charged with public relations could have become privy to such information. As the testimony of numerous Farben executives at Nuremberg unanimously attests, the Kränzchen operated behind a heavy veil of secrecy that excluded even those senior executives not in Kalle's circle.[72]

Since Gattineau enjoyed, so far as is known, no close ties with any of the much more senior members of that circle, it would seem extraordinary for him to have gained precise knowledge of the most sensitive actions of the Kränzchen. The principal figure in the circle, Kalle himself, later gave testimony that casts added doubt on Gattineau's story, since Kalle denied any knowledge of contributions to the Nazis prior to their take-over in 1933.[73] A left-wing DVP Reichstag deputy who struggled within that party to uphold the liberal heritage of Stresemann, Kalle would seem an unlikely proponent of aid to the NSDAP. His political corre-spondence of 1932 reveals him as a man who deeply mistrusted Na-zism.[74] Kalle's steadfast contention at Nuremberg that his Kränzchen had given no funds to the NSDAP, which was backed up by testimony of his private secretary of 1932, thus carries considerable weight.[75] An-other member of the Kränzchen, Clemens Lammers, who also denied at Nuremberg that any of the funds administered by that group went to the Nazis, seems equally unlikely to have agreed to aid for that party.[76] In June 1932, at just about the time Gattineau's story has the Kränzchen allocating a portion of its political funds to the NSDAP, Lammers deliv-ered the speech before the industrial Reichsverband in which he point-edly warned against the peril represented by that party.[77] Still further doubt is cast on Gattineau's story by the participation in the Kränzchen of at least one Farben executive of Jewish ancestry, who presumably would have resisted support for such a rabidly anti-Semitic party.[78] For all these reasons Gattineau's story cannot simply be accepted at face value. Even if the story should prove true, that would not mean that Farben was seeking to bring the NSDAP to power. It would instead merely reveal that Germany's largest corporation, like the upstart Fried-rich Flick, suffered in 1932 from a degree of political insecurity that led those of its executives responsible for relations with the parties to broaden Farben's political insurance coverage by according to the coun-try's most rapidly growing political movement a share of the premiums they paid in an attempt to secure their firm against a future shift in power.

Some of the Farben money handled by the Kränzchen apparently reached the Nazis in 1932 indirectly and without the knowledge of the chemical trust's executives. In November 1931 General Schleicher wrote to Kalle, requesting a contribution of 10,000 marks for the army's pro-gram of clandestine quasi-military training for civilians, which operated under the name Wehrsport.[79] Through the Interior Ministry the army financed such training by the *Wehrverbände,* the rightist paramilitary or-ganizations that flourished under the Republic.[80] Kalle quickly re-sponded by agreeing to provide the requested 10,000 marks.[81] Since the Schleicher papers, in which these letters were found, are incomplete, it remains conceivable that further contributions ensued from the side of Farben. Other documents in those papers reveal that Schleicher bestowed a share of the money he collected for Wehrsport on the leader of the Berlin SA, Count Helldorf.[82] Presumably, the secretive general neither limited his solicitations for Wehrsport purposes to Farben nor disclosed to that firm's executives or other industrial contributors that he was passing along some of their money to Nazi storm trooper units. Big business funds reaching the NSDAP in such fashion must therefore be regarded as involuntary contributions that reveal nothing more than the eagerness of some business executives to cultivate power holders such as Schleicher, as well as the susceptibility of those executives to patriotic appeals.

Very different circumstances gave rise to another, more substantial contribution to the Nazi cause in the spring or early summer of 1932. The key role in that transfer of funds was played by Ludwig Grauert, the managing director of the employers' association of the iron and steel industry in the Ruhr, Arbeitnordwest. As already noted above, Grauert had by 1931 become a fellow traveler of National Socialism, making the acquaintance of such Nazis as Wilhelm Frick, Hermann Göring, Gregor Strasser, and Otto Wagener. With the concurrence of his superior, the chairman of Arbeitnordwest, Ernst Poensgen of United Steel, Grauert had arranged in 1931 for a "loan" via Wagener in support of launching a new Nazi newspaper in Essen, the National-Zeitung.[83] By early 1932 Grauert's sympathy for National Socialism had become widely known.[84] That fact did not escape another Nazi sympathizer in the camp of Ruhr heavy industry, Fritz Thyssen. Under repeated interrogation after the war, Grauert later consistently told a story whose main outlines Poensgen corroborated.[85] Thyssen had invited him to the Düsseldorf Park Hotel, Grauert related, where he found Walther Funk with the industrialist. Funk, who disclosed at Nuremberg that he sometimes solicited funds at the request of Rudolf Hess, who managed the finances of Hitler and his entourage, expressed a need for money at the meeting with Thyssen and Grauert. Thyssen, maintaining that he had no immediate access to funds of the needed magnitude, urged Grauert to make available 100,000 marks from the treasury of Arbeitnordwest. Since his boss, Poensgen, was away on a trip, Grauert obtained the approval of Ernst Borbet, another United Steel director, who served as deputy chairman of Arbeitnordwest. He took the 100,000 marks he gave to Funk, Grauert testified at Nuremberg, from the fund designed to support employers whose plants were under strike.

As Grauert quickly discovered, he had seriously misperceived the attitudes of the leading men of Arbeitnordwest. When Poensgen returned and learned that organization's manager had given money to a Nazi, he objected strenuously.[86] Poensgen had reacted angrily at about the same time to press rumors to the effect that some of the Industrialists who belonged to Arbeitnordwest had financed the Nazis.[87] To his chagrin he now discovered that his own subordinate had used funds for which he, as that organization's chairman, bore responsibility. When Gustav Krupp von Bohlen heard what Grauert had done, he became so irate that he demanded the manager's dismissal. According to Grauert, he learned to his dismay that the attitude of his employers toward National Socialism had changed since the "loan" for the *National-Zeitung* the previous year. The leading men of the Ruhrlade had, unbeknownst to him, decided not to permit any iron and steel organization funds to go to the NSDAP and took bitter exception to his action, he later recalled.[88] Only intervention by Fritz Thyssen saved Grauert his job, the latter explained at Nuremberg. Having learned of the indignant reaction of such important steel men as Poensgen and Krupp, Thyssen informed them that he had merely asked Grauert for a temporary loan to cover a personal contribution of his own. To substantiate that claim, Thyssen reached into his pocket and reimbursed Arbeitnordwest for the full 100,000 marks.[89] The chastened Grauert, now apprized of the growing coolness of his employers toward National Socialism, was allowed to keep his job but showed himself much more circumspect with regard to his new political friends until the Nazi acquisition of power.

The coffers of the Ruhr magnates may not have remained entirely closed to the Nazis in the spring of 1932. Whereas some of the leading iron and steel men had, as Grauert discovered, developed grave reservations about National Socialism, the political spokesmen for the coal operators seem to have suffered from no preclusive inhibitions. As a consequence of dissension in the Ruhrlade because of the Gelsenkirchen transaction and other disagreements, the leaders of the Bergbauverein had successfully asserted its control over political funds deriving from the Ruhr coal industry.[90] According to the fellow-traveling journalist August Heinrichsbauer, who performed various tasks for the leadership of the Bergbauverein, 100,000 marks of coal industry money went to the Nazis in the spring of 1932.[91] This would appear compatible with what is known of the political attitudes of the chairman of the Bergbauverein, Ernst Brandi. On his return from a visit to the United States in early 1932, Brandi informed the board of the organization that he had told curious Americans that National Socialism represented a movement of malcontents but that he regarded Hitler as "a man of great stature."[92] An editor of the *Münchner Neuesten Nachrichten,* on whose advisory board Brandi served, later recalled that the industrialist had identified himself with the "Harzburg Front" after attending the Bad Harzburg meeting and had displayed a "slight inclination toward Hitler."[93] After attending Hitler's Industry Club speech in January 1932 Brandi had, the editor recalled, prophesied that Hitler was the coming man.[94] In February 1933, after Hitler's appointment as chancellor, Brandi boasted to editor Fritz Klein of the *Deutsche Allgemeine Zeitung* that he had the previous summer argued within that business-controlled paper's advisory body that the NSDAP must be viewed positively and that the only way out lay in assigning Hitler the chancellorship.[95]

Despite all this evidence, there are grounds for doubting whether the political spokesmen of the Ruhr coal operators sought in the spring of 1932 to bring the Nazis to power. Heinrichsbauer, the only source for the story of the 100,000-mark contribution to the NSDAP, specified that it represented only a fraction of their total political expenditures at that time. He recalled that two to three times that amount had gone to each of the "three large bourgeois parties."[96] Here Heinrichsbauer's memory does not entirely accord with the record, for a host of other evidence reveals that by the time of the campaign for the July Reichstag election Brandi had decided to withhold support from the DVP in an effort to consolidate the bourgeois right.[97] That same evidence does, on the other hand, bear out the substance of Heinrichsbauer's contention since the vehicle for that consolidation was, in Brandi's plan, the DNVP. Insofar as evidence exists of Brandi's desire to intervene to influence the course of politics, the beneficiary was to be Hugenberg, not Hitler. Even as late as February 1933 Brandi backed not the Nazis but "the non-Nazi component" of what he perceived as the "national unification" effected under Hitler's chancellorship.[98] During the previous spring and summer all indications pointed to the DNVP as the recipient of the lion's share of Ruhr coal's political money. As for the motive behind the contribution of 100,000 marks to the NSDAP remembered by Heinrichsbauer, only speculation remains possible in the absence of conclusive documentation. One possibility is that Brandi and his associates may have wanted to promote the Nazis so as to prepare the way for an alliance between Hugenberg and Hitler on the basis of a renewed "Harzburg Front." But given the dynamism and prosperity of the NSDAP, as compared to the declining strength and straitened circumstances of the DNVP—the party to which their primary allegiance went—Brandi and his associates would surely have concentrated their resources on Hugenberg if only such a consideration had played a role. That they chose instead, if Heinrichsbauer's memory serves, to include the NSDAP suggests another line of reasoning on their part, namely, that they may have numbered among those men of big business who responded to the mounting Nazi tide by expanding their political insurance through a diversion to that party of a share of the "premiums" they had grown accustomed to paying in order to obtain coverage in the event of a change of regime. A further recollection of Heinrichsbauer raises still another possibility. As he recalled, the coal operators had made their contribution of 100,000 marks primarily in order to bolster the position within the NSDAP of Walther Funk.[99] If so, they, like so many others, had fallen victim to the fallacious notion that one could alter Nazism by subsidizing particular Nazis who seemed "reasonable" or "moderate."

Very different motives played a role in the flow of certain other money from the business community to National Socialism. Evidence of those payments could not be kept secret; it appeared daily in black and white in the form of big advertisements by large corporations in the Nazi press. The party's newspapers had in earlier years caused great financial difficulties for those Nazis who published them. With the possible exception of the *Völkischer Beobachter*, they rarely if ever received material help from the party proper. Party officials applied the abundant income that derived from dues, rallies, and other grass-roots sources to more directly political ends. Denied access to the mainstream of party funds, Nazi newspapers and magazines had to rely financially on the entrepreneurial ingenuity of their promoters and on the income those publications generated from sales and from advertising.[100] In the 1920s advertising in even the national organ, the *Völkischer Beobachter*, came mainly from retail merchants, including department stores—non-Jewish—with the occasional addition of ads from producers of such mass-consumption household products as soap powders and coffees. By 1932, however, that had changed. Readers of the *Völkischer Beobachter* now found its pages adorned with large, splashy advertisements paid for by such companies as Daimler-Benz (for its Mercedes-Benz cars), the Ford Motor Company, the Auto-Union corporation, and the German branches of the Continental and Dunlop tire companies.[101] Without question, the income from such advertisements helped the Nazi press and hence the party's cause. But can that income be regarded as subsidization arising from political motives? The records that might permit a conclusive answer to that question remain to be located. Circumstantial evidence strongly suggests, however, that the placing of large, presumably expensive ads in Nazi publications in 1932 cannot be regarded as proof of a desire to help the NSDAP in its quest for power. That circumstantial evidence can be found in the pages of the official daily organ of the Social Democratic Party, *Vorwärts*. There, too, one finds large, presumably expensive ads, paid for by capitalist corporations, offering automobiles (including Mercedes-Benz), auto tires, and radios (then still a luxury item).[102] Conceivably, the executives of those corporations might have contracted to pay for advertisements in the organ of a party officially committed to the socialization of industry in order to ingratiate themselves with the leaders of that party. But although at least a few of Germany's capitalists apparently contributed some occasional funds to the SPD, that hypothesis seems of very limited plausibility in view of the prevalent hostility toward that party in business circles. It seems much more likely that corporations paid for ads in *Vorwärts* because their advertising departments informed them that the Social Democratic paper commanded a large readership that included many potential purchasers of their products. By the spring of 1932, with nearly thirteen and a half million voters having cast their ballots for Adolf Hitler in the second round of the presidential election, the same reasoning presumably applied to advertisements in the *Völkischer Beobachter*.

In at least one case, to be sure, the decision to pay for large advertisements in the *Völkischer Beobachter* involved more than merely commercial calculations. In that case, the decision rested with Philipp Reemtsma, Germany's foremost cigarette producer. Reemtsma's Hamburg firm did not qualify as part of big business since producing cigarettes did not involve huge amounts of capital investment. But by 1932 the Reemtsma firm had, through a succession of mergers, come to dominate a lucrative consumer market. By virtue of having absorbed most of its major competitors, it sold at least two-thirds of the approximately forty million cigarettes bought by the country's smokers.[103] Since cigarettes were subject to excise taxes amounting to roughly a third of their sales prices, Reemtsma devoted considerable attention to the politicians who could shape tax legislation to his favor or disadvantage. His political activities seem to have focused primarily on the middle of the Weimar party spectrum. He had since the 1920s aligned himself with the Democratic Party and supported it financially.[104] After World War II he claimed also to have aided the ill-fated Conservative People's Party when its leaders broke with Hugenberg's DNVP and attempted unsuccessfully to establish themselves as a force in the Reichstag at the time of the 1930 elections.[105] For the 1932 presidential election Reemtsma contributed 25,000 marks to the Hindenburg campaign before each of the rounds of balloting.[106] Reemtsma and his firm had by that time long since become a favorite target of Nazi invective.[107] This hostility on the part of the NSDAP resulted less from Reemtsma's moderate politics than from his firm's success in swallowing up competitors and cornering a large portion of a conspicuous consumer-item industry, a success that made it the kind of *Konzern* many Nazi spokesmen liked to blame for the depressed economic plight of many small manufacturers.[108] Reemtsma's products aroused especially strong hostility within the SA since the brands of cigarettes endorsed by the storm-trooper organization, for a share of the profits, found in Reemtsma just the sort of formidable competitor the packages of their own brands warned against with the slogan *"Gegen Trust und Konzern!"* By 1932 the SA's cigarette factory was circulating a vituperative tract directed against Reemtsma.[109]

Also by 1932, with the National Socialists scoring one election gain after another, Reemtsma began, like Friedrich Flick and possibly Otto Wolff, to regard them with grave concern as possible future rulers. In an effort to counteract the hostility toward him and his firm in the NSDAP, Reemtsma adopted a direct approach, inviting three local Hamburg Nazi leaders to dinner in the spring of 1932. He failed, one of the three later reported, to convince them of the benignity of his enterprise. He did, however, make clear to his guests his misgivings about the goals and aims of National Socialism and of Hitler.[110] Nevertheless, Reemtsma arranged to meet Hitler not long thereafter, reportedly sometime in July 1932.[111] Exactly what course their conversation took remains undocumented. Hitler later scornfully recalled Reemtsma as a crass businessman: "If I agree to be photographed with a cigar between my teeth, I believe Reemtsma would immediately offer me a half a million marks!"[112] Regardless of the opinions the two men formed of each other, the result of their meeting becomes evident to anyone who inspects the pages of the *Völkischer Beobachter*. There, starting on July 20, eleven days before the Reichstag election that would provide the NSDAP with its greatest electoral triumph, elaborate half-page ads for Reemtsma cigarettes suddenly began appearing almost every day until the election, and thereafter at intervals of two or three weeks.[113] Later in the year the irate Nazi proprietor of a small snuff factory in the Bavarian town of Landshut, who also dealt in cigarettes, complained to the party's national headquarters about acceptance by the *Völkischer Beobachter* of advertisements from a rapacious trust of the very kind National Socialism had pledged to break up.[114] He and the other Nazis who complained received by way of explanation a curt notification that "acceptance of the Reemtsma advertisement in the *Völkischer Beobachter* took place at the order of the Führer after personal consultation with Herr Reemtsma, following thoroughgoing scrutiny by the central National Socialist advertising office."[115] Neither such letters nor the continuing appearance of Reemtsma ads sufficed to overcome hostility to that firm in the ranks of the NSDAP, and after Hitler's acquisition of power Reemtsma reportedly survived a Nazi onslaught, aimed at consigning him to prison, only by cultivating the favor of Hermann Göring through generous application of under-the-table funds toward the costly material needs of that expansive party chieftain.[116] His payments for advertisements in 1932 certainly helped the NSDAP—or at least the *Völkischer Beobachter*—financially, but that would hardly seem to have been his intention. If his talk with Hitler had converted him to the Nazi camp, he would presumably have simply given money directly to the party leader or one of his aides since that would have occasioned fewer difficulties within the NSDAP from Nazis like the Landshut snuff processor. Yet no evidence suggests that Reemtsma made any such contributions or abandoned his aloofness toward National Socialism. Instead, he apparently struck a bargain with Hitler in an effort to gain both immediate commercial advantages and, he seems to have hoped, a lessening of hostility on the part of a potential wielder of political power. Like so many others, he sought political insurance for future eventualities, not a Nazi triumph.

Advertisements in the *Völkischer Beobachter* by a large international corporation probably contributed to the early development of one of the most persistent canards about the relations between National Socialism and big business. That canard had its origins in rumors that circulated in

Berlin in the spring of 1932 linking to the Nazis Sir Henri Deterding, the head of Royal Dutch Shell Oil Company, who according to some versions was supplying Hitler's party with large amounts of money.[117] These rumors may have been triggered by the friendly treatment accorded to Deterding's views in the Nazi press, where his ardent anti-bolshevism and his unorthodox proposals for combating the depression were sympathetically reported.[118] But it seems more likely that his firm's practice of placing large, conspicuous ads in the *Völkischer Beobachter* set in motion the rumor mills of the capital. When apprized of those rumors at the time, Deterding flatly denied them.[119] They have nevertheless proved irrepressible, spreading through the literature on Hitler's rise and becoming ever more elaborate without the benefit of any proof whatever.[120] One East German historian has placed the amount of money Deterding allegedly gave to the NSDAP prior to Hitler's appointment as chancellor at ten million marks.[121]

The legend of Deterding's aid to the NSDAP prior to 1933 has in some versions been bolstered by confusing his attitudes and actions then with those of a period well after the Nazi takeover. Deterding did indeed manifest a strong interest in Germany's internal affairs, but only several years after Hitler had become dictator. After his retirement from Shell in 1936 he moved to Germany, taking up residence with his third wife, a young German woman, on an estate in Mecklenburg, a province to which he could trace his ancestry on his father's side.[122] There Deterding developed cordial relations with the local Nazi leaders, contributing generously to Nazi-sponsored charities and developing a plan to donate part of his estate to provide model farms for homesteaders.[123] When Deterding died in 1939, an official of the party-operated charity, Winterhilfswerk, served as one of his pallbearers, having been officially designated as a representative of the Führer.[124] Hitler himself, to be sure, later referred disparagingly to Deterding, linking him with former Economics Minister Hjalmar Schacht, and imputing bribery to him.[125] Still, if Deterding had, in fact, bankrolled Hitler or the party before 1933, surely that information would not have gone unmentioned in the eulogistic obituaries that appeared in the press of the Third Reich. Yet none of those make mention of any aid by the oil executive prior to his retirement to Mecklenburg,[126] nor is any such mention to be found in the protest of the gauleiter of Mecklenburg against a Nazi magazine's denunciation of Deterding in 1941 as a greedy English plutocrat.[127]

As for the Shell ads of 1932 in the *Völkischer Beobachter*, no more grounds exist for attaching political motives to them than to those of other large firms that advertised there. Shell motor oil and gasoline were consumer products whose sales might be expected to improve if attractive ads reached the large readership of a paper addressed to the followers of a party that could mobilize millions of voters and hundreds of thousands of members. As in the case of Reemtsma, Sir Henri Deterding could have spared the leaders of the NSDAP considerable disaffection among their rank-and-file followers by simply giving cash if he had intended to aid the Nazi cause. In the event, the appearance of Shell ads in the party organ occasioned the same sort of indignant outcries as did the Reemtsma ads. One such protest from a Nazi district organization led the director of the party publishing house, Max Amann, to lose his temper. "We accept Shell ads," Amann wrote in his reply, "because not even we National Socialists can drive with water."[128] Presumably, the advertising division of the German branch of Shell believed that their company could not sell its products without convincing consumers—regardless of their political proclivities—of the merits of these products. Even in the midst of Germany's catastrophic "year of elections," politics did not wholly displace business considerations.

VI
Big Business and the Triumph of Nazism

1. Nazis as Champions of Parliament and the Workers— The Capitalists Find Their Chancellor

During the late summer and autumn of 1932 the NSDAP followed a course that alienated virtually all of big business. Even some of those business executives who had shown themselves favorably disposed toward the National Socialists recoiled when they suddenly transformed themselves into advocates of parliamentary democracy and champions of the laboring masses. Those who had hoped for a government of "national opposition" that would unite the Nazis with politicians of the traditional right looked on in dismay as the NSDAP turned ferociously against those politicians, including a chancellor who came to enjoy enthusiastic support in the business community. As Germany approached its fifth national election of 1932, the reputation of the NSDAP in business circles was sinking rapidly.

The Reichstag election of July 31, 1932, further eroded the initially precarious parliamentary position of the Papen cabinet by virtually obliterating the non-Catholic parties of the middle. Only the DNVP, which held its own by retaining 40 seats, offered the prospect of reliable support in the chamber. The day after the election Papen reaffirmed his resolve to keep his government free of all formal ties to the parliament. He expressed the hope, however, that a collision with the Reichstag could be averted by means of a working arrangement between his cabinet and the two parties that together controlled a majority in the new chamber, the Center with its 75 seats and the NSDAP with its 230.[1] The leaders of the Center quickly disabused the chancellor of the notion that they would cooperate with a renegade from their ranks who seemed bent on establishing a dictatorial regime, as evidenced by his deposition of the Prussian government, in which the Center had been represented. The Catholic leaders preferred a return to parliamentary government, including the NSDAP if necessary, to a continuation of Papen's rule by presidential decree in defiance of the Reichstag.[2] In mid-August Papen turned to the Nazis and offered Hitler the nominal post of vice-chancellor in his cabinet, the most President Hindenburg was willing to allow the Nazi leader. But at meetings with both Papen and Hindenburg during the second week of August Hitler rejected such an arrangement. As the leader of the largest party in the new Reichstag, he stubbornly insisted on the chancellorship. When Hindenburg would not give way, the negotiations collapsed. In mid-August Hitler proclaimed the NSDAP's opposition to the Papen cabinet.[3]

From all indications big business exercised little or no influence on these abortive negotiations with Hitler. A month later August Heinrichsbauer, the fellow-traveling journalist and lobbyist with ties to Ruhr industrialists, wrote to Gregor Strasser that some unspecified executives from the *Revier* had in August communicated to key people in Berlin their support for Hitler's appointment as chancellor.[4] But even if that was true, advice from industrial quarters clearly carried insufficient weight to overcome the objections of Hindenburg. The president still objected to Hitler so strongly that he rejected out of hand even the advice of one of his closest advisers, General von Schleicher, to make Hitler chancellor and surround him with conservative ministers.[5] Moreover, even if a man like Fritz Thyssen had made his support for Hitler's designs on the chancellorship known in Berlin, he could not claim to speak for the whole of Ruhr industry. Opinion in those circles varied widely as to the most desirable resolution to the political situation. Thyssen, Ernst Brandi of the Bergbauverein, and Ludwig Grauert of Arbeitnordwest argued that the Nazis, as the largest party, deserved to form a cabinet with Hitler as chancellor.[6] The *Deutsche Führerbriefe*, a publication addressed to business executives, called for a grant of presidential emergency powers to a cabinet headed by Hitler.[7] Other voices from the business community took a more cautious approach. Baron Tilo von Wilmowsky, brother-in-law and close adviser of Gustav Krupp von Bohlen und Halbach, was willing to see the Nazis brought into the government only as part of a parliamentary coalition in which the NSDAP, even with Hitler as chancellor, would be checked by the Center and the DNVP.[8] A well-connected observer in Berlin reported in early August that business circles in the capital wanted no change at all in the cabinet.[9] Nor did the most politically active and influential of the Ruhr industrialists, Paul Reusch. Throughout the spring Reusch had striven to minimize friction between the Nazis and the other components of the "national opposition" in order to facilitate inclusion of the NSDAP in a government of that complexion at the state level. He still favored their entry into the governments of the smaller states—though no longer that of Prussia—in coalition with the Catholic and bourgeois parties.[10] Admitting the Nazis to the national government was, however, a very different matter for Reusch. In August he instructed the newspapers he controlled not to advocate the appointment of Hitler or any other National Socialists to the Reich cabinet. He had taken offense at the Nazis' behavior during the negotiations with Papen and Hindenburg, and he ordered criticism of it in his press.[11] But Reusch's main consideration in wishing the Nazis excluded from the national government derived from his desire to see the Papen cabinet get on with its promised constitutional and economic "reforms." That, he judged, could best be accomplished if the government remained unencumbered by ties to any party, including the NSDAP.[12]

In making his calculations, Reusch failed to take into account Hitler's relentless drive for power and his readiness to resort to any means in order to destroy an obstacle, such as the Papen cabinet, that blocked his path. Reusch was therefore unprepared for the sudden shift in the Nazi leader's strategy that led the NSDAP into postures that he, like most big businessmen, found extremely alarming. Hitler, having failed to secure the chancellorship from Hindenburg following his stunning election triumph of July, now embarked on a course of all-out opposition calculated to overcome the president's opposition to Nazi leadership of the national government by demonstrating the vulnerability of the Papen cabinet because of its lack of popular support. Failing that, Hitler intended to isolate and humiliate Papen in the Reichstag and expose his unpopularity in another test of strength at the polls.

In pursuit of these strategic goals, Hitler adopted tactics that involved audacious and utterly cynical reversals of long-standing Nazi positions. Most strikingly, he began to use Papen's pledge to govern without regard to the Reichstag as a cudgel against the cabinet. Overnight the NSDAP became a zealous defender of the parliamentary democracy Hitler had hitherto excoriated. In the Prussian Landtag the Nazi deputies joined in late August with the Social Democrats and Communists in passing bills aimed at restoring the authority of the state parliament and ending Papen's emergency rule in that state.[13] The Nazi deputies in the Landtag then went on to introduce a series of bills of their own that ran directly counter to the policies of the Papen cabinet by calling for government aid to various categories of persons suffering from the depression.[14] When the Reichstag convened at the beginning of September, the Nazis collaborated with the Center Party to elect the chamber's officers. Hermann Göring thus became president of the body he had so long derided. Immediately on assuming his new office Göring cautioned the Papen cabinet against dissolving the newly elected parliament. A working majority existed, he proclaimed, as demonstrated by the vote that had bestowed his new dignity on him. To send home the deputies under such circumstances would amount, Göring sanctimoniously warned, to a violation of the constitution.[15] For those big businessmen who, like Reusch, had assumed with relief that the Papen cabinet had put an end, once and for all, to parliamentary democracy as practiced during the Republic, the sudden enthusiasm of Göring and other Nazi leaders for representative government could only seem an ominous development.

Big business also found very disturbing the composition of the potential Reichstag majority alluded to by Göring. By the time Göring spoke, everyone who read a newspaper knew that well-publicized negotiations were under way between the Nazis and the Center. In retrospect it appears clear that Hitler never seriously contemplated forming a coalition cabinet on a parliamentary basis with the Catholic party. He seems merely to have encouraged the negotiations in order to bring to bear his party's powerful position in the new Reichstag in maximal fashion, so as to make untenable Papen's claim to authority.[16] But as the business community could not know this, it viewed the apparently real prospect of a "black-brown" government with great apprehension. Business circles had long feared that, given the strength of the Christian trade unions in the Center Party, these would collude with left-wing elements of the NSDAP if that party entered into a coalition with the Center, producing a pro-labor, anti-business government. When prominent Catholic labor leaders greeted the prospect of a coalition with the Nazis warmly during early September, setting off rumors about Nazi-Centrist plans for socialization of basic industries, those fears seemed confirmed.[17] Information on those negotiations reaching Reusch convinced him that the socialistic elements in the NSDAP were growing ever stronger.[18] Meanwhile, mounting friction between the NSDAP and the DNVP, which had rallied to Papen's defense, made any notion of a united "national opposition" appear fanciful.[19]

In the midst of this mounting Nazi assault on the Papen cabinet, the chancellor and his associates unveiled constitutional and economic plans that removed the lingering reservations of most big businessmen about his government. In mid-August Papen's interior minister, Baron Wilhelm von Gayl, used a commemoration of the thirteenth anniversary of the Weimar constitution's ratification to announce the cabinet's intention to seek changes in that document. He proposed to restrict the right to vote, which the constitution bestowed on all twenty-year-old men and women, to abolish proportional representation so as to diminish the role of political parties, and to establish an appointive or indirectly elected upper chamber as a counterweight to the Reichstag.[20] These plans greatly bolstered the prestige of the cabinet in those big business circles that had long entertained similar schemes for reducing the power of the popularly elected national parliament. Such was the case with Reusch, who favored replacing the republican Reichsrat, in which representatives of state governments sat, with an appointive upper chamber.[21]

Of even more immediate interest to big business was the long-awaited announcement of the cabinet's economic program. That came in a speech Papen delivered in Münster on August 28, and a week later the chancellor implemented what came to be known as the Münster Program by means of emergency decrees. In drafting its plans the cabinet had preserved strict secrecy, so that speculation about the forthcoming measures had become rampant. Only two days before Papen's Münster speech the press carried rumors to the effect that the government would launch a large-scale, state-administered program of work-creation for Germany's army of unemployed, financed by a special tax on private property or compulsory loans to the state by owners of capital.[22] Great relief therefore spread through big business circles when Papen announced his actual program, which sought to create work for the jobless by stimulating economic activity in the private sector. To encourage the expansion of production and the employment of more workers, the Münster Program provided businesses with a form of tax relief that would also inject fresh credit into the economy. Additional tax relief went to firms hiring workers directly from the ranks of the unemployed. Moreover, the Münster Program allowed employers who hired new workers to reduce a substantial portion of the weekly contract wages of all their employees. Only a minor portion of the government's efforts were to take the form of direct work-creation through government-financed public works.[23]

Papen's Münster Program met the most optimistic hopes of big business, which responded with enthusiastic approbation.[24] By according primacy in its recovery program to the private sector, it seemed to mark the clean break with "collectivism" that most of the business community had hoped for in vain from Brüning. The emphasis on tax relief appeared to be a vindication of the contention that excessive taxation had crippled the economy in the first place and must be ended before recovery could take place. The provision permitting the reduction of contract wages was particularly welcome, representing the first significant breach in the body of post-revolutionary law and practice that had made labor contracts virtually inviolable. It held out the prospect of the general wage reduction that virtually all of big business believed must come about if prices were to be lowered sufficiently to rekindle the investment necessary for recovery. Also, coupled with the Papen cabinet's earlier immobilization of the state arbitration system and its reduction of unemployment and social insurance benefits, the provision for contract-wage reduction seemed to herald an intention to dismantle the measures enacted during the Republic to protect the rights and welfare of the working people of Germany. That was a welcome prospect for most big businessmen, who remained convinced that excessive *Sozialpolitik* had crippled the economy and caused the special severity of the depression in their country. Now, at last, a government was summoning up the wisdom and courage to dismantle both these misguided measures and the political order that had given rise to them. In Franz von Papen, the business community belatedly realized, it had found a chancellor to whom it could accord its full and enthusiastic allegiance.

Nazi attacks on that same chancellor quickly cast the NSDAP in an increasingly unfavorable light so far as the business community was concerned. In early September the party's Reichstag deputies, who were conferring with Centrist deputies about a possible coalition, joined with their Catholic negotiating partners in condemning the cabinet's new measures as unfair to Germany's workers.[25] Shortly thereafter three Nazi heads of state governments issued a public statement denouncing the cabinet for reducing unemployment benefits and state pensions.[26] These and similar stands on the part of the Nazis made difficult the position of those political observers who contended that the best way to check the Nazis was to saddle them with governmental responsibility, a view held by, among others, such respected and politically moderate Jewish figures as the banker Carl Melchior and Hans Schäffer, former state secretary in the Finance Ministry under Brüning. When presented by Schäffer and Melchoir with this argument in early September, Ludwig Kastl, executive director of the industrial Reichsverband, demurred; the damage the NSDAP would do to the economy made any such move unacceptable, Kastl insisted.[27]

The Nazis' opposition to the economic policies of the Papen cabinet also caused problems for the Keppler circle. During early September Keppler and another member of the circle, Karl Vincent Krogmann, found that the businessmen with whom they came into contact showed themselves ill disposed toward National Socialism, having closed ranks behind the chancellor.[28] Business executives feared, Krogmann explained in a letter to Keppler, that if the NSDAP got into power, economic policy would be dictated by men lacking any practical experience who would act solely on the basis of theories.[29] Krogmann complained particularly about a recent three-day economic conference at the Brown House that had received much publicity in the Nazi press. Under the auspices of Gottfried Feder's Engineering-Technical Section of the Reichsleitung, that conference provided a forum for two speeches by Feder, in which he reiterated his monetary theories and demanded nationalization of money and credit institutions. Also at the conference Nazi Reichstag deputy Fritz Reinhardt announced that the NSDAP would stand for no further reductions in wages or social benefits. Adrian von Renteln, the official of the Economic Policy Section designated as responsible for the Immediate Economic Program of July, pronounced capitalism incapable of coping with the depression. Another member of the Economic Policy Section, Werner Daitz, again spelled out the countercyclical, deficit-spending proposals of that program.[30] Such statements and the positive publicity accorded them in the Nazi press aroused mistrust in the business community, Krogmann informed Keppler. The apparently official endorsement of the views of such theoreticians could only cast doubt, Krogmann added, on Hitler's repeated assurances to the effect that upon attaining power he would content himself with establishing overall goals and then leave economic decisions to businessmen. Developments like the three-day economic conference, Krogmann continued, undercut the line of argument he used in approaching business executives. Whereas he sought to convince them that a circle of leading figures from the business community was forming around Hitler in order to prevent any stupidities in the economic sphere, the enthusiastic reports on the Munich economic conference in the Nazi press made his arguments seem implausible.[31]

The parliamentary tactics of the NSDAP provided further cause for alarm in the business community. Once Papen had made clear his intention to deal with an implacably hostile Reichstag majority by using a dissolution decree granted him by Hindenburg, Hitler began taunting the chancellor with charges of unconstitutionally flouting the democratically expressed will of the populace. He himself remained, by contrast, "strictly constitutional," Hitler proclaimed; the NSDAP planned to alter the constitution, but only by constitutional means.[32] When the newly elected parliament convened for its first business session on September 12, Göring used his position as president of the chamber to humiliate the chancellor on whom the business community had placed its hopes. By ignoring Papen's attempts to read into the record the dissolution decree signed by Hindenburg, he permitted the deputies to ballot on a Communist motion of no confidence. With the votes of the Nazis and others, the motion carried by 513 to 42. Only the shrunken DVP and DNVP backed Papen, who suffered the most crushing parliamentary defeat ever inflicted on a German chancellor. Not until after the vote did he succeed in dissolving the chamber.[33]

The NSDAP's anti-Papen stance quickly put it on a collision course with big business, as the party's assault on the chancellor and his cabinet set loose a torrent of Nazi anti-capitalism. On the very day of the no-confidence vote and dissolution, the Nazis launched an abrasive election campaign that left no doubt about their decision to resort to demagogic socio-economic radicalism. To open the campaign, they had ready for release that day a pamphlet that branded as reactionary both Papen and his cabinet.[34] The chancellor had, it charged, aligned himself completely with the "private capitalistic system" by issuing emergency decrees that "lacked any spark of social justice." The pamphlet pilloried the cabinet's efforts to reduce wages and undermine the sanctity of contract wages, pledging the NSDAP to resist both. It described Papen's reductions in social benefits as "social robbery" perpetrated against "the mass of working people" in order to bestow a gift on a "small gang" of big business entrepreneurs. Papen's close and one-sided ties with the business community revealed, the pamphlet announced, that his entire economic policy amounted to nothing more than a throwback to *Manchestertum* (a derisive term for laissez-faire economic policies) designed to fill the bank accounts of those "gentlemen." In keeping with the tone of this pamphlet, Gottfried Feder took to the hustings, denouncing the Papen cabinet's tax-relief measures as a fraudulent trick designed to benefit the country's "big shots." Such measures only prepared the way for communism, Feder warned. But the workers would not be fooled, he added. Germany's voters would see that only the work-creation plans of National Socialism, based on his monetary theories, offered a sure way out of the depression.[35] Other Nazi campaign orators delivered stump speeches with titles such as "Down with the Dictatorship of the Moneybags," promising that the NSDAP would repel Papen's "class war party of capitalism."[36] A Nazi who inquired during the campaign about the NSDAP's policy toward large corporations received notification that these would be socialized.[37]

This pronounced Nazi turn to socio-economic radicalism did not escape notice in the business community. The Ruhr steel executive Fritz Springorum, who had established friendly relations with Papen, spoke in early September disparagingly of the "violent agitation and incitement" directed against the chancellor by the NSDAP.[38] Martin Blank, one of Paul Reusch's political agents, reported to him from Berlin at about the same time that the radicalization of the NSDAP, together with Hindenburg's aversion to that party, ruled out any possibility of including the Nazis in the government.[39] Another of Reusch's informants in the capital, Erich von Gilsa, noted during the third week of September that the Nazis' campaign was marked by extraordinary demagogy and a recourse to "purely socialist ideas" in order to entice votes from the camp of the "Marxist workers." He added that it had become fashionable among National Socialist leaders to look and behave like proletarians in keeping with their party's increasingly socialistic line; even Göring, whom such a role ill suited, conformed to the new Nazi style. Of the large parties, Gilsa concluded, only the DNVP remained committed to private enterprise.[40] The DNVP, for its part, responded to the NSDAP's radical campaign by abandoning all talk of collaboration with Hitler and his party. The Nationalists vigorously parried the thrusts of the Nazis, charging them with betrayal of the "national opposition," abandonment of presidential government, and defense of the democratic "system" of Weimar.[41]

The attitude of the business press toward the NSDAP cooled still further under the onslaught of that party's radical campaign. The rightist *Deutsche Allgemeine Zeitung* of Berlin expressed alarm at reports of a speech in which Gregor Strasser advocated a "German socialism." The socialist Strasser, the paper noted, demanded a state takeover of all financial and credit institutions, well aware that such a move would give the government so much power over the economy that it would, in effect, mean state socialism. The bourgeois friends and voters of the NSDAP could hardly find edifying Nazism's open commitment to the goal of socialism, the *DAZ* editorial concluded.[42] In Düsseldorf the *Deutsche Bergwerks-Zeitung* observed in the midst of the election campaign that if a reader did not immediately recognize a Nazi newspaper from its masthead, he would often have difficulty deciding whether what he read had been written by a Communist, a Social Democrat, or a Nazi.[43]

The direction taken by the NSDAP's leadership and the negative response to it of the business community greatly hampered efforts by the Keppler circle to reassure businessmen that Nazi economic policy was in good hands. The irrepressible Gottfried Feder proved a particularly troublesome problem. To Keppler's distress, Feder discoursed at length in late October on his idiosyncratic economic views before an invited audience in Berlin that included a number of businessmen. Keppler termed the speech the next day a "catastrophe" and asked the party headquarters to forbid Feder to hold any more such talks.[44] During the following week the Brown House received a flow of letters from other persons in Feder's audience, protesting that his remarks had harmed the party. As a result, Hitler's deputy, Rudolf Hess, wrote to Feder, reminding him of the party leader's request that he refrain in his speeches from going into details about economic policies. He instructed Feder to cancel any such scheduled speeches. Feder protested vehemently, but on November 9 Hess informed the chief economic theorist of the NSDAP that Hitler did not want him to give any more speeches about economic questions to select audiences.[45] By that time, however, Feder's damage had been done, for the fall election campaign was over.

Nor did the Nazis limit their socio-economic radicalism during the fall election campaign to words. To an unprecedented degree they actively involved themselves in strike activity on behalf of workers. In September the party upgraded the Nazi Factory Cell Organization (NSBO), which received enhanced status in the Reichsleitung, an enlarged staff, and subsidies from the party treasurer.[46] That organization, which had an estimated membership of about 40,000 in 1931, claimed to number over 300,000 by the autumn of 1932.[47] In one of its publications its leader proclaimed capitalism "immoral" and declared trade unions a necessity.[48] An article widely disseminated in the Nazi press during October reminded Papen that the party had never foresworn the strike as the most important means for dealing with greedy employers. Strikes were rare in the depression-ridden Germany of late 1932, but where they occurred, usually in response to wage cuts, the Nazis lent them support whenever possible.[49] Party newspapers proudly proclaimed the participation of NSBO men in strikes and announced that they received strike-support compensation from the party equal to that distributed by the trade unions to their members. In mid-October the *Deutsche Bergwerks-Zeitung* of Düsseldorf detected a Nazi-planned wave of wildcat strikes sweeping across Germany and noted that a party paper in Düsseldorf spoke in terms of a general strike. The Nazi gauleiter in Munich, Adolf Wagner, had recently proclaimed the NSDAP the only truly revolutionary party in Germany, the *Deutsche Bergwerks-Zeitung* added, not challenging the accuracy of that assertion.[50] Such a claim, coupled with the Nazis' active support of labor, could only bode ill for the future so far as business was concerned.

To their distress, the men of the Bergbauverein discovered that this new party line led the NSDAP to ignore vital interests of the Ruhr coal operators, despite their past aid to various Nazis and the party membership of Erich Winnacker, the regional coal executive of the United Steel Works who had left the DNVP to join the NSDAP in April. During September Winnacker joined in the deliberations of Nazis in the Ruhr regarding the party's stance on issues pending in the coal industry, one of the most important of which turned on a controversy over Social Democratic and trade union demands for a shortening of the mining workday from eight to seven hours. Drawing on data supplied him by the Bergbauverein, Winnacker argued against Nazi support for the seven-hour day, insisting that adoption of such a measure would make it economically unfeasible to operate the mines. Nazis employed in the mines vigorously challenged Winnacker's position, contending that technical advances made it possible to accomplish in seven hours what had formerly taken eight.[51] When the local gauleiter referred the question to Gregor Strasser for a ruling, identifying Winnacker and setting forth his views as well as those of his opponents, Strasser brushed the operators' contentions aside and informed the gauleiter he had no objections to Nazi support for the seven-hour day.[52] For the Nazi hierarchy, the interests of coal operators obviously carried less weight in the fall of 1932 than did those of coal miners, who after all had many more ballots to cast on November 6. The men of the Bergbauverein quickly drew their conclusions from the NSDAP's shift to a radical socio-economic course. During the summer that organization's chairman, Ernst Brandi, had favored the appointment of Hitler as chancellor. Now, in September, Brandi shifted his ground, falling in behind Chancellor Papen, who had taken him into his confidence.[53] Departing from its customary practice of refraining from political commentary, the house organ of the Bergbauverein contemptuously dismissed in September the plans of Feder and other Nazis for job creation through large-scale investment in a hydroelectric power system that would—among other things— threaten the primacy of coal as Germany's energy source.[54] Then, during the second week of September, Brandi joined with the other members of the board of advisers of the business-controlled *Rheinisch-*

Westfälische Zeitung of Essen to fire its editor, the fellow-traveling Theodor Reismann-Grone, rather than allow him to align the paper editorially with the NSDAP.[55]

Almost as disconcerting to big business as the Nazis' espousal of the
cause of industrial workers was the NSDAP's agrarian radicalism during
the autumn election campaign. This support for agrarian interests came
as no surprise since the party had, with notable success, concentrated
much of its attention on the rural population ever since 1930, when its
inroads into the countryside had contributed importantly to its electoral
gains of that year. But by the fall of 1932 the demands of Germany's
agrarian organizations had become more radical and threatening from
the standpoint of industry and banking. The Nazis themselves had a
hand in that process of radicalization, as they had infiltrated the largest
and most vocal of the agrarian organizations, the Reichslandbund,
within which their spokesmen consistently assumed extreme positions.[56]
When, in the fall of 1932, the Reichslandbund and the other organizations comprising the "Green Front" that championed agrarian interests
demanded a thoroughgoing system of stringent import quotas for agricultural products and a downward adjustment of the interest rates on
outstanding farm mortgages, the Nazis emphatically endorsed their demands.[57] Seeking to mobilize discontent in the countryside against the
Papen cabinet, the Nazis accused the government of indifference toward
Germany's farmers. To the distress of industrial and commercial interests, which feared that import quotas would provoke retaliation abroad
against German industrial exports, and to the alarm of financial circles,
which objected to tampering with mortgage terms, Papen retreated before this barrage of Nazi agrarian agitation. Late in September his minister of agriculture endorsed in principle both reduced interest rates on
farm mortgages and import quotas on foodstuffs.[58] But since the cabinet moved only dilatorily on those matters, that commitment did not still
Nazi accusations that Papen was doing too little for agriculture. Nor did
the commitment ever result in any drastic governmental measures, as
initially feared by industry, commerce, and banking. Still, the impact of
Nazi agrarian agitation became a source of mounting concern in business circles. Wilhelm Keppler, sensitive to the negative effects in
business circles of the NSDAP's demands for increased agrarian protectionism, informed a member of his circle early in October that he had
just talked with Hitler and learned that the party leader rejected such a
one-sided anti-industrial policy. In an obvious effort to spread this report, Keppler added that he would not object if his correspondent
passed that information along whenever an opportunity presented itself.[59] Much more than the dissemination of such purported inside
information would have been needed, however, to counteract the
damaging effects in business circles of the NSDAP's massive propaganda
campaign in favor of tight import quotas on agricultural products.

At least one attempt at conciliation between the NSDAP and the business community took place in the midst of the party's shift to socio-economic radicalism. That effort began when Adrian von Renteln, the young assistant of Otto Wagener, head of the party's Economic Policy Section, paid a visit, while in Berlin in mid-July, to a boyhood friend who worked on the staff of the industrial Reichsverband. Renteln presented himself as a key figure in the formulation of Nazi economic policy and requested from the Reichsverband a list of industrialists who would be interested in cooperating with the NSDAP in that regard. He planned, he told his friend, to approach them personally and then arrange for them consultations with such Nazis as Hitler and Gregor Strasser. Neither Walther Funk nor Wagener, but rather Strasser alone, was the decisive figure with regard to the party's position on economic questions, Renteln asserted.[60] When apprized of this development, the staff manager of the Reichsverband, Jakob Herle, agreed, after consulting with Reusch and presumably other major figures in the organization, to meet with Renteln when he next visited Berlin in early August. On that occasion Renteln repeated to Herle most of what he had told his friend and held out the prospect of ongoing direct communications between the Economic Policy Section of the party and the Reichsverband. By way of initiating such a dialogue, he suggested a written exchange of views. Herle acceded to that suggestion, as well as to Renteln's request for information from the Reichsverband on pending economic issues. Herle stressed, however, that the commitment of the Reichsverband to a nonpartisan political stance ruled out anything beyond the sort of exchange of ideas and information which his organization always stood willing to undertake with all parties. He accordingly left unmet Renteln's original request for the names of industrialists who might be prepared to meet with him and other Nazis. Instead, Herle proposed that Renteln set in motion a dialogue by sending him a statement of the NSDAP's most important economic policy demands. Renteln agreed, and they parted company in amicable fashion.[61] When informed of what had happened, Reusch applauded Herle for at last establishing contact between the Reichsverband and the Economic Policy Section of the NSDAP.[62]

Despite this promising beginning, the dialogue with the Reichsverband initiated by Renteln proved one-sided and of extremely brief duration. Instead of the sort of letter he had expected, Herle received from Renteln merely a copy of the Immediate Economic Program issued by the NSDAP at the height of the campaign for the July Reichstag election.[63] At the time of its appearance, that pamphlet's socio-economic demagogy and its commitment of the party to a far-reaching job-creation program financed by deficit spending and higher taxes on the rich had occasioned widespread alarm in business circles.[64] To Herle's obvious dismay, he now discovered that the Nazi designated on the back of the title page as responsible for that offending publication was none other than the eager young man who had visited him at the offices of the Reichsverband. Attempting to make the best of a disappointing situation, Herle responded to the contents of the pamphlet in restrained fashion in a thirty-page letter to Renteln, which he immediately circulated to the leading members of the Reichsverband along with a covering note explaining what had led up to that communication.[65] Herle's letter to Renteln amounted to a devastating critique of the July pamphlet. Herle informed Renteln at the outset that he regarded the Immediate Economic Program as political *Agitationsmaterial,* unsuitable as the basis for an exchange of views with members of the business community. He nevertheless felt obliged, he wrote, to supply his own personal views in hopes that Renteln might take these into consideration in his further work.

Herle then proceeded to dissect the Nazis' July pamphlet, patiently correcting factual errors and pointing out the pamphlet's failure to face up to the undesirable econonomic consequences of slogans such as agricultural autarky through protectionism and government control of all foreign trade and international transactions. He objected to the pamphlet's disparaging references to businessmen, accusing Renteln of displaying prejudice against industrial entrepreneurs and favoring farmers and members of the *Mittelstand.* While the pamphlet nowhere rejected private enterprise, Herle observed, its particular points called for a degree of state intervention in the economy that could only end in socialization and a kind of state capitalism. As for the central policy thrust of the Immediate Economic Program—its call for a large-scale government program of job-creation through deficit spending—Herle rejected any move in that direction as a resort to the very methods of wasteful government spending that had gotten Germany into its economic difficulties in the first place. He branded as particularly counterproductive the demand for stiffer taxes on the rich, contending that such a move would stifle investment and therefore economic recovery. In line with the business community's view of the depression as a crisis of production rather than of consumption, he warned Renteln that only measures designed to spur capital formation and investment could pull the country out of the depression. He therefore rejected the July pamphlet's call for stiffer taxation of the propertied. Only a return to economic freedom, to a system that allowed responsible, self-reliant entrepreneurs to achieve profits through hard work and skillful management, could produce the desired results. If Renteln would agree to that—but only then—the way to discussions with prominent men of industry would stand open, Herle concluded.

Herle never received an answer to his letter. At the time he was writing, the NSDAP's economic policy personnel was on the verge of a major shake-up. An indication of this came a few days later, when Schacht wrote Reusch that Hitler had disclosed to him that he had withdrawn the

Immediate Economic Program of July from circulation.[66] Then, in the middle of September, reports began to reach the business community to the effect that Renteln's immediate superior, Otto Wagener, was leaving the Economic Policy Section and taking his assistant with him.[67] These reports were soon confirmed by official party announcements of a thoroughgoing reorganization of that section.[68] On hearing of these developments, Herle led Reusch to believe that Wagener and Renteln had been removed because of the NSDAP's July pamphlet.[69] The true reasons for their ouster remain unclear, but it is obvious that long-standing intrigues in the Nazi hierarchy certainly also played a part. Ever since the spring Wagener had increasingly come into conflict with both Feder and Funk. Despite their differences, those two had united in opposition to the publication of a pamphlet in which Wagener had set forth his understanding of Nazi economic policy. As chairman of the party's Economic Council, Feder claimed the right to veto any such publication.[70] Wagener, for his part, regarded Feder's Economic Council, which led at best a shadowy existence, as a mere subordinate adjunct to his Economic Policy Section.[71] Faced with this dispute, Hitler typically avoided a clearcut decision by turning the question over to a special commission. As a result of its deliberations, publication of Wagener's already printed pamphlet was withheld, and it was downgraded to an internally circulated document.[72] Wagener's ouster, and that of his assistant, Renteln, thus represented at least in part the denouement of a decline in influence that had begun considerably earlier as a consequence of internal rivalries and Hitler's aversion to a clear statement of the party's economic policies.

The removal of Wagener and Renteln did not improve the standing of the NSDAP in the business community. In place of Wagener an unlikely duo took over what remained of his Economic Policy Section. That organization was now divided into two parts: one, charged with the "private economy," headed by Funk, and a second, designated "state economy," under the leadership of Feder. Two men known to differ sharply on basic economic issues now jointly chaired the NSDAP's Economic Council, which became the party's supreme body for economic questions.[73] Faced with this bewildering development, Herle and Reusch agreed that no further contacts with the NSDAP on the part of the Reichsverband seemed worthwhile.[74] Even before the announcement of the appointments of Funk and Feder, Reusch had revealed dismay at the radical socio-economic course pursued by the Nazis. In writing to inform him of Hitler's statement about withdrawing the Immediate Economic Program, Schacht had chided Reusch about what he characterized as the proclivity of the leaders of the business community "to chase after whatever government is in power."[75] In his response Reusch angrily denied that this applied to him. "I make no secret," he added, "of the fact that the National Socialists, toward whom I was quite sympathetic, have disappointed me sorely during the past weeks. Quite apart from their other gaucheries, they have lost much sympathy through their collaboration with the Communists."[76] Not all industrialists shared Reusch's negative reaction to the course pursued by the NSDAP. In mid-September one of Reusch's political informants, Erich von Gilsa, reported to him in disgust that some executives remained favorably disposed to Nazism despite its radical anti-Papen and anti-business stance. According to one rumor, an industrialist whose name Gilsa did not learn had reportedly said that he had invested too much money in the NSDAP to give up on it now.[77] That man presumably dismissed as political rhetoric and parliamentary tactics the developments that so disturbed Reusch. This appears also to have been the case with the Berlin banker Otto Christian Fischer. In a speech to a closed business gathering in September, Fischer reassured his audience that the Nazis' leadership principle would in the end leave them no choice but to accept a capitalist economic order.[78] Reusch, for his part, began to think of ways to remove Hugenberg from the chairmanship of the DNVP so as to attract Nazi voters to that party in the November balloting.[79]

From all indications, most Ruhr industrialists reacted very much like Reusch to the turn taken by the NSDAP at the end of the summer of 1932. A lengthy letter, sent to Gregor Strasser from Essen by August Heinrichsbauer on September 20, provides evidence of this.[80] Heinrichsbauer reported that he had the previous day brought Walther Funk together in Essen with a group of Ruhr businessmen whose names he did not supply but whom he characterized as previously very supportive of the NSDAP. In contrast to earlier occasions, those men had roundly criticized the behavior of the party and asked Heinrichsbauer to make their objections known to Strasser. They took particular issue with the NSDAP's abandonment of its anti-parliamentary principles in cooperating with the Communists in the Reichstag against the Papen cabinet and entering into coalition negotiations with the Center Party. Whereas Nazism had, as a "movement," previously held aloof from partisan maneuvering, it now seemed to Heinrichsbauer's informants bent on sinking to the level of merely another political party. They objected as well to Hitler's all-or-nothing stance during the post-election negotiations with Papen and Hindenburg, predicting that such an attitude would lead to the NSDAP's self-isolation and self-exclusion from the government. They found distressing the NSDAP's defamation of Hugenberg, fearing that the resulting mutual alienation would destroy the cohesion of the "national" camp, thereby aiding and abetting its enemies. They also took extreme offense at the Nazis' "Marxist" agitation against the Papen cabinet, despite the NSDAP's earlier agreement to tolerate that cabinet and despite Papen's many accomplishments, not the least of which lay, in their eyes, in his economic program. Such resort to demagogy would, they feared, deprive National Socialism of its "spiritual" qualities and contribute to a general proletarianization that would drive the Nazis to

Marxist-like policies in the future. The businessmen believed, Heinrichsbauer reported to Strasser, that sooner or later the Nazis must reach an agreement with the Papen cabinet. The latter, they asked the party to remember, had done away with the Weimar "system," so that Nazi attacks on the old political order no longer had validity. As Heinrichsbauer left no doubt in his letter to Strasser, the businessmen he and Funk had talked with on September 19 wanted the party to abandon the course it had entered on in August, when Hitler had vainly demanded the chancellorship for himself.

The publication during the late summer and autumn of 1932 of the most devastating critique of Nazi economic policies yet printed in a major business organ further revealed the mounting disapproval in business circles. That critique appeared in the weekly publication of the national organization of chambers of commerce and industry, *Deutsche Wirtschafts-Zeitung*, in the form of six lengthy articles during August, September, and October.[81] The author reviewed with care the economic provisions of the twenty-five-point program of 1920 and the various programmatic publications by Feder, Rosenberg, and other Nazis, most of which the NSDAP was still distributing. He dissected these thoroughly, exposing their lack of clarity, their inconsistencies and contradictions, and stressing their threatening implications for private enterprise. While recognizing that Hitler and other Nazi leaders had pledged themselves to uphold the rights of private property and individual initiative, the author reviewed the many other party pronouncements that indicated a Nazi state would severely infringe in numerous ways on those rights. He especially emphasized the threat represented by Nazi proposals for "breaking the thralldom of interest payments," for socializing banking, for government issuance of unbacked fiat currency, and for deficit spending to combat unemployment. The author also documented the NSDAP's commitment to economic autarky, spelling out its implications for German industrial exports and for trade in general. To all this he appended an imposing list of bills introduced by Nazi parliamentarians, including a recent one that called for doubling the tax on high incomes. In general, the author of the articles in the *Deutsche Wirtschafts-Zeitung* characterized Nazi attitudes toward economic matters as nostalgic and romantic, full of longing for a return to simpler times, preferably the Middle Ages. The Nazis, he noted, preferred simply to ignore most of the realities produced by the enormous changes that had taken place in the economy over the previous century. Instead of an economic policy, they had only "an aggregation of demands, devoid of any system, arising from resentments and lack of clarity." The Nazis, he concluded, had neglected to think through economic questions thoroughly, with the consequence that their positions on economic matters must remain a source of grave concern to the business community. Any businessmen not already uncritically committed to National Socialism who read these well-documented articles must have found it difficult to escape a similar conclusion.

Other business-oriented publications reacted negatively to the radicalized election campaign of the NSDAP. The liberal *Frankfurter Zeitung* proclaimed that the Nazis were attacking the economic program of the Papen cabinet in a manner indistinguishable from that of the Marxists. *Der Angriff*, Goebbels's Berlin organ, had accused the cabinet of "social robbery." The *Völkischer Beobachter* had protested against violations of the sanctity of collective-bargaining contracts. Revealingly, the Frankfurt daily observed, the Nazis attacked Papen's economic policy precisely because of its liberal, capitalist orientation. The article then proceeded to expose the contradictions in the publications of Gottfried Feder.[82] The rightist *Deutsche Bergwerks-Zeitung* of Düsseldorf warned that hoping the Nazis would abandon their "impossible economic views and demands" amounted to a head-in-the-sand political stance. If the Nazis continued, through their subversive activity, to spread further "the Marxist pestilence," they would have to be resisted with determination and without fear. Holding to the fiction of a "national front" that would bring together the Nazis and bourgeois forces made no sense since such a front had never really existed. If it were ever to be realized, it would come about only because the Nazis had become wiser through losses. The Düsseldorf paper therefore urged its readers to vote to strengthen the economically reasonable bourgeois wing of a potential "national front." Businessmen could not let Papen's cabinet collapse since it represented, as the chancellor had proclaimed, the last chance. If it went under, the most probable result would be a socialistic dictatorship of one coloration or another.[83]

Such criticism of the NSDAP probably contributed to the reactivation, late in the fall election campaign, of the conciliatory fork of the Nazi tongue employed so often in the past to placate business fears. That side of Nazism found partial expression in a new pamphlet on Nazi economic policy released in October. This *Wirtschaftliches Aufbauprogramm*, or Constructive Economic Program, seemed to reflect the growing influence of Funk as a result of his advancement to the head of one of the two new divisions of what had formerly been Wagener's Economic Policy Section. Funk's enhanced standing also found expression in his participation in drafting the speech in which Gregor Strasser announced the new program on October 20.[84] In its published form that program omitted the strident rhetorical anti-capitalism of the previous summer's Immediate Economic Program and revised some of its proposals that had proved so objectionable to business circles. In place of heavier taxation of the rich, the October program called for a general reduction of taxes, especially those which impeded production. In place of price controls, it proposed a freeing of prices. While endorsing agrarian protectionism and priority for the home market in general, the new program specified that Germany's essential exports must not be impeded. But while it modified these features of the July pamphlet, it did not amount to a reversal of course. The October pamphlet retained the demands for abandonment of the gold standard, state takeover of banking and currency, and large-scale deficit spending to finance public work-creation programs. It also repeated the promise that the Nazis would substitute the principles of German socialism for those of liberal capitalism. Moreover, the October program continued the NSDAP's assault on the economic measures of the Papen cabinet, branding these as plutocratic in their orientation and totally inadequate to the task of recovery. After analyzing the new Nazi program, Paul Reusch's economic adviser informed his employer that despite many objectionable features, it represented undeniable progress when compared with earlier Nazi statements about economic policy.[85] However, there remained the problem of establishing the status of the *Aufbauprogramm*, for as that same adviser had recently pointed out to Reusch, it was very difficult to establish who spoke with final authority for the NSDAP on matters of economic policy.[86]

The conciliatory fork of the Nazi tongue presumably made itself heard again when Funk, Strasser, and Hitler himself met with groups of industrialists in the Ruhr in October 1932. No record seems to have survived of who attended or what Strasser and Funk said in talks on October 28 before "a small invited circle" in Essen.[87] A bit more is known about Hitler's visit to Fritz Thyssen's country house, Schloss Landsberg, near Essen on October 21. Thyssen had sent out in advance formal invitations to what he described as a "discussion" (*Aussprache*) with the Nazi leader.[88] To his distress a number of the most important figures in the Ruhr did not accept. Thyssen was particularly angered when the chairman of the industrial Reichsverband, Gustav Krupp von Bohlen und Halbach, responded to his invitation with a curt note of declination.[89] Hans von Loewenstein, the executive director of the Bergbauverein, also declined.[90] Nor did Paul Reusch attend.[91] In fact, Thyssen later named as participants in the meeting with Hitler at his house only two prominent figures from the Ruhr, the venerable Emil Kirdorf and Albert Vögler, the general director of United Steel, the firm whose supervisory board Thyssen chaired.[92] Vögler had expressed his intention to attend two days earlier at a meeting in Berlin at which, as will be explained below, he and other major figures from German industry agreed to raise a large amount of money to help the parties backing the Papen cabinet. Vögler told those present that he intended to go to the meeting at Thyssen's in hopes of effecting a reconciliation between the NSDAP and the Papen cabinet. That would be easier before the election than afterwards, he reasoned, when Hitler would, regardless of the outcome of the balloting, have to become more radical.[93] Vögler presumably came away from the gathering at Thyssen's house with his hopes disappointed, as no conciliatory approaches reached the

Reich Chancellery from the Brown House in the final weeks of the election campaign. As to what did happen at Thyssen's, very little is known. Thyssen later remembered only that Hitler had reassured those present of his intention to restore the monarchy.[94] Under the circumstances, that scarcely sufficed to dispel the widespread mistrust which his party's radical behavior had engendered in big business circles. Overall, the meeting at Thyssen's seems to have been far less important than the Communist journalists who traced Hitler there assumed to have been the case.[95]

Nor did anything the Nazis said during the remainder of the election campaign dispel the prevailing mistrust of their party in business circles. Down to election day, November 6, the radical fork of Nazism's tongue dominated its public image. The tide of invective against Papen and his "cabinet of barons" continued unabated as the Nazis held to their defense of parliamentary democracy against a "reactionary clique" that included Hugenberg and his DNVP. They also persisted in their promises to defend Germany's workers against exploitative capitalists. The climax of the NSDAP's campaign came in early November, just prior to the balloting, when the Nazis openly collaborated with the Communists to incite a strike of Berlin's transport workers, immobilizing public conveyances in the capital for nearly a week.[96] In September Alfred Sohn-Rethel, a resourceful young Communist economist, who managed to conceal his political affiliation from the business association for which he worked in Berlin, succeeded in planting a lengthy, anonymous two-part, article about National Socialism in the *Deutsche Führerbriefe*, a newsletter that enjoyed a following in big business circles.[97] Sohn-Rethel's article portrayed the NSDAP as the potential savior of a capitalist economic system plagued by dwindling support from the masses. In keeping with the Communist line on the SPD, he argued that the Social Democrats had rescued capitalism after 1918 by renewing its mass basis at that time. Now, however, the economic crisis was undercutting the SPD by bringing about a curtailment of the *Sozialpolitik* with which that party had appeased the artistocracy of labor, thereby keeping the working class divided and powerless. The new mass party of 1932, which also brandished anti-capitalist slogans—the NSDAP—therefore offered the only hope for a "reconsolidation of capitalism" that would avert a resort to military dictatorship and, ultimately, a Communist revolution. The business community must, Sohn-Rethel's article strongly implied, rally behind National Socialism and tame it, just as earlier it had tamed and exploited the SPD. In publishing his article Sohn-Rethel acted as an *agent provocateur*, seeking to aid the Communist Party in the upcoming election by discrediting the SPD and heightening fears of social reaction. As soon as he learned that his article would appear in print in the *Deutsche Führerbriefe*, he at once sent a copy to the Communist newspaper *Die Rote Fahne* so that it could be ready with an immediate exposé of the devious machinations of the masterminds of capitalism.[98] When the article appeared, the Communist propaganda machine at once began to make use of it. For nearly four decades thereafter many writers of history continued to cite Sohn-Rethel's words as proof of the espousal of the Nazi cause by big business in the fall of 1932.[99] Only his own disclosure in 1970 of his authorship and motives necessitated abandonment of what had long been regarded as a key piece of evidence in a widespread version of National Socialism's rise.[100] If at the time Sohn-Rethel had hoped by means of his article to tempt Germany's capitalists to conform during the autumn of 1932 to Marxist analysis by aligning themselves with the NSDAP, his hopes went unrealized. His article found no resonance whatever in the business community. Apprizing the performance of the Nazis, the *Deutsche Bergwerks-Zeitung* of Düsseldorf observed on election day: "Anyone who thinks in terms of private enterprise can give his vote only to the parties that stand behind the government. National Socialism, which has once again cast itself in a reprehensible light by collaborating with the Communists in the Berlin transport strike, is following the same false paths as Marxism."[101] A few days earlier the *Vossische Zeitung* of Berlin had noted, "The boundaries between National Socialism and Bolshevism have lately become even more hazy than before."[102]

2. Political Money in the Fall Election Campaign— Maneuvers in the Twilight of Weimar

The Nazis' radical socio-economic line during the autumn election campaign, their strident anti-capitalist rhetoric, and their unrelenting onslaught on a chancellor who had gained the enthusiastic backing of the men of big business had a profound effect on the political behavior of the latter. Both during the campaign and after, most of the business community displayed a pronounced aversion to National Socialism. If any doubt existed about this, it was dispelled when the Nazis and their fellow travelers sought, during the maneuvering for advantage that followed the November election, to enlist big business support for the appointment of Hitler as chancellor.

Not surprisingly, the behavior of the Nazis during the fall campaign served as a brake on financial contributions to the NSDAP from big business sources. According to two men closely connected with Ruhr industry, Ludwig Grauert and August Heinrichsbauer, its politically active leaders decided to allow none of their political money to go the Nazis.[1] This would seem borne out by Otto Steinbrinck's recollection of a visit he received in Berlin in the fall of 1932 from Walther Funk. Steinbrinck recalled that Funk expressed to him on that occasion discouragement at the unresponsiveness he had encountered on a recent trip through the western industrial region. As an outsider in Ruhr circles, Steinbrinck's employer, Friedrich Flick, remained unaffected by this ban, so that Steinbrinck adhered to Flick's practice of paying insurance premiums to the Nazis, providing Funk on that occasion with what he later estimated at between 20,000 and 30,000 marks.[2] No evidence has come to light about the disposition of IG Farben's political funds in the fall of 1932, but there were indications of increasingly negative attitudes toward the Nazis from that side, too. In a pamphlet widely distributed in industrial circles, Carl Bosch, chairman of Farben's managing board, issued a sharp warning against the idea of economic autarky, then an increasingly prominent theme in the progaganda of the NSDAP, which sought to capitalize on mounting agrarian demands for high protectionist tariffs and other barriers to foreign trade.[3] Max Ilgner, the young executive in charge of Farben's Berlin office, later testified that he terminated in the fall of 1932 the monthly subsidies he had paid to Funk since the spring.[4] Sometime during the latter part of 1932 the sole Farben executive who had joined the NSDAP, Wilhelm Rudolf Mann, submitted his resignation from the party, a step perhaps not unrelated to efforts by the NSBO to link together Nazi factory cells in all of Farben's plants so as to form a trade-union type structure in that firm.[5]

The curtailment of financial aid from big business occurred just as the NSDAP was experiencing its first serious money problems since its rapid expansion had begun more than two years earlier.[6] After the party's failure to gain a place in the government despite its landslide electoral triumph of July, the yield from its internal sources of funds fell off. The sustained growth in membership that had fed large amounts of money, in the form of registration fees and dues, into the Nazi organization at the grass roots slackened. Some members dropped out, others simply ceased to pay their dues. The transmission system that had moved money from the local units upward to the regional organizations and on to the national headquarters faltered in some parts of the country and generally delivered less than before. Weariness with the fifth major election campaign of 1932 reduced the heavy attendance at Nazi rallies that had hitherto proved such a lucrative source of funds.[7] Profits from the party's commercial efforts also declined.[8] Party papers found their circulation, and hence their revenues, contracting.[9] The non-Nazi press carried rumors of mounting unpaid party debts.[10]

Despite all this, it would be misleading to speak of a crippling financial crisis of the NSDAP in the fall of 1932. The party seems to have experienced only the kind of difficulties common among rapidly expanding organizations that suffer a contraction of income and discover the pains of overextension as a consequence of having habitually relied on growth to meet their material needs. That is, the Nazis still had plenty of money, although their practice of spending without thought to priorities now put their resources under considerable strain. They continued to raise millions of marks from internal sources, and the availability of an abundance of volunteers and of contributions in kind from members and sympathizers of moderate means kept the NSDAP free from dependence on major financial contributions from outside sources during the autumn election campaign. This involved some activities not wholly in keeping with the party's carefully cultivated image of self-sufficiency, such as sending into the streets of Germany uniformed SA men who, tin boxes in hand, solicited passersby for contributions.[11] Thanks to such efforts, and the credit rating it still commanded among many merchants, the party managed to mount its usual massive campaign. Still, the decision to adopt a posture in the fall campaign that would predictably offend big business came at an inopportune time in terms of the financial needs of the NSDAP. Yet that was clearly a price Hitler was willing to pay, along with a general diminution of sympathy for his party in business circles. In the fall of 1932 he obviously attached far less importance to the money and favor of big business than to his strategy of discrediting the Papen cabinet and resorting to intensified demagogic propaganda in an effort to hold his increasingly restive supporters in line and to attract new followers as replacements for those who defected.

Disturbed by the Nazis' radicalism and intransigence and concerned about the precarious position of the Papen cabinet, the politically active components of German industry once more assumed an active role in the autumn election campaign. In contrast to the resignation and pessimism that had gripped large parts of the business community during the campaigns of the spring and summer, renewed energy and determination became evident. Symptomatic of this was the leadership exerted by Carl Friedrich von Siemens, who had withdrawn from political activity in the spring. In October Siemens joined with steelmen Fritz Springorum and Albert Vögler and textile executive Abraham Frowein to issue invitations to a special nationwide meeting in Berlin of politically active industrialists and industrial agents.[12] The resulting gathering included such major figures of Ruhr industry as Krupp von Bohlen, Paul Silverberg, Fritz Springorum, Albert Vögler, and Hans von Loewenstein of the Bergbauverein. Siemens was joined by Hermann Bücher, chief executive of the other large electro-technical firm, AEG. The chemical industry was represented by the executive director of its national association. Paul Reusch did not attend, but his Berlin agent, Martin Blank, took part, sending Reusch a full report afterwards. The pro-Nazi Fritz Thyssen was conspicuous by his absence. Most of the major industrial branch and regional associations sent their top officials. With the consent of its chairman, Krupp, even the industrial Reichsverband abandoned its traditional non-partisan stance by permitting its senior staff officials to participate under the pretext that they were acting solely as private individuals. In reality German industry convened its first national political conclave when these men gathered at the Club of Berlin on the afternoon of October 19, 1932.[13]

As became immediately evident at a conference of the organizers of this conclave just before the full group convened on the nineteenth, they were acting in collusion with the Papen cabinet. The state secretary in the Reich Chancellery, Erwin Planck, joined them and reiterated what he had already told them earlier: The cabinet, and especially Chancellor Papen, wanted the establishment of a centralized election fund for use in accordance with the wishes of the Reich government. Money would go only to parties and organizations that were neither radical nor potential components of a "black-brown" coalition of Center Party and NSDAP. That is, the cabinet wanted industry to aid only parties that stood politically between those two. It recognized that achievement of a Reichstag majority lay beyond its grasp, but a return to parliamentary rule had, in any case, no place in its plans. The cabinet nevertheless hoped to avoid conflict with the Reichstag. It was not the cabinet's fault, but rather that of the Nazis, that no cooperation had been possible. The cabinet still stood ready to reach agreement with the NSDAP. But the task at hand was to cut back the votes for the NSDAP and the Center Party, which together threatened the cabinet by virtue of holding, between them, a mathematical majority. The cabinet did not think it advisable, Planck went on, to expend all the money industry raised on the November election; it intended to save some for use afterwards for propaganda on behalf of its planned constitutional reforms and a restoration of a more tranquil public atmosphere. In response to Planck's presentation, Vögler proposed, to the general agreement of those present, that industry seek with all the means at its disposal to keep the present cabinet in power. The organizers then designated Siemens to preside over the full gathering when it began in a few minutes. Siemens emphasized the desirability of giving those who came to that gathering the impression that the initiative had originated with industry, not with the cabinet. State Secretary Planck then departed, and the organizers went to receive their guests.[14]

When the twenty-one participants in the full conclave of October 19 convened at 4 P.M., Ludwig Kastl, managing director of the Reichsverband, laid before them the organizers' proposals. Kastl prefaced that presentation by reporting that attempts to unify the bourgeois forces between the Catholic Center and the NSDAP had again failed, principally because of Hugenberg's unwillingness to step down as leader of the DNVP. Since no consolidation of the bourgeois camp would be possible prior to the election, he continued, it had become all the more necessary to concentrate the available financial resources of industry. General agreement prevailed about the desirability of keeping the current non-party cabinet in office, Kastl asserted without drawing any dissent from those present. Industry had a particular interest in preserving the cabinet's authority so that Papen and his ministers could proceed with the implementation of their reforms, he observed. With regard to the finances of the election campaign, Kastl announced that the cabinet had proposed establishment of a fund of two million marks from private sources, to be administered jointly by a group of industrialists and State Secretary Planck. Kastl then repeated Planck's proposal that only part of the two million marks be spent before the election. The need to bolster the bourgeois parties was so great, Kastl added, that industry must aid the DNVP despite Hugenberg's recent endorsement of drastic import quotas for agricultural products. In the ensuing discussion, several of those present emphasized that a generous portion of the funds must go to revive the DVP. No one dissented from the prevailing consensus that no money at all should go to the NSDAP, and that, indeed, the whole purpose of the fund-raising effort lay in strengthening other parties in hopes of attracting voters away from National Socialism.[15]

The conclave produced the desired results. In a lengthy discussion the participants departed radically from previous practice by revealing to one another the techniques their various organizations had hitherto used in raising money for political purposes. The picture that emerged was one of multiple but uncoordinated systems, with each organization having previously guarded its secrets jealously from the others but at the same time having shared a general feeling of frustration, if not futility, at what was regarded by all those who spoke about the past as a disappointing impact by industry on electoral politics. Repeatedly, those who spoke out attested to a diminishing interest in participation by the industrialists belonging to their organizations. They accordingly resolved to establish after the election a centralized, national organization for raising and bringing to bear political money. In October 1932 German industry at last belatedly sought to transcend its many internal and regional divisions in order to cooperate politically.

More immediately, the participants in the conclave agreed to raise at once a political fund of two million marks, as proposed by the Papen cabinet. However, some of those present questioned the wisdom of placing such a fund even partially under the authority of the cabinet; its composition, they pointed out, might change at any time. Accordingly, the gathering appointed, for the purpose of administering the funds, a Kuratorium consisting of Siemens, Springorum, and Willy Tischbein, general director of the German Continental Rubber Works and spokesman of the industrialists' association of Hanover. Several of those present suggested raising the funds through the Reichsverband, but that organization's leaders rejected that as too flagrant a departure from its traditional non-partisan position on politics. Instead, collection of the two million marks was left to the discretion of those present, with a guideline of forty pfennigs per employed worker demarcating the level of contribution expected from industrial employers.[16] By the time Siemens sent a circular letter a few days later to those who had attended the meeting at the Club of Berlin, he could report that of the one million marks needed immediately, only 600,000 to 700,000 marks remained to be raised.[17] Since all those present on the nineteenth had agreed that two million marks presented no problem, they presumably had no difficulty in raising the targeted sum.[18] Nor were the Papen cabinet's funds from industrial sources limited in the fall of 1932 to those agreed on at the conclave of October 19. At Nuremberg after the war Friedrich Flick told of a separate meeting organized by Otto Wolff, who invited a group of industrialists to his house to hear Papen request funds with which "to fight Hitler."[19] In support of that testimony Flick submitted documentation showing that he alone contributed 100,000 marks to Papen's undertaking in October 1932.[20]

Further evidence of the business community's support of the Papen cabinet appeared in an election appeal issued on the eve of the November 6 balloting.[21] Sponsored by a DNVP group, the "German Committee 'Hindenburg for Volk and Reich'," it identified the Papen cabinet as President Hindenburg's solution to the divisive "party rule" of the republican era and urged support for the chancellor and his ministers. The cabinet would give the country what it needed: a fundamental reordering of national life, guided by German and Christian beliefs, socially organic thought, and respect for the family. The cabinet stood for the principles of private property, personal initiative and responsibility, accomplishment, attainment, and just rewards. By way of aiding the chancellor and the president in the realization of these goals, the signatories urged voters to cast their ballots for the DNVP. Among the 339 signatures affixed to the appeal readers found those of several dozen prominent figures from big business. These included Ernst Brandi and Hans von Loewenstein of the Bergbauverein; Ernst von Borsig, chairman until a few months earlier of the national association of industrial employers; Konrad Piatscheck of the lignite-mining industry; Ruhr steel executive Fritz Springorum and Carl Hoeppe, one of the coal-mining directors of the Hoesch firm headed by Springorum; two coal-mining executives of United Steel, Adolf Hueck and Gustav Knepper; Friedrich Funcke, another mining executive who served on United Steel's supervisory board; and two prominent Berlin bankers, Georg Solmssen and Oskar Wassermann. The name from the business community that stood out as most notable was, however, that of the general director of United Steel, Albert Vögler. His signature vexed Wilhelm Keppler, who believed that he had enlisted Vögler earlier in the year for his circle of economic advisers to the NSDAP.[22] Other notable industrialists found it impossible to sign the appeal because of their objections to Hugenberg and his party. That appears to have been the case with Krupp von Bohlen and Paul Reusch, both of whose long-standing opposition to Hugenberg was well known.[23] Reusch raised no objections, however, when his employee and political adviser, Erich von Gilsa, signed the appeal. He also instructed the newspapers controlled by his firm to desist from attacks on the DNVP during the final stages of the campaign, and he let it be known that he himself intended to vote for that party.[24] Others, such as Siemens and Abraham Frowein, two of the organizers of the conclave of October 19 at the Club of Berlin, mounted separate efforts on behalf of the Papen cabinet by publishing their own statements in the press.[25]

By virtue of the determination of all these men to aid the forces aligned behind the Papen cabinet and deal a setback to those, including the Nazis, who opposed that cabinet, the politically active men of German industry stood united as never before on the eve of the November election of 1932. For the first time, they had become sufficiently motivated politically to coordinate their political funding at the national level. In an effort to strengthen and preserve the existing government, they placed their money squarely behind the parties aligned with Papen and his cabinet. How much effect this had on the outcome of the balloting of November 6 cannot be determined, but the returns do show that the two parties that received most of the funds raised by big business, the DVP and the DNVP, together tallied in excess of a million votes more than they had in July. The Nazis, by contrast, suffered their greatest losses ever. Their tally decreased by more than two million votes as compared to July, and their Reichstag delegation fell from 230 to 196. As the Papen cabinet had hoped, the threat of a "black-brown" majority vanished, as the Center Party also suffered losses. Many factors contributed to this outcome, among them the widespread disapproval for the imperious demands Hitler had addressed in August to President Hindenburg and the alarm occasioned by the radical policies that had plunged the Nazis into acrimonious conflict with a cabinet that many Germans on the political right found appealing and identified with the revered Hindenburg. Nor did the Nazis' new-found enthusiasm for parliamentary democracy and the well-being of Germany's workers help them. At the time of the election of November 1932, big business formed merely one part of a general reaction against a National Socialism that seemed to be moving rapidly to the left. In response to the Nazis' setback, a sense of relief prevailed in business circles and the stock market staged a rally.[26]

Encouraged by the outcome of the balloting, virtually all of the business community wanted the Papen cabinet to remain in power. That was, however, not a simple matter. Despite the massive setback suffered by the Nazis and the gains of the parties aligned with the cabinet, the chancellor still lacked anything remotely approaching a parliamentary majority. If another crisis were to be averted, he would have to reach some sort of *modus vivendi* with the Reichstag. The hostilities generated by Papen's acceptance of the chancellorship in defiance of his own former party, the Center, and his deposition of the SPD-led Prussian cabinet in July ruled out any expansion of the government's parliamentary basis to the left. There remained only the possibility of an expansion to the right by means of some sort of accommodation with the NSDAP.

Until the balloting, hope lingered in business circles that the losses suffered by the Nazis would sober them and lead them to accept a role subordinate to Papen.[27] Hitler quickly dashed such hopes by repeating immediately after the election his demand for the chancellorship and renewing his attacks on the Papen cabinet. The political situation reverted essentially to that of the summer, except that the threat of a "black-brown" coalition no longer existed and the cabinet could not again so easily resort to a dissolution of the Reichstag. As a result, the unnerving sense of instability that had pervaded Germany's public life before the election returned in still greater force. Desperate for the predictability that all capitalists long for, but seeing that goal again recede, most of the country's men of big business looked on with feelings of helplessness and pessimism. Some, however, sought to influence the course of events despite all past discouragements.

One of those who did not abandon efforts to shape political developments was Paul Silverberg, the prominent Cologne industrialist. He had begun his career in lignite mining and then branched out into electricity and, finally, into bituminous-coal mining.[28] An energetic man, he played a leading part in the industrial Reichsverband from the very outset and belonged to the inner circle of numerous other industrial associations, including the elite Ruhrlade. In their councils his resourcefulness combined with an eloquence rare among industrial executives to make Silverberg one of the best known and most respected spokesmen of industry. During the late 1920s he had championed a course of accommodation toward the Social Democrats without, however, advocating any fundamental departure from industry's defense of its interests.[29] As became apparent in the early 1930s, that position was merely tactical. By 1932 Silverberg was exerting himself to defend the position of the rightist, anti-labor Papen cabinet.[30] A recent study has portrayed Silverberg as an advocate of installing Hitler in the chancellorship from the late summer of that year on, despite his Jewish parentage.[31] Aside from its inherent implausibility, that interpretation rests on two very questionable assumptions: first, that the words of Werner von Alvensleben, secretary of the Berlin Herrenklub, can be accepted as wholly trustworthy information; and, second, that the views voiced in the *Deutsche Führerbriefe*, a twice-weekly newsletter for executives, reflected Silverberg's thinking. The first of these assumptions is undermined by Alvensleben's well-deserved reputation as an irresponsible gossip and notorious political intrigant, as well as by contemporaneous documentation on Silverberg's attitudes.[32] The second assumption collapses under a close examination of the *Deutsche Führerbriefe*, the publication whose editorials of August and September 1932 in favor of bringing the Nazis into the government have been invoked as evidence of a decision on Silverberg's part to rely on National Socialism to prop up German capitalism. A four-page current events newsletter, it went twice a week to about 1,000 subscribers from a small office in Berlin.[33] Behind it stood two young men who in 1928 recognized that businessmen and others in decision-making positions would pay a sizeable subscription fee for a publication that promised to provide them with inside information about happenings in the capital. One of those young men, Otto Meynen, also worked as the Berlin representative of Silverberg, who occasionally contributed an anonymous article to the newsletter. There are no grounds, however, for believing that Silverberg attempted, from his business headquarters in Cologne, to determine consistently the content of a newsletter hurriedly put to press twice a week in Berlin as a profit-making venture by his representative there and a partner. Silverberg was especially unlikely to have dictated the positions adopted in editorials in the *Führerbriefe* that dealt with political affairs. They fell not within the purview of the economist Meynen but rather within that of his partner, Franz Reuter, a political scientist by training. Reuter, who also held a second job, as an industrial public relations man, had ties to Hjalmar Schacht, about whom he had for some time been collecting material for what would eventually become an admiring biography.[34] Insofar as the anonymous editorials in the *Führerbriefe* about the political situation in the later summer of 1932 might have reflected outside influence, Schacht, rather than Silverberg, seems the prime suspect.

As for Silverberg's politics during the late summer and early autumn of 1932, firsthand evidence shows him to have been concerned above all about the possibility of a coalition between the NSDAP and the Center Party. He feared that such a combination would propel into decisive positions anti-capitalist elements in those parties that would strive for the socialization of major industries such as chemicals, coal, and iron and steel. Faced with such demands from a "black-brown" coalition, the parties on the left would have no alternative but to go along, an alarmed Silverberg warned Reusch in early September. In order to forestall the formation of Nazi-Center coalition, he continued, he had sought contacts in all directions.[35] As a consequence, he had come together with Werner von Alvensleben on the evening of August 31. The only record of that encounter stems from Alvensleben.[36] It seems clear from Alvensleben's report to General von Schleicher, which he claimed to have sent to Hitler as well, that Silverberg sought to exploit Alvensleben's access to high-ranking Nazis in order to convey to them a message he hoped might deter them from the alliance with the Center Party. He warned, according to Alvensleben, that such an alliance would move the NSDAP in the direction of Marxism and bring it into competition with the SPD and KPD on terms that would place it at a great disadvantage. As Alvensleben reported Silverberg's remarks, the industrialist then held out the prospect of big business cooperation with National Socialism if it would only turn its back on the Center Party. How much of Alvensleben's report stemmed from Silverberg and how much he himself added, or altered, either intentionally or unintentionally, remains unclear. It would be mistaken, however, simply to interpret that report as evidence of determination on Silverberg's part to support Hitler's drive for power. Even granting a high degree of accuracy to Alvensleben's version of Silverberg's remarks, these can just as plausibly be interpreted as a tactical move designed to serve the immediate, temporary purpose of throwing obstacles in the path of a possible development that preoccupied and worried Silverberg greatly, namely a "black-brown" alliance of the NSDAP and the Center Party. Silverberg's participation in the conclave of October 19, at which the participants agreed on a fund-raising drive to bolster Papen and deal a setback to the NSDAP, does not suggest that he viewed the political situation in an entirely different manner from most of the elite of German industry.

Fragmentary records permit reconstruction of what appears to have been the aftermath of Silverberg's gambit of late August 1932. In the middle of September Alvensleben reported to Hitler that the *Führerbriefe* was calling for his appointment to head the government and that Meynen, whom he identified as the right hand of Silverberg, was responsible for this. In that same report, however, Alvensleben contradictorily claimed credit himself for the appearance of pro-Hitler articles in the *Führerbriefe*. He then warned Hitler that the Papen cabinet was pressuring the publication to alter its line. By way of thwarting that effort, Alvensleben urged Hitler to receive Meynen—a Westphalian Protestant, he specified.[37] Despite a second letter to Hitler a week later, in which Alvensleben praised Silverberg as an extraordinarily accomplished businessman whose sole fault lay in being a *Judenabkömmling* (a Jewish offspring), nothing came of Alvensleben's proposal for a meeting between Hitler and Meynen during the election campaign.[38] After the November 6 balloting, however, Hitler did receive both Meynen and Reuter. By that time there was no longer any need for Silverberg's tactic of seeking to entice the NSDAP away from a possible alliance with the Center Party, since the results of the election had erased the threat of a "black-brown" coalition. As a result, the meeting of Meynen and Reuter with Hitler took a non-political tack, with the Nazi leader discussing economic portents with his young journalist visitors.[39] With Hitler still unyieldingly opposed to any cooperation with the Papen cabinet, Silverberg turned his attentions to another Nazi, Gregor Strasser. Through Alvensleben, Strasser had approached Meynen after the election and asked for help in building up the elements in the NSDAP which, like himself, questioned Hitler's all-or-nothing strategy and favored some compromise with Papen. According to Meynen, Silverberg at once responded favorably to Strasser's overture and began channeling subsidies to him via Meynen.[40] As events would soon prove, Silverberg had bet on a loser.

Another attempt from the side of big business to bring the NSDAP behind the Papen cabinet by surmounting the obstacle posed by Hitler's obstinancy also occurred soon after the November election. It was undertaken by Max Schlenker, manager of the largest association of businessmen in the northern Rhineland and the Ruhr, the Langnamverein, and also of the northwestern branch of the iron and steel industrialists' association. Following the election Schlenker went to Berlin to consult with officials of the Papen cabinet, among them Prussian commissar Franz Bracht.[41] As a result of these consultations Schlenker wrote a letter on November 10 to steel executive Fritz Thyssen, whose advocacy of Nazism was by that time well known. Schlenker's letter has not survived, but the content of Thyssen's response of the next day makes clear that Schlenker had, without disclosing his collaboration with the Berlin officials, proposed that the industrialist circumvent Hitler by urging other Nazi leaders, such as Strasser, to effect a compromise accommodation with the Papen cabinet. Schlenker's effort came to naught, as Thyssen— by then a loyal Nazi if not yet an official party comrade—parroted the party line about Hitler's sole authority and the united will of the NSDAP.[42] But unsuccessful as Schlenker's venture proved, it revealed the strong desire in Rhenish-Ruhr industrial circles late in 1932 to preserve the Papen cabinet in the expectation that the chancellor and his ministers would, with the backing of the president, subordinate and contain Nazism by harnessing it to their conservative purposes.

To the consternation of the business community, hopes placed on the Papen cabinet soon proved considerably less than well founded. When Papen wrote to invite Hitler to discuss participation by the NSDAP in his cabinet after the election, the Nazi leader accused the chancellor of bad faith in a letter that the NSDAP promptly published.[43] Nor did the Center Party relent in its opposition to the cabinet. Papen might again have defied the hostile Reichstag majority except for the sudden withdrawal of support by the man who had masterminded his appointment five months earlier, Kurt von Schleicher. Displeased by the independence the chancellor had displayed and convinced that he could not "tame" the Nazis, Schleicher prevailed on Hindenburg to call for Papen's resignation and open negotiations with the parties aimed at achieving a parliamentary basis for a new government. The president reluctantly complied, accepting Papen's resignation on November 17. He nevertheless at once commissioned the chancellor, who remained in office in a caretaker capacity, with the formation of a new cabinet. Since none of the parties altered its position, Papen's efforts in that direction came to naught. During the ensuing week the press of Germany carried one report after another of fruitless efforts by the chancellor to break what had become a gridwork of hardened deadlocks among the parties and between the parliament and the executive. The remnants of the political system established with such high hopes at Weimar some thirteen years earlier had begun to sink into what would soon prove its death agony.

Germany was beginning to experience the full effects of the power vac-
uum that would eventuate in one of history's greatest catastrophes.[44]

In this atmosphere of uncertainty and mounting pessimism, the Langnamverein held a much-publicized meeting of its membership in Düsseldorf on November 23.[45] That gathering had originally been planned
as a triumphant celebration of the "new state" proclaimed by spokesmen
of the Papen cabinet, at which some of its representatives would appear
to set forth their plans for constitutional reform. Instead, the 1,500
members convened with no spokesmen of the cabinet on hand, just as
hopes for Papen's survival had begun to dwindle rapidly. As a consequence an atmosphere of deep pessimism pervaded the gathering. One
observer reported afterwards that most of the industrialists he had
talked with favored Hitler's appointment as chancellor. Whereas those
same men had extolled Papen only a few weeks earlier, the observer
noted, they now felt it would be the greatest mistake not to commission
Hitler with formation of a cabinet. This had not resulted from any shift
in sentiment in favor of the Nazi, he added. Instead, the men who now
advocated Hitler's appointment had come to the conclusion that it was
simply no longer to be avoided. Under these circumstances, they felt it
was advisable to appoint Hitler as quickly as possible. The observer
found among those who held such views no expectation that Hitler
would succeed in solving Germany's problems. He also added that skep-
tics among them assumed that a cabinet formed by the Nazi leader
would last only a few weeks.[46] Much the same sort of attitude was expressed by an editorial that appeared in the *Rheinisch-Westfälische Zeitung*
of Essen just after Papen submitted his resignation to Hindenburg.
Praising Papen, that newspaper regretted his failure to secure a popular
basis for his cabinet. The editorial recalled that since August it had
urged inclusion of the Nazis in the Papen cabinet. Now the only solution
lay in calling on Hitler to form a government. It was too late for anything
else.[47] Presumably these views were not too far removed from those held
by the men at the helm of the Bergbauverein who exercised financial
control over the Essen daily.

Not all of the business community lapsed into passive resignation in
November 1932. A much more upbeat tone prevailed in the talks that
came from the podium of the Langnamverein gathering.[48] The principal speakers were that association's manager, Max Schlenker, its chairman, Fritz Springorum, and political theorist Carl Schmitt, who served
as the featured guest in place of the spokesmen of the Papen cabinet,
who had declined to come. Schlenker opened the proceedings by extolling the achievements of the Papen cabinet, particularly its preparations
for constitutional and administrative reform. "The western German
business community is prepared", he announced, "to follow any government that continues courageously with the recent beginnings at reform and grants the business community new scope for the unfolding

of its own unbroken strengths." In his address Springorum praised Papen's achievements and, without expressly commiting himself or the Langnamverein, strongly suggested that the chancellor should continue in office, even in the face of popular opposition. In remarks that revealed concern about National Socialism, Springorum cautioned against experiments with the currency and against government job-creation programs. The best way to generate employment opportunities lay in the sort of return to the sound methods of private capitalism that Papen had upheld. From Carl Schmitt the members of the Langnamverein heard an address in which he inveighed against a return to the "party state" of Weimar. Schmitt's call for a "strong state" that would take charge and govern without regard to popular sentiment or election outcomes also amounted, under the circumstances of the moment, to a plea for the retention of Papen. Some of the business press also advocated Papen's continuation in office and backed up that stand with warnings about the unreliability of the Nazis on economic questions.[49]

The really important figures in big business remained unwilling to advocate Hitler's appointment to the chancellorship in November. That became apparent from the response to a petition that called on Hindenburg to install the Nazi leader at the head of a cabinet equipped with presidential emergency powers. The idea for that petition originated in late October with the Nazi Wilhelm Keppler, who used his circle to draw up the statement and collect signatures.[50] The undertaking was orchestrated in close consultation with Heinrich Himmler, who acted as liaison to the Brown House. Drafted with the help of Schacht, the petition was designed to give the impression that it represented a spontaneous appeal on the part of men prominent in German economic life, including agriculture. By placing such a petition before the president after the November balloting, the Nazi organizers hoped to overcome his long-standing resistance to the appointment of Hitler as chancellor. Early in November they started approaching the three dozen or so men they hoped would sign.[51] The results proved very disappointing, especially with regard to the industrialists on the list. By November 12 an annoyed Schacht informed Hitler that the effort appeared not entirely in vain, despite the unwillingness to participate of heavy industry, *Schwerindustrie*, which, he complained, deserved its name because of its *Schwerfälligkeit*, its sluggishness.[52] When the petition reached the president a week later, it bore only nineteen signatures.[53] Eight belonged to members of the Keppler circle itself: Ewald Hecker, Emil Helferrich, Karl-Vincent Krogmann, Friedrich Reinhart, August Rosterg, Schacht, Kurt von Schröder, and Franz Heinrich Witthoeft. Only one really prominent industrialist signed, Fritz Thyssen, but his support of Hitler scarcely amounted to news by November 1932. Two signatures stemmed from insignificant men in Hamburg, an Erwin Merck, who appears to have been a banking acquaintance of Kurt von Schröder, and merchant-shipper Kurt Woermann, who had for some time identified himself with National Socialism.[54] Four others signing were a Senator Beindorff, a manufacturer of inks and artists' supplies in Hanover; Erich Lübbert, head of a construction firm in Berlin; Rudolf Ventzki, a provincial manufacturer of farm equipment; and Kurt von Eichborn, a partner in a private bank in Breslau who in 1931 had become one of the many lesser businessmen drawn to Nazism.[55] The remaining five signatures belonged to agrarians. In a letter to President Hindenburg's secretary, Friedrich Reinhart of the Keppler circle, who delivered the petition, claimed that Paul Reusch, Fritz Springorum, and Albert Vögler also "fully and completely" endorsed the petition but had not signed only because they did not wish to become active politically.[56] Other evidence belies that claim, however.[57] The petition of the Nazi-controlled Keppler circle went to Hindenburg, despite energetic recruitment efforts on the part of its organizers, with no big business support beyond its own membership aside from that of Fritz Thyssen, whose enthusiastic pro-Nazi views represented a long-standing exception in the camp of industry.

Even if Hindenburg believed the misleading information that Reusch, Springorum, and Vögler had endorsed the petition of the Keppler circle, neither that report nor the petition itself sufficed to overcome his resistance to Hitler. After the president had established that no workable combination of parties existed, he turned again to Papen. The caretaker chancellor requested presidential backing for an indefinite suspension of the Reichstag and for revision of the constitution in an authoritarian direction by unconstitutional means. In the face of objections from Defense Minister Schleicher that the army could not simultaneously defend Germany's borders with Poland and cope with civil disturbances resulting from the chancellor's proposed extreme course, Hindenburg rejected Papen's terms. Instead, he named Schleicher to the chancellorship on December 2.[58] Throughout these events, as at the time of the appointments of Brüning and Papen, big business remained a passive, poorly informed bystander. Again, the decisive impetus for a change of national political leadership came from the military.

3. Capitalists Adjust to a "Red General" in the Chancellery

If they had been consulted, virtually none of Germany's business leaders would have favored assigning the chancellorship to Kurt von Schleicher. In their circles he had come to be regarded as a questionable figure. Because he enjoyed cordial relations with trade union leaders, he had gained a reputation for being soft on labor.[1] In July, after taking over the Defense Ministry under Papen, he had reinforced that image in a radio address by proclaiming a social role for the army, especially on behalf of the poor. The military, he announced on that occasion, would not serve as a protective force for "outdated economic forms or indefensible distributions of property."[2] Some big businessmen regarded Schleicher, probably erroneously, as the driving force, during the summer and fall of 1932, behind the project for a Center-NSDAP coalition, which they feared would result in anti-capitalist policies.[3] The manager of the national organization of chambers of industry and commerce, Eduard Hamm, expressed the fears of many when he spoke of the possibility that the new chancellor might establish, on a parliamentary basis, a regime with a soldier-worker orientation.[4] In short, much of big business tended initially to view Schleicher as a potential quasi-socialist in military garb, or even, as one of his intellectual admirers put it, a "red general."[5] Yet within only six weeks most of the business community had decided that it would prefer to live with Schleicher rather than face another governmental crisis with all the economically disruptive uncertainties that would entail.

As soon as Schleicher's appointment became known, fears spread through the business community that the new chancellor would break with Papen's policies. On the one hand, Schleicher's retention of most of Papen's cabinet, including Economics Minister Hermann Warmbold, appeared a reassuring sign. On the other hand, his appointment, as special commissioner for job creation, of Günther Gereke, an outspoken advocate of large-scale, government-administered public works projects as a remedy for unemployment, raised alarm signals for *die Wirtschaft*. That alarm quickly found pointed expression in an editorial in the Düsseldorf business newspaper *Deutsche Bergwerks-Zeitung*. Papen's reliance on private enterprise had produced the first encouraging signs of economic recovery in years, that paper maintained. A relapse into the statist experiments of the past decade in an effort to generate jobs artificially would undo all the good Papen had achieved, it warned. The editorial expressed concern about rumors to the effect that the new cabinet stood ready to seek political support by making concessions to the trade unions and to the political parties in the spheres of economic and social policy. The editorial also deplored the new cabinet's apparent lack of interest in the constitutional reforms projected by the Papen cabinet. The departure of Papen's interior minister, Baron Wilhelm von Gayl, who had taken the lead in planning for constitutional changes, struck the Düsseldorf paper as a very disturbing development.[6] Its editors, along with the men of big business who shared their views, would have felt even greater concern if they had known of Schleicher's overall political strategy. He aimed at nothing short of a far-reaching political realignment by bringing behind his government the trade unions and at least part of the NSDAP. He had for some time cultivated relations with Gregor Strasser and hoped to entice the NSDAP into backing his cabinet by offering Strasser the posts of vice-chancellor and minister-president of Prussia.[7] If Schleicher's strategy had succeeded, the business community would have found itself confronted by a hostile political phalanx headed by the chancellor. But he failed to put that strategy into operation, primarily because of Strasser's unwillingness to defy Hitler's ban on any Nazi involvement in the government short of his own appointment as chancellor. Unaware of the full extent of Schleicher's plans, most of the press and the public viewed the chancellor's negotiations with Strasser merely as an attempt to revive Papen's efforts to bring the Nazis behind the government in a subordinate role.

The men of the Ruhrlade harbored a special mistrust for Schleicher. Even before his appointment as chancellor they had come to suspect him of misappropriating part of the funds they had placed at his disposal for support of the Papen cabinet in the campaign for the July Reichstag election. The purchase during August of a Berlin newspaper, *Tägliche Rundschau,* by a group of intellectuals associated with the magazine *Die Tat* aroused their suspicions in that regard. As Schleicher had ties to that group and especially to its leader, Hans Zehrer, some observers assumed that the general had supplied part of the money used for the purchase. Rumors reaching the men of the Ruhrlade led them to believe Schleicher had used for that purpose some of the funds they had given him to aid the parties sympathetic to the Papen cabinet. Zehrer's use of the *Tägliche Rundschau* to advocate the development of a trade union axis that would include pro-labor elements of the Nazi Party and prepare the way for a "German revolution" added to their chagrin. When they confronted Schleicher with their suspicions in the autumn, a rancorous exchange of communications via Schleicher's industrialist friend Otto Wolff ensued. Schleicher vehemently denied that he had diverted funds, but the men of the Ruhrlade remained unconvinced and embittered.[8] Now, to their distress, they found in the Reich Chancellery a man whom they not only regarded as unreliable on economic and social policy but whom they also suspected of having bilked them financially for his own political purposes. In issuing instructions at the beginning of December 1932 to the editors of newspapers owned by his firm, Paul Reusch, the leading figure in the Ruhrlade, ordered the editors to adopt a reserved attitude toward the new cabinet and to bestow no laurels on it in advance. He did not believe Schleicher's cabinet would last long, Reusch confided to one editor.[9] At least in part under the impact of the concern they shared about the new government, the members of the Ruhrlade managed during December to surmount that group's internal differences sufficiently to schedule for early January 1933 its first meeting since the previous summer.[10]

While Schleicher occupied himself with his ultimately futile efforts to forge a popular basis for his cabinet, big business interests launched a campaign aimed at exerting pressure on the chancellor to retain Papen's economic program. That undertaking assumed added urgency when the new Reichstag convened on December 6 and, before adjourning three days later, revealed hostility toward many aspects of Papen's economic decrees on the part of a large majority that encompassed the KPD, the SPD, and the NSDAP. At meetings held during the first half of December, the national organization of chambers of industry and commerce, the national association of industrial employers, and the industrial Reichsverband responded to the new situation by reiterating their endorsement of the Papen program. All three issued warnings that any abandonment of the sound principles upheld by the former chancellor would jeopardize the economic recovery just beginning to make itself felt.[11] At a meeting of the Reichsverband on December 14 its chairman, Krupp von Bohlen, bluntly warned the Schleicher cabinet to follow in the path of Papen by relying on the initiative and responsibility of private entrepreneurs. He cautioned the cabinet against any experiments with Germany's currency and credit system and urged it to draw a sharp line between the state's sphere of responsibility and that of the private economy. The country's political leaders, Krupp exhorted, must cease placing chains on the business community. Following Krupp's remarks two holdovers from the Papen cabinet, Finance Minister Count Schwerin von Krosigk and Economics Minister Warmbold, assured the Reichsverband gathering that no radical departures were in the offing. Both pledged continuation of the Papen cabinet's efforts to reduce unemployment by stimulating private enterprise through tax relief. In addition, Warmbold spoke out against obstacles to international trade, with obvious reference to mounting agrarian demands for import quotas on foodstuffs.[12]

Hardly had the business community registered these reassuring statements when quite different utterances began emanating from the Schleicher cabinet. The very day Krosigk and Warmbold spoke before the Reichsverband, the chancellor announced he had decided to restore the inviolability of wage contracts, which Papen had breached by using presidential emergency powers to permit employers to reduce contract-wage rates if they hired additional workers.[13] Schleicher thus erased a measure universally applauded in business circles as a step toward the restoration of sound economic principles. On that same day the cabinet approved a greatly expanded job-creation program that relied heavily on public works projects of the sort favored by Gereke, thereby calling into question the new government's commitment to Papen's policy of seeking recovery by stimulating the private sector.[14] Rumors also circulated to the effect that the "armistice" between the cabinet and the parties that permitted the adjournment of the Reichstag on December 9 until mid-January prefigured an agreement that would give Schleicher a working majority in the chamber.[15] Parliamentary rule, presumed by many in the business community to have been dead—at least in its Weimar form—since the summer, now threatened to reassert itself under a highly unorthodox Prussian general.

Additional doubts about Schleicher's commitment to the policies of Papen arose as a consequence of a radio address by the chancellor on December 15, one day after the Reichsverband gathering.[16] In that speech Schleicher proclaimed as the sole program of his cabinet the slogan "Create work!" Cheerfully accepting the label "social general" coined by his critics, he announced that he felt no commitment to either capitalism or socialism. Such concepts as private enterprise and planned economy had lost their terror for him, he added, as those abstractions did not exist in real life. He therefore intended simply to do in the economic sphere whatever seemed reasonable at the moment and most likely to yield the best results for the people and the country. There was no point in Germans breaking each other's heads about doctrinal matters, he added. In keeping with that position the chancellor vigorously defended his action in restoring the inviolability of contract wages; workers' wages had sunk so low that any further reduction would simply be intolerable, he explained. Schleicher also justified the newly announced government work-creation program as a pragmatic emergency measure that might not entirely conform to the laws of economics but would provide a much needed stimulus to the economy and a way to help those who could not continue to go without incomes until recovery set in. He thus seemed to commit himself to Gereke's well-known plans for extensive government-financed public works projects. Some voices in the business community responded with guarded optimism to the chancellor's speech, applauding his energetic approach to the country's economic troubles.[17] Others reacted angrily to both Schleicher's policies and to his whole attitude toward the economy.[18]

Paul Reusch took sharp, if private, exception to the chancellor's eschewal of any allegiance to either capitalism or socialism. For Reusch one of life's certitudes lay in the existence of unshakable economic principles that had to be upheld under all conditions. He feared inflationary effects from Schleicher's program of job-creation and charged that while Schleicher talked about continuing Papen's efforts to reduce governmental intervention in the economy, the new chancellor did nothing along those lines. Reusch further regretted the absence in Schleicher's address of any commitment to constitutional reforms. Overall, he found Schleicher disturbingly accommodating in his attitude toward the political parties and the trade unions. Reusch expressed special concern lest the chancellor give way to mounting agrarian demands for import restrictions on foodstuffs so high as to provoke certain retaliation against German industrial exports.[19] Schleicher's radio address to the nation struck Reusch as devoid of any program and consisting merely of "bows to all sides" designed to heighten the personal political popularity of the chancellor. He feared that Schleicher would, when the Reichstag reconvened in January, seek to ingratiate himself with the political parties by making sweeping concessions at the expense of *die Wirtschaft*, thereby hampering economic recovery.[20]

In his actions, as opposed to his words, Schleicher failed to bear out the worst fears of the business community. His cabinet's actual efforts to combat the depression turned out to involve merely some relatively modest modifications of Papen's program.[21] The cabinet retained and even expanded the tax-relief measures with which Papen had sought to fuel investment by the private sector. Plans for direct work-creation by the government had to be curtailed because of resistance on the part of Reichsbank president Hans Luther to any large-scale extension of credit to the government. The 500-million-mark credit Luther finally granted to the Schleicher cabinet for public works projects hardly represented a quantum leap beyond the approximately 300 million marks the Papen cabinet had earmarked for similar use. To the relief of the business community, the new cabinet displayed no interest in fundamentally revising the relationship between the economy and the government. To the pleasant surprise of industrial and commercial interests, Schleicher showed no inclination either to knuckle under to the increasingly insistent demands of agrarian interests for drastic import quotas on foodstuffs. Indeed, in regard to trade policy the new cabinet came down more squarely on the side of *die Wirtschaft* than had Papen's, which had vacillated on agricultural protection.

As for the cabinet's efforts to secure for itself a working-class political basis cutting across the parties, events soon consigned all such aspirations to the realm of empty speculation. In early December Gregor Strasser's flirtation with Schleicher brought him into a collision with Hitler that resulted in Strasser's resignation from his party posts.[22] His departure left National Socialism, under Hitler's reasserted authority, in a posture of uncompromising opposition to Schleicher and his cabinet. The chancellor's efforts to cultivate support on the left also came to naught. Initially at least, Schleicher found some receptivity toward collaboration among the leadership of the socialist trade union movement, but the Social Democratic Party quashed any serious moves toward cooperation with a chancellor who had played a key role in deposing the SPD-led government of Prussia and now seemed intent on ruling without regard for the parliament, possibly by unconstitutionally postponing new elections in the wake of another dissolution of the Reichstag.[23] Unable to find a popular political following, Schleicher and his ministers pulled back from far-reaching measures of any sort, lest these offend potential supporters. In the economic sphere the cabinet quickly developed into a do-nothing regime that essentially continued, with insignificant modifications, the policies of its predecessor.

As 1933 began, opinion in the business community divided on the Schleicher cabinet. Some, such as Carl Duisberg of IG Farben and Jakob

Herle, staff manager of the industrial Reichsverband, remained disturbed by the chancellor's statements during his first weeks in office.[24] Others began to view the new cabinet in a more positive light during January 1933. Such was the case with Krupp von Bohlen's brother-in-law and political confidant, Baron Tilo von Wilmowsky, who established a cordial personal relationship with Schleicher.[25] The chancellor made himself available to other leaders from the business community as well, leaving them with a generally encouraging impression of his attitudes toward economic policy.[26] Such supportive consultations came as a welcome development at a time when the paramount agricultural organization, the Reichslandbund, was mounting increasingly intemperate attacks on the "allmighty moneybag interests of internationally oriented export industry." In increasingly hostile tones, that organization charged industrial interests with blocking the import quotas on foodstuffs which its spokesmen insisted were desperately needed to restore the well-being of the agrarian sector.[27] The rejection of those claims by the Schleicher cabinet in mid-January, which led to a rupture in the government's relations with the Reichslandbund, thus came as a welcome development for industry. Eduard Hamm, managing director of the national organization of chambers of industry and commerce, spoke out approvingly about the cabinet's trade policies at a meeting of that organization's directorate a few days later. With regard to overall economic policy as well, Hamm pointed out, the Schleicher cabinet had yet to depart in any significant respect from the course charted by Papen. Its program of job-creation through public works had turned out very differently than originally projected, failing to bear out the fears in business circles that Schleicher sought some sort of economic planning or would neglect the "driving forces" of private enterprise. Dangers of those sorts could still not be dismissed altogether, Hamm warned, in appealing for continued vigilance.[28] But his remarks unmistakably signaled an increasingly positive assessment of the six-week-old cabinet.

This shift derived at least in part from a widespread desire in business circles for a period of political stability after the repeated upheavals of 1932. As one business leader after another had observed since the previous autumn, the uncertainty arising from political instability posed a serious handicap to recovery.[29] Lacking confidence, because of political instability, about continuity in national economic policy or even in such everyday matters as the varieties and levels of taxation, businessmen in late Weimar Germany—as in most places at most times—felt reluctant to commit large amounts of capital to long-range projects. As signs of recovery proliferated in late 1932 and early 1933 after long years of depression, continuing with the Schleicher cabinet, even if it left something to be desired, seemed at the minimum to represent a lesser evil when compared to the uncertainties of a renewed governmental crisis, which might possibly eventuate in still another rancorous and indecisive national election.[30]

There seemed, in any event, little in the way of realistic alternatives to the Schleicher cabinet in January 1933. The business community's favorite, Papen, appeared abandoned by Hindenburg and still without any popular following. The Catholic Center Party was viewed with mistrust in business circles because of its opposition to the Papen cabinet and because of the assertiveness of its trade union wing. Despite the gains of the DVP in the November election, it remained a negligible factor, now little more than a mere satellite of the DNVP. Hugenberg had made the latter party unpalatable even to some of his formerly most loyal industrial supporters by endorsing the extreme protectionist demands of the agrarians. Even Albert Vögler of United Steel, until recently one of Hugenberg's faithful followers, now joined in the efforts to persuade him to step down as DNVP chairman that preoccupied Paul Reusch and other politically active Ruhr industrialists in January 1933.[31] Nor did the breach between the DNVP and the Nazis appear to narrow appreciably. Conciliatory gestures to Hitler on the part of Hugenberg met with no reciprocation, so that a recrudescence of the "national opposition" seemed no more likely than during the fall. In fact, no alternative to the Schleicher cabinet appeared very feasible as the day of reckoning approached when the government would have to go before the reconvened Reichstag with its hostile majority. With the acquiescence of the Nazis that day was twice put off, until January 31 finally became the date set for the chamber to convene again. On January 23 the big-business-owned *Deutsche Allgemeine Zeitung*, after surveying all the possibilities, concluded that the only way out of the political deadlock lay in a suspension of the Reichstag by the Schleicher cabinet and rule by it in defiance of the constitution.[32]

As for the NSDAP, it seemed both in decline and committed to policies unacceptable to big business. On the heels of their losses in the November Reichstag election, the Nazis suffered during the ensuing month even greater setbacks in local elections held in areas where they had previously done well at the polls.[33] In addition, their financial problems showed no signs of resolution. Strasser's resignation of his party offices following his unsuccessful attempt to bring Hitler to abandon his all-or-nothing "policy of catastrophe" seemed to end all hope of bringing the Nazis behind a broad rightist government. By ousting Strasser, Hitler reinforced his growing reputation for intransigent obstructionism. From the business community's point of view, the eclipse of Strasser marked the triumph of extremism over moderation in the NSDAP.[34] In spite of his occasional advocacy of Nazi economic policies they deeply mistrusted, some businessmen had come to see Strasser as a potentially reasonable Nazi who might one day bring his party, with its mass following, behind a conservative regime.[35] Hitler, once viewed as a moderate, had now cast himself in the role of an unreasonable, uncompromising obstacle to a rightist coalition. The departure of Strasser made it appear more doubtful than ever that the NSDAP would consent to participate in the government on anything except Hitler's publicly stated terms, which now included a demand for presidential emergency powers in addition to the chancellorship for himself. Since Hindenburg had long since firmly rejected both of those demands, a Nazi entry into the government seemed a very remote possibility at best. Nor did the Nazis abandon their socio-economic demagogy, despite their cultivation of a red scare in the wake of the KPD's gains in the November Reichstag election.[36] In mid-November their delegation in the Bavarian Landtag introduced with much fanfare a bill instructing the Munich government to call on the Reichstag to pass a law dissolving all trusts, concerns, and cartels.[37] Nazi speakers and newspapers attacked Schleicher vigorously but on very different grounds than did his business critics, characterizing his government as simply a revised edition of Papen's "cabinet of barons." With particular vitriol the Nazis denounced the man to whom big business looked for protection of its interests in the cabinet, Economics Minister Warmbold. Siding with the agrarians, whose demands for drastic foodstuff import quotas Warmbold resisted, the Nazis labeled the minister an agent of IG Farben and "large-scale industrial interests linked with international finance capital."[38] During the Reichstag session of December 1932 Nazi deputies competed with Social Democrats and Communists in denouncing Papen's economic program as unsocial, voting with those parties to strike down some of Papen's measures most disliked by labor.[39] When a mining company announced its intention late in 1932 to close a coal mine that was losing money, the Nazi press sided—to the consternation of Hans von Loewenstein of the Bergbauverein—with the miners' demand that the government forbid the operators to shut down the mine.[40] Even the elderly renegade Nazi, Emil Kirdorf, whose favor Hitler had continued to cultivate, held aloof from supporting the NSDAP and demonstratively distanced himself from that party by publicly reaffirming his allegiance to the DNVP on the first day of 1933.[41]

As Hitler began his final drive for power, relations between the NSDAP and the business community seemed to have reached an all-time low. The Social Democratic daily, *Vorwärts*, noticed this. At the beginning of January 1933 it observed, in words highly uncharacteristic for its pages, "Hitlerism has long since lost all credit with high finance, heavy industry, and the large landowners."[42] The liberal *Frankfurter Zeitung*, which enjoyed considerable respect in business circles, drew an optimistic conclusion from the situation. Surveying the apparent disarray of the NSDAP's leadership, its seemingly ebbing popular appeal, and what appeared to be its increasingly desperate demagogy, the Frankfurter paper expressed in its new year's edition a view that enjoyed wide currency at the time: "The mighty National Socialist assault on the democratic state has been repulsed. . . ." [43]

4. Big Business Experiences the Birth of the Third Reich

Unfortunately, the *Frankfurter Zeitung*'s political obituary proved premature by twelve years. Within less than a month of its appearance, Adolf Hitler stood at the head of the German government. The story of that unexpected and calamitous turn of events has been so often told that a brief sketch will suffice here. Schleicher, although he held both the chancellorship and the Ministry of Defense, occupied a position more precarious than appearances indicated. Like Papen, he had to face up to the problem of an implacably hostile Reichstag majority. He displayed considerable imagination and audacity in attempting to marshal parliamentary support, or at least toleration, on the part of politicians ranging from the SPD on the left to the NSDAP. But in the end all his stratagems failed. Even the DNVP went into opposition, leaving Schleicher with a still narrower basis of support than Papen had commanded. With the chamber scheduled to reconvene at the end of January, Schleicher, like Papen before him, called on President Hindenburg to dissolve the Reichstag and postpone new elections indefinitely so that the cabinet could rule by means of presidential emergency powers without interference from the parliament. However, Hindenburg, under the influence of the camarilla around him, had soured on Schleicher. He refused a dissolution decree to the chancellor, who submitted his resignation on January 28. The president then assigned the task of sounding out the parties about a new government to Papen, with whom he had parted only reluctantly in December and who hungered both for a return to power and for revenge on Schleicher. On the basis of negotiations with Hitler and other foes of Schleicher that had begun in early January, Papen held out to Hindenburg the prospect of a broad nationalist government that would encompass the DNVP, the NSDAP, and the Stahlhelm veterans' organization. After several days of elaborate intrigue, during which even Schleicher swung behind Hitler's candidacy in hopes of blocking a return to power by Papen, a new cabinet took office on January 30, 1933. Hitler became chancellor, with Papen as vice-chancellor and commissar for Prussia, while Hugenberg took over both the Economics and Agriculture ministries. Werner von Blomberg, a general favorably inclined to the new combination, replaced Schleicher as defense minister. Besides Hitler, the cabinet included only two other Nazis, Wilhelm Frick as interior minister and Hermann Göring as minister without portfolio, charged with the duties of the Prussian minister-presidency. It at once proclaimed itself a "government of national concentra-

tion." Two days later, after negotiations between Hitler and the Center
Party collapsed, thereby ruling out a parliamentary basis for the new
cabinet, the Reichstag was dissolved by presidential decree and a new
national election scheduled for March 5.

Many aspects of these momentous developments have ever since remained the subject of controversy, but none more so than the role of big
business. Numerous contemporary observers immediately attributed to
it an important, even crucial, part in the events that led to the installation
of Hitler in the chancellorship. With variations, countless subsequent
treatments of the subject have echoed that allegation. The generalized
indictment falls, under scrutiny, into three component parts. First, it is
alleged that big business played a vital part in effecting the reconciliation
between Papen and Hitler that made possible their intrigues against
Schleicher and their cooperation in forging the cabinet of January 30.
Second, it is contended that big business rescued the NSDAP from financial ruin after Hitler and Papen became reconciled, just in time to make
possible a Nazi electoral triumph in a state election that rallied Nazism
for its final, successful bid for power. Third, it is maintained that big
business helped to turn Hindenburg against Schleicher and to overcome
his resistance to making Hitler chancellor. In the light of the evidence
that has accrued over a half century, each of these three allegations
proves untenable.

The charge that big business was instrumental in bringing Hitler and
Papen together turns on the role of Baron Kurt von Schröder, the Cologne banker at whose home the two politicians met on January 4, 1933.
That meeting is rightly regarded as a major juncture since on that occasion those two conspirators put aside their past differences and began
intriguing to replace Schleicher's cabinet with one each hoped to control.
The scene of their meeting, Schröder's presence, and his role in the
arrangements to bring the two politicians together have led many to assume that the banker—and therefore big business—had a vital hand in
effecting the collaboration between Papen and Hitler that eventuated in
the cabinet of January 30.[1] This assumption involves a number of mis-
conceptions. Schröder's house became the site of the meeting because its
location made it convenient for Papen and Hitler, both of whom had
plans for travel in the Rhineland. They sought a secret, confidential ren-
dezvous, and Schröder was among the few persons who knew of their
intention to meet.[2] As for Schröder's participation in the meeting, both
Schröder and Papen later agreed that the banker played no part, and
Papen maintained that Schröder had been present for only part of his
lengthy conference with Hitler.[3] It would seem farfetched, to say the
least, to suggest that such a political outsider as Schröder could have
influenced the decisions of men like Papen and Hitler in January 1933.
Schröder could not, in any event, speak for big business, as is often implied. He was merely a partner in a medium-sized provincial bank whose

personal involvement with large-scale industry consisted of holding seats on the largely honorific supervisory boards of several industrial firms. He had little contact with the important figures of big business and remained unknown to most of them until he became politically involved on behalf of the NSDAP during the latter half of 1932.[4] He did not become their agent or spokesman even then.

Schröder could play his role not because he enjoyed any great importance as a business figure but rather because he formed a key link in a fortuitous chain of personal relationships by means of which communications could develop between two men who wanted to meet: Papen and Hitler. Schröder's contact with Hitler went back to the banker's enlistment, in late May, by Nazi Wilhelm Keppler for the circle of economic advisers that erstwhile small entrepreneur was then setting up at Hitler's behest. As already mentioned, Schröder knew Keppler as a result of the latter's unsuccessful efforts a few years earlier to raise a loan for a business venture. Not long after Schröder agreed to join the Keppler circle, a politician with whom he shared a mutual acquaintance unexpectedly assumed a new importance: Franz von Papen became Reich chancellor. Soon thereafter Schröder met Papen through their mutual acquaintance.[5] As one of the few persons with entrée to both Papen and Hitler, two men separated by a wide social chasm, Kurt von Schröder thus fortuitously became a man with potentially very useful connections. These connections took on great significance when Schröder encountered Papen on December 16, 1932, at the Berlin Herrenklub, where he had just heard the former chancellor reveal in a speech his displeasure with the Schleicher cabinet and his favorable inclination toward inclusion of the NSDAP in the government.[6] Schröder had a month earlier been led by Keppler to hope that Papen might look with favor on Hitler's appointment to the chancellorship and might possibly even intercede with Hindenburg on the Nazi leader's behalf. The former chancellor's speech consequently quickened his interest and led to a conversation with Papen afterwards.[7] Papen, whose accounts of the events leading to Hitler's appointment are notoriously untrustworthy, later claimed Schröder first broached the subject of a meeting with Hitler on that occasion.[8] At the time Schröder publicly claimed responsibility for initiating the meeting.[9] After the war he repeatedly testified that the initiative came from Papen.[10] There is no way to determine which version is true, but it seems just as likely that Papen, rather than Schröder, first raised the possibility of a meeting with Hitler.

Even if Schröder took the initiative to bring Papen and Hitler together, no evidence supports the widespread assumption that he acted on behalf of big business. He may have been convinced, as he implied after the war at Nuremberg, that he acted in the interests of the business community, but its leaders remained unaware of his actions. None of the important industrialists whose views and activities for that period are documented had any recorded contact with Schröder in December 1932 or January 1933, or showed any signs of knowing about his activities.[11] Not even the Nazi Fritz Thyssen knew what Schröder was up to until after the meeting of January 4.[12] In an affidavit that Schröder submitted at Nuremberg in 1947, and which has received much attention in writings about the Papen-Hitler meeting, the banker stated that before complying with Papen's wish for a talk with Hitler he had consulted with "a number of gentlemen from the business community" (die Wirtschaft) and informed himself about the attitude of the business community toward a collaboration between Papen and Hitler, which he found to be favorable.[13] That statement has been portrayed as indisputable proof that Schröder acted on behalf of big business.[14] Those who take that position have, however, left unmentioned a lengthy interrogation of Schröder at Nuremberg during which he was pressed to identify those businessmen with whom he consulted.[15] Asked whether he had spoken with men such as IG Farben's Carl Duisberg or Carl Bosch, Schröder explained that he had not since he had virtually no contact with Duisberg and had not at that time even met Bosch. Asked whether he had consulted anyone at the industrial Reichsverband, Schröder replied that he had in 1932 "nothing to do with industry" and knew nothing about the workings of the Reichsverband. When the interrogator continued to press him about the identity of the businessmen he claimed to have spoken with in December 1932, Schröder admitted that his soundings had gone no further than the Keppler circle. As mentioned earlier, the members of that Nazi-inspired and Nazi-led group in no sense constituted, as is so often alleged, an impressive or representative array of executives. Their encouragement of Schröder hardly amounted to support on the part of German big business for his role in bringing together Papen and Hitler. Schröder's testimony under interrogation about the importance for him of the Keppler circle would seem borne out by his having immediately turned over arrangements for the Papen-Hitler meeting to the leader of the circle, Nazi Wilhelm Keppler. In making the arrangements, Keppler used Schröder merely as an intermediary to Papen and as a convenient host for what proved a momentous exchange between two unscrupulous politicians eager to collaborate on the basis of one of politics' most primitive formulas, namely, my enemy's enemy is my friend.[16] Compared with the roles played by Franz von Papen and Adolf Hitler on January 4, 1933, Kurt von Schröder's amounted to that of a mere spear holder on the stage of history.

When a Berlin newspaper, which had somehow got wind of Papen's assignation with Hitler in time to post a reporter outside of Schröder's house, quickly broke the sensational story of Papen's meeting with the Nazi leader, that news at once gave rise to a legend that has since become firmly entrenched in historical accounts of the event: that large-scale big business financial aid flowed to the Nazis as a consequence of a deal reached during the meeting of January 4, 1933, at Schröder's house.[17] No evidence whatever underlay the reports to that effect, which immediately proliferated in the leftist press. Hitler, Papen, and Schröder all later denied that money had even been mentioned, and no evidence has since come to light to contradict their denials.[18] The political logic of the situation militated, in any case, against any attempt by Hitler to raise funds for the NSDAP in such fashion. In order to do so he would have had to admit, at least tacitly, that his movement was in need, an admission that could only have weakened his bargaining position in pursuit of his paramount goal, the chancellorship. No such obvious considerations occurred to the leftist journalists of Germany, however. As soon as they heard the meeting had taken place at the house of the "big banker" Schröder, as the Communist daily *Die Rote Fahne* described him with obvious relish and an exclamation mark in parentheses, they knew with certainty its true significance.[19] "Since Hitler has been heavily financed by many groups within Rhenish-Westphalian industry," the readers of *Die Rote Fahne* now learned, "and since such subventions are customarily channeled through private bankhouses, the background of this meeting becomes clear."[20] The capitalists who all along had lurked in the shadows behind National Socialism had at last been surprised at their dirty work. Or, as in some versions, the discovery of the meeting meant that Hitler, the "agent of big industry," as the SPD's organ *Vorwärts* labeled him, had been caught *"in flagrante"* with his big-business patrons.[21]

For those who jumped to such conclusions, no doubt remained about the true nature of Nazism. It stood revealed as the demagogic tool of the same exploiters of the people who also manipulated such more conspicuous political puppets as Schleicher, Papen, and Hugenberg. In numerous imaginatively elaborated versions, this message multiplied in the left-wing publications of Germany during the final, crucial weeks of January 1933. While Hitler moved toward his goal of the chancellorship with a sure sense for the realities of power, his opponents on the left exultantly proclaimed an ultimately despairing and incapacitating message, which they insisted the meeting of January 4 had verified: Whether the Reich chancellor was named Schleicher, Papen, or Hitler made no difference since all were mere tools of the capitalists.[22] The analysts of the left had convinced themselves that by bringing to the attention of the German people this incontestable corroboration of their ideologically based interpretation of National Socialism, they could set off a massive popular revulsion that would somehow sweep Nazism into oblivion. Those among them who survived the ghastly consequences of their rapidly approaching political debacle may presumably later have found at least some consolation in the many triumphs achieved in subsequent history books by their willful, biased interpretation of the Hitler-Papen meeting, according to which Kurt von Schröder, not Franz von Papen or Adolf Hitler, loomed as the key participant.[23]

Some writers of the history of the period, unable to accept the full-blown leftist version of the meeting of January 4, have, while leaving the matter of causation vague, alleged that large amounts of capitalist money flowed to the NSDAP immediately in the aftermath of that event.[24] But no persuasive evidence has been adduced to support that allegation either. Nothing indicates that the Nazis received any notable infusion of funds in January 1933 from any source, much less from big business. Goebbels's published diaries, repeatedly cited in support of such allegations, reveal nothing of the sort.[25] Nor did the NSDAP's campaign for the election of January 15 in the state of Lippe-Detmold. What proved a successful strategy there involved virtually total reliance on the customary Nazi technique of making campaigning pay for itself.[26] In pursuit of Lippe-Detmold's 100,000 voters, the NSDAP blanketed that tiny state with no fewer than thirty-eight mass rallies during the twelve days preceding the balloting. To rekindle the electorate's interest, the Nazis mobilized most of the oratorical "big guns" of the party, including Hitler, who himself addressed no fewer than seventeen rallies within ten days. To cover their expenses, the Nazis charged those who came to hear such celebrities admission fees considerably in excess of the normal rates. The strategy worked. The NSDAP regained in Lippe-Detmold enough of the votes it had lost in November to proclaim the outcome as a victory. But the campaign there proved a near thing financially. On at least one occasion, a bailiff sequestered the box office receipts for a party rally to meet the claim of impatient creditors.[27] In his sober postwar memoir Otto Dietrich, who served as Hitler's press agent in January 1933, recalled that the party leader's adjutant had at one point in the Lippe campaign urgently requested a personal loan of 2,000 marks from him, explaining that there was not enough money on hand to pay the rental fee demanded in advance for the hall in which Hitler was scheduled to speak the next day.[28]

Money had in any event very limited significance during January 1933. The key to power lay in influence with Hindenburg, who alone possessed the constitutional authority to appoint a chancellor and authorize or deny the dissolution of the Reichstag. Thus, by far the most serious of all the charges against big business is that it helped to turn the president against Schleicher and toward Hitler. No evidence of appeals to Hindenburg from the business community for the removal of Schleicher or the appointment of Hitler has ever been adduced to support this charge, however.[29] Quite to the contrary, the only documented high-level attempt at intervention with Hindenburg from the *die Wirtschaft* during January 1933 was aimed at cautioning the President against installing a right-wing cabinet including the NSDAP. That intervention, which came from the side of the industrial Reichsverband, must be viewed in the light of a letter of January 26, 1933, in which Ludwig Kastl, the executive director of that organization, reported on political matters to its chairman, Gustav Krupp von Bohlen, then on vacation in Switzerland.[30] The situation in Berlin had become impenetrable, Kastl informed Krupp. He noted that the DNVP's decision to come out against the Schleicher cabinet was generally deplored, and he found alarming the speculation that the DNVP might seek to form a new government with the Nazis. He had that same day learned from Schleicher's state secretary, Erwin Planck, of talk about a Papen-Hitler-Schacht cabinet. Papen would, according to that rumor, reassume the chancellorship; Hitler would become minister of defense and the interior; Schacht would be named finance minister; and Hugenberg would take over both the Economics and the Agriculture ministries. Kastl left no doubts about his negative assessment of such a cabinet. Granting Hugenberg control over both ministries concerned with economic matters would, he feared, result in a triumph, in the sphere of trade policy, of the agrarian protectionism so dreaded by industry. Kastl further feared that such a cabinet would amount to a declaration of hostilities against the larger part of the population—by which he clearly meant organized labor—and would therefore lead to civic disorder. Such a cabinet was being proclaimed as a *Bombenkabinett,* Kastl reported, but he felt that the emphasis lay more heavily on the word *Bomben* than on the *Kabinett.* He found consolation, however, in his belief that such a combination had little chance of success. The Social Democrats would strenuously oppose it; the Center Party would never support it; and it was highly unlikely that Hindenburg would accept it. Having consigned the disturbing possibility of a Papen-Hitler-Schacht cabinet based on the NSDAP and DNVP to the realm of improbability, Kastl went on to sketch out what he regarded as the most desirable political solution from the standpoint of *die Wirtschaft.* The best way out of the present predicament, he explained to Krupp, lay in retaining the Schleicher cabinet. That would avoid the economically disruptive effects of another change of government and new elections. If the Reichstag proved rebellious, then it should be dissolved and efforts made to obtain the parties' acquiescence in a postponement until the autumn of the new election, which the constitution called for within sixty days of a dissolution. Interestingly, Kastl's formula coincided closely with the one favored by Schleicher himself in late January 1933, a fact probably not unrelated to Kastl's cordial relations with State Secretary Planck.[31]

When Kastl wrote his letter to Krupp on January 26, he saw no immediate need for political intervention on the part of the Reichsverband, but the accelerating pace of events led him to reconsider only two days later. When, at midday on January 28, the news of Schleicher's resignation became public, Kastl at once joined with Eduard Hamm, the chief official of the national organization of chambers of industry and commerce, in submitting a brief letter to President Hindenburg's state secretary, Otto Meissner. Later Kastl reported that he had taken this step at the urging of United Steel's Albert Vögler.[32] Writing in what they described as a personal capacity, but on the basis of broad soundings in business circles, Kastl and Hamm emphasized the indispensability for economic recovery of calm and stability. They urged that the current "political difficulties" be dealt with in such a fashion as to occasion the least possible disturbance for the country.[33] In a separate letter of the same day to Meissner, Kastl reported that since dispatching his and Hamm's letter he had spoken by telephone with Krupp and established that the chairman of the Reichsverband fully endorsed the position he and Hamm had taken.[34] Meissner replied, also on the twenty-eighth, acknowledging that he had brought the two letters to the attention of Hindenburg, who, he wrote, also wished to resolve the pending political problems with as little disruption as possible for the business community.[35] Later, after Hitler had become chancellor, rumors about these letters of January 28 formed the basis for angry accusations that Kastl and Krupp had at the last minute intervened with Hindenburg in the name of the Reichsverband in an attempt to block the appointment of the Nazi leader to the chancellorship.[36] The actual wording of those very brief letters did not substantiate that accusation, so Kastl and Krupp could safely deny it. But if the letters are placed in the context of the views Kastl expressed in his letter of January 26 to Krupp and of Krupp's unconcealed distaste for National Socialism, the accusation takes on considerable validity.[37] It also seems highly unlikely that Meissner, that well-informed busybody, would have remained so ignorant of the attitudes of prominent men such as Kastl and Krupp as not to grasp the warning against a *Bombenkabinett* including the Nazis that lay between the lines of the letters submitted to him on January 28. The possibility of such ignorance on Meissner's part diminishes further in light of the later recollection by Schleicher's commissar for work-creation, Günther Gereke, that Krupp's brother-in-law and confidant, Tilo von Wilmowsky, who seldom if ever disagreed with Krupp on political matters, had spoken out during the last week of January 1933 against tampering with the Schleicher cabinet.[38] The stand taken at that same time by Kastl and Krupp on behalf of the Reichsverband, cautiously worded as it was, represented an unprecedented break with past practice. Throughout the republican era that organization's leaders had studiously avoided attempts to influence the formations of cabinets, recognizing the unpleasant consequences of having to deal, in the event of failure, with chancellors and ministers whose appointment they had opposed.[39] Yet on January 28, 1933, the chief executive officer of the Reichsverband, along with his counterpart at the national organization of chambers of commerce and industry, became sufficiently alarmed to go at least to the very verge of attempting to influence President Hindenburg's choice of a new government. And in the light of what is known of Kastl's and Krupp's views, their messages to the president amounted to a warning against putting Hitler and his party into power.[40]

As for Hitler's partisans and sympathizers in big business circles, no evidence even suggests that they intervened on his behalf with Hindenburg in January 1933. The ardor of some Nazi fellow travelers from big business had in any case cooled by January 1933. The banker Emil Georg von Stauss became less enthusiastic about the NSDAP after a Nazi press attack on him during the summer of 1932; his recorded political activities thereafter centered on efforts to shore up his old party, the DVP.[41] The journalist and lobbyist August Heinrichsbauer continued to promote the ousted Gregor Strasser after the latter's break with Hitler. So did Hans Reupke, the Nazi admirer of Italian Fascism who worked as a legal expert for the industrial Reichsverband. During January Reupke and Heinrichsbauer, both of whom had come to view a Hitler cabinet as a menace to the economy, collaborated secretly on schemes for a comeback within the NSDAP by Strasser.[42] Fritz Thyssen remained loyal to Hitler but also ignorant of the intrigues of late January, receiving no call to bring to bear whatever influence he had in Berlin.[43] Presumably Hitler had by late January 1933 realized that an endorsement from a businessman like Thyssen would be of little use in overcoming the only remaining obstacle to his capturing the chancellorship, the resistance of Hindenburg. Quite clearly Hitler had concluded that success depended on his ability to pit rivals like Papen and Schleicher against each other and to mobilize on his behalf those persons who, like Hindenburg's son and certain key generals, could exert direct influence on the president. With regard to the military, Hitler's ties to the wealthy Wagnerians who had befriended and patronized him during the party's early years in Munich assumed at one key juncture in late January 1933 far greater significance than anything that can be attributed to big business. Edwin and Helene Bechstein, by making their Berlin home available on January 29 for a secret meeting between Hitler and another friend of theirs, Chief of the Army Command General Kurt von Hammerstein-Equord, rendered vital aid to the Nazi leader in his ultimately successful effort to win the backing of the military establishment for his candidacy as chancellor.[44]

When some of the most politically active Ruhr industrialists thought, in January 1933, of a replacement for Schleicher as chancellor, their candidate was not Hitler but Papen. They did not, however, envisage any swift change of governments. Papen himself nourished hopes that he might return to office when he met, at his request, on January 7 in Albert Vögler's Dortmund home with Krupp von Bohlen, Reusch, Springorum, and Vögler.[45] Papen led that group to believe that Hitler had abandoned his demands for the chancellorship and would be willing to serve as a junior partner in a "cabinet of national concentration" within which Nazism would be checked by strong bourgeois forces.[46] In

an apparent effort to counter press reports of a conspiracy on his part
with Hitler against Schleicher, Papen gave the industrialists to understand that the meeting in Cologne had not been directed against the
chancellor and had produced no definite plans. However, he indicated
his intention to assume an active role in rallying the bourgeois camp as a
counterweight to National Socialism. He also left his industrial friends
with the impression that he would eventually make himself available to
head a "cabinet of national concentration." Papen's news proved welcome to the Ruhr industrialists with whom he spoke in Dortmund on
January 7. They had serious reservations about Schleicher's economic
policies and—at least in the case of Reusch—still mistrusted the chancellor because of the suspicion that he had used for his own purposes some
of the Ruhrlade funds channeled to him during the summer election
campaign of 1932. The industrialists gathered in Dortmund responded
positively to Papen's project for yoking the Nazis to a conservative-
dominated government. Reusch regarded the inclusion of the Nazis in
the government as very desirable since he believed that the formation of
a strong nationalist government, based on a majority of the people,
would strengthen Germany's foreign policy hand in the year ahead,
when he expected major diplomatic developments that could possibly
lead to significant revisions of the Versailles settlement. Reusch believed
that such a government would also bolster Germany's position at the
World Economic Conference scheduled for the summer. He welcomed
Papen's Dortmund announcement that Hitler was now willing to forgo
the chancellorship, but he expressed concern at reports that the Nazi
leader had designs on the Defense Ministry, an arrangement Reusch
regarded as out of the question.

While the industrialists who met with Papen on January 7 agreed with
him as to goals, they came to differ with him about the best way to
achieve those goals. They left the meeting in Dortmund under the impression that the former chancellor would lay the basis for a comeback
by setting out to capture the leadership of the DNVP. For some time
sentiment had grown in industrial circles in favor of replacing the abrasive and obdurate Hugenberg with a more attractive leader who would
show greater responsiveness to the interests of *die Wirtschaft.* Those who,
like Reusch, favored that step expected the DNVP to become under new
leadership a magnet for bourgeois voters left politically homeless by the
decline of the old middle parties as well as for those who had earlier
defected to the NSDAP but now showed signs of disillusionment with
that movement. Under the impression that Papen stood ready to take
over the DNVP, Reusch and his friends set out during January to mobilize the anti-Hugenberg forces within the DNVP.[47] Even Vögler, previously a loyal Hugenberg follower, agreed to this plan in the wake of
the Dortmund meeting with Papen. He undertook to prevail on the stiff-
necked leader of the DNVP at least to accept Papen as his deputy and

heir apparent.[48] The plan to replace Hugenberg with Papen might have made sense at some earlier date, although its feasibility even then remains doubtful. But the notion that Franz von Papen's capturing control of the battered and depleted party of the old right could represent a significant step toward resolving the political crisis of January 1933 testifies eloquently to an astonishing lack of acumen on the part of some of Germany's most politically active industrialists as well as to their remoteness from reality.

Nothing whatever came of the DNVP project since Papen showed no interest in pursuing it. When he wrote to Springorum on January 20, he made no mention of it.[49] Instead, he reassured the industrialist of his continuing efforts to bring about a "national concentration." He was meeting with resistance, Papen wrote, from Hitler, who showed a renewed unwillingness, following the NSDAP's strong showing in the election in Lippe-Detmold, to resign himself to the position of a "junior partner" in a cabinet based on such a formula. Only two possibilities remained, Papen continued. One of these obviously amounted to Papen's predictions in the event the Schleicher cabinet remained unaltered, although Papen did not mention the chancellor's name. That course would lead, Papen warned, to a dissolution of the Reichstag and new elections, developments he characterized as highly injurious for *die Wirtschaft* and unlikely to bring about a resolution of the political impasse.

The second possibility, which Papen clearly favored, involved a parliamentary enabling act for a cabinet reconstructed "with Hitler," a formulation so worded as to leave unclear who would occupy the chancellorship. Regardless of which of these two possibilities eventuated, Papen emphasized that Germany's bourgeois political forces must be rallied "as a counterweight against Hitler." Papen then requested help with his efforts in that regard, repeating a proposal he had earlier made to Springorum, the treasurer of the Ruhrlade, presumably at the Dortmund meeting of January 7. He asked for a monthly subsidy, for a month or two, of 5,000 marks, with which he proposed to set up a small office in Berlin that would keep him informed by surveying the provincial press and spotting opportunities for intervention. In replying to Papen's letter on January 24, Springorum observed that a stiffening of the NSDAP's position after the Lippe-Detmold elections had been predictable, but that he had since then detected once more a greater inclination by the Nazis to cooperate with the bourgeois right.[50] He assured Papen of his support for efforts to unite the bourgeois political forces as preparation for a "national concentration." Springorum saw no value, however, in setting up a small office of the sort Papen had proposed, which he argued would "float in the air." He had come away from their earlier talk, Springorum continued, believing that Papen intended to obtain a firm organizational basis for his undertaking by personally entering the

DNVP. Only that step, the industrialist insisted, held out hope for the creation of a strong national movement that could guarantee a stable national government including the NSDAP. By the time Springorum's letter reached Papen in Berlin, the former chancellor was playing for far higher stakes and much quicker results than he had intimated to his industrialist friends. He was preparing the way, behind the scenes and by means of intrigue, for the volcanic eruption that would very soon radically transform Germany's political landscape. With a return to power apparently within his grasp, Papen not too surprisingly left in the dark the narrow-minded, unimaginative men of the Ruhr, who could still think only in conventional terms of political parties and so remained mired at a level of political strategy he had now transcended as he proceeded with his plan to harness Adolf Hitler for his own purposes.

An economic interest group contributed to the realization of Papen's scheme, but it was not *die Wirtschaft*. That help came instead from the agrarians of Germany.[51] Led by the well-organized Reichslandbund, in which Nazi infiltration had by then assumed large proportions, the spokesmen of Germany's "Green Front" directed an increasingly clamorous chorus of complaints at the Schleicher cabinet in January 1933. The cabinet's unwillingness to suspend foreclosures on agricultural land had offended virtually all of the country's agricultural interests. Its refusal to impose stringent import quotas on foodstuffs had further alienated many agrarian groups. The Junkers and other landowners in East Prussia nursed a special grievance of their own, arising out of the cabinet's plans to divide large bankrupt estates in that backward province into family farms as part of a plan to resettle unemployed people on the land. These East Elbians became further outraged when the cabinet made no effort to squelch the findings of a parliamentary inquiry that had uncovered numerous instances of landowners' misuse of government funds disbursed under the Osthilfe program instituted under Brüning to aid the ailing agriculture of the eastern provinces. By the middle of January the Schleicher cabinet had in effect broken off relations with the Reichslandbund in protest against its demagogic agitation, and the agrarians had gone into all-out opposition. That opposition carried special political force by virtue of the alignment of some of President Hindenburg's oldest and closest friends with the Reichslandbund. East Elbian landowners such as Elard von Oldenburg-Januschau commanded, by virtue of their privileged and private access to the presidential ear, a particularly potent weapon, and all signs indicate that they did not shrink from employing it against Schleicher.

The agrarians sought no help from big business in their onslaught against the Schleicher cabinet, nor would they likely have received a positive response if they had done so in January 1933. By then relations between *die Wirtschaft* and the Reichslandbund had sunk to an all-time low. The escalating demands of the agrarian spokesmen for higher tariffs and lower import quotas for foreign foodstuffs had awakened dire fears in industrial and financial circles of a shift to outright agricultural autarky with ruinous consequences for Germany's manufacturing exports. These fears had become sufficiently pressing by January to bring about a renewal of collaboration between industry and the trade unions, as spokesmen for those two interest groups joined forces to urge the Schleicher cabinet not to capitulate to the agrarians' trade policy demands.[52] Communication between the industrial organizations and the Reichslandbund had by then taken on a tone of outright hostility. During December 1932 the leaders of the Reichslandbund had further exacerbated the frictions arising from their head-on clash of interests with industry by authorizing public attacks in their organization's press on the chairman of the Reichsverband, Krupp von Bohlen, and a spokesman of the chemical industry, Edmund Pietrkowski.[53] The deterioration in relations which resulted from that breach of accepted lobbying practice precluded the sort of collaboration between big business and Junkers against Schleicher that leftist journalists conjured up at the time without benefit of evidence and numerous writers of history have since perpetuated.[54]

The climax of the political drama of January 1933 caught the political leaders of big business unawares. Krupp von Bohlen, who had not joined in the efforts of Springorum, Reusch, and Vögler to promote a comeback by Papen, remained isolated at his Swiss vacation retreat, where he had fallen ill. A letter he wrote to the Reichsverband from there on January 30 reveals that he had no notion of the great events under way in the capital.[55] Fritz Springorum also departed on a trip in late January, having put off a personal meeting requested by Schleicher until the second week of February. He left with assurances from a seasoned Berlin lobbyist for Ruhr industry that he need expect no fundamental political changes before his scheduled return on February 7.[56] On the twenty-eighth, the day Schleicher fell, Reusch could report to Krupp only that great confusion reigned in Berlin and that Schleicher would probably "disappear."[57] Despite his many sources of information, Reusch appears to have remained ignorant of the machinations in Berlin that would install Hitler at the head of the government on the thirtieth. Certainly neither he nor the other leaders of the business community could have gained a clear picture of events in the capital from the press.[58] Contradictory rumors abounded in the conservative business newspapers, which displayed no clear consensus about the most likely or desirable outcome of the crisis. On the twenty-ninth the right-wing *Rheinisch-Westfälische Zeitung* of Essen concluded that Schleicher's failure and the overall political constellation ruled out any solution other than a cabinet of "national concentration" under Hitler. But that same day the *Deutsche Allgemeine Zeitung* of Berlin held that Hitler's long-standing demand for the chancellorship might exclude such a solution in view of

Hindenburg's well-known opposition to giving him that post. If that should prove to be the case, the Berlin daily predicted that another Papen cabinet was likely, but it warned readers not to expect a swift resolution of the crisis. Also on the twenty-ninth the *Deutsche Bergwerks-Zeitung* of Düsseldorf expressed hope for a cabinet led jointly by Papen and Hitler, which it portrayed as the only means of avoiding an open break with the parliament. But the same editorial voiced misgivings about recent Nazi legislative proposals that ran counter to Papen's formula for economic recovery through stimulation of the private sector. On the morning of the thirtieth, only hours before Hitler became chancellor, the liberal *Frankfurter Zeitung* reported continuing uncertainty about whether that post would go to him or to Papen. At midday, when the members of the new cabinet arrived at the presidential palace for the customary formalities, not even all the ministers-designate knew for certain whether Papen or Hitler would stand at the head of the government.[59] Only a small circle was privy to the bargains that produced the Hitler cabinet, and from all indications it did not include any spokesmen of big business.

In line with customary practice, the business community responded to the change of cabinets by adopting a cautious posture and attempting to discern the new regime's economic policies. Paul Reusch gave expression to the prevailing attitude when he instructed the editor of a newspaper owned by his firm to "adopt, as usual, a reserved and calm attitude toward the government." He then added, "For the time being, enthusiasm would be inappropriate."[60] Reusch's calm masked grave concern on his part, however, about the political consequences of the latest turn of events. He feared that in the newly scheduled Reichstag elections the NSDAP would swamp the bourgeois forces so thoroughly as to deny them a voice in national affairs for the foreseeable future. In hopes of stemming the Nazi tide, Reusch continued to nurse his long-standing project for a single, united bourgeois party and to voice his unrealistic desire to see Hugenberg remove a major obstacle to that project by stepping down as chairman of the DNVP.[61] Ludwig Kastl, of the industrial Reichsverband, also displayed grave concern about the cabinet that took office on January 30, 1933.[62] He took the unusual step of participating the following day in a Berlin summit conference with the managing directors of the other major national associations of industry, commerce, and finance. They had decided for the time being, Kastl wrote to Krupp in Switzerland, not to seek an audience with Hitler or Hugenberg, at least not so long as no other interest group did so, lest they appear importunate. His immediate concern, Kastl's letter makes clear, centered on Hugenberg. He expressed the fear that the new minister for economics and agriculture might purge a senior official in the Economics Ministry who was favorably inclined to industry or, still worse, might submerge the whole ministry in a new one encompassing the existing

Agriculture and Labor ministries as well. Either of those developments would have highly unpleasant consequences for industry, Kastl informed Krupp. He therefore urged that the Reichsverband do something to head them off. Kastl's wary attitude toward the new cabinet seems to have been widely shared by investors, as stock-market prices wavered unsteadily during the early days of the Hitler government. An analyst writing in the liberal *Frankfurter Zeitung* explained that the flatness (*Lustlosigkeit*) of the market resulted from the vagueness of the new cabinet's initial statements, from concern about possible experiments with the currency and with economic policy, and from worry about the effects of the new election campaign on the economy.[63] Another report in the same paper attributed the absence of alarm among investors to the "antiseptic" effect of the new cabinet's mixed composition, that is, the numerical preponderance of conservative ministers.[64] Three weeks after the cabinet took office stock prices remained at about the same level as at the end of January, whereas bond prices had dipped somewhat.[65]

The failure of even politically aware men like Reusch and Kastl to take note of the implications of Adolf Hitler's installation in the Reich Chancellery reflected a widespread myopia on the part of Germany's big businessmen. To some extent that could be attributed to their preoccupation with matters which seem trivial in retrospect but which loomed large for them at the time, as is so often the case in human affairs. But to a considerable degree they were, like many stock-market investors and other contemporaries, misled by the composition of the new cabinet, in which nine conservative ministers far outnumbered the three Nazis. Ernst Brandi, of United Steel and the Bergbauverein, expressed confidence in February that the experienced men of the old right would soon prevail over Hitler. He therefore urged that the *Münchner Neuesten Nachrichten*, on whose advisory board he served, support the new cabinet editorially.[66] Karl Haniel, a member of the Ruhrlade who also sat on the advisory board of the *MNN*, predicted that Hitler would quickly be pushed aside but that in the meantime National Socialism would free the Ruhr from the specter of Communism. Haniel therefore agreed with Brandi that the Munich daily should support the new cabinet editorially, despite the grave reservations he and other members of the advisory board harbored about Nazism.[67] A special importance attached, in the eyes of many in the business community, to the prominent place apparently occupied in the cabinet by the man who, more than any other politician of the whole republican era, had won their confidence: Franz von Papen. As vice-chancellor, Papen seemed, especially because of his well-known close and cordial relations with President Hindenburg, to represent a guarantee against any radical policies. Ludwig Grauert, whose role as managing director of the industrial employers' association of the Ruhr iron and steel industry brought him into contact with many executives, later observed that the new government had initially seemed to most merely a revived Papen cabinet with a few Nazis added.[68] Papen himself fed such misapprehensions by telling acquaintances, "I have Hindenburg's confidence. Within two months we will have pushed Hitler so far into a corner that he'll squeak."[69]

Only a few men of big business saw through these illusions and immediately recognized the implications of Hitler's elevation to the chancellorship. When the news of that development reached Hermann Bücher, of the electrical equipment firm AEG at a Franco-German conference in Paris, he left no doubt about his reaction, exclaiming, "Et maintenant, tout est fini . . ." ("Now it is all over . . .").[70] Otto Wolff, the Cologne iron merchant and industrialist who had aligned himself with Schleicher, argued on the evening of January 29 that reports of Hitler's pending appointment called for extreme actions on the part of the general, who had remained chancellor on a caretaker basis following his resignation the day before. Wolff urged Schleicher to undertake what would have amounted to a coup d'etat by declaring a state of emergency, removing Hindenburg under guard to his estate in East Prussia, and arresting General Werner von Blomberg, who was on his way to Berlin to replace Schleicher in his capacity as defense minister.[71] Unfortunately, such advice seemed too extreme at the time, even for Schleicher, who would die less than a year and a half later at the hands of Nazi gunmen in a house outside Berlin owned by Otto Wolff.[72]

Although a strong longing within the business community for a period of sustained political stability that would foster economic recovery worked in favor of acceptance of the Hitler-Papen regime, its initial measures occasioned grave misgivings in business circles. In the sphere of trade the cabinet quickly granted far-reaching concessions to the protectionist demands of the agrarians, moving in February to impose higher import duties on meat, livestock, and fats as well as to extend additional price support to grain crops.[73] Protests against this greatly expanded protection for agriculture that leading figures of die Wirtschaft directed to Hugenberg, sometimes personally, proved unavailing.[74] Businessmen also found unsettling the wave of Nazi vigilantism that swept Germany in the aftermath of Hitler's appointment to the chancellorship. Although Nazi acts of intimidation were directed primarily against "Marxists," trade unionists, and other political foes, owners and managers of businesses discovered that they enjoyed no immunity. Some employers found themselves threatened with political retaliation, or even force, unless they complied with peremptory demands for raises, promotions, or even a voice in management posed by Nazi employees.[75] The Nazi Factory Cell Organization proved particularly assertive, as the coal operators of the Ruhr discovered in February when they announced their intention not to renew the existing contract with the miners when it expired at the end of March. Injecting a massive dose of politics into labor-management relations, the Ruhr branch of the NSBO publicly denounced the operators' action as "sabotage of national and social reconstruction" and warned that if they did not heed the new times, Adolf Hitler would teach them that "to think nationally meant to act socially."[76] Developments such as that cast a pall over the presidium of the industrial Reichsverband when it met on February 16 and 17 to assess the situation. In the first public statement about the Hitler cabinet issued in the name of the Reichsverband, the presidium adopted the sort of curt, admonitory tone it had so often employed during the Republic. Industry's attitude toward the new cabinet would, the statement warned, depend on its economic policy measures. If economic conditions were to improve, the statement pointedly added, "disturbances of civil order and social peace" must be avoided, lest the basis for recovery be destroyed.[77]

As the leaders of German industry soon discovered, admonitions proved of little value in dealing with the Hitler cabinet. While the presidium of the Reichsverband was meeting, its chairman, Krupp von Bohlen, and several dozen other prominent industrialists received telegrams from Hermann Göring, inviting them to attend a conference at his official residence on February 20 at which Hitler would explain his policies.[78] Expecting a discussion of the sort he had participated in with previous chancellors, Krupp prepared to explain to Hitler industry's misgivings about his government's policies. His notes show that he intended to lay particular stress on the positive effects for economic recovery of furthering exports and the negative effects of a protectionist trade policy that favored agriculture.[79] One of the memoranda Krupp prepared for the conference at Göring's residence called for a return to the clear demarcation between the state and the economy that the Reichsverband had applauded as one of the notable attainments of the Papen cabinet. It also expressed concern lest the purge of the state bureaucracy launched by the new regime become merely a transfer of government jobs from one political party to another.[80] Krupp went to the February 20 conference well prepared to speak out for industry, but he never got to present its misgivings or engage in an exchange of views of the sort he had taken part in with previous chancellors.

When Krupp and some two dozen other invited industrialists arrived at Göring's residence late on the afternoon of February 20, they had the unusual experience of being kept waiting by government officials.[81] Not until a quarter of an hour after the scheduled beginning of the "conference" did their host, Göring, appear, along with Walther Funk, now press spokesman of the cabinet. Hitler came still later, accompanied by Otto Wagener, whose role as head of the Economic Policy Section of the NSDAP until the previous September had made his name anathema in big business circles. After shaking hands with all those present, Hitler subjected them to one of his lengthy monologues. Dismissing as rumors reports that the new government planned bold experiments in the economic sphere, he quickly moved to the level of generalizations, again extolling, as so often before business audiences, the virtues of private property, inheritance rights, individual initiative, and personal responsibility. He repeated his statement of a year earlier at the Düsseldorf Industry Club about the incompatibility of political democracy with private enterprise. He spelled out once more his arguments about the primacy of politics over economics and elaborated on the Social Darwinist interpretation of society and history that underlay those arguments. Again he proclaimed the necessity of extirpating Marxism at home so that a united German people could face its enemies abroad. Only after that would Germany be able to decide on its own about its armed forces, he added in an obvious allusion to the deadlocked disarmament negotiations in Geneva. Only a martially prepared nation could, he explained, have a flourishing economy.[82] Returning to domestic politics as he neared the end of his long, rambling presentation, Hitler announced that the country stood before a "last election," one that offered a final chance to reject Communism by means of the ballot box. But even if the election failed to provide a majority for his cabinet, Hitler served notice, he had no intention of surrendering power. Either Communism would perish by constitutional means or "other weapons," entailing "greater sacrifices," would be employed. The only remaining choices lay between his regime and Communism, and the fight must be to the death. The outcome would determine Germany's fate for 10 or even 100 years.

When Hitler finally concluded his remarks, he had spoken for roughly an hour and a half without even alluding to any of the concrete questions of economic policy that so interested the men of industry who formed his select audience. He had instead delivered his customary didactic lecture on the determinants of human history and their proper application to Germany's political affairs, to which he as usual subordinated the whole sphere of economics. He had, furthermore, threatened a resort to force if the forthcoming election failed to return a parliament supportive of his regime, in effect confronting those present with a choice between a victory of his cabinet at the polls or a civil war. Under the circumstances Krupp decided after Hitler had finished that it would be imprudent to challenge the views he had expressed on the relationship between politics and economics or to express industry's misgivings about the new government's policies. Putting aside his memorandum, the chairman of the Reichsverband stated that a detailed discussion did not seem desirable and improvised polite words of thanks and some innocuous generalizations about the need for a strong and independent state that would clarify the domestic political situation and impartially serve the general welfare.[83] Having listened to Krupp's brief remarks, Hitler departed.

After Hitler left, the industrialists present at Göring's residence learned that the gathering had a concealed agenda that would make their visit extremely expensive for them. Their host took the floor and assured them that no experiments with the economy need be feared.[84] Political pacification would, Göring predicted, exercise a calming effect on the economy. He then reiterated Hitler's statement that, regardless of the outcome of the election, the present "distribution of forces" would remain unaltered. Göring nevertheless insisted on the importance of the election and, after mentioning the NSDAP's need for money, observed that those who did not stand in the forefront of the political battle had an obligation to make at least financial sacrifices. Such sacrifices could be borne more easily, he concluded, if one kept in mind that the balloting of March 5 would be "the last for the next five years, probably even for the next hundred years." Having left his guests with that arresting thought, Göring, too, departed. By obvious prearrangement Hjalmar Schacht stepped forward and announced that the time had arrived for a trip to the cashbox. He presented what amounted to a bill for three million marks, a sum he had already allocated among the various branches of industry. Although most of the executives present proved, under examination, considerably less than major figures in German industry, the group to whom Schacht addressed this surprising plan included a sufficient number meeting that description to make possible its success. Spokesmen for the major branches of industry he had targeted for contributions complied, some at once, others after consulting with absent associates or superiors. Together, they pledged the stipulated three million marks and delivered it during the subsequent weeks to Schacht, who administered it.[85]

What took place at the gathering of February 20, 1933, in Göring's residence is significant on several counts. For one thing, none of the several eyewitness accounts makes any mention of Hitler's saying anything about suppressing the trade unions or even curtailing their rights. A statement of that sort would certainly have strengthened his appeal under the circumstances and would hardly have gone unnoted by those who were present. But Hitler was apparently not yet ready to take the political risks involved in divulging his intentions along those lines. The very fact that the meeting took the course it did dispels the claims, made at the time and repeated ever since, that the coffers of industry had long since opened to the Nazis, either after Hitler's Industry Club speech, or during the election campaigns of 1932, or following the Nazi leader's meeting with Papen at banker Kurt von Schröder's house in early January 1933. If those coffers had already swung open, Hitler and his accomplices would scarcely have had to stage their elaborate ruse to assemble the industrialists at Göring's residence in order to extract money from them. Nothing in the surviving accounts of that gathering by participants suggests that what happened there represented merely a continuation of an established pattern of subsidization of Hitler and his movement. Instead, all the evidence indicates that the gathering amounted to a milestone: the first significant material contribution by organized big business interests to the Nazi cause. That contribution unquestionably helped the Nazis to tighten their grip on power. The industrialists who complied with Schacht's specifications thus assumed a share of responsibility for the consolidation of Hitler's regime, if not for its creation.

That responsibility is somewhat mitigated, however, by the failure of some to realize that they were dealing with an incipient one-party dictatorship. A sufficient number of those who contributed to Schacht's levy still believed that the Hitler cabinet represented a coalition for the group to insist that Schacht assign a quarter of the yield to the Kampffront-Schwarz-Weiss-Rot, an election alliance formed by Vice-Chancellor Papen, the Stahlhelm veterans' organization, and the DNVP.[86] Some, including the leading men of the Ruhrlade, Springorum and Reusch, still clung to the belief that Papen was the decisive figure in the new government and channeled additional campaign contributions to him.[87] Some gave money, above and beyond that pledged on February 20, directly to Hugenberg's DNVP in an obvious effort to strengthen it as opposed to the NSDAP.[88] On behalf of those who contributed funds as a result of the gathering at Göring's residence, it should be further noted that under the circumstances of February 20, 1933, their payments represented something less than a wholly voluntary action, for that gathering amounted to a shakedown. During the Republic big businessmen had on occasion given financial support to those in power, but—as in the case of their generous support for the Papen cabinet at the time of the autumn election campaign of 1932—they had done so in response to requests and had raised and administered the money in question as they saw fit. Now, in February 1933, they got a mild foretaste of the political extortion that soon became one of the hallmarks of Adolf Hitler's Third Reich.

Despite the new government's widespread intimidation of political foes and the industrial funds that flowed to the political forces backing it as a result of the gathering of February 20, Hitler's party failed to secure a parliamentary majority in the March election. Contrary to what Hitler had predicted to the industrialists gathered at Göring's residence, no open civil war followed, mainly because the division and irresoluteness of the leftist parties paralyzed them and so ruled out any significant opposition to the regime. By making use of the presidential emergency powers bestowed on the cabinet after the Reichstag fire in late February, the Nazis began the piecemeal "revolution by installments" that would progressively subvert the civil and political rights Germans had enjoyed under the Republic. In order to lessen his dependence on President Hindenburg, Hitler successfully demanded after the March balloting that the new Reichstag grant him dictatorial powers for four years by passing a parliamentary enabling act that would free him from having to rely on the president's emergency powers under Article 48 of the constitution. At the final, turbulent Reichstag session, conducted on March 23 in the absence of scores of Communists and Social Democrats who had been arrested or had fled to escape arrest, Hitler finally delivered the long-awaited speech setting forth the program of his cabinet.[89] When he touched briefly on economic matters, he uttered words calculated to still fears in the business community. He restated the Nazi slogan to the effect that the *Volk* did not live for the economy, nor the economy for capital, but that capital must serve the economy and the economy the *Volk*. He then proclaimed that his government did not intend to direct the economy by means of a state-organized economic bureaucracy but would instead give every possible encouragement to private initiative while upholding the principle of private property. He promised a reduction of government expenditures and of the cost of government itself, as well as administrative reform and a revision of the tax system that would simplify it and reduce the burden it imposed. With regard to the sensitive question of trade policy, Hitler stated that Germany's situation ruled out any full autarky and promised that his cabinet harbored no hostility toward exports. Finally, he promised to avoid any experiments with the currency, thereby apparently renouncing the monetary schemes of Gottfried Feder, which had so long occasioned concern about National Socialism among Germany's business leaders. After reading the new chancellor's words, which a great many people mistakenly assumed represented sincere commitments on his part, many men of big business undoubtedly shared the reaction of Jakob Wilhelm Reichert, executive director of the national association of iron and steel industrialists, who concluded that the "long guessing game" about where Nazism stood with regard to the economy had at last come to a happy end on March 23, 1933.[90]

Doing business in the Third Reich proved, however, more complex than Hitler's programmatic speech of March 23 had suggested. This became evident to the members of the presidium of the industrial Reichsverband that very day. When they assembled for one of their ordinarily cordial, collegial meetings, which were usually structured from the outset to produce a consensus, they experienced a turbulent session that revealed to the members that their own organization would not be unaffected by the political changes Germany was undergoing.[91] An exultant Fritz Thyssen lectured them in no uncertain terms about the implications of recent developments for the Reichsverband: "The national revolution has still not ended. It has not stumbled over Communism and it will not stumble over a straw like the Reichsverband. . . . In the future care must be taken to prevent any oppositional tendencies from arising against the national movement." The era of liberalism had been vanquished once and for all, Thyssen informed his fellow industrialists, and therefore the time had come for a new spirit to prevail in the Reichsverband. As a first step in this direction he demanded that all the officers of the Reichsverband step down to make way for the election of successors more in tune with the times. Thyssen then proceeded to denounce the leadership of the organization for serving as "trainbearer" to the republican system. He angrily recalled that his attempts two and a half years earlier to rebut remarks made by Brüning before the Reichsverband and to speak out for the "national movement" had met with hisses. He had not forgotten the sneers from the ranks of the Reichsverband that had greeted his efforts to establish contacts between industry and the NSDAP, such as the speech he had arranged for Hitler before the Industry Club in Düsseldorf, or the refusal of Krupp, the chairman of the Reichsverband, to meet with Hitler at Thyssen's home the previous autumn. Thyssen also protested against the removal by the association's leadership of a Nazi flag hoisted atop the headquarters of the Reichsverband a few days earlier by some of its "national" employees. He applauded, on the other hand, the Nazi storm troopers who had afterwards forced their way into the building and raised the swastika banner again in order to teach the Reichsverband respect for the new flag. Turning his fire on Kastl, Thyssen denounced the executive director for using sessions of the association to equate Nazism with Communism. On the very day Hitler became chancellor, Thyssen charged, Kastl had gone so far as to intervene with President Hindenburg in an effort to block his appointment. Thyssen then concluded by accusing the leadership of the Reichsverband of plotting with the trade unions to form a conspiracy against the new government.

In making this last accusation, Thyssen shifted his attack from Kastl to the chairman of the Reichsverband, Krupp von Bohlen himself. Nor was that accusation without basis. During the previous weeks Krupp had in fact joined with several other industrialists in meeting with trade union officials. Frustrated by the cabinet's apparent commitment to an autarkic trade policy favorable to agriculture but damaging to industrial exports, and alarmed at reports that the regime intended to substitute an Italian-style corporatist structure for the existing interest-group organizations, Krupp and other industrialists had reached out to the trade union leaders, who shared their views on foreign trade and their opposition to corporatism. In the resulting talks the participants had explored the possibility of reviving the Zentralarbeitsgemeinschaft established by labor and management in 1918 by the terms of the Stinnes-Legien Agreement.[92] Nothing could better reveal how far removed from reality the leaders of German industry were in March 1933 or could more effectively refute the contention that they knew of and endorsed from the outset the new regime's intention to destroy the trade unions. Krupp's participation in these industry–trade-union talks placed him in a very uncomfortable position on March 23 since Thyssen used it to accuse him of plotting against the cabinet headed by the man who had that very day received dictatorial powers from the Reichstag. While admitting to the talks with the trade unionists, Krupp claimed he and the others had decided to ask the chancellor whether it would be advisable to lay the basis for cooperation with labor. He and Carl Friedrich von Siemens had made an appointment with Hitler for that very day to discuss this with him, but the appointment had been cancelled by the chancellor's office, Krupp added. He then dealt with other accusations by Thyssen. He had declined Thyssen's invitation to meet with Hitler the previous October because the invitation had been directed to him in his official capacity as chairman of the Reichsverband rather than privately and because, as a non-party man, he saw no reason to attend a meeting of Nazis.[93] He had not authorized display of the swastika flag at the headquarters of the Reichsverband because it was still not the national flag.[94] Finally, Krupp denied Thyssen's charge that Kastl had intervened with Hindenburg at the end of January against Hitler. Kastl, taking advantage of the cautious and ambiguous wording of the letter he and Hamm had sent to State Secretary Meissner on January 28, also denied that accusation. He and Hamm had merely urged that the political crisis be resolved as swiftly as possible, Kastl stated in his defense. He added that he later telephoned Meissner to tell him that it was impossible to govern against the opposition of a party that had twelve million voters behind it. Kastl left unspecified, however, whether he had made that telephone call before or—as seems more likely—after Hitler had become chancellor. The ensuing heated discussion, during which several members of the presidium denounced Thyssen and defended Krupp and Kastl, came to an end only when Paul Reusch provided a face-saving formula. By a unanimous vote, in which even Thyssen joined, the presidium expressed its confidence in Krupp, who in turn agreed to the new elections of officers Thyssen had demanded. The presidium also publicly proclaimed its support of the new government, even while continuing to express its concern about trade protectionism.[95]

The Reichsverband never recovered from the presidium's stormy session on the day the Reichstag bestowed dictatorial powers on Hitler. In order to sound out the dictator before proceeding further, Krupp arranged for an appointment with him, in the company of Carl Friedrich von Siemens, on April 1. But on the day Krupp and Siemens appeared at the Reich Chancellery for what proved an inconclusive audience with Hitler, the Reichsverband, like so many German institutions in the spring of 1933, lost its independence. A Nazi vigilante squad led by Otto Wagener, the former head of the Economic Policy Section of the NSDAP, invaded the organization's Berlin headquarters.[96] The Reichsverband had failed, Wagener announced, to take any notice of the revolution taking place in Germany and had continued to operate as though nothing had changed. By way of rectifying this situation, Wagener insisted on the immediate dismissal of Kastl, whose opposition to

National Socialism and support of the Young Plan made him unacceptable. Wagener further called for the dismissal of the Jewish members of the staff and the removal of all Jewish industrialists from the presidium. To "insure agreement between the economic policy of the Reichsverband" and the economic policy and *Weltanschauung* of the National Socialist movement, he installed at the head of the organization two unknown outsiders who, he certified, enjoyed the confidence of the movement. To the consternation of the leadership of the Reichsverband, all protests to high officials of the government, including Hindenburg and Hugenberg, about Wagener's takeover proved unavailing. During the first days of April Krupp entered into "negotiations" with Wagener that resulted in a capitulation to that Nazi's plans for dissolution of economic interest-group organizations such as the Reichsverband and their replacement by a corporatist structure. Kastl was dismissed, as were the Jewish employees. When the industrialists who made up the presidium learned of Krupp's acceptance of Wagener's demands, they protested by an overwhelming majority vote that included even Fritz Thyssen, for whom Krupp's servility went too far. But that protest, too, remained without effect since conservatives in the cabinet proved powerless to resist Nazi pressure. In May the Reichsverband "voluntarily" dissolved itself, and in June what remained of its organization was swallowed up, along with other industrial associations, into the Nazi-sponsored Reichsstand der Deutschen Industrie. In July Paul Reusch wrote resignedly to a held-over staff member about the prospects of the Reichsstand: "Any possibility of influencing legislation or the organs of administration seems to me now impossible. What is there, then, to do?"[97] One historian has recently characterized the relations between German industry and the Nazi regime as "a long process of mutual accommodation."[98] During the first months of the Third Reich, however, changes took place quite abruptly, and the accommodation came from the side of the industrialists.

Beginning with the takeover of the Reichsverband, the industrialists of Germany, whom Marxists have ever since identified as the decisive behind-the-scenes authorities in the Third Reich, learned repeatedly during the spring of 1933 just how much weight their wishes carried under the new political dispensation. Their knowledge on that score expanded appreciably when they sought to protect their Jewish colleagues from the anti-Semitism unleashed on the country by its new rulers. Whatever limitations Germany's men of big business may have had in other regards, their ranks had remained uncontaminated by anti-Semitism. Viewing that form of prejudice as a benighted and plebeian phenomenon, virtually all gentile big businessmen accepted their Jewish counterparts on a basis of equality. They regarded themselves as hardheaded, forward-looking realists for whom such questions as religious affiliation or ancestry had no relevance. Although many of their number had not espoused fully the political tenets of liberalism, virtually all partook of this feature of the liberal outlook. They failed to take Nazi anti-Semitism seriously, dismissing it, as did so many Germans, as mere demagogic phrase-mongering. Yet beginning with Nazi Otto Wagener's demand for an anti-Semitic purge of the Reichsverband on April 1, the day the Nazis launched their first national boycott of Jewish businesses, the business community saw some of its most respected Jewish members subjected to public calumny, physical and psychic harassment, and peremptory dismissal from positions they had held in the Reichsverband, chambers of commerce and industry, and other business associations. Some prominent businessmen sought to help mitigate the effects of these developments by supporting an organization established by well-known German Jews in an effort to counter the effects of the regime's measures.[99] Others, among them Emil Kirdorf, protested to the new holders of power against actions directed against the Jews of Germany.[100] But such protests met with no responsiveness. The chemist Carl Bosch, head of IG Farben's board of directors, discovered this when he attempted to use an audience with Hitler in the summer of 1933 to impress on the chancellor the costs to the country of policies that made conditions unbearable for some of its leading scientists simply because they were Jewish. According to Bosch's biographer, an increasingly impatient Hitler finally interrupted the venerable scientist and Nobel Prize winner to inform him that he understood nothing about the matter. Germany would, if necessary, get along for a hundred years without physics and chemistry, the chancellor of the Reich assured his astonished guest before having him peremptorily shown the door.[101] Not long thereafter IG Farben inaugurated a practice of quietly transferring Jewish executives to subsidiaries abroad in order to shield them from Nazi anti-Semitism.[102]

Despite these and other humbling experiences, the men of big business accommodated themselves, as did most Germans, to the Third Reich. Not to do so would have been extraordinary since business firms virtually always try to make their peace—if they are allowed—with any and all regimes, including those controlled by Communists. To do otherwise would have been unthinkable for businessmen, who could not move their factories, mines, and banks to another country. One industrialist who protested in April 1933 against the capitulation of the Reichsverband and against anti-Semitic measures gave expression to this when he nevertheless added, "Political opposition would, for an economic association, be utter madness."[103] Acceptance of the regime became easier when its early months brought or, more properly, coincided with the long hoped-for return of prosperity. Beginning in 1933 economic activity picked up rapidly until, only three years later, Germany became the first country to shake off the Great Depression and achieve full employment again. This improvement in economic conditions brought with it the profits that ultimately serve as the measure of success or failure in the business world. And the reappearance of black ink in ledgers where much red had appeared in previous years stilled objections to less pleasant concomitants of the Nazi regime, such as price and wage controls, tight limitations on the use of profits, high taxes, increased government spending, stringent foreign exchange controls, rationing of raw materials, and imperious bureaucratic intervention in the private sphere that made the *Zwangswirtschaft* of World War I and the immediate post-war period seem trivial by comparison. Able again to produce and sell profitably, Germany's businessmen experienced little difficulty in adapting to a regime that, even though it gave them no voice in its decisions, held labor in check and, on the whole, respected private property. They took their profits, paid the financial tribute extorted from them by the new rulers, and asked no questions. They did what was demanded of them by a regime that needed their expertise, even during a war they had not been consulted about and whose criminally utopian aims few comprehended. Some eventually became implicated in the horrendous crimes against humanity committed by the regime during that war.

As to the dictator who determined not only the fate of *die Wirtschaft* but of Germany as a whole, he never abandoned his hopes of transforming the country's economic life so as to facilitate the rise of a new meritocratic elite. Hitler merely adjourned the whole subject of the economy's future shape until the day when he would realize his grandiose plans for conquest of vast territories. He thus demonstrated sufficient realism to recognize that he could not prepare Germany for a great war while undertaking a fundamental reorganization of its economy. Accordingly, he left in place the economic elite he had inherited and harnessed its talents for his purposes. Some observers have taken this as proof that he never seriously intended to tamper with the existing social order. But if one reads the monologues to which Hitler subjected his private entourage during the early phases of World War II, when his armies seemed invincible and victory appeared within his grasp, one must come to a different conclusion. For in those monologues Hitler affirmed his intention to alter Germany's economic life after the war so as to do away with what he condemned as the flaws that permitted too much wealth to accumulate in the hands of too few, and too often in what he regarded as undeserving hands.[104] To the end Adolf Hitler held to his quest for a "third way" between capitalism and socialism.

The men of big business who figure prominently in this book fared variously in the Third Reich. Most remained at their posts and prospered; but some fared less well. The "non-Aryan" Paul Silverberg, after vainly attempting to placate the Nazis with public expressions of loyalty to the new regime, had to relinquish all of his many positions in 1933. At the end of the year he went into exile in Switzerland, where Gustav Krupp von Bohlen made a point of visiting his old colleague.[105] Krupp, who had not concealed his dislike of Nazism before Hitler attained power, did an about-face and abased himself before the new ruler. After two of his sons died in the war and the Gestapo imprisoned both his sister-in-law and her husband, his confidant Tilo von Wilmowsky, for subversive activities, Krupp lost his mind.[106] Paul Reusch was forced by the regime to relinquish control of his industrial empire in 1942 after repeated clashes with the authorities.[107] Eventually he gravitated to the fringes of the ill-fated resistance movement around Carl Goerdeler.[108] Fritz Springorum, unable to prevent the removal, under Nazi pressure, of Max Schlerker, the veteran business manager of the Langnamverein, resigned his position as chairman of that once proud Ruhr business association in the spring of 1933.[109] To an acquaintance Springorum explained resignedly (at the age of forty-six), "We have to accept the fact that we are played out and leave the field to youth."[110] Fritz Thyssen, who briefly succeeded Springorum as figurehead chairman of the Langnamverein, proclaimed himself the supreme economic authority in the Ruhr and tried to promote corporatism as the basis for the Third Reich's social and economic order. He quickly lost favor with Hitler, however. When Thyssen complained to Hitler in 1934 about this ingratitude, the dictator's reply provided a revealing glimpse of his opinion of a big businessman who had helped him on his way to power: "I never made you any promises. . . . I've nothing to thank you for. What you did for my movement you did for your own benefit, and wrote it off as an insurance premium."[111] On realizing in 1939 that Hitler's policies were leading Germany into war, Thyssen belatedly recognized the folly of his earlier support of Nazism. He fled abroad, denounced the regime publicly, saw his property expropriated, and, when the Vichy authorities turned him over to the Nazis, found himself in one of the Third Reich's concentration camps.[112] The full story of how big business and the executives who ran it fared during the twelve years of tyranny imposed upon Germany by the Nazis cannot, however, be told here. That is a story in its own right and still awaits its historian.[113]

Conclusions

1. *Capitalists, Nazis, and Guilt*

What can be said, in the light of the findings presented here, by way of answering the questions posed at the outset of this volume? To what extent did the men of German big business undermine the Weimar Republic? To what extent did they finance the Nazi Party and use their influence to boost Hitler into power? As should be evident by this point, the answer in both cases is: a great deal less than has generally been believed.

Only through gross distortion can big business be accorded a crucial, or even major, role in the downfall of the Republic. The business community displayed, to be sure, little enthusiasm for the new democratic state, and very few major executives could be termed democrats by conviction. Particularly at the outset of the republican period they felt jeopardized by a political system that assigned ultimate authority over national policy to a mass electorate. They also deplored many republican policies, especially the rapid expansion of *Sozialpolitik*—welfare state legislation—and direct governmental intervention in labor-management relations. But once the difficulties of the Republic's first five years had been overcome and a measure of prosperity restored, most men of big business reconciled themselves to the new state, if not always to its policies. So long as the country prospered, they saw little chance for a change of regime. Most remained frustrated politically, having discovered that economic potency did not translate readily into political effectiveness in a democratic polity, where ballots weighed more than money and where blocs of disciplined interest-group voters counted for more than did financial contributions.

Big businessmen did, to be sure, play a part in causing the crisis that eventuated in the paralysis of the Republic's parliamentary system in 1930. The insistence by some sectors of big business on curtailment of the capstone of republican *Sozialpolitik,* the national unemployment insurance program, helped at that time to precipitate what in retrospect emerges as one of the earliest of the now familiar fiscal crises of twentieth-century capitalist welfare states. The outcome of that crisis was, however, determined not by the business community but rather by the political spokesmen of organized labor. Also, the resulting parliamentary deadlock did not in itself put an end to Weimar democracy. That stalemate assumed fateful proportions only because it triggered a fundamental shift of authority to the presidency through use of the emergency powers assigned to that office by the constitution. Behind that move stood not Germany's capitalists but rather its military leadership. Generals, not corporation executives, effected the establishment of presidential rule in 1930. As a consequence of that development—which initially made some of the leading figures in the business community very uneasy because of their concern about the reaction of credit markets abroad—they and their compeers found themselves with even less political influence than they had enjoyed earlier. As long as the parliamentary system functioned, the politically active elements of big business had frequently managed to combine their small parliamentary bloc with other interest groups through horse trading of the usual sort so as to influence the shape of legislation. The links between big business and those bourgeois parties that regularly received subsidies from it had enabled its political spokesmen to exert pressure, if not always successfully, on government policies when those parties participated in ruling coalitions. Under the governmental system that began to take shape in 1930, however, the wishes of the business community carried little or no weight with the decisive source of authority, President Hindenburg, or with the military men who served as his counselors. During the period of presidential rule, men chosen by those counselors, men not beholden to big business, determined national policy. And it was those men—Brüning, Papen, and Schleicher—and not Germany's capitalists who set the disastrous political and economic course that destroyed what remained of the Weimar Republic and fostered the growth of the Nazi Party.

If the role of big business in the disintegration of the Republic has been exaggerated, such is even more true of its role in the rise of Hitler. While a significant part of the business community contributed materially—if less than wholly voluntarily—to the consolidation of Hitler's regime after he had become chancellor, he and his party had previously received relatively little support from that quarter. The early growth of the NSDAP took place without any significant aid from the circles of large-scale enterprise. Centered in industrially underdeveloped Bavaria, tainted with illegality as a consequence of the failed beer hall putsch of 1923, saddled with a program containing disturbingly anti-capitalist planks, and amounting only to a raucous splinter group politically, the NSDAP languished in disrepute in the eyes of most men of big business throughout the latter part of the 1920s. The major executives of Germany proved, with rare exception, resistant to the blandishments of Nazis, including Hitler himself, who sought to reassure the business community about their party's intentions. Only the Nazi electoral breakthrough of 1930, achieved without aid from big business, drew attention to it from that quarter. Those businessmen who attempted to assess the suddenly formidable new movement encountered a baffling riddle. The closer they scrutinized the NSDAP, the more difficult it became to determine whether it supported or opposed capitalism and, more specifically, the large-scale, organized enterprise to which capitalism had given rise in Germany. That riddle was not a chance occurrence. Hitler wanted things just that way. By cultivating a strategy of calculated ambiguity on economic matters, he sought to enable the appeals of his party to transcend the deep-seated social divisions in the country. That strategy led to puzzlement and wariness among the politically active components of big business, who wanted above all to establish the NSDAP's position on the economic issues that preoccupied them and assumed ever more urgency as the Great Depression deepened.

For nearly two years—from the autumn of 1930 until the summer of 1932—elements within or close to big business engaged in flirtations of varying intensity and duration with National Socialism. Some saw in Nazism a potential ally against the political left and organized labor, which many in the business community blamed for much of the country's misfortune, including the depression. Some of those who harbored such hopes set out, often with the help of opportunistic intermediaries, to cultivate prominent figures in the leadership ranks of the NSDAP. On the Nazi side, Hitler and certain of his lieutenants appear to have operated initially on the same assumption that colored leftist analyses, namely, that capitalists amounted to an important factor in politics. But whereas the parties of the left sought to mobilize mass support against big business in order to break the alleged control of the capitalists over the state, Hitler and his accomplices set out merely to neutralize the business community politically in order to keep Germany's capitalists from obstructing the Nazis' grasp for power.

Hitler and other Nazi spokesmen therefore sought repeatedly to convince those capitalists whose ears they could gain that there was no need to fear socialism from National Socialism. In a strict sense that was true, since the Nazis did not seek government ownership of the means of production. But Hitler and other Nazi emissaries revealed only highly selective versions of their movement's aims to members of the business community. They omitted mention of the aspirations of many Nazis, including Hitler himself, for far-reaching changes in German social and economic relationships that would, among other things, have drastically impinged on the position of capitalists. Nor did they, as has often been alleged, promise to dissolve the trade unions, hold out the prospect of lucrative armaments contracts, or project a war of exploitative conquest. The Nazi leaders may have secretly harbored such aims, but to divulge them at a time when the NSDAP was striving to attract voters from all possible quarters and gain admission to the national government would have been out of keeping with their opportunistic tactics. Instead, most portrayed Nazism to the business community as primarily a patriotic movement that would undercut the political left by wooing the wage earners of Germany back into the "national" political camp. Ignoring the concrete economic issues that preoccupied businessmen, Hitler held out to those with whom he came into contact the prospect of a political panacea that would sweep away Germany's mundane problems by unifying it domestically and strengthening it internationally. He also soft-pedaled or left altogether unmentioned his anti-Semitism when speaking to men of big business, having recognized its unpopularity in those circles. Such reassuring versions of the NSDAP's goals generally produced skeptical reactions among members of the business community, however, for those reassurances were offset by clamorous anti-capitalist rhetoric on the part of other Nazis and by the NSDAP's frequent alignment with the political left on concrete socio-economic issues. Right down to Hitler's installation in the chancellorship, Nazism spoke with a forked tongue and behaved duplicitously in the eyes of most capitalist magnates. As a consequence, only rarely did relations between the NSDAP and big business progress beyond the level of flirtation prior to the Nazi takeover. Despite repeated blandishments from Hitler himself and some members of his entourage, most politically active figures in the business community remained confused by the contradictory utterances about economic matters emanating from the NSDAP and uneasy about what direction that party would finally take. Aside from a few minor executives who belonged, for the most part, to the younger generation of Germans so strongly attracted to the Nazi movement, only one capitalist of note, Fritz Thyssen, became a loyal adherent of Nazism before 1933.

Much confusion has arisen in publications dealing with the subject of this book because of a failure to distinguish between the men of big business and lesser businessmen. The prevalent categories of big business (or "monopoly capital") and lower middle class (or "petite bourgeoisie") have obscured the existence of a large number of substantial entrepreneurs who presided over often appreciable firms but who occupied a place in the economy substantially different from that of the great capitalists of Germany. Consequently, support for Nazism from such lesser businessmen has frequently been mistaken as evidence of complicity on the part of big business. The susceptibility of such entrepreneurs to National Socialism is not difficult to understand. As the depression tightened its grip on the economy, many of them found themselves and their firms exposed to increasingly cutthroat competition for shrinking markets. Few could rely on the cartels and other types of price-setting arrangements with which many big producers shielded themselves against the rapid decline in prices. Nor could they expect support from the great national business associations, such as the industrial Reichsverband, which were dominated by an elite drawn from big business. The large-scale enterprises that made up big business could also count upon restraint on the part of creditors and on various forms of aid from the government, since the prospect of their insolvency posed an intolerable threat to the whole economic, social, and political order. The failure of lesser firms, by contrast, awakened no such solicitude. Such firms could, and did, sink with scarcely a ripple. As a result, much hostility toward big business existed among the businessmen who presided over the often sizeable firms which, although dwarfed by the great new corporations and conglomerates of the twentieth century, nevertheless comprised a significant part of the German economy. Caught between what they perceived as predatory big business, on the one side, and assertive big labor in league with "Marxist" mass political organizations, on the other, such men did not feel threatened by Nazi denunciations of *Konzerne* and other great concentrations of capital. Those who found themselves in truly desperate economic straits were also less likely than executives of mammoth corporations to look askance at such Nazi panaceas as the "breaking of the thralldom of interest payments" or economic autarky. From the vantage point of such men, Nazi proposals for large-scale deficit spending could seem a ray of hope rather than a threat to sound governmental monetary and fiscal policies. For them, Nazi schemes for corporatist organization of the economy could appear to hold out the promise of greater representation for their interests than was possible within the existing structure of trade associations dominated by big business interests. It was, as a consequence, among such lesser businessmen, not among the great capitalists of Germany, that Nazism made inroads during its rise to power. Most of those hard-pressed men were in no position during the Great Depression, however, to extend large-scale financial assistance to the NSDAP, and none of their number commanded sufficient influence in political circles to facilitate Hitler's quest for high office.

As for big business, a graph of its relations with the NSDAP along the lines of a fever chart would show a steep, if uneven, rise from virtually zero prior to the September Reichstag election of 1930 to a high point in the spring or early summer of 1932, followed by a precipitous decline through the autumn of 1932 that continued until Hitler's appointment as chancellor. At the high point in 1932 the NSDAP seemed well-nigh unstoppable, having scored one election gain after another. Despite mounting dissension between the Nazis and the traditional right, and despite the waning political strength of the latter, hopes lingered in some big business circles for an alliance that would subordinate the NSDAP, with its mass following, to conservative forces in a nationalistic, rightist regime. During the second half of the summer of 1932, the Nazis dashed such hopes. By launching a sustained and unbridled assault on the Papen cabinet, which had come to enjoy the virtually unanimous and enthusiastic support of big business, Hitler demonstrated that he attached less significance to the opinions of the business community than he did to the removal of the obstacle to his quest for power posed by a government of the traditional right. In championing the prerogatives of the parliament and the interests of workers as part of an offensive designed to discredit Papen's presidential "cabinet of barons," the NSDAP seemed to swerve sharply leftward and so to confirm the worst suspicions of many big businessmen about Nazi social and economic radicalism. Nazi advocacy of a sweeping government program of job creation through deficit spending on an unprecedented scale indicated the triumph of those "fiscally irresponsible" elements within the NSDAP that had long aroused apprehensions in business circles. The party's espousal of the drastic trade restrictions demanded by agrarian interests gave rise to fears of extreme autarkic policies that would provoke retaliation abroad against the exports on which a large part of German industry had become increasingly dependent as the domestic market shrank under the impact of the depression. By late 1932 past efforts to cultivate "moderate" Nazis seemed in vain. The fall of Gregor Strasser removed a man who had come to be widely perceived in big business circles as a Nazi advocate of accommodation with the traditional elite. Hitler, once viewed in some business quarters as a moderating influence within the party, now seemed an intransigent opponent of any such accommodation.

Quite contrary to the widespread impression that Hitler gained power in January 1933 with strong backing from big business, his appointment to the chancellorship came just when relations between his movement and the business community had reached the lowest point since the NSDAP's election gains of 1930 had forced it upon the attention of the politically engaged men of big business. Germany's leading capitalists remained passive, ill-informed bystanders during the backroom intrigues in the circles around President Hindenburg that resulted in Hitler's installation as chancellor. By that time the business community was recovering from its initial apprehensions about the cabinet of Kurt von Schleicher. His government had failed to follow the leftward course many had initially feared it would; to the relief of the business community, Schleicher upheld most of the Papen cabinet's policies. While few of the country's capitalists harbored any real enthusiasm for the enigmatic general who stood at the head of the government, an inclination to prefer his continuation in office prevailed in late January 1933. The alternative of still another cabinet crisis would, most of the political leadership of big business feared, once more give rise to the uncertainties about economic policy that they believed had thwarted recovery during the politically turbulent year just past. Rather than risk a disruption of the economic upturn widely detected since late 1932, it seemed preferable to hope for a period of stability under the general. When the most prominent industrial association, the Reichsverband, broke with previous practice and attempted to intervene with President Hindenburg as the final cabinet crisis of Weimar Germany broke out at the end of January 1933, it did so to warn against according Adolf Hitler a prominent place in a new, provocatively rightist cabinet. However, that effort to wield the influence of the business community for political purposes proved, like so many undertaken during the Weimar period, in vain.

Contrary to another long-standing misapprehension, spokesmen of the business community did not collude with those of agriculture in agitating for Hitler's installation as chancellor in January 1933. By that time relations between those two interest groups had deteriorated to the breaking point because of increasingly irreconcilable and acrimonious disagreements over trade policy. Whatever took place in early 1933 by way of a recrudescence, in support of Hitler's appointment, of the alliance between traditional elites of the Empire, one important element— big business—was conspicuous by its absence. The often-invoked continuity between the imperial and Nazi regimes thus suffers from a crucial gap.

If big business did not, as is so often maintained, help boost Hitler into the chancellorship by throwing its influence behind him, how much effect did the political money have that flowed from the business community to various Nazis? How much help to Hitler and his party in their quest for power were the contributions and subsidies accounted for here, as well as similar ones that presumably went undocumented? That question can obviously not be answered definitively since the evidence remains incomplete. Some observations can be made, however, on the basis of patterns of behavior that have emerged from this study. First of all, the multi-million-mark contributions from big business that allegedly fueled the Nazi juggernaut existed only in the imaginations of certain contemporary observers and, later, of some writers of history. Those firms and organizations that regularly engaged in large-scale political funding continued—right down to the last election prior to Hitler's appointment as chancellor—to bestow the bulk of their funds on opponents or rivals of the Nazis. The few sizeable contributions that appear to have reached the Nazis from big business sources shrink in significance when compared to the amounts that went to the bourgeois parties and to the campaign to re-elect President Hindenburg. With rare exceptions such contributions to Nazis were not given primarily for the purpose of strengthening the NSDAP or boosting it into power but rather in pursuit of a variety of essentially defensive strategies. They usually went to individual Nazis, not to the party as such. Some of the donors looked upon financial support for prominent Nazis as insurance premiums designed to assure them friends in power if the new movement should succeed in capturing control of the state. Others, who felt that their firms had special grounds to fear the NSDAP if it should come to power, paid out what can only be characterized as protection money to potential rulers. Still others sought to reshape Nazism in line with their wishes by strengthening, through financial subsidies, the position within the party of individual Nazis they regarded as exponents of "moderate" or "reasonable" economic policies. A portion of the subsidies doled out to individual Nazis by men of big business for such reasons may have been used by the recipients for party purposes, but from all indications a considerable share went toward enhancing their personal living standards.

Discussions of financial assistance to the Nazis from big business have usually been based on a false assumption, namely, that the NSDAP, like the bourgeois parties of the Weimar Republic, depended on subsidies from large contributors. This simply was not the case. Just as the Nazi leaders proudly proclaimed at the time, their party financed itself quite handsomely through its own efforts, at least down to the autumn of 1932. The NSDAP proved, in fact, an unprecedentedly effective forerunner of those highly organized fund-raising associations that have since become familiar features of liberal, democratic societies. In contrast to the bourgeois parties of the Republic, whose top echelons solicited large contributions and then distributed funds to the lower echelons, money flowed upward within the NSDAP from the grass roots, through the regional organizations, and to the national leadership in Munich. Compared to the sustained intake of money raised by membership dues and other contributions of the Nazi rank and file, the funds that reached the NSDAP from the side of big business assume at best a marginal significance. As the relations between leading Nazis and members of the business community abundantly reveal, the former rarely adopted the pose of supplicants seeking material aid, at least not until their party experienced its first serious financial difficulties during the autumn of 1932. By that time, however, deteriorating relations had made members of the business community less disposed than ever to contribute to the NSDAP. The Nazis themselves, not Germany's capitalists, provided the decisive financing for Hitler's rise to power.

More important than any financial aid that reached the Nazis from big business or any influence brought to bear in their favor from that quarter was the help rendered them indirectly and inadvertently by politically active elements in the business community. Most conspicuously, support for individuals and organizations such as Papen, Schleicher, Hugenberg, the DNVP, and the Stahlhelm strengthened political forces that would eventually play key roles in installing Hitler in power. At the time that support was given, these men and organizations seemed to their business backers to represent not stirrup holders for Hitler but rather bulwarks against a Nazi takeover, with the prospect of taming the NSDAP for the purposes of the traditional right. In failing to recognize their irresponsible nature, their patrons in big business made themselves unwitting accessories to their follies, which were to cost Germany and much of the rest of Europe dearly. In other ways, too, men of big business lent indirect aid to the Nazis. By inviting Hitler and other party spokesmen to address their gatherings, they bestowed a degree of social acceptability upon them that may have influenced other Germans to vote for, or join, the NSDAP. Even abstinence from political activity by the men of big business could inadvertently redound to the advantage of the Nazis. The businessmen who at the time of the Prussian and national elections of the spring and summer of 1932 withheld their customary subsidies from the traditional parties indirectly aided the Nazi cause, although such was not their intention. While some who withheld their contributions wanted to express disillusionment with partisan politics in general, most wanted to coerce the traditional right-of-center parties into resolving their differences and merging into a single organization, or at least a firm bloc, that would defend the interests of the business community against political extremism of both the right and the left. Withholding those contributions had the effect, however, of further weakening parties whose voters the Nazis were vigorously courting. In view of the already depleted strength of those parties, it seems improbable that they could have escaped unscathed even if their former big business backers had provided the usual subsidies or even increased them. But, as it turned out, withholding those subsidies only imposed an added handicap on the efforts of those besieged parties to hold on to their voters. In that instance, too, political ineptitude rather than design led some of the business community to render indirect and unintentional aid to Hitler and his party. That aid hardly amounted, however, to a major contribution to Hitler's rise.

If the political record of big business is sadly lacking in political acumen, it is even more sorely devoid of public morality and civil courage. Most of the leaders of the business community were never tempted to become Nazis. The NSDAP's promise to destroy the existing elite and impose a new one in its place held little allure for men already at the top of their society. Its plebeian tone offended their taste. So did its anti-Semitism, for whatever other prejudices the leading men of German big business harbored, that form of bigotry was rare in their ranks. Most also found disturbing Nazism's demand for total power and its voluble strain of anti-capitalism, which focused predominantly on large-scale enterprise. Almost as alarming were the unorthodox fiscal and monetary schemes put forward by prominent Nazis as remedies for the depression. Still, most men of big business viewed Nazism myopically and opportunistically. Like many other Germans whose national pride had been wounded by the unexpected loss of the war and by a humiliating peace treaty, they admired Nazism's defiant nationalism and hoped it could be used to help reassert what they regarded as their country's rightful place among the great powers. Preoccupied as they were with domestic economic issues, they also hoped Nazism could be used against their long-standing adversaries, the socialist parties and the trade union movement. That hope waxed and waned as the Nazis shifted their political tactics. During the last half year preceding Hitler's appointment as chancellor, it subsided to low ebb. But few spokesmen of big business spoke out publicly against the NSDAP. Viewing it in terms of narrow self-interest, most failed to perceive the threat it posed to the very foundations of civilized life. Therein lay their heaviest guilt, one they shared, however, with a large part of the German elite.

To be realistic, it is probably unfair to place a heavy burden of guilt on the men of big business for their failings in the face of a political movement that swept through their society like an elemental force. Businessmen, after all, seldom take the lead politically. As a knowledgeable and perceptive observer, Joseph Schumpeter, commented not long after the events chronicled in this book, "The attitudes of capitalist groups toward the policy of their nations are predominantly adaptive rather than causative, today more than ever." Rather than shaping events, Schumpeter noted, even the mightiest of businessmen merely respond to events shaped by others. By way of explaining this he further observed that the kind of economic leadership exercised by the modern capitalist "does not readily expand, like the medieval lord's military leadership, into the leadership of nations. On the contrary, the ledger and the cost calculation absorb and confine."[1] The leaders of German big business were, for all their pretensions, such absorbed and confined men, preoccupied with the management of large, complex organizations. They could at most dabble in politics. They could not commit their energies in a sustained fashion to that sphere of activity, so that they remained part-time amateurs, operating only sporadically, and usually ineffectually, on the periphery of politics. As such, they were sorely ill-suited to deal with a phenomenon like Nazism.

2. Myths, Preconceptions, and the Misuse of History

This has become, of necessity, a book that deals not only with the past but also with myths about that past. In order to tell its story, numerous myths had to be refuted. Such is, of course, generally the case with the writing of history, but the sheer volume of myths in this instance and their stubborn persistence call for an attempt at explanation.

Even in otherwise carefully researched works on the rise of Nazism, the most threadbare of tales have frequently served to indicate or imply complicity on the part of big business. Anyone even slightly familiar with the historical literature will have been well acquainted, at the very least, with the oft-told tales of a Ruhr coal levy for the NSDAP, of the business community's representation at the Bad Harzburg meeting, of its response to Hitler's Düsseldorf Industry Club speech, of its participation in the petition of November 1932 to Hindenburg, and of the allegedly central role of the banker Kurt von Schröder at the Hitler-Papen meeting of January 4, 1933. Such myths have repeatedly been presented as established facts. Allegations about financial support of the NSDAP by big business abound in works on that party's rise. By way of documentation, one repeatedly finds cited such dubious sources as the ghostwritten memoir attributed to Fritz Thyssen, or the propagandistic Third Reich memoir of Otto Dietrich, or simply unsubstantiated press reports. Emil Kirdorf's membership in the NSDAP long served as proof of big business support even though public statements on his part at the time revealed his resignation from the party only a year after he had joined. Other men of big business who had no known involvement whatever with Nazism before the Nazi takeover have been repeatedly portrayed as supporters and financiers of Hitler. The notion that Germany's capitalists contributed significantly to Hitler's rise has become something of a truism. More often than not, that is the message conveyed by American textbooks for students of European history and by other instructional works. With astonishing frequency, in short, evidence and purported evidence bearing on the subject of this book has been dealt with by historians in a fashion marked by a striking suspension of professional standards.

Even solid evidence has frequently been interpreted in such a manner as to distort it. The same historians who carefully present public pronouncements of other interest groups as bargaining positions subject to revision through negotiation have portrayed those of the business community as non-negotiable demands. Statements by men of big business advocating admission of the Nazis to the government have been interpreted as conclusive proof of their desire for a Nazi regime, although scrutiny of those statements in context often reveals that those who uttered them merely shared with many others, including some staunch foes of Nazism, the belief that the best hope of discrediting the NSDAP lay in saddling it with a share of governmental responsibility in a time of economic distress. Bias, in short, appears over and over again in treatments of the political role of big business even by otherwise scrupulous historians.

That bias should not come as a surprise. Professional historians generally have little or no personal contact with the world of business. Like so many intellectuals, they tend to view big business with a combination of condescension and mistrust. Relatively few of their number find it a congenial subject for research. As a consequence, most of what historians have written about the political role of German big business in the period dealt with in this book has been largely uninformed by knowledge about businessmen or their institutions. Since almost all of those who have concerned themselves with the relationship between the business community and Nazism have, to one degree or another, stood left or at least left of center in their political sympathies, a great many have found it difficult to resist the temptation to implicate big business, which clearly belonged on the right, in the rise of Nazism. Although deliberate distortion figures in some publications on the subject, the susceptibility of most historians to the myths dealt with in this volume is attributable not to intellectual dishonesty but rather to the sort of preconceptions that hobble attempts to come to grips with the past.

In a rare instance where such preconceptions gained explicit expression, an influential left-liberal historian made clear in the summer of 1932 his firm conviction, even at that early point, about the complicity of big business in the onrush of Nazism. In a letter to his friend George W. F. Hallgarten, who would later author a study of the subject that long enjoyed authoritative status, Eckart Kehr wrote, "In thirty years we shall, I hope, have enough material to show in detail what whores Adolf and his thirteen million rampaging *Idiotenbürger* were to Thyssen, etc." [1] When Kehr wrote those words they could have had no more basis than allegations gleaned from the press and from the political polemics of the day. Yet even at that point, before the Nazis had attained power, Kehr found it congenial, as have so many intellectuals since, to attribute both sinister aims and great political potency to the capitalists of Germany. He felt no need for further enlightenment. The task of research would lie, so far as he was concerned, merely in substantiating what he already believed, in confirming what he had prejudged. Preconceptions of this kind have too often impaired the judgment of those who have sought to explain Hitler's rise to power. All too often writers dealing with that subject have disregarded one of the fundamental principles of historical scholarship, namely, that historians must exercise the utmost of critical vigilance precisely when they find that a proposition about the past conforms with their own previous beliefs.

The perpetuation of the many specific myths addressed in this book has been fostered by the cultivation, for more than a half century, of a more comprehensive myth. According to one of the most persistent schools of interpretation, Germany's capitalists were not merely implicated in Nazism's rise but indeed played *the* decisive role in bringing it about. That interpretation had its origins in intellectual circles that saw during the 1920s Mussolini's imposition of dictatorship on Italy as confirmation of predictions made earlier by secular prophets of considerable renown. According to those predictions, an increasingly beleaguered bourgeoisie could be expected, as the proletarian revolution approached, to make a desperate but ultimately vain attempt to stave off its inevitable doom by breaching the legal and constitutional forms that had hitherto masked its dominance in order to impose an openly tyrannical regime. Like Italian Fascism, Nazism was a vehicle of bourgeois repression. Behind its ludicrous leaders, as behind Mussolini, lurked mighty capitalists who bankrolled the NSDAP and otherwise opened for it the way to power. First applied to Italy, this formula made of Nazism merely one manifestation of a generic phenomenon designated by its proponents as fascism. At a time when no consensus prevailed among other observers about the reasons for Nazism's successes, that interpretation enabled its adherents to set, as it were, the initial agenda for inquiries into the causes of the Third Reich. And, as is often the case with the development of historical scholarship, that initial agenda has continued to influence discussion of the subject.

Historical writing based on the proposition that capitalists or, more broadly, capitalism played the decisive role in bringing the Nazis to power has produced several variations on that basic theme. The earliest and simplest of these, the agent theory, holds that Germany's "monopoly capitalists" collectively brought to bear their economic potency so as to nurture the NSDAP and install it in power in order to exploit the working class at home and unleash an imperialistic war of aggression abroad. Because of the obvious implausibility of ascribing such uniform political behavior to the business community as a whole, recourse was had to more elaborate theories. Most of these are structural in nature. They seek to explain political developments in terms of relationships among socio-economic groupings. According to the most active school of structural interpretation, the Third Reich came into being as a consequence of a titanic struggle that took place out of public view in the economic sphere between great capitalist blocs, or "monopoly groups," locked in combat in defense of conflicting economic interests. The Nazis took over the government when the "monopoly group" with which they were aligned won out in that struggle in the economic sphere.[2] According to another line of structural interpretation, Nazism gained control over the state when "contradictions" among the "dominant classes and class fractions" (which are portrayed as extending beyond the business community) made it impossible for any of those forces to establish "hegemony" over the others, a situation that produced a crisis that led to the establishment of the dominance of "big monopoly capital."[3] Other variations on the same basic proposition, known as Bonapartist theories, are less rigidly structural. Proponents of Bonapartist theories maintain that Hitler, like Emperor Napoleon III of France, came to power because the bourgeoisie had lost its capacity to rule but managed to retain its economic position by relinquishing management of the state to a dictator of its choice because the proletariat was not yet ready to carry out its own revolution.[4]

Quite aside from the mutual incompatibilities of these variations on the basic thesis of capitalism as the cause of Nazism, attempts to account for the rise of Hitler and his party by using that thesis as the point of departure have produced a badly flawed body of historical writing. The simplistic agent theory, which portrays Germany's capitalists as having acted in concert to bring Hitler to power, requires such flagrant distortions of the historical record that it has become reserved for indoctrination propaganda of a primitive variety. It is now mainly employed by regimes that find it a useful means of warning those over whom they rule that all capitalist societies contain an inherent potentiality for murderous destructiveness that only a total transformation of their economic and social systems can dispel. As for structural interpretations, they have produced little agreement as to the composition of the groups whose alleged struggles with one another supposedly determined the course of events that resulted in the Third Reich. The most frequently employed categories in "monopoly group" interpretations are, moreover, of very questionable validity. Despite the process of diversification that saw some of the most prominent German iron and steel firms branching out into the manufacture of finished products by the 1920s, those interpretations anachronistically posit the continuing existence of an essentially monolithic "heavy industry" bloc. They also assume the existence of an opposing bloc composed of the chemical industry and producers of electrical equipment, even though evidence of collaboration between these rather different branches of production has yet to be adduced. Otherwise, "monopoly group" interpretations vary widely on particulars. So do Bonapartist theories of Nazism's rise. All these interpretations display, in fact, much the same elasticity as do psychoanalytic interpretations of Hitler and so result in a similar lack of agreement on specifics as well as on conclusions. Whereas valid hypotheses tend to generate consensus, versions of Nazism's rise to power based on the assumption that capitalism accounts for its triumph have given rise to such a high degree of arbitrariness and disagreement as to result in utter inconclusiveness.

One reason for this inconclusiveness is that works embodying the agent theory, structural theories, and the Bonapartist theories have been long on thesis and short on evidence. Much of what passes for evidence consists of myths of the sort mentioned above. Inventively embellished and tendentiously interpreted, these and other often dubious scraps of information are ceaselessly repeated. Evidence that might contradict or cast doubt on the interpretation being presented is simply ignored. Almost never is an effort made to document carefully the relationship between alleged cause and alleged effect. That relationship is instead suggested impressionistically by means of a loose array of circumstantial and often questionable evidence. In countries with repressive regimes that have incorporated explanations of Nazism as a manifestation of capitalism into their indoctrination systems, unfettered inquiry has long since ceased. Where regimes that control historians' access to publication have bestowed official approval on such an interpretation of the Third Reich's origins, one of the most fruitful avenues for the advance of knowledge—the correction of error—remains sealed off. Under such circumstances historical writing becomes merely an exercise in confirming the validity of official doctrine, and scholastic debate about abstract concepts such as "state monopoly capitalism" is substituted for scholarly investigation.

Most publications that explain the rise of Nazism in terms of capitalism have no need to rely heavily on evidence. They take as their point of departure a reductive assumption that obviates the necessity for a tightly argued and closely documented analysis of the causes of events: the primacy of economics. If that assumption is granted, the traditional focuses of inquiry into the origins of the Third Reich—intellectual traditions, government policies, national elections, the political behavior of social groups, and the actions of parties and politicians, including Hitler and the Nazis—become relegated to the status of mere epiphenomena located in the "superstructure" of society. Far from determining the course of events, such epiphenomena at most reflect developments taking place in the decisive economic sphere. Since most of what occurs in the economic sphere is assumed to remain concealed from the public and even from the historian, much must be surmised from a few clues rather than demonstrated by a sustained marshaling of evidence, as in traditional historical scholarship. By proclaiming, through reliance on such clues, confirmation of the economic sphere's decisive role, the case is proven. In numerous instances, however, the authors of such interpretations betray something less than complete confidence in their method by propping up their arguments through recourse to fallacious reasoning. Quite commonly, that which was to be explained—the triumph of Hitler—becomes itself the ultimate proof of the validity of those interpretations. That is, through circular reasoning the Nazis' acquisition of power is presented as proof that the forces at work in Germany's capitalist economy had of necessity to eventuate in the creation of the Third Reich. Alternatively, recourse is had to a functionalist, or "cui bono," argument basically similar to that employed by nineteenth-century anti-Semites who insisted that the Jews must have caused the French Revolution since they benefited so greatly from it: Since the capitalists profited under the Third Reich, they must surely have been behind its creation. The "function" of Nazism must, according to such reasoning, therefore have been to rescue German capitalism.

This book proposes no new explanation for the rise of Hitler. Instead, it confirms the judgment of those historians who have concentrated on the political sphere. The ill-fated Weimar Republic was a fragile democratic polity that labored throughout its brief existence under the taint of association with the humiliating defeat in World War I. From the outset it encountered unrelenting hostility from many citizens imbued with beliefs incompatible with democracy. The defenders of the Republic sought to legitimize it in the eyes of the country's wage earners by establishing the most advanced welfare state of the day, the economic burdens of which may well have undermined Germany's economic vitality and certainly alienated most of the business community. The Republic also had to wrestle with a host of intractable problems that would have made it difficult for any regime to gain general popularity: reparations for a war lost by the previous regime, hyper-inflation, an agrarian crisis, the fiscal difficulties of an advanced welfare state and, finally, the crushing effects of the Great Depression. The Republic also suffered from a fatal constitutional flaw that permitted a transfer of authority in 1930 from the paralyzed parliament to the presidency through recourse to the sweeping emergency powers invested in that office. In the person of the aged Hindenburg, the presidency came increasingly under the influence of an irresponsible camarilla in which the military leadership played a key role, making and unmaking a succession of cabinets that governed by presidential emergency decrees. Discontent with the inability of those cabinets to cope with the effects of the depression fostered the growth of political extremism, one expression of which was Nazism. By combining the charismatic appeal of its leader with remarkably effective organization and by appealing to prejudice and xenophobia, the NSDAP had marshaled a hard core of militant activists even before the depression struck. By promising to undo the Versailles settlement and by exploiting social tensions and the economic grievances of numerous elements of society through resort to appeals of calculated ambiguity and unscrupulous mendacity, the Nazis put together a formidable coalition of malcontents. By exploiting the unpopular policies of the presidential regime, as well as the deprivation and insecurity resulting from the depression, the NSDAP cut ever more deeply into the electorate, emerging by mid-1932 as the country's largest party. Stymied by Hindenburg's unwillingness to entrust the chancellorship to Hitler, it slipped into decline. In what proved to be the last free election it suffered heavy losses at the polls in the fall of 1932. Within the NSDAP internal strife broke out. Only when the members of the camarilla around Hindenburg fell out among themselves did one faction of presidential advisers rescue the faltering NSDAP by sabotaging their rivals and prevailing on the president to appoint Hitler chancellor of a coalition cabinet they expected to control. But the Nazis quickly outmaneuvered the conservative members of the coalition and imposed their dictatorial rule within a matter of months.

The striking feature of this explanation for the rise of Hitler, which appears here in greatly simplified form, is that it requires little or no mention of big business. Only at the time of the parliamentary crisis of 1930 did the business community play anything approaching a crucial role in shaping the course of events, and, as had been shown above, its role was not ultimately decisive in determining the outcome of that crisis. Otherwise, the men of German big business and their institutions shrink to insignificance in comparison with the politicians and military men whose blunders and miscalculations made possible Hitler's attainment of power. A primacy of politics, not a primacy of economics, marked the realities of late Weimar Germany. Among those who understood this was Adolf Hitler. For a time he appears to have shared, at least to some extent, the belief that economic might amounted to political potency, but he learned better. During his final, successful drive for power he concentrated his efforts exclusively on the electorate and on those political figures who held the keys to state power, and he did so in a fashion bound to alienate much of the business community. One of the reasons for Hitler's success lay in his recognition of the primacy of politics and his astuteness in acting on that principle.

The sustained appeal of interpretations of Hitler's rise in terms of a primacy of economics poses a historical problem that deserves fuller elucidation than is possible here. Until fairly recently the popularity of such interpretations could, in considerable measure, be explained in terms of a paucity of information: In the absence of knowledge, myth flourishes. But the persistence of such interpretations even in the face of mounting evidence of their fallaciousness calls for a broader explanation. As already mentioned, preconceptions about businessmen among intellectuals have obviously played an important role. Still another factor lies in the promise of such interpretations to reveal deeper, more profound causes than those visible to the uninitiated. Whether in the form of theories about forces working behind the scenes in the economic sphere to produce the Third Reich or in the form of the occult, the prospect of attaining to special knowledge otherwise hidden from view holds a strong attraction for certain types of people. An interpretation of history that places the blame for disastrous events on the rich provides another form of gratification. The proposition that big business or, more broadly, capitalism played the decisive role in the rise of Hitler also obviously appeals to some as corroboration of a body of doctrine.

Above all, however, the appeal of that proposition derives from its political usefulness. Since the collapse of the Third Reich, interpretations of its origins based on that proposition have been used in an effort to discredit and undermine societies with capitalist economies and to legitimize repressive anti-capitalist regimes. In the early 1930s the identification of capitalism with Nazism (usually apostrophized as fascism) seemed an expedient means of rallying the masses simultaneously against two enemies, or so many leaders of the political left in Germany appear to have believed. Identifying Nazism with capitalism may possibly have helped at the time to hold some German voters behind the parties of the left, but that same identification may also partially explain the curious passivity that gripped so much of the left's leadership and rendered it ineffectual in the face of Nazism's drive for power. Depicting Hitler—as did many spokesmen of the left—as just another lackey of capitalism, essentially similar to Brüning, Papen, and Schleicher, amounted to a reckless trivialization of a lethal political phenomenon. But just as trivializing the Nazis in that fashion may have induced complacency in some of their opponents, portraying Nazism as a manifestation of the "monopoly stage" of capitalism may have made it appear so formidable to others on the left as to induce despair, if not paralysis. For how could one combat the NSDAP with any hope of success if it amounted not just to another political party striving for power but to an expression of the final stage of a whole phase of history, perhaps destined to shape the course of events, at least until the eventual victory of the working class? Coping with the day-to-day onslaught of Nazism posed challenge enough, but the odds against stemming the underlying forces of history must have seemed daunting indeed to those who believed in such forces. No one can say with any confidence that the leaders of the political left in Weimar Germany might, had they acted differently, have halted the Nazi advance. But much speaks for the proposition that their chances would have improved if more of them had realistically assessed the reasons why the NSDAP proved so attractive for millions of voters, and if they had sought ways to compete for those ballots rather than attempting, in line with an ideological preconception, to "unmask" Nazism as a tool of the capitalists.

The reaction to this book on the part of those who posit the primacy of economics—and therefore attribute the triumph of Hitler to Germany's capitalists or, more generally, to that country's capitalist economy—is quite predictable. Some will dismiss it as an apology for capitalism and its author as a lackey of powerful vested economic interests. Some will contend that the book is directed at a straw man and that no one worthy of note has ever seriously argued that anything so crude as direct financial aid or influence from the side of big business played a decisive, or even major, role in Nazism's rise to power. Others will condescendingly observe that the author is a mere positivist, a vulgar factologist who lacks any comprehension of the underlying motive forces of human events. Still others will contend that the larger picture is hopelessly lost in a mass of detail, the forest being obscured by the trees; that the author has concerned himself with mere questions on the order of who said what to whom and what happened when; that he has focused excessively on the actions of individuals, thus omitting more fundamental determinants. Analysis must take place, it will be announced, on a "higher plane" and be informed by conceptualization and theory. Such strictures have a superficial ring of profundity that will doubtless impress many. But the deficiencies of the body of historical writing produced by those who have relied on such formulas undercut the plausibility of these particular strictures. Objections of that sort have no validity unless it can be demonstrated by those who raise them that history can be written on the terms they propose without reliance on the impressionistic use of a smattering of evidence, without the misconstrual and omission of evidence, and without the use of fabricated or otherwise invalid evidence. It does not suffice to retreat to a "higher plane" where hypotheses take on such an abstract quality as to rule out either confirmation or refutation. Nor does it suffice to posit processes of causation different from those normally employed to explain human affairs. One of the most basic premises of the professional study of history is that events are not directly caused by abstract concepts, whether those be "the hand of God," "manifest destiny," or "monopoly capital." The concrete events of history occur because of the actions of human beings, who often carry out their will, to be sure, through institutions of their own creation. Unless this proximate form of causation can be convincingly demonstrated, the invocation of more remote levels of causation remains empty speculation, bereft of any foundation in the realities of history.

Reflecting in 1940 upon his experiences in seeking to identify the reasons for the collapse of the Third French Republic in the face of the onslaught of the Third Reich, the brilliant historian Marc Bloch, who himself soon fell victim to Nazism, wrote these words: ". . . the ABC of my trade consists in avoiding big-sounding abstract terms. Those who teach history should be continually concerned with the task of seeking the solid and the concrete behind the empty and the abstract. In other words, it is on men rather than functions that they should concentrate their attention."[5] Those intellectuals who have explained the rise of Adolf Hitler and his party by recourse to "higher planes" of analysis have long displayed, and continue to display, great reluctance to think in such concrete terms. According to one of the most quoted maxims bearing on the subject of this book, it is impossible to speak about fascism without also speaking about capitalism. The author of that now famous dictum, Max Horkheimer, enunciated that formulation as an exile who had been forced to flee Nazi-ruled Germany.[6] He and the others who had applied that formula had been mistaken about the nature of Nazism at the time, but most learned nothing from their defeat. Nor have their latter-day disciples, who continue to subordinate the study of Nazism to a crusade against capitalism. As always when the writing of history is made subservient to some other goal, the result has been poor history. The Third Reich is, however, too appalling a manifestation of our species' capacity for evil to be left to flawed diagnoses that engender the sort of false security inspired, in the days before modern medical science, by the nostrums our ancestors devised to protect themselves against debilitating diseases. With history, as with medicine, a false diagnosis can have disastrous consequences. If a repetition of anything resembling the murderous regime headed by Adolf Hitler is to be prevented, its causes must be subjected to the most rigorous possible study. In the case of this book's subject, that involves close, empirical investigation of the relationships between actual capitalists and actual Nazis rather than reliance upon grandiose theories about capitalism and fascism. The findings of this study indicate that such investigation can only lead to the conclusion that although there are many legitimate reasons for faulting the large-scale, organized industrial capitalism of the twentieth century, responsibility for the Third Reich is not a valid cudgel with which to belabor that economic system.

Abbreviations Used in Notes

JBIDG	*Jahrbuch des Instituts für Deutsche Geschichte* (Tel-Aviv)
JBWG	*Jahrbuch für Wirtschaftsgeschichte*
JCH	*Journal of Contemporary History*
JEH	*Journal of Economic History*
JMH	*Journal of Modern History*
JSH	*Journal of Social History*
KA	Krupp-Archiv, Essen
KP	Klein Papers (These are in the personal possession of Dr. Fritz Klein, East Berlin.)
LAB	Landesarchiv Berlin
LC	Library of Congress, Washington, D.C.
LHAK	Landeshauptarchiv Koblenz
NA	National Archives, Washington, D.C.
NPL	*Neue Politische Literatur*
NSDAP HA	NSDAP Hauptarchiv (Hoover Institution Microfilm)
NSHSAH	Niedersächsisches Hauptstaatsarchiv Hannover
NSSAO	Niedersächsisches Staatsarchiv Osnabrück
P & P	*Past & Present*
PVJS	*Politische Vierteljahresschrift*
RG	Record Group (classification in U.S. National Archives)
RVB	*Rheinische Vierteljahrsblätter*
SA	Siemens-Archiv, Werner-von-Siemens-Institut für Geschichte des Hauses Siemens, Munich
SAD	Stadtarchiv Düsseldorf
SAE	Stadtarchiv Essen
SAM	Staatsarchiv Münster
SEG	*Schulthess' Europäischer Geschichtskalender*
SGB	Archiv, Spruchkammergericht, Bielefeld
SH	*Social History*
T/RP	Thyssen/Reves Papers (Copies deposited by author in archive of Institut für Zeitgeschichte, Munich.)
VB	*Völkischer Beobachter*
VDAV	Vereinigung der Deutschen Arbeitgeberverbände
VDESI	Verein Deutscher Eisen- und Stahlindustrieller
VfZ	*Vierteljahrshefte für Zeitgeschichte*
VSWG	*Vierteljahrschrift für Sozial- und Wirtschaftsgeschichte*
WA	*Wissenschaftliche Annalen* (East Berlin)
WLB	*Wiener Library Bulletin*
WP	Westarp Papers, Gaertringen
WWB	Weltwirtschaftsbücherei, Kiel
WWR	*Wehrwissenschaftliche Rundschau*
ZAP	Zentralarchiv der DDR, Potsdam
ZARB	Zentralarchiv Rheinische Braunkohlenwerke, Pfaffendorf
ZfG	*Zeitschrift für Geschichtswissenschaft*
ZfU	*Zeitschrift für Unternehmensgeschichte*

Notes

Introduction, section 1: The Issues and the Sources

1. Such was long the case with the article by George W. F. Hallgarten, "Adolf Hitler and German Heavy Industry," *JEH* 12 (1952): 222–46. It went through three printings in German translation as part of Hallgarten's book, *Hitler, Reichswehr und Industrie* (Frankfurt, 1st and 2nd eds. 1955; 3rd ed. 1962). See also the apologetic book by Louis P. Lochner, *Tycoons and Tyrant* (Chicago, 1954).

2. This is particularly the case with the scores of party-line publications from East Germany or the Soviet Union. For a recent example, see Kurt Pätzold and Manfred Weissbecker, *Geschichte der NSDAP 1920–1945* (Cologne, 1981), a book first published in East Berlin under the title *Hakenkreuz und Totenkopf.*

3. See, for example, James and Suzanne Pool, *Who Financed Hitler?* (New York, 1978), translated into German as *Hitlers Wegbereiter zur Macht* (Munich, 1979); among other things, its authors cited documents from archives they had never visited. For a different but even more disqualifying example, see David Abraham, *The Collapse of the Weimar Republic* (Princeton, 1981); Abraham's use of evidence is discussed in *AHR* 88 (1983): 1143–49; for a detailed analysis, see Ulrich Nocken, "Weimarer Geschichte[n]. Zum neuen amerikanischen Buch 'Collapse of the Weimar Republic'," *VSWG* 71 (1984). For an example of still another sort, see Ekkehard Franke-Gricksch (ed.), *So wurde Hitler finanziert* (Leonberg, 1983); this recent publication rests upon a fabricated document that was conclusively discredited thirty years ago: Hermann Lutz, "Fälschungen zur Auslandsfinanzierung Hitlers," *VfZ* 2 (1954): 586–96.

4. See, for some examples, Udo Wengst, "Unternehmerverbände und Gewerkschaften in Deutschland im Jahre 1930," *VfZ* 25 (1977): 99–119; idem, "Der Reichsverband der Deutschen Industrie in den ersten Monaten des Dritten Reiches," *VfZ* 28 (1980): 94–110; Bernd Weisbrod, *Schwerin-*

dustrie in der Weimarer Republik (Wuppertal, 1978); Reinhard Neebe, *Grossin-dustrie, Staat und NSDAP 1930–1933* (Göttingen, 1981).

5. Kurt Gossweiler, *Kapital, Reichswehr und NSDAP 1919–1924* (Cologne, 1982), pp. 321f. Gossweiler, a faculty member at the East Berlin university, addressed these remarks to my *Faschismus und Kapitalismus in Deutschland* (Göttingen, 1972; 2nd edition, 1980).

6. See the affidavit (NI-9126) of Karl von Heider, the counterintelligence of-ficer at Farben's Frankfurt headquarters, July 25, 1947: *Trials of War Crimi-nals before the Nuernberg Military Tribunals under Control Council Law No. 10*, 15 vols. (Washington, D.C., 1949–53), VII, pp. 446–60.

7. Peter Hayes, "The *Gleichschaltung* of IG Farben" (diss., Yale University, 1982); Helmuth Tammen, "Die I.G. Farbenindustrie Aktiengesellschaft (1925–1933). Ein Chemiekonzern in der Weimarer Republik" (diss., Freie Universität Berlin, 1978). See also Rudolf Schröder, "Die Aus-schussprotokolle der IG-Farben als Quelle zur Betriebsgeschichtsforschung über die Zeit des Kapitalismus," *JBWG* (1967), Teil 1: 250–69.

Introduction, section 2: Big Business in the Weimar Context

1. See, for examples, Alfred L. Bernheim (ed.), *Big Business: Its Growth and its Place* (New York, 1937); Survey Research Center, University of Michigan, *Big Business from the Viewpoint of the Public* (Ann Arbor, 1951); David E. Lilienthal, *Big Business: A New Era* (New York, 1952); A. D. H. Kaplan, *Big Enterprise in a Corporative System* (Washington, D.C., 1954); Neville Abra-ham, *Big Business and Government* (London, 1974).

2. See Hans-Joachim Winkler, *Preussen als Unternehmer 1923–1932* (Berlin, 1965).

3. Hannes Siegrist, "Deutsche Grossunternehmen vom späten 19. Jahrhun-dert bis zur Weimarer Republik," *G & G* 6 (1980): 84, 93–99.

4. Statistisches Reichsamt, *Wirtschaft und Statistik* 8 (1928): 251.

5. For the following, I have relied on Siegrist, "Grossunternehmen," pp. 60–102, which covers only industrial corporations, and on the more compre-hensive coverage, but of only the largest corporations, in Statistisches Reichsamt, *Wirtschaft und Statistik* 8 (1928): 250–54.

6. George Stocking and Myron Watkins, *Cartels in Action* (New York, 1947), pp. 413–14.

7. Peter Czada, *Die Berliner Elektroindustrie in der Weimarer Zeit* (Berlin, 1969), still provides the best study of this industry.

8. Hans Pohl, "Die Konzentration in der deutschen Wirtschaft vom aus-gehenden 19. Jahrhundert bis 1945," in *Die Konzentration in der deutschen Wirtschaft seit dem 19. Jahrhundert*, ed. by Hans Pohl and Wilhelm Treue (Wiesbaden, 1978), p. 21.

9. See Erich Maschke, *Es entsteht ein Konzern. Paul Reusch und die GHH* (Tübingen, 1969). For other examples, see Statistisches Reichsamt, *Konzerne, Interessengemeinschaften und ähnliche Zusammenschlüsse im Deutschen Reich Ende 1926* (Berlin, 1927). See also the short survey with useful bibli-ography by Hartmut Pogge von Strandmann, "Entwicklungsstrukturen der

Grossindustrie im Ruhrgebiet," in Karl Rohe and Herbert Kühr (eds.), *Politik und Gesellschaft im Ruhrgebiet* (Königstein/Ts., 1979), pp. 142–61.

10. I have relied for the following on Statistisches Reichsamt, *Deusche Wirtschaftskunde. Ein Abriss der deutschen Reichsstatistik,* 2nd. ed. (Berlin, 1933), pp. 6 and 110.

11. On the Ruhr's development, see Wilfried Feldenkirchen, *Die Eisen- und Stahlindustrie des Ruhrgebiets, 1879–1914* (Wiesbaden, 1982).

12. See the useful symposium, *Organisierter Kapitalismus,* ed. by Heinrich August Winkler (Göttingen, 1974).

13. See Erich Maschke, *Grundzüge der deutschen Kartellgeschichte bis 1914* (Dortmund, 1964).

14. A government survey estimated the number of industrial cartels in 1925 at 2,500: Horst Wagenführ, *Kartelle in Deutschland* (Nuremberg, 1931), p. xiii; Rudolf K. Michels, *Cartels, Combines and Trusts in Post-War Germany* (New York, 1928), pp. 172f. The more conservative figure used here is drawn from Wolfram Fischer, "Bergbau, Industrie und Handwerk, 1914–1970," in *Handbuch der deutschen Wirtschafts- und Sozialgeschichte,* ed. by Hermann Aubin and Wolfgang Zorn, 2 vols. (Stuttgart, 1971–76), II, p. 811.

15. For an overview, see Alfred Kuhlo, *Die Organisation der deutschen Industrie* (Berlin, 1928); for more comprehensive information, see *Handbuch wirtschaftlicher Verbände und Vereine des deutschen Reiches,* 3rd ed. (Berlin and Vienna, 1928).

16. See Helge Pross, *Manager und Aktionäre in Deutschland* (Frankfurt, 1965). The description of post-war German firm structure in Heinz Hartmann, *Authority and Organization in German Management* (Princeton, 1959), pp. 16–20, applies almost as well to the only slightly more complex corporate patterns of Weimar. IG Farben, which was run by an elaborate system of committees, represented an exception to the overall pattern; see Hayes, "The *Gleichschaltung* of IG Farben," ch. 1.

17. Statistisches Reichsamt, *Wirtschaft und Statistik* 11 (1931): 710.

18. Kurt Wiedenfeld, "Führer der Wirtschaft," in *Die deutsche Wirtschaft und ihre Führer,* ed. by Kurt Wiedenfeld, vol. I (Gotha, 1925), pp. xi–xii.

Chapter I, section 1: German Capitalism Survives a Revolution

1. On this less well-known aspect of the imperial period, see Klaus Saul, *Staat, Industrie, Arbeiterbewegung im Kaiserreich* (Düsseldorf, 1974).

2. See Agnes M. Prym, *Staatswirtschaft und Privatunternehmung in der Geschichte des Ruhrkohlenbergbaus* (Essen, 1950), pp. 31–44; Charles Medalen, "State Monopoly Capitalism in Germany: The Hibernia Affair," *P & P* no. 78 (Feb. 1978): 82–112.

3. See James J. Sheehan, *The Career of Lujo Brentano* (Chicago, 1966).

4. See Kenneth D. Barkin, *The Controversy over German Industrialization, 1890–1902* (Chicago, 1970).

5. See Helga Nussbaum, *Unternehmer gegen Monopole* (East Berlin, 1966); Hartmut Kaelble, *Industrielle Interessenpolitik in der wilhelminischen Gesellschaft* (Berlin, 1967); Fritz Blaich, *Kartell- und Monopolpolitik im kaiserlichen Deutschland* (Düsseldorf, 1973); Siegfried Mielke, *Der Hansa-Bund für*

Gewerbe, Handel und Industrie 1909–1914 (Göttingen, 1976); Hans-Peter Ullmann, *Der Bund der Industriellen* (Göttingen, 1976).

6. Ralf Dahrendorf, *Society and Democracy in Germany* (New York, 1967), p. 43.

7. Still among the most perceptive observations on this subject are those of a contemporary, Moritz Julius Bonn, *Das Schicksal des deutschen Kapitalismus* (Berlin, 1930). See also Saul, *Staat, Industrie, Arbeiterbewegung*, esp. pp. 54ff.

8. See Wolfgang Hock, *Deutscher Antikapitalismus* (Frankfurt, 1960); Armin Mohler, *Die konservative Revolution in Deutschland* (Stuttgart, 1950); Klemens von Klemperer, *Germany's New Conservatism* (Princeton, 1957); Herman Lebovics, *Social Conservatism and the Middle Classes in Germany* (Princeton, 1969).

9. On the climate of opinion in Germany before World War I, see Fritz Fischer, *Krieg der Illusionen* (Düsseldorf, 1969), and Klaus Wernecke, *Der Wille zur Weltgeltung* (Düsseldorf, 1970).

10. Wolfgang J. Mommsen, "Domestic Factors in German Foreign Policy before 1914," *CEH* 6 (1973): 10. On the role of a major businessman who sought to be a peacemaker, see Lamar Cecil, *Albert Ballin* (Princeton, 1967).

11. The role of big business during the war remains largely unstudied. On the annexationist movement and the part businessmen played in it, see the still valuable study by Hans W. Gatzke, *Germany's Drive to the West* (Baltimore, 1950).

12. On the following, see Gerald D. Feldman, *Army, Industry and Labor in Germany, 1914–1918* (Princeton, 1966); idem, "German Business between War and Revolution," in Gerhard A. Ritter (ed.), *Entstehung und Wandel der modernen Gesellschaft* (Berlin, 1970), pp. 312–41; idem, "The Origins of the Stinnes-Legien Agreement: A Documentation," *Internationale Wissenschaftliche Korrespondenz zur Geschichte der deutschen Arbeiterbewegung* 19/20 (1973): 45–103. See also Jürgen Kocka, *Klassengesellschaft im Krieg 1914–1918* (Göttingen, 1973), esp. p. 126; Friedrich Zunkel, *Industrie und Staatssozialismus. Der Kampf um die Wirtschaftsordnung in Deutschland, 1914–1918* (Düsseldorf, 1974).

13. See SA, 4/Lf 646, Anlage, for a breakdown of the sources and uses of more than sixteen million inflated marks contributed by business interests for these purposes, apparently in 1919, a year when one of the principal political funding organizations of big business, the Kuratorium für den Wiederaufbau des deutschen Wirtschaftslebens, expended only somewhat more than three million marks in support of candidates for the National Assembly that would write a constitution while governing the country. On big business support of anti-Bolshevik propaganda, see Eduard Stadtler, *Als Antibolschewist 1918/19* (Düsseldorf, 1935), pp. 46–49, 56–60, 70f.

14. The failure of attempts at socialization has attracted curiously little attention from historians. The fullest account is still provided by an unpublished dissertation: Hans Schieck, "Der Kampf um die deutsche Wirtschaftspolitik nach dem Novemberumsturz 1918" (diss., Universität Heidelberg, 1958); excerpt, "Die Behandlung der Sozialisierungsfrage in den Monaten nach dem Staatsumsturz," in Eberhard Kolb (ed.), *Vom Kaiserreich zur Republik* (Cologne, 1972); see also Peter Wulf, "Die Auseinandersetzung um die Sozialisierung der Kohle in Deutschland, 1920/1921," *VfZ* 25 (1977): 46—

98. For an East German interpretation, see Gerhard Brehme, *Die sogenannte Sozialisierungsgesetzgebung der Weimarer Republik* (East Berlin, 1960).

15. Gerald D. Feldman, "The Social and Economic Policies of German Big Business, 1918–1929," *AHR* 75 (1969): 48.

16. Feldman, *Army, Industry and Labor*, pp. 59f.; Kocka, *Klassengesellschaft*, p. 28f.

17. Richard Lewinsohn, *Die Umschichtung des europäischen Vermögens* (Berlin, 1925), pp. 117ff.

18. See the interesting perspective on the impact of this settlement on one firm in Edgar Salin, "Paul Reusch," *Mitteilungen der List-Gesellschaft* 8 (1957): 197.

19. Gerald D. Feldman, "Economic and Social Problems of the German Demobilization, 1918–19," *JMH* 47 (1975): 1–47; idem, "Die Demobilmachung und die Sozialordnung der Zwischenkriegszeit in Europa," *G & G* 9 (1983): 156–77.

20. Quoted in Feldman, "Social and Economic Policies," p. 48.

21. Quoted in Theodor Heuss, *Robert Bosch* (Stuttgart, 1946), p. 371.

22. See Gerald D. Feldman, "Big Business and the Kapp Putsch," *CEH* 4 (1971): 99–130.

23. Minutes of the Hauptvorstand of the Verein Deutscher Eisen- und Stahlindustrieller, Oct. 5, 1923, in BAK, R13 I/98.

24. Peter Wulf, *Hugo Stinnes: Wirtschaft und Politik 1918–1924* (Stuttgart, 1979), pp. 452–65.

25. See Ludwig Kastl, of the industrial Reichsverband, to Silverberg, Dec. 30, 1925, with an attached copy of the memorandum submitted to Hindenburg the day before, both in BAK, Silverberg Papers, 235. According to Kastl's account of the meeting, Hindenburg and possibly also Reusch displayed confusion about presidential emergency powers under Article 48 of the constitution on the one hand and a parliamentary enabling act on the other. Kastl reported that the president had agreed with Reusch's proposal for "stronger use of Article 48 on the basis of an enabling act." The Chancellery minute of the audience of Dec. 29 contains no mention of Reusch's proposal, nor could the editor find any evidence in the Chancellery files that Hindenburg took any actions in response to his visitors' pleas: Karl-Heinz Minuth (ed.), *Akten der Reichskanzlei. Weimarer Republik. Die Kabinette Luther I und II*, 2 vols. (Boppard, 1977), II, pp. 1021–27. On this incident, see also Weisbrod, *Schwerindustrie*, pp. 243f.

26. See his farewell speech as chairman of the industrial Reichsverband on Sept. 25, 1931, quoted in Hans-Joachim Flechtner, *Carl Duisberg: Vom Chemiker zum Wirtschaftsführer* (Düsseldorf, 1959), p. 402.

27. Letter to Walther Bernhard, Oct. 23, 1931: KP.

Chapter I, section 2: *Money Versus Votes*

1. For all the recent scholarly attention to German big businessmen, their ideological orientation has received surprisingly little systematic attention. On the attitudes of the early entrepreneurial elite of western Germany, see Friedrich Zunkel, *Der Rheinisch-Westfälische Unternehmer 1834–1879* (Cologne and Opladen, 1962), pp. 133ff; also the occasional observation about these matters in the almost exclusively quantitative sociological study, Toni Pierenkemper, *Die westfälischen Schwerindustriellen 1852–1913* (Göttingen,

1979). See, for the late Empire, Hans Jaeger, *Unternehmer in der deutschen Politik (1890–1918)* (Bonn, 1967), pp. 293–305. Michael Schneider, *Unternehmer und Demokratie* (Bonn-Bad Godesberg, 1975), offers a frequently polemical interpretation of the outlook of the business community during the Republic. See also the temporally more general, if mainly organizational, interpretation in Hartmann, *Authority and Organization*, pp. 22–50. The trenchant observations of a critical contemporary are still enlightening: Götz Briefs, *Betriebsführung und Betriebsleben in der Industrie* (Stuttgart, 1934).

2. On these and subsequent developments, see Feldman, "German Big Business Between War and Revolution"; idem, "Die Freien Gewerkschaften und die Zentralarbeitsgemeinschaft," in Heinz Oskar Vetter (ed.), *Vom Sozialistengesetz zur Mitbestimmung* (Cologne, 1975), pp. 229–52. Still useful is Heinrich Kaun, *Die Geschichte der Zentralarbeitsgemeinschaft der industriellen und gewerblichen Arbeitgeber und Arbeitnehmer Deutschlands* (Jena, 1938).

3. See Feldman, "Economic and Social Problems of the German Demobilization."

4. See Carl-Ludwig Holtfrerich, *Die deutsche Inflation, 1914–1923* (Berlin and New York, 1980), pp. 242–45. For detailed studies that challenge some of Holtfrerich's interpretations, see the contributions by Rudolf Tschirbs and Andreas Kunz in Gerald D. Feldman et al. (eds.), *The German Inflation Reconsidered* (Berlin and New York, 1982).

5. See Jaeger, *Unternehmer in der deutschen Politik*, pp. 31ff.

6. This terminology is used here in conformity with the usage of the Weimar period, not in a descriptive sense, since none of the parties in question was in any sociological sense purely "bourgeois."

7. Karl Zell, member of the Vorstand of Kronprinz A. G. für Metallindustrie, to Witkugel, Apr. 27, 1933: ZAP, papers of the DVP, file 151.

8. See Charles S. Maier, *Recasting Bourgeois Europe* (Princeton, 1975), p. 247; Lothar Albertin, *Liberalismus und Demokratie am Anfang der Weimarer Republik* (Düsseldorf, 1972), pp. 397f.

9. Hugo Stinnes's career as a DVP Reichstag deputy provides a well-documented example: Wulf, *Stinnes*, esp. pp. 526f.

10. A subject of much speculation, the participation of big business in the bourgeois parties has yet to be examined with precision or thoroughness. For attempts in that direction, see Manfred Dörr, "Die Deutschnationale Volkspartei 1925 bis 1928" (diss., Universität Marburg, 1964); Lothar Döhn, *Politik und Interesse: Die Interessenstruktur der Deutschen Volkspartei* (Meisenheim am Glan, 1970); Albertin, *Liberalismus und Demokratie;* Konstanze Wegner (ed.), *Linksliberalismus in der Weimarer Republik* (Düsseldorf, 1980). See also the still noteworthy contemporary exploration by Richard Lewinsohn, *Das Geld in der Politik* (Berlin, 1931).

11. Hayes, "The *Gleichschaltung* of IG Farben," pp. 67–70.

12. On the DNVP budget, see the report of the party treasurer, Sept. 18, 1931: NSSAO, Erw. C 1, DNVP, Bd. 23. On the cost of an electoral district campaign, see the estimate of the Prussian police that referred to the Ruhr: Report of the Polizeipräsident, Essen, to the Regierungspräsident, Düsseldorf, Nov. 28, 1930: HSAD, Regierung Düsseldorf, folder 30653.

13. Such seems to have been the case with Peter Klöckner, head of the steel firm of the same name with headquarters in Duisburg. Even as a member of the

Ruhrlade (see below), Klöckner maintained close ties to the Center Party, which his brother Florian represented in the Reichstag from 1920 to 1933. On Klöckner, see Volkmar Muthesius, *Peter Klöckner und sein Werk*, 2nd ed. (Essen, 1959).

14. See the speech by Carl Duisberg of IG Farben, chairman of the industrial Reichsverband, to a gathering of industrialists in Berlin, Nov. 26, 1926, reported in *Das Deutsche Volk. Katholische Wochenzeitung für das gesamte deutsche Volkstum*, Dec. 5, 1926 (#40); and *Der Deutsche. Tageszeitung für deutsche Volksgemeinschaft und für ein unabhängiges Deutschland*, Dec. 4, 1926 (#284).

15. Misleading on this count are the assertions in Döhn, *Politik und Interesse*, pp. 368f.

16. The full record of the Kuratorium remains to be established. It is misidentified as a creation of the industrial Reichsverband and the union of Arbeitgeberverbände in Arnold J. Heidenheimer and Frank C. Langdon, *Business Associations and the Financing of Political Parties* (The Hague, 1968), p. 37. The following account is based on the papers of its founder, Carl Friedrich von Siemens: SA, esp. files 4/Lf 519 and 646; also the papers of the organization's treasurer, Eduard Mosler of the Disconto-Gesellschaft: DWI, file 6872 of the records of the Deutsche Bank und Disconto-Gesellschaft. See, in addition, Albertin, *Liberalismus und Demokratie*, pp. 189–90; Werner Schneider, *Die Deutsche Demokratische Partei in der Weimarer Republik 1924–1930* (Munich, 1978), pp. 71f., 234.

17. Information on these organizations is contained in a lengthy memorandum on the meeting of a sizeable number of politically active big businessmen and agents of the political organizations of big business in Berlin on Oct. 19, 1932, at which they exchanged reports on their past activities: enclosure in letter, Martin Blank to Paul Reusch, Oct. 20, 1932: GHH, file 4001012024/10.

18. See the documents on the Kommission published in Kaelble, *Industrielle Interessenpolitik*, pp. 215–22; and in Werner Müller and Jürgen Stockfisch, "Borsig und die Demokratie," *Beiträge, Dokumente, Informationen des Archivs der Hauptstadt der Deutschen Demokratischen Republik* 4 (1967): 19–23. See also the correspondence between Carl Friedrich von Siemens of the Kuratorium and the director of the Kommission, Johannes Flathmann, during 1919: SA, 4/Lf 646. See, in addition, Heidenheimer and Langdon, *Business Associations*, pp. 31f., 39f.

19. On Hugenberg's career, see Dankwart Guratzsch, *Macht durch Organisation: Die Grundlegung des Hugenbergschen Presseimperiums* (Düsseldorf, 1974); Klaus-Peter Hoepke, "Alfred Hugenberg als Vermittler zwischen grossindustriellen Interessen und Deutschnationaler Volkspartei," in Hans Mommsen et al. (eds.), *Industrielles System und Politische Entwicklung in der Weimarer Republik* (Düsseldorf, 1974), pp. 907–19. Heidrun Holzbach, *Das 'System Hugenberg': Die Organization bürgerlicher Sammlungspolitik vor dem Aufstieg der NSDAP* (Stuttgart, 1981); John A. Leopold, *Alfred Hugenberg: The Radical Nationalist Campaign against the Weimar Republic* (New Haven, 1977).

20. See H. A. Turner, Jr., "The *Ruhrlade:* Secret Cabinet of Ruhr Heavy Industry in the Weimar Republic," *CEH* 3 (1970): 203.

21. For the following, see Turner, "The *Ruhrlade*," pp. 195–228. Until one member died in late 1932, the Ruhrlade consisted of the twelve charter members: Erich Fickler, managing director of the Dortmund coal-mining firm Harpener Bergbau AG and chairman of the supervisory board of the Rhenish-Westphalian bituminous-coal cartel; Karl Haniel, chairman of the supervisory board of the Gutehoffnungshütte conglomerate; Peter Klöckner, founder and head of Klöckner-Werke AG, a coal and steel combine in Duisburg; Arthur Klotzbach, a director of Fried. Krupp AG; Gustav Krupp von Bohlen und Halbach; Ernst Poensgen, former managing director of Phönix AG and first deputy director of the United Steel trust, into which Phönix had been absorbed; Paul Reusch, de facto presiding officer of the Ruhrlade and managing director of the Gutehoffnungshütte conglomerate; Paul Silverberg, chairman of the supervisory board of Germany's largest lignite-mining firm, Rheinische AG für Braunkohlenbergbau und Brikettenfabrikation, and of the major bituminous-coal-mining firm Harpener Bergbau, as well as chairman of the Rhenish lignite cartel; Fritz Springorum, managing director of the Eisen- und Stahlwerk Hoesch AG of Dortmund and treasurer of the Ruhrlade; Fritz Thyssen, chairman of the supervisory board of United Steel; Albert Vögler, presiding director of United Steel; and Fritz Winkhaus, managing director of the Köln-Neuessener Bergwerksverein, a coal-mining subsidiary of the Hoesch firm.

22. The well-documented experiences of the lavishly financed Ruhrlade bear out the following observations: Turner, "The *Ruhrlade*."

23. See Michael Stürmer, *Koalition und Opposition in der Weimarer Republik 1924–1928* (Düsseldorf, 1967), pp. 285f.; Carl Böhret, *Aktionen gegen die 'kalte Sozialisierung' 1926–1930* (Berlin, 1966), pp. 117f., 222–35. Business interests were even less well represented in the parliament of the largest and most important federal state, Prussia: Horst Möller, "Parlamentarisierung und Demokratisierung im Preussen der Weimarer Republik," in Gerhard A. Ritter (ed.), *Gesellschaft, Parlament und Regierung* (Düsseldorf, 1974), p. 380.

24. Stürmer, *Koalition und Opposition*, p. 285.

25. Lewinsohn, *Geld in der Politik*, p. 112. The largest of the half-dozen organizations of civil servants could alone account for thirty-one deputies, or 5.4 percent of the chamber elected in 1930: Karl Dietrich Bracher, *Die Auflösung der Weimarer Republik*, 2nd ed. (Stuttgart and Düsseldorf, 1957), p. 178, n. 24.

26. Counting only officials of the "free" or socialist unions and Christian blue-collar unions (thus omitting the Christian white-collar unions and the liberal Hirsch-Duncker unions), Michael Schneider found representation averaging 12 percent in the national parliaments between 1919 and 1932: *Die Christlichen Gewerkschaften, 1894–1933* (Bonn, 1982), p. 629. On the importance of the union membership of most SPD deputies, see Richard Hunt, *German Social Democracy* (New Haven, 1964), p. 172.

27. On the following, see Kurt Koszyk, *Deutsche Presse 1914–1945* (Berlin, 1972); idem, "Zum Verhältnis von Industrie und Presse," in Mommsen et al. (eds.), *Industrielles System*, pp. 704–16. Modris Eksteins, *The Limits of Reason: The German Democratic Press and the Collapse of the Weimar Republic* (New York, 1975), pp. 160–79.

28. The editor of the *DAZ*, Fritz Klein, conspired in 1931 with Chancellor Brüning to deceive the businessmen who owned his paper: Turner, "The *Ruhrlade*," p. 213.

29. See the revealing documents on Paul Reusch's efforts to exercise control over the *Münchner Neuesten Nachrichten*, one of the several papers in which his firm owned a controlling interest: Kurt Koszyk, "Paul Reusch und die Münchner Neuesten Nachrichten," *VfZ* 20 (1972): 75–103. Ultimately, in the spring of 1932, Reusch gave up and resigned his position on the paper's administrative committee.

30. The tardy emergence and ineffectuality of public relations efforts by German industry have generally been overlooked. See the exaggerated description of one such endeavor in Hans Radandt, *Kriegsverbrecherkonzern Mansfeld* (East Berlin, 1958), pp. 68–73. For a firsthand assessment, see the observations of a man directly involved in the attempts to improve the image of Ruhr heavy industry: August Heinrichsbauer, *Schwerindustrie und Politik* (Essen, 1948), p. 13.

31. See, for example the *FZ* article cited by Bernd Weisbrod, *Schwerindustrie*, pp. 211f.

32. Leopold, *Hugenberg*, passim; see also chapter VI, section 4.

33. See H. A. Turner, Jr., *Stresemann and the Politics of the Weimar Republic* (Princeton, 1963).

34. Weisbrod, *Schwerindustrie*, pp. 386f., 428.

35. On Moldenhauer's background, see Paul Steller, *Führende Männer des rheinisch-westfälischen Wirtschaftslebens* (Berlin, 1930), p. 167. On his relations with Farben, see the correspondence of that firm's Carl Duisberg with him; also Duisberg to W. F. Kalle, May 29, 1922: BAL, Autographensammlung Dr. Carl Duisberg. On Moldenhauer's difficulties with industrial interests as economics minister, see Ilse Maurer, *Reichsfinanzen und grosse Koalition. Zur Geschichte des Reichskabinetts Müller, 1928–1930* (Bern and Frankfurt, 1973), and the excerpts from Moldenhauer's unpublished memoirs in Ilse Maurer and Udo Wengst (eds.), *Politik und Wirtschaft in der Krise 1930–1932: Quellen zur Ära Brüning*, 2 vols. (Düsseldorf, 1980), I, pp. 98–102, 121–24, 205–12, 243–46.

Chapter I, section 3: Assets

1. Schieck, "Die Behandlung der Sozialisierungsfrage," p. 145.

2. Peter Krüger, *Deutschland und die Reparationen 1918/19* (Stuttgart, 1973); idem, "Die Rolle der Banken und der Industrie in den deutschen reparationspolitischen Entscheidungen nach dem Ersten Weltkrieg," in Mommsen et al. (eds.), *Industrielles System*, pp. 568–82; Hermann Rupieper, "Industrie und Reparationen: Einige Aspekte des Reparationsproblems 1922–1924," ibid., pp. 582–92; idem, *The Cuno Government and Reparations, 1922–1923* (The Hague, 1979), pp. 55ff.

3. For examples, see Maier, *Recasting Bourgeois Europe*, esp. pp. 249–72.

4. Gerald D. Feldman and Irmgard Steinisch, "Die Weimarer Republik zwischen Sozial- und Wirtschaftsstaat," *AfS* 18 (1978): 353–439.

5. On the following, see Gerald D. Feldman and Heidrun Homburg, *Industrie und Inflation* (Hamburg, 1977); Holtfrerich, *Die deutsche Inflation;* Karsten

Laursen and Jørgen Pedersen, *The German Inflation 1918–1923* (Amsterdam, 1964); Gerald D. Feldman, *Iron and Steel in the German Inflation 1916–1923* (Princeton, 1977). That not all of industry profited from the inflation is the contention of a recent study of the machine-building branch: Dieter Lindenlaub, "Maschinenbauunternehmen in der Inflation 1919 bis 1923," in Feldman et al. (eds.), *The German Inflation Reconsidered*, pp. 49–106.

6 On the following, see Claus-Dieter Krohn, *Stabilisierung und ökonomische Interessen. Die Finanzpolitik des Deutschen Reiches 1923–1927* (Düsseldorf, 1974); idem, "Steuerpolitik und Industrie in der Stabilisierungsphase," in Mommsen et al. (eds.), *Industrielles System*, pp. 426–38; Karl Bernhard Netzband and Hans-Peter Widmaier, *Währungs- und Finanzpolitik der Ära Luther 1923–1925* (Basel and Tübingen, 1964).

7. Larry Eugene Jones, "Inflation, Revaluation, and the Crisis of Middle-Class Politics: A Study in the Dissolution of the German Party System, 1923–28," *CEH* 12 (1979): 143–68.

8. Still the best survey of this development is Robert A. Brady, *The Rationalization Movement in German Industry* (Berkeley, 1933).

9. Dirk Stegmann, "Deutsche Zoll- und Handelspolitik 1924/25-1929 unter besonderer Berücksichtigung agrarischer und industrieller Interessen," in Mommsen et al. (eds.), *Industrielles System*, pp. 499–513.

10. Karl Heinrich Pohl's *Weimars Wirtschaft und die Aussenpolitik der Republik 1924–1926* (Düsseldorf, 1979) unconvincingly portrays the Foreign Ministry as subservient to industrial interests; for a more balanced and precise study, see Ulrich Nocken, "Das Internationale Stahlkartell und die deutsch-französischen Beziehungen 1924–1932," in *Konstellationen internationaler Politik 1924–1932*, ed. by Gustav Schmidt (Bochum, 1983), pp. 165–202. Many of the major figures of the business community publicly endorsed Stresemann's Locarno policy in 1925; see Ernst W. Hansen, "Zur Wahrnehmung industrieller Interessen in der Weimarer Republik," *VfZ* 28 (1980): 495, n. 41.

11. Aside from one compendium of basic institutional information—Walther Hubatsch, *Entstehung und Entwicklung des Reichswirtschaftsministerium* (Berlin, 1978)—the Economics Ministry remains largely unexamined by historians. The following observations are based on records from its files, now in the West German Bundesarchiv in Koblenz and the East German Zentralarchiv in Potsdam, as well as on the private papers of such leading industrialists as Gustav Krupp von Bohlen und Halbach, Paul Reusch, Paul Silverberg, and Fritz Springorum, cited elsewhere in this volume.

12. Krohn, *Stabilisierung und ökonomische Interessen*, p. 94; Pohl, *Weimars Wirtschaft und die Aussenpolitik*, pp. 182f.; Weisbrod, *Schwerindustrie*, pp. 366 ff.; Fritz Blaich, *Staat und Verbände in Deutschland zwischen 1871 und 1945* (Wiesbaden, 1979), pp. 69–72.

13. On this point, see the perceptive observations of a shrewd contemporary: Bonn, *Schicksal*, esp. pp. 54f., 128f.

14. The Reichsverband still lacks an adequate study. On its beginnings, see Friedrich Zunkel, "Die Gewichtung der Industriegruppen bei der Etablierung des Reichsverbandes der Deutschen Industrie," in Mommsen et al. (eds.), *Industrielles System*, pp. 637–47; and Gerhard Schulz, "Räte, Wirtschaftsstände und die Transformation des industriellen Ver-

bandswesens am Anfang der Weimarer Republik," in Ritter (ed.), *Gesellschaft, Parlament und Regierung*, pp. 355-66. See also the articles in the in-house publication of the West German successor organization, Bundesverband der deutschen Industrie, *Der Weg zum industriellen Spitzenverband* (Darmstadt, 1956).

15. See Roswitha Leckebusch, *Entstehung und Wandlungen der Zielsetzungen, der Struktur und der Wirkungen von Arbeitgeberverbänden* (Berlin, 1966); Gerhard Erdmann, *Die deutschen Arbeitgeberverbande im sozialgeschichtlichen Wandel der Zeit* (Neuwied and Berlin, 1966). See also the in-house publications: Alfred Kuhlo, *Die Organisation der deutschen Industrie* (Berlin, 1928); Fritz Tänzler, *Die deutschen Arbeitgeberverbände, 1904-1929* (Darmstadt, 1929); Dieter Schäfer, *Der Deutsche Industrie- und Handelstag als politisches Forum der Weimarer Republik* (Hamburg, 1966); see also the in-house publication of the successor organization in West Germany: Deutscher Industrie- und Handelstag, *Die Verantwortung des Unternehmers in der Selbstverwaltung* (Frankfurt, 1961).

16. See, for example, Stürmer, *Koalition und Opposition*, esp. pp. 223f.

17. Ulrich Nocken, "Inter-Industrial Conflicts and Alliances as Exemplified by the AVI-Agreement," in Mommsen et al. (eds.), *Industrielles System*, pp. 693-704.

18. See Wilfried Gottschalch, *Strukturveränderungen der Gesellschaft und politisches Handeln in der Lehre von Rudolf Hilferding* (Berlin, 1962); Robert A. Gates, "German Socialism and the Crisis of 1929-33," *CEH* 7 (1974): 343-48; Heinrich August Winkler, "Einleitende Bemerkungen zu Hilferdings Theorie des Organisierten Kapitalismus," in Winkler (ed.), *Organisierter Kapitalismus* (Göttingen, 1974), pp. 9-18; Richard Breitman, *German Socialism and Weimar Democracy* (Chapel Hill, 1981), pp. 114-30.

19. Dietmar Petzina, "Gewerkschaften und Monopolfrage vor und während der Weimarer Republik," *AfS* 20 (1980): 195-217.

Chapter I, section 4: Liabilities

1. Still the best chronicle of this development is Ludwig Preller, *Sozialpolitik in der Weimarer Republic* (Stuttgart, 1949).

2. Count Kuno von Westarp to Emil Kirdorf, Mar. 10, 1927: WP.

3. For the details of the system, see Hans-Hermann Hartwich, *Arbeitsmarkt, Verbände und Staat 1918-1933* (Berlin, 1967), esp. pp. 28-42.

4. Ibid., pp. 380-88; Weisbrod, *Schwerindustrie*, esp. pp. 395ff.

5. Peter Flora, Jens Alber, Jürgen Kohl, "Zur Entwicklung der westeuropäischen Wohlfahrtsstaaten," *PVJS* 18 (1977): 728-29.

6. See Böhret, *Aktionen gegen die 'kalte Sozialisierung.'*

7. See Michael Schneider, *Das Arbeitsbeschaffungsprogramm des ADGB* (Bonn-Bad Godesberg, 1975), pp. 53-59.

8. Denunciations of Weimar Sozialpolitik formed a staple of the speeches by business leaders at the meetings of the major associational organizations of the time as well as in the publications of those organizations. See, for example, the speech by the managing director of the Reichsverband, Ludwig Kastl, on Sept. 14, 1928: *Veröffentlichungen des Reichsverbandes der Deutschen Industrie*, no. 42 (1928): 13-36.

9. Schneider, *Unternehmer und Demokratie*, pp. 168f.

10. For an illuminating summary, see Weisbrod, *Schwerindustrie*, pp. 52–92.

11. See Fritz Blaich, "'Garantierter Kapitalismus': Subventionspolitik und Wirtschaftsordnung in Deutschland zwischen 1925 und 1932," *ZfU* 22 (1977): 50–70.

12. Gerhard Kroll, *Von der Weltwirtschaftskrise zur Staatskonjunktur* (Berlin, 1958), pp. 131–93. See also the polemical work by Claus-Dieter Krohn, *Wirtschaftstheorien als politische Interessen* (Frankfurt, 1981).

13. See the articles of Knut Borchardt, now collected in his *Wachstum, Krisen, Handlungsspielräume der Wirtschaftspolitik* (Göttingen, 1982), pp. 165ff. Cf. the critique by Claus-Dieter Krohn, "'Ökonomische Zwangslagen' und das Scheitern der Weimarer Republik," *G & G* 8 (1982): 415–26.

14. On the attitudes of the Ruhr industrialists, see Weisbrod, *Schwerindustrie*. For a useful summary in English of Weisbrod's interpretation of Ruhr heavy industry's role, see his article, "Economic power and political stability reconsidered: heavy industry in Weimar Germany," *SH* 4 (1979): 241–63.

15. Weisbrod, *Schwerindustrie*, pp. 31–51.

16. Ibid., pp. 145–214.

17. On the following, see Ursula Hüllbüsch, "Der Ruhreisenstreit in gewerkschaftlicher Sicht," in Mommsen et al. (eds.), *Industrielles System*, pp. 271–89; Michael Schneider, *Auf dem Weg in die Krise* (Wentorf bei Hamburg, 1974); Weisbrod, *Schwerindustrie*, pp. 415–56. A recent study shows a majority of the industrial backers of the lockout unwilling to push it to a confrontation with governmental authority, see Gerald D. Feldman and Irmgard Steinisch, "Notwendigkeiten und Grenzen sozialstaatlicher Intervention," *AfS* 20 (1980): 57–117.

18. On the following, see Jörg-Otto Spiller, "Reformismus nach rechts," in Mommsen et al. (eds.), *Industrielles System*, pp. 593–602; Weisbrod, *Schwerindustrie*, pp. 273–98.

19. Leopold, *Hugenberg*, pp. 55–67. Among Germany's nationally prominent industrialists, only two endorsed the plebiscite against the Young Plan: Emil Kirdorf and Fritz Thyssen. Some press reports linked Albert Vögler of the United Steel Works to it as well, but he publicly denied those reports: *Berliner Tageblatt*, Nov. 13, 1929 (#537). Paul Reusch privately denounced the plebiscite as a "great stupidity," and two other prominent industrialists, Robert Bosch and Hermann Bücher (AEG), signed a public protest against it that was promoted by the Social Democratic minister of the interior, Carl Severing: Spiller, "Reformismus nach rechts," pp. 597f.

20. On the following, see Helga Timm, *Die deutsche Sozialpolitik und der Bruch der grossen Koalition im März 1930* (Düsseldorf, 1952); Weisbrod, *Schwerindustrie*, pp. 457–77; Albin Gladen, "Probleme staatlicher Sozialpolitik in der Weimarer Republik," in Mommsen et al. (eds.), *Industrielles System*, pp. 248–59.

21. "Aufstieg oder Niedergang?," *Veröffentlichungen des Reichsverbandes der Deutschen Industrie*, no. 49 (1929); "Wirtschafts- und Sozialpolitik. Steuer- und Finanzpolitik," ibid. no. 50 (1930).

22. See, for example, the remarks by the steel industrialist Albert Vögler at a meeting of the Reichsverband in 1924 in which he lamented the loss of the

"überparteilicher Staat" of the past and expressed hope it could be re-covered in the future: Schneider, *Unternehmer und Demokratie,* p. 55.

23. This was succinctly articulated by a spokesman of IG Farben, Hermann Hummel, at a meeting of the Reichsverband in 1925 when he stated that if the country's entrepreneurs accepted the new form of government, then the state and the citizenry should accept the existing economy: Weisbrod, *Schwerindustrie,* p. 247.

24. Schneider, *Unternehmer und Demokratie,* pp. 85–92, 149f.

25. Ibid. Also Heinrich August Winkler, "Unternehmer und Wirtschafts-demokratie in der Weimarer Republik," *PVJS* 11 (1970): 308–22, Son-derheft 2.

26. Schneider, *Unternehmer und Demokratie,* pp. 166f.; Döhn, *Politik und Interesse,* p. 383.

27. Heinrich August Winkler, "Unternehmerverbände zwischen Stände-ideologie und Nationalsozialismus," *VfZ* 17 (1969): 341–71. See also Ulrich Nocken, "Corporatism and Pluralism in Modern German History," in *Indus-trielle Gesellschaft und politisches System,* ed. by Dirk Stegmann, Bernd-Jürgen Wendt, and Peter-Christian Witt (Bonn, 1978), pp. 37–56.

28. Plans for constitutional alterations were developed by the Bund zur Er-neuerung des Reiches, formed in 1928 under the leadership of former chancellor Hans Luther. See Luther's memoir, *Vor dem Abgrund 1930–1933* (Berlin, 1964); also the tendentious sketch by Kurt Gosweiler, "Bund zur Erneuerung des Reiches (BER)," in Dieter Fricke et al. (eds.), *Die bür-gerlichen Parteien in Deutschland,* 2 vols. (East Berlin, 1968), I, pp. 195–200.

29. "Industrie-Politik," issue of Sept. 23, 1929 (#710). For the full text of the speech by Duisberg quoted therein, see *Veröffentlichungen des Reichsverbandes der Deutschen Industrie,* no. 48 (1929), pp. 10–23.

Chapter II, section 1: Patrons of the Fledgling Movement

1. For the founding and early period of the party, see Dietrich Orlow, *The History of the Nazi Party,* 2 vols. (Pittsburgh, 1969–73), I, pp. 11ff.; also the apologetic but informative book by Georg Franz-Willing, *Die Hitlerbewegung. Der Ursprung, 1919–1922* (Hamburg and Berlin, 1962). For a statistical analysis of the early membership, see Donald M. Douglas, "The Parent Cell," *CEH* 10 (1977): 55–72.

2. An English translation of the 1920 program is in Jeremy Noakes and Geof-frey Pridham (eds.), *Documents on Nazism* (New York, 1975), pp. 38–40.

3. These rumors are alluded to in the articles cited in n. 7, below.

4. "Emil Gansser," obituary by Hans-Heinrich Lammers, *VB,* Jan. 17, 1941 (#17); for further information on the origins of Hitler's appearance before the club see the recollections of one of Gansser's friends: Wilhelm Weicher to Lammers, Jan. 18, 1941, in NSDAP HA, roll 52, folder 1223. In 1942 Hitler recalled his appearance but erroneously placed it in 1921: *Hitler's Secret Conversations, 1941–1944* (New York, 1953), p. 509. For a summary of the talk based on the recollections of three men who had attended, see Julius Karl von Engelbrechten and Hans Volz, *Wir wandern durch das nation-alsozialistische Berlin* (Munich, 1937), pp. 15f., 53. The unedited text of the summary is printed in Hitler, *Sämtliche Aufzeichnungen 1905–1924,* ed. by

Eberhard Jäckel (Stuttgart, 1980), pp. 642f. A later account by a man who attended provides little information about the content of Hitler's speech, but depicts the club and its members: Wilhelm Weicher, "Wie ich Adolf Hitler kennenlernte," *Der Türmer* 36 (Apr., 1934), pp. 90f. On Gansser, see *Hitler's Secret Conversations*, p. 179; Franz-Willing, *Hitlerbewegung . . . 1919–1922*, pp. 137, 184f. 196f.; Ernst Hanfstaengl, *Zwischen Weissem und Braunem Haus* (Munich, 1970), pp. 66, 69f., where Gansser is erroneously identified as a board member at Siemens; Albrecht Tyrell, *Vom 'Trommler' zum 'Führer'* (Munich, 1975), p. 259, n. 440. Werner Jochmann (ed.), *Nationalsozialismus und Revolution* (Frankfurt, 1963), pp. 98, 139, which documents his career as a Nazi Reichstag deputy from May to Dec. 1924; BDC, Partei Kanzlei Korrespondenz: Dr. Emil Gansser. See the text of Gansser's invitation in Albrecht Tyrell (ed.), *Führer befiehl . . .* (Düsseldorf, 1969), p. 46.

5. Engelbrechten und Volz, *Wir wandern*, p. 54.

6. Aust testified at length about these events in a slander trial brought by Hitler in 1929; see NSDAP HA, 69/1507, Privatklagesache Hitler/Dr. Strausse wegen Beleidigung. See also Aust's testimony before the commission investigating the antecedents of the beer hall putsch of 1923, reprinted in part in Ernst Deuerlein (ed.), *Der Hitler-Putsch* (Stuttgart, 1962), p. 63.

7. "Die Geldgeber der Nationalsozialisten," *Fränkische Tagespost*, Dec. 16, 1922 (#295); "Die Geldgeber der Nationalsozialisten," *Frankfurter Zeitung*, Dec. 21, 1922 (#916); "Die Geldgeber des Herrn Hitler," *Münchener Post*, Dec. 21, 1922 (#297).

8. See n. 6, above.

9. *Hitler's Secret Conversations* (1953), p. 67. He had received more financial aid in the early years of the party from Berlin and Württemberg than from Munich, he maintained in these remarks of 1941.

10. Müller and Stockfisch, "Borsig und die Demokratie," pp. 1–44; Eduard Stadtler, *Antibolschewist*, pp. 48f. ZAP, Alldeutscher Verband, file 202; Fritz Detert, Borsig's private secretary, to Borsig's son, Oct. 23, 1937: DWI, Records of the Deutsche Bank und Disconto-Gesellschaft, Generalsekretäriat Dr. von Stauss, Part of this letter is quoted in Radandt, *Kriegsverbrecherkonzern*, pp. 12–15.

11. For this and much of the following, see the letter by Detert cited in the previous note. No evidence supports the contention that Borsig arranged for Hitler's second appearance: Dirk Stegmann, "Zwischen Repression und Manipulation," *AfS* 12 (1972): 413, n. 256.

12. "'Hitlers Gönner.' Eine Zuschrift des Herrn v. Borsig," *Berliner Tageblatt*, Mar. 12, 1927 (#120).

13. See Burhenne's letter to Hans-Heinrich Lammers, Jan. 30, 1942, and Gansser's letters to Burhenne, in NSDAP HA, 52/1223. Three of those letters appear in Kurt Gossweiler, *Kapital, Reichswehr und NSDAP 1919–1924* (Cologne, 1982), pp. 558–60, where Burhenne is identified as a "Direktor" at Siemens, a post he attained only later: Gossweiler, *Kapital*, p. 346. On Burhenne's role at Siemens, see Jürgen Kocka, *Unternehmensverwaltung und Angestelltenschaft am Beispiel Siemens 1847–1914* (Stuttgart, 1969), p. 447.

14. Burhenne to Lammers, Jan. 30, 1942: NSDAP HA, 52/1223.

15. Fritz Detert to Borsig's son, Oct. 23, 1937 (see n. 10, above).

16. "Hitlers Geldgeber," *Bayerischer Kurier*, Jan. 5, 1928 (#5); "'Hitlers Gönner,' Eine Zuschrift des Herrn v. Borsig," *Berliner Tageblatt*, Mar. 12, 1927 (#120).

17. Hanfstaengl, *Zwischen Weissem und Braunem Haus*, pp. 69f.

18. Engelbrechten and Volz, *Wir wandern*, pp. 10f. This party publication explains the late beginnings of the Berlin organization in terms of the Prussian government's ban on Nazi activities. That ban did not, however, prevent the NSDAP from organizing in other parts of Prussia.

19. Alexander Glaser to Reusch, Apr. 18, 1921: GHH, 30019393/5. Reusch to Glaser, Apr. 23, 1921, ibid.

20. Reusch to Glaser, May 8, 1921, ibid.

21. "'Kapital' und 'Arbeiter,'" *Berliner Tageblatt*, Dec. 30, 1922 (#594), quoting from *Die württembergische Industrie*.

22. See Hitler's memorandum of Oct. 22, 1922, one of whose purposes was clearly fund-raising: Tyrell (ed.), *Führer befiehl . . .* , pp. 47–55. See also the secondhand account of Hitler's efforts to raise funds in Berlin, written in September 1933 by W. von Zezschwitz, a friend of Hitler's companion on that trip, Dietrich Eckart: BAK, NS 26/1308.

23. See the biographical sketch by Kurt Roselius in Wilhelm Lührs (ed.) *Bremische Biographien 1912–1962* (Bremen, 1969), pp. 420f. Also, Hans-Otto Wesemann, "Schöpfer der Böttcherstrasse," in Gustav Stein (ed.), *Unternehmer in der Politik* (Düsseldorf, 1954), pp. 203–13.

24. Roselius, *Briefe und Schriften zu Deutschlands Erneuerung* (Oldenburg, 1933), pp. 5f.

25. See the excerpt from a report on his speech of Jan. 18, 1923, in Hitler, *Sämtliche Aufzeichnungen*, p. 797.

26. Rumors about aid from Stinnes for the Nazis had first surfaced as early as 1920: Franz-Willing, *Hitlerbewegung . . . 1919–1922*, pp. 90, 189.

27. The most thorough study of Stinnes's career finds no basis for the allegations of aid for the NSDAP either by him or by his ambitious subordinate, Friedrich Minoux, who broke with Stinnes early in October 1923 and was frequently mentioned in conservative circles prior to the beer hall putsch as a candidate for a dictatorial directorate that would replace the Republic: Wulf, *Stinnes*. For a recent portrayal of Stinnes as a Nazi, see Hans-Hermann Hartwich, "Parteien und Verbände in der Spätphase der Weimarer Republik," in Volker Rittberger (ed.), *1933: Wie die Republik der Diktatur erlag* (Stuttgart, 1983), p. 87. Among East German historians Stinnes still ranks as a significant financier of Nazism: Pätzold and Weissbecker, *Geschichte der NSDAP*, p. 69.

28. See his speeches of November 1921 and February 1923 in Hitler, *Sämtliche Aufzeichnungen*, pp. 521, 836; also *Mein Kampf*, 11th ed. (Munich, 1933), I, p. 257.

29. On Thyssen's background, see Wilhelm Treue and Helmut Uebbing, *Die Feuer verlöschen nie. August Thyssen-Hütte 1926–1966* (Düsseldorf and Vienna, 1966), esp. pp. 198ff.; also Harold J. Gordon, *The Reichswehr and the German Republic, 1919–1926* (Princeton, 1957), pp. 255f.

30. Thyssen, *I Paid Hitler* (New York, 1941), p. 82. On the origins and limitations of this volume, see my article, "Fritz Thyssen und 'I paid Hitler,'" *VfZ* 19 (1971): 225–44.

31. T/RP (IfZ), stenogram, sheet 278; NA, RG 238, NI-042, "Interview with Mr. Thyssen," Mar. 1, 1946; ibid., Pre-Trial Interrogations, Thyssen, Sept. 4, 1945.

32. For the vain efforts of the police to find records of the party's finances, see NSDAP HA, 26A/1765 and 68/1497.

33. See Franz-Willing, *Hitlerbewegung . . . 1919–1922*, pp. 187, 190; Harold J. Gordon, "Ritter von Epp und Berlin, 1919–1923," *WWR* 9 (1959): 333f.

34. Alfred Kruck, *Geschichte des Alldeutschen Verbandes, 1890–1939* (Wiesbaden, 1954), pp. 192f. Also, memorandum in a Partei-Kanzlei file for 1932 about a conversation between Paul Bang of the league and a Dr. Keller, in NA, RG 242, Microcopy T-81, roll 1, frame 11317. See also the undocumented assertions by Georg Franz-Willing in his *Krisenjahr der Hitlerbewegung* (Preussisch Oldendorf, 1975), pp. 203f.

35. On the noblemen, see *Hitler's Secret Conversations* (1953), pp. 180, 498. On the White Russians, see Robert C. Williams, *Culture in Exile: Russian Emigres in Germany, 1881–1941* (Ithaca, 1972), p. 167, where the author fails to provide conclusive documentation. On the Swiss sympathizers, whom Hitler visited during the summer of 1923 in one of his rare trips outside Germany, see Beat Glaus, *Die Nationale Front. Eine Schweizer faschistische Bewegung* (Zurich, 1969), pp. 27f.; Franz-Willing, *Hitlerbewegung . . . 1919–1922,* pp. 196f. On the widow from Finland, who was apparently Gertrud von Sedlitz, see ibid., p. 187; also her deposition of Feb. 2, 1929, in NSDAP HA, 69/1507. There were repeated rumors during 1923 that the French government subsidized the NSDAP in order to disrupt the German state; Hitler responded with two libel suits, both of which he won: Franz-Willing, *Hitlerbewegung . . . 1919–1922*, p. 189; and "Eine Abrechnung," *VB*, Apr. 20, 1926 (#89). Much information on the party's early benefactors was brought to light by a Bavarian parliamentary investigating committee in early 1924, excerpts from whose findings were published in SPD Landesausschuss Bayern, *Hitler und Kahr: Die Bayerischen Napoleonsgrössen von 1923* (Munich, 1928), esp. part II, pp. 98–105.

36. See the police interrogation of Eckart, Nov. 15, 1923: LC, Manuscript Division, Rehse Collection; also Eckart's boast in the *Völkischer Beobachter* in 1922 that a considerable portion of the party's early financial resources were attributable to him, quoted in Konrad Heiden, *Hitler: Das Zeitalter der Verantwortungslosigkeit* (Zürich, 1936), p. 250. Eckart also proved valuable as a go-between to others: Margarete Plewnia, *Auf dem Weg zu Hitler. Der 'völkische' Publizist Dietrich Eckart* (Bremen, 1970), pp. 69–71.

37. The German version of Hanfstaengl's memoirs, *Zwischen Weissem und Braunem Haus*, is more detailed than the earlier English-language version.

38. Hanfstaengl, *Zwischen Weissem und Braunem Haus*, pp. 60, 66, 188.

39. See Ludecke's memoirs, *I Knew Hitler* (New York, 1937), esp. pp. 101–8.

40. Günter Schubert, *Anfänge nationalsozialistischer Aussenpolitik* (Cologne, 1963), pp. 148–50.

41. Ludecke, *I Knew Hitler*, pp. 69, 139, 141, 145, 191–201. His account of his mission to Italy has been corroborated by other evidence: Walter Werner Pese, "Hitler und Italien, 1920–1926," *VfZ* 3 (1955): 117. Rumors of subsidies from Ford for the NSDAP spread from the German press to *The New York Times* in 1922 (ed. of Dec. 20). The American diplomat assigned the

task of tracking down these rumors asked Hitler in early 1923 whether there was any truth to them and received a negative answer: Robert D. Murphy, *Diplomat Among Warriors* (New York, 1964), p. 23. Hitler was scarcely a reliable source of information, of course, but in this instance he apparently spoke the truth; no scrap of evidence has ever been found to corroborate the persistent rumor that Ford subsidized the NSDAP. Nor do the efforts of Ludecke and others to obtain aid from Italian Fascists seem to have produced any yield: Schubert, *Anfänge,* pp. 206–19; Alan Cassels, "Mussolini and German Nationalism," *JMH* 25 (1963): 137ff.

42. On the Munich backers of the party, see *Hitler's Secret Conversations* (1953), pp. 179f.; and Ludecke, *I Knew Hitler,* pp. 92f. The lower Bavarian farmer was Simon Eckart (no relation to Dietrich Eckart), who supplied security for a bank loan that enabled the *Völkischer Beobachter* to weather one of its early crises: see his obituary in *VB*, (Bayerische Ausgabe), Apr. 23, 1936 (#114); and the letter to Simon Eckart from Bernhard Schick, former director of the Munich Hansa-Bank, June 6, 1935, now in BAK, NS 26/1218. The Augsburg spice and cooking-oil processor was Gottfried Grandel, who also provided security for a key loan to the early party and claimed to have made good on it when the Nazis defaulted: see Tyrell, *Vom 'Trommler zum 'Führer,'* p. 255; also Grandel's lengthy letter of Oct. 22, 1941, to the Nazi Hauptarchiv, in NSDAP HA, 26/514; also his letter to Hitler, Oct. 27, 1920, in NA, RG 242, Microcopy T-84, 5/4337–38; also letter to author from Assessor Geislinger, deputy Hauptgeschäftsführer, Industrie- und Handelskammer Augsburg, Sept. 6, 1971. Grandel took an active part in radical *völkisch* politics and was indicted for an attempt on the life of General Hans von Seeckt in 1924, but acquitted in the subsequent trial: see Cuno Horkenbach (ed.), *Das Deutsche Reich von 1918 bis heute* (Berlin, 1930), p. 194. The Swabian undergarment manufacturer was Heinrich Becker of the town of Geislingen, an active SA member; see anon., *Hitler und sein Anhang,* pp. 15–22; also NSDAP HA, 69/1507, Dr. Landmann to Polizeidirektion München, Apr. 15, 1930. The Ersatz coffee partner was Richard Franck; see *Hitler's Secret Conversations* (1953), p. 179 (where the name is misspelled and Franck is erroneously characterized as the "wheat man," presumably a mistaken translation of Kornfranck, a nickname alluding to his firm's coffee substitute, which was made from grains; also Franz-Willing, *Hitlerbewegung . . . 1919–1922,* pp. 184, 192f.; also Alfred Marquard, *100 Jahre Franck, 1828–1928* (n.p., n.d.), pp. 14, 51f., 94f.

43. One such financial crisis threatened to shut down the *Völkischer Beobachter* as late as the autumn of 1921; see telegram from Dietrich Eckart to Emil Gansser, Nov. 28, 1921, now in BAK, NS 26/1317.

44. See the police report of Jan. 26, 1923, in NSDAP HA, 69/1507; also Franz-Willing, *Krisenjahr,* pp. 158f.

45. Franz-Willing, *Hitlerbewegung . . . 1919–1922,* pp. 192f.

46. Just when Hitler met the Bechsteins and Bruckmanns remains unclear. Frau Bechstein testified in 1924 to having been introduced to Hitler by the *völkisch* poet and dramatist Dietrich Eckart: SPD Landesausschuss Bayern, *Hitler und Kahr,* II, p. 102. In his memoirs the Munich historian Karl Alexander von Müller maintained that Frau Bruckmann met Hitler only in 1924: *Im Wandel einer Welt* (Munich, 1966), p. 300. However, this is contra-

dicted by other evidence; see Hellmuth Auerbach, "Hitlers politische Lehrjahre und die Münchener Gesellschaft 1919–1923," *VfZ* 25 (1977): 34, n. 152.

47. An habitué of Frau Bruckmann's salon later described such an arrival by Hitler, which he placed at Hanfstaengl's house, however: Müller, *Im Wandel einer Welt,* p. 129; see also Müller's description of how Hitler captured and held the attention of the other guests at Frau Bruckmann's salon, in ibid., pp. 301–3. See also the description of Hitler's relationship with Frau Bruckmann in Ulrich von Hassell, *Vom andern Deutschland* (Frankfurt and Hamburg, 1964), pp. 24, 36, 97f., 184, 242.

48. Baldur von Schirach, *Ich glaubte an Hitler* (Hamburg, 1967), pp. 66f.

49. Georg Wenzel (ed.), *Deutscher Wirtschaftsführer* (Hamburg, 1929), col. 122. *Handbuch der Deutschen Aktien-Gesellschaften,* Ausgabe 1926, vol. 4 (Berlin and Leipzig, 1927), pp. 6001f.

50. SPD Landesausschuss Bayern, *Hitler und Kahr,* II, p. 102. This claim would seem substantiated by Hitler's reference in 1942 to Bechstein's aid for the newspaper in 1923: *Hitler's Secret Conversations (1953),* p. 179.

51. Hanfstaengl, *Zwischen Weissem und Braunem Haus,* p. 76.

52. SPD Landesausschuss Bayern, *Hitler und Kahr,* II, p. 102.

53. Statement by Karl Rosenhauer, Director of Deutsche Hansabank, to Amtsgericht München, Jan. 14, 1929, in NSDAP HA, 69/1507.

54. *Das Deutsche Führerlexikon 1934/1935* (Berlin, 1934), pp. 75f.

55. *Handbuch der Deutschen Aktiengesellschaften,* Ausgabe 1926, vol. 2, pp. 3314f.

56. Müller, *Im Wandel einer Welt,* p. 307.

57. For the following, see Schirach, *Ich glaubte an Hitler,* pp. 54f. Friedrich Christian Prinz zu Schaumburg-Lippe, *Zwischen Krone und Kerker* (Wiesbaden, 1952), pp. 74ff.

58. Müller, *Im Wandel einer Welt,* p. 301.

59. Winfried Schüler, *Der Bayreuther Kreis von seiner Entstehung bis zum Ausgang der wilhelminischen Ära* (Münster, 1971), p. 85.

60. Roderick Stackelberg, "Houston S. Chamberlain: From Monarchism to National Socialism," *WLB* 31 (1978): 124.

61. See chapter II, section 4.

62. See chapter VI, section 4.

63. Hildegard Brenner, *Die Kunstpolitik des Nationalsozialismus* (Hamburg, 1963), pp. 7–10.

64. This is apparent from Bruckmann's correspondence in 1932 with Alfred Rosenberg about the Kampfbund, in NA, RG 242, Microcopy T-454, 71/1402–11.

65. Jeremy Noakes, *The Nazi Party in Lower Saxony, 1921–1933* (Oxford, 1971), p. 17; Franz-Willing, *Krisenjahr,* p. 162. Hitler in *VB,* Feb. 14, 1923, reprinted in Hitler, *Sämtliche Aufzeichnungen,* p. 831.

66. Martin Vogt, "Zur Finanzierung der NSDAP zwischen 1924 und 1928," *GWU* 21 (1970): 238.

67. Franz-Willing, *Hitlerbewegung . . . 1919–1922,* p. 182.

68. Heinrich Hoffmann, *Hitler Was My Friend* (London, 1955), p. 62.

69. Franz-Willing, *Hitlerbewegung . . . 1919–1922,* p. 186.

70. NSDAP HA, 69/1507, report of Polizeidirektion, Munich, on NSDAP, Feb. 6, 1923.

Chapter II, section 2: The Cacophony of Nazi Economic Policies

1. Rosenberg, *Wesen, Grundsätze und Ziele der Nationalsozialistischen Deutschen Arbeiterpartei* (Munich, 1923). Although dated 1923, the publication actually appeared in November 1922: Hans Volz, *Daten aus der Geschichte des Nationalsozialismus*, 9th ed. (Berlin and Leipzig, 1939), p. 10.
2. Rosenberg, *Wesen*, pp. 8–9.
3. Ibid., pp. 27f.
4. Ibid.
5. Ibid., pp. 28f.
6. Ibid., p. 25.
7. Ibid., pp. 28f.
8. *Der Deutsche Staat auf nationaler und sozialer Grundlage. Neue Wege in Staat, Finanz und Wirtschaft* (Munich, 1923). All citations here are from the second edition, also issued in 1923. On Feder's career, see Albrecht Tyrell, "Gottfried Feder and the NSDAP," in Peter Stachura (ed.), *The Shaping of the Nazi State* (London, 1978).
9. Feder, *Staat*, p. 43. It was symptomatic of how casually programmatic matters were regarded in the NSDAP that a typographic error in the 1923 edition of Feder's book that misdated the adoption of the Twenty-Five Points of 1920 as "24. Februar 1923" had still not been corrected in the fifth edition, which appeared in 1932 (p. 40).
10. Ibid., pp. 45–49.
11. Feder, *Das Programm der N.S.D.A.P. und seine weltanschaulichen Grundgedanken* (Munich, 1927).
12. Feder, *Staat*, pp. 21f.
13. Ibid., p. 23.
14. Ibid.; the quoted portion appears on p. 16.
15. Ibid., p. 45.
16. Ibid., p. 76.
17. Ibid., pp. 22f.
18. Ibid., p. 23.
19. Ibid., p. 45.
20. Feder, *Programm*, p. 37f.
21. Ibid., p. 47.
22. Ibid., p. 52.
23. Feder, *Das Programm*, 16th ed. (Munich, 1930), p. 24.
24. Issue of March 18, 1930, quoted in Reinhard Kühnl, *Die nationalsozialistische Linke 1925–1930* (Meisenheim am Glan, 1966), pp. 235f.
25. Ibid. Also Max Kele, *Nazis and Workers. National Socialist Appeals to German Labor, 1919–1933* (Chapel Hill, 1972).
26. Kele, *Nazis and Workers*, pp. 40f., 119f.
27. These ideas received their fullest articulation in the draft program that originated with Gregor Strasser in late 1925 and was quashed by Hitler a few months later. See Reinhard Kühnl, "Zur Programmatik der nationalsozialistischen Linken: Das Strasser-Programm von 1925–26," *VfZ* 14 (1966): 317–33.
28. Quoted in Kele, *Nazis and Workers*, p. 119.

29. Quoted in Kühnl, *Linke*, p. 72.

30. Ibid., p. 73.

31. Ibid., p. 72.

32. Ibid., p. 15f.

33. "Warum Arbeiterpartei?" *Der Angriff*, July 23, 1928 (#30).

34. See, for example, the letter from one of IG Farben's parliamentary spokesmen, Paul Moldenhauer, to the chairman of that firm's supervisory board, Carl Duisberg, July 9, 1924; BAL, Autographensammlung Duisberg. For an example of the press coverage, see an article in the conservative *Deutsche Allgemeine Zeitung* of Oct. 16, 1930 (#484): "Die Flut der Agitationsantrage."

35. Wilhelm Frick, *Die Nationalsozialisten im Reichstag 1924–1931* (Munich, 1932), pp. 93, 100f.

36. See, for example, the draft bill presented by the Nazi deputies in May 1929: *Verhandlungen des Reichstages* (Anlagen), vol. 436, #1034. That same bill was reintroduced in October 1930: Frick, *Reichstag*, p. 94.

37. Frick, *Reichstag*, p. 124.

38. See, for examples, *Verhandlungen*, vol. 423, pp. 775f., 811–14.

39. Horkenbach (ed.), *Das Deutsche Reich* (1930), p. 214.

40. *Verhandlungen*, vol. 394, p. 12221.

41. Ibid., vol. 393, pp. 11359, 11380–83.

42. Ibid., vol. 234, pp. 215–18; vol. 424, pp. 1946–50.

43. Ibid., vol. 423, pp. 304f, 399–410.

44. Ibid., vol. 393, pp. 10610, 10634–37; Frick, *Reichstag*, p. 134.

45. *Verhandlungen*, vol. 387, pp. 4281–89.

46. Ibid., vol. 423, pp. 305, 400.

47. Ibid., vol. 424, pp. 1126ff.

48. Kühnl, "Zur Programmatik," pp. 318–23.

49. Volz, *Daten*, p. 22. See also Tyrell, "Gottfried Feder and the NSDAP," p. 85, n. 111.

50. Kele, *Nazis and Workers*, pp. 149–51.

51. Ibid., pp. 156–60.

52. Tyrell (ed.), *Führer befiehl . . .* , pp. 294–96.

53. Buchner, *Grundriss einer nationalsozialistischen Volkswirtschaftstheorie* (Munich, 1930).

54. Ibid., pp. 10, 19–21.

55. Ibid., p. 43.

56. Ibid., p. 22.

57. *Verhandlungen*, vol. 427, p. 4766.

58. See, for an example, the discrepancies in two editions of Feder, *Programm*, mentioned above. For alterations in Rosenberg, *Wesen*, compare the 1933 edition with the original.

59. Rosenberg, *Das Wesensgefüge des Nationalsozialismus. Grundlagen der deutschen Wiedergeburt* (Munich, 1932); Feder, *Was will Adolf Hitler? Das Programm der N.S.D.A.P.* (Munich, 1931).

60. Alfred Pfaff, *Der Wirtschafts-Aufbau im Dritten Reich* (Munich, 1932); Ottokar Lorenz, *Die Beseitigung der Arbeitslosigheit* (Berlin, [1932]).

Chapter II, section 3: Hitler's Economics

1. See the memoirs of Lutz Graf Schwerin von Krosigk, *Staatsbankrott* (Göttingen, 1974), pp. 189f.; also those of Albert Krebs, *Tendenzen und Gestalten*. (Stuttgart, 1959), pp. 149f.; also Hermann Rauschning, *Gespräche mit Hitler* (Zurich, 1940), pp. 26f. Hitler's ignorance of economics has been analyzed by Wilhelm Treue in "Hitlers Denkschrift zum Vierjahrsplan 1936," *VfZ* 3 (1955): 196–202; and by Burton H. Klein, *Germany's Economic Preparations for War* (Cambridge, Mass., 1959), p. 170. Despite its title, John D. Heyl's article, "Hitler's Economic Thought: A Reappraisal," *CEH* 6 (1973): 83–96, deals mainly with the relationship between political authority and economic policy during the Third Reich, rather than with Hitler's attitudes toward economic matters. I have dealt more extensively with the matters treated here in an article, "Hitlers Einstellung zu sozial-ökonomischen Fragen vor der 'Machtergreifung,'" *G & G* 2 (1976): 89–117. For two responses to that article, see Avraham Barkai, "Sozialdarwinismus und Antiliberalismus in Hitlers Wirtschaftskonzept," in *G & G* 3 (1977): 406–17; and Peter Krüger, "Zu Hitlers 'nationalsozialistischen Wirtschaftserkenntnissen'," in *G & G* 6 (1980): 263–82. See also Barkai's *Das Wirtschaftssystem des Nationalsozialismus* (Cologne, 1977), esp. pp. 25–30.
2. Speech of Sept. 18, 1922, quoted—along with other examples—in Turner, "Hitlers Einstellung," p. 90. Despite this conviction, Hitler confessed to the fear that if a party of Weltanschauung took up economic issues, these would drain away energy from the political tasks at hand: *Mein Kampf*, 2 vols. (Munich, 1933), II, p. 680.
3. *Mein Kampf*, I, pp. 164f.
4. Turner, "Hitlers Einstellung," pp. 91f.
5. *Mein Kampf*, I, pp. 166–68.
6. Turner, "Hitlers Einstellung," p. 91.
7. *Mein Kampf*, I, pp. 166ff.
8. Ibid., pp. 255, 257.
9. Ibid., p. 168.
10. Turner, "Hitlers Einstellung," p. 92f.
11. *Hitlers zweites Buch* (Stuttgart, 1961), p. 53.
12. The development of Hitler's ideas on foreign policy has been most thoroughly examined in Axel Kuhn, *Hitlers aussenpolitisches Programm* (Stuttgart, 1970).
13. Hitler, "Warum musste ein 8. November kommen?" in *Deutschlands Erneuerung* 8 (1924): 205.
14. See, for example, Rauschning, *Gespräche*, (Zurich, 1940), pp. 35–47; see also H. A. Turner, Jr., "Fascism and Modernization," *World Politics* 24 (1972): 547–64.
15. See Barkin, *Controversy*.
16. This theme appeared in Hitler's speeches as early as 1921: Hitler, *Sämtliche Aufzeichnungen*, p. 505; see also Hitler, "Warum musste ein 8. November kommen?" pp. 199f.; *Mein Kampf*, I, pp. 255f.
17. *Hitlers zweites Buch*, pp. 61f.; see also *Mein Kampf*, I, pp. 47, 288–92; H. A. Turner, Jr., "Hitler's Secret Pamphlet for Industrialists, 1927" *JMH* 40 (1968): 359; Rauschning, *Gespräche*, p. 56.

18. *Mein Kampf*, I, pp. 49f., 370.

19. Ibid., p. 257.

20. *Mein Kampf*, II, p. 776. See also, for his denunciations of Cuno in speeches, Hitler, *Sämtliche Aufzeichnungen*, pp. 922f., 930f., 981–87, 1003f.

21. Rauschning, *Gespräche*, p. 26. For the dating of this passage I have relied on Theodor Schieder, *Hermann Rauschnings "Gespräche mit Hitler" als Geschichtsquelle* (Opladen, 1972), p. 63.

22. *Hitlers Secret Conversations* (1953), p. 60; cf. the German text, from which the translation departs: Hitler, *Monologe im Führerhauptquartier 1941–1944*, edited by Werner Jochmann (Hamburg, 1980), pp. 93f.

23. Turner, "Hitlers Einstellung," p. 95f. This theme runs consistently through Otto Wagener's recapitulations of his many conversations with Hitler: H. A. Turner, Jr., (ed.), *Hitler aus nächster Nähe. Aufzeichnungen eines Vertrauten, 1929–1932* (Berlin and Frankfurt, 1978).

24. *Mein Kampf*, II, pp. 570f.; *Hitlers zweites Buch*, p. 55.

25. *Mein Kampf*, II, p. 421; Hitler, "Warum musste ein 8. November kommen?" pp. 200, 203.

26. "Warum musste ein 8. November Kommen?" pp. 200f.; *Mein Kampf*, II, pp. 420, 498f.

27. Early in his political career he publicly called for socialization measures, but only for natural resources and banking: Hitler, *Sämtliche Aufzeichnungen*, pp. 177, 218 (speeches of Aug. 1920). Those proposals soon dropped out of his repertoire.

28. Tyrell, *Vom 'Trommler' zum 'Führer,'* pp. 84f.

29. *Mein Kampf*, II, p. 511.

30. Quoted in the fictionalized memoirs of a Nazi who claimed to have been present: Bodo Uhse, *Söldner und Soldat*, 2nd ed. (East Berlin, 1956), p. 180. A much more extensive attack on socialism was attributed to Hitler by Otto Strasser after he broke with the NSDAP in 1930: Otto Strasser, *Aufbau des deutschen Sozialismus*, 2nd ed. (Prague, 1936), pp. 116–36. Strasser's writings are, however, highly polemical, and he cannot be regarded as a reliable source of information.

31. Krebs, *Tendenzen*, p. 143.

32. Ernst Boepple (ed.), *Adolf Hitlers Reden* (Munich, 1934), p. 25.

33. Ibid., p. 32.

34. Report on Hitler's speech of Jan. 29, 1923: "Die Delegiertenversammlung," *VB*, Jan. 31, 1923 (#9).

35. Rauschning, *Gespräche*, pp. 179–81.

36. Norbert Schausberger, "Österreich und die deutsche Wirtschaftsexpansion nach dem Donauraum," in *Österreich in Geschichte und Literatur* 16 (1972): 197. I am indebted to Prof. Peter Hayes for bringing this metaphor to my attention.

37. *Mein Kampf*, II, p. 451.

38. Ibid., pp. 480–85.

39. Ibid., I, pp. 232f.

40. Hitler, *Sämtliche Aufzeichnungen*, passim.

41. *Mein Kampf*, I, pp. 256f, 369f; II, pp. 485f. See also "Nazi Economic Policy. Hitler Interviewed. Share of Wealth for All," *The Manchester Guardian*, Aug. 20, 1932.

42. *Mein Kampf,* I, pp. 366f., 369–73.

43. Ibid., II, pp. 672–77. See also his speech in Zwickau on July 15, 1925, in the anonymous leaflet, *Rede eines Mannes, dem das Reden verboten wird* (Zwickau, 1925). I am indebted to Dr. Axel Kuhn for providing me with a copy of the latter document.

44. *Mein Kampf,* II, p. 774; speech to Hamburg National Club on February 28, 1926, published in Werner Jochmann (ed.), *Im Kampf um die Macht* (Frankfurt, 1960), pp. 102, 116.

45. Goebbels, *Das Tagebuch von Joseph Goebbels 1925/26,* ed. by Helmut Heiber (Stuttgart, 1960), p. 72.

46. This and the following is based on my edition of Wagener's memoirs, *Hitler aus nächster Nähe.*

47. See chapter VI, section 1.

48. Rauschning, *Gespräche,* pp. 25ff.

49. "Um die Enteignung," *VB,* Feb. 19, 1926 (#41); "Die Bamberger Tagung," ibid., Feb. 25, 1926 (#46). See also Ulrich Schüren, *Der Volksentscheid zur Fürstenenteignung 1926* (Düsseldorf, 1978), pp. 154–58.

50. Turner, "Hitlers Einstellung," pp. 106–11.

51. Turner (ed.), *Hitler aus nächster Nähe,* p. 444.

52. Hitler apparently announced in the wake of the Bamberg Conference of February 1926 that he had assigned final authority over programmatic matters to Gottfried Feder. This proved only a tactical move designed to deflect discontent with the program from him to Feder. In actuality Feder never enjoyed such authority: Wolfgang Horn, *Führerideologie und Parteiorganisation in der NSDAP* (Düsseldorf, 1972), p. 242. Feder nevertheless lay claim to that authority: *Programm,* 1st ed. (Munich, 1927), p. 10.

53. "Hitler zwischen Arbeitern und Unternehmern," *Frankfurter Zeitung,* Nov. 6, 1930 (#828).

Chapter II, section 4: An Abortive Courtship of Ruhr Industry— Nazism in Disrepute

1. NSDAP HA, 5/136, Deputy Gauleiter Schlessmann of Gau Essen-Ruhr to Reichspressestelle, Munich, May 17, 1943; also letter, Polizei-Präsident of Essen to Gauleiter Josef Terboven, May 28, 1926 (this document, now in BAK, was used while still at BDC, in the collection Reichsschatzmeister, Ordner 155).

2. The other Essen speeches took place on Dec. 3, 1926; Apr. 27, 1927; and Dec. 5, 1927 (for sources, see n. 3, below). The Königswinter speech, which seems not to have been attended by the press, took place on Dec. 1, 1926; see the photocopy of the invitation issued by the Rhenish gauleiter, Robert Ley, on Nov. 21, 1926, in Ley, *Deutschland ist schöner geworden* (Munich, 1940), opposite p. 54. Rudolf Hess later mentioned it in a letter to a Nazi living abroad, Walther Hewel, dated Mar. 30, 1927: NA, RG 238, 3753-PS, published in English translation by Gerhard Weinberg, "National Socialist Organization and Foreign Policy Aims in 1927," *JMH* 36 (1964): 428–33.

3. For the speech of June 18, 1926, which took place in a room at the Essen Vereinhaus, see: "Deutsche Wirtschafts- und Sozialpolitik. Ein Vortrag Hitlers," *Rheinisch-Westfälische Zeitung,* June 20, 1926 (#422), a report re-

printed in full in *VB*, June 24, 1926 (#142), and partially in anon., *Adolf Hitler und seine Bewegung im Lichte neutraler Beobachter und objektiver Gegner* (Munich, 1927), pp. 12–15. For the speech of Dec. 3, 1926, held in the Kammermusiksaal of the Städtischer Saalbau, see: "Volksgesundung auf nationaler Grundlage. Adolf Hitlers 2. Vortrag," *Essener Anzeiger*, Dec. 5, 1926 (#285), reprinted in *Adolf Hitler und seine Bewegung*, pp. 17–20; also "Hitler vor westdeutschen Wirtschaftlern," *Rheinisch-Westfälische Zeitung*, Dec. 4, 1926 (#850); also "Adolf Hitler vor den Wirtschaftsführern," *VB*, Dec. 8, 1926. On Hitler's speech of Apr. 27, 1927, held in the Kruppsaal of the Städtischer Saalbau, see "'Führer und Masse'. Ein Vortrag Hitlers im Essener Saalbau," *Rheinisch-Westfälische Zeitung*, Apr. 29, 1927 (#299), reprinted in full in *VB*, May 3, 1927 (#100), and partially in *Adolf Hitler und seine Bewegung*, pp. 26–27. See also the brief account in "Hitler vor den Wirtschaftsführern des Ruhrgebiets," *VB*, Apr. 29, 1927 (#97). On the speech of Dec. 5, 1927, see "Hitler sprach in Essen," *Essener Anzeiger*, Dec. 7, 1927 (#286); "Adolf Hitler spricht zu 800 Vertretern der deutschen Wirtschaft," *VB*, Dec. 10, 1927 (#285), reprinting excerpts from the *Rheinisch-Westfälische Zeitung*, the *Essener Allgemeine Zeitung*, and *Der Mittag* of Düsseldorf; see the reprinted portions of some of these accounts in Tyrell (ed.), *Führer befiehl . . .* , pp. 189f.

4. See Jochmann (ed.), *Im Kampf um die Macht*.

5. On the size of the first audience, see the letter from the Polizeipräsident of Essen to Gauleiter Terboven, May 28, 1926 (cited in n. 1, above) and the excerpt from the *Rheinisch-Westfälische Zeitung* quoted in The *Völkischer Beobachter* of Dec. 10, 1927 (cited in n. 3, above). The *VB* set attendance at Hitler's speech of Dec. 1926 at 400 (issue of Dec. 8), while Rudolf Hess later estimated it at 500 in his letter of Mar. 30, 1927, to Walther Hewel (see n. 2, above); a police agent, who could not gain entry but observed those arriving, set the gathering at 200: report of the Polizeipräsident of Essen to the Regierungspräsident, Düsseldorf, Feb. 5, 1927: HSAD, Regierung Düsseldorf, folder 16738. A police report of May 3 estimated that about 200 persons had attended Hitler's talk on April 27 (ibid.), but the *Rheinisch-Westfälische Zeitung* claimed twice as many had attended (issue of Apr. 29). The *Völkischer Beobachter* boasted that 800 heard its party leader in Dec. 1927 (issue of Dec. 10), but the other press reports agreed on the figure 600.

6. GHH, 400101290/37, letter to Vögler, Dec. 8, 1927.

7. The man in question, who remains wrapped in obscurity, was variously referred to by other Nazis as "Gauwirtschaftsberater Arnold" (Schlessmann to Reichspressestelle, May 17, 1943—see n. 1, above) and "Hüttendirektor Arnold": Friedrich Alfred Beck, *Kampf und Sieg. Geschichte der Nationalsozialistischen Deutschen Arbeiterpartei im Gau Westfalen-Süd von den Anfängen bis zur Machtübernahme* (Dortmund, 1938), p. 221; see also the report on his efforts on behalf of the local party organization, "Kampfabschnitt Gau Westfalen-Süd," *VB*, Dec. 31, 1931 (#365); also, Goebbels, *Tagebuch . . . 1925/26*, pp. 22, 53, 66f., 84, 109. The editor of the Goebbels *Tagebuch*, Helmut Heiber, has speculated that Arnold might in reality have been Robert Karl Arnhold, director of the Deutsches Institut für technische Arbeitsschulung (ibid., p. 22, n. 3). The East German historian Kurt Goss

weiler converts that speculation into a certainty without benefit of evidence, in the process shifting Arnhold's residence from Düsseldorf some thirty kilometers to the northeast to Hattingen: "Hitler und das Kapital (II)," *Blätter für deutsche und internationale Politik* 23 (1978): 1002f. On the Henrichshütte, see Paul Wiel, *Wirtschaftsgeschichte des Ruhrgebietes* (Essen, 1970), p. 254. On Arnhold's later agitation against the great firms of the Ruhr, see Ludwig Grauert to Gottfried Feder, July 14, 1933: GSAD, Rep. 77, Nr. 39, Bl. 126–27. (I am indebted to Prof. Ernst Nolte for supplying me with a copy of this document.)

8. In 1926 Goebbels mistook Friedrich Carl vom Bruck, the director of a modest metal fittings manufacturing company in Velbert, a town between Düsseldorf and Essen, for "a leading industrialist of the Ruhr": Goebbels, *Tagebuch . . . 1925/26*, pp. 57, 63. On Bruck's background, see IDW, Funcke Papers, vol. 6, part 1, "Vergangene Zeiten," section "Der Eisen und Stahlwaren-Industriebund 1919"; also BAK, Silverberg Papers, vol. 258, p. 148, letter from Kurt Sorge and Hermann Bücher of the industrial Reichsverband to Bruck, May 31, 1924, at a time when the latter was involved in a secessionist organization, the Industriellen Vereinigung. (I am indebted to Dr. Ulrich Nocken for this documentation on Bruck, who is erroneously identified in Heiber's edition of the Goebbels diary, p. 57, n. 3, as Fritz vom Bruck, a banker who was only thirty years old in 1926.) Bruck helped Gregor Strasser to launch his publishing house, the Kampfverlag, by extending him a loan of four thousand marks, against the security of Strasser's apothecary shop (Goebbels, *Tagebuch . . . 1925/26*, pp. 130–33). Bruck is thoroughly misidentified as "one of the leading men in the Hoesch-Concern" in Gossweiler, "Hitler und das Kapital (II)," p. 1003.

9. Hess to Walther Hewel, Dec. 8, 1928, which stems from the same repository as the letter by Hess cited in n. 2, above; report of *Essener Allgemeine Zeitung*, quoted in *VB*, Dec. 10, 1927 (#285). Goebbels confided to his diary that the small audience that heard Hitler's first Essen speech included a down-and-out writer friend of his who hawked sausages in Cologne: *Tagebuch . . . 1925/26*, pp. 34f., 84.

10. *Rheinisch-Westfälische Zeitung*, Apr. 29, 1927 (#299).

11. *VB*, Dec. 10, 1927 (#285).

12. Hess to Hewel, Mar. 30, 1927 (see n. 2, above).

13. *Essener Allgemeine Zeitung*, quoted in *VB*, Dec. 10, 1927 (#285).

14. The following is based on my article, "Emil Kirdorf and the Nazi Party," *CEH* 1 (1968): 324–44.

15. Albert Speer, *Spandauer Tagebücher* (Frankfurt, 1975), pp. 122f. Speer conceded that one could never be sure about the accuracy of Hitler's reminiscences, p. 123.

16. From all indications, the financial circumstances of the party in the Ruhr posed continual difficulties throughout the 1920s: Wilfried Böhnke, *Die NSDAP im Ruhrgebiet 1920–1933* (Bonn-Bad Godesberg, 1974), pp. 114–16, 158–62; also, Goebbels, *Tagebuch . . . 1925–26*, passim.

17. August Heinrichsbauer, a journalist with close ties to the industry of the Ruhr, stated in a postwar memoir that Kirdorf contributed one hundred thousand marks to the NSDAP on joining: *Schwerindustrie und Politik* p. 38. Heinrichsbauer made that statement, however, more than two decades after

the events in question and offered no source of information. Moreover, since he had testified only a short time earlier under oath that he had never met either of the two persons purportedly involved—Kirdorf and Hitler—his statement can, at best, have rested on no more than secondhand information: NA, RG 238, Pre-Trial Interrogations, Heinrichsbauer, Jan. 9, 1947.

18. See my article, which includes the full text of the pamphlet in German and English translation: "Hitler's Secret Pamphlet."

19. He confused foreign loans with foreign ownership of German firms, for example, and suggested that failures of small businesses were a major source of unemployment: ibid.

20. That copy is in the possession of the Bücherei, GHH.

21. Turner, "Emil Kirdorf and the Nazi Party," pp. 332f.

22. GHH, 400101290/37, Reusch to Vögler, Oct. 27, 1927.

23. Ibid., 4001012024/6, Reusch's secretariat to Martin Blank, Nov. 24 and 29, 1929.

24. Friedrich Bucher to Hitler, July 20, 1929. This document, now in the BAK, was used while still at BDC, where it was located in the Reichsleitung collection, Personalakte Hüttmann. The banker in question was Maximilian von Schinckel, who had retired as head of the Norddeutsche Bank of Hamburg in 1919 at the age of seventy.

25. Krebs, *Tendenzen*, pp. 174f.

26. See, for the following, Turner, "Emil Kirdorf and the Nazi Party," pp. 333–39.

27. NSDAP HA, 56/1358a, Ley to Hitler, Dec. 21, 1927; Grohé to Reichsleitung, Dec. 21, 1927; also NA, RG 238, Case 6, Dokumentenbuch Schmitz I, affidavit of Wilhelm Kalle, an IG Farben director, Oct. 4, 1947; also "Jüdische Kampfmittel gegen Nationalsozialisten. Pg. Dr. Ley auf die Strasse gesetzt," *VB*, Jan. 5, 1928 (#4). See, in addition, Albrecht Tyrell, "Führergedanke und Gauleiterwechsel," *VfZ* 23 (1975): 360f. Relying on allegations made by a renegade Nazi in 1932 and Communist party boss Walter Ulbricht in 1956, the East German historian Kurt Gossweiler has contended that Farben continued, after Ley's dismissal, to give money to him and hence to his Nazi newspaper in Cologne: "Hitler und das Kapital (II)," pp. 1005f.

28. Heuss, *Bosch*, pp. 628f.

29. "Zum Tage," issue of Apr. 26, 1928 (#196).

30. "Der völkische 'Seniorchef,'" *Berliner Tageblatt*, Aug. 18, 1926 (#387).

31. "'Hitlers Gönner'. Eine Zuschrift des Herrn v. Borsig," *Berliner Tageblatt*, Mar. 12, 1927 (#120). On the background to Borsig's statement, see Ernst Feder, *Heute sprach ich mit . . . Tagebücher eines Berliner Publizisten 1926–1932* (Stuttgart, 1971), pp. 107f.

32. The man in question, Paul Hoffmann, held managerial posts with a number of medium-size manufacturing firms in the Ruhr. In the early 1930s he resumed his open activities for the party after a number of setbacks in his business career. Through his activities as chairman of an organization seeking restitution for small manufacturers for losses suffered during the Ruhr occupation, Hoffmann had come to be regarded as anti-big industry: Gilsa to Reusch, July 8, 1932: GHH, 400101293/4. Hoffman's personnel file in

the Berlin Document Center contains information on his business career as well as on his activities for the NSDAP. The East German historian Kurt Gossweiler has numbered Hoffmann among the *Ruhrmagnaten:* "Hitler und das Kapital (II)," p. 1003.

33. Kirdorf's stepson, Wilhelm Wessel, explained this in a letter to Rudolf Hess, Apr. 28, 1932. His version was subsequently confirmed, presumably by Hitler: BDC, Partei Kanzlei correspondence on Kirdorf. Otto Wagener, who himself came to the NSDAP from business, later recalled the difficulties experienced in the early 1930s by businessmen known to be sympathetic to National Socialism: Turner (ed.), *Hitler aus nächster Nähe,* p. 337.

34. "Adolf Hitler vor den Wirtschaftsführern," *VB,* Dec. 8, 1926 (#284). After Hitler's Essen speech in December 1927 the party organ betrayed even greater defensiveness. The many wage-earning Nazis who had hitherto suffered disadvantages because of their employers' hostility toward the NSDAP stood to gain, it asserted, from their leader's efforts to overcome prejudices about the party cultivated by "Jewish news agencies": "Adolf Hitler spricht zu 800 Vertretern der deutschen Wirtschaft," ibid., Dec. 10, 1927 (#285).

35. NSDAP HA, 70/1516, police report on the Landesparteitag of the NSDAP in Stuttgart, May 7 and 8, 1927. Hitler assured his followers that he had no intention of asking for financial aid from industry; the movement knew those "big shots" (*Herrschaften*) much too well to get involved with them. "We are just as opposed to the political goals of the men of industry," a police report quoted him saying, "as we are to those of the Marxists."

36. See Joachim Petzold, *Die Demagogie des Hitlerfaschismus* (Frankfurt, 1983), pp. 256f.

37. "Aus der Bewegung. Erklärung," *VB,* Apr. 19, 1928 (#91).

38. Orlow, *History,* I, pp. 117f. Kele, *Nazis and Workers,* p. 126.

39. Horn, *Führerideologie und Parteiorganisation,* pp. 254f.

40. "Program des F.K.," enclosed in letter, Reusch to Ludwig Endres, Oct. 20, 1929, regarding the policies of the *Fränkischer Kurier* of Nuremberg: GHH, 4001012007/15.

41. Testimony of Wilhelm Keppler at Nuremberg, Aug. 18, 1947, NA, RG 238, Case 5, vol. 17a, p. 5593.

*Chapter III, section 1: The Great Coalition Gives Way
to Presidential Rule*

1. See Timm, *Die deutsche Sozialpolitik und der Bruch der grossen Koalition,* pp. 149–207; Werner Conze, "Die politischen Entscheidungen in Deutschland 1929–1933," in Conze and Hans Raupach (eds.), *Die Staats- und Wirtschaftskrise des Deutschen Reichs 1929/33* (Stuttgart, 1967), p. 207; Maurer, *Reichsfinanzen;* Martin Vogt, "Die Stellung der Koalitionsparteien zur Finanzpolitik 1928–1930," in Mommsen et al. (eds.), *Industrielles System,* pp. 439–62; Weisbrod, *Schwerindustrie,* pp. 457–77; idem., "Economic power and political stability reconsidered," pp. 260f.; idem, "The Crisis of German Unemployment Insurance in 1928/1929 and its Political Repercussions," in Wolfgang J. Mommsen (ed.), *The Emergence of the Welfare State in Britain and Germany* (London, 1981), pp. 188–204.

2. See, for example, Paul Reusch to Erich von Gilsa, March 25, 1930: Maurer and Wengst (eds.), *Politik und Wirtschaft*, I, p.97.

3. In his memoirs Paul Moldenhauer, the DVP finance minister in the Müller cabinet, wrote that the oppositional right wing of the party's delegation seldom numbered more than fifteen. He set the hard-core oppositionalists at eight, among whom he included five deputies with ties to Ruhr industry: ibid.,I, p. 99.

4. See Maurer and Wengst (eds.) *Politik und Wirtschaft*, I, pp. 33ff.; Maurer, *Reichsfinanzen*, pp. 113ff.; Martin Vogt (ed.), *Akten der Reichskanzlei. Weimarer Republik. Das Kabinett Müller II*, 2 vols. (Boppard, 1970), II, pp. 1429ff.

5. See the excerpt from his memoir cited in 3, above.

6. Quoted in Maurer, *Reichsfinanzen*, p. 137. See also Ursula Hüllbüsch, "Die deutschen Gewerkschaften in der Weltwirtschaftskrise," in Conze and Raupach (eds.), *Die Staats- und Wirtschaftskrise*, pp. 143–45.

7. Bracher, *Auflösung*, p. 303. See also Timm, *Bruch*, p. 201.

8. See Volker Berghahn, "Das Volksbegehren gegen den Young-Plan und die Ursprünge des Präsidialregimes, 1928–1930," in Dirk Stegmann et al. (eds.), *Industrielle Gesellschaft*, p. 445.

9. Reusch to Gilsa, Oct. 25 and Nov. 9, 1929: GHH, 400101293/4.

10. See the memorandum on a conversation with Luther on March 9, 1930, by Walther Jänecke, publisher of the *Hannoverscher Kurier* and prominent figure in the DVP, in Maurer and Wengst (eds.), *Politik und Wirtschaft*, I, pp. 78–82.

11. See Maurer, *Reichsfinanzen*, pp. 121–28; Thilo Vogelsang, *Reichswehr, Staat und NSDAP* (Stuttgart, 1962), pp. 65ff.; Edward W. Bennett, *German Rearmament and the West, 1932–1933* (Princeton, 1979), pp. 22–47.

12. Maurer, *Reichsfinanzen*, p. 117. On rightist speculations about Article 48, see Maurer and Wengst (eds.), *Politik und Wirtschaft*, I, pp. 11, 23.

13. Maurer, *Reichsfinanzen*, p. 124.

14. Ibid., p. 134; Maurer and Wengst (eds.), *Politik und Wirtschaft*, I, pp. 87f., Gilsa to Reusch, Mar. 18, 1930.

15. Horkenbach (ed.), *Das Deutsche Reich* (1930), pp. 305f.

16. On this legislation, see *SEG* 71 (1930): 110–12.

17. On this so-called Oeynhausen arbitration verdict, see Preller, *Sozialpolitik*, p. 409; Hartwich, *Arbeitsmarkt, Verbände und Staat*, p. 162.

18. See the article by Ludwig Grauert, executive manager of the employer association of Ruhr iron and steel producers: "Der Oeynhausener Schiedsspruch," *Stahl und Eisen*, June 26, 1930 (Jg. 50, Nr. 26), pp. 913–15.

19. See Maurer and Wengst (eds.), *Politik und Wirtschaft*, I, p. 70; Vogt (ed.), *Kabinett Müller II*, II, p. 1517. Bernd Weisbrod mistakes this for a call for use of Article 48: *Schwerindustrie*, p. 474.

20. Neebe, *Grossindustrie*, p. 67.

21. Gilsa to Reusch, July 17, 1930: GHH, 400101293/4.

22. On the following, see Wengst, "Unternehmerverbände und Gewerkschaften," pp. 99–119; Neebe, *Grossindustrie*, pp. 67–72. Among those who regretted the break with the SPD was Albert Vögler of United Steel; he expressed this in a letter of July 16, 1930, to Fritz Klein, editor of the *Deutsche Allgemeine Zeitung*: KP.

23. For the following, see Leopold, *Hugenberg*, pp. 73–80; Friedrich Freiherr Hiller von Gaertringen, "Die Deutschnationale Volkspartei," in Erich Matthias and Rudolf Morsey (eds.), *Das Ende der Parteien 1933* (Düsseldorf, 1960), pp. 544–53.

24. Ibid.

25. Andreas Dorpalen, *Hindenburg and the Weimar Republic* (Princeton, 1964), pp. 168ff.

26. Blank to Reusch, July 23, 1930: GHH, 4001012024/7. In this letter Blank, Reusch's agent in Berlin, reported on the recommendations along those lines made by Roland Brauweiler of the league of industrial employers (VDAV) to Labor Minister Adam Stegerwald and on Blank's own plans to join with another official of the VDAV the next day in recommending a similar course to General Schleicher.

27. Heinrich Brüning, *Memoiren 1918–1934* (Stuttgart, 1970), pp. 181f.

28. Erasmus Jonas, *Die Volkskonservativen 1928–1933* (Düsseldorf, 1965).

29. See, for example, the letter from Gottfried von Dryander, a DNVP defector to the KVP, to Reusch, undated but received Sept. 3, 1930, and Reusch's reply of Sept. 4: GHH, 400101293/1.

30. The most prominent of these was Jakob Wilhelm Reichert, executive manager of the association of iron and steel producers (VDESI) and a former DNVP Reichstag deputy, who not only stood as a candidate for the KVP but also served as chairman of the new party's finance committee: printed appeal for funds, Aug. 20, 1930: GHH, 400101293/10. At the request of Ernst Poensgen, the chairman of the employer association of the Ruhr iron and steel producers (Arbeitnordwest), that association's executive manager, Ludwig Grauert, stood as a KVP candidate; see the interrogation of Grauert at Nuremberg, Aug. 23, 1946: NA, RG 238, Pre-Trial Interrogations. Similarly, Heinrich Gattineau, then an assistant to Carl Duisberg, chairman of IG Farben's board of directors and also of the industrial Reichsverband, ran as a KVP Reichstag candidate: Gattineau's testimony on Apr. 24, 1948, at Farben trial at Nuremberg: ibid., Case 6, vol. 34a, pp. 12400f.

31. Ludwig Grauert (see previous note) later estimated that his campaign for the KVP had cost 380,000 marks and that about 300,000 had come from industrial sources: Grauert's testimony at the de-nazification trial of Fritz Thyssen HHSA, Spruchkammerverfahren gegen Dr. Fritz Thyssen in Königstein, Obertaunus, 1948, Verhandlungsprotokolle, Aug. 24, 1948; interrogation of Grauert at Nuremberg, Aug. 23, 1946, NA, RG 238, Pre-Trial Interrogations. See also the affidavit of Feb. 19, 1948, by Martin Blank, Reusch's Berlin agent, for the Krupp trial at Nuremberg: ibid., Case 10, Dokumentenbuch Bülow II, doc. 80. Gottfried Treviranus, of the KVP later estimated that only about a fourth of its funds consisted of subsidies such as those from business: Jonas, *Volkskonservativen*, p. 138. Treviranus probably lacked knowledge, however, of party finances at the local level, to which Grauert referred in his testimony.

32. The following is based on the extensive documentation in the Reusch Papers, especially the correspondence between Reusch and Blank: GHH, 4001012024/7. See also Turner, "*Ruhrlade*," pp. 209–11; Larry Eugene Jones, "'The Dying Middle,'" *CEH* 5 (1972): 44–53.

33. Ibid.

34. Blank to Springorum, July 29, 1930: GHH, 4001012024/7.

Chapter III, section 2: The Wherewithal of the Nazi Breakthrough

1. See the article in the Communist daily in Berlin, *Welt am Abend*, of July 22 (#168), reprinted in *Geschäftliche Mitteilungen für die Mitglieder des Reichsverbandes der Deutschen Industrie*, Aug. 5, 1930 (Jg. 12, Nr. 19), p. 171. For a liberal view, see "Bemerkungen," *Frankfurter Zeitung*, Aug. 20, 1930 (#617). The views of Bavarian Minister President Heinrich Held were reported by the envoy of Württemberg in Munich: Wolfgang Benz (ed.), *Politik in Bayern, 1919–1933* (Stuttgart, 1971), p. 238. For the analysis of the American chargé, see *Foreign Relations of the United States*, 1930, vol. III, p. 84.

2. Kurt Hiller, "Warnung vor Koalitionen," *Die Weltbühne*, Sept. 23, 1930 (Jg. 26, Nr. 39).

3. Quoted in *Internationale Presse-Korrespondenz*, Sept. 16, 1930, p. 1940.

4. "Eine Erklärung Kirdorfs," *Berliner Lokal-Anzeiger*, Aug. 23, 1930 (#397).

5. Berghahn, "Volksbegehren gegen den Young-Plan," pp. 444f.

6. Timm, *Die deutsche Sozialpolitik und der Bruch der grossen Koalition*, pp. 138f.

7. Kühnl, *Linke*, pp. 292–97.

8. Kele, *Nazis and Workers*, p. 143.

9. Feder, "Nationalsozialismus und Privateigentum," *VB*, Aug. 27, 1930 (#203).

10. Quoted in David A. Hackett, "The Nazi Party in the Reichstag Election of 1930" (diss., University of Wisconsin, 1971), pp. 282f.

11. Ibid., p. 286.

12. See, for example, "Sozialismus in Theorie und Praxis," *VB*, July 24, 1930 (#174).

13. Kele, *Nazis and Workers*, pp. 161f.

14. Georg Schröder, "Das nationalsozialistische Wirtschaftsprogramm," *Der Arbeitgeber*, July 15, 1930 (Jg. 20, Nr. 14), pp. 404–06.

15. "Falschmeldungen über die Beteiligung des Reichsverbandes der Deutschen Industrie am Wahlkampf," *Geschäftliche Mitteilungen für die Mitglieder des Reichsverbandes der Deutschen Industrie*, Aug. 5, 1930 (#19), p. 171.

16. "Industrie und Reichstagswahlen," ibid., Aug. 25, 1930 (#21), p. 187. That statement had been released to the press a week earlier, according to an appended preamble.

17. Martin Blank to Reusch, Aug. 28, 1930: GHH, 4001012024/7.

18. Ibid., Blank to Springorum, July 29, 1930: cf. chapter III, section 1.

19. Letter of Sept. 13, 1930, quoted in Hackett, "The Nazi Party in the Reichstag Election of 1930," pp. 274f.

20. "Finanzierung der NSDAP," report by the Prussian minister of the interior, submitted to the Foreign Ministry on Sept. 16, 1930: NA, RG 242, Microcopy T-120, 4763/192210–15. See also the report of the Oberpräsident of the Province of Westphalia to the Oberpräsident of the Province of the Rhineland, Oct. 15, 1930: LHAK, 403/16733, Bl. 297. The Oberpräsident of Westphalia reported, among other things, that one of his agents had gained access to the files of the Bergbauverein, the organization of bituminous-coal operators, and established that it had not contributed money

to the NSDAP. The same held true, he reported, of the Northwest German branch of the Verein Deutscher Eisen und Stahlindustrieller.

21. See the report by the Polizeipräsident of Cologne to the Regierungspräsident of Cologne, Jan. 23, 1931: LHAK, 403/16740.

22. These aspects of National Socialism have yet to be fully charted and analyzed. They are best grasped through the chronicles of local party units published during the Third Reich, for example: Franz Buchner, *Kamerad! Halt aus! Aus der Geschichte des Kreises Starnberg der NSDAP* (Munich, 1938). On the free leaflets, see Thomas Schnabel, "Die NSDAP in Württemberg 1928–1933," in idem (ed.), *Die Machtergreifung in Südwestdeutschland* (Stuttgart, 1982), p. 55.

23. See, for example, "Hitlers Privatarmee," *Kölnische Volkszeitung*, Mar. 18, 1932 (#78), in which the author reckoned that it cost between 200,000 and 250,000 marks a day to maintain the SA.

24. See Conan Fischer, *Stormtroopers* (London, 1983), pp. 110–42, and William Sheridan Allen, *The Nazi Seizure of Power*, rev. ed. (New York, 1984), p. 79. See also Richard Bessel, *Political Violence and the Rise of Nazism* (New Haven and London, 1984), pp. 54–57.

25. Adolf Dresler, *Das Braune Haus und die Verwaltungsgebäude der Reichsleitung der NSDAP*, 3rd ed. (Munich, 1939), pp. 51f.; Julius Karl von Engelbrechten, *Eine braune Armee entsteht* (Munich and Berlin, 1937), p. 95. See also NSDAP HA, 73/1549.

26. See the advertisement for the razor blades in *VB*, October 6–7, 1929 (#232). On the margarine, see NA, RG 242, Microcopy T-81, 91/105161, SA unit Hesse-Kassel-Nord to all Dienststellen, Sept. 1, 1932; also Fischer, *Stormtroopers*, p. 114.

27. Turner (ed.), *Hitler aus nächster Nähe*, pp. 61f.; Fischer, *Stormtroopers*, pp. 128f.

28. SA order of Feb. 27, 1930: NSDAP HA, 89/1849.

29. Heinrich Bennecke, *Hitler und die SA* (Munich, 1962), p. 204. Also NA, RG 242, Microcopy T-81, 91/105070, SA Gruppen-Führer West to Chef des Stabes, Sept. 21, 1932.

30. See, for example, the letter of Carl Raegener, Generalvertreter of Kameradschaft-Zigaretten-Speditionsgesellschaft m.b.H., to Gauleiter Weinrich of Hessen-Nassau-Nord, Aug. 17, 1932, in which Raegener protested against coercive obstruction of sales of his firm's cigarettes: NA, RG 242, T-81, 91/105147f. On the firm, see the announcement of the Nazi Bezirksleitung in Gera, May 20, 1932: ibid., 91/105151.

31. Oren James Hale, "Adolf Hitler: Taxpayer," *AHR* 60 (1955): 837.

32. "Finanzierung der NSDAP" (see n. 20); Hans-Georg Rahm, "'Der Angriff' 1927–1930" (diss., Universität Berlin, 1938), p. 223. In contrast to Goebbels's successful venture in Berlin, Gauleiter Robert Ley's attempt to found a party organ in Cologne proved a financial fiasco: Friedrich Christian Prinz zu Schaumburg-Lippe, . . . *Verdammte Pflicht und Schuldigkeit . . . Weg und Erlebnis, 1914–1933* (Leoni am Starnberger See, 1966), pp. 171f., 249; also the documentation in NSDAP HA, 56/1358a.

33. See, for example, Franz Josef Heyen, *Nationalsozialismus im Alltag* (Boppard, 1967), pp. 33ff.

34. See the accounts in the classic study of small-town Nazism: Allen, *Nazi Seizure*.

35. The Prussian Political Police, who carefully monitored the Nazis' rallies, made this observation; see, for example, Die Nationalsozialistische Deutsche Arbeiterpartei. Referentendenkschrift, Mai 1930: LHAK, 403/16742.

36. These figures come, respectively, from Gerhard Bry, *Wages in Germany, 1871–1945* (Princeton, 1960), p. 381; Statistisches Reichsamt, *Deutsche Wirtschaftskunde* (Berlin, 1933), p. 291; *VB*, Sept. 27, 1930 (#230), advertisement of Knagge & Peitz, men's furnishing store in Munich; *VB*, Sept. 25, 1930 (#228), advertisement for Horn, a Munich department store.

37. Walter Oehme and Kurt Caro, *Kommt 'Das Dritte Reich'?* (Berlin, 1931), p. 92.

38. Report of the Polizeipräsident, Essen, to the Regierungspräsident, Düsseldorf, November 28, 1930: HSAD, Regierung Düsseldorf, 30653.

39. Buchner, *Kamerad! Halt aus!*, p. 398.

40. "Finanzierung der NSDAP" (see n. 20, above).

41. Hackett, "The Nazi Party in the Reichstag Election of 1930," pp. 295f. See also Allen, *Nazi Seizure*, pp. 8of.

42. Tyrell (ed.), *Führer befiehl . . .* , pp. 257–61.

43. Jeremy Noakes, *The Nazi Party in Lower Saxony 1921–1933* (London, 1971), pp. 142ff.

44. "Finanzierung der NSDAP" (see n. 20, above).

45. For documentation of the following, see Horst Matzerath and Henry A. Turner, Jr., "Die Selbstfinanzierung der NSDAP," *G & G* 3 (1977): 59–92.

46. For an example, see the warning by Rudolf Hess to the Ortsgruppe Nürnberg on July 26, 1926, that Hitler would refuse to speak there unless the local organization paid the national headquarters its share of past dues: now at the BAK, this document was used while still in the BDC, Sammlung Schumacher 199b.

47. See the report of the Oberpräsident of the Rheinprovinz to the Prussian minister of the interior, Dec. 15, 1930: LHAK, 403/16733.

48. For the following, see Matzerath and Turner, "Selbstfinanzierung."

49. See Hitler's official proclamation: "Aufruf!" *VB*, Feb. 9–10, 1930 (#35).

50. Hackett, "The Nazi Party in the Reichstag Election of 1930," pp. 162–64. After the election the insurance arrangement was converted into a charitable one that relieved the party of obligations to those members who contributed to what became known as the SA-Hilfskasse.

51. See the Rundschreiben of the Gau Westfalen, Oct. 27, 1930: SAM, Regierung Münster, Abt. VII, Nr. 67, Bd. 1; also the excerpt from the financial agreement between the Gau and the local SA, Nov. 19, 1930: ibid., Bd. 2. See also Allen, *Nazi Seizure*, p. 79.

52. See Polizeidirektion München to Reichskommissar für Überwachung der öffentlichen Ordnung, Sept. 28, 1928: BAK, R 43 I/2252, Bl. 259 (reverse side). In this case, those who joined such a circle pledged to pay fifty pfennigs a month in addition to their dues.

53. Geoffrey Pridham, *Hitler's Rise to Power* (New York, 1973), p. 99; Böhnke,

NSDAP im Ruhrgebiet, p. 147; Oehme and Caro, *Kommt 'Das Dritte Reich'?,* p. 22.

54. Wolfgang Schäfer, *NSDAP, Entwicklung und Struktur der Staatspartei des Dritten Reiches* (Hanover and Frankfurt, 1957), p. 17.
55. "Die NSDAP erwirbt ein Parteihaus!" *VB,* May 25–26, 1930 (#123).
56. See the speech by Treasurer Schwarz to the party congress of 1935, on Sept. 13, 1935; copy used in BDC, Non-Biographic Collection, Ordner 266 (now located in BAK).
57. "Die NSDAP erwirbt ein Parteihaus!," *VB,* May 25–26, 1930 (#123).
58. "Parteihaus-Sonderumlage," *VB,* June 22–23, 1930 (#147).
59. On the following, see Matzerath and Turner, "Selbstfinanzierung."
60. The party numbers assigned to members of the NSDAP had reached 293,000 at the time of the 1930 election, but that figure fails to take into consideration the memberships that had lapsed by then. The Nazis themselves used the probably more realistic figure of 200,000 members for internal purposes in mid-Sept. 1930: Hackett, "The Nazi Party in the Election of 1930," p. 137. The expenditures of the SPD for the campaign were recorded in SPD, *Jahrbuch der Deutschen Sozialdemokratie für das Jahr 1930* (Berlin, 1931), p. 209.
61. Matzerath and Turner, "Selbstfinanzierung," p. 67.
62. This very approximate extrapolation assumes that the NSDAP's membership averaged about 250,000 during Sept., Oct. and Nov. of 1930. By the end of the year the party numbers assigned to members had reached 389,000, but that figure certainly exaggerated the size of the membership for the reasons mentioned in n. 60. The income of the SPD at the Bezirk level, which corresponded roughly to that of the NSDAP's Gau, totaled 12,846,337.94 marks during 1930: SPD, *Jahrbuch . . . 1930,* p. 196.
63. Report of the treasurer, Sept. 18, 1931, in NSSAO, Erw. C1, DNVP, Bd. 23.
64. One documented exception came in the form of a subsidy of 30,000 marks from the rightist union of retail clerks to support the candidature of one of its employees who ran on the Nazi ticket: Krebs, *Tendenzen,* p. 144.

Chapter III, section 3: A "Long Guessing Game" Begins

1. Karl Erich Born, *Die deutsche Bankenkrise 1931* (Munich, 1967), pp. 57f.; Rolf Lüke, *Von der Stabilisierung bis zur Krise* (Zurich, 1958), pp. 262f.; Borchardt, *Wachstum,* p. 168. See also the data in Horkenbach (ed.), *Das Deutsche Reich* (1930), pp. 324f.
2. Horkenbach (ed.), *Das Deutsche Reich* (1930), p. 321.
3. Josef Winschuh, "Sozialpolitik und Nationalsozialismus," *Deutsche Wirtschafts-Zeitung,* Sept. 25, 1930 (#39), pp. 911–13. This publication was the official organ of the national organization of chambers of commerce and industry, the Deutscher Industrie- und Handelstag.
4. Carl Landauer, "Das nationalsozialistische Wirtschaftsprogramm," *Der deutsche Volkswirt,* Sept. 26, 1930 (#52), pp. 1764–68.
5. "Erwerbslosenwahl 1930," *Ruhr und Rhein Wirtschaftszeitung,* September 19, 1930 (#38), pp. 1233f.
6. Hansa-Bund, *Geschäftsbericht 1930* (Berlin, n.d.), p. 7.

7. Gilsa to Reusch, Sept. 15, 1930: GHH, 400101293/4.

8. See the memorandum by Brüning's secretary, Hermann Pünder, of Sept. 15, 1930: BAK, R 43 I/1308, Bl. 597–99.

9. Ibid.; also Papen to Schleicher, Sept. 24, 1930: BA/MA, Schleicher Papers, N 42/80.

10. Neebe, *Grossindustrie*, pp. 81f.

11. Ibid., p. 76.

12. Wengst, "Unternehmerverbände und Gewerkschaften," pp. 109–15; Reinhard Neebe, "Unternehmerverbände und Gewerkschaften in den Jahren der grossen Krise 1929–33," *G & G* 9 (1983): 315f.

13. Paul Reusch's not untypical views appeared in an article, "Alle Mann an Deck!" which the editor of a newspaper controlled by his firm, the *Schwäbischer Merkur*, wrote at his direction; see Reusch's instructions to the editor: Reusch to Dörge, Sept. 5, 1930: GHH, 4001012007/12; also Reusch's letter to Otto Weinlig, Sept. 5, 1930, in Maurer and Wengst (eds.) *Politik und Wirtschaft*, I, pp. 377f. See also the notes by Brüning's secretary on the chancellor's meeting with Albert Vögler, managing director of the United Steel Works, on Nov. 18: Hermann Pünder, *Politik in der Reichskanzlei* (Stuttgart, 1961), p. 75.

14. Karl Haniel to Paul Reusch, Oct. 16, 1930: Maurer and Wengst (eds.), *Politik und Wirtschaft*, I, pp. 419–21.

15. For the views of Brüning and his cabinet, see Michael Grübler, *Die Spitzenverbände der Wirtschaft und das erste Kabinett Brüning* (Düsseldorf, 1982), p. 219. This useful volume reached me too late to allow its findings to be fully incorporated into this study. For the views of other moderate rightists, see Bracher, *Auflösung*, p. 372; Martin Schumacher, *Mittelstandsfront und Republik, 1919–1933* (Düsseldorf, 1972), pp. 163f. See also Hans von Lindeiner-Wildau to Martin Blank, Oct. 1, 1930: Maurer and Wengst (eds.), *Politik und Wirtschaft*, I, pp. 402f.

16. On the evening of Nov. 18 Albert Vögler of the United Steel Works called on Brüning and told him that eight leading bankers and industrialists had that day sought in vain for eight hours to bring Hugenberg to support the cabinet on the grounds that such a step was urgently needed to staunch the flow of foreign capital out of the country: Pünder, *Politik in der Reichskanzlei*, p. 75.

17. Maurer and Wengst (eds.), *Politik und Wirtschaft*, I, p. 431, n. 1.

18. Goebbels, "Das Wirtschaftsprogramm," *Der Angriff*, Oct. 12, 1930 (#82).

19. Frick, *Nationalsozialisten im Reichstag*, pp. 93f., 122f. Similar bills were introduced by Nazi delegations in state parliaments: Hans-Willi Schondelmaier, "Die NSDAP im Badischen Landtag 1929–1933," in Schnabel (ed.), *Machtergreifung in Südwestdeutschland*, p. 93.

20. See the issue of Oct. 16, 1930 (#246). Contrary to an oft-repeated story, the Nazis did not withdraw these bills, nor did the Communists reintroduce them and maneuver the Nazis into voting against their own proposals; cf. Gerhard Granier, *Magnus von Levetzow* (Boppard, 1982), pp. 280f., n. 2.

21. Magnus von Levetzow to Beno Freiherr von Herman, Nov. 4, 1930: Granier, *Levetzow*, p. 285.

22. Article entitled "Hitlerfreundliche," quoted in "Krach zwischen Schwerindustrie und Naziführern," *Dortmunder Generalanzeiger*, Oct. 22, 1930 (#291).

23. "Die Flut der Agitationsanträge," issue of Oct. 16, 1930 (#484). See also the similar protest in the financial newspaper *Berliner Börsen-Zeitung* of Nov. 11, 1930 (#527), quoted in Klaus Wernecke and Peter Heller, *Der vergessene Führer. Alfred Hugenberg* (Hamburg, 1982), p. 161.

24. See the summary of a conversation of a high Prussian official with a Berlin banker in the report of the Oberpräsident of the Province of Saxony to the Prussian interior minister, Oct. 20, 1930: LHAK, Koblenz, 403/16733.

25. See Hartwich, *Arbeitsmarkt, Verbände und Staat*, pp. 169–75.

26. "Nationalsozialisten zum Metallarbeiterstreik," *Frankfurter Zeitung*, Nov. 9, 1930 (#837).

27. "N.S.D.A.P. solidarisch mit den Metallarbeitern," *VB*, Oct. 17, 1930 (#247); "Der Metallarbeiterstreik als Protest gegen die Tributpolitik der Wirtschaft," ibid., Nov. 5, 1930 (#263).

28. "Wenn Herr Goebbels Innenminister wird," Nov. 6, 1930 (#828).

29. "Der Metallarbeiterstreik als Protest gegen die Tributpolitik der Wirtschaft," *VB*, Nov. 5, 1930 (#263). I have translated *die Wirtschaft* here as "big business" when Hitler clearly used it in that sense, although that translation obscures the ambiguity of his words.

30. "Hitler zwischen Arbeitern und Unternehmern," *FZ*, Nov. 6, 1930 (#828). Hitler again invoked the multiplier effect a year later in an interview with a reporter for the *New York Herald Tribune:* "Private Debts to be First if Hitler is Ruler," issue of Dec. 5, 1931.

31. Granier, *Levetzow*, pp. 145–49. The project foundered during 1931 because of the discovery of Cuno's membership in the Rotary Club, which upheld the Versailles Treaty, and because of suspicions about his links, as a Catholic, to the Center Party and the Bavarian People's Party: ibid., pp. 162, 167–70. Cuno died, a politically forgotten man, on Jan. 5, 1933.

32. On the following, see Granier, *Levetzow*, esp. pp. 276–78, Levetzow's letter to Beno Freiherr von Herman, Oct. 3, 1930, and the excerpt from Levetzow's letter to Prinz Heinrich XXXIII. Reuss of Oct. 23, 1930, in n. 7, p. 278. Cf. Holger H. Herwig, "From Kaiser to Führer: The Political Road of a German Admiral, 1923–33," *JCH* 9 (1974): 112–13.

33. Jochmann (ed.), *Im Kampf um die Macht.*

34. Ibid., p. 38; Ursula Büttner, *Hamburg in der Staats- und Wirtschaftskrise 1928–31* (Hamburg, 1982), p. 419. The resulting controversy in the club continued into late December, when some members threatened to resign in order to register their dissatisfaction: "Hitlers Hamburger Gastspiel," *Vossische Zeitung*, Dec. 30, 1930 (#310).

35. See the summary, by an anonymous author who was present, in Jochmann (ed.), *Nationalsozialismus und Revolution*, pp. 309–14; cf. the account in a report by Kohlbach, an official of the Stahlhelm Landesamt Nordmark, to that organization's Bundesamt, Dec. 4, 1930: ZAP, Stahlhelm, 25. On the preparations for the speech by Cuno, see his letter to Fritz Klein of the *Deutsche Allgemeine Zeitung*, Nov. 29, 1930: KP. The speech received widespread advance publicity: "Hitler sucht Anschluss an die Wirtschaft," *Frankfurter Zeitung*, Nov. 29, 1930 (#889).

36. Jochmann (ed.), *Nationalsozialismus und Revolution*, p. 313. Rudolf Blohm, the shipbuilder, told the historian Alfred Vagts of having heard Hitler speak in Hamburg, probably on the occasion of his talk before the National

Club. Vagts later wrote to this writer: "According to Blohm, quite a number in the audience were taken in while the meeting lasted. But most of them recovered, sooner or later. It was, as he put it . . . , like resuming their sales resistance. . . ." (Vagts to HAT, Sept. 8, 1972).

37. Büttner, *Hamburg*, pp. 419, 642, n. 113.

38. Later press reports placed the meeting in November: "Nationalsozialistische Werbung um die Schwerindustrie," *Frankfurter Zeitung*, Jan. 24, 1931 (#64). This seems borne out by the date of the report on Ernst Poensgen's reaction, cited in n. 40, below.

39. See Wilhelm Tengelmann's written statement of 1945: NA, RG 238, NI-635.

40. Shortly after the gathering, Poensgen described what had happened there to Jakob Wilhelm Reichert, manager of the national organization of iron and steel industrialists (VDESI), who recorded Poensgen's report in a letter to Max Schlenker, manager of the Langnamverein, on Dec. 4, 1930: BAK, R13 I/602. After the war, from exile in Switzerland, Poensgen recalled the gathering at Kirdorf's, estimating the number of those present at about thirty, but without naming any: "Hitler und die Ruhrindustriellen. Ein Rückblick," NA, RG 238, Case 10, Documentenbuch Bülow I. Rumors to the effect that Hitler had made a "strong impression" among the Ruhr industrialists led Ludwig Kastl, manager of the industrial Reichsverband, to suspect that the Nazi leader's influence lay behind the threat on the part of the leaders of the principal organization of Ruhr coal industrialists, the Bergbauverein, to secede from the Reichsverband; see Reichert's letter to Schlenker of Dec. 4, 1930, cited above. That threat arose, however, from long-standing dissatisfaction in Ruhr coal circles with the moderate and conciliatory policies of the Reichsverband as well as with what they saw as their inadequate representation in its councils. The threat represented, in any event, nothing more than a bluff since those behind it had no serious intent to secede; see the remarks of the chairman of the Bergbauverein, Ernst Brandi, to the board of the Fachgruppe Bergbau beim Reichsverband der Deutschen Industrie, Jan. 16, 1931: BBA, Bestand 15, Bd. 13. The iron and steel industrialists of the Ruhr quashed even such a gesture by threatening to withdraw the mines they controlled from the Bergbauverein if it adopted a resolution in favor of secession from the Reichsverband; see Reusch to Blank, Jan. 28, 1931: GHH, 4001012024/8. Kastl's suspicions reveal more about the deteriorating relations between the Reichsverband and the coal operators than about the influence of Hitler among Ruhr industrialists.

41. For the following, see Levetzow's letter to Herman, Nov. 4, 1930: Granier, *Levetzow*, pp. 280–85.

42. Blank to Reusch, Nov. 23, 1929: GHH, 4001012024/6.

43. Feder, "Nationalsozialismus und Privateigentum," Aug. 27, 1930 (#203).

44. Feder spoke in the Reichstag on Dec. 4, 1930: *Verhandlungen*, vol. 444, pp. 242–50.

45. Kele, *Nazis and Workers*, p. 179.

46. *Verhandlungen*, vol. 444, pp. 485–91.

47. Ibid., pp. 633–36.

48. "Die Nationalsozialisten fordern eine Aufsichtsrats- und eine Dividen-densteuer," Dec. 16, 1930 (#298).

49. "Der nationalsozialistische Eigentumsbegriff," ibid.

50. "Führer," *DAZ*, Dec. 15, 1930 (#584).

51. Reusch to Edgar J. Jung, Dec. 27, 1930, and Jan. 2, 1931: GHH, 400101293/11.

52. Rademacher to Count Kuno von Westrap, Jan. 5, 1931: WP.

53. Speech to the DVP Vereinigung für Handel und Industrie, Dec. 18, 1930: BAK, Dingeldey Papers, 83.

54. "Nationalsozialistische Werbung um die Schwerindustrie," *Frankfurter Zeitung*, Jan. 24, 1931 (#64).

55. Wilhelm Steinberg, manager of the Pressestelle Eisen in Düsseldorf, to August Heinrichsbauer, Jan. 15, 1931: IDW, papers of the Wirtschafts-vereinigung Eisen und Stahl, P2154.

56. "'Froh, kein Wirtschaftsprogramm zu haben' sagt Herr Staatsminister Frick," Jan. 24, 1931 (#64); Horkenbach (ed.), *Das Deutsche Reich* (1931), p. 29.

57. A copy of the directive is attached to the carbon of Reusch's letter to Her-mann Saemann, Feb. 5, 1931: GHH, Allgemeine Verwaltung, 4001015/31; copies of the letters to other prominent industrialists, also dated Feb. 5, 1931, are in file 400101293/11 of the Reusch Papers, ibid. In his covering letter to Nazi sympathizer Fritz Thyssen, Reusch deviated from this word-ing and wrote, "I recommend that you subject the enclosed guidelines to close scrutiny."

58. Reupke later testified that his trip had been partially subsidized by five hun-dred to one thousand marks given to him by August Heinrichsbauer, who frequently served as a courier for Ruhr industrialists: Klaus-Peter Hoepke, *Die deutsche Rechte und der italienische Faschismus* (Düsseldorf, 1968), p. 150, n. 60.

59. *Das Wirtschaftssystem des Faschismus* (Berlin, 1930). See also his article, "Der Faschismus—warum kein Exportartikel?" *Der Tag*, Sept. 9, 1930 (#215).

60. Heinrich August Winkler, "Unternehmer und Wirtschaftsdemokratie," p. 313. For a particularly scathing denunciation of Italian Fascism, see the pamphlet by Hugo Kanter, Syndikus of the Braunschweig chamber of com-merce, *Staat und berufsständischer Aufbau* (n.p., 1932). See also the excerpt from the favorable assessment of May 1930 by Max Schlenker, executive director of the Langnamverein, quoted in Werner Sörgel, *Metallindustrie und Nationalsozialismus* (Frankfurt am Main, 1965), p. 23.

61. Hoepke, *Faschismus*, p. 181, n. 150; *Geschäftliche Mitteilungen für die Mitglieder des Reichsverbandes der Deutschen Industrie*, June 21, 1930 (#15), p. 150; ibid., July 10, 1930 (#17), p. 4.

62. See the excerpt from Vögler's letter to Jakob Herle of the Reichsverband in Reupke's letter to Martin Blank, July 1, 1930: GHH, 4001012024/7. It is not known whether Vögler's recommendation was acted on.

63. *Der Nationalsozialismus und die Wirtschaft* (Berlin, 1931). Reupke was suffi-ciently obscure that the generally well-informed economic editor of the *Berliner Tageblatt*, Felix Pinner, wondered about his background in a critical review of the book: "Geläuterte Phraseologie?" Feb. 21, 1931 (#89). There

is extensive documentation on Reupke, who was expelled from the party in 1934, in the files of the Oberstes Parteigericht in the BDC.

64. "Nationalsozialismus und Wirtschaft," *Deutsche Führerbriefe*, Mar. 10, 1931 (#20).

65. "Wirtschaft und Nationalsozialismus," *Ruhr und Rhein Wirtschaftszeitung*, Mar. 6, 1931 (#10).

66. Scherer to Kellermann, May 9, 1931: GHH, Kellermann Papers, 40010137/12.

67. "Hans Reupke: Der Nationalsozialismus und die Wirtschaft," Mar. 10, 1931 (#69).

68. "Jüdisches Allerlei," in *Berliner Beobachter*, supplement to issue of Mar. 15–16, 1931 (#74/75). Reupke's book was denounced as "Rome-subservient" by dissident left-wing Nazis in Hamburg; see Jochmann (ed.), *Nationalsozialismus und Revolution*, p. 340.

69. "Sind wir Faschisten? Ein paar notwendige Bemerkungen," *Arbeitertum*, July 1, 1931.

70. Ruprecht Schotte to Hans von und zu Loewenstein, July 31, 1931: BBB, Loewenstein Papers, Allgemeiner Schriftwechsel.

71. A typewritten copy of Wagener's draft is located in the archive of FSGNSH, file 916. It bears the title "National-Sozialistische Wirtschaftsaufgaben"; the foreword is dated Sept. 14, 1930.

72. Blank to Reusch, June 19, 1931: GHH, 4001012024/8.

73. Agenda for Ruhrlade meeting of July 6, 1931: ibid., 400101124/14.

74. Blank to Reusch, June 19, 1931: ibid., 4001012024/8.

75. On Heinrichsbauer's background, see Koszyk, *Deutsche Presse, 1914–1945* pp. 176–78; Turner, "Grossunternehmertum und Nationalsozialismus, 1930–1933," *HZ* 221 (1975): 47–50; Neebe, *Grossindustrie*, pp. 117, 250.

76. See section 4 of this chapter.

77. Blank to Reusch, June 19, 1931: GHH, 4001012024/8.

78. Avraham Barkai has assumed that Blank's letter referred to the draft circulated by Hierl, but the express citation in the letter of the title "nationalsozialistisches Wirtschaftsmanifest" in quotation marks casts doubt on this, since the Hierl draft bore a quite different title: Barkai, "Wirtschaftliche Grundanschauungen und Ziele der NSDAP," *JBIDG* 7 (1978): 355–85.

79. Blank to Reusch, June 19, 1931: GHH, 4001012024/8.

80. Dirk Stegmann has uncritically accepted Heinrichsbauer's claim, as reported to Reusch by Blank, as conclusive proof that the "right wing of Ruhr industry" could force the NSDAP to suppress views unpalatable to it: Stegmann, "Zum Verhältnis," pp. 416f., 448, n. 240.

81. See the counter-draft by Albert Krebs, also entitled "Nationalsozialistische Wirtschaftsaufgaben," in FSGNSH, file 913.

82. Turner (ed.), *Hitler aus nächster Nähe*, pp. 478–81.

83. On the rebellion, see Orlow, *History*, I, pp. 216–19.

84. See the positive evaluation in "Die Vorgänge im Nationalsozialismus," *Deutsche Führerbriefe*, Apr. 10, 1931 (#28). According to Paul Reusch's political agent, Martin Blank, who also evaluated the suppression of the rebellion

85. positively, if not so wholly optimistically, August Heinrichsbauer was the author of this article: GHH, 4001012024/8, Blank to Reusch, Apr. 13.

85. Bücher was the source of funds that reached Stennes through the industrialist's old friend Forstrat Georg Escherich; see Paul Reusch's correspondence with Bücher: GHH, 400101290/5. On Bücher's friendship with Escherich, see Heuss, *Bosch*, p. 557.

86. See "Wo steht der Nationalsozialismus?" *Deutsche Führerbriefe*, June 19, 1931 (#47). It seems likely that this article, like that cited in n. 84, was written by August Heinrichsbauer, since both were attributed to a "Kenner" of the Nazi party. See also "Wirtschaft und Nationalsozialismus," *Ruhr und Rhein Wirtschaftszeitung*, Mar. 6, 1931 (#10).

87. See, for example, the speech by former chancellor Wilhelm Cuno of the Hamburg-Amerika shipping line before the Düsseldorf Industry Club on Apr. 17, 1931: "Der Krieg nach dem Kriege. Wirtschaftspolitische Reminiszenzen und Ausblicke" (als Stenogramm gedruckt), copy in WWB. See also "Wirtschaft und Nationalsozialismus," *Ruhr und Rhein Wirtschaftszeitung*, Mar. 6, 1931 (#10).

88. See n. 86, above.

89. Minutes of meeting of Verein Deutscher Eisen- und Stahlindustrieller, May 3, 1933: BAK, R13 I/1078.

Chapter III, section 4: Capitalist Fellow Travelers and Subsidized Nazis

1. On Stauss' background, see Friedrich Glum, *Zwischen Wissenschaft, Wirtschaft und Politik* (Bonn, 1964), pp. 165, 260f.; Erich Achterberg and Maximilian Müller-Jabusch, *Lebensbilder deutscher Bankiers aus fünf Jahrhunderten*, 2nd ed. (Frankfurt am Main, 1963), pp. 255–61; Ernst Wilhelm Schmidt, *Männer der Deutschen Bank und der Disconto-Gesellschaft* (Düsseldorf, 1957), p. 120.

2. Döhn, *Politik und Interesse*, p. 360.

3. Granier, *Levetzow*, p. 310.

4. "Löbe Reichstagspräsident," *Berliner Tageblatt*, Oct. 16, 1930 (#458); "Stauss und Hitler," *Vorwärts*, Oct. 18, 1930 (#490); Ernst Feder, *Heute sprach ich mit*, p. 275.

5. "Armer Herr von Stauss!" *Berliner Tageblatt*, Oct. 16, 1930 (#489); "Der enttäuschte Bankfürst," ibid., Oct. 17, 1930 (#491).

6. Richard Kohn to Stauss, Nov. 1, 1930: DWI, records of Deutsche Bank und Disconto-Gesellschaft, file A23/4, No. 58.

7. Turner (ed.), *Hitler aus nächster Nähe*, pp. 455–60.

8. IfZ, ED 60, Aufzeichnungen des Gen. Maj. a.D. Dr. h. c. Otto Wagener, Heft 16, p. 1033. On Stauss' role in the DVP, see his letter to its chairman, Eduard Dingeldey, July 21, 1932: BAK, Dingeldey Papers, 25.

9. Hans Radandt, "Das Monopolkapital und der deutsche Faschismus," *WA*, Beiheft 1956, p. 78.

10. Hans Radandt, "'100 Jahre Deutsche Bank'. Eine typische Konzerngeschichte," *JBWG*, 1972, Teil 3, p. 55; Karl Erich Born, *Die deutsche Bankenkrise* (Munich, 1967), p. 171.

11. See the biographical data in file no. 673, papers of the Generalsekretariat, records of Deutsche Bank und Disconto-Gesellschaft: DWI, A23/22.

12. Hans Buchner, *Die goldene Internationale* (Munich, 1928), p. 43.

13. Alfred Rosenberg, *Freimauerische Weltpolitik im Lichte der kritischen Forschung* (Munich, 1929), p. 63.

14. See the police dossier on Feder: NSDAP HA, 56/1346.

15. See the report on his speech of Dec. 7, 1930, to the Wirtschaftsbeirat of the Bayerische Volkspartei: *SEG* 71 (1930): 239–41; also his "Die Nation will nicht zugrundegehen," *Deutsche Allgemeine Zeitung*, Dec. 25, 1930 (#601).

16. Schacht, *76 Jahre meines Lebens* (Bad Wörishofen, 1953), p. 350f.; Fanny Gräfin von Wilamowitz-Moellendorf, *Carin Göring* (Berlin, 1934), p. 140.

17. See the interrogation of Schacht, July 20, 1945: NA, RG 238, 3725-PS.

18. "Hjalmar Schacht beim Kaiser in München," *Das Nationalsozialistische Montagsblatt*, June 22, 1931 (#18).

19. "Schacht und die Nationalsozialisten," *Berliner Tageblatt*, July 3, 1931 (#308).

20. Leopold, *Hugenberg*, p. 59.

21. "Hugenbergs Kampffront," *Deutsche Allgemeine Zeitung*, July 10, 1929 (#314).

22. Thyssen told of his belief in the corporatist tenets in Nazism in the interviews with the journalist who became the ghost-writer for his purported memoir, *I Paid Hitler* (New York, 1941): T/RP, stenogram, sheets 281, 284f., 292, 295f.

23. Neebe, *Grossindustrie*, pp. 85f.

24. Otto Schmidt-Hannover, *Umdenken oder Anarchie* (Göttingen, 1959), p. 276.

25. Turner, "Fritz Thyssen und 'I paid Hitler,'" pp. 238f.

26. Schacht, *76 Jahre*, p. 351; Wilamowitz-Moellendorf, *Carin Göring*, p. 140.

27. Thyssen's wife Amélie joined the party considerably earlier, on March 1, 1931: BDC, Parteikanzlei Korrespondenz, Mitgliedschaftsamt, Munich, to Gauschatzmeister des Gaues Essen, Wilhelm Beyer, June 24, 1940.

28. Udo Kissenkoetter, *Gregor Strasser und die NSDAP* (Stuttgart, 1978), p. 125.

29. Neebe, *Grossindustrie*, pp. 117f.

30. Kissenkoetter, *Strasser*, p. 126.

31. Gerhard Schulz, *Aufstieg des Nationalsozialismus* (Frankfurt, Berlin, Vienna, 1975), pp. 623f., 873; see also the official Nazi biography of Funk: Paul Oestreich, *Walther Funk. Ein Leben für die Wirtschaft* (Munich, 1940).

32. According to Funk's written statement of June 28, 1945, through Heinrichsbauer he met Paul Schulz, a friend of Strasser's, who then introduced him to the latter: NA, RG 238, EC-440.

33. International Military Tribunal, *Trial of the Major War Criminals Before the International Military Tribunal, Nuremberg, 14 November 1945–1 October 1946*, 42 vols. (Nuremberg, 1947–49), XIII, p. 82, testimony of Funk on May 4, 1946.

34. Under interrogation on June 4, 1945, Funk specified that Albert Vögler, general director of the United Steel Works, and Gustav Knepper, head of the coal-mining division of that combine, had urged him to join the NSDAP; asked for names of others with whom he was in contact, Funk mentioned Ruhr steel industrialist Peter Klöckner as well as August Diehn and August Rosterg, two executives in the potash industry, but he did not specify that these men had urged him to enter the party: NA, RG 238, 2828-PS. Interrogated again a year and a half later, Funk named as members of

the group that had encouraged him to join the party Vögler; Knepper; Fritz Springorum, general director of the Hoesch steel works in the Ruhr; and a member of the Tengelmann family, presumably the elderly Ernst Tengelmann, general director of a coal-mining firm Essener Steinkohlenbergwerke until its absorption into the Gelsenkirchener Bergwerks-AG in 1930. In this later interrogation, Funk stated that Klöckner had not belonged to the group that had propelled him into the NSDAP: ibid., Pre-Trial Interrogations, Funk, Dec. 2, 1946.

35. See Funk's written statement of June 28, 1945: NA, RG 238 (Nuremberg documents) EC-440. See also the record of Funk's membership: BDC, Parteikanzlei Korrespondenz.

36. Funk's interrogation of Dec. 2, 1946 (see n. 34).

37. On Reismann-Grone's background, see Lothar Werner, *Der Alldeutsche Verband 1890–1918* (Berlin, 1935), p. 31; Kruck, *Alldeutschen Verbandes*, pp. 110f. Fritz Pudor, *Nekrologe aus dem rheinisch-westfälischen Industriegebiet, Jahrgang 1939–51* (Düsseldorf, 1955), pp. 174f. Kurt Koszyk, *Deutsche Presse*, pp. 170f. According to the membership records of the NSDAP, Reismann-Grone became a Nazi Party member on Jan. 1, 1930, but it seems likely that he actually entered considerably later: Turner (ed.), *Hitler aus nächster Nähe*, p. 494, n. 6.

38. See the analysis of the paper's coverage of the NSDAP in Richard F. Hamilton, *Who Voted for Hitler?* (Princeton, 1982), pp. 162–67.

39. Klaus Werner Schmidt, "Die 'Rheinisch-Westfälische Zeitung' und ihr Verleger Reismann-Grone," *Beiträge zur Geschichte Dortmunds und der Grafschaft Mark* 69 (1974): 364.

40. Turner (ed.), *Hitler aus nächster Nähe*, pp. 215–18.

41. Edgar von Schmidt-Pauli, *Die Männer um Hitler* (Berlin, 1932), pp. 120f.

42. Turner (ed.), *Hitler aus nächster Nähe*, p. 229.

43. Schmidt, "Die 'Rheinisch-Westfälische Zeitung,'" p. 357; idem, "Rheinisch-Westfälische Zeitung (1883–1944)," in *Deutsche Zeitungen des 17. bis 20. Jahrhunderts*, ed. by Heinz-Dietrich Fischer (Pullach, 1972), p. 376.

44. Grauert consistently gave the same account of this episode during post-war interrogations: NA, RG 238, Pre-Trial Interrogations, Sept. 28, 1946; Dec. 5, 1946; Jan. 15, 1947. For Wagener's account, see Turner (ed.), *Hitler aus nächster Nähe*, p. 219.

45. Even during the first year of the Third Reich, the *National-Zeitung* adhered to a deviant line under Terboven's direction: Koszyk, *Deutsche Presse*, pp. 384f. The documents cited by Koszyk do not substantiate his assertion that Fritz Thyssen subsidized the Essen paper.

46. Grauert was a follower of Othmar Spann, the Austrian theorist of corporatism. See Walter Ferber, "Othmar Spann und der Nationalsozialismus," *Civitas. Monatsschrift des schweizerischen Studentenvereins* 15 (1960): 547–50. See also the post-war interrogations of Grauert (n. 44, above).

47. Grauert interrogation of Sept. 28, 1946 (see n. 44, above).

48. "Nationalsozialistische Werbung um die Schwerindustrie," *Frankfurter Zeitung*, Jan. 24, 1931 (#64).

49. Grauert interview by Fritz Tobias, Oct. 3, 1957, who kindly sent me a copy.

50. Turner (ed.), *Hitler aus nächster Nähe*, p. 460.

51. Ibid., p. 219.

52. Ibid., p. 220.

53. On the following, see Turner, "Fritz Thyssen und 'I paid Hitler.'"

54. Turner (ed.), *Hitler aus nächster Nähe*, pp. 226–29. This account is confirmed by a post-war interrogation of Grauert, who figures prominently in it: NA, RG 238, Pre-Trial Interrogations, Grauert, Sept. 28, 1946.

55. Heinrichsbauer, *Schwerindustrie*, pp. 40–42; NA, RG 238, Pre-Trial Interrogations, Heinrichsbauer, Jan. 9 and 13, Nov. 20, 1947.

56. Kissenkoetter, *Gregor Strasser*, pp. 125f.

57. Ibid., p. 126.

58. Turner, "*Ruhrlade*," p. 216; also HAD, Personen Konten 1931/33, p. 743.

59. Kissenkoetter, *Gregor Strasser*, p. 126.

60. For the following, see Turner (ed.), *Hitler aus nächster Nähe*, pp. 368ff.

61. Ibid., p. 379.

62. NA, RG 238, Funk interrogation of June 4, 1945, 2828-PS. Copies of the newsletter, *Wirtschaftspolitischer Informationsdienst*, with which Funk supplemented the Nazi *Wirtschaftspolitischer Pressedienst*, may be found in NA, RG 242, Microcopy T-81, roll 714.

63. See the account of his dealings with Max Ilgner and Heinrich Gattineau of IG Farben in chapter V, below.

64. NA, RG 238, Pre-Trial Interrogations, Funk, Dec. 2, 1946; ibid., 2828-PS, interrogation of June 4, 1945.

65. Turner (ed.), *Hitler aus nächster Nähe*, pp. 389f.

66. Turner, "Fritz Thyssen und 'I paid Hitler,'" pp. 236f.

67. Turner (ed.), *Hitler aus nächster Nähe*, p. 227.

68. See Otto Wagener's recollection of a conversation during which party treasurer Schwarz explained these matters in the early thirties: Turner (ed.), *Hitler aus nächster Nähe*, pp. 239f. A statement written by Schwarz for the Nuremberg war crimes tribunal confirms Wagener's account: BDC, Non-Biographic Collection, Ordner 266, Schwarz statement of May 15, 1945. In one of his monologues during World War II, Hitler described the administration of the NSDAP's dues collection system in a manner that left no doubt of his ignorance of its niceties: *Secret Conversations* (1953), p. 268.

69. Oren James Hale, "Adolf Hitler Taxpayer," *AHR* 60 (1955): 830–42.

70. Turner (ed.), *Hitler aus nächster Nähe*, p. 240.

71. See the 1945 statement by Schwarz cited in n. 68, above.

72. Funk himself testified at Nuremberg that such was his understanding at the time: NA, RG 238, 2828-PS, interrogation of June 4, 1945.

73. Hale, "Adolf Hitler: Taxpayer," pp. 833f.

74. Ibid., p. 833.

75. See the facsimile of the letter from Hitler to Prince Friedrich Christian of Schaumburg-Lippe, Feb. 7, 1929, in the latter's memoir, *Pflicht und Schuldigkeit*, p. 159.

76. Hale, "Adolf Hitler: Taxpayer," p. 837.

77. NA, RG 238, 2828-PS, interrogation of Funk, June 4, 1945.

78. Turner (ed.), *Hitler aus nächster Nähe*, p. 239.

79. Roland V. Layton, "The *Völkischer Beobachter*, 1920–1933: The Nazi Party Newspaper in the Weimar Era," *CEH* 3 (1970): 362.

80. Schirach, *Ich glaubte an Hitler*, p. 112.

81. Ibid., p. 113.

82. *Hitler's Secret Conversations* (New York, 1953), pp. 457f.
83. Dietrich, *Zwölf Jahre mit Hitler*, p. 187; Schirach, *Ich glaubte an Hitler*, p. 162; Hanfstaengl, *Hitler—The Missing Years*, pp. 153f.; idem, *Zwischen Weissem und Braunem Haus*, pp. 216f. Sefton Delmer, *Trail Sinister* (London, 1961), p. 143. According to Delmer, the Hearst correspondent in Berlin paid Hitler a dollar a word for articles he wrote for the Hearst papers: Delmer to the author, May 2, 1969.
84. Hanfstaengl, *Hitler—The Missing Years*, p. 154.
85. *Secret Conversations* (1953), p. 457.
86. LC, Manuscript Division, Adolf Hitler Collection: Kaiserhof bill dated Mar. 2, 1932, and paid that day.
87. Ibid., bill for stay of Sept. 1–4, 1931, paid on the fourth.
88. "Adolf Hitler gegen die neuesten Verleumdungen," issue of Aug. 1, 1931 (#213).
89. Turner (ed.), *Hitler aus nächster Nähe*, p. 314.
90. Heinrichsbauer, *Schwerindustrie*, p. 43; see also Heinrichsbauer's affidavit of Jan. 31, 1948: NA, RG 238, Case 10, Dokumentenbuch Bülow II, #68.
91. Heinrichsbauer, *Schwerindustrie*, p. 43.
92. Heinrichsbauer's statement of Jan. 9, 1947: NA, RG 238, Pre-Trial Interrogations. Winnig told of the lectures in his memoirs: *Vom Proletariat zum Arbeitertum* (Hamburg, 1933), p. 167. At the time Winnig was an editorial writer for the *Berliner Börsen-Zeitung:* Wilhelm Ribhegge, *August Winnig* (Bonn, 1973), p. 268.

Chapter IV, section 1: Disillusionment with Brüning— The "Harzburg Front"—Capitalists in Fear of the Ruler

1. An unusually full and clear articulation of the business community's view of the causes of the depression and the proper response to it can be found in the printed text of a speech delivered on July 1, 1931, to the Vereinigung von Banken und Bankiers in Rheinland und Westfalen e. V. by an executive of the Cologne banking house Salomon Oppenheim Jr. & Cie. who later served as a close adviser to West German Chancellor Konrad Adenauer: Robert Pferdmenges, *Die deutsche Wirtschaft—wie sie ist und wie sie sein sollte* (Cologne, n.d.). See also the speech by Paul Silverberg before the Hauptausschuss of the Reichsverband der Deutschen Industrie, June 19, 1931: BAL, Reichsverband, 62/10, 5b.
2. Gustav Krupp von Bohlen und Halbach et al. to Brüning, July 30, 1931: Maurer and Wengst (eds.), *Politik und Wirtschaft*, I, pp. 800–806.
3. These recommendations and those spelled out below found expression in numerous submissions to the chancellor. See, for example, the report on a meeting of a group of industrialists with Brüning on Jan. 26, 1931, in the minutes of the Ruhrlade meeting of Feb. 2, 1931, enclosed in a letter from Ernst Poensgen to Krupp von Bohlen of Feb. 3, 1931: KA, IV E 152; also the report on that same meeting in the letter from Martin Blank to Paul Reusch, Jan. 31, 1931: Maurer and Wengst (eds.), *Politik und Wirtschaft*, I, pp. 543f. See also the public statement of the industrial Reichsverband of Apr. 25, 1931, summarized in Horkenbach (ed.), *Das Deutsche Reich* (1931), p. 145; letter from Ernst Brandi to Brüning, Aug 14, 1931: BBB, Loewen

stein Papers, Allgemeiner Schriftwechsel. See also Fritz Springorum to Fritz Winkhaus, Sept. 4, 1931: HAD, Springorum Papers, B1a 51/28.

4. Documentation on this and the following may be found in Maurer and Wengst (eds.), *Politik und Wirtschaft*.

5. Hans Mommsen, "Heinrich Brünings Politik als Reichskanzler: Das Scheitern eines poltischen Alleinganges," in Karl Holl (ed.), *Wirtschaftskrise und liberale Demokratie* (Göttingen, 1978), p. 24.

6. For some informative observations on Brüning's policies, see Gerhard Schulz, "Reparationen und Krisenprobleme nach dem Wahlsieg der NSDAP 1930: Betrachtungen zur Regierung Brüning," *VSWG* 67 (1980): 200–22.

7. See, for example, Fritz Springorum to Blank, May 15, 1931: GHH, 4001012024/8; Fritz Klein to Walther Bernhard, May 18, 1931: KP. In June 1931 Brüning allowed Albert Vögler of the United Steel Works to believe he was considering him as economics minister, but apparently without actually offering the post to Vögler: Aktennotiz by Eduard Dingeldey, June 13, 1931: BAK, Dingeldey Papers, 38, Bl. 79–85. This incident is inaccurately portrayed in Döhn, *Interesse und Politik*, pp. 201–3, where Vögler is alleged to have made his entry into the cabinet conditional on its adoption of dictatorial methods.

8. Gilsa to Reusch, Aug. 6, 1931: Maurer and Wengst (eds.), *Politik und Wirtschaft*, II, p. 872.

9. See the account of the meeting of the Langnamverein on June 1, 1931, in Horkenbach (ed.), *Das Deutsche Reich* (1931), p. 190. See also the report on the meeting of the Verein Deutscher Eisen- und Stahlindustrieller of June 17, 1931: BAK, R13 I/130.

10. Duisberg explained his support for Brüning in a letter of June 26, 1931, in which he replied to Emil Kirdorf's denunciation of the chancellor: BAL, Autographensammlung Duisberg. See also the report on his speech to the Industrie- und Handelskammer of Düsseldorf on June 23, 1931: "Duisberg für Brüning," *Berliner Börsen-Courier*, June 24, 1931.

11. See the minutes of the confidential conferences of major industrialists held in Bochum on Apr. 1 and May 5, 1931, where these matters were discussed with unusual frankness: BBB, Loewenstein Papers, B 1.

12. Reusch to Krupp, May 5, 1931; Krupp to Duisberg, June 10, 1931: GHH, 400101290/27.

13. See Born, *Bankenkrise*.

14. Döhn, *Politik und Interesse*, pp. 193–95; Michael Grübler, *Spitzenverbände*, pp. 451f. See also Blank to Reusch, June 12, 1931: GHH, 4001012024/8.

15. For this and the following, see the minutes of Brüning's tense meeting with spokesmen of the Reichsverband on Sept. 18, 1931: Maurer and Wengst (eds.), *Politik und Wirtschaft*, II, pp. 967–75.

16. For an example of the misgivings these measures produced, see Peter Klöckner to Krupp von Bohlen, July 31, 1931: KA, E IV 841. Also, the letter from Walther Bernhard, a director of the Darmstädter und Nationalbank, to Fritz Klein, editor of the business-owned *Deutsche Allgemeine Zeitung* of Berlin, Nov. 11, 1931: KP.

17. See Berenice A. Carroll, *Design for Total War* (The Hague, 1968), pp. 66–71.

18. See Ernst Willi Hansen, *Reichswehr und Industrie* (Boppard, 1978).

19. See Bennett, *German Rearmament.*

20. Maurer and Wengst (eds.), *Politik und Wirtschaft,* esp. II, pp. 908–12, 961f., 967–75, 1452; Gert von Klass, *Albert Vögler* (Tübingen, 1957), pp. 197–207. Eventually the Brüning cabinet did arrange for the railway system to obtain credits that enabled it to place extensive orders with the iron and steel industry during the latter months of 1931, but only after considerable friction between the latter and the cabinet: Michael Wolffsohn, *Industrie und Handwerk im Konflikt mit staatlicher Wirtschaftspolitik?* (Berlin, 1977), pp. 242–47.

21. Vermerk über eine Besprechung mit Geheimrat Klöckner, Dr. Poensgen und Dr. Reichert, am 14. August 1931 vormittags 10 Uhr im Reichswirtschaftsministerium: ZAP, Reichswirtschaftsministerium, 20470.

22. Eventually the Reichsbank's acceptance of Russian notes made possible further expansion of credits to the Soviet Union: Fritz Springorum to Fritz Winkhaus, Sept. 4, 1931: HAD, Springorum Papers, B1a 51/28; Manfred Pohl, "Die Finanzierung der Russengeschäfte zwischen den beiden Weltkriegen," in Beiheft 9 of *Tradition. Zeitschrift für Firmengeschichte und Unternehmerbiographie* (Frankfurt, 1975); Wolffsohn, *Industrie und Handwerk,* pp. 237–41; Dietmar Petzina, "Elemente der Wirtschaftspolitik in der Spätphase der Weimarer Republik," *VfZ* 21 (1973): 130f.; Hartmut Pogge von Strandmann, "Grossindustrie und Rapallopolitik," *HZ* 222 (1976): 331–33.

23. Maurer and Wengst (eds.), *Politik und Wirtschaft,* II, pp. 974f.

24. See the observations about Luther in Schulz, "Reparationen und Krisenprobleme," pp. 214–18; also the letter, Gilsa to Reusch, Aug. 6, 1931: Maurer and Wengst (eds.), *Politik und Wirtschaft,* II, pp. 871–73; also, the report on meeting of presidium of Reichsverband, Nov. 26, 1931, in Richard Buz to Reusch, Nov. 27, 1931: GHH, 4001012010/17.

25. Schlenker to Reusch, Sept. 21, 1931: GHH, 400101221/11. See also Fritz Springorum to Fritz Winkhaus, Sept. 4, 1931: HAD, Springorum Papers, B1a 51/28.

26. See the exchange of letters between Reusch and Kastl in mid-September: Maurer and Wengst (eds.), *Politik und Wirtschaft,* II, pp. 944f., 950f., 963. See also Reusch's letter of Sept. 21, 1931, to Fritz Büchner, editor of the *Münchner Neuesten Nachrichten:* GHH, 4001012007/6.

27. Horkenbach (ed.), *Das Deutsche Reich* (1931), pp. 318–20.

28. Fritz Klein, "Zweites Kabinett Brüning?" issue of Oct. 5, 1931 (#458). Another editorial in the same paper—"Vorfrucht der nationalen Diktatur?" by Otto von Sethe, issue of Oct. 4, 1931 (#457)—is mistakenly described in Bracher, *Auflösung,* p. 415, as a call for dictatorship; in actuality the author expressed regret about talk of dictatorship and defended the principle of democracy. Bracher's version apparently derives from the misconstrual by selective quotation in Fritz Klein, "Zur Vorbereitung der faschistischen Diktatur durch die deutsche Grossbourgeoisie (1929–1932)," *ZfG* 1 (1953): 895f.

29. See the Aktennotiz prepared by Otto Steinbrinck for Friedrich Flick, Oct. 5, 1931: NA, RG 238, NI-3615, printed in Dietrich Eichholtz and Wolfgang Schumann (eds.), *Anatomie des Krieges* (East Berlin, 1969), pp. 89f. See also "Unsere Meinung," *Deutsche Allgemeine Zeitung,* Oct. 6, 1931 (#459).

30. On Hindenburg's wishes for a cabinet revamping, see Brüning's report to his party's Reichstag deputies in Rudolf Morsey (ed.), *Die Protokolle der Reichstagsfraktion und des Fraktionsvorstandes der Deutschen Zentrumspartei 1926–1933* (Mainz, 1969), p. 545.

31. See the diary entry for Oct. 9, 1931, by Fritz Klein, in which the editor of the *Deutsche Allgemeine Zeitung* recorded a conversation of that evening with Brüning: KP. See also Silverberg to Krupp von Bohlen, Oct. 12, 1931, in Maurer and Wengst (eds.), *Politik und Wirtschaft*, II, pp. 1035–38.

32. This is reflected in the press reports of the day: "Brüning verhandelt," *Deutsche Allgemeine Zeitung*, Oct. 8, 1931 (#463); "Enttäuschte Erwartungen," ibid., Oct. 10, 1931 (#467). Otto Stark, "Die Kraftprobe," *Berliner Tageblatt*, Oct. 10, 1931 (#479): "Die neuen Männer," *Frankfurter Zeitung* Oct. 11, 1931 (#757–58); "Kabinett Brüning," ibid., Oct. 11, 1931 (#759). Warmbold later reported that when he received the summons to the Chancellery, he had expected to be offered the Agriculture Ministry: Warmbold, "Irrtümer in Brünings Memoiren," *Frankfurter Allgemeine Zeitung*, Jan. 15, 1971 (#12).

33. On Cuno's initiative, see Fritz Klein's diary for Oct. 5, 1931, and "Denkschrift Cuno/Meibom/Klein für Hindenburg 5.10.31," both in: KP. See also Henning von Meibom to Cuno, Oct. 6, 1931: in HLH, Cuno Papers, "Politik von February 1931 bis Januar 1933." Cf. the slanted version of this episode in Fritz Klein, "Zur Vorbereitung," pp. 896–901.

34. For the text of his speech, see Schacht's *Nationale Kreditwirtschaft* (Berlin, 1934), pp. 5–11. On the furor it occasioned in Oct. 1931, see *SEG* 72 (1931): 227–29.

35. "Es geht ums Ganze," *Vorwärts*, Oct. 12, 1931 (#478).

36. Schacht to Reusch, Oct. 20, 1931; Reusch to Schacht, Oct. 23, 1931: GHH, 400101290/33. Reusch to Krupp, Oct. 20, 1931, and Krupp to Reusch, Oct. 22, 1931: KA, R 216¹.

37. For this list, with attribution, see "Grosse und kleine Leute," *Frankfurter Zeitung*, Oct. 13, 1931 (#761–62); for another report using it, with minor variations, see "Auftakt in Harzburg," *Deutsche Allgemeine Zeitung*, Oct. 11, 1931 (#469); for still another version, based on its use in Hugenberg's *München-Augsburger Abendzeitung*, see Leopold, *Hugenberg*, p. 103.

38. "'Kein Mensch hat sich erschreckt,'" *Berliner Tageblatt*, Oct. 13, 1931 (#482); "Die Tagung der nationalen Opposition," *Kölnische Zeitung*, Oct. 12, 1931 (#556). The former mentioned no businessmen, the latter only the Syndikus Max Schlenker (see below, n. 42) and Louis Ravené, a Berlin iron wholesaler and active Stahlhelm member (see n. 44).

39. "Geheimrat Kreth" appears in some versions as a "Geheimrat Kreht"; a "Krieger-Wintershall" sometimes as a "Krüger-Wintershall"; a "Gen.-Dir. Heugst" sometimes as a "Gen.-Dir. Heubst"; a "Geheimrat Böringer" as a "Geheimrat Böhlinger"; a "Hüttendirektor Cubier" as "Cuber" or "Qubier" or "Kubier"; a "Paul Rohde" proved unaccountably interchangeable in some versions with a "Paul Huth."

40. In addition to those mentioned in n. 42, this applies, because in the frequency of common names, to "Dir. Grosse," "Gen.-Dir. Möllers," and "Gen.-Dir. Hohn." Other names come from recognizable provincial families of local commercial or manufacturing importance, but the omission of first

names or positions makes it impossible to identify individuals: "Dr. Mees-mann (Mainz)," "Delius (Bielefeld)."

41. "Gen.-Dir. Gottstein" was presumably Hans Gottstein of the Feldmühle, Papier- und Zellstoffwerke AG of Stettin (Wenzel, *Wirtschaftsführer*, col. 757); "Gen.-Dir. Meydenbauer" was in all probability the Berlin attorney Hans Meydenbauer, who did not hold that lofty title but rather served on the supervisory boards of a number of enterprises controlled by Hugenberg himself (ibid., col. 1485); "Dr. Regendanz" was probably Wilhelm G. Regendanz, a German-born Dutch banker and colonial enthusiast who in 1931 held the post of administrateur délégué of the Amstelbank in Amsterdam (ibid., col. 1777); "Geheimrat Dr. Reinecker" (Chemnitz) was most likely the seventy-year-old Geheimer königlicher sächsischer Kommerzienrat Dr. Johannes Reinecker, director of the J. E. Reinecker AG, a tool manufacturing firm in Chemnitz (ibid., col. 1791); a merchant named Paul Rohde headed the Berlin sales division of a medium-size steel rolling mill in the Ruhr, the Rheinisch-Westfälische Stahl- und Walzwerke AG (ibid., col. 1854).

42. This applies to Max Schlenker of the Langnamverein and the northwest group of the association of iron and steel industrialists, Ludwig Grauert of the Ruhr industrial employers organization (Arbeitnordwest), and Hans von und zu Loewenstein, the manager of the Bergbauverein, whose attendance escaped the notice of the press; see his reflections on the gathering in his letter to Bergrat Professor Böker, Oct. 26, 1931: BBB, Loewenstein Papers, Allgemeiner Schriftwechsel, Verschiedenes A 1. Martin Sogemeier was the Syndikus of the Zweckverband Nordwestdeutscher Wirtschaftsvertretungen (Wenzel, *Wirtschaftsführer*, col. 2161). "Geheimrat Kreth" (sometimes Kreht) may have been Regierungsrat a.D. Hermann Kreth of the Verwertungsverband Deutscher Spiritusfabrikanten (ibid., col. 1246); "Gen.-Dir. Möllers" may have been Gustav Möllers of the Verkaufsvereinigung für Teererzeugnisse (ibid., col. 1520); "Gen.-Dir. Hohn" was identified in some versions of the Telegraphen-Union list as being with the Langnamverein (Leopold, *Hugenberg*, p. 103).

43. Rudolf Blohm and Gottfried Gok, both directors of the Hamburg shipbuilding firm of Blohm & Voss, bulked much larger as longtime Pan-Germans and activist DNVP supporters of Hugenberg than as members of the business community: Leopold, *Hugenberg*, passim; the same applied to Erich Winnacker, one of the fifty-some directors of United Steel, who was an active member of the right wing of the DNVP; see his correspondence with Kellermann of the Gutehoffnungshütte, cited in n. 45. The same would have been the case if the Poensgen listed among those in attendance was Hellmuth (see n. 48).

44. Such was the case with Martin Blank, the Berlin representative of Reusch's firm, Gutehoffnungshütte; on his activities in the Stahlhelm, see GHH, 4001012024/7, letter to Reusch, Sept. 5, 1930; on his plans to attend the meeting, see GHH, 4001012024/9, letter to Reusch, Oct. 5, 1931. Another of those present, Erich von Gilsa, the former DVP deputy closely associated with Reusch, was also a member of the Stahlhelm: Volker Berghahn, *Der Stahlhelm* (Düsseldorf, 1966), pp. 117ff., 122, 174. Still another figure present (although this escaped the attention even of Hugenberg's Telegraphen-

Union) with ties to the Stahlhelm was Hans von Loewenstein, executive director of the organization of Ruhr coal operators, the Bergbauverein: BBB, Loewenstein Papers, Anordnungen der Militärregierung für den Bereich Essen, Loewenstein to Friedrich Christian Prinz zu Schaumburg-Lippe, Oct. 8, 1931. One of the active businessmen listed as present by the Telegraphen-Union was also an active Stahlhelmer, Louis Ravené, a Berlin iron wholesaler: BAL, Autographen-Sammlung Duisberg, Ravené to Duisberg, Mar. 11, 1932. So, according to August Heinrichsbauer, was Hellmuth Poensgen (see n. 48).

45. GHH, 400101293/4, Gilsa to Kellermann, March 21, 1931; Reusch to Gilsa, Mar. 23, 1931; ibid., Kellermann Papers, 40010137/12, Erich Winnacker (a director of United Steel who was active in the DNVP) to Kellermann, Mar. 18, 1931; Kellermann to Winnacker, Mar. 31, 1931; Winnacker to Kellermann, Apr. 1, 1931. As a result of this correspondence, Reusch's firm, the Gutehoffnungshütte, contributed the modest sum of five hundred marks each to the Stahlhelm and the local units of the DVP and DNVP in support of their efforts on behalf of the referendum.

46. See Berghahn, *Stahlhelm,* pp. 179–86.

47. For such reports, which specified only the name of Fritz Springorum, managing director of the Hoesch steel firm and treasurer of the Ruhrlade, see Blank to Reusch, Oct. 5, 1931, and Blank to Springorum, Oct. 5, 1931: Maurer and Wengst (eds.), *Politik und Wirtschaft,* II, pp. 1017–19.

48. Bracher, *Auflösung,* p. 410, adds names to the Telegraphen-Union list and omits others, giving no source whatever for any of that information, not even a reference for the original list. One name added there is that of Fritz Thyssen, whose ghostwritten memoir places him at Bad Harzburg (*I Paid Hitler,* p. 97), but who could not possibly have attended since he was on an extended trip to the United States at the time; see the report on his speech at Columbia University on Oct. 21: "Thyssen sees Reich Balked by the Mark," *The New York Times,* Oct. 22, 1931. The reporter for the *Berliner Tageblatt* commented on the absence of Thyssen and also that of Kirdorf: "'Kein Mensch hat sich erschreckt,'" issue of Oct. 13, 1931 (#482). In numerous versions of the gathering Albert Vögler and Ernst Poensgen, chairman and vice-chairman, respectively, of the board of directors of United Steel, appear among those allegedly present. But in "'Kein Mensch hat sich erschrekt'" the reporter for the *Berliner Tageblatt* commented expressly on Vögler's absence. If he had been present, moreover, he would have been identified, as was customary, as Generaldirektor, the most prestigious title in German industry; the "Dr. Vögler" listed as present by Hugenberg's wire service was in all likelihood his younger brother, Dr. Eugen Vögler, an executive of a construction firm: Klass, *Vögler,* p. 20; Wenzel, *Deutscher Wirtschaftsführer,* col. 2341. As the reporter for the *Berliner Tageblatt* specified, "a Poensgen" was present at Bad Harzburg, but he would hardly have expressed his information in that fashion if the member of that large family on hand had been Ernst, one of Germany's foremost industrial executives: "'Kein Mensch hat sich erschreckt!'" issue of Oct. 13, 1931 (#482). The Telegraphen-Union list included a "Geheimrat Poensgen," but Ernst did not bear that honorific title from imperial times. Conceivably that title may have erroneously been applied to Kommerzienrat Rudolf Poensgen, a re-

tired elderly relative of Ernst Poensgen: Wenzel, *Wirtschaftsführer*, col. 1721. But it seems most likely that the Poensgen at Harzburg was Ernst's younger cousin, Hellmuth, whom August Heinrichsbauer later specified as one of those present: NA, RG 238, Case 10, Dokumentenbuch Bülow I, Heinrichsbauer's affidavit of Jan. 31, 1948. According to Heinrichsbauer, Hellmuth Poensgen attended as a representative of the Stahlhelm. One of the fifty-some members of United Steel's board of directors, Hellmuth Poensgen was also active in the DNVP and proclaimed his endorsement of the "national opposition" at a Düsseldorf rally of that party just days before the Bad Harzburg conclave: "Kampf der Erfüllungspolitik," *Tempo*, Oct. 10, 1931; a Berlin daily, *Tempo* mistakenly identified the speaker as Ernst Poensgen, but the announcements of the meeting by the DNVP explicitly identify him as Hellmuth: SAD, Nachlass Lehr, vol. 7, announcements dated Oct. 5, 1931; see also Gisbert Gemein, "Die DNVP in Düsseldorf 1918–1933" (diss., Universität Köln, 1969), pp. 97f.; Hellmuth is incorrectly identified there as Ernst's brother; on the familial relationship, see the letter from Albert Wiedemann to Hellmuth Poensgen, Nov. 8, 1929: BA/MA, Wiedemann Papers, N 158/17.

49. See, for examples, Arthur Schweitzer, *Big Business in the Third Reich* (Bloomington, 1964), pp. 34, 96f.; Michael Schneider, *Unternehmer und Demokratie*, p. 106; Dirk Stegmann, *Die Erben Bismarcks* (Cologne and Berlin, 1970), p. 521; Joachim C. Fest, *Hitler* (Frankfurt, 1973), p. 419. Pätzold and Weissbecker, *Geschichte der NSDAP*, p. 149. In one version of the Harzburg meeting, rumors about businessmen allegedly invited or planning to attend that circulated a week prior to the gathering serve as evidence about those who actually attended: Dirk Stegmann, "Zum Verhältnis von Grossindustrie und Nationalsozialismus 1930–1933," *AfS* 13 (1973): 420f., esp. n. 102. The list of participants, expanded in this fashion, has now become the basis for a still further version: Schulz, *Aufstieg*, p. 662.

50. "'Kein Mensch hat sich erschreckt,'" issue of Oct. 13, 1931 (#482).

51. Gilsa to Reusch, Oct. 13, 1931: Maurer and Wengst (eds.), *Politik und Wirtschaft*, II, pp. 1043f. On Reusch's absence, see GHH, 4001012024/9, Reusch to Blank, Oct. 6, 1931.

52. Schacht to Reusch, Oct. 20, 1931: GHH, 400101290/33.

53. Gilsa to Reusch, Oct. 13, 1931: Maurer and Wengst (eds.), *Politik und Wirtschaft*, II, pp. 1043f.

54. Blank to Springorum, Oct. 5, 1931: ibid., II, pp. 1018f.

55. Gilsa to Reusch, Oct. 13, 1931: ibid., II, pp. 1043f.

56. Reusch to Gilsa, Oct. 14, 1931: GHH, 400101293/4.

57. Schacht to Hitler, Apr. 12, 1932: text in Fritz Klein, "Neue Dokumente zur Rolle Schachts bei der Vorbereitung der Hitlerdiktatur," *ZfG* 5 (1957): 821. Fritz Klein, editor of the *Deutsche Allgemeine Zeitung* and father of the author of the above article, was well aware that the big businessmen who owned his paper were at the mercy of the chancellor, whose confidence he enjoyed. When some of the industrialists involved in the consortium behind the *DAZ* considered selling it to Hugenberg in late 1931, Klein rested secure in the knowledge that Brüning could quash any such deal by exploiting the dependency of industry on his government; see his diary entries for Nov. 16 and Dec. 21, 1931: KP.

Chapter IV, section 2: Ruhr Coal: Canards and Calculations

1. See, for example, Bullock, *Hitler*, pp. 156f.; Fest, *Hitler*, p. 418; Schweitzer, *Big Business*, p. 100.

2. Otto Dietrich, *Mit Hitler in die Macht* (Munich, 1934), pp. 45f.

3. Otto Dietrich, *Zwölf Jahre mit Hitler* (Cologne, n.d. [1955]), p. 185.

4. Blank to Reusch, Sept. 4, 1931; Reusch to Blank, Sept. 5, 1931: GHH, 4001012024/9. NA, RG 238, NI-446, Heinrichsbauer to Krupp, Sept. 3, 1931; NI-443, Krupp's secretary to Heinrichsbauer, Sept. 8, 1931. Invitation from Prince and Princess Wied to Loewenstein (undated), and reply by Loewenstein's secretariat, Sept. 9, 1931: BBB, Loewenstein Papers, Allgemeiner Schriftwechsel. On the Wieds' relationship to Göring, see Wilamowitz-Moellendorff, *Carin Göring*, pp. 126–28.

5. "Hitler als Gast in Essen. Finanzielle Hintergründe," *General-Anzeiger für Dortmund und das gesamte rheinisch-westfälische Industriegebiet*, Jan. 15, 1931 (#15).

6. See, for example, "Zechengeld für Hitler," *Vorwärts*, May 28, 1931 (#243); "Gelbe Garde vom Hakenkreuz," *Münchener Post*, May 29, 1931 (#121); also the denial by the Bergbauverein, "Kein Industriegeld für Hitler," *Deutsche Allgemeine Zeitung*, May 28, 1931 (#236).

7. *Verhandlungen des Reichstages*, vol. 446, p. 2082, Breidscheid's speech of Oct. 14, 1931. The Social Democratic press immediately published his remarks: "Sozialismus, nicht Reaktion!" *Vorwärts*, Oct. 14, 1931 (#482).

8. "Unsere Meinung," *Deutsche Allgemeine Zeitung*, Oct. 16, 1931 (#477).

9. "Durch Industriegelder werden die Nazi grossgezogen," *Münchener Post*, Nov. 14–15, 1931 (#204).

10. Fritz Küster, *Die Hintermänner der Nazis. Von Papen bis Deterding* (Hanover, 1946), p. 15. Thirty-five years later that version of the tale was still an article of faith not only in Communist circles in East Germany but also among Social Democrats in the Federal Republic; see the speech by SPD treasurer Alfred Nau: *Parteitag der Sozialdemokratischen Partei Deutschlands vom 1. bis 5. Juni 1966 in Dortmund* (Bonn, 1966), p. 225. The East German version appears in the widely distributed indoctrination publication: Institut für Gesellschaftswissenschaften beim ZK der SED, *Imperialismus heute*, 5th ed. (East Berlin, 1968), p. 56.

11. Report of the Polizeipräsident of Essen to the Regierungspräsident in Düsseldorf, Jan. 15, 1931: LHAK, 403/16734, Bl. 283–5. Cf. Böhnke, *Die NSDAP im Ruhrgebiet*, p. 160.

12. Report of Polizeipräsident in Essen to the Regierungspräsident in Düsseldorf, Jan. 22, 1931: HSAD, Regierung Düsseldorf, 17251. Cf. "In eigener Sache. Zurückweisung einer schmutzigen Verleumdung," *National-Zeitung*, Jan. 19, 1931 (#15).

13. Report of the Oberpräsident in Koblenz to the minister of the interior, July 25, 1931: LHAK, 403/16734, Bl. 347.

14. Kurt Koszyk, "Jakob Stöcker und der Dortmunder 'General-Anzeiger' 1929–1933," *Publizistik. Zeitschrift für die Wissenschaft von der Presse* 8 (July–Aug. 1963), pp. 282–95.

15. Communication of Bergbauverein to its members, Feb. 4, 1930: copy in HHSA, records of de-nazification trial of Fritz Thyssen, Hauptakte 287.

16. Gustav Deschamps, General Direktor of Concordia-Bergbau A.G., to Brandi, Sept. 22, 1930: BBB, Loewenstein Papers, Allgemeiner Schriftwechsel, Brandi.

17. Loewenstein to Brandi, Sept. 30, 1930: Brandi to Deschamps, Oct. 1, 1930; staff memorandum for their replies, Sept. 22, 1930: BBB, Loewenstein Papers, Allgemeiner Schriftwechsel, Brandi.

18. See Turner, "The *Ruhrlade.*"

19. All three coal-mining operations of the Prussian state belonged to the Bergbauverein; two, Steinkohlenbergwerk Hibernia and Bergwerks-Aktiengesellschaft Recklinghausen, also belonged to the Zechenverband; the general director of the latter two operations, Otto von Velsen, sat on the managing boards and executive committees of both organizations: *Jahrbuch für den Ruhrkohlenbezirk,* herausgegeben vom Verein für die bergbaulichen Interessen, Jg. 30 (Essen, 1932), pp. 405–9. See also Paul Osthold, *Die Geschichte des Zechenverbandes 1908–1933* (Berlin, 1934); and Winkler, *Preussen als Unternehmer.*

20. Brandi to Oberberghauptmann Ernst Flemming, Aug. 15, 1932; copy, with notation, to General Director Otto von Velsen: BAK, Hugenberg Papers, 36.

21. Helmut Lüthgen, *Das Rheinisch-Westfälische Kohlensyndikat in der Vorkriegs-, Kriegs- und Nachkriegszeit und seine Hauptprobleme* (Leipzig and Erlangen, 1926); *Handbuch der Deutschen Aktien-Gesellschaften,* Jg. 37, Bd. 4 (Berlin, 1932), pp. 5411–13. See also the affidavit of Dec. 29, 1947, in which the veteran general secretary of the cartel, Albert Janus, categorically denied any contributions by it to the NSDAP prior to the Nazi takeover in 1933: NA, RG 238, Case 10, Dokumentenbuch II Bülow, #14.

22. Hugenberg to Loewenstein, May 29, 1931: BAK, Hugenberg Papers, 192.

23. Loewenstein to Brandi, June 5, 1931: BBB, Loewenstein Papers, Allgemeiner Schriftwechsel, Brandi.

24. See, for examples, Max Koch, *Die Bergarbeiterbewegung im Ruhrgebiet zur Zeit Wilhelms II., 1889–1914* (Düsseldorf, 1954). For an interesting comparison of the determinants of management attitudes in coal and in iron and steel, see Elaine Glovka Spencer, "Between Capital and Labor: Supervisory Personnel in Ruhr Heavy Industry before 1914," *JSH* 9 (1975): 182–84.

25. See Prym, *Staatswirtschaft,* pp. 31–44; Medalen, "State Monopoly Capitalism," pp. 82–112.

26. Hugo Bonikowski, "Die öffentliche Bewirtschaftung der Kohle," *Handbuch der Kohlenwirtschaft,* ed. by Karl Borchardt (Berlin, 1926), pp. 369–81. See also Peter Wulf, "Regierung, Parteien, Wirtschaftsverbände und die Sozialisierung des Kohlenbergbaues 1920–1921," in Hans Mommsen et al. (eds.), *Industrielles System,* pp. 647–57.

27. Hans Mommsen, "Sozialpolitik im Ruhrbergbau," in idem et al. (eds.), *Industrielles System,* pp. 303–21; see also Gerald D. Feldman, "Arbeitskonflikte im Ruhrbergbau 1919–1922," *VfZ* 28 (1980): 168–223.

28. On Brandi, see the obituary in *Stahl und Eisen,* Nov. 11, 1937 (Jg. 57, #45), pp. 1291f.; also Walter Bacmeister, *Nekrologe aus dem rheinisch-westfälischen Industriegebiet. Jahrgang 1937* (Essen, 1940), pp. 12–14.

29. According to Walter Serlo, *Die Preussischen Bergassessoren*, 4th ed. (Essen, 1933), only 1,750 men had qualified for the title since 1850.

30. Brandi to Walther Bernhard, Oct. 23, 1931: KP.

31. Brandi to Hans von Loewenstein, Feb. 21, 1931: BBB, Loewenstein Papers, file "Anordnungen der Militärregierung für den Bereich Essen."

32. On Loewenstein, see Fritz Pudor, *Lebensbilder aus dem rheinisch-westfälischen Industriegebiet. Jahrgang 1958–1959* (Düsseldorf, 1962), pp. 82–84.

33. Hans Mommsen, "Der Ruhrbergbau im Spannungsfeld von Politik und Wirtschaft in der Zeit der Weimarer Republik," *Blätter für deutsche Landesgeschichte* 108 (1972): 166f.

34. Since 1921 Loewenstein had promoted the Bund für Ständischen Aufbau, which published the periodical *Blätter für Ständischen Aufbau:* BBB, Loewenstein Papers, Ständischer Aufbau.

35. Ibid., Allgemeiner Schriftwechsel, Loewenstein to Reupke, Nov. 9, 1931; see also the file "Anordnungen der Militärregierung für den Bereich Essen," Loewenstein to Schaumburg-Lippe, Oct. 8, 1931, and Feb. 11, 1932.

36. Ibid., Allgemeiner Schriftwechsel, Verschiedenes A 1, Loewenstein to Bergrat Prof. Dr.-Ing. Böker, Aachen, Oct. 26, 1931.

37. Ibid., Loewenstein to Hitler, Oct. 13, 1931. The book was vol. 5 of Hans Spethmann, *Zwölf Jahre Ruhrbergbau*, 5 vols. (Essen, 1928–1931), a work sponsored by the Bergbauverein.

38. Horkenbach (ed.), *Das Deutsche Reich* (1931), p. 193.

39. On the Ruhrlade, see Brandi to Springorum, Mar. 1, 1930: HAD, Springorum Papers, B1a 84.

40. Niederschrift über die Vorstandssitzung der Fachgruppe Bergbau am 16. Januar 1931: BBA, Bestand 15, Bd. 13; Blank to Reusch, Jan. 27, 1931, and Reusch to Blank, Jan. 28, 1931: 4001012024/8.

41. Letter of Dec. 4, 1934: BBA, Zechen-Verband, 13/703.

42. NA, RG 238, NI-12850, affidavit of Jan. 29, 1947; see also Pre-Trial Interrogations, Heinrichsbauer, Jan. 9, 1947.

43. Turner (ed.), *Hitler aus nächster Nähe*, p. 229.

44. See, for example, "An unsere Angestellten und Arbeiter," a joint protest against alleged Social Democratic attempts to stir up class conflict issued by the Bergbauverein and the northwest group of the iron and steel industrialists' association, *National-Zeitung*, Essen, issue of July 18–19, 1931 (#166).

45. On the attitudes and actions of Brandi and Loewenstein during 1932, see below, chapter V, section 4, and chapter VI, section 2.

Chapter IV, section 3: The Proliferating Forks of Nazism's Tongue

1. Hans-Gerd Schumann, *Nationalsozialismus und Gewerkschaftsbewegung* (Hanover and Frankfurt, 1958), pp. 30 ff.

2. For the following, see Kele, *Nazis and Workers*, pp. 168–98; see also an East German interpretation: Hermann Roth, "Die nationalsozialistische Betriebszellenorganisation, (NSBO) von der Gründung bis zur Röhm-Affäre (1928 bis 1934)," *JBWG*, 1978, Teil 1, pp. 49–66.

3. "Theaterdonner der Gewerkschaften für den 1. Dez.," *Betriebsarbeiter und Hakenkreuz. Kampfblatt der National-Sozialistischen-Betr. Zellen-Organisation,*

Wanne, issue of Nov. 21, 1931, copy enclosed in report of the Polizeipräsident of Bochum to the Oberpräsident in Münster, Nov. 26, 1931: SAM, Regierung Münster, Abt. VII, Nr. 67, Band 3.

4. Otto Wagener, head of the Economic Policy Section of the Reichsleitung, announced this campaign in a Rundschreiben to his organization on Sept. 13, 1931: Maurer and Wengst (eds.), *Politik und Wirtschaft*, II, pp. 954–56.

5. See the report on Funk's talk, which took place on Oct. 16, "Nationalsozialismus und Wirtschaft," by J. W. Reichert, manager of the national organization of iron and steel industrialists, enclosed with his letter to the industrialist Friedrich Flick, Oct. 19, 1931: NA, RG 238, NI-8316.

6. Feder spoke on Oct. 22: Report of Regierungspräsident, Düsseldorf, to Oberpräsident, Koblenz, Nov. 17, 1931: LHAK, 403/16735. *Vorwärts*, the SPD daily, later listed some of those present in an article characteristically entitled "Hitlers Geldgeber": issue of Nov. 14, 1931 (#536). Of the sixteen men listed, including a man identified as a local brewery director, only two, possibly three, merited entries in a directory of more than 13,000 prominent businessmen, Wenzel, *Wirtschaftsführer:* Karl Storkebaum, director of the association of steel cable manufacturers (ibid., cols. 2233f.); Eugen Wiskott, a sixty-four-year-old former general director of a defunct coal-mining firm, who sat on the supervisory boards of a number of other mining enterprises (ibid., col. 2479); and a member of the Tengelmann family of Essen, listed without first name or title, who may have been Ernst or Fritz, executives of the Essener Steinkohlenbergwerke AG, which was swallowed up in the Gelsenkirchener Bergwerks-AG in 1930 (ibid., cols. 2264f.); but the Tengelmann in question may also have been one of the younger generation of that family, who were still only junior coal executives in 1931.

7. See the program for the "conference" of Nov. 7, 1931, and the report on it by the Polizeipräsident, Düsseldorf, to the Regierungspräsident, Düsseldorf, Nov. 10, 1931: LHAK, 403/16736.

8. In a letter to Hans von Loewenstein of the Bergbauverein of Nov. 28, 1931, Gustav Knepper, head of the coal-mining operations of the United Steel Works, invited Loewenstein to a "simple supper" at the Kaiserhof Hotel on the evening of Dec. 7, after which Gregor Strasser would join in a discussion with "a small circle of representatives of the coal industry": BBB, Loewenstein Papers, Allgemeine Schriftwechsel, A 1. Loewenstein accepted in a letter of Dec. 2 to Knepper: ibid. After the war Ludwig Grauert, manager of the Ruhr industrial employers' association (Arbeitnordwest), recalled hearing Strasser address a gathering of thirty-some coal operators at the Kaiserhof at the end of 1931 or the beginning of 1932: NA, RG 238, Pre-Trial Interrogations, Grauert, Oct. 8, 1946.

9. Turner (ed.), *Hitler aus nächster Nahe*, pp. 441–43.

10. "Hitler's Geldgeber," issue of Nov. 14, 1931 (#536).

11. Reichert widely circulated his report, which has turned up not only in the Flick documents at Nuremberg (see n. 5, above) but also in the Westarp Papers at Gaertringen (with Reichert's letter of Oct. 19 to Count Kuno von Westarp); in addition, Funk's reply of Nov. 1 to Fritz Springorum's letter to him of Oct. 24 makes clear that Springorum's information about his speech derived from Reichert (see n. 12).

12. HAD, Springorum Papers, 337o/6, Funk to Springorum, Nov. 1, 1931. Springorum's letter to Funk of Oct. 24 has apparently not survived.

13. NA, RG 238, Pre-Trial Interrogations, Ludwig Grauert, Sept. 2, 1946.

14. LHAK, 403/16735, report of Regierungspräsident, Düsseldorf, to Oberpräsident, Koblenz, Nov. 17, 1931.

15. "Wirtschaftspolitische Unklarheit im Nationalsozialismus," *Deutsche Führerbriefe*, Nov. 15, 1931 (#89).

16. This was the conclusion of one man after hearing a talk, to a "small circle" that included some businessmen, by Joachim Haupt, editor of a Nazi newspaper in Lower Saxony and head of the Organisationsabteilung II of the Gau Hannover-Süd Braunschweig: copy of letter, with salutation "Sehr geehrter Herr Doktor," undated, without signature, located in Paul Reusch's correspondence with Max Schlenker of the Langnamverein and northwest group of the Verein Deutscher Eisen- und Stahlindustrieller for 1931–32, in GHH, 400101221/11.

17. Gilsa to Reusch, Aug. 6, 1931: Maurer and Wengst (eds.), *Politik und Wirtschaft*, II, p. 871.

18. Blank to Reusch, Aug. 11, 1931: ibid., II, p. 883.

19. "Nationalsozialismus," in Hansa-Bund, *Wirtschaftspolitisches ABC-Buch* (Berlin, n.d. [1931]), pp. 138–42.

20. Siemens, *Die gegenwärtige Lage Deutschlands. Rede gehalten auf dem Frühstück des Bond-Club in New York am 30. Oktober 1931* (n.p., n.d.).

21. BBB, Loewenstein Papers, Allgemeine Wirtschaftsfragen, Bd. 3, file on Geschäftsführervereinigung der landschaftlichen Industrieverbände im Reichsverband der Deutschen Industrie, Niederschrift for the meeting of Oct. 30, 1931.

22. This view was made explicit a year earlier by the young Hermann Winkhaus, son of a member of the Ruhrlade who served in a junior position in the management of the coal-mining operations of Paul Reusch's Gutehoffnungshütte: letter to Fritz Springorum, Dec. 8, 1930: HAD, Springorum Papers, 337o/1.

23. Gilsa to Reusch, Dec. 18, 1931: GHH, 400101293/4. See also "Hitler soll kapitalistischer werden. Herr von Gilsa will dafür sorgen," *Frankfurter Zeitung*, Feb. 12, 1932 (#113–114), quoting the part of the memo cited here from the organ of the Christian trade union movement, *Der Deutsche*, of Feb. 11, 1932.

24. See Leopold, *Hugenberg*, p. 105; Berghahn, *Stahlhelm*, pp. 187–90; Ernst-August Roloff, *Bürgertum und Nationalsozialismus 1930–1933. Braunschweigs Weg ins Dritte Reich* (Hanover, 1961), pp. 73–75.

25. Hindenburg's memo of Feb. 25, 1932: Maurer and Wengst (eds.), *Politik und Wirtschaft*, II, p. 1307.

26. Eberhart Schön, *Die Entstehung des Nationalsozialismus in Hessen* (Meisenheim am Glan, 1972), p. 195.

27. Ibid., pp. 194f. Krebs, *Tendenzen*, p. 32; Horkenbach (ed.), *Das Deutsche Reich* (1931), pp. 339, 344.

28. Döhn, *Politik und Interesse*, p. 204; Maurer and Wengst (eds.), *Politik und Wirtschaft*, II, pp. 1085–87, Gilsa to Reusch, Nov. 3, 1931; ibid., pp. 1137f.,

Gilsa to Reusch, Dec. 3, 1931; Gilsa to Kellermann, Nov. 3, 1931: GHH, Kellermann Papers, 400101308/9.

Chapter IV, section 4: Nazis and Lesser Businessmen

1. *Wirtschaft und Statistik*, Mar. 14, 1930 (Jg. 10, Nr. 5), p. 214.
2. See, for example, Helmut Schwarzbach, "Die Differenzen zwischen dem Verband Sächsischer Industrieller und dem Reichsverband der Deutschen Industrie 1931," in *JBWG*, 1971, Teil 3, pp. 75–93.
3. "Der nationalsozialistische Kämpfer Martin Mutschmann 60 Jahre," *VB*, Mar. 9, 1939 (#68); Peter Hüttenberger, *Die Gauleiter* (Stuttgart, 1969), p. 217; SPD, *Reichstagswahl 1930. Referentenmaterial* (Berlin, [1930]), p. 48.
4. On the Heidelberg speech, see Petzold, *Demagogie*, pp. 256f. On Keppler's background, see Turner, "Grossunternehmertum und Nationalsozialisms," p. 34; Johnpeter Horst Grill, *The Nazi Movement in Baden, 1920–1945* (Chapel Hill, 1983), pp. 154–57.
5. "Albert Pietzsch," *Deutsche Zeitung*, Nov. 21, 1941; *Das Deutsche Führerlexikon*, p. 355. Pietzsch's firm was capitalized at only three million marks when it became an Aktiengesellschaft in 1928: Hans Radandt, "'100 Jahre Deutsche Bank,'" p. 57; see also the unpublished memoir by Alfred Vagts, who met Pietzsch as a student in Munich: "Adolf Hitlers Maler—Adolf Ziegler" (manuscript made available by Dr. Vagts).
6. Turner (ed.), *Hitler aus nächster Nähe*, pp. II, 13.
7. See the excerpt from the favorable review in *Die Deutsche Arbeitgeber-Zeitung* of Alfred Rosenberg's *Der Mythos des 20. Jahrhunderts*, reprinted in Hans Reupke, *Der Nationalsozialismus und die Wirtschaft*, p. 26, n. 5a; also "Wirtschaft und Wahlen," in *Die Deutsche Arbeitgeber-Zeitung*, Nov. 20, 1932 (Jg. 31, Nr. 47). The editor of the paper, Friedrich Fikentscher, first applied for membership in the NSDAP in 1927 and finally joined in 1932: BDC, personnel records. The paper, rather than *Der Arbeitgeber*, is erroneously identified as the organ of the Vereinigung der Deutschen Arbeitgeberverbände in Gerhard Jeschke, "Vom 'Neuen Staat' zur 'Volksgemeinschaft'. Unternehmerverbände und Reichspolitik vom Sturz Brünings bis zu den Märzwahlen 1933," in *Ergebnisse. Hefte für historische Öffentlichkeit*, Heft 8 (Oct. 1979): 11–96. See also Jürgen John, "Die Faschismus-'Kritik' in der Zeitschrift 'Der Arbeitgeber,'" *ZfG* 30 (1982): 1072–86.
8. On the following, see Fritz Dickmann, "Die Regierungsbildung in Thüringen als Modell der Machtergreifung," *VfZ* 14 (1966): 454–64; "Die Regierungsbildung," *Weimarische Zeitung*, Jan. 10, 1930 (#9); "Noch keine Entscheidung im Landtag," ibid., Jan. 11, 1930 (#10).
9. Turner (ed.), *Hitler aus nächster Nähe*, pp. 312f.
10. "Adolf Hitler über Politik und Wirtschaft," *Weimarische Zeitung*, Jan. 11, 1930 (#10); see also "Die Volkspartei gegen Frick," *Vossische Zeitung*, Jan. 12, 1930 (#11); also "Adolf Hitler vor geladenen Gäste in Weimar," *VB*, Jan. 17, 1930 (#13).
11. Dickmann, "Regierungsbildung," p. 462.
12. Rudolf Ludloff, *Kasernen statt Wohnungen. Zur Geschichte der deutschen Zementindustrie im Imperialismus bis 1945* (East Berlin, 1963), p. 182.

13. Johannes Müller, *Die Industrialisierung der deutschen Mittelgebirge* (Jena, 1938).

14. Ludloff, *Kasernen,* pp. 181f.

15. "Ein Schritt näher. Die Regierungsbildung in Thüringen," *Weimarische Zeitung,* Jan. 9, 1930 (#8).

16. Ludloff, *Kasernen,* pp. 181–86.

17. NA, RG 242, Microcopy T-81, 116/136685-7, Carl Hoesrich, Roda bei Ilmenau, to Gauleitung, Weimar, Mar. 1, 1932.

18. Ibid., frame 136992, Verband der Mitteldeutschen Industrie e.V. to Fraktion der NSDAP, Weimar, Sept. 28, 1931.

19. On the banks, see Born, *Bankenkrise.* The story of Borsig has yet to be fully recounted or analyzed; see the information on the government's advance of 1.2 million marks to Borsig in July 1931 in Fritz Blaich, "'Garantierter Kapitalismus'. Subventionspolitik und Wirtschaftsordnung in Deutschland zwischen 1925 und 1932," *ZfU* 22 (1977): 62f. After further aid from the Reich during the summer, the firm finally declared its insolvency in December 1931, but its operations were salvaged by means of a receivership subsidized in part by the Reich. I am grateful to Dr. Dieter Lindenlaub for alerting me to the documentation on Borsig in the records of the Reichsfinanzministerium, BAK, R2/14.968–14.973, 14.975, 17.237–17.239, and the records of the Deutsche Revisions- und Treuhand AG, BAK, R84, Borsig 1930 und 1931.

20. In September 1931 Brüning told a group of industrialists that the government had to intervene to avert the damage that the collapse of large enterprises entailed for the economy: Maurer and Wengst (eds.), *Politik und Wirtschaft,* II, p. 972.

21. Paul Kleinewefers, *Jahrgang 1905. Ein Bericht* (Stuttgart, 1977), pp. 83–85.

22. Hansa-Bund, *Jahresbericht 1931. Heft 29 der Flugschriften des Hansa-Bundes* (Berlin, n.d. [1932]), pp. 5f.; Kleinewefers, *Jahrgang 1905,* pp. 76f.

23. See, for example, the revealing observations about the "Jewish problem" in Kleinewefers, *Jahrgang 1905,* p. 78.

24. "Wirtschaftsdiktator Feder," *Vorwärts,* May 23, 1931 (#236).

25. Report of Oberpräsident of the Rhineland to the Prussian minister of the interior, Jan. 16, 1932: LHAK, 403/16736.

26. "Die Wirtschaftspolitik des Nationalsozialismus," *Der Tag,* Nov. 23, 1931 (#280).

27. Lutz Graf Schwerin von Krosigk, *Die grosse Zeit des Feuers: Der Weg der deutschen Industrie,* 3 vols. (Tübingen, 1957–59), III, pp. 251, 274.

28. Report of Oberregierungsrat Peters to Oberpräsident of the Rhineland, May 4, 1931: LHAK, 403/16734.

29. Ibid., report of Oberpräsident of the Rhineland to the Prussian minister of the interior, July 25, 1931. On the Schoellers and Schulls, see Zunkel, *Unternehmer,* pp. 15f., 29, 111. Schwerin von Krosigk, *Zeit des Feuers,* III, p. 274.

30. On Peill, see Schwerin von Krosigk, *Zeit des Feuers,* III, p. 173; also Feder to Organisationsabteilung II, Feb. 1, 1932, announcing Peill's appointment to the NSDAP's Wirtschaftsrat: BAK, NS 22/11. On the Peill family, see Zunkel, *Unternehmer,* p. 114.

31. Schwerin von Krosigk, *Zeit des Feuers,* I, pp. 293f.

32. Friedrich Zunkel, "Die Gewichtung der Industriegruppen bei der Etablierung des Reichsverbandes der Deutschen Industrie," in Mommsen et al. (eds.), *Industrielles System*, p. 640.

33. On the following, see Ulrich Nocken, "Inter-Industrial Conflicts and Alliances as Exemplified by the AVI-Agreement," Mommsen et al. (eds.), *Industrielles System*, pp. 693–704. See also Oscar Funcke, *Der Kampf in der Eisenindustrie* (Hagen, 1934); Gerald D. Feldman, *Iron and Steel in the German Inflation*, pp. 457f.; Fritz Ulrich Fack, "Die deutschen Stahlkartelle in der Weltwirtschaftskrise" (diss., Freie Universität Berlin, 1957), pp. 31f.; Weisbrod, *Schwerindustrie*, p. 482.

34. Abraham Frowein's remarks to the Hauptausschuss of the Reichsverband on Sept. 19, 1930, quoted in Grübler, *Spitzenverbände*, p. 178.

35. "Nazis arbeiten mit Industriellen," *Dortmunder Generalanzeiger*, Jan. 13, 1931 (#13); "Ein I.G. Farben-Syndikus rührt die Trommel für Hitler," ibid., Jan. 14, 1931 (#14); "IG-Farbentrust wirbt für NSDAP," *Sozialistische Republik*, Jan. 15, 1931 (#12); report of Polizeipräsident, Wuppertal, to Regierungspräsident, Düsseldorf, Jan. 16, 1931: LHAK, 403/16733.

36. On Klein, see his Führerfragebogen, dated Feb. 2, 1933, in BDC; *Das Deutsche Führerlexikon*, p. 235; see also the description of his post with Farben in K. Krekeler, for the Direktorium, to Abteilungsvorstände and Betriebsführer, Dormagen, Jan. 28, 1927: BAL, 221/5, Rundschreiben der Sozialabteilung.

37. See Hans-Peter Görgen, *Düsseldorf und der Nationalsozialismus* (Düsseldorf, 1969), pp. 47, 49, 68, 105f. Klein's commitment to corporatism won him appointment in 1933 as head of the Institut für Ständewesen in Cologne, which Fritz Thyssen supported. But his role there got him into trouble with other elements in the party; he was eventually expelled in 1944; see the Gestapo report, "Der Spannkreis. Gefahren und Auswirkungen.Ende Mai 1936," IfZ, 413/52, p. 15; BDC, Partei Korrespondenz on Klein.

38. Report, Regierungspräsident, Düsseldorf, to Oberpräsident of Rhineland, Dec. 21, 1931: LHAK, 403/16736.

39. Nocken, "Inter-Industrial Conflicts and Alliances," pp. 700–3.

40. Ibid., p. 702.

41. See Pleiger's brief autobiography, prepared on Nov. 3, 1947, for the American military tribunal at Nuremberg: NA, RG 238, NI-12222.

42. See the affidavit of Adolf von Carlowitz, Jan. 30, 1948, ibid., NI-13990.

43. See Matthias Riedel, *Eisen und Kohle für das Dritte Reich. Paul Pleigers Stellung in der NS-Wirtschaft* (Göttingen, 1973).

44. See his memoirs, *Krisenmanager im Dritten Reich* (Düsseldorf, 1973).

45. On Daitz, see Wenzel, *Wirtschaftsführer*, col. 419f.; *Das Deutsche Führerlexikon*, p. 89. He became a member of the party on Feb. 1, 1931, according to the membership file in the BDC. In 1932 Daitz, who served as a regional commissioner of the Economic Policy Section of the NSDAP, contributed to one of the party's theoretical tracts on job creation through deficit spending: Karl Dietrich Bracher, Wolfgang Sauer, Gerhard Schulz, *Die nationalsozialistische Machtergreifung* (Cologne, 1960), p. 401. On his career in the Third Reich, when he held a position in the Foreign Ministry, see Hans-Adolf Jacobsen, *Nationalsozialistische Aussenpolitik 1933–1938* (Frankfurt and Berlin, 1968), pp. 61ff. The East German historian Kurt Gossweiler has

unaccountably portrayed Daitz as an IG Farben man: "Hitler und das Kapital," p. 1008.

46. Wirtschaftspolitische Vereinigung, Frankfurt am Main, to Hindenburg, July 17, 1931: ZAP, Büro des Reichspräsidenten, 46. This document has been cited in numerous East German publications as proof of big business support for the NSDAP despite the fact that none of the signatories were important executives. Wilhelm Traupel, for example, has been identified in those publications as an official of Krupp, but actually served merely as head of Krupp's sales division for agricultural machines, with his office in Frankfurt, not at the Essen headquarters of the firm: Wenzel, *Deutscher Wirtschaftsführer*, col. 2303. Another, Hans Geisow, has been identified as an IG Farben executive even though he worked for that firm in a technical capacity as a chemist only until 1931, when he resigned to promote the NSDAP: Hermann A. L. Degener (ed.), *Wer ist's*, 10th ed. (Berlin, 1935), p. 479; Hans Geisow, *So wurde ich Nationalsozialist. Ein Bekenntnis* (Munich, 1931). The misidentification of Geisow with IG Farben derives from the cover letter of July 24, 1931, with which the Präsidium of the Vereinigten Vaterländischen Verbände forwarded the petition to the president. That misidentification has now become an accepted fact in East German publications; cf. Wolfgang Ruge in Hans-Joachim Bartmuss et al., *Deutsche Geschichte in drei Bänden*, 3 vols. (East Berlin, 1968), III, pp. 137f.

47. Turner (ed.), *Hitler aus nächster Nähe*, pp. 314, 385–88.

48. On the banking house, see Kurt von Eichborn, *Das Soll und Haben von Eichborn & Co. in 200 Jahren* (Munich and Leipzig, 1928). On Eichborn himself, see Albert Pietzsch to Major Buch, Apr. 9, 1936: BDC, Oberstes Parteigericht.

49. See the revealing identifications of the businessmen who assumed leadership of the chambers of industry and commerce in Bavaria after the Nazi takeover in Fritz Blaich, "Die bayerische Industrie 1933–1939," in *Bayern in der NS-Zeit*, ed. by Martin Broszat et al., 6 vols. (Munich, 1977–83), II, pp. 241–44.

Chapter V, section 1: Hitler's Industry Club Speech and Its Aftermath

1. A Communist newspaper in Düsseldorf, *Freiheit*, somehow obtained a copy of the invitation and printed it in facsimile on Jan. 25, 1932 (#20).

2. The following is based on the account that Thyssen later consistently gave: Turner, "Fritz Thyssen und 'I paid Hitler,'" p. 232. That version received confirmation from the chairman of the club, Karl Jarres, who was away on a trip when the speech took place, in an affidavit dated Mar. 9, 1948: NA, RG 238, Case 10, Dokumentenbuch Bülow II.

3. "Hitler Pledges to Pay Berlin's Debts to World," *Chicago Tribune*, Dec. 5, 1931; "Private Debts to be First if Hitler is Ruler," *New York Herald Tribune*, Dec. 5, 1931. Hitler gave similar assurances in private to the American ambassador on the same visit to Berlin: Werner Link, *Die amerikanische Stabilisierungspolitik in Deutschland 1921–32* (Düsseldorf, 1970), p. 534.

4. The diplomat, First Secretary of the Embassy Kliefoth, relayed Hanfstaengl's remarks to Hans Schäffer, state secretary in the Finance Ministry: IfZ, Schäffer diary ED 93, entry of Jan. 26, 1932.

5. See, for the following, NA, RG 238, NI-4092, Bericht des Hausvorstandes zur ordentlichen Mitglieder-Versammlung des Industrie-Clubs am Montag, den 31. Oktober 1932; KA, E789, correspondence between Karl Haniel and Krupp, Jan. 1932; "Hitler in Düsseldorf," *Kölnische Volkszeitung*, Jan. 27, 1932 (#27); "'Heil Hitler', der Held der Schwerindustrie in Düsseldorf," *Volkszeitung* (Düsseldorf), Jan. 27, 1932 (#22); Polizeipräsident, Düsseldorf, to Regierungspräsident, Düsseldorf, January 27, 1932: LHAK, 403/16736; Görgen, *Düsseldorf und der Nationalsozialismus*, pp. 26f.

6. See the text in *Vortrag Adolf Hitlers vor westdeutschen Wirtschaftlern im Industrie-Klub zu Düsseldorf am 27. [sic] Januar 1932* (Munich, 1932).

7. Ernst Poensgen, "Hitler und die Ruhrindustriellen. Ein Rückblick," in NA, RG 238, Case 10, Dokumentenbuch Bülow I. Also Max Schlenker's letter of Sept. 1, 1948, to the presiding judge at Thyssen's de-nazification trial: HHSA, Hauptakte, 431.

8. See the mayor's account of 1955, quoted in Walter Först, *Robert Lehr als Oberbürgermeister* (Düsseldorf, 1962), pp. 235f.; also Bericht des Hausvorstandes. . . . (see n. 5, above).

9. See, for example, the report in the SPD *Volkszeitung* of Düsseldorf, Jan. 29, 1932 (#24).

10. "Hitler vor den Industriellen," *Kölnische Volkszeitung*, Jan. 28, 1932 (#28); "Thyssen als Hitlers Schrittmacher," *Vossische Zeitung*, Jan. 27, 1932 (#45); "Industrielle Reverenz," *Berliner Tageblatt*, Jan. 27, 1932 (#45).

11. Report of Kriminal-Kommissar Dr. Meyer, enclosed in report of the Polizeipräsident, Düsseldorf, to the Regierungspräsident, Düsseldorf, Jan. 27, 1932: LHAK, 403/16736.

12. The impressions of the mayor, Dr. Rosendahl, are recorded in the report of the Oberpräsident, Koblenz, to the Prussian Interior Ministry, Feb. 3, 1932: LHAK, 403/16736. The mayor's analysis does not accord entirely with the instances of applause recorded in the printed version of the full speech (see n. 6). That version was, however, published by the Nazis themselves several months after the speech, so that the notations of applause are not above suspicion, especially since they do not appear in excerpts from the speech published in the *Völkischer Beobachter*, Apr. 19, 1932 (#110). The version of the speech printed by the Nazis apparently derived from a stenogram made by the club, which has not survived.

13. Konrad Heiden, *Geburt des Dritten Reiches* (Zurich, 1934), pp. 40f.

14. The following is based on the report of the club's Hausvorstand to its meeting of Oct. 31, 1932 (see n. 5); also the extensive report of the Regierungspräsident, Düsseldorf, to the Oberpräsident, Koblenz, Feb. 5, 1932: LHAK, 403/16736.

15. This is evident from the correspondence of Carl Duisberg, Gustav Krupp von Bohlen und Halbach, Paul Reusch, Paul Silverberg, and Fritz Springorum, cited elsewhere.

16. The following is drawn from the report of the Hausvorstand of Oct. 31, 1932 (see n. 5), and NA, RG 238, NI-10492.

17. Anton Betz, "Die Tragödie der 'Münchner Neuesten Nachrichten' 1932/33," *Journalismus* 2 (1961): 29.

18. The list is in the report of the Regierungspräsident, Düsseldorf, to the Oberpräsident, Koblenz, Feb. 5, 1932: LHAK, 403/16736. The only really

prominent figures mentioned from big industry were Jakob Hasslacher of the Rheinische Stahlwerke, Heinrich Pattberg, a retired coal-mining director, and Wolfgang Reuter of the Demag machine-building firm. On the other hand, the presence of numerous officials of industrial associations was registered.

19. Ibid. Krupp was interested to the extent of sending an observer: letter to Karl Haniel, Jan. 19, 1932: KA, E 789.

20. Neebe, *Grossindustrie*, p. 120.

21. Kleinewefers, *Jahrgang 1905*, pp. 74–76. His memory of the speech's content does not coincide with the surviving text.

22. Diary of Hans Schäffer, entry for Feb. 4, 1932; IfZ, ED 93, vol. 18. See also Brecht's privately printed *Erinnerungen* (Munich, n.d.), p. 49.

23. See n. 12.

24. Regierungspräsident, Düsseldorf, to Oberpräsident, Koblenz, Feb. 5, 1932: LHAK, 403/16736.

25. NA, RG 238, Pre-Trial Interrogations, Aug. 23, 1946. Grauert identified the industrialist as Georg Talbot of Gustav Talbot & Co., a firm that produced railway cars in Aachen: cf. Wenzel, *Wirtschaftführer*, col. 2260. Grauert was interrogated about the gathering again on Sept. 2, 1946, but added little to what he had said earlier about the speech and the audience.

26. The *Deutsche Führerbriefe*, a newsletter for businessmen, soon thereafter erroneously reported that Hitler had spoken out sharply against the trade unions: "Hitler in Düsseldorf," Feb. 5, 1932 (#10). That false rumor has since found its way into the scholarly literature: cf. Schweitzer, *Big Business*, p. 100; Helmut Heiber, *Die Republik von Weimar* (Munich, 1966), p. 242. William Carr, *A History of Germany, 1815–1945* (New York, 1969), p. 347.

27. Krupp to Karl Haniel, Jan. 19, 1932: KA, E 789.

28. NA, RG 238, Case 10, Wilmowsky's testimony of Mar. 31, 1948, vol. 14a, pp. 5305f.

29. Krupp's correspondence with Karl Haniel made it clear that the firm would receive a ticket for only one of its executives, and Janssen was repeatedly specified as the recipient: Krupp to Haniel, Jan. 19, 1932; Haniel to Krupp, Jan. 20 and 23, 1932: KA, E 789. For Janssen's background, see his curriculum vitae in NA, RG 238, NI-9223; see also *Jahrbuch für den Ruhrkohlenbezirk*, herausgegeben vom Verein für die bergbaulichen Interessen, Jg. 30 (Essen, 1932), pp. 147f. See also the Krupp-inspired book by Gert von Klass, *Die drei Ringe* (Tübingen, 1953), p. 413.

30. For Wilmowsky's testimony, see n. 28. Wilmowsky commanded wide respect as a man of integrity who had rejected any involvement with National Socialism before or during the Third Reich. The substance of his testimony about the Krupp executive who attended the Industry Club speech is grossly misconstrued in William Manchester, *The Arms of Krupp* (Boston, 1968), p. 360.

31. Dietrich, *Mit Hitler*, pp. 46–48.

32. Bullock, *Hitler*, pp. 177–79; Bracher, *Auflösung*, p. 441. The repetitions of these accounts are too numerous to cite here fully. They have produced many inventive variations, including one according to which "German industry" resolved on the occasion of the "secret" Düsseldorf gathering of January 1932 to "lend financial aid to Hitler's presidential campaign against

Hindenburg," even though Hitler did not become a candidate until almost a month later: Karl A. Schleunes, *The Twisted Road to Auschwitz* (Urbana, 1970), p. 63. For typical versions, see Schweitzer, *Big Business*, p. 100; George H. Stein, *Hitler* (Englewood Cliffs, 1968), pp. 54f.; Erich Eyck, *A History of the Weimar Republic*, 2 vols. (New York, 1970), II, pp. 359f.; A. J. Ryder, *Twentieth-Century Germany* (New York, 1973), p. 279. For a version still current in West German leftist circles, see Eugen Eberle, "Der Nationalsozialismus aus lebensgeschichtlicher Perspektive," in Volker Rittberger (ed.), *1933. Wie die Republik der Diktatur erlag* (Stuttgart, 1983), p. 170.

33. Dietrich, *Mit Hitler*, p. 49.

34. Dietrich, *Zwölf Jahre mit Hitler*, pp. 185f.

35. Thyssen, *I Paid Hitler*, pp. 100ff. Cf. Turner, "Fritz Thyssen und 'I paid Hitler,'" pp. 231f.

36. Poensgen, "Hitler und die Ruhrindustriellen," p. 6; Thyssen's testimony at his de-nazification trial, August 18, 1948: HHSA, Spruchkammerverfahren gegen Dr. Fritz Thyssen in Königstein, Obertaunus.

37. For Poensgen's critical views on corporatism, see his letter to Jakob Wilhelm Reichert of Nov. 23, 1932, in BAK, R 13 I/105; for Grauert's enthusiasm for Spann's brand of corporatism, see his letter to Göring of Sept. 13, 1932, which he accompanied with a book by one of Spann's disciples, Walter Heinrich: LC, Rare Books Division, Hitler Library. (I am indebted to Professor John Haag for bringing this document to my attention.) On Poensgen's attitude toward Nazism, see the records of his de-nazification trial, HSAD, NW 1002, I 70 908.

38. Diary of Hans Schäffer, recording a conversation with Gustav Brecht on Feb. 4, 1932: IfZ, ED 93.

39. See, for examples, "Hitler an der Festtafel des Kapitals," *Die Rote Fahne*, Jan. 27, 1932 (#21); "Hitler bei den Industriellen" (Cartoon) and "Zehn Fragen der Trustherren und die Antworten Hitlers," ibid., Jan. 28, 1932 (#22); "Wie Hitler mit Krupp und Thyssen schlemmt," ibid., Jan. 30, 1932 (#24).

40. "Adolf Hitler vor der westdeutschen Industrie," *Westdeutscher Beobachter*, Jan. 27, 1932 (#22).

41. "Hitler wirbt für den Sozialismus," *Westdeutscher Beobachter*, Jan. 28, 1932 (#23). See also "Was wollte Adolf Hitler in Düsseldorf?" *National-Zeitung* (Essen), Jan. 29, 1932 (#24).

42. Dr. Liebernickel, Geschäftsführendes Vorstandsmitglied des Wirtschaftsbundes Niedersachsen-Kassel, to Hitler, Jan. 29, 1932: NSHSAH, Hann. 310, 1A 35.

43. "Verleumder am Pranger! Die Wahrheit über Hitlers Vortrag vor den westdeutschen Industriellen," *VB*, Feb. 18, 1932 (#49).

44. "Adolf Hitlers grosse Düsseldorfer Rede vor den Führern der Wirtschaft," *VB*, Apr. 19, 1932 (#110).

45. See n. 6. The authenticity of the text, as printed by the Nazis, went unchallenged by those who heard the speech.

46. Quoted in "Front gegen das Unternehmertum," *Deutsche Bergwerks-Zeitung*, Feb. 4, 1932 (#29).

47. Ottokar Lorenz, *Die Beseitigung der Arbeitslosigkeit* (Berlin, 1932). Internal evidence makes it clear this pamphlet was issued in late January or early February.

48. "Front gegen das Unternehmertum," *Deutsche Bergwerks-Zeitung*, Feb. 4, 1932 (#29).

49. "Zehn Fragen und Antworten," *Nationalsozialistischer Parlamentsdienst*, Ausgabe A, Feb. 4, 1932.

50. "Wirtschaftssätze des Nationalsozialismus," *Kölnische Zeitung*, Feb. 23, 1932 (#107); "Zehn Fragen an Hitler—sozialistische Antworten," *Der Ring*, Feb. 26, 1932.

51. Wilmowsky to Reusch, Mar. 18, 1932; Reusch to Wilmowsky, Mar. 20, 1932: GHH, 400101290/39.

*Chapter V, section 2: Big Business Approaches
the Political Maelstrom in Disarray*

1. "Unsere Meinung," issue of Mar. 13, 1932 (#123).

2. See the list of some of the 430 signatories to the Hindenburg Aufruf of February: *Berliner Börsen-Courier*, Feb. 23, 1932 (#89).

3. The funds were never fully accounted for, and estimates of the amount raised range as high as 7.5 million marks. See the records of the trial of Günther Gereke, chairman of the Arbeitsausschuss of the Kuratorium of the Hindenburgausschüsse and later Reichskommissar für Arbeitsbeschaffung under Schleicher, who was accused, after Hitler's takeover, of embezzling from the funds: LAB, Gereke Prozess, esp. vol. I, pp. 1–14, vol. II, pp. 143–44. See also Gereke's memoirs, *Ich war königlich-preussischer Landrat* (East Berlin, 1970). The documents used in a recent dissertation seem to cover only a small period of the fund-raising effort for Hindenburg: Tammen, "I.G. Farbenindustrie Aktiengesellschaft," pp. 178–82.

4. See, for examples, Duisberg's correspondence during March and April with Fritz Springorum, Paul Reusch, Ernst Tengelmann, and Albert Vögler: BAL, Autographensammlung Duisberg and 76/9.

5. The pamphlet distributed by Thyssen, *Der Sozialismus der Hitlerbewegung im Lichte Spenglerscher Geschichtsforschung oder die tiefste Ursache für den Aufstieg des Nationalsozialismus in Deutschland*, by Rechtsanwalt Dr. Paul Krumm (Geldern, 1932), argued that Hitler, like Spengler, was a spiritual descendant of Frederich the Great; Nazism's "socialism" was, Krumm maintained, rooted in the "collective instinct" of the German *Volk*, which yearned to subordinate the individual voluntarily to the well-being of the whole, something quite contrary to the regimentation of Marxism. At Thyssen's request, Paul Reusch distributed copies to the members of the Ruhrlade; see the correspondence in GHH, 40010124/14. Thyssen had copies sent to other businessmen as well; see the acknowledgment from the secretary of Oscar Schlitter, a director of the Deutsche Bank und Disconto-Gesellschaft, to August Thyssen-Hütte, Apr. 1, 1932: DWI, records of DB & DG, Generalsekretariat Dr. Schlitter, A20/30. Thyssen explained his endorsement of Hitler in his answer to the question "Warum nicht Hindenburg, sondern Hitler?" in *VB*, Mar. 13–14, 1932 (#73/74).

6. Reusch to Bavarian Hindenburg-Ausschuss, Mar. 24, 1932: GHH, 400101293/12. In that letter Reusch announced that the *Fränkischer Kurier*, a Nuremberg daily he controlled, would observe neutrality prior to the second round of balloting. He himself reportedly abstained from casting a second ballot: Franz Mariaux, "Einleitung" to Paul Silverberg's *Reden und Schriften* (Cologne, 1951), p. LXXVI.

7. Leopold, *Hugenberg*, pp. 110f.

8. Springorum to Duisberg, April 14, 1932: BAL, 76/9; Springorum to Wilmowsky, March 22, 1932: GHH, 400101290/36.

9. Gottfried Treviranus, *Das Ende von Weimar* (Düsseldorf, 1968), pp. 296f.; Brüning, *Memoiren*, pp. 531f. The rumors that reached Brüning, to the effect that United Steel, which gave 5,000 marks to the Hindenburg campaign, according to Brüning, also gave a half million marks to Hitler, remain unsubstantiated. In view of United Steel's mounting financial difficulties and its increasing dependence on the Brüning cabinet through the Gelsenkirchen affair (see below), those rumors seem highly implausible. On the contradictions between Brüning's memoirs and his earlier writings on this point, see Rudolf Morsey, *Zur Entstehung, Authentizität und Kritik von Brünings 'Memoiren 1918–1934'* (Opladen, 1975), p. 18.

10. For a sample of the business community's attitude toward the Braun cabinet on the day of the election, see the diatribe in "Die Woche," *Deutsche Bergwerks-Zeitung*, Apr. 24, 1932 (#96).

11. See chapter IV, section 1.

12. See Springorum's letter to Tilo von Wilmowsky of Mar. 22, 1932: Maurer and Wengst (eds.), *Politik und Wirtschaft*, II, pp. 1352–54. See also the confidential minutes of the meeting of the Wirtschaftsverband der Hannoverschen Industrie on Apr. 15, 1932: BBB, Loewenstein Papers, Allgemeine Wirtschaftsfragen, Bd. 3. That organization resolved to aid the DVP and the DNVP in the Prussian election campaign. See also the reports of a meeting in March of Ruhr Syndizi Grauert, Loewenstein, and Schlenker with spokesmen of the Hanover industrialists in Schlenker to Springorum, Mar. 23, 1932, and Schlenker to Reusch, Mar. 22, 1932: GHH, 400101221/11.

13. Maurer and Wengst (eds.), *Politik und Wirtschaft*, II, p. 1354, Reusch to Wilmowsky, Mar. 23, 1932; p. 1363, Wilmowsky to Reusch, Mar. 25, 1932; pp. 1366f., Wilmowsky to Goerdeler, Apr. 1, 1932; Leopold, *Hugenberg*, p. 113.

14. See, for an articulation of this position, Springorum to Wilmowsky, Mar. 22, 1932, Maurer and Wengst (eds.), *Politik und Wirtschaft*, II, pp. 1352–54.

15. Springorum to Reusch, Apr. 12, 1932, ibid., pp. 1373f.; Reusch to Springorum, Apr. 15, 1932: GHH, 400101290/36; Turner, "The *Ruhrlade*," pp. 214f.

16. See Springorum's letters to Reusch of Mar. 26 and Apr. 12, 1932, Maurer and Wengst (eds.), *Politik und Wirtschaft*, II, pp. 1364, 1373f.

17. At the time of the campaign for the July Reichstag election, Oscar Schlitter, a director of the Deutsche Bank und Disconto-Gesellschaft who had long been active in politics, responded to a request for funds on behalf of a DNVP candidate with a donation of only 1,000 marks: DWI, records of DB

& DG, Generalsekretariat Schlitter, 6469, Max Schlenker to Schlitter, July 13, 1932; Schlitter to Schlenker, July 13, 1932.

18. Gilsa to Kellermann, Apr. 6, 1932: GHH, Allgemeine Verwaltung, 400106/84.

19. Duisberg to Siemens, Feb. 25, 1932; Siemens to Duisberg, Mar. 1, 1932; Duisberg to Siemens, Mar. 7, 1932; Duisberg to Siemens, Mar. 24, 1932; Siemens to Duisberg, Apr. 5, 1932, all in SA, 4/Lf 670.

20. On the actions of the Wirtschaftsverband der Hannoverschen Industrie, see n. 12. No record has been found of contributions by IG Farben, but several officials testified after the war that the practices begun in the 1920s continued throughout the republican period: Hayes, "The *Gleichschaltung* of IG Farben," pp. 67–70.

21. Horkenbach (ed.), *Das Deutsche Reich* (1932), pp. 30, 48.

22. Brandi explained his plans in a letter of Mar. 7, 1932, to Karl Jarres, the DVP mayor of Duisberg and unsuccessful presidential candidate of 1925: BAK, Jarres Papers, 44. On the Bergbauverein's support of the DNVP, see Hugenberg to Mann, May 7, 1932: BAK, Hugenberg Papers, 38. On Brandi's resentment at his exclusion from the political decisions of the Ruhrlade, see the diary of Fritz Klein, editor of the *Deutsche Allgemeine Zeitung,* entry for May 13, 1932: KP.

23. Horst Romeyk, "Die Deutsche Volkspartei in Rheinland und Westfalen 1918–1933," *RVB* 39 (1975): 231f. See also BAK, Dingeldey Papers, 58, Dingeldey to Thiel, Feb. 26, 1932; ibid., report on meeting of Geschäftsführender Ausschuss and Hauptvorstand of DVP Wahlkreisorganisation Westfalen-Süd in Dortmund, Feb. 26. 1932. See also the record of a meeting in which Brandi urged another DVP deputy to break with that party before the Landtag elections: diary of Fritz Klein, entry of Apr. 21, KP. The man in question, Fregattenkapitän a.D. Ernst Hintzmann, resigned—as Brandi had urged—amidst maximum publicity just before the balloting: *Stuttgarter Neues Tageblatt,* Apr. 23, 1932 (#187).

24. "Gelsenkirchen bleibt fest," *Nationalliberale Correspondenz,* Mar. 1, 1932 (#43). See also the informative retrospective account "Bericht über Vorbereitung und Ergebnis der Reichstagswahlen vom 6. November 1932 im Wahlkreis 23 (Düsseldorf-West)," by Generalsekretär Krüger, dated Dec. 6, 1932, and conveyed by Krüger to Dingeldey on Dec. 7, 1932: BAK, Dingeldey Papers, 97b.

25. On the troubles of the DVP, see Döhn, *Politik und Interesse,* pp. 200ff.; Roloff, *Bürgertum und Nationalsozialismus,* pp. 105ff. See also Heinemann (DVP secretary in Westfalen-Süd) to Dingeldey, June 2, 1932, BAK, Dingeldey Papers, 16; "exposé" by Hermann of the Reichsgeschäftsstelle, submitted to party leader Dingeldey on Dec. 2, 1932: ibid., 96a.

26. "Von den Börsen," Apr. 26, 1932 (#308–309).

27. As late as 1932 the DVP had no reliable system for collecting dues or even registering members. The party secretary of the DVP organization in the Dresden-Bautzen Wahlkreis, Johannes Dieckmann, later recalled issuing lists of addresses of persons believed sympathetic to the party to unemployed persons, who were supposed to divide with the party whatever

money they managed to collect by door-to-door solicitation: interview with Dieckmann, East Berlin, Apr. 5, 1966.

28. Leopold, *Hugenberg*, pp.117, 122f.

29. "Das Zentralkomitee der KPD. zum Sturz der Brüningregierung," *Die Rote Fahne*, May 31, 1932 (#117); "Natürlich wieder die Industrie," *Deutsche Bergwerks-Zeitung*, June 1, 1932 (#126), reporting on allegations by an organ of the Christian trade unions.

30. For a succinct, well-documented account of these events, see Vogelsang, *Reichswehr*, pp. 166-202: for important additions, see Bennett, *German Rearmament*, pp. 70-77. See also Udo Wengst, "Schlange-Schöningen, Ostsiedlung und die Demission der Regierung Brüning," *GWU* 30 (1979): 538-51.

31. Support for Brüning within the Reichsverband came particularly from its executive director, Ludwig Kastl, who had become a close unofficial adviser to the chancellor, especially on international economic affairs; see Brüning's *Memoiren*, passim; for an example of Kastl's efforts to dampen criticism of the chancellor by the Ruhr industrialists, see Blank to Reusch, May 18, 1932: Maurer and Wengst (eds.), *Politik und Wirtschaft*, II, pp. 1460f.

32. Kroll, *Von der Weltwirtschaftskrise*, p. 98.

33. William Lewis Patch, Jr., "Christian Trade Unions in the Politics of the Weimar Republic, 1918-1933 "(diss., Yale University, 1981). p. 311.

34. See the protest sent to Brüning by the Reichsverband on May 3, 1932: Maurer and Wengst (eds.), *Politik und Wirtschaft*, II, pp. 1431f. The similar protest from the league of industrial employers is cited there in a footnote.

35. In explanations of his resignation, Warmbold cited a number of grounds, including basic disapproval of Brüning's deflationary policies; see his letter of resignation to Hindenburg: ibid., pp. 1423f.; also his Nuremberg affidavit of Oct. 5, 1947: NA, RG 238, Case 6, Dokumentenbuch Schmitz II; also his letter to the *Frankfurter Allgemeine Zeitung*, Oct. 17, 1968 (#242). Warmbold's resignation was not accepted by Hindenburg until May 6.

36. See Max Schlenker, "Deutschlands Wirtschaftslage und ihre Zukunftsaussichten," *Stahl und Eisen*, May 12, 1932 (Jg. 52, Nr. 19), pp. 465–68. See also the attacks on the cabinet in the *Berliner Börsenzeitung* during May, quoted in Helmut J. Schorr, *Adam Stegerwald* (Recklinghausen, 1966), p. 242.

37. Kastl to Reusch, Sept. 11, 1931: Maurer and Wengst (eds.), *Politik und Wirtschaft*, II, p. 950.

38. A copy of the invitation to the banquet on Sept. 18, 1925, sent to sixteen industrialists, plus some prominent politicians, including the Social Democratic minister president of Prussia, Otto Braun, and his interior minister, Carl Severing, may be found in the Autographensammlung of Carl Duisberg: BAL.

39. Letter to Jakob Herle, June 3, 1932: KA, IV E 178.

40. See, for example, the observations of Paul Reusch, usually the country's politically best-informed industrialist, in a letter to Fritz Schäffer, July 1, 1932: GHH, 400101293/12; also the reaction of Robert Bosch, as recorded in Heuss, *Bosch*, p. 522.

41. See the agenda prepared for the Ruhrlade meeting of Nov. 3, 1930, by its treasurer, Fritz Springorum, in his papers: HAD, F1i 3; ibid., file B1a 84;

also Herbert Gottwald, "Franz von Papen und die 'Germania,'" *JBG* 6 (1972): 539–604; Jürgen A. Bach, *Franz von Papen in der Weimarer Republik* (Düsseldorf, 1977), pp. 265ff.

42. See the report on the new chancellor's speech to the Deutscher Landwirtschaftsrat on June 11: *SEG* 73 (1932): 105–07. Also, the report of Ludwig Kastl, managing director of the industrial Reichsverband, to its chairman, Krupp von Bohlen, on June 20, 1932, about the concerned inquiries from members of that organization after the speech: KA, IV E 178.

43. Preller, *Sozialpolitik*, pp. 448–50. See the favorable response by the industrial Reichsverband: Horkenbach (ed.), *Das Deutsche Reich* (1932), p. 210.

44. Bernd Weisbrod, "The Crisis of German Unemployment Insurance," p. 190.

45. Richard Meine to Präsidium of Reichsbürgerrat, July 11, 1932: SA, 4/Lf 646; Oskar Schlitter to Schlenker, July 13, 1932: DWI, records of Deutsche Bank und Disconto-Gesellschaft, Generalsekretariat Schlitter, 6469.

46. Larry Eugene Jones, "Sammlung oder Zersplitterung?" *VfZ* 25 (1977): 285f. On Farben's part in this undertaking, see Kalle to Jarres, June 5, 1932, and Jarres to Kalle, June 11, 1932: BAK, Jarres Papers, 44.

47. Turner, "The *Ruhrlade*," pp. 214ff.

48. See the note to Loewenstein by Ernst Brandi, July 9, 1932, written on a letter from Hans Humann to Brandi, Springorum, Hugo Stinnes, July 7: BBB, Loewenstein Papers, Allgemeiner Schriftwechsel, Brandi; also Loewenstein to Gutehoffnungshütte, Oct. 22, 1932, and memo by Kellermann, Oct. 26, 1932: GHH, Allgemeine Verwaltung, 400106/104; also Bericht über Vorbereitung und Ergebnis der Reichstagswahlen vom 6. November 1932 im Wahlkreis 23 (Düsseldorf-West) by Generalsekretär Krüger, dated Dec. 6, 1932, and conveyed by Krüger to Dingeldey on Dec. 7, 1932: BAK, Dingeldey Papers, 97b.

49. Wenderoth to Dingeldey, Aug. 3, 1932, ibid., vol. 16; Spangenberg to Hermann, Aug. 4, 1932: ZAP, Deutsche Volkspartei Papers, 117.

50. Wenderoth to Dingeldey, July 10, 1932: BAK, Dingeldey Papers, 16.

51. Roloff, *Bürgertum und Nationalsozialismus*, pp. 105ff.

52. See file 149 of the Deutsche Volkspartei Papers: ZAP.

53. Dingeldey to Schleicher, July 12 and 18, 1932: BA/MA, Schleicher Papers, N 42/22.

54. Vögler to Schleicher, July 25, 1932; Springorum to Schleicher, July 23, 1932: ibid.

55. Schleicher (draft) to Vögler, Nov. 9, 1932: ibid.

56. Telegram, Dingeldey to Schleicher, July 25, 1932; Vögler to Schleicher, Nov. 14, 1932: ibid.

57. "Von den Börsen," Aug. 2, 1932 (#569–70).

Chapter V, section 3: Attempts at Dialogue with the Nazi Hydra

1. Turner, "Fritz Thyssen und 'I paid Hitler,'" p. 239.

2. Thyssen sometimes indulged in a kind of political buffoonery that elicited more hilarity than support from his listeners; see, for example, his remarks and the response to them in the minutes of the Vorstand meeting of the Reichsverband on June 19, 1931: BAL, Reichsverband der Deutschen

Industrie collection. Thyssen's advocacy of corporatism also won him little or no support in industrial circles; see the minutes of the Hauptvorstand of the Verein Deutscher Eisen- und Stahlindustrieller for Nov. 17, 1932: BAK, R 13 I/105.

3. See their Nazi personnel files in the BDC; also Wilhelm Tengelmann's written statement of 1945 for the Nuremberg war crimes trials, NA, RG 238, NI-635; also Walter Tengelmann's testimony at Nuremberg, Oct. 9, 1947, NA, RG 238, Case 5, vol. 25a, pp. 8265f., 8361. Ernst Tengelmann joined his sons' party only in 1933, after the Nazi takeover: BDC, Parteikartei.

4. Aktenvermerk in file of correspondence between Reusch and Erich von Gilsa, recording telephone mesage from Gilsa on Apr. 11, 1932, about Winnacker's change of parties: GHH, 400101293/4. On Winnacker's position at United Steel, see *Jahrbuch für den Ruhrkohlenbezirk*, herausgegeben vom Verein für die bergbaulichen Interessen, Jg. 30 (Essen, 1932), pp. 248, 265. In March 1931 Winnacker sought in vain to get coal operators in the Ruhr to subsidize a newspaper of "a certain party" by buying subscriptions so as to gain leverage with which to prevent undesirable policies on its part: GHH, Kellermann Papers, 40010137/12, exchange of letters with Winnacker (see esp. Winnacker to Kellermann, Mar. 12, 1931).

5. See above, chapter V, section 2.

6. See the party correspondence on Winnacker in BDC, Parteikanzlei Korrespondenz and Gauleitung München-Oberbayern.

7. See Mann's autobiographical summary of 1947: NA, RG 238, NI-5167; also his party records in the BDC.

8. Testimony at Nuremberg, Mar. 31, 1948: NA, RG 238, Case 6, vol. 29a, pp. 10434–38.

9. Kassenverwaltung, Reichsleitung München, to Gauleitung Köln-Aachen, Apr. 5, 1932: BDC, Parteikanzlei Korrespondenz.

10. NA, RG 238, Case 5, vol. 10a, pp. 3176–79, testimony of July 2, 1947; ibid., NI-3122, Flick affidavit of Nov. 29, 1946. On Steinbrinck's acquaintanceship with Funk, see Steinbrinck to Funk, Dec. 11, 1931: NA, RG 238, NI-3218.

11. NA, RG 238, Case 5, vol. 15a, pp. 5058f., testimony of Aug. 7, 1947.

12. See chapter V, section 4, esp. n. 9.

13. Reusch's views found expression in an editorial which the editor of the Stuttgart daily *Schwäbischer Merkur*, Georg Dörge, wrote at his instruction: G.D., "National-bürgerlich!" issue of Apr. 27, 1932 (#97). For Reusch's role in the preparation of the editorial, see his letter to Springorum, Apr. 27, 1932: GHH, 400101290/36.

14. Reusch enjoyed especially good relations with the chairman of the BVP, Fritz Schäffer; see their correspondence in GHH, 400101293/12. The BVP had received subsidies from the Ruhrlade since 1928: Turner, "The *Ruhrlade*," p. 207. On Reusch's involvement in Bavaria, see Falk Wiesemann, *Die Vorgeschichte der nationalsozialistischen Machtübernahme in Bayern 1932/1933* (Berlin, 1975), pp. 64–67.

15. Reusch told of his meeting with Hitler in three letters written the next day, carbons of which were retained for his files, now in GHH: to Schacht, 400101290/33; to Wilmowsky, 400101290/39; to Rudolf Kötter,

4001012007/15. The text of the letter to Schacht appears in Stegmann, "Zum Verhältnis," pp. 451f.

16. On the following, see the documents from the Reusch Papers printed in Kurt Koszyk, "Paul Reusch und die 'Münchner Neuesten Nachrichten,'" *VfZ* 20 (1972): 75–103. Koszyk offers no evidence for his assertion that Reusch had also met with Hitler earlier, on Feb. 23, 1932 (p. 79).

17. Letter to Kötter, Mar. 20 (see note 15, above).

18. Turner, *"Ruhrlade,"* p. 218; Anton Betz, director of the *MNN*, to Reusch, Apr. 8 and 14, 1932: GHH, 4001012007/6; Reusch's secretary to Richard [sic] Hess, Munich, Apr. 6, 1932: ibid., 400101293/12.

19. See Koszyk, "Paul Reusch"; Erwein von Aretin, *Krone und Ketten* (Munich, 1955), pp. 70f. These developments were seriously distorted in Willi Kinnigkeit, "Was hinter der Zeitung steht . . . ," *Süddeutsche Zeitung*, Feb. 14/15, 1959 (#39).

20. See the new information on Schacht's meetings with Hitler and his entourage in the summer and fall of 1931 in Granier, *Levetzow*, pp. 299f., 316.

21. Schacht to Reusch, Mar. 18, 1932: GHH, 400101290/33.

22. Reusch to Schacht, Mar. 20, 1932: ibid.

23. For the favorable response of Fritz Springorum, see his letter to Reusch, Mar. 22, 1932: HAD, Springorum Papers, B1a 78/42c. Schacht indicated in a letter to Reusch of June 6, 1932, that Reusch had given him to expect that Krupp and Albert Vögler would probably join him and Springorum in financing the Arbeitsstelle: GHH, 400101290/33, Schacht to Reusch, June 6, 1932, text in Koszyk, "Paul Reusch," pp. 99f.

24. Schacht to Hitler, Apr. 12, 1932, text in Klein, "Neue Dokumente zur Rolle Schachts," p. 821.

25. On Keppler's background, see Turner, "Grossunternehmertum und Nationalsozialismus," p. 34; Grill, *Nazi Movement in Baden*, pp. 154–57; Reinhard Vogelsang, *Der Freundeskreis Himmler* (Göttingen, 1972), pp. 22f., 30.

26. On this and the following, see Keppler's testimony at Nuremberg: NA, RG 238, Pre-Trial Interrogations, Keppler, Nov. 24, 1945, Aug. 13 and 30, 1946; NI-903, affidavit by Keppler, Sept. 24, 1946; also his testimony, ibid., Case 5, vol. 17a, pp. 5591–93 (Aug. 18, 1947); ibid., Case 11, vol. 30a, pp. 12688–99 (July 16, 1948); ibid., vol. 45a, pp. 19219–21 (Sept. 1, 1948).

27. Testimony of Aug. 18, 1947, at Nuremberg, p. 5593 (see n. 26).

28. That meeting, on Apr. 30, 1932, at the Kaiserhof Hotel, is recorded in the memoirs of Emil Helfferich, a future member of Keppler's circle who was present: *1932–1946 Tatsachen* (Jever, 1969), p. 8.

29. Fritz Kranefuss (Keppler's nephew and assistant) to Helfferich, May 14, 1932: ibid., p. 10.

30. Keppler met with Schacht on May 18, 1932: ibid., p. 10.

31. Ibid., pp. 10f.

32. Schacht to Keppler, May 27, 1932: ibid., p. 12.

33. Ibid., pp. 11f., especially Keppler's letter to Schröder, June 1, 1932.

34. Hitler's letter, which seems not to have survived, was mentioned in Keppler's letter to Schröder of June 1, 1932, and in Schacht's letter to Keppler, of May 27, 1932: ibid., pp. 11f.

35. Rudolf Hess to Gauleiter Bernhard Rust of Hannover-Süd-Braunschweig, May 31, 1932: NSHSAH, Hann. 310, 1A, 37 [1].
36. Helfferich, *1932–1946*, p. 12, Schacht to Keppler, May 27, 1932.
37. Ibid., pp. 12f., especially the text of Keppler's letter to Emil Helfferich, June 5, 1932.
38. GHH, 400101290/33, Schacht to Reusch, June 6, 1932, text in Koszyk, "Paul Reusch," pp. 99f.
39. On July 18, Schacht sent Krupp von Bohlen a copy of a paper by Krämer on the effects of the pound devaluation of the previous autumn on Britain's economic and financial situation, which Schacht described in his accompanying letter to Krupp as the first product of the Arbeitsstelle: KA, IV E 1124. Krupp, along with Reusch, Springorum, and Thyssen, contributed financially to support the Arbeitsstelle: GHH, 400101290/33, Reusch to Schacht, June 25, 1932. On Krämer's background, see Kroll, *Von der Weltwirtschaftskrise*, p. 376; Schneider, *Arbeitsbeschaffungsprogramm*, p. 39, n. 56.
40. KA, IV E 202, Krupp to Herle, Dec. 26, 1932.
41. See Schacht's letter to Keppler of May 27, 1932: Helfferich, *1932–1946*, p. 12. Schacht seems to have regarded Helfferich as the decisive figure at that point. Otto Steinbrinck, who joined the circle later in the summer of 1932, later reported he had at first assumed that Schacht was in charge: NA, RG 238, NI-5962, interrogation, Jan. 23, 1947.
42. See Schröder's testimony at his de-nazification trial on Nov. 18, 1948: SGB, records of Spruchkammerverfahren gegen Kurt von Schröder, 1947, 1948, 1950, trial transcript, vol. II, pp. 65f. See also the interrogation of Schröder at Nuremberg, Mar. 10, 1947: NA, RG 238, Pre-Trial Interrogations.
43. Helfferich, *1932–1946*, p. 7.
44. Ibid., pp. 13ff.; Krogmann, *Es ging um Deutschlands Zukunft, 1932–1939* (Leoni am Starnberger See, 1976), p. 10. This memoir must be used with caution, as Krogmann misrepresented some of the documents from his private papers now available in FSGNSH.
45. Helfferich, *1932–1946*, p. 13.
46. NA, RG 238, Pre-Trial Interrogations, Keppler, Aug. 13, 1946.
47. Vogelsang, *Freundeskreis*, pp. 22–28.
48. See Keppler's letters of May 3 and 20, 1932, to Helfferich, in the latter's memoir, *1932–1946*, pp. 9–11, and Keppler's letter to Schacht of June 1, 1932, ibid., pp. 11f.
49. Ibid., pp. 13f. Cf. Vogelsang, *Freundeskreis*, passim. If Vögler had actually actively joined the Keppler circle, some mention of its activities would almost certainly have reached Reusch through Vögler, despite their temporary estrangement during the summer of 1932 over the Gelsenkirchen affair; but this appears from Reusch's papers not to have been the case. Emil Helfferich explicited noted in his memoirs that Vögler did not attend the group's meeting with Hitler on June 20, 1932: *1932–1946*, p. 14. Otto Steinbrinck recalled at Nuremberg not encountering Vögler at the circle's meetings: NA, RG 238, NI-5962, interrogation, Jan. 23, 1947. On one occasion Keppler stated at Nuremberg that Hitler had originally proposed Vögler in addition to Schacht as a member of his group: testimony of Aug.

18, 1947 (see n. 26), p. 5592; in an affidavit of Sept. 24, 1946, he expressed uncertainty, writing that Hitler "possibly" also named Vögler: ibid., NI-903. Yet on Aug. 30, 1946, Keppler specified that Hitler had nominated no one other than Schacht (see n. 26).

50. See, for example, his article, "Wann kommt der deutsche Wirtschaftsaufstieg?" issue of July 22, 1932 (#170). Another article by Rosterg for the *Deutsche Bergwerks-Zeitung*, which was reprinted by the *Völkischer Beobachter* in Aug. 1931, has been cited by a Soviet historian, without mention of its original place of publication or of the Nazi paper's disagreement with Rosterg's views, as an indication of his political allegiance: Lev Israelevic Ginzberg, "Auf dem Wege zur Hitlerdiktatur," *ZfG* 17 (1969): 829f.

51. There is documentation in the records of the Ilseder Hütte in Peine on Hecker's rise within the firm after his marriage to Emilie Meyer in 1912; see IHP, files WA 107 and 108. From 1921 to 1924 Hecker represented the DVP in the Prussian Landtag, thereafter remaining active in the local party; see his letter to Stresemann, Feb. 24, 1929: NA, RG 242, Microcopy T-120, 3164/103/174668–70. His rightist political views were expressed in his letter of May 12, 1930, to Generaldirektor Albrecht: IHP, WA 1600. See also *Das Deutsche Führerlexikon*, p. 176f.

52. On Bingel's background, see Georg Siemens, *Geschichte des Hauses Siemens*, 3 vols. (Freiburg and Munich, 1947–51), III, pp. 146, 344; Wenzel, *Wirtschaftsführer*, col. 197.

53. Helfferich was not even listed in the authoritative national directory of more than 13,000 business executives: Wenzel, *Wirtschaftsführer*. Krogmann, the son of a prominent Hamburg merchant, ranked, at age forty-three, as something of an impetuous youth in the gerontic Hamburg chamber of commerce after his admission in 1931: Büttner, *Hamburg*, pp. 48, 356f. Witthoefft's background makes him seem an unlikely member, at sixty-nine, of a group assembled on behalf of the NSDAP. A leading member of the liberal Hansa-Bund since before World War I, he stood on the left wing of Stresemann's DVP afterward, representing it in the National Assembly and in the Hamburg parliament, where he outspokenly denounced chauvinistic nationalism: ibid., pp. 49, 359, 365–68; Mielke, *Hansa-Bund*, p. 191.

54. Karl was the oldest of six brothers, Emil the youngest: John G. Williamson, *Karl Helfferich, 1872–1924* (Princeton, 1971), p. 7.

55. See the reply to an article by Reinhart in the *Berliner Börsen-Courier:* "Herrn Reinharts falsches Ziel," *Frankfurter Zeitung*, Jan. 9, 1932 (#21/22); also "Das deutsche Währungsproblem," *Deutsche Bergwerks-Zeitung*, July 16, 1932 (#165), where mention is made of Reinhart's stand on currency problems.

56. See Wenzel, *Wirtschaftsführer*, col. 1795f.

57. For some of the abundant evidence of Schröder's obscurity, see Turner, "Grossunternehmertum und Nationalsozialismus," pp. 32f.; Born, *Bankenkrise*, p. 182. On his firm, see the in-house version in Christian Eckert, *J. H. Stein. Werden und Wachsen eines Kölner Bankhauses in 150 Jahren* (Berlin, 1941); for a more critical view, see Willi Strauss, *Die Konzentrationsbewegung im deutschen Bankgewerbe* (Berlin and Leipzig, 1928), p. 127.

58. In informing Reusch of the businessmen who had expressed readiness to support his Arbeitsstelle financially, Schacht referred to all but one of his prospective backers solely by last names; the one exception was Schröder, whose full name Schacht thought it advisable to include, along with the name of Schröder's firm in parentheses: letter of Schacht to Reusch, June 6, 1932, in GHH, 400101290/33. Otto Steinbrinck, deputy to the industrialist Friedrich Flick, similarly identified Schröder when he wrote on Dec. 11, 1931, to Walther Funk, whose background as a former editor of a major financial newspaper would have made such an identification unnecessary in the case of an important banker: NA, RG 238, NI-3218.

59. Because of an apparent lapse of memory on Keppler's part during interrogation at Nuremberg, this meeting has often erroneously been dated as May 18, which would place it prior to completion of the circle's formation. See, for example, Vogelsang, *Freundeskreis*, pp. 28f. Using Goebbels's published diary, Vogelsang argues that Hitler could not have been in Berlin on June 20. However, Hitler met in the capital that day with Papen's interior minister, Baron Wilhelm von Gayl: Horkenbach (ed.), *Das Deutsche Reich* (1932), p. 204. Also, an official of the Reich Finance Ministry who went to the Kaiserhof that day recorded in his diary having seen the uniformed Nazi guards who usually stood watch while Hitler was in residence, as well as Keppler circle member Friedrich Reinhart and "a number of very bourgeois-looking gentlemen" waiting in the antechamber to Hitler's suite: diary of Hans Schäffer, June 20, 1932, IfZ, ED 93, Bd. 21, Bl. 601.

60. Keppler recalled the meeting twice at Nuremberg, each time falsely dating it at as May 18, 1932: NA, RG 238, NI-903, affidavit of Sept. 24, 1946; ibid., Case 5, vol. 17a, pp. 5614f., testimony of Aug. 18, 1947. Schröder responded to questions about the meeting three times, placing it correctly in June 1932: ibid., NI-246, interrogation of Dec. 1, 1945; Pre-Trial Interrogations, Mar. 10, 1947; Case 5, vol. 13a, pp. 4408f., testimony of July 28, 1947. Helfferich's memory of the meeting appears in his memoir, *1932-1946*, p. 14.

61. Helfferich, *1932-1946*, p. 14.

62. See his testimony, as cited in n. 60.

63. NA, RG 238, Pre-Trial Interrogations, Mar. 10, 1947.

64. "*Lobrede*"—this passage in the manuscript of Helfferich's memoir, now in FSGNSH, was omitted from the published version; cf. Helfferich, *1932-1946*, p. 14. For Schacht's later denial of his role in the Keppler circle, of which he claimed to have only a "vague notion," see NA, RG 238, Case 5, vol. 12a, p. 3943, testimony of July 21, 1947.

65. See Keppler's affidavit of Sept. 24, 1946, and his testimony of Aug. 18, 1947 (citations in n. 60).

66. NA, RG 238, Pre-Trial Interrogations, July 2, 1947.

67. Helfferich, *1932-1946*, pp. 14f.

68. On Steinbrinck's entry into the circle, see Helfferich, *1932-1946*, p. 17; Vogelsang, *Freundeskreis*, p. 32; at Nuremberg Steinbrinck testified consistently on repeated occasions that the initiative for his contact with the circle had come from Keppler and his nephew, Fritz Kranefuss, whom Vögler, whose Berlin office was in the same building as Flick's, had referred to him; they had come, he recalled, at the suggestion of Schacht; he re-

sponded positively, Steinbrinck maintained, in keeping with the Flick firm's defensive strategy of establishing contact with as broad a range of politicians as possible: NA, RG 238, Pre-Trial Interrogations, Jan. 25, 1947; Case 5, vol. 15a, pp. 4998–5000, 5067, testimony of Aug. 6 and 7, 1947; vol. 16a, pp. 5103f., testimony of Aug. 8, 1947.

69. See correspondence between Keppler and Krogmann in the latter's papers: "Keppler-Kreis," 913, FSGNSH; also Hecker's letter of July 22, 1932, to Julius Fromme: IHP, WA 13. On Keppler's move to Berlin, see his letter to Krogmann, Sept. 4, 1932: Krogmann Papers.

70. Keppler to Krogmann, Aug. 24, 1932: Krogmann Papers (see n. 69).

71. Kranefuss later became the "spiritus rector" of the circle when it was appropriated, during the Third Reich, by Heinrich Himmler, who displaced Keppler: Vogelsang, *Freundeskreis*, passim.

72. This becomes apparent from his correspondence with Krogmann: Krogmann Papers (see n. 69).

73. See Keppler's testimony on Aug. 18, 1947: NA, RG 238, Case 5, vol. 17a, p. 5597.

74. See Krogmann's letters to Keppler of July 25 and Aug. 17, 1932: Krogmann Papers (see n. 69).

75. See Krogmann to Keppler, Aug. 22, 1932; Keppler to Krogmann, Aug. 24, and Dec. 29, 1932: ibid.

76. Keppler to Krogmann, Aug. 6, 1932: ibid. On Schacht's absence from meetings, see NA, RG 238, NI-5962, Steinbrinck interrogation, Jan. 23, 1947; he stated that Rosterg had also taken no part.

77. See Steinbrinck's testimony at Nuremberg, Aug. 6, 1947: NA, RG 238, Case 5, vol. 15a, p. 4999.

78. Ibid.; Krogmann to Keppler, Sept. 11, 1932: Helfferich, *1932–1946*, p. 15.

79. Steinbrinck's Nuremberg testimony of Aug. 6, 1947: NA, RG 238, Case 5, vol. 15a, p. 4999.

80. Cf. Stegmann, "Zum Verhältnis," p. 428. See also the sweeping claims about the role of the circle in the formulation of Nazi economic policy, without benefit of evidence, in Schweitzer, *Big Business*, pp. 34, 102, 359. Contrary to the unanimous testimony of participants, Schweitzer asserts that the circle aided the NSDAP financially before 1933 (cf. n. 84, below).

81. Krogmann to Helfferich, Aug. 22, 1932: Krogmann Papers (see n. 69).

82. GHH, 400101220/13a, Reusch to Herle, Sept. 22, 1932; Herle to Reusch, Sept. 23, 1932.

83. See Vogelsang, *Freundeskreis*; Michael H. Kater, "Heinrich Himmler's Circle of Friends 1931–1945," *MARAB—A Review* 2 (Winter 1965–66): 74–93, which errs in dating the formation of the circle. See also the unreliable article by Klaus Drobisch, "Der Freundeskreis Himmler," *ZfG* 8 (1960): 304–28.

84. All those members later asked whether the circle had raised funds for the NSDAP prior to Hitler's acquisition of power consistently replied in the negative; those who spoke of the beginning of that practice set it in 1935 or 1936: NA, RG 238, NI-246 and NI-247, interrogations of Schröder, Dec. 1 and 3, 1945; PS-3337, Schröder's affidavit of Dec. 5, 1945; Schröder's denazification trial statement of June 3, 1948, in the trial proceedings, vol. I,

pp. 202f., Spruchkammerverfahren gegen Kurt von Schröder, 1947, 1948, 1950, in SGB. NA, RG 238, Pre-Trial Interrogations, Steinbrinck, Jan. 25, 1947; NI-5962, interrogation of Steinbrinck, Jan. 23, 1947. See also Helfferich, *1932–1946*, p. 26. These statements are corroborated by the absence, in the contemporary correspondence of the members of the circle cited above, of any mention of fund-raising activities. Nevertheless, the legend that the Keppler circle raised funds for the NSDAP before 1933 persists without any supporting evidence: Schweitzer, *Big Business*, p. 102; George W. F. Hallgarten and Joachim Radkau, *Deutsche Industrie und Politik von Bismarck bis heute* (Frankfurt, 1974), p. 207. In a recent publication the East German historian Joachim Petzold has revived this legend: "Grossbürgerliche Initiativen für die Berufung Hitlers zum Reichskanzler," *ZfG* 31 (1983): 42f. From mention of "das Finanz-Gremium" in a letter from Keppler to Schröder of Oct. 21, 1932, Petzold concludes that Keppler was referring to a special "Finanzierungskonsortium" established for the purpose of raising money for the NSDAP. However, it seems far likelier that Keppler was merely referring to the committee of the circle charged with considering plans for national financial policy.

85. This becomes obvious from a reading of the correspondence between Eduard Dingeldey, chairman of the DVP, and Wilhelm Kalle, a Farben director who served as a DVP Reichstag deputy from 1924 to 1932: BAK, Dingeldey Papers, 34, especially Kalle to Dingeldey, Mar. 7, 1932. See also Karl Holdermann, *Im Banne der Chemie. Carl Bosch. Leben und Werk* (Düsseldorf, 1953), p. 268.

86. Hayes, "*Gleichschaltung* of IG Farben," pp. 62–66.

87. Ibid., pp. 52–60; see also Thomas Parke Hughes, "Technological Momentum in History: Hydrogenation in Germany 1898–1933," *P & P* No. 44 (Aug. 1969): 106–32. For a less reliable presentation, see Tammen, "Die I.G. Farbenindustrie," pp. 94–112.

88. Feder, *Programm* (1927), p. 47f.

89. "Jüdische Kampfmittel gegen Nationalsozialisten," Jan. 5, 1928 (#4).

90. See, for example, "Volkswirtschaft und Handel: Goldschmidt und Schlitter in den [sic] I.G. Farben," *VB*, June 7, 1930 (#134).

91. The article in question, "Moloch I.G." by K. E. Weiss, was distributed by the Nazi press service Grossdeutscher Pressedienst of Berlin in early June 1931 and appeared in numerous Nazi publications; see the text in NA, RG 242, Microcopy T-253, 57/1513252f.

92. NA, RG 238, NI-15257, "Bericht über den Besuch der Leuna-Werke durch Presse und Politik (1.-9.10.1931)," by Heinrich Gattineau, Oct. 12, 1931; RG 242, Microcopy T-81, 116/136985, Konstantin Hierl and Otto Wagener to Fritz Sauckel, Sept. 30, 1931. At Nuremberg Gattineau mistakenly placed the visits in 1932: ibid., RG 238, Case 6, vol. 34a, p. 12382, testimony of Apr. 22, 1948.

93. Gattineau, "Bericht" (see n. 92).

94. "Interessenten-Interesse am 'Einheitstreibstoff,'" *VB*, Feb. 10, 1932 (#41).

95. "Leunabenzin—ein deutscher Treibstoff," Apr. 13, 1932 (#104).

96. "I.G. Farben und Oppau!" Mar. 11, 1932 (#71).

97. See, for example, "Treibstoffpreiskandal," *Der Führer* (Karlsruhe), Jan. 21, 1932.

98. NA, RG 238, Pre-Trial Interrogations, Gattineau interrogation of Apr. 14, 1947; Case 6, vol. 34a, p. 12437, Gattineau testimony of Apr. 22, 1948; NI-8788, Gattineau affidavit, June 12, 1947.

99. NA, RG 242, Microcopy T-253, 57/1513247–49, Gattineau to Haushofer, June 6, 1931.

100. NA, RG 238, Case 6, vol. 25a, pp. 8976-81, Bütefisch testimony, Mar. 10, 1948; vol. 34a, p. 12437, Gattineau testimony, Apr. 22, 1948. Bütefisch is misidentified as "Direktor" of the Leuna synthetic-gasoline plant in Tammen, "I.G. Farbenindustrie," p. 282.

101. NA, RG 238, Pre-Trial Interrogations, Gattineau, Nov. 21, 1946, and Apr. 14, 1947; NI-4833, Gattineau affidavit, Mar. 13, 1947 (in NI-5170 Gattineau later sought to disavow this affidavit, but it was corrected in his own hand); NI-8637, Bütefisch interrogation, Apr. 16, 1947. Under interrogation at Nuremberg Gattineau displayed obvious uncertainty about when the meeting had taken place, dating it variously as the middle or end of 1932 when questioned on April 14, 1947 (see above). Nevertheless, the interrogators began placing the meeting in the fall of 1932 or at the end of the year. No evidence was ever produced to support that dating, however. The earliest documented mention of the meeting quotes Bütefisch to the effect that it occurred in June; see the official firm history of the main synthetic-gasoline plant written in 1940 on the basis of interviews with Bütefisch and others: "25 Jahre Leuna-Werke," by Walter Greiling, vol. III, p. 155, typed copy in NA, RG 238, NI-14304. Greiling stated at Nuremberg that Bütefisch had seen and corrected his manuscript: ibid., NI-14508, affidavit by Greiling, Jan. 14, 1948. Although printed, the history was never released. According to Bütefisch, the author had indulged in too much literary license, by which Bütefisch very likely meant that it seemed imprudent to publish verbatim quotations attributed to the man who had become the all-powerful dictator of Germany since meeting with the two young emissaries of Farben: ibid., Case 6, vol. 25a, pp. 8976–81, Bütefisch testimony of Mar. 10, 1948. Significantly, Bütefisch did not challenge Greiling's dating of his and Gattineau's visit to Hitler. The account of the meeting in Joseph Borkin, *The Crime and Punishment of I.G. Farben* (New York, 1978), pp. 55f., draws on Greiling's work but ignores its dating.

102. NA, RG 238, Case 6, vol. 34a, p. 12439, Bütefisch testimony of Apr. 22, 1948; NI-8637, Bütefisch interrogation, Apr. 16, 1947.

103. Ibid., Case 6, vol. 24a, p. 8747, testimony of Mar. 8, 1948.

104. The prosecution at Nuremberg sought to establish a connection between the 1932 meeting of Gattineau and Bütefisch with Hitler and an agreement consummated between the Reich government and Farben in December 1933 that provided price supports for synthetic gasoline. That interpretation was emphatically rejected by Gattineau and Bütefisch. It was also refuted by affidavits from officials in the Economics Ministry who had negotiated and drawn up the 1933 agreement, all of whom denied that any political influence had been involved: NA, RG 238, Case 6, Doku-

mentenbuch Bütefisch IV, affidavits by Ernst Fischer, Botho Mulert, and Hermann Petri.

105. "I.G. Farben vorläufig behauptet," *National-Zeitung* (Essen), Dec. 4, 1932 (#320).

106. See Carl Bosch's eloquent defense of liberal trade policy in his pamphlet of Nov. 1932: *Handelspolitische Notwendigkeiten* (copy in KA, IV C 205).

107. "Adolf Hitler: Mein Programm," *VB*, Apr. 5, 1932 (#96).

108. "Was ist Kapitalismus?" (#1, Feb. 15, 1932), Rednerinformation distributed by Reichspropagandaleitung: NSHSAH, Hann. 310 I A, Nr. 35.

109. Ibid., "Handelspolitik," excerpt from Rednerinformation Nr. 2, Mar. 1, 1932, Reichspropaganda-Abteilung der NSDAP; "Sozialpolitik," Rednerinformation Nr. 5, Apr. 15, 1932; "Stegerwald lässt die Sozialversicherung zusammenbrechen," Rednerinformation Nr. 6, May 1, 1932. On autarky, see Hitler's statement prior to the July Reichstag balloting in Werner Siebarth (ed.), *Hitlers Wollen*, 8th ed. (Munich, 1940), p. 152.

110. "Nationalsozialistische Steuerakrobatik," *Deutsche Wirtschafts-Zeitung*, July 14, 1932 (#28).

111. Böhnke, *NSDAP im Ruhrgebiet*, p. 188.

112. See the report on Strasser's radio speech of July 29, 1932, which left a much more radical impression than his better-known Reichstag speech of May 10: "Der Wahlkampf im Sender," *Frankfurter Zeitung*, July 30, 1932 (#564).

113. *Wirtschaftliches Sofortprogramm der N.S.D.A.P.*, Broschürenreihe der Reichspropaganda-Leitung der NSDAP, Kampfschrift, Heft 16 (Munich, 1932), with foreword by Strasser and with notation: "Verantwortlich Dr. A. von Renteln, Munchen." Its publication was announced in *VB*, July 17/18 (#199/200).

114. NA, RG 238, Pre-Trial Interrogations, Heinrichsbauer, Jan. 9 and Feb. 6, 1947. In the first of these interrogations Heinrichsbauer said he did not know who had invited Göring; in the second he specified that the chairman of the club, Ernst Brandi, had invited him.

115. GHH, 400101293/2, Franz von Gebsattel to Reusch, Apr. 19, 1932; see also the remarks on the talk by Josef Pschorr at meeting of Vorstand of Deutscher Industrie- und Handelstag, May 10, 1932: BAK, Silverberg Papers, 641.

116. Funk, "Die Lüge von der Wirtschaftsfeindlichkeit des Nationalsozialismus," *Unser Wille und Weg*, April 1932, pp. 105–10; Wilmowsky to Reusch, June 27, 1932: GHH, 400101290/39.

117. This is revealed by two reports on the talks by the Nazis Josef Klein and Otto Wagener at a meeting of the Gauwirtschaftsrat in Düsseldorf on July 23, 1932, attended by 700 to 800 persons, including industrialists and bankers: GHH, Kellermann Papers, 400101308/9, Gilsa to Reusch, July 25, 1932; BAK, Jarres Papers, 43, Heinrich Philippi to Karl Jarres, July 27, 1932.

118. Maurer and Wengst (eds.), *Politik und Wirtschaft*, II, p. 1363, Wilmowsky to Reusch, Mar. 25, 1932.

119. Wilmowsky to Reusch, June 27, 1932: GHH, 400101290/39.

120. Lammers, *Autarkie, Planwirtschaft und berufsständischer Staat?* (Berlin, 1932).

121. See his report on a speech on economic issues in Sterkrade on July 7, 1932, by Paul Hoffmann, chairman of the local Nazi Gauwirtschaftsrat: GHH, 400101293/4, Gilsa to Reusch, July 8, 1932; also his report on the meeting of the Gauwirtschaftsrat in Düsseldorf on July 23, 1932, at which Josef Klein and Otto Wagener spoke: ibid., Kellermann Papers, 400101308/9, Gilsa to Reusch, July 25. A manufacturing executive who attended the latter meeting reacted similarly to Gilsa: Heinrich Philippi to Karl Jarres, July 27, 1932: BAK, Jarres Papers, 43.

122. Reusch to Schacht, July 27, 1932: GHH, 400101290/33.

123. Schacht to Gilsa, July 12, 1932: ibid., Kellermann Papers, 400101308/9.

124. Gilsa to Reusch, July 15, 1932: ibid.

125. Diary of Hans Schäffer, Jan. 15, 1932: IfZ, ED 93.

126. Reusch to Ludwig von Bomhard of the *Fränkischer Kurier,* July 7, 1932: GHH, 4001012007/15.

127. "Die Woche," *Deutsche Bergswerks-Zeitung,* Mar. 20, 1932 (#68).

128. Funke, "Freiheit stirbt nicht!" *Westfälisches Tageblatt,* June 25, 1932.

129. Lammers, *Autarkie,* pp. 42–45.

Chapter V, section 4: Insurance Premiums and Protection Money for Potential Rulers

1. Schäffer Diary, entry for Feb. 11, 1932: IfZ, ED 93.

2. Matzerath and Turner, "Die Selbstfinanzierung der NSDAP."

3. See the announcement, with photograph, in *VB,* July 9, 1932 (#191).

4. The metaphor—*Versicherungsprämien*—was employed at Nuremberg by Heinrich Gattineau to explain IG Farben's distribution of political money across the party spectrum: NA, RG 238, Case 6, vol. 34a, p. 12405, testimony of Apr. 22, 1948.

5. See Gerhard Volkland, "Hintergründe und politische Auswirkungen der Gelsenkirchen-Affäre im Jahre 1932," *ZfG* 11 (1963): 289–318; Henning Köhler, "Zum Verhältnis Friedrich Flicks zur Reichsregierung am Ende der Weimarer Republik," in Mommsen et al. (eds.), *Industrielles System,* pp. 878–83.

6. See Steinbrinck's affidavit of Jan. 28, 1947: NA, RG 238, NI-3508. The Papen cabinet referred the matter to a special investigating committee, which announced on June 21 that no grounds existed for questioning the legality of the transaction: "Untersuchung der Gelsenberg-Transaktion," *Deutsche Bergwerks-Zeitung,* July 2, 1932 (#153). A month later, in a radio speech the day before the Reichstag balloting, Papen indicated his cabinet's disapproval of government aid to imperiled private enterprises and pledged to return to private ownership any firms the government felt compelled, for the good of the whole, to take over: Horkenbach (ed.), *Das Deutsche Reich* (1932), p. 263. His cabinet did nothing, however, toward reversing the Gelsenkirchen transaction.

7. Turner, *Stresemann,* p. 158.

8. See the interrogation of Steinbrinck on Jan. 23, 1947: NA, RG 238, NI-5962; also Steinbrinck's affidavit of Jan. 28, 1947: ibid., NI-3508; also

the biography of Flick by his associate Konrad Kaletsch, dated Feb. 7, 1947: ibid., NI-5212.

9. Flick claimed at Nuremberg to have given 450,000 marks to the Hindenburg campaign and supplied records of bank withdrawals in that amount by way of substantiation: ibid., Case 5, Dokumentenbuch Flick I, doc. 2. His claim has been substantiated by one of those in charge of the Hindenburg funds: Gereke, *Landrat,* pp. 177, 184. Flick also claimed he had made another contribution of 500,000 marks to the fund on the basis of a statement by a former official of his firm's Silesian office: affidavit by Konrad Gehlofen, June 25, 1947: NA, RG 238, Case 5, Dokumentenbuch Flick I, doc. 3. Gereke, however, reported in his memoirs that Flick refused a plea for a second contribution of 450,000 marks: *Landrat,* p. 184. On the other hand, Brüning's transport minister, Gottfried Treviranus, who also took part in the Hindenburg campaign, recalled in his memoirs that Flick had given one to one and a half million marks: *Ende von Weimar,* p. 297.

10. NA, RG 238, Case 5, Dokumentenbuch Flick I, doc. 2.

11. Ibid.

12. NA, RG 238, Pre-Trial Interrogations, Flick, Jan. 8, 1947; Case 5, vol. 10a, p. 3165f., Flick's testimony of July 2, 1947.

13. Flick to Hugenberg, July 19, 1932: ibid., Dokumentenbuch Flick I, doc. 2.

14. Ibid., vol. 10a, p. 3197, Flick's testimony of July 2, 1947; Pre-Trial Interrogations, Steinbrinck, Jan. 23, 1947. A subordinate of Flick, Odilo Burkart, claimed in a letter in 1940 that Göring had, after viewing Flick's books, submitted a report to Hitler and secured his personal approval for the transaction: Burkart to Grillitzer, Sept. 17, 1940: ibid., NI-5432. This claim appears to have been a matter of boasting for tactical advantage, since if Hitler had in fact accorded his personal approval to the deal, Flick would have scarcely felt the need to placate, at considerable expense, the lesser Nazis on whom he subsequently bestowed money. George W. F. Hallgarten's contention, in his *Hitler, Reichswehr und Industrie* (1955), pp. 107–13, that the Nazis extorted financial support from Flick and other steel executives by blocking a parliamentary investigation of the Gelsenkirchen transaction has proved untenable; cf. Volkland, "Hintergründe," pp. 311–13. In a later publication Hallgarten abandoned key points of his contention: Hallgarten and Radkau, *Deutsche Industrie,* pp. 205–07.

15. Wilhelm Sollmann, former Reich interior minister, examined Flick's books for the SPD: NA, RG 238, Case 5, vol. 10a, pp. 3196f., Flick's testimony of July 2, 1947. See also NA, RG 238, Pre-Trial Interrogations, Steinbrinck, Jan. 23, 1947. For the criticism of the transaction by the SPD, see Volkland, "Hintergründe," pp. 314f.

16. The article, by A. Reinhold and entitled "Der Flick-Skandal," appeared in the July 1932 issue of the Nazi periodical *Deutsche Volkswirtschaft;* for the excerpts quoted here, see Volkland, "Hintergründe," pp. 310f.

17. Steinbrinck told of this episode on several occasions at Nuremberg: NA, RG 238, NI-5962, interrogation of Jan. 23, 1947; Pre-Trial Interrogations, Steinbrinck, Jan. 25, 1947; see also his testimony of Aug. 6, 7, and 8, 1947, in Case 5, vol. 15a, pp. 4998, 5067, vol. 16a, pp. 5103f. On Steinbrinck's

background, see Bodo Herzog, *Kapitänleutnant Otto Steinbrinck* (Krefeld, 1963).

18. NA, RG 238, Case 5, vol. 15a, p. 5000, Steinbrinck's testimony of Aug. 6, 1947. Steinbrinck had known Walther Funk at least since late 1931; see his letter to Funk, Dec. 11, 1931: NA, RG 238, NI-3218.

19. Ibid., NI-5962, interrogation of Steinbrinck, Jan. 23, 1947; Pre-Trial Interrogations, Steinbrinck, Jan. 25, 1947; Case 5, vol. 15a, p. 4999, Steinbrinck testimony of Aug. 6, 1947.

20. See n. 19. Steinbrinck told of the gathering at a small "Weinrestaurant" in testimony at Nuremberg on Aug. 8, 1947: NA, RG 238, Case 5, vol. 16a, p. 5102.

21. Ibid., Pre-Trial Interrogations, Keppler, Jan. 10, 1947.

22. Ibid., Case 5, vol. 15a, pp. 5087f., Steinbrinck's testimony of Aug. 7, 1947.

23. Ibid.; also NI-3508, Steinbrinck's affidavit of Jan. 28, 1947.

24. Ibid., NI-5962, Steinbrinck interrogation, Jan. 23, 1947.

25. Ibid.

26. Ibid.

27. Ibid. See also Steinbrinck's testimony of Aug. 6, 1947: ibid., Case 5, vol. 15a, p. 4981.

28. See ibid., NI-3508, Steinbrinck's affidavit of Jan. 28, 1947; see also Case 5, vol. 15a, p. 5087, Steinbrinck's testimony of Aug. 7, 1947. Steinbrinck placed the first contact with Ley and Reischach, which came about via Flick's public relations office in Düsseldorf, at the end of 1931.

29. Ibid., pp. 4981f.; NI-3508, Steinbrinck's affidavit of Jan. 28, 1947.

30. Ibid., NI-5962, interrogation of Steinbrinck, Jan. 23, 1947.

31. Ibid. See also Pre-Trial Interrogations, Steinbrinck, Jan. 24, 1947; NI-3508, Steinbrinck's affidavit of Jan. 28, 1947. In 1938 Steinbrinck placed this agreement in 1931 in a letter to a Flick executive who had been approached by Nazis for a contribution: NI-3454, Steinbrinck to Karl Raabe, Dec. 28, 1938. Under repeated interrogation at Nuremberg, however, Steinbrinck insisted the agreement could not have come into being until 1932. That tallies with the other evidence, for if the agreement had been effected in 1931, Flick presumably would have been spared the contributions he made to other Nazis during 1932.

32. Ibid., NI-5962, interrogation of Steinbrinck, Jan. 23, 1947.

33. Ibid., Case 5, vol. 15a, p. 4981, Steinbrinck's testimony of Aug. 6, 1947.

34. Ibid., vol. 10a, pp. 3171f., Flick's testimony of July 2, 1947; Dokumentenbuch Flick I, doc. 1, "Zahlungen und Spenden für politische Zwecke," June 6, 1947. In another affidavit Flick entered the figure "100,000 marks" under NSDAP in a listing of his 1932 political contributions, but he qualified this with a footnote stating that some of that estimated sum was probably given later, that is, after the Nazi takeover: NI-3122, affidavit of Nov. 29, 1946. That qualification is ignored in an East German publication making use of that affidavit: Klaus Drobisch, "Flick und die Nazis," *ZfG* 14 (1966): 379. A similar distinction between contributions made before and after the Nazi takeover in the document of June 6, 1947 (cited in this note, above), is also ignored by Drobisch (p. 381). The same sort of oversight marks the figures on Flick's contributions to the Nazis in Günter Ogger,

Friedrich Flick der Grosse (Bern and Munich, 1971), pp. 130–33. Relying in all probability on Drobisch, Ogger places Flick at Hitler's Industry Club speech (pp. 130f). Drobisch gives as his sole source for that information a publication by East German Communist party boss Walter Ulbricht ("Flick und die Nazis," p. 379). Flick denied, under repeated interrogation at Nuremberg, either being present at Hitler's speech or receiving an invitation: NA, RG 238, Pre-Trial Interrogations, Flick Jan. 6, 1947; Case 5, vol. 10a, p. 3197, testimony of July 2, 1947. Nor did any of those eyewitnesses who reported on persons seen at the speech mention Flick (see above, section 1 of this chapter).

35. Flick said as much in his explanation of how the payments had been made: NA, RG 238, Case 5, vol. 10a, p. 3171, testimony of July 2, 1947.

36. On Wolff's business career, see Paul Ufermann, *Könige der Inflation*, 3rd ed. (Berlin, 1924), pp. 35–41; Felix Pinner, *Deutsche Wirtschaftsführer* (Charlottenburg, 1925), pp. 58–65; Walther Hermann, "Otto Wolff," *Rheinisch-westfälische Wirtschaftsbiographien*, vol. 8 (Münster, 1962), pp. 123–56; Richard Lewinsohn, *Das Geld in der Politik*, pp. 171f.

37. Paul Ufermann, *Der deutsche Stahltrust* (Berlin, 1927), pp. 56, 79, 112, 144, 164. On Wolff's role in copper mining, see the tendentious East German publication: Radandt, *Kriegsverbrecherkonzern*.

38. See Wolff's correspondence with Oscar Schlitter in the latter's papers: DWI, records of the Deutsche Bank und Disconto-Gesellschaft, file 4751, esp. Schlitter to Wolff, June 25, 1929, and Wolff to Schlitter, July 22, 1929.

39. Wolff, *Die Geschäfte des Herrn Ouvrard* (Frankfurt am Main, 1932); idem, *Ouvrard: Speculator of Genius* (London, 1962).

40. Wolff's role in financing Stresemann's ill-fated newspaper, *Die Zeit*, is recorded in part in a letter from Carl Duisberg to Wilhelm Kalle, Jan. 3, 1923: BAL, Autographensammlung Duisberg.

41. Brüning, *Memoiren*, p. 508.

42. Two men active in the Hindenburg fund-raising effort agreed in their memoirs on Wolff's generous participation. Günther Gereke characterized his contribution as a large sum: *Landrat*, p. 184; Gottfried Treviranus set Wolff's contribution at a million marks: *Ende von Weimar*, p. 297. According to Flick, Wolff was instrumental in moving him to contribute to the Hindenburg fund: NA, RG 238, Case 5, vol. 11a, pp. 3573f., Flick's testimony of July 14, 1947.

43. How and when Wolff came to befriend Schleicher remains unclear, but by May 1932 Chancellor Brüning was learning of the general's views via Wolff: Brüning, *Memoiren*, p. 576.

44. Albert Vögler to Schleicher, Nov. 14, 1932; Wolff to Vögler, Nov. 17, 1932: BA/MA, Schleicher Papers, N 42/22.

45. NA, RG 238, Case 5, vol. 10a, p. 3165, testimony of Flick, July 2, 1947; IfZ, ED 93, diary of Hans Schäffer, entry of Dec. 1, 1932.

46. For some revealing insights into Wolff's business circumstances, see the records of a lawsuit lodged against his company by Paul Rohde, which was in the courts from 1930 to 1933, in the papers of Wolff's attorney, Walter Luetgebrune: NA, RG 242, Microcopy T-253, roll 2.

47. Brüning, *Memoiren*, pp. 365, 448.

48. According to Gottfried Treviranus's memoirs, Brüning consoled Wolff with the prospect of aid after the Lausanne conference on reparations, scheduled to begin in June, had taken place: *Ende von Weimar*, p. 215.

49. See, for example, "Die Kriegsgewinnler melden sich," *National-Zeitung* (Essen), Sept. 15, 1932 (#240). Otto Wagener, head of the Economic Policy Section of the NSDAP, used Wolff as an example of how a businessman could damage the economy: Wagener's memorandum to commissioners of his organization and to Gauwirtschaftsberater, Dec. 17, 1931: NSHSAH, Hann. 310, 1A 35. Some Nazis regarded Wolff as Jewish; see the letter, Arno Schickedanz to Rudolf Hess, Dec. 22, 1931: NSDAP HA, B/1533.

50. See the memo by Scholtz for Prussian Commissar Franz Bracht, Oct. 20, 1932: ZAP, Bracht Papers, Bd. 2, Bl.183.

51. In April 1932, Hans Schäffer, state secretary in the Reich Finance Ministry, recorded in his diary after a conversation with Wolff the latter's opposition to including Nazis in the government: IfZ, ED 93, entry for Apr. 28. At Nuremberg Jakob Wilhelm Reichert of the Verein Deutscher Eisen- und Stahlindustrieller, remembered Wolff as very anti-Nazi: NA, RG 238, NI-11594, affidavit of July 7, 1947.

52. Schäffer diary: IfZ, ED 93, entry of Aug. 13, 1932.

53. Pünder, *Politik in der Reichskanzlei*, p. 147.

54. According to the excerpt from a financial statement by Wolff of Oct. 20, 1933, printed in an East German collection of documents, Wolff reported having made political contributions totaling 290,000 marks in 1932, of which 160,800 had gone to the NSDAP: Wolfgang Ruge and Wolfgang Schumann (eds.), *Dokumente zur deutschen Geschichte 1929–1933* (East Berlin, 1975), p. 89. The listed contributions do not, however, add up to 290,000 marks, nor is his contribution to the Hindenburg campaign fund included. Another East German writer has reported that in 1935 Wolff informed the tax authorities in Cologne that he had given at least 180,000 marks to the NSDAP in 1932: Eberhard Czichon, *Wer verhalf Hitler zur Macht?* (Cologne, 1967), p. 54.

55. See the memo by Scholtz for Prussian Commissar Franz Bracht, Oct. 20, 1932: ZAP, Bracht Papers, Bd. 2, Bl.183.

56. NA, RG 238, EC-440, Funk statement of June 28, 1945.

57. On the joint office in Düsseldorf, see ibid., Case 5, vol. 15a, p. 5087, Steinbrinck's testimony of Aug. 7, 1947.

58. Czichon, *Wer verhalf Hitler?* p. 54. That story does not appear in the published version of Gereke's memoirs, *Landrat*.

59. See Peter Hayes, "'A Question Mark with Epaulettes'? Kurt von Schleicher and Weimar Politics," *JMH* 52 (1980): 51–59.

60. See the autobiographical information composed by Ilgner at Nuremberg and dated Oct. 23, 1945: NA, RG 238, NI-712. See also the biographical sketch by Walter Bachem, Jan. 29, 1947: NI-5125.

61. On the plans of the "Wagemann-Kreis," see Kroll, *Von der Weltwirtschaftskrise*, pp. 396ff.; Wilhelm Grotkopp, *Die grosse Krise* (Düsseldorf, 1954), pp. 24f.; Claus-Dieter Krohn, "Autoritärer Kapitalismus," in Dirk Stegmann et al. (eds.), *Industrielle Gesellschaft*, pp. 123f. For Ilgner's recol-

lections of the circle, see his affidavit of Dec. 7, 1946: NA, RG 238, NI-6677.

62. NA, RG 238, NI-6677 (see note 61) and NI-6699, Ilgner's affidavit, Apr. 25, 1947; ibid., Pre-Trial Interrogations, Ilgner, Apr. 10, 1947; ibid., Case 6, vol. 26a, p. 9411, Ilgner's testimony of Mar. 16, 1948.

63. Ibid., NI-6677.

64. Ibid., Case 6, Dokumentenbuch Ilgner I, doc. 4, Ilgner's affidavit of Feb. 27, 1948.

65. Ibid., NI-6677.

66. Ibid., Case 6, Dokumentenbuch Ilgner I, doc. 4, Ilgner's affidavit of Feb. 27, 1948.

67. Ibid. See also Pre-Trial Interrogations, Ilgner Apr. 10, 1947; NI-6677 and NI-7082.

68. Ibid. See also Ilgner's affidavit of June 30, 1945: NI-1304.

69. Ibid., NI-4833, Gattineau's affidavit of Mar. 13, 1947. See also his interrogation of Jan. 17, 1947: ibid., Pre-Trial Interrogations.

70. Ilgner related this story in a statement he prepared at Nuremberg, "Papers about various questions," dated June 21, 1945: ibid., NI-1293. He repeated the story many times at Nuremberg in other statements and under interrogation, not always mentioning Gattineau as the source.

71. Ibid., Pre-Trial Interrogations, Gattineau, Jan. 17, 1947, and Mar. 5, 1947; ibid., NI-4833, Gattineau's affidavit of Mar. 13, 1947.

72. See, for example, the affidavit of Georg von Schnitzler, July 5, 1945: ibid., NI-2696.

73. See Kalle's affidavit of Sept. 8, 1947: ibid., Case 6, Dokumentenbuch Schmitz I, doc. 4.

74. See his correspondence with Eduard Dingeldey, leader of the DVP: BAK, Dingeldey Papers 34.

75. See the affidavit of Ernst Pfeiffer, Sept. 8, 1947: NA, RG 238, Case 6, Dokumentenbuch Schmitz II, doc. 24.

76. Ibid., vol. 17a, pp. 5713ff., Lammers' testimony of Jan. 20, 1948.

77. See section 3 of this chapter.

78. According to Kalle, the firm's legal adviser, Professor Julius Flechtheim, counted among the occasional participants in the circle's deliberations: NA, RG 238, Case 6, Dokumentenbuch Schmitz I, doc. 5, Kalle's affidavit of Oct. 4, 1947.

79. Schleicher to Kalle, Nov. 25, 1931: BA/MA Schleicher Papers, N 42/26.

80. See Bennett, German Rearmament, pp. 44–46, 62–69.

81. Kalle to Schleicher, Nov. 30, 1931: BA/MA, Schleicher Papers, N 42/26.

82. Ibid., N 42/22, Colonel Kurt von Bredow to Schleicher, Oct. 21 and 25, 1932. These communications reveal that subsidies had been paid to the Berlin SA at some earlier time, then interrupted.

83. See chapter III, section 4.

84. See "Schwerindustrie und Adolf Hitler," Frankfurter Zeitung, Jan. 19, 1932 (#49).

85. NA, RG 238, Pre-Trial Interrogations, Grauert, Aug. 23, 1946, Dec. 5, 1946, and Jan. 5, 1947; NI-3747, Grauert's affidavit of Jan. 14, 1947; Case 10, Dokumentenbuch von Bülow II, doc. 94, excerpt from testimony of Grauert before the International Military Tribunal, Mar. 13, 1946.

Grauert gave essentially the same testimony at the de-nazification trial of Fritz Thyssen on Aug. 24, 1948: HHSA, Thyssen trial records, Verhandlungsprotokolle, In a letter of Aug. 30, 1948, to the presiding judge at Thyssen's trial, Ernst Poensgen confirmed Grauert's story: ibid., Hauptakte, p. 472. Under interrogation at Nuremberg, Jakob Wilhelm Reichert of the Verein Deutscher Eisen- und Stahlindustrieller recalled the same events: ibid., Klageschrift, pp. 216f.

86. See, in addition to the documents cited in the previous note, Heinrichsbauer, *Schwerindustrie*, p. 56.

87. On seeing such rumors in the press, Poensgen inquired about them of Krupp von Bohlen, who had been mentioned as their source: KA, IV E 914, Poensgen to Krupp, Apr. 13, 1932. Krupp denied any validity to such reports: ibid., Krupp to Poensgen, Apr. 15, 1932.

88. Grauert's testimony of Mar. 13, 1946, Aug. 23, 1946, and Aug. 24, 1948 (see n. 85).

89. See Grauert's testimonies cited in n. 85, especially that of Aug. 23, 1946.

90. See section 2 of this chapter.

91. Heinrichsbauer, *Schwerindustrie*, p. 44.

92. See Brandi's report to the Vorstand of Jan. 28, 1932: BBA, Verein für die bergbaulichen Interessen, Vorstand 1930–34.

93. Betz, "Tragödie," p. 27.

94. Ibid., p. 29.

95. Quoted by Fritz Klein in a book review in *ZfG* 21 (1973): 1523.

96. Heinrichsbauer, *Schwerindustrie*, p. 44.

97. See section 2 of this chapter.

98. Klein in *ZfG* 21 (1973): 1524 (see n. 95).

99. Heinrichsbauer, *Schwerindustrie*, p. 44.

100. The economics of the Nazi press prior to 1933 still await full exploration and analysis. See, in the meantime, on the tribulations of Robert Ley's Cologne daily, *Westdeutscher Beobachter*, Schaumburg-Lippe, *Pflicht und Schuldigkeit*, pp. 171f., 249; also the documentation on the same paper in NSDAP HA, 56/1358a. See also the information on the *Hamburger Tageblatt* in Krebs, *Tendenzen*, esp. pp. 98–100.

101. See, for examples, the following issues of the 1932 Munich edition: July 15 (Continental tires), Aug. 6 (Daimler-Benz), Aug. 10 (Dunlop tires and Auto Union), and Aug. 14/15 (Ford), Sept. 4/5 (Telefunken), Sept. 24 (Adlerwerke automobiles).

102. See, for example, the following issues of 1929: Feb. 4 and Mar. 1 (Daimler-Benz), Mar. 3 (Telefunken), Mar. 5 (Opel); and 1932: Mar. 12 (Opel), Mar. 14 (Dunlop tires), Mar. 20 (Adlerwerke automobiles).

103. Schwerin von Krosigk, *Die grosse Zeit*, III, pp. 399f.; "Der Reemtsma-Konzern," in Deutsches Wirtschaftsinstitut (East Berlin), *Berichte* 11, no. 3 (1960): 2–7.

104. Armin Behrendt, *Wilhelm Külz* (East Berlin, 1968), pp. 100, 275, n. 72.

105. NA, RG 238, Pre-Trial Interrogations, Reemtsma, Apr. 8, 1947.

106. Reemtsma to Carl Duisberg, Mar. 9 and 29, 1932: BAL, 76/9.

107. See, for example, the attack on Reemtsma before the Reichstag on Dec. 21, 1929, by Franz Stöhr of the NSDAP: *Verhandlungen*, vol. 426, p. 3791. See also Krebs, *Tendenzen*, p. 105.

108. See the letter of a snuff manufacturer, Emil Weiss, to the Nazi judicial office, USCHLA, Sept. 30, 1932: NA, RG 242, Microcopy T-81, 91/105164–66.

109. See the report of the SA-Gruppenführer Hochland, Sept. 26, 1932: ibid., 91/105193. See also the ad for Trommler, Alarm, Sturm, and Neue Front cigarettes, all produced by the Sturm Zigarettenfabrik under an agreement with the SA: *VB*, Sept. 11/12, 1932 (#255/256); cf. Turner (ed.), *Hitler aus nächster Nähe*, pp. 60–63.

110. Krebs, *Tendenzen*, pp. 105f.

111. Grimm, for Reichsleitung, to Emil Weiss, Sept. 27, 1932: NA, RG 242, Microcopy T-81, 91/105163. The date July appears, without documentation, in "Der Reemtsma-Konzern," Deutsches Wirtschaftsinstitut (East Berlin), *Berichte* 11, no. 3 (1960): 6f.

112. *Hitler's Secret Conversations* (1953), entry for Jan. 4, 1942, p. 145.

113. See the following issues of the Munich edition: July 20, 22, 23, 26, 27, 28, 29, 30, 31, August 1/2, 19, 23, 26, and 30.

114. Emil Weiss to USCHLA, Sept. 30, 1932 (see n. 108); an earlier complaint of Sept. 12 had preceded this letter, in which the despairing Weiss announced his intention to abandon his active role for the party.

115. Grimm to Weiss, Sept. 30, 1932 (see n. 111).

116. Schwerin von Krosigk, *Die grosse Zeit*, III, pp. 399f.; "Der Reemtsma-Konzern," in Deutsches Wirtschaftsinstitut (East Berlin), *Berichte* 11, no. 3 (1960): 7. Otto Wagener's placement prior to 1933 of a conversation in which Franz Pfeffer von Salomon told him of payments by Reemtsma to Wagener's hated rival, Hermann Göring, appears to be an anachronism: Turner (ed.), *Hitler aus nächster Nähe*, p. 287.

117. See Schulz, *Aufstieg*, pp. 636, 875–77; also Quietus, "Hitler's Finanzen," *Die Weltbühne* Apr. 19, 1932 (Jg. 28, Nr. 16): 585. One such rumor, recorded by an American journalist who spent part of 1932 in Berlin, has become a favorite source for writers bent on linking Deterding to the Nazis before 1933: Edgar Ansel Mowrer, *Germany Puts the Clock Back* (New York, 1933), pp. 144f. Cf. Glyn Roberts, *The Most Powerful Man in the World* (New York, 1938), p. 322.

118. See the article about Deterding's views, "Absatzvergrösserung ist das Ziel der Wirtschaftsführung," *VB*, Feb. 10, 1931 (#41).

119. Schulz, *Aufstieg*, p. 875, n. 240.

120. See, for examples, Küster, *Hintermänner der Nazis*, p. 24; Hallgarten, *Hitler, Reichswehr und Industrie* (1955), p. 127, n. 34; Hallgarten and Radkau, *Deutsche Industrie*, p. 203; Czichon, *Wer verhalf Hitler*, p. 33; Czichon, *Hermann Josef Abs* (East Berlin, 1969), p. 46. No substantiation has ever been found for the story of a link between Deterding and Ernst Röhm submitted at Nuremberg by Erich Fürst Waldburg zu Zeil: Schulz, *Aufstieg*, p. 875, n. 241, and Hermann Lutz, *German-French Unity* (Chicago, 1957), pp. 114–17. For an exposé of two fabricated versions of Deterding's purported contributions to Hitler's rise, see Lutz, "Fälschungen," p. 391. Deterding figures prominently in the fanciful tales of international conspiracies by the propaganda chief of the East German Communist regime, Albert Norden, *Fälscher* (East Berlin, 1960), where he is portrayed as hav-

ing made the Nazi party into his willing tool as early as the 1920s (p. 102). See also n. 117.

121. Wolfgang Ruge, *Weimar—Republik auf Zeit* (East Berlin, 1969), p. 262.

122. Rudolph Blauert, "Dr. Deterding, seine Bedeutung für Mecklenburg und Deutschland," *Mecklenburgische Monatshefte* 15 (1939): 182–88; E. H. Bull, "Erinnerungsblätter aus der Lebensbeschreibung der gelehrten Familie Detharding (Deiterding, Deterding) und deren kulturelles Wirken in Mecklenburg," ibid., pp. 189–95; Emil Georg von Stauss, "Abschied von Sir Henri Deterding," ibid., pp. 196–98.

123. See the memorandum on Deterding's contributions to the Winterhilfswerk by Emil Georg von Stauss, Mar. 17, 1937 (photocopy opposite p. 97 of Norden, *Fälscher*), and Stauss's letter of Oct. 4, 1937, to Dr. Sippell, both in DWI, file A23/5 of the records of the Deutsche Bank und Disconto-Gesellschaft. Revealingly, correspondence in that same file between Stauss and Deterding during 1931 and 1932 contains no references to German domestic politics, much less to National Socialism.

124. See "Trauerfeier für Sir Henry Deterding," *VB*, Feb. 11, 1939 (#42).

125. Hitler, *Monologe im Führerhauptquartier*, p. 239, entry for Jan. 27, 1942.

126. "Henry Deterding," *VB*, Feb. 10, 1939 (#41); see also n. 124.

127. The article "Flüssiges Gold" appeared in *Deutsche Illustrierte*, July 8, 1941; the gauleiter of Mecklenburg, Friedrich Hildebrandt, set forth his defense of Deterding in a letter of July 7, 1941, to Justizrat Dr. Blauert of Güstrow: DWI, file A 23/5, records of the Deutsche Bank und Disconto-Gesellschaft.

128. Amann to NSDAP Bezirk Dresden, Feb. 11, 1932: BDC, Oberstes Parteigericht.

Chapter VI, section 1: Nazis as Champions of Parliament and the Workers— The Capitalists Find Their Chancellor

1. *SEG*, 73 (1932): 136.

2. Detlev Junker, *Die Deutsche Zentrumspartei und Hitler 1932/33* (Stuttgart, 1969), pp. 86f.

3. Bracher, *Auflösung*, pp. 612–17.

4. Heinrichsbauer to Strasser, Sept. 20, 1932: NA, RG 242, Microcopy T-81, 1/11436–45.

5. Hayes, "'Question Mark with Epaulettes?'" pp. 49f.

6. On Thyssen and Grauert, see the latter's testimony at Thyssen's denazification trial: HHSA, Verhandlungsprotokoll, Aug. 24, 1948. On Brandi, see the excerpt from his letter to Fritz Klein, editor of the *Deutsche Allgemeine Zeitung*, Feb. 6, 1932, quoted in a book review by Klein's son Fritz, *ZfG* 21 (1973): 1523.

7. "Hitler in Front," issue of Aug. 12, 1932 (#62).

8. Wilmowsky to Reusch, Aug. 9, 1932: GHH, 400101290/39.

9. Kurt von Lersner to Kurt von Schröder, Aug. 2, 1932: NA, RG 238, NI-200.

10. Reusch to Georg Dörge, Aug. 4, 1932: GHH, 4001012007/13.

11. Reusch to Kötter, Aug. 14, 1932: ibid., 4001012007/15.

12. Reusch to Kötter, Aug. 8, 1932: ibid.

13. Horkenbach (ed.), *Das Deutsche Reich* (1932), pp. 294, 300f.

14. "Soziale Anträge unserer preussischen Landtagsfraktion," *VB*, Sept. 9, 1932 (#253).

15. Horkenbach (ed.), *Das Deutsche Reich* (1932), p. 300.

16. Junker, *Zentrumspartei*, p. 108; Rudolf Morsey, *Der Untergang des politischen Katholizismus* (Zurich, 1977), pp. 56ff.

17. Horkenbach (ed.), *Das Deutsche Reich* (1932), p. 318; Silverberg to Reusch, Sept. 5, 1932: GHH, 400101290/35.

18. Reusch to Kötter, Sept. 25, 1932: GHH, 4001012007/15b.

19. Leopold, *Hugenberg*, pp. 121ff.

20. Horkenbach (ed.), *Das Deutsche Reich* (1932), p. 284f.

21. Minutes of the meeting of the Arbeitsausschuss of the Verfassungs-ausschuss of the Deutscher Industrie- und Handelstag, Aug. 17, 1932: BAK, R11/377.

22. See the confidential communication of the industrial Reichsverband to the members of its Präsidium and Vorstand, Aug. 26, 1932: GHH, 400101220/13b.

23. See the summary of Papen's speech at Münster in Horkenbach (ed.), *Das Deutsche Reich* (1932), p. 296.

24. See the telegram sent to Papen on Aug. 28, 1932, by the chairman of the industrial Reichsverband, Krupp von Bohlen: NA, RG 238, NI-6723; also telegram of Bundesführung of Hansa-Bund, same date, *Jahresbericht 1932* (Berlin, n.d.), pp. 15f. Also, Hermann Röchling, "Nur keine voreilige Kritik," *Deutsche Bergwerks-Zeitung*, Oct. 16, 1932 (#144); editorial in *Deutsche Führerbriefe*, Sept. 2, 1932 (#68); confidential communication of Reichsverband to members of its Präsidium and Vorstand, Sept. 16, 1932: GHH, 400101220/13; "Das Programm von Münster," *Ruhr und Rhein Wirtschaftszeitung*, Sept. 2, 1932 (Heft 36), pp. 573f.

25. Junker, *Zentrumspartei*, p. 98.

26. Horkenbach (ed.), *Das Deutsche Reich* (1932), p. 285.

27. Schäffer's diary, entry for Sept. 9, 1932: IfZ, ED 93.

28. Krogmann to Keppler, Sept. 2, 1932; Keppler to Krogmann, Sept. 4, 1932: FSGNSH, Krogmann Papers, 913.

29. Krogmann to Keppler, Sept. 11, 1932: ibid.

30. See the three reports, all headlined "Nationalsozialismus und Ar-beitsbeschaffung," in *VB*, Sept. 7 (#251), Sept. 8 (#252), and Sept. 9 (#253); see also the critical response in "Das Wirtschaftsprogramm des Nationalsozialismus," *Deutsche Wirtschafts-Zeitung*, Sept. 22, 1932 (#38).

31. Krogmann to Keppler, Sept. 11, 1932: FSGNSH, Krogmann Papers, 913.

32. Horkenbach (ed.), *Das Deutsche Reich* (1932), p. 317.

33. Bracher, *Auflösung*, pp. 627–29.

34. *Reichskanzler von Papen im Lichte seiner Politik*, Reichspropagandaleitung der NSDAP, München, den 12. September 1932.

35. "Dr. Feder über das Wirtschaftsprogramm der NSDAP," *Koblenzer General-Anzeiger*, Sept. 28, 1932 (#225).

36. Allen, *Nazi Seizure*, p. 134.

37. Emil Weiss to USCHLA, Sept. 20, 1932: NA, RG 242, Microcopy T-81, 91/105164–66.

38. Springorum to Fritz Winkhaus, Sept. 10, 1932: HAD, B1a 51/2; see also Springorum to Papen, Aug. 29, 1932: ibid., B1a 82/16.

39. Blank to Reusch, Sept. 10, 1932: GHH, 4001012024/10.

40. Gilsa to Reusch, Sept. 19, 1932: ibid., 400101293/4.

41. Leopold, *Hugenberg*, pp. 123f.

42. "Unsere Meinung," issue of Oct. 23, 1932 (#499).

43. "Die Woche," issue of Oct. 16, 1932 (#244).

44. Keppler to Emil Helfferich, Oct. 29, 1932: FSGNSH, Krogmann Papers, 913.

45. See Joachim Petzold, "Monopole—Mittelstand—NSDAP," *ZfG* 28 (1980): 867–75.

46. Orlow, *History*, I, p. 275.

47. Hermann Roth, "Die nationalsozialistische Betriebszellenorganisation (NSBO) von der Gründung bis zur Röhm-Affäre (1928 bis 1934)," *JBWG*, 1978, Teil 1, p. 54.

48. Reinhold Muchow, in *Nationalsozialismus und 'freie' Gewerkschaften*, quoted in ibid., p. 53.

49. Ibid. See also Gunther Mai, "Die nationalsozialistische Betriebszellen-Organisation," *VfZ* 31 (1983): 585f., 603; Klaus Schaap, *Die Endphase der Weimarer Republik im Freistaat Oldenburg* (Düsseldorf, 1978), p. 217.

50. "Die Woche," issue of Oct. 16, 1932 (#244). This informative article includes numerous quotations from the Nazi press, including statements about NSBO strike-support compensation as well as news of expulsion of strikebreakers from the party. See also Mai, "Betriebszellen-Organisation," p. 586.

51. Winnacker to Bergassessor Goethe of Bergbauverein, Sept. 9, 1932; Goethe to Winnacker, Sept. 12, 1932: BBB, Loewenstein Papers, Allgemeiner Schriftwechsel.

52. Gauleiter Alfred Meyer to Strasser, Sept. 17, 1932; Strasser to Meyer, Sept. 23, 1932: ibid.

53. See the memorandum on a lengthy conference Papen held at Neu-babelsberg on Aug. 16 with Brandi, Hans Humann of the *Deutsche Allgemeine Zeitung*, the banker Jacob Goldschmidt, and the steel executive Fritz Springorum: SAE, Reismann-Grone Papers, vol. 15, pp. 17–19.

54. See the review of *Technik und Wirtschaft im Dritten Reich* by Franz Lawaczeck, a protégé of Gottfried Feder, in *Glückauf*, Sept. 10, 1932 (#37), pp. 830f.

55. Schmidt, "Die 'Rheinisch-Westfälische Zeitung,'" pp. 361–63; Heinrichsbauer, *Schwerindustrie*, p. 20; "Dr. Reismann-Grone zum Abschied," *National-Zeitung*, Apr. 29, 1937 (#117).

56. See Horst Gies, "The NSDAP and Agrarian Organizations in the Final Phase of the Weimar Republic," in H. A. Turner, Jr. (ed.), *Nazism and the Third Reich* (New York, 1972), pp. 45–88.

57. See, for example, the final part of Feder's speech in Koblenz, Sept. 27, 1932 (cf. n. 35, above).

58. Horkenbach (ed.), *Das Deutsche Reich* (1932), p. 335.

59. Keppler to Krogmann, Oct. 8, 1932: FSGNSH, Krogmann Papers, 913.

60. See Herle's letter to Reusch of Aug. 3, 1932, with enclosed memorandum, "Mitteilung meines Mitarbeiters, Herrn von Buxhoeveden, an mich betreffend eine Besprechung mit Herrn Dr. Adrian von Renteln, Stellvertreter des Herrn Wagener in der Wirtschaftspolitischen Abteilung des Braunen Hauses": GHH, 400101220/13.

61. See Herle's letter to Reusch, Aug. 3, 1932, with enclosure, "Betr.: Besprechung zwischen Herrn von Renteln und den Herren Dr. Herle und Dr. von Buxhoeveden," dated Aug. 1, 1932: ibid.

62. Reusch to Herle, Aug. 4, 1932: ibid.

63. See Herle's communication to members of the Reichsverband, "Nur zur persönlichen Information! Nicht zur Weitergabe!" Sept. 8, 1932: ibid.; also in BAK, Silverberg Papers, 232, with Herle's letter to Silverberg of Sept. 9, 1932.

64. See chapter V, section 3; also "Der Zwiespalt in der nationalsozialistischen Wirtschaftspolitik," Deutsche Führerbriefe, Aug. 26, 1932 (#66).

65. Herle to Renteln, Sept. 8, 1932, copies in GHH, 400101220/13, BAK, Silverberg Papers, 232. The text appears in Stegmann, "Zum Verhältnis," pp. 452–65. For an abbreviated and tendentious treatment of Herle's response, see the East German publication ed. by Wolfgang Schumann, Gerhart Hass, et al. Deutschland im zweiten Weltkrieg, 4 vols. (East Berlin, 1974–81), I, p. 63.

66. Schacht to Reusch, Sept. 12, 1932: GHH, 400101290/33. There is evidence that Hitler did in fact order the Sofortprogramm withdrawn from circulation: Barkai, Wirtschaftssystem, p. 39. The pamphlet was, however, still being sold at Nazi rallies as late as September 27; see "Einnahmebelege der Ortsgruppe Braunschweig-Fallerslebertor von 1.9.1932 bis 31.1.1933" NSHSAH, Hann. 310, I E 5, Bl. 292.

67. Heinrichsbauer to Pinkerneil, Sept. 15, 1932: Fachgruppe Bergbau beim Reichsverband der Deutschen Industrie, file 258 (these records, in the possession of the Wirtschaftsvereinigung Bergbau, Bad Godesberg, when used, are now in the Bergbau Archiv, Bochum). See also "Informationen des Tages," Deutsche Führerbriefe, Sept. 16, 1932 (#72), p. 4; Hugo Kanter, Syndikus of the Braunschweig Handelskammer, to Hamm of the Deutscher Industrie- und Handelstag, Sept. 21, 1932: BAK, R11/377.

68. See Hitler's Verfügung of Sept. 22, 1932: BDC, Sammlung Schumacher, Ordner 212.

69. Herle to Reusch, Sept. 23, 1932: GHH, 400101220/13.

70. See "Bericht über die Sitzung des Reichswirtschaftsrates am 27. April 1932 vormittags 11 Uhr im Braunen Haus," BAK, NS 22/11.

71. Ibid.; also "Sonderanweisungen des Leiters der Hauptabteilung IV (Wirtschaft)," signed by Wagener, VB, July 13, 1932 (#195); Karl-Heinz Ludwig, Technik und Ingenieure im Dritten Reich (Düsseldorf, 1974), p. 92; Tyrell, "Gottfried Feder," pp. 75f.; Barkai, Wirtschaftssystem, p. 31.

72. Turner (ed.), Hitler aus nächster Nähe, pp. 478–81.

73. Martin Broszat, Der Staat Hitlers (Munich, 1969), p. 78. On Funk's well-known aversion to Feder and his ideas, see the letter of Hugo Kanter, Syndikus of the Braunschweig Handelskammer, to Eduard Hamm of the Deutscher Industrie- und Handelstag, Sept. 21, 1932: BAK, R11/377.

74. Reusch to Herle, Sept. 22, 1932; Herle to Reusch, Sept. 23, 1932: GHH, 400101220/13.

75. Schacht to Reusch, Sept. 12, 1932: ibid., 400101290/33.

76. Reusch to Schacht, Sept. 21, 1932: ibid.

77. Gilsa to Reusch, Sept. 19, 1932: ibid., 400101293/4.

78. Quoted in "Nationalkapitalismus tut Not," *Deutsche Führerbriefe*, Oct. 4, 1932 (#77).

79. Reusch to Gilsa, Sept. 21, 1932: GHH, 400101293/4.

80. Heinrichsbauer to Strasser, Sept. 20, 1932: NA, RG 242, Microcopy T-81, 1/11436–45; the text of this letter appears in full in Günter Plum, *Gesellschaftsstruktur und politisches Bewusstsein in einer katholischen Region 1928–1933* (Stuttgart, 1972), pp. 301–04. Only a few weeks earlier Heinrichsbauer had displayed a much more optimistic assessment of the NSDAP; see Blank to Reusch, Sept. 3, 1932: GHH, 4001012024/10; also memo for Hugenberg by Otto Schmidt-Hannover, Sept. 5, 1932: BAK, Hugenberg Papers, 38.

81. "Das Wirtschaftsprogramm des Nationalsozialismus," Aug. 18 and 25, Sept. 8, 22, 29, and Oct. 6. The articles were later republished, with minor changes, as a pamphlet by the author, Karlheinz Rieker, *Das Wirtschaftsprogramm des Nationalsozialismus* (Berlin, 1933).

82. "Das nationalsozialistische Dilemma. I. Planwirtschaft oder Kapitalismus?" Sept. 18, 1932 (#700).

83. "Die Woche," Oct. 16, 1932 (#244).

84. *Das Wirtschaftliche Aufbauprogramm der NSDAP. Eine Rede Gregor Strassers gehalten vor 15 000 nationalsozialistischen Betriebszellenmitgliedern am 20, Oktober 1932 im Berliner Sportpalast* (Berlin, 1932). Feder proclaimed the new program in advance: "Die wirtschaftliche Aufbauarbeit des Nationalsozialismus. Gottfried Feder verkündet das Aufbauprogramm der N.S.D.A.P.," *VB*, Oct. 18, 1932 (#292). In a later published form, the authorship was attributed to Funk "in Zusammenarbeit mit Gottfried Feder": Feder, *Kampf gegen die Hochfinanz* (Munich, 1934), p. 371. At Nuremberg Funk claimed sole authorship: *Trial of the Major War Criminals*, XIII, p. 85, testimony of May 4, 1946. For an analysis of the program, see Barkai, *Wirtschaftssystem*, pp. 41–43.

85. Memorandum by Scherer for Reusch, Oct. 24, 1932: GHH, 400127/3 (I am indebted to Dr. Reinhard Neebe for bringing this document to my attention).

86. Scherer to Reusch, Sept. 21, 1932: ibid., 400101220/13.

87. Heinrichsbauer to Kellermann of the Gutehoffnungshütte, Oct. 22, 1932: ibid., Kellermann Papers, 40010137/4. In a note to Heinrichsbauer on Oct. 24, Kellermann declined: ibid.

88. See the invitation to Krupp von Bohlen, undated: KA, IV E 1129

89. Krupp to Thyssen, Oct. 20, 1932: ibid. An observer in the Ruhr who provided information for Franz Bracht, the Prussian commissar installed by Papen, reported that the turnout had proved disappointing, producing strained relations between the men of United Steel, who attended, and those of Krupp, Hoesch, and the Gutehoffnungshütte, who had not. Except possibly for Thyssen, no one had contributed money to Hitler, the

observer added: ZAP, Bracht Papers, vol. 2, Bl. 178f., Scholtz to Minis-
terialrat Dr. Gritzbach, Oct. 24, 1932, and Scholtz's memo for Bracht,
"Vertraulich!" bearing the stamped date of Oct. 29, 1932.

90. Loewenstein to Thyssen, Oct. 20, 1932: BBB, Loewenstein Papers, Allgemeiner Schriftwechsel.

91. Reusch to Gebsattel, Nov. 23, 1932: GHH, 400101290/15.

92. See his reponse during an interview in 1940 by Emery Reves, the ghost-
writer author of *I Paid Hitler,* a book attributed to Thyssen: T/RP, sheet
270. Cf. Turner, "Fritz Thyssen und 'I paid Hitler.'"

93. "Aufzeichnung über eine Besprechung im Klub von Berlin am Mittwoch,
den 19. Oktober 1932, nachm. 4 Uhr," enclosure in Blank to Reusch, Oct.
20, 1932: GHH, 4001012024/10. Vögler was at the time communicating
closely with Hugenberg and sought in vain to arrange a meeting between
Hitler and Hugenberg: see Vögler to Hugenberg, Sept. 22, 1932, and
Hugenberg to Vögler, Oct. 19, 1932: BAK, Hugenberg Papers, 39.

94. T/RP, sheet 270 (cf. n. 92, above).

95. "Hitler bei Thyssen," *Die Rote Fahne,* Oct. 25, 1932 (#194); "Geheimkon-
ferenz Hitler-Thyssen-Bracht," *Freiheit* (Düsseldorf), Oct. 23, 1932 (clipping with letter, Scholtz to Gritzbach, Oct. 24, 1932, cited in n. 89, above).
Prussian Commissar Bracht did not attend.

96. Bracher, *Auflösung,* p. 644.

97. "Die Soziale Rekonsolidierung des Kapitalismus," *Deutsche Führerbriefe,*
Sept. 16, 1932 (#72) and Sept. 20, 1932 (#73).

98. See Sohn-Rethel, "Die soziale Rekonsolidierung des Kapitalismus (September 1932)," *Kursbuch,* Sept. 1970 (#21), pp. 23–26, 29–34.

99. See, for some examples, World Committee for the Victims of German Fas-
cism, *The Brown Book of the Hitler Terror* (New York, 1933), pp. 30–33; E.
Palme Dutt, *Fascism and Social Revolution* (New York, 1935), pp. 170–74;
Ernst Fischer, *Das Fanal* (Vienna, 1946), pp. 58–61; Richard Sasuly, *IG
Farben* (New York, 1947), pp. 68f.; Joachim Streisand, *Deutsche Geschichte
von den Anfängen bis zur Gegenwart. Eine marxistische Einführung* (Cologne,
1972), pp. 348f.; Amos Simpson, *Hjalmar Schacht in Perspective* (The
Hague, 1977), pp. 77f.; Jürgen Kuczinski, *Klassen und Klassenkämpfe im
imperialistischen Deutschland und in der BRD* (Frankfurt am Main, 1972), p.
473.

100. An East German propaganda organ published in West Germany even
went so far as to impugn Sohn-Rethel's claim to having been a Communist
in 1932 and to portray him as a lackey of the capitalists: E. Berliner, "Das
monopolistische Problem der Massenbasis, die 'Deutschen Führerbriefe'
und Alfred Sohn-Rethel. Anmerkungen und Dokumentation zu einer un-
vollkommenen Enthüllung," *Blätter für deutsche und internationale Politik* 19
(Feb. 1974): 154–74. In an angry reply Sohn-Rethel sought to refute the
aspersions cast on his credentials as a loyal Communist: "Zum Artikel von
E. Berliner: Das monopolkapitalistische Problem der Massenbasis, die
'Deutschen Führerbriefe' und Alfred Sohn-Rethel. Die vollkommene
Selbtsenthüllung eines Anonymous," ibid. (Dec. 1974): 1285–1296. See
also the rejoinder of E. Berliner, "Anmerkungen zu Sohn-Rethels Philip-
pika," ibid., pp. 1297-1301. Sohn-Rethel republished his 1932 article in his

Ökonomie und Klassenstruktur des deutschen Faschismus (Frankfurt, 1973), pp. 165–72.

101. "Die Woche," Nov. 6, 1932 (#262).

102. "Politische Hintergründe," Nov. 3, 1932 (#528).

Chapter VI, section 2: Political Money in the Autumn Election Campaign—
Maneuvers in the Twilight of Weimar

1. Heinrichsbauer, *Schwerindustrie*, p. 48; NA, RG 238, Case 10, Dokumenten-buch Bülow II, doc. 70, Heinrichsbauer's affidavit of Jan. 31, 1948; Pre-Trial Interrogations, Heinrichsbauer, Jan. 9, 1947; Grauert, Dec. 5, 1946.

2. NA, RG 238, Case 5, vol. 15a, p. 4981, testimony of Aug. 6, 1947.

3. Bosch, *Handelspolitische Notwendigkeiten*, als Manuskript gedruckt, November 1932: KA, IV C 205.

4. NA, RG 238, NI-6677, Ilgner's affidavit, Dec. 7, 1946; NI-7082, same of May 1, 1947; Pre-Trial Interrogation of Ilgner, Apr. 10, 1947.

5. See the correspondence on Mann in BDC, Parteikanzlei Korrespondenz, especially Kassenverwaltung, Gauleitung Köln-Aachen, to Kassenver-waltung Reichsleitung, Mar. 29, 1933, at which point Mann applied for readmission. On the NSBO's efforts, see Kele, *Nazis and Workers*, p. 199.

6. This chapter of the finances of National Socialism still awaits full explora-tion. See, in the meantime, Matzerath and Turner, "Selbstfinanzierung," p. 68; Allen, *Nazi Seizure*, pp. 132f.; Noakes, *Lower Saxony*, pp. 235f.; Fischer, *Stormtroopers*, pp. 110–42; Bessel, *Political Violence*, p. 94; Stimmungs-berichte from the autumn of 1932 in NA, RG 242, Microcopy T-81, 91/105058–246.

7. Allen, *Nazi Seizure*, pp. 132ff.; Noakes, *Lower Saxony*, p. 235.

8. See the report on the conference between the office of the party treasurer and Reichszeugmeister Richard Büchner, Oct. 24 and 25, 1932, dated Nov. 7, 1932: BDC, Reichsschatzmeister, Ordner 101 (this collection is now in BAK).

9. Oren J. Hale, *The Captive Press in the Third Reich* (Princeton, 1964), pp. 59f.

10. One widespread rumor had the party in debt to the extent of twelve million marks by December 1932: *A-Brief. Vertraulicher Informationsdienst*, Dec. 16, 1932 (#315), copy in IfZ, 102/2; "12 Millionen Schulden," *Kölnische Volks-zeitung*, Dec. 18, 1932 (#348). The source of the rumor seems to have been an allegation published in mid-December by Otto Strasser, who had had nothing to do with the party for more than two years: "Der Konflikt in der NSDAP," *Frankfurter Zeitung*, Dec. 17, 1932 (#940/41). This rumor has often been repeated in later publications, despite the absence of any eviden-tial basis. The decentralized structure of the NSDAP's finances makes the availability of such a global figure unlikely in any event. In 1942 Hitler did, however, speak of having signed many notes for loans in 1932: Henry Picker, *Hitlers Tischgespräche*, ed. by Gerhard Ritter (Bonn, 1951), entry for May 6, 1942, p. 280.

11. Noakes, *Lower Saxony*, p. 236.

12. See Siemens's circular letter of Oct. 24, 1932: SA, 4/Lf 670.

13. See the minutes of the meeting prepared by Martin Blank, enclosed with his letter to Reusch, Oct. 20, 1932: GHH, 4001012024/10. Present, aside from those mentioned here, were Hans Berckemeyer, representing Silesian industry; Ernst von Borsig; Konrad Piatscheck of the lignite industry; Rudolf Funke, representing the brewers of Germany; Edmund Pietrkowski, managing director of the Verein zur Wahrung der Interessen der chemischen Industrie; Hans Vögele, representing the industrialists of Baden; Max Schlenker of the Langnamverein; Philipp Helfferich, a textile executive representing the industry of the Palatinate; Jakob Herle and a Dr. Heinecke of the Reichsverband; and Wolf-Dietrich von Witzleben, Siemens's secretary. Blank's minutes have been published: Stegmann, "Zum Verhältnis," pp. 468-75.

14. Minutes by Blank (see n. 13).

15. Ibid.

16. Ibid.

17. See the circular letter by Siemens, Oct. 24, 1932: SA, 4/Lf 670.

18. On the implementation of the fund-raising campaign, see the appeal for contributions circulated by Pietrkowski in a circular letter of Oct. 29 on behalf of the national organization of the chemical industry, published in Hans Radandt, "'Freie Wahlen' und Monopolkapital," ZfG 9 (1961): 1321f. See also the appeals sent by Siemens to some two dozen Berlin industrialists on Oct. 27: SA, 4/Lf 670. Siemens's office referred all requests for funds, from the Deutsche Staatspartei and the Wirtschaftspartei as well as from the DVP and DNVP, to Martin Blank, who administered the money on behalf of the three-man Kuratorium: ibid.

19. NA, RG 238, Case 5, vol. 10a, p. 3165, testimony of July 2, 1947; Case 10, vol. 15a, p. 5554, testimony of Apr. 2, 1948.

20. Ibid., Case 5, Dokumentenbuch Flick I, doc. 2, Planck to Flick, Oct. 7, 1932; Flick to Planck, Oct. 10, 1932; receipt from Dresdner Bank, Oct. 10, 1932. Max von der Porten, the industrialist charged with overseeing the government-controlled Gelsenkirchen stock, told former State Secretary Hans Schäffer that Otto Wolff had brought Flick, Krupp, and Vögler to contribute 100,000 marks each to an election fund for the fall campaign: IfZ, ED 93, Schäffer diary, entry for Dec. 1, 1932.

21. See "Aufruf zum 6. November 1932": ZAP, Büro des Reichspräsidenten, 47. George W.F. Hallgarten mistakenly assumed that the appeal was in support of the NSDAP: Hitler, Reichswehr und Industrie (1955), p. 115 (cf. note 23).

22. Keppler to Krogmann, Oct. 26, 1932: FSGNSH, Krogmann Papers, 913.

23. Krupp to Prince Otto zu Salm-Horstmar, Oct. 12, 1932, in response to Salm-Horstmar's letter of the eleventh: NA, RG 238, NI-444 and NI-445; Reusch to Salm-Horstmar, Oct. 13, 1932: GHH, 400101293/12.

24. Reusch to Kötter, Oct. 2, 1932: GHH, 4001012007/15; Reusch to Salm-Horstmar, Oct. 13, 1932: ibid., 400101293/12.

25. Siemens, "Die Wirtschaft verlangt Stetigkeit des Regierungskurses," Ostpreussische Zeitung, Oct. 28, 1932; Frowein, "Wahlpflicht der Wirtschaft," Kölnische Zeitung, Nov. 3, 1932 (#602).

26. See the report of an American observer who spoke with German industrialists after the election: Calvin B. Hoover, Germany Enters the Third Reich

(New York, 1933), p. 64. On the stock market, see "Nach der Wahl," *Ruhr und Rhein Wirtschaftszeitung*, Nov. 11, 1932 (#46); "Die Börse auf den Wahlausgang fest und lebhafter," *Deutsche Bergwerks-Zeitung*, Nov. 8, 1932 (#263).

27. On Nov. 4, two days before the election, for example, Reusch cautioned Rudolf Kötter, editor of the *Fränkischer Kurier*, one of the newspapers controlled by his firm, to print nothing that might impede negotiations among the parties after the balloting: GHH, 4001012007/15.

28. Still useful on Silverberg's business career is the introduction by Franz Mariaux to Silverberg, *Reden und Schriften*.

29. See Dirk Stegmann, "Die Silverberg-Kontroverse 1926," in *Sozialgeschichte Heute*, ed. by Hans-Ulrich Wehler (Göttingen, 1974), pp. 594–610; Weisbrod, *Schwerindustrie*, pp. 246–72.

30. Silverberg to Reusch, Sept. 5, 1932: GHH, 400101290/35.

31. Neebe, *Grossindustrie*, pp. 153–68.

32. On Alvensleben, see Bracher, *Auflösung*, pp. 722f.; Vogelsang, *Reichswehr*, pp. 392–94. For the documentation on Silverberg's attitudes, see n. 35.

33. The following is based on letters to this writer from Meynen of Apr. 15 and June 11, 1969, as well as in an interview in Baden-Baden on June 6, 1970. The publication was indirectly subsidized by industrialists such as Paul Reusch, who paid for multiple subscriptions at the yearly price of seventy-five marks; cf. Neebe, *Grossindustrie*, p. 154. See also the information brought to light about the *Führerbriefe* in the controversy bearing on the articles planted there in September 1932 by the covert Communist provocateur Alfred Sohn-Rethel (cf. section 1 of this chapter). Editorials in the *Führerbriefe* did not consistently call for a government led by the Nazis, as Neebe infers: cf. editorial of Sept. 6, 1932 (#69), which proposed the appointment as chancellor of neither Papen nor Hitler but rather of some unspecified person previously uninvolved in the dispute between those two.

34. Reuter's principal job was as Berlin representative of the Pressestelle Kohle und Eisen. On his relations with Schacht, see the foreword to his biography, dated Dec. 1933: *Schacht* (Berlin, 1934), p. 5.

35. Silverberg to Reusch, Sept. 5, 1932: GHH, 400101290/35. See also "Dr. Silverberg zu Fragen der Wirtschaftspolitik," *Deutsche Wirtschafts-Zeitung*, Oct. 27, 1932 (#43).

36. "Notiz über den Abend vom 31. August 1932," enclosed with Alvensleben's letter to Schleicher of Sept. 2, 1932: BA/MA, Schleicher Papers, N 42/22, Bl. 125–27.

37. Alvensleben to Hitler, Sept. 15, 1932: NA, RG 242, Microcopy T-81, 1/11338–39.

38. Alvensleben to Hitler, Sept. 21, 1932: ibid., frames 11334–36.

39. This account is based on Meynen's letter to me of Apr. 15, 1969, and my interview with him of June 6, 1970. The Berlin magazine *Welt am Montag* reported on the meeting afterwards, setting it on about Nov. 9, according to "Hitler und die Schwerindustrie," *Münchner Zeitung*, Nov. 21, 1932 (#321). That report gave no particulars except that Meynen and Reuter had come away convinced that Hitler knew the limits of his power. Doubt is cast on the knowledgeability of the report, however, by its inclusion of the news that Hitler had recently apologized to Reusch for the NSDAP's cooperation with

the Communists in supporting strikes in the Ruhr and the strike of the Berlin transport workers. Reusch at once branded that unlikely allegation as "wholly fabricated": Reusch to Gebsattel, Nov. 23, 1932: GHH, 400101290/15. The report on Meynen and Reuter's meeting with Hitler by an informant of Prussian Commissar Franz Bracht seems equally without benefit of knowledge; see Scholtz to Bracht, stamped with the date Nov. 9, 1932: ZAP, Bracht Papers, Bd. 2, Bl. 177. Scholtz attributed the meeting to Silverberg's "burning wish" to regain the status of influential business advisor he had enjoyed under Brüning, but that interpretation must be viewed in the light of Scholtz's employment by Otto Wolff, Silverberg's archenemy in Cologne, to direct the public relations office Wolff jointly maintained in Düsseldorf with Friedrich Flick (see chapter V, section 4).

40. See Otto Meynen, "Dr. Paul Silverberg," *Der Volkswirt* 5 (1951): 11. Meynen told of the subsidies to Strasser in his interview with this writer on June 6, 1970.

41. Schlenker to Bracht, Nov. 15, 1932: DZAP, Bracht Papers, Bd. 2, Bl. 129. This document is printed in Czichon, *Wer verhalf*, p. 66.

42. Thyssen to Schlenker, ZAP, Bracht Papers, Bd. 2, Bl. 130–31. Cf. the published text in Czichon, *Wer verhalf*, p. 67.

43. Bracher, *Auflösung*, pp. 656–60.

44. Ibid., pp. 660–69.

45. See the official record in *Mitteilungen des Vereins zur Wahrung der gemeinsamen wirtschaftlichen Interessen in Rheinland und Westfalen* (Jg. 1932, n.F., Heft 21). See also the report in *Stahl und Eisen*, Dec. 8, 1932 (Jg.52, Nr. 49), pp. 1226ff. The motto of the meeting was "Gesunde Wirtschaft im starken Staat." On the unsuccessful effort to have Interior Minister Gayl and Prussian commissar Bracht address the gathering, see Springorum to Reusch, Nov. 10, 1932: GHH, 400101290/36.

46. Scholtz to Bracht, undated but received on Nov. 26, 1932: ZAP, Bracht Papers, Bd. 2, Bl. 169. Only the first two sentences of this document from the East German archives have been published or cited in East German publications; the subsequent sentences, in which Scholtz (a journalist hired to report to Prussian Commissar Franz Bracht on developments in the Ruhr) qualified his statement by specifying the grounds for the opinions he had encountered, have been systematically omitted: Czichon, *Wer verhalf*, p. 73; Ruge, *Weimar*, p. 345.

47. "Die Tagesfrage," *Rheinisch-Westfälische Zeitung*, Nov. 18, 1932 (#589).

48. The texts of the speeches are in the official report of the association (cf. n. 45). Schlenker published the same week a much more extensive version of his views in which he identified himself more explicitly with the Papen cabinet: "Gesunde Wirtschaft im starken Staat," *Stahl und Eisen*, Nov. 24, 1932 (Jg. 52, Nr. 47), pp. 1168–71.

49. "Die Woche," *Deutsche Bergwerks-Zeitung*, Nov. 20, 1932 (#273).

50. This emerges clearly from the correspondence of the circle, especially Keppler to Krogmann and to Helfferich, Oct. 29, 1932; Krogmann to Keppler, Nov. 4, 1932: FSGNSH, Krogmann Papers, 913. Cf. Turner, "Grossunternehmertum," pp. 58–60.

51. Keppler to Krogmann, Nov. 12, 1932: FSGNSH, Krogmann Papers, 913. Keppler sent a similar letter to Helfferich the same day: Helfferich, *Tatsachen*, p. 17. Also, Keppler to Schröder, Nov. 13, 1932: NA, RG 238, NI-209. The list of those targeted was found in a vault at Schröder's bank after the war and used at Nuremberg on the assumption that all those named had signed: ibid., 3901-PS. The limited number of actual signatures became public only with the appearance of an East German publication that misidentified some of the signatories: Albert Schreiner, "Die Eingabe deutscher Finanzmagnaten, Monopolisten und Junker an Hindenburg für die Berufung Hitlers zum Reichskanzler (November 1932)," *ZfG* 4 (1956): 366–69. Despite the publication therein of the essential documentation from the East German archives, some historians in that state long continued to allege support for the petition by industrialists whose names were on the original list but who did not sign; see, for example, Helmut Eschwege, *Kennzeichen J* (East Berlin, 1966), pp. 29f.; Institut für Gesellschaftswissenschaften beim ZK der SED, *Imperialismus heute*, 5th ed. (East Berlin, 1968), p. 56; Klaus Drobisch et al., *Juden unterm Hakenkreuz* (Frankfurt, 1973), p. 66. This is corrected in the latest East German publication on the subject, which otherwise adds nothing new: Petzold, "Grossbürgerliche Initiativen," pp. 38–54.

52. Schacht to Hitler, Nov. 12, 1932: NA, RG 238, EC-456 (printed in Czichon, *Wer verhalf*, p. 64).

53. The original signed copies of the petition are in ZAP, Büro des Reichspräsidenten, 47.

54. On Merck, see NA, RG 238, NI-246 interrogation of Schröder, Dec. 1, 1945; Pre-Trial Interrogations, Schröder, Mar. 10, 1947. The first name Erwin was not specified by Schröder, and since there were several Mercks in Hamburg, it is possible Schröder was referring to another one. Erwin Merck was not significant enough to appear among the more than 13,000 businessmen listed in Wenzel, *Wirtschaftsführer*. On Woermann, who was in business independently of the prominent branch of his old Hamburg family, see Wenzel, *Wirtschaftsführer*, col. 2486; Krebs, *Tendenzen*, p. 105; Büttner, *Hamburg*, p. 624; Klaus Hildebrand, *Vom Reich zum Weltreich* (Munich, 1969), pp. 157–65. See also Woermann's article, "Die soziale Befreiung," in *Was wir vom Nationalsozialismus erwarten*, ed. by Albrecht Erich Günther (Heilbronn, 1932), pp. 138–48.

55. Since no first name was used, it is unclear whether the Beindorff who signed was the father, Fritz, then seventy-two, or his son, Günther, since both were senators in Hanover: Wenzel, *Wirtschaftsführer*, cols. 143f. On Lübbert, see ibid., cols. 1395f. A Stahlhelmer, Lübbert had long been active politically on the right: Berghahn, *Stahlhelm*, p. 164; Lewinsohn, *Das Geld*, p. 138. On Ventzki, see Wenzel, *Wirtschaftsführer*, col. 2333. On Eichborn, see n. 48 in chapter IV, section 4.

56. Reinhart to Otto Meissner, Nov. 21, 1932: ZAP, Büro des Reichspräsidenten, 47.

57. Writing to Schröder on Nov. 21, 1932, Vögler reported that Reusch and Springorum had refused to sign: NA, RG 238, N1-210. Both had informed him, he reported, that on the whole (*an und für sich*) they shared the view

expressed in the petition and saw its recommendation as the only real solution to the present crisis. Neither would sign, however, since they wanted to
refrain from taking any position politically. They also did not want to exac-
erbate the divisions that had developed in the *Revier* by speaking out politically. Aside from being much more qualified in characterizing the views of
Reusch and Springorum than Reinhart's, Vögler's letter does not tally with
the recorded attitudes of Reusch and Springorum at the time. In his letter
of Nov. 20 to Vögler declining to sign (GHH, 400101290/37), Reusch expressed no approval whatever and explained his negative response merely
in terms of "the existing circumstances" *(nach Lage der Verhältnisse)*, a phrase
that might well have referred to the national political situation. Reusch is
not known, moreover, to have advocated Hitler's appointment on any other
occasion. When that question next came up in his correspondence, he expressed clear opposition to the idea: Reusch to Kötter, Jan. 8, 1933: GHH,
4001012001/16. There are no other records of Springorum's ever favoring
Hitler's appointment to the chancellorship either. Additional doubt is cast
on Vögler's version by the fact that, far from avoiding a public political
stand, Springorum had placed his signature on the DNVP election appeal
on behalf of the Papen cabinet only a few weeks earlier (see above). Having
taken that public stand, it is difficult to grasp why he would have balked, in
principle, at a private communication to Hindenburg. It seems more likely
that he objected to its content. In light of these facts, the suspicion arises
that Vögler was seeking to turn Schröder down gently by making excuses
for the refusal of Reusch and Springorum to sign the petition Schröder was
promoting. Perhaps most significant of all, Vögler, who had also signed the
appeal on behalf of the Papen cabinet, withheld his own signature. Schacht
later recalled talking to Vögler at the time and discovering that he had refused to sign: NA, RG 238, Case 5, vol. 12a, p. 3992, testimony of July 21,
1947. An East German historian has asserted that Vögler issued a point-
blank *(unverblühmt)* demand for a Hitler cabinet in a speech to the Verein
Deutscher Eisenhüttenleute on Nov. 26, 1932: Czichon, *Wer verhalf*, p. 49.
That claim is, however, borne out neither by the cited source nor by the
published text of the speech in *Stahl und Eisen*, Dec. 15, 1932 (Jg. 52, Nr.
50), p. 1238. Keppler's claim that Paul Silverberg unhesitatingly stood ready
to sign the petition despite his Jewish ancestry seems based on a report that
reached Keppler at second or third hand and must be regarded as an uncorroborated, quite implausible rumor: Keppler to Krogmann, Nov. 14,
1932: FSGNSH, Krogmann Papers, 913 (cf. Neebe, *Grossindustrie*, p. 167).
After the war Silverberg reported knowing of the petition but stated that his
ancestry ruled out any possibility of his signing: ZARB, 219/201, Silverberg to
Wolf-Dietrich von Witzleben, Sept. 28, 1953. (I am indebted to Dr. Reinhard Neebe for bringing this document to my attention.)

58. Bracher, *Auflösung*, pp. 670–76.

Chapter VI, section 3: Capitalists Adjust to a "Red General"
in the Chancellery

1. See Blank to Reusch, Sept. 10, 1932: GHH, 4001012024/10; Hugo Stinnes,
Jr., to Fritz Klein, Dec. 3, 1932: KP.

2. *SEG* 73 (1932): 128–31, speech of July 26, 1932.

3. Silverberg to Reusch, Sept. 5, 1932: GHH, 400101290/35; Reusch to Kötter, Sept. 25, 1932: ibid., 4001012007/15.

4. See Hamm's draft of a letter to Most, Dec. 10, 1932: BAK, R11/10.

5. That appellation was bestowed on Schleicher by Hans Zehrer, editor of the magazine *Die Tat*, in its issue of Dec. 4, 1932: Ebbo Demant, *Von Schleicher zu Springer. Hans Zehrer als politischer Publizist* (Mainz, 1971), p. 101.

6. "Die Woche," *Deutsche Bergwerks-Zeitung*, Dec. 4, 1932 (#285).

7. Hayes, "'A Question Mark with Epaulettes?'" pp. 57f.

8. Reusch to Springorum, Oct. 12, 1932: GHH, 400101290/36. See also Ernst Poensgen to Vögler, Oct. 8, 1932; Paul Beeck, Chefbüro Otto Wolff, to Schleicher, Nov. 3, 1932; and Wolff to Vögler, Nov. 17, 1932: BA/MA, Schleicher Papers, N 42/22. Cf. Turner, "The *Ruhrlade*," p. 222. On the relationship between Zehrer and Schleicher, see Demant, *Von Schleicher zu Springer*.

9. Reusch to Kötter, Dec. 3, 1932: GHH, 4001012007/15; Reusch to Dörge, Dec. 5, 1932: ibid., 4001012007/13.

10. Turner, "The *Ruhrlade*," p. 224.

11. See the report on the meeting of the Hauptausschuss of the Deutscher Industrie- und Handelstag, Dec. 7, 1932, in *Westdeutsche Wirtschafts-Zeitung*, Dec. 16, 1932 (#51). For the meeting on Dec. 14, 1932, of the Vereinigung der Deutschen Arbeitgeberverbände, see "Vom Tage," *Der Arbeitgeber*, Dec. 15, 1932, p. 549. On the Reichsverband meeting, see n. 12.

12. See the Reichsverband report on the meeting of its Hauptausschuss on Dec. 14, 1932, in Rundschreiben 584/VIII, circulated with letter, Herle to members of Präsidium and Fachgruppen, Dec. 15, 1932, copy in GHH, 400101220/13. Krupp's speech received wide exposure in the business press; see, for example, "Mehr Gradlinigkeit," *Ruhr und Rhein Wirtschafts-zeitung*, Dec. 23, 1932 (#52).

13. Horkenbach (ed.), *Das Deutsche Reich* (1932), p. 418.

14. Ibid., p. 418f.

15. "Rückfall?" *Ruhr und Rhein Wirtschaftszeitung*, Dec. 16, 1932 (#51).

16. See the excerpts in *SEG* 73 (1932): 223–31.

17. See the editorial "Die Woche," *Deutsche Bergwerks-Zeitung*, Dec. 18, 1932 (#297); see also Rundschreiben P. 310/32 of the Deutscher Industrie- und Handelstag, Dec. 19, 1932: GHH, 40010123/25.

18. See, for example, "Der Taktiker," *Rheinisch-Westfälische Zeitung*, Dec. 18, 1932 (#645).

19. Reusch to Eduard Hamm, Dec. 22, 1932: GHH, 40010123/25.

20. Reusch to Hamm, Dec. 31, 1932: ibid.

21. On the following, see Wolffsohn, *Industrie und Handwerk*, pp. 98–106; Dieter Petzina, "Hauptprobleme der deutschen Wirtschaftspolitik 1932/33," *VfZ* 15 (1967): 18–55.

22. Kissenkoetter, *Strasser*, pp. 162ff. See also Peter D. Stachura, *Gregor Strasser and the Rise of Nazism* (London, 1983), pp. 103ff.

23. Richard Breitman, "On German Social Democracy and General Schleicher 1932–33," *CEH* 9 (1976): 352–78.

24. See the excerpts from Herle's speech at Neuss on Jan. 2, 1933, enclosed with his letter to Reusch of Jan. 4, 1933: GHH, 400101220/14. See also

Duisberg's approving reaction to that speech in his letter to Herle of Jan. 9, 1933: BAL, Reichsverband, Allgemeiner Schriftwechsel mit der Geschäftsführung.

25. See Wilmowsky's letter to Schleicher of Feb. 1, 1933: BA/MA, N 42/92 (I am indebted to Dr. Reinhard Neebe for bringing this document to my attention); see also Gereke, *Landrat*, p. 215.

26. See the report on one such meeting by the chairman of the Deutscher Industrie- und Handelstag, Bernhard Grund, to that organization's directorate on Jan. 18, 1933: BAK, Silverberg Papers, 642.

27. Horkenbach (ed.), *Das Deutsche Reich* (1933), p. 17.

28. Sitzung des Vorstandes des Deutschen Industrie- und Handelstags am 18. Januar 1933 vorm. 10 Uhr: BAK, Silverberg Papers, 642.

29. See, for examples, Carl Friedrich von Siemens, "Die Wirtschaft verlangt Stetigkeit des Regierungskurses," *Ostpreussische Zeitung*, Oct. 28, 1932; telegram of the Hansa-Bund to Hindenburg, Nov. 28, 1932, in that organization's *Jahresbericht 1932* (Berlin, n.d.), p. 16; resolution of the Präsidium of the industrial Reichsverband, Nov. 25, 1932: BAL, 62/10.4e; speech by Bernhard Grund to the Hauptausschuss of the Deutscher Industrie- und Handelstag, Dec. 7, 1932, reported in *Westdeutsche Wirtschafts-Zeitung*, Dec. 16, 1932 (#51); speech by Carl Köttgen, chairman of the Vereinigung der Deutschen Arbeitgeberverbände, Dec. 14, 1932, as reported in "Vom Tage," *Der Arbeitgeber*, Dec. 15, 1932; resolution of Präsidium of industrial Reichsverband, Jan. 19, 1933: Horkenbach (ed.), *Das Deutsche Reich* (1933), p. 21.

30. See, on the signs of economic recovery, the report on Silverberg's speech to the Vollversammlung of the Industrie- und Handelskammer of Cologne, Jan. 9, 1933, in *Westdeutsche Wirtschafts-Zeitung*, Jan. 13, 1933 (#2). On the fear of new elections in business circles, see the lead editorial in *Tägliche Rundschau*, Jan. 18, 1933, and the editorial in the Düsseldorf *Deutsche Bergwerks-Zeitung*, "Die Woche," Jan. 29, 1933 (#25).

31. See Reusch's letters to Vögler of Jan. 10, 18, and 23, 1933: GHH, 400101290/37; see also Reusch's letters to Robert Lehr, the DNVP mayor of Düsseldorf, Nov. 28, 1932, and Jan. 10, 1933: ibid., 400101293/12. Cf. Leopold, *Hugenberg*, pp. 127ff.

32. "Der Gordische Knoten," Jan. 23, 1933 (#38).

33. Horkenbach (ed.), *Das Deutsche Reich* (1932), pp. 378f., 411. According to Kissenkoetter, *Strasser*, p. 171, the Nazi tally in the Thuringian communal elections of Dec. 4, 1932, represented a loss of 40 percent as compared to the July 1932 Nazi vote.

34. This becomes abundantly apparent from a reading of the reports and commentary in the business-oriented press: "Unsere Meinung," *Deutsche Allgemeine Zeitung*, Dec. 10, 1932 (#579); "Strasser legt sämtliche Aemter nieder," *Frankfurter Zeitung*, Dec. 9, 1932 (#920); "Gregor Strassers Abschiedsbrief," ibid., Dec. 10, 1932 (#921/22). See also the editorial and the article "Gregor Strasser" in *Deutsche Führerbriefe*, Dec. 9, 1932 (#96). Reusch assessed Strasser similarly in two letters to the editor of the *Fränkischer Kurier*, Rudolf Kötter, Jan. 8 and 12, 1933: GHH, 4001012007/16. Initial reports indicated that Gottfried Feder had joined Strasser in resigning: "Der Konflikt in der NSDAP," *Frankfurter Zeitung*, Dec. 10, 1932 (#921/22).

Feder, however, immediately issued a denial: "Eine Erklärung Feders," ibid., Dec. 10, 1932 (#923). A week later Hitler seemingly reaffirmed Feder's position in the Nazi leadership ranks by naming him, along with Funk, to head a reorganized economic section of the Reichsleitung: "Weitere Verfügungen des Führers zur Herstellung einer erhöhten Schlagkraft der Bewegung," *VB*, Dec. 17, 1932 (#352). Cf. Tyrell, "Gottfried Feder," p. 78.

35. The East German historian Kurt Gossweiler has gone rather too far in arguing for Strasser's good standing in business circles. Gossweiler has identified Strasser as an agent of IG Farben on the basis of Strasser's career as an apothecary before joining the NSDAP and his employment after leaving the party by a pharmaceutical firm: "Die Rolle des Monopolkapitals bei der Herbeiführung der Röhm-Affare" (diss., Humboldt Universität, East Berlin, 1963), pp. 287–89.

36. On the Nazis' red-scare tactics, see Kele, *Nazis and Workers*, p. 209.

37. "Nationalsozialisten fordern Auflösung der Trusts," *Deutsche Bergwerks-Zeitung*, Nov. 20, 1932 (#273).

38. "IG Farben vorläufig behauptet," *National-Zeitung* (Essen), Dec. 4, 1932 (#320).

39. *SEG* 73 (1932): 215–20; cf. Bracher, *Auflösung*, p. 679. See also the angry reaction of the business-oriented *Deutsche Bergwerks-Zeitung*, "Die Woche," Dec. 11, 1932 (#291).

40. See the letter sent on Dec. 7, 1932, by Loewenstein's Sekretariat, at his instruction, to Wilhelm Hölling, Geschäftsführer of the Fachgruppe Bergbau beim Reichsverband der Deutschen Industrie, requesting correction of the erroneous statements in the article, "Vertreter der Belegschaft Zeche Sachsen bei der Reichsregierung," in the Nazi daily in Essen, *National-Zeitung*, Dec. 2, 1932 (#318): BBB, Loewenstein Papers, Allgemeiner Schriftwechsel, Bergassessor Hölling.

41. *Berliner Lokal-Anzeiger*, Jan. 1, 1933 (#1), as quoted in Gossweiler, "Die Rolle," vol. II, B 20f., Anlage XI.

42. "Der Weg eines Jahres: Hitlers Aufstieg und Niedergang," Jan. 1, 1933 (#1).

43. "Ein Jahr deutscher Politik," Jan. 1, 1933 (#1/2).

Chapter VI, section 4: Big Business Experiences the Birth of the Third Reich

1. This assumption pervades not only the Marxist publications on the subject but also a large number of non-Marxist works. For a few examples, see Konrad Heiden, *Der Fuehrer* (Boston, 1944), pp. 520–22; Bullock, *Hitler*, p. 221; Karl Dietrich Bracher, *The German Dictatorship* (New York, 1970), p. 200; Schweitzer, *Big Business*, p. 104; Fest, *Hitler*, p. 496; A. J. Ryder, *Twentieth-Century Germany* (New York, 1973), p. 275. On the fiftieth anniversary of Hitler's appointment as chancellor, a well-known British historian explained it in these terms: "Urged on by Ruhr capitalists, von Papen struck a bargain with Hitler. . . .": A. J. P. Taylor, "Jan. 30, 1933," *The New York Times*, Jan. 30, 1983. Much the same contention, equally without benefit of evidence, appears in Axel Kuhn, "Die Unterredung zwischen Hitler

und Papen im Hause des Barons von Schröder," *GWU* 24 (1973): 709–22;
I have criticized Kuhn's study and discussed other aspects of the meeting
in my article, "Grossunternehmertum und Nationalsozialismus 1930–
1933," esp. pp. 20–39.

2. In his letter of Dec. 19, 1932, in which he informed Hitler of Schröder's
talk with Papen on Dec. 16, Keppler proposed the banker's house as the
best place for a confidential meeting: NA, RG 242, Microcopy T-81,
1/11318–19. This eventually proved convenient for Hitler, who was
scheduled to begin his series of campaign speeches in nearby Lippe-
Detmold on the evening of Jan. 4, and for Papen, who planned at that time
to be on his way back to Berlin from a visit to his family's home in the Saar;
cf. Jutta Ciolek-Kümper, *Wahlkampf in Lippe* (Munich, 1976), p. 313; Franz
von Papen, *Vom Scheitern einer Demokratie, 1930–1933* (Mainz, 1968), p.
336.

3. Papen, *Vom Scheitern*, p. 337; idem, *Der Wahrheit eine Gasse* (Munich, 1952),
p. 255; NA, RG 238, Pre-Trial Interrogations, Papen, Sept. 10, 1946; ibid.,
NI-246, interrogation of Schröder, Dec. 1, 1945. Hess, Himmler, and Keppler accompanied Hitler to Schröder's house, but all accounts agree that
they were not present at the talk between Hitler and Papen.

4. On Schröder's background, see section 2 of this chapter.

5. That mutual acquaintance was Baron Kurt von Lersner, the former diplo-
mat and DVP Reichstag deputy: NA, RG 238, NI-249, "Translation of
Statement Prepared by von Schroeder on his Political Activities" (1945).
Lersner and Schröder belonged to the same university fraternity; see
Lersner's letters of 1932 to Schröder: ibid., NI-200, NI-202, NI-203. See
also Papen's reply of Oct. 1 to a letter from Schröder, relayed to him by
Lersner: ibid., NI-201.

6. Papen, *Gasse*, p. 254; idem, *Scheitern*, p. 334; Schröder's statement of 1945
in NI-249 (cf. n. 5, above). For a description of the evening at the Herrenklub by one of those present, see Theodor Eschenburg, "Franz von
Papen," *VfZ* 1 (1953): 163f.

7. NA, RG 238, NI-209, Keppler to Schröder, Nov. 13, 1932; when Keppler
wrote to Schröder two weeks later, on Nov. 28, the hopes he had raised
had proved illusory, and he made no further mention of them: ibid.,
NI-211.

8. Papen, *Gasse*, p. 254; idem, *Scheitern*, p. 334.

9. "Eine Auslassung des Freiherrn von Schröder," *Frankfurter Zeitung*, Jan. 7,
1933 (#19).

10. See, for some examples, NA, RG 238, NI-246, interrogation of Schröder,
Dec. 1, 1945; ibid., 3337-PS, Schröder's affidavit of Dec. 5, 1945; ibid.,
NI-7990, Schröder's affidavit of July 21, 1947. The records of Schröder's
post-war statements at Nuremberg show that he deviated from that account only once, during a Pre-Trial Interrogation on June 18, 1947 (ibid).
The transcript for that interrogation has Schröder contradicting himself
by first stating that the initiative for the meeting had come from Papen and
then that he, Schröder, had inquired of Papen through Keppler whether
he would be ready to meet with Hitler; apparently either Schröder or the
stenographer became confused at that point since Keppler and Papen did
not know each other at that time.

11. That is the case with Krupp von Bohlen, Fritz Springorum, Paul Reusch, Paul Silverberg, and Albert Vögler. Papen was, by prearrangement, Silverberg's guest for dinner in Cologne on the evening of the former chancellor's meeting with Hitler at Schröder's house. This gave rise, after the meeting became known, to speculation in the press that Silverberg had somehow been involved. He denied this at the time and later insisted that Papen had not even mentioned to him his meeting with Hitler; cf. Neebe, *Grossindustrie*, pp. 171–73, where an unconvincing attempt is made to call Silverberg's denials into doubt.

12. See Thyssen's account in the 1940 interviews with the journalist Emery Reves, who served as ghost-writer for his purported memoir, *I Paid Hitler:* T/RP, sheet 271. See also Hermann Rauschning's report on his interview with Thyssen in the spring of 1934, in Rauschning's *Men of Chaos* (New York, 1942), p. 220.

13. NA, RG 238, NI-7990, affidavit of July 21, 1947.

14. See, for example, the assertion, on the basis of Schröder's affidavit, by Arthur Schweitzer, in his *Big Business*, p. 104: "Turning against the new government of General von Schleicher, the business leaders consulted each other and came to the conclusion that they had to arrange for a direct reconciliation between von Papen and Hitler." See also Stegmann, "Zum Verhältnis," p. 439; Hallgarten and Radkau, *Deutsche Industrie*, pp. 215f., where an English version of the affidavit is quoted at length, apparently in re-translation, with numerous deviations from the original German text.

15. NA, RG 238, Pre-Trial Interrogations, Schröder, June 18, 1947.

16. On Dec. 19, Keppler confirmed, in a letter to Schröder, the latter's telephone message the previous day about Papen's readiness to meet with Hitler. He approved heartily of the idea, Keppler wrote, and had placed a letter addressed to Hitler recommending that course in the hands of Himmler, who also favored it and was on his way to Munich: NA, RG 238, NI-212. Keppler's letter to Hitler, dated Dec. 19, is in NA, RG 242, Microcopy T-81, 1/11318–19. On the subsequent arrangements, see NA, RG 238, NI-213 (Keppler to Schröder, Dec. 26); NI-215 (Keppler to Schröder, Dec. 29); NI-214 (Papen to Schröder, Dec. 28); NI-216 (Keppler to Schröder, Jan. 2, 1933).

17. This contention has long been a staple of Marxist-Leninist publications; see, for some examples, Isakhar M. Faingar, *Die Entwicklung des deutschen Monopolkapitals* (East Berlin, 1959; trans. of original Russian pub., Moscow, 1958), p. 103f.; Czichon, *Wer verhalf*, p. 51; Wolfgang Ruge in Bartmuss et al., *Deutsche Geschichte*, III, p. 160; Streisand, *Deutsche Geschichte*, p. 371. The story of a "deal" also appears in numerous non-Marxist works; see, for example, A. J. P. Taylor, *The Course of German History* (London, 1945), pp. 210f.; John W. Wheeler-Bennett, *The Nemesis of Power* (New York, 1954), p. 273; William L. Shirer, *The Rise and Fall of the Third Reich* (New York, 1960), p. 179. In some of these accounts, the meeting of Jan. 4 led to the formation of a big business "consortium" established expressly for the purpose of aiding the Nazis financially: cf. Faingar, *Entwicklung*, p. 103; Ruge in Bartmuss et al., *Deutsche Geschichte*, III, p. 160. That tale, in support of which no evidence has ever been adduced, was in circulation, at the latest, three years after the event: Heiden, *Hitler*, p. 314. By 1952 it had

become embellished with the additional "information" that the alleged "consortium" had, immediately on its formation, paid the Nazis' election debts and raised a million marks for the SS: Hallgarten, "Adolf Hitler and German Heavy Industry," pp. 242f. (reprinted in the 1955 edition of Hallgarten's *Hitler, Reichswehr und Industrie*, p. 116). The figure of a million marks has since been repeated in countless Marxist publications; see, for examples, the citations of the volumes by Bartmuss et al. and Streisand, above; also Ulrike Hörster-Philipps, *Konservative Politik in der Endphase der Weimarer Republik* (Cologne, 1982), p. 367. According to one East German version, intended for students at Parteihochschule "Karl Marx," no less than ten million marks came to the NSDAP from big business in the aftermath of the Papen-Hitler meeting: Siegfried Vietzke and Heinz Wohlgemuth, *Deutschland und die deutsche Arbeiterbewegung in der Zeit der Weimarer Republik* (East Berlin, 1966), p. 290. An imaginatively embellished version of the legend has now appeared, for over twenty years, uncorrected through five editions, in a textbook for American college students: "At this point German business came to the rescue. At a meeting of Rhine-Ruhr industrialists held on January 4, 1933, in the house of the Cologne banker Curt von Schroeder [*sic*], Hitler received a promise to pay the party's election debts and the wages of the Storm Troopers. In return, the Nazi leader implicitly undertook to maintain a hands-off policy toward German industry": H. Stuart Hughes, *Contemporary Europe: A History*, 5th ed., (Englewood Cliffs, 1981), p. 237.

18. Hitler issued his denial in the form of a public statement on Jan. 13, two days before the balloting in Lippe-Detmold, in an effort to counter the rumors discussed below: Horkenbach (ed.), *Das Deutsche Reich* (1933), p. 18. For Papen's denial, see his memoir, *Gasse*, pp. 256f.; for Schröder's, see NA, RG 238, Case 5, vol. 13a, pp. 4440f., testimony of July 28, 1947.

19. "Geheime Verhandlungen Hitler-Papen bei rheinischem Bankfürsten," *Die Rote Fahne*, Jan. 6, 1933 (#5).

20. "Bei den 'feinen Leuten,'" *Die Rote Fahne*, Jan. 6, 1933 (#5). These words were attributed to *Der Jungdeutsche*, an organ of the Jungdeutsches Orden.

21. "Hitler beim Herrenklub. In flagranti ertappt," *Vorwärts*, Jan. 6, 1933 (#10); "Der Agent der Grossindustrie," *Vorwärts*, Jan. 7, 1933 (#11). A similar but less ideologically phrased report appeared in the *Frankfurter Zeitung*: "Die Lage des Kabinetts Schleicher," Jan. 10, 1933 (#26).

22. See, for example, Carl von Ossietzky, "Der Flaschenteufel," *Die Weltbühne*, Jan. 10, 1933 (Jg. 29, Nr.2), p. 42.

23. The article on National Socialism in the authoritative East German reference work on German political history portrays the Cologne meeting, solely on the basis of Schröder's role, as a decisive turning point. "Hitler and the Nazi Party had now become the political agents (*Exponenten*) of a majority of German monopolists": Manfred Weissbecker, "Nationalsozialistische Deutsche Arbeiterpartei (NSDAP) 1919–1945," in Fricke (ed.), *Die bürgerlichen Parteien*, II, p. 414. See also Kurt Gossweiler, "Kurt von Schröder: Das Bankkapital stellt die Weichen," in Helmut Bock, Wolfgang Ruge, Marianne Thoms (eds.), *Sturz ins Dritte Reich* (East Berlin, 1983), esp. pp. 70f.

24. S. William Halperin, *Germany Tried Democracy* (New York, 1946), p. 524; Bullock, *Hitler*, p. 221; Dorpalen, *Hindenburg*, pp. 410f.; Carr, *History of Germany*, p. 357; Hajo Holborn, *A History of Modern Germany, 1840–1945* (New York, 1969), p. 705; Schulz, *Aufstieg*, p. 747.

25. In one passage frequently cited in this connection, Goebbels noted on Jan. 5 that the finances of the Berlin Gau had somewhat improved. But an infusion of capitalist funds, even if almost immediately after the end of the Papen-Hitler meeting the previous afternoon, could scarcely have affected the local organs of the party so quickly. In any event, Goebbels coupled that entry of Jan. 5 with the complaint (unmentioned by those who cited only the first part of the entry) that no financial resources existed for a renewal of the political struggle: *Vom Kaiserhof zur Reichskanzlei* (Munich, 1934), p. 235. On the next day, Jan. 6, the entry again shows Goebbels complaining about the poor financial situation: ibid., p. 236. On Jan. 16 Goebbels's entry stated that the situation of the party had been fundamentally altered overnight, but he obviously referred to its electoral success in Lippe-Detmold, not to its finances: ibid., p. 243. A day later, on Jan. 17, he noted that the finances of his Gau had suddenly improved but attributed this explicitly to economy measures, not to new sources of income: ibid. Goebbels's book cannot, in any case, be regarded as an incontrovertibly authentic diary; see Helmut Heiber, *Goebbels* (New York, 1972), pp. 91f. A passage in a post-war volume of Goebbels's diary involving an exchange with tax officials has been erroneously interpreted as reflecting the party's finances: Bracher, *Auflösung*, p. 694; Fest, *Hitler*, p. 497. Since the NSDAP was, as a non-profit organization, not liable for taxes, that exchange clearly bore only on Goebbels's personal finances.

26. See Ciolek-Kümper, *Wahlkampf in Lippe*, pp. 88–91, 139–43, 313–15; Arno Schröder, *'Hitler geht auf die Dörfer'. Der Auftakt zur nationalen Revolution. Ergebnisse und Bilder von der entscheidenden Januarwahl 1933 in Lippe* (Detmold, 1938), pp. 13–18, 46, 64f., 70, 79, 86, 104f., 113f., 184f., 209.

27. Ciolek-Kümper, *Wahlkampf in Lippe*, p. 142.

28. Dietrich, *Zwölf Jahre*, p. 187.

29. On the basis of highly questionable sources, Dirk Stegmann has contended in his "Verhältnis," p. 439, that on Jan. 30 Hindenburg repeatedly asked to see the petition that the Keppler circle had submitted to him the previous November; cf. my critique of this most improbable story in "Grossunternehmertum und Nationalsozialismus," p. 62.

30. NA, RG 238, Case 10, Dokumentenbuch Bülow I (this document was confiscated from a file in the KA, Reichsverband, KC—1084, Bd. V). Kastl's letter is partially printed in Neebe, *Grossindustrie*, p. 152.

31. On Schleicher's position, see Vogelsang, *Reichswehr*, pp. 372f.

32. Kastl made this statement at the meeting of the presidium of the industrial Reichsverband on Mar. 23, 1933: minutes in KA, IV E 885.

33. The letter of Kastl and Hamm is in ZAP, Büro des Reichspräsidenten, 47.

34. Ibid.

35. Ibid.

36. Fritz Thyssen made this charge at the meeting of the presidium of the Reichsverband on Mar. 23, 1933 (see n. 32, above), a development dealt with below.

37. On Krupp's dislike and mistrust for Nazism, see his letter to Herr von Brackel, Dec. 29, 1932: NA, RG 238, Case 10, Dokumentenbuch Bülow III. See also the interview of Thyssen by his ghost-writer, Emery Reves, in France in 1940: T/RP, sheet 261.

38. Gereke, *Landrat*, p. 225. Gereke's memory seems corroborated by Wilmowsky's cordial letter to Schleicher of Feb. 1, 1933, in which he warmly recalled an evening they had recently spent together and regretted Schleicher's removal from office: BA/MA, Schleicher Papers, N42/92.

39. As late as Jan. 14, 1933, Hermann Loening, one of the soon-to-be dismissed Jewish members of the senior staff of the Reichsverband, wrote to Krupp to inform him that an official in the Economics Ministry had called him to ask whether the industrial organization did not wish to undertake measures against Chancellor Schleicher's reported plan to install Hugenberg as both minister of economics and minister of agriculture. The official had recognized, Loening added, that "we make it a point to remain very reticent about cabinet changes." Krupp, in his reply to Loening of Jan. 16, 1933, wrote: "Like you, I see no way to respond to this suggestion." KA, IV E 203.

40. The East German historian Wolfgang Ruge, who gives the correct archival citation for the letters of Kastl and Hamm, which are located in an East German archive, misrepresents those documents as evidence that Kastl and Krupp "insisted" on the immediate appointment of Hitler as chancellor: Ruge, *Hindenburg*, pp. 474f.

41. On Stauss, see Stauss to Dingeldey, July 21, 1932; Dingeldey to Stauss, Aug. 29, 1932: BAK, Dingeldey Papers, 25. Stauss aligned himself in the fall of 1932 with the Papen cabinet: DWI, records of the Deutsche Bank und Disconto-Gesellschaft, A23/1, Generalsekretariat v. Stauss, letter to J. O. Coff, Oct. 1, 1932. Before the March Reichstag election of 1933 Stauss secured financial support for the DVP from Carl Friedrich von Siemens; see Wolf-Dietrich von Witzleben to Dingeldey, Mar. 2, 1933: SA, 4/Lf 670.

42. See the copies of their correspondence made by the police and used in the party trial of Repuke in 1934, in the records of the Oberstes Parteigericht, BDC. Reinhard Neebe has argued that Fritz Springorum's proposal in his letter to Papen of Jan. 24, 1933, that the former chancellor receive Heinrichsbauer, reveals an attempt to bring Papen to collaborate with Strasser instead of Hitler: *Grossindustrie*, pp. 145f., 152. That view presumes, however, full knowledge on the part of Springorum (and those industrialists with whom he worked in January 1933, such as Reusch) about the machinations of the often very secretive Heinrichsbauer, a presumption that remains uncorroborated.

43. See the interview of Thyssen by his ghost-writer, Emery Reves, in France in 1940: T/RP, sheet 170.

44. Vogelsang, *Reichswehr*, p. 393; Kunrat von Hammerstein, *Spähtrupp* (Stuttgart, 1963), p. 49; cf. Gordon A. Craig, *The Politics of the Prussian Army, 1640–1945* (New York, 1955), pp. 465f.

45. See the correspondence of Springorum, who arranged the meeting at Papen's request: HAD, Springorum Papers, B1a 82/12b, Springorum to Papen, Dec. 23, 1932; ibid., B1a 82/12, Springorum to Papen, Dec. 27, 1932; Papen to Springorum, Dec. 29, 1932; ibid., B1a 75/21, Springorum to Krupp, Dec. 28, 1932; Krupp to Springorum, Dec. 30, 1932; GHH, 400101290/36, Springorum to Reusch, Dec. 28, 1932, and Reusch to Springorum, Dec. 30, 1932. In his letters to the others Springorum expressed the intention to invite also Erich Fickler, managing director of the Harpener Bergbau AG of Dortmund and a member, like the others, of the Ruhrlade, but it remains unclear whether Fickler attended. Papen's meeting with the industrialists in Dortmund on the seventh quickly became known as a result of a report in the *Dortmunder General-Anzeiger,* cited in "Papens nachträglicher Kölner Bericht," *Tägliche Rundschau,* Jan. 10, 1933 (#8). See also "Papen in Dortmund," *Vorwärts,* Jan. 9, 1933 (#14). East German historians have invented a meeting between Hitler and a group of industrialists, often set at Emil Kirdorf's home in Mülheim, but sometimes in Cologne, on January 5, in some versions on January 7: Institut für Marxismus-Leninismus beim ZK der SED, *Geschichte der deutschen Arbeiterbewegung,* 8 vols. (East Berlin, 1966), IV, p. 382; Kuczynski, *Klassen und Klassenkämpfe,* p. 471; Wolfgang Ruge, *Hindenburg* (East Berlin, 1974), p. 467; Karl Nuss, *Militär und Wiederaufrüstung in der Weimarer Republik* (East Berlin, 1977), p. 291; Pätzold and Weissbecker, *Geschichte der NSDAP,* p. 199.

46. No record of the meeting seems to have been made, so this reconstruction of what took place is based on the following correspondence of the participants: GHH, 4001012007/16, Reusch to Rudolf Kötter, Jan. 8, 1933; ibid., 400101293/12, Reusch to Robert Lehr, Jan. 10, 1933; ibid., 400101290/37, Reusch to Vögler, Jan. 10, 18, and 23, 1933. HAD, Springorum Papers, B1a 76/50, Springorum to Robert Lehr, Jan. 13, 1933; ibid., B1a 82/11, Springorum to Papen, Jan. 14, 1933; ibid., B1a 82/9a, Papen to Springorum, Jan. 20, 1933; ibid., B1a 82/9, Springorum to Papen, Jan. 24, 1933. In his second volume of memoirs Papen erroneously placed the meeting in Dortmund on Jan. 4 and wrote only of complaints from the industrialists about policies of the Schleicher cabinet, making no mention of what he told them: *Scheitern,* pp. 343f.

47. This emerges from the January letters of Springorum and Reusch to Robert Lehr (see n. 46). On Lehr's role in the anti-Hugenberg faction of the DNVP, see Först, *Robert Lehr,* and Gemein, "Die DNVP in Düsseldorf," esp. pp. 66–75 and 187–93.

48. Reusch discussed this project in his January letters to Vögler (see n. 46).

49. See n. 46.

50. The citation of Springorum's letter is given in n. 46.

51. See, on the following: Otto Meissner, *Staatssekretär unter Ebert—Hindenburg—Hitler* (Hamburg, 1950), pp. 265f.; Bruno Buchta, *Die Junker und die Weimarer Republik* (East Berlin, 1959), pp. 145–60; Vogelsang, *Reichswehr,* pp. 358f., 375; Friedrich Martin Fiederlein, "Der deutsche Osten und die Regierungen Brüning, Papen, Schleicher" (diss., Universität Würzburg,

1966), pp. 434–54. On Nazi infiltration of the Reichslandbund, see Gies, "The NSDAP and Agrarian Organizations."

52. Reinhard Neebe, "Unternehmerverbände und Gewerkschaften in den Jahren der Grossen Krise 1929–33," *G & G* 9 (1983): 327.

53. Some of the key evidence on these developments is summarized in Leopold, *Hugenberg*, pp. 243f., n. 155. Alfred Sohn-Rethel has assigned an important role in Schleicher's fall and Hitler's appointment to an alleged acceptance in early December 1932 by IG Farben's Carl Bosch of a scheme put forward by the Mitteleuropäischer Wirtschaftstag, which called for a complex system of agricultural cartels and import quotas on foodstuffs calculated to impose "imperialistic" designs on southeastern Europe: Sohn-Rethel, *Ökonomie und Klassenstruktur*, p. 94. Nothing in the voluminous industrial documentation supports this story or the significance Sohn-Rethel attributes to the Mitteleuropäischer Wirtschaftstag, where he worked at the time; cf. Bosch's denunciation of "all quotas and barriers to trade" in the speech he delivered in Vienna in mid-December: Werksarchiv der Badischen Anilin- und Soda-Fabrik, Sig. W 1, "Carl Bosch—Abschrift eines handschriftlichen Entwurfes zum Wiener Vortrag bei Verleihung der Exner Medaille am 16. Dez. 1932" (I am indebted to Professor Peter Hayes for bringing this document to my attention).

54. See "Sie wollen Papen wieder," *Vorwärts*, Jan. 10, 1933 (#16); Carl von Ossietzky, "Kamarilla," *Die Weltbühne*, Jan. 31, 1933 (Jg. 29, Nr. 5). According to the standard East German interpretation, Hitler was installed in power by an unscrupulous camarilla "at the direct order of monopoly capital and the Junkers": Ruge, *Hindenburg*, p. 476. See also Jürgen Kuczynski, *Die Geschichte der Lage der Arbeiter unter dem Kapitalismus,* vol. V (East Berlin, 1966), p 134; Vietzke and Wohlgemuth, *Deutschland*, p. 293; and Lotte Zumpe, *Wirtschaft und Staat in Deutschland 1933 bis 1945* (East Berlin, 1980), p. 41. Even an East German monograph that persuasively documents the crucial role of the agrarians in turning Hindenburg against Schleicher concludes by dividing the responsibility between them and "the most reactionary parts of the *Grossbourgeoisie*," despite having presented no evidence implicating the latter: Buchta, *Junker*, p. 167. The legend of Junker-capitalist collaboration in felling Schleicher and installing Hitler in the chancellorship also appears in non-Marxist works: Dieter Petzina, "Germany and the Great Depression," *JCH* 4 (1974): 70f.; Shirer, *Rise and Fall*, pp. 179–80; Carr, *History*, p. 357; Norman Stone, *Hitler* (Boston, 1980), pp. 27, 35.

55. In that letter Krupp asked the headquarters of the Reichsverband to remind Work-Creation Commissar Günther Gereke that he had not replied to a letter sent him by Krupp: KA, IV E 203.

56. Martin Sogemeier, manager of the Zweckverband Nordwestdeutscher Wirtschaftsvertretungen e.V., Berlin, to Springorum, Jan. 25, 1933: HAD, Springorum Papers, F115.

57. Reusch to Krupp, Jan. 28, 1933: KA, R216¹.

58. On the following, see "Jetzt nationale Sammlung!" *Rheinisch-Westfälische Zeitung*, Jan. 29, 1933 (#53); "Unsere Meinung" and "Doppelverhandlungen mit den Nationalsozialisten," *Deutsche Allgemeine Zeitung*, Jan.

29, 1933 (#49); "Die Woche," *Deutsche Bergwerks-Zeitung*, Jan. 29, 1933 (#25); "Hitler oder Papen?" *Frankfurter Zeitung*, Jan. 30, 1933 (#80).

59. See the diary of Count Lutz Schwerin von Krosigk, who was continued as finance minister: IfZ, Zs/A-20, Band 4, entries for Jan. 30 and Feb. 5, 1933.

60. Reusch to Kötter, Feb. 3, 1933: GHH, 4001012007/16.

61. Reusch to Eduard Hamm of Deutscher Industrie- und Handelstag, Feb. 4, 1933: ibid., 40010123/25.

62. The following is based on Kastl's letter to Krupp of Jan. 31, 1933: KA, IV E 203.

63. "Die Börse in der politischen Krise," Feb. 5, 1933 (#96/97).

64. "Regierungswechsel und Börse," Jan. 31, 1933 (#83).

65. "Stille Börsen," *Frankfurter Zeitung*, Feb. 19, 1933 (#134/135).

66. Anton Betz, "Die Tragödie," p. 34. Betz, one of the editors of the *MNN*, was present at the meeting of its advisory board on Feb. 11, 1933, at which Brandi and Karl Haniel (see n. 67, below) spoke. See also the similar position adopted by Brandi in a letter of Feb. 6, 1933, to Fritz Klein, editor of the *Deutsche Allgemeine Zeitung*, quoted by Klein's son, also Fritz, in *ZfG* 21 (1973), pp. 1523f.

67. Betz, "Tragödie," p. 34.

68. NA, RG 238, Pre-Trial Interrogations, Grauert, Dec. 5, 1946.

69. Quoted in Bracher, *Dictatorship*, p. 195.

70. Wladimir d'Ormesson, "Une tentative de rapprochement franco-alle-mand entre les deux guerres," *Revue de Paris* 69 (Feb. 1962): 27. A liberal-minded man, Bücher had deplored the passivity of the trade unions after Papen's deposition of the Prussian cabinet in July 1932 and proposed a meeting of leading industrialists with union leaders: diary of Hans Schäffer, IfZ, ED 93, entry for July 22, 1932.

71. Hammerstein, *Spähtrupp*, p. 53; Schwerin von Krosigk, *Staatsbankrott*, p. 167.

72. H. R. Berndorff, *General zwischen Ost und West* (Hamburg, [1951]), p. 268.

73. Udo Wengst, "Der Reichsverband der Deutschen Industrie in den ersten Monaten des Dritten Reiches," *VfZ* 28 (1980): 95.

74. Ibid., pp. 95f.; also Neebe, *Grossindustrie*, pp. 176f. See also the reports on meetings with Hugenberg made at the session of the Deutscher Industrie- und Handelstag on Mar. 1, 1933: GHH, 40010123/33b.

75. Wengst, "Reichsverband," pp. 96f. These incidents, which persisted into the spring, remain to be examined; for a firsthand account of one, see Ludecke, *I Knew Hitler*, pp. 620–22. See also the speech in which Bernhard Grund, president of the national organization of chambers of industry and commerce, deplored the shutdown of the Breslau stock exchange following its invasion by "unauthorized persons," enclosed with a letter from the organization's executive director, Eduard Hamm, to members, Mar. 14, 1933: BAK, Silverberg Papers, 644. On other such incidents, see Timothy W. Mason, *Sozialpolitik im Dritten Reich* (Opladen, 1977), p. 103.

76. "Nationalsozialistischer Kampfruf gegen den Zechenverband," *Frankfurter Zeitung*, Feb. 12, 1933 (#117).

77. *SEG* 74 (1933): 48.

78. NA, RG 238, D-201, Göring's telegram of Feb. 16, 1933, to Krupp.

79. Krupp summarized the views he intended to express in a set of handwritten notes, to which the date 22.II.33 (Feb. 22, 1933) was later appended: KA, IV E 203.

80. NA, RG 238, Case 10, Dokumentenbuch Bülow II, Aufzeichnung für die Besprechung bei Reichsminister Göring am 20. Februar 1933 (originally in KA, KC-1084, Bd. V).

81. The following account of the session of Feb. 20, 1933, is based on these contemporary documents: NA, RG 238, D-203, an anonymous contemporary record of the speeches of Hitler and Göring, confiscated for the Nuremberg war crimes trials from the files of Gustav Krupp von Bohlen's private correspondence; GHH, 4001012024/11, a report prepared by Martin Blank on the basis of information from a participant and dated Feb. 21, 1933; ibid., 400101290/36, Fritz Springorum's eyewitness account in his letter to Reusch of Feb. 21, 1933. The testimonies of participants more than a decade later at Nuremberg are much less reliable and informative than these contemporaneous accounts; cf. NA, RG 238, EC–439, affidavit of Georg von Schnitzler, Nov. 10, 1945; NI-3243, Friedrich Flick's affidavit of Jan. 14, 1947; NI-9550, Schacht's affidavit of Aug. 12, 1947. Martin Blank's informant listed the following eighteen men as present: Brandi (almost certainly Ernst, of United Steel and Bergbauverein), Büren (presumably Karl, general director of Braunkohlen- und Brikett-Industrie AG, Berlin), Diehn (presumably August, of the potash cartel), Grauert (Ludwig, of the Ruhr industrial employers' association), Heubel (presumably Günther, of the F.C. Th. Heye Braunkohlenwerke G.m.b.H., Saxony), Krupp von Bohlen, v. Loewenstein (Hans, of the Bergbauverein), v. Opel (presumably a member of the family that had sold the Opel automobile works to General Motors of the United States in 1929), Quandt (probably Günther, of the Wintershall potash-mining firm), Reuter (probably Wolfgang, Demag machine-building firm, Duisburg), v. Schnitzler (Georg, of IG Farben), Schulte (Eduard, of Georg von Giesche's Erben, a holding company with interests in mining and banking, Breslau), Springorum (Fritz, of Hoesch steel), Hugo Stinnes (the son of the famous Stinnes), Tengelmann (which member of that family remains uncertain), Vögler (Albert), v. Winterfeld (presumably Ludwig, a director of Siemens & Halske), and v. Witzleben (presumably Wolf-Dietrich, Carl Friedrich von Siemens's private secretary). In addition Georg von Schnitzler, in the affidavit listed above, remembered that Paul Stein, general director of the Auguste Viktoria coal-mining firm of Recklinghausen, and a von Loewenfeld from an industrial enterprise in Essen had been present. How many of those invited attended remains uncertain. Reusch declined, explaining that he had to be out of the country on the twentieth: telegram to his secretary, Wagner, Feb. 17, 1933, GHH, 400101293/12. Robert Bosch declined his invitation, complaining that he would have no opportunity at a large gathering to speak personally with the new chancellor: Heuss, *Bosch*, p. 633.

82. Despite allegations that Hitler proclaimed his intention to launch a massive rearmament program on this occasion, these elliptical comments about military matters were the only ones attributed to him by eyewitnesses after

the session; cf. Stegmann, "Verhältnis," p. 440; Bernd Engelmann, *Einig gegen Recht und Freiheit* (Munich, 1975), pp. 272.

83. NA, RG 238, D-204, Krupp's minutes of his remarks, dated Feb. 22, 1933.

84. For Göring's talk and the subsequent course of the meeting, see the contemporary accounts cited in n. 81, above.

85. For the records of the *Nationale Treuhand*, as Schacht designated the resulting fund, see the bank records in NA, RG 238, NI-391; see also BAK, Hugenberg Papers, 38, Scheibe to Hugenberg, Mar. 1, 1933; Hugenberg to Schacht, Mar. 2, 1933; Schacht to Hugenberg, Mar. 3, 1933; Scheibe to Hugenberg, Mar. 15, 1933.

86. Schacht at first claimed that only a fifth had been allotted to the Kampffront, but the DNVP successfully contested this; see the correspondence in the Hugenberg Papers cited in the previous note.

87. Papen to Springorum, Mar. 14, 1933: HAD, Springorum Papers, B1a 82/7a; Springorum to Papen, Mar. 25, 1933, ibid., B1a 82/7; Reusch to Kurt von Lersner, Mar. 4, 1933: GHH, 400101293/12.

88. Scheibe to Siemens, Feb. 28, 1933; Witzleben to Scheibe, Mar. 10, 1933: SA, 4/Lf 670; NA, RG 238, Pre-Trial Interrogations, Flick, Dec. 30, 1946, and Jan. 8, 1947; Reusch to Major General Count von der Goltz, Mar. 4, 1933: GHH, 400101293/12.

89. For the text of the speech, see Horkenbach (ed.), *Das Deutsche Reich* (1933), pp. 131–36.

90. Minutes of meeting of Verein Deutscher Eisen- und Stahlindustrieller, May 3, 1933: BAK, R 13 I/1078.

91. The highly revealing minutes of this meeting are located in the KA, IV E 885: "Vertraulich! Betr.: Präsidialsitzung am 23. März 1933," enclosure in letter to Krupp from Ludwig Kastl, Mar. 27, 1933.

92. Neebe, "Unternehmerverbände und Gewerkschaften," pp. 327–29, where Carl Friedrich von Siemens and Clemens Lammers are mentioned along with Krupp; see also August Heinrichsbauer's affidavit of Jan. 31, 1948, in which he told of a discussion in his presence by Ernst Brandi, Fritz Springorum, and Albert Vögler about a letter in which Krupp proposed a revival of the ZAG: NA, RG 238, Case 10, Dokumentenbuch Bülow I.

93. Either Krupp's memory failed him or he elaborated the facts by contending that Thyssen's invitation had come to him in his official capacity, for the invitation contained no such specification: KA, IV E 1129.

94. Here Krupp is corroborated by a letter he sent to Jakob Herle of the Reichsverband about the flag question on Mar. 13, 1933; NA, RG 238, Case 10, Dokumentenbuch Bülow III.

95. See Neebe, *Grossindustrie*, pp. 181f.

96. On this and the following, see ibid., pp. 182–88; Wengst, "Reichsverband," pp. 101–10.

97. Reusch to Herle, July 20, 1933: GHH, 400101220/14.

98. Joachim Radkau in Hallgarten and Radkau, *Deutsche Industrie und Politik*, p. 237.

99. Hans Schäffer, the widely respected state secretary in the Reich Finance Ministry under Brüning, and Carl Melchior, a partner in the M. M. Warburg banking house of Hamburg, secured aid for the Reichsvertretung der Juden from Carl Bosch, Gustav Krupp von Bohlen, Carl Friedrich von

Siemens, Albert Vögler, among others: Eckhard Wandel, *Hans Schäffer. Steuermann in wirtschaftlichen und politischen Krisen* (Stuttgart, 1974), p. 244.

100. According to Fritz Thyssen, Kirdorf asked him to deliver to Hitler personally a letter in which Kirdorf "protested against the persecutions of the Jews which went on in Germany in 1933": *I Paid Hitler*, p. 99 (this passage corresponds to one in Thyssen's interviews with his ghost-writer, Emery Reves, in 1940: T/RP, sheet 267). That Kirdorf actually did write at least one letter protesting against anti-Semitism in 1933 is demonstrated by its mention in a letter from Ernst Brandi to Hermann Olfe of December 15, 1933: GBW, Kirdorf Papers, 2 00 01/1/10. In his *Tycoons and Tyrants*, p. 173, Louis P. Lochner gives the text of such a letter of protest, which he attributes to Kirdorf and which he reports appeared in the *Rheinisch-Westfälische Zeitung* in 1933; but since Lochner provides no date for its publication, I have been unable to locate any such letter in that paper. Lochner further reports that Kirdorf "invited himself as Silverberg's house guest for a number of days, thereby demonstrating his disagreement with Nazi anti-Semitism" (ibid.); in a letter to Krupp von Bohlen of July 22, 1933, Silverberg spoke of spending the previous Saturday with the Kirdorfs, but at their home: KA, IV E 894.

101. Holdermann, *Im Banne der Chemie*, p. 272.

102. Hayes, *"Gleichschaltung* of IG Farben," p. 123.

103. Georg Müller-Oerlinghausen to Jakob Herle of the Reichsverband, Apr. 13, 1933, quoted in Neebe, *Grossindustrie*, p. 187.

104. See Henry Picker, *Hitlers Tischgespräche im Führerhauptquartier 1941–1942* (Stuttgart, 1963), pp. 169, 203ff., 476f.

105. Neebe, *Grossindustrie*, p. 196; Silverberg to Krupp von Bohlen, Feb. 14, 1934, and Krupp to Silverberg, Feb. 16, 1934: KA, IV E 894.

106. Klass, *Die drei Ringe*, pp. 436ff.

107. Maschke, *Konzern*, pp. 204f.; NA, RG 238, NI-10773, affidavit by Jakob Wilhelm Reichert, Sept. 6, 1947; NI-11594, same of July 7, 1947.

108. Gerhard Ritter, *Carl Goerdeler und die deutsche Widerstandsbewegung* (Stuttgart, 1955), p. 413; *Spiegelbild einer Verschwörung. Die Kaltenbrunner-Berichte an Bormann und Hitler über das Attentat vom 20. Juli 1944*, herausgegeben vom Archiv Peter für historische und zeitgeschichtliche Dokumentation (Stuttgart, 1961), pp. 348, 546, 552–54; Hassell, *Vom andern Deutschland*, pp. 94, 96f.

109. Neebe, *Grossindustrie*, pp. 187f.

110. Quoted in the memoirs of that acquaintance, Glum, *Zwischen Wissenschaft, Wirtschaft und Politik*, p. 410.

111. Hermann Rauschning, *Makers of Destruction* (London, 1942), p. 163. Rauschning reported hearing this directly from Thyssen on the latter's return from his meeting with Hitler. On Thyssen's pretensions during the first year of the regime, see Horkenbach (ed.), *Das Deutsche Reich* (1933), p. 293.

112. Turner, "Fritz Thyssen und 'I Paid Hitler,'" p. 225; the de-nazification court which tried Thyssen in 1948 classified him as only slightly tainted, fined him, but allowed him to emigrate to Argentina, where he died in 1951 (ibid., p. 228). On Hitler's rejection of the corporatism promoted by Thyssen, see Broszat, *Staat Hitlers*, pp. 225–27.

113. Schweitzer, *Big Business in the Third Reich,* neither covers that topic adequately nor provides a reliable treatment of the points it does address. By far the best overview is provided by David Schoenbaum in his *Hitler's Social Revolution* (New York, 1966), pp. 119–58; see also Broszat, *Staat Hitlers,* pp. 218–30. Gerhard Schulz, "Die Diktatur in der Wirtschaft," in Bracher et al., *Machtergreifung,* pp. 627–71.

Conclusions, section 1: Capitalists, Nazis and Guilt

1. *Capitalism, Socialism and Democracy,* 3rd ed. (New York, 1950), pp. 55 and 137.

Conclusions, section 2: Myths, Preconceptions, and the Misuse of History

1. Quoted in the introduction to Eckart Kehr, *Der Primat der Innenpolitik,* ed. by Hans-Ulrich Wehler (Berlin, 1965), p. 20, n. 47.
2. See Eike Hennig, "Materialien zur Diskussion der Monopolgruppentheorie," *NPL* 18 (1973): 170–93.
3. See, for example, the heralded book by Nicos Poulantzas, *Fascism and Dictatorship* (London, 1974); cf. the critique by Jane Caplan, "Theories of Fascism: Nicos Poulantzas as Historian," *History Workshop,* no. 3 (Spring 1977): 83–100.
4. See Jost Dülffer, "Bonapartism, Fascism and National Socialism," *JCH* 11 (1976): 109–28.
5. Bloch, *Strange Defeat* (New York, 1968), p. 27.
6. "Die Juden und Europa," *Zeitschrift für Sozialforschung* 8 (1939): 115.

Bibliography

Achterberg, Erich, and Maximilian Müller-Jabusch. *Lebensbilder deutscher Bankiers aus fünf Jahrhunderten.* 2nd ed. Frankfurt, 1963.

Adolf Hitler und seine Bewegung im Lichte neutraler Beobachter und objektiver Gegner. Munich, 1927.

Albertin, Lothar. *Liberalismus und Demokratie am Anfang der Weimarer Republik.* Düsseldorf, 1972.

Allen, William Sheridan. *The Nazi Seizure of Power. The Experience of a Single German Town, 1922–1945.* Rev. ed. New York, 1984.

Angell, James W. *The Recovery of Germany.* New Haven, Conn., 1929.

Aretin, Erwein von. *Krone und Ketten.* Munich, 1955.

Aubin, Hermann, and Wolfgang Zorn, eds. *Handbuch der deutschen Wirtschafts- und Sozialgeschichte.* 2 vols. Stuttgart, 1972–76.

Auerbach, Hellmuth. "Hitlers politische Lehrjahre und die Münchener Gesellschaft 1919–1923," *Vierteljahrshefte für Zeitgeschichte* 25 (1977): 1–45.

Bach, Jürgen A. *Franz von Papen in der Weimarer Republik.* Düsseldorf, 1977.

Bacmeister, Walter. *Emil Kirdorf.* 2nd ed. Essen, 1936.

———, *Nekrologe aus dem rheinisch-westfälischen Industriegebiet. Jahrgang 1937.* Essen, 1940.

Barkai, Avraham. "Sozialdarwinismus und Antiliberalismus in Hitlers Wirtschaftskonzept," *Geschichte und Gesellschaft* 3 (1977); 406–17.

———. "Die Wirtschaftsauffassung der NSDAP," *Aus Politik und Zeitgeschichte. Beilage zur Wochenzeitung Das Parlament,* Mar. 1, 1975, pp. 3-39.

———. "Wirtschaftliche Grundanschauungen und Ziele der NSDAP," *Jahrbuch des Instituts für Deutsche Geschichte* [Tel-Aviv] 7 (1978): 355–85.

———. *Das Wirtschaftssystem des Nationalsozialismus.* Cologne, 1977.

Barkin, Kenneth. "Adolf Wagner and German Industrial Development," *Journal of Modern History* 41 (1969): 144–59.

———. *The Controversy over German Industrialization, 1890–1902.* Chicago, 1970.

Bartmuss, Hans Joachim, et al. *Deutsche Geschichte in drei Bänden*. 3 vols. East Berlin, 1965–68.

Beck, Friedrich Alfred. *Kampf und Sieg. Geschichte der Nationalsozialistichen Deutschen Arbeiterpartei im Gau Westfalen-Süd von den Anfängen bis zur Machtübernahme*. Dortmund, 1938.

Beckenbach, Ralf. *Der Staat im Faschismus. Ökonomie und Politik im Deutschen Reich 1920 bis 1945*. Berlin, 1974.

Behrendt, Armin. *Wilhelm Külz*. East Berlin, 1968.

Bennecke, Heinrich. *Hitler und die SA*. Munich, 1962.

Bennett, Edward W. *German Rearmament and the West, 1932–1933*. Princeton, N.J., 1979.

Benz, Wolfgang, ed. *Politik in Bayern, 1919–1933*. Stuttgart, 1971.

Berghahn, Volker. *Der Stahlhelm. Bund der Frontsoldaten, 1918–1935*. Düsseldorf, 1966.

———. "Das Volksbegehren gegen den Young-Plan und die Ursprünge des Präsidialregimes, 1928–1930." In *Industrielle Gesellschaft und politisches System*, ed. by Dirk Stegmann, Bernd-Jürgen Wendt, and Peter-Christian Witt. Bonn, 1978, pp. 431–46.

Berndorff, H. R. *General zwischen Ost und West* (Hamburg, [1951]).

Bessel, Richard. *Political Violence and the Rise of Nazism*. New Haven and London, 1984.

Betz, Anton. "Die Tragödie der 'Münchner Neuesten Nachrichten' 1932/33." *Journalismus* 2 (1961): 22–46.

Blaich, Fritz. "Die bayerische Industrie 1933–1939," In *Bayern in der NS-Zeit*, ed. by Martin Broszat et al. 6 vols. Munich, 1977–83, 2, pp. 237–80.

———. "'Garantierter Kapitalismus.' Subventionspolitik und Wirtschaftsordnung in Deutschland zwischen 1925 und 1932." *Zeitschrift für Unternehmensgeschichte* 22 (1977): 50–70.

———. *Kartell- und Monopolpolitik im kaiserlichen Deutschland*. Düsseldorf, 1973.

———. *Staat und Verbände in Deutschland zwischen 1871 und 1945*. Wiesbaden, 1979.

Bock, Helmut, et al., eds. *Sturz ins Dritte Reich*. Leipzig, 1983.

Böhnke, Wilfried. *Die NSDAP im Ruhrgebiet 1920–1933*. Bonn-Bad Godesberg, 1974.

Böhret, Carl. *Aktionen gegen die 'kalte Sozialisierung' 1926–1930*. Berlin, 1966.

Bonikowski, Hugo. "Die öffentliche Bewirtschaftung der Kohle." *Handbuch der Kohlenwirtschaft*, ed. by Karl Borchardt. Berlin, 1926, pp. 369–88.

Bonn, Moritz Julius. *Das Schicksal des deutschen Kapitalismus*. Berlin, 1930.

Borchardt, Knut. *Wachstum, Krisen, Handlungsspielräume der Wirtschaftspolitik*. Göttingen, 1982.

Borkin, Joseph. *The Crime and Punishment of I.G. Farben*. New York, 1978.

Born, Karl Erich. *Die deutsche Bankenkrise 1931*. Munich, 1967.

Bracher, Karl Dietrich. *Die Auflösung der Weimarer Republik*. 2nd ed. Stuttgart and Düsseldorf, 1957.

———. *The German Dictatorship*. New York, 1970.

Bracher, Karl Dietrich, Wolfgang Sauer, and Gerhard Schulz. *Die nationalsozialistische Machtergreifung*. Cologne and Opladen, 1960.

Brady, Robert A. *The Rationalization Movement in German Industry*. Berkeley, Calif., 1933.

————. *The Spirit and Structure of German Fascism.* London, 1937.

Brecht, Gustav. *Erinnerungen.* Munich: privately printed, 1964.

Brehme, Gerhard. *Die sogenannte Sozialisierungsgesetzgebung der Weimarer Republik.* East Berlin, 1960.

Breiting, Rupert. "Das Geld in der deutschen Parteipolitik." *Politische Vierteljahresschrift* 2 (1961): 348–63.

————. "Unternehmerische Meinungspolitik in der Weimarer Republik." In *Sprache und Politik. Festgabe für Dolf Sternberger,* ed. by Carl-Joachim Friedrich and Benno Reifenberg. Heidelberg, 1968, pp. 364–99.

Breitman, Richard. *German Socialism and Weimar Democracy.* Chapel Hill, N.C., 1981.

————. "On German Social Democracy and General Schleicher 1932–33." *Central European History* 9 (1976): 352–78.

Brenner, Hildegard. *Die Kunstpolitik des Nationalsozialismus.* Hamburg, 1963.

Bombach, Gottfried, et al., eds. *Der Keynesianismus.* 2 vols. Berlin and New York, 1976.

Briefs, Götz. *Betriebsführung und Betriebsleben in der Industrie.* Stuttgart, 1934.

Broszat, Martin. "Die Anfänge der Berliner NSDAP 1926/27." *Vierteljahrshefte für Zeitgeschichte* 8 (1960): 85–118.

————. *Der Staat Hitlers.* Munich, 1969.

Brüning, Heinrich. *Memoiren 1918–1934.* Stuttgart, 1970.

Bry, Gerhard. *Wages in Germany, 1871–1945.* Princeton, N.J., 1960.

Buchner, Franz. *Kamerad! Halt aus! Aus der Geschichte des Kreises Starnberg der NSDAP.* Munich, 1938.

Buchner, Hans. *Die goldene Internationale.* Munich, 1928.

————. *Grundriss einer nationalsozialistischen Volkswirtschaftstheorie.* Munich, 1930.

Buchta, Bruno. *Die Junker und die Weimarer Republik.* East Berlin, 1959.

Büttner, Ursula. *Hamburg in der Staats- und Wirtschaftskrise 1928–31.* Hamburg, 1982.

Bullock, Alan. *Hitler. A Study in Tyranny.* London, 1952.

Bundesverband der Deutschen Industrie. *Der Weg zum industriellen Spitzenverband.* Darmstadt, 1956.

Carr, William. *A History of Germany, 1815–1945.* New York, 1969.

————. *Hitler. A Study in Personality and Politics.* New York, 1979.

Carroll, Berenice A. *Design for Total War.* The Hague, 1968.

Cassels, Alan. "Mussolini and German Nationalism." *Journal of Modern History* 35 (1963): 137–57.

Cecil, Lamar. *Albert Ballin.* Princeton, N.J. 1967.

Ciolek-Kümper, Jutta. *Wahlkampf in Lippe.* Munich, 1976.

Conze, Werner, and Hans Raupach, eds. *Die Staats- und Wirtschaftskrise des Deutschen Reichs 1929/33.* Stuttgart, 1967.

Craig, Gordon A. *The Politics of the Prussian Army, 1640–1945.* New York, 1955.

Czada, Peter. *Die Berliner Elektroindustrie in der Weimarer Zeit.* Berlin, 1969.

Czichon, Eberhard. *Wer verhalf Hitler zur Macht? Zum Anteil der deutschen Industrie an der Zerstörung der Weimarer Republik.* Cologne, 1967.

————. "Wer verhalf Hitler zur Macht? Zur politischen Funktion des Keppler-Kreises innerhalb der deutschen Industrie im Jahre 1932." *Blätter für deutsche und internationale Politik* 11 (1966): 873–908.

Delmer, Sefton. *Trail Sinister.* London, 1961.

Demant, Ebbo. *Von Schleicher zu Springer. Hans Zehrer als politischer Publizist.* Mainz, 1971.

Das Deutsche Führerlexikon 1934/1935. Berlin, 1934.

Deutscher Industrie- und Handelstag. *Die Verantwortung des Unternehmers in der Selbstverwaltung.* Frankfurt, 1961.

Dietrich, Otto. *Mit Hitler in die Macht.* 5th ed. Munich, 1934.

———. *Zwölf Jahre mit Hitler.* Munich, [1955].

Döhn, Lothar. *Politik und Interesse. Die Interessenstruktur der Deutschen Volkspartei.* Meisenheim am Glan, 1970.

Dörr, Manfred. "Die Deutschnationale Volkspartei 1925 bis 1928." Diss., Universität Marburg, 1964.

Dorpalen, Andreas. *Hindenburg and the Weimar Republic.* Princeton, N.J., 1964.

Douglas, Donald M. "The Parent Cell." *Central European History* 10 (1977): 55–72.

Dressler, Adolf. *Das Braune Haus und die Verwaltungsgebäude der Reichsleitung der NSDAP.* 3rd ed. Munich, 1939.

Drobisch, Klaus. "Flick und die Nazis." *Zeitschrift für Geschichtswissenschaft* 14 (1966): 378–97.

———. "Der Freundeskreis Himmler." *Zeitschrift für Geschichtswissenschaft* 8 (1960): 304–28.

———. "Hindenburg-, Hitler-, Adenauerspende." *Zeitschrift für Geschichtswissenschaft* 15 (1967): 447–58.

——— et al. *Juden unterm Hakenkreuz.* Frankfurt, 1973.

Dülffer, Jost. "Bonapartism, Fascism and National Socialism." *Journal of Contemporary History* 11 (1976): 109–28.

Dutt, E. Palme. *Fascism and Social Revolution.* New York, 1935.

Eberle, Eugen, and Peter Grohmann. *Die schlaflosen Nächte des Eugen E. Erinnerungen eines neuen schwäbischen Jacobiners.* Stuttgart, 1982.

Eckert, Christian. *J. H. Stein. Werden und Wachsen eines Kölner Bankhauses in 150 Jahren.* Berlin, 1941.

Eichborn, Kurt von. *Das Soll und Haben von Eichborn & Co. in 200 Jahren.* Munich and Leipzig, 1928.

Eichholtz, Dietrich. "Probleme einer Wirtschaftsgeschichte des Faschismus in Deutschland." *Jahrbuch für Wirtschaftsgeschichte* 1963, Teil 3, 97–127.

———, and Wolfgang Schumann, eds. *Anatomie des Krieges.* East Berlin, 1969.

Eksteins, Modris. *The Limits of Reason: The German Democratic Press and the Collapse of the Weimar Republic.* New York, 1975.

Engelbrechten, Julius Karl von. *Eine braune Armee entseht.* Munich and Berlin, 1937.

———, and Hans Volz. *Wir wandern durch das nationalsozialistische Berlin.* Munich, 1937.

Engelmann, Bernd. *Einig gegen Recht und Freiheit.* Munich, 1975.

Erdmann, Gerhard. *Die deutschen Arbeitgeberverbände im sozialgeschichtlichen Wandel der Zeit.* Neuwied and Berlin, 1966.

Eschenburg, Theodor. "Franz von Papen." *Vierteljahrshefte für Zeitgeschichte* 1 (1953): 153–69.

Eschwege, Helmut. *Kennzeichen J.* East Berlin, 1966.

Eyck, Erich. *A History of the Weimar Republic.* 2 vols. New York, 1970.

Faingar, Isakhar M. *Die Entwicklung des deutschen Monopolkapitals.* East Berlin, 1959; transation of Russian edition, Moscow, 1958.

Feder, Ernst. *Heute sprach ich mit . . . Tagebücher eines Berliner Publizisten 1926–1932.* Stuttgart, 1971.

Feder, Gottfried. *Der Deutsche Staat auf nationaler und sozialer Grundlage.* Munich, 1923.

———. *Das Programm der N.S.D.A.P. und seine weltanschaulichen Grundgedanken.* Munich, 1927.

———. *Was will Adolf Hitler? Das Programm der N.S.D.A.P.* Munich, 1931.

Feldenkirchen, Wilfried. *Die Eisen- und Stahlindustrie des Ruhrgebiets 1879–1914.* Wiesbaden, 1982.

Feldman, Gerald D. "Arbeitskonflikte im Ruhrbergbau 1919–1922." *Vierteljahrshefte für Zeitgeschichte* 28 (1980): 168–223.

———. *Army, Industry and Labor in Germany, 1914–1918.* Princeton, N.J., 1966.

———. "Aspekte deutscher Industriepolitik am Ende der Weimarer Republik 1930–1933." In *Wirtschaftskrise und liberale Demokratie,* ed. by Karl Holl. Göttingen, 1978, pp. 103–25.

———. "Big Business and the Kapp Putsch." *Central European History* 4 (1971): 99–130.

———. "Die Demobilmachung und die Sozialordnung der Zwischenkriegszeit in Europa." *Geschichte und Gesellschaft* 9 (1983): 156–77.

———. "Economic and Social Problems of the German Demobilization, 1918–19." *Journal of Modern History* 47 (1975): 1–47.

———. "Die Freien Gewerkschaften und die Zentralarbeitsgemeinschaft 1918–1924." In *Vom Sozialistengesetz zur Mitbestimmung. Zum 100. Geburtstag von Hans Böckler,* ed. by Heinz Oskar Vetter. Cologne, 1975, pp. 229–52.

———. "German Business between War and Revolution: The Origins of the Stinnes-Legien Agreement." In *Entstehung und Wandel der modernen Gesellschaft. Festschrift für Hans Rosenberg zum 65. Geburtstag,* ed. by Gerhard A. Ritter. Berlin, 1970, pp. 312–41.

———. *Iron and Steel in the German Inflation 1916–1923.* Princeton, N.J., 1977.

———. "The Origins of the Stinnes-Legien Agreement: A Documentation." *Internationale Wissenschaftliche Korrespondenz zur Geschichte der deutschen Arbeiterbewegung* 19/20 (1973): 45–103.

———. "The Social and Economic Policies of German Big Business, 1918–1929." *American Historical Review* 75 (1969): 47–55.

——— et al., eds. *The German Inflation Reconsidered.* Berlin and New York, 1982.

Feldman, Gerald D., and Heidrun Homburg. *Industrie und Inflation. Studien und Dokumente zur Politik der deutschen Unternehmer 1916–1923.* Hamburg, 1977.

Feldman, Gerald D., and Ulrich Nocken. "Trade Associations and Economic Power: Interest Group Development in the German Iron and Steel and Machine-Building Industries, 1900–1933." *Business History Review* 49 (1975): 413–45.

Feldman, Gerald D., and Irmgard Steinisch. "Notwendigkeiten und Grenzen sozialstaatlicher Intervention." *Archiv für Sozialgeschichte* 20 (1980): 57–117.

———. "Die Weimarer Republik zwischen Sozial- und Wirtschaftsstaat. Die Entscheidung gegen den Achtstundenstag." *Archiv für Sozialgeschichte* 18 (1978): 353–439.

Ferber, Walter. "Othmar Spann und der Nationalsozialismus." *Civitas. Monatsschrift des schweizerischen Studentenvereins* 15 (1960): 547–50.

Fest, Joachim. *Hitler. Eine Biographie.* Frankfurt and Berlin, 1973.

Fiederlein, Friedrich Martin. "Der deutsche Osten und die Regierungen Brüning, Papen, Schleicher." Diss., Universität Würzburg, 1966.

Fischer, Conan. *Stormtroopers.* London, 1983.

Fischer, Ernst. *Das Fanal. Der Kampf Dimitroffs gegen die Kriegsbrandstifter.* Vienna, 1946.

Fischer, Fritz. *Krieg der Illusionen.* Düsseldorf, 1969.

Fischer, Wolfram. *Deutsche Wirtschaftspolitik 1918–45.* 3rd. ed. Opladen, 1968.

Flechtner, Hans-Joachim. *Carl Duisberg: Vom Chemiker zum Wirtschaftsführer.* Düsseldorf, 1959.

Flora, Peter, Jens Alber, and Jürgen Kohl. "Zur Entwicklung der westeuropäischen Wohlfahrtsstaaten." *Politische Vierteljahresschrift* 18 (1977): 707–72.

Först, Walter. *Robert Lehr als Oberbürgermeister.* Düsseldorf, 1962.

Franz-Willing, Georg. *Die Hitlerbewegung. Der Ursprung 1919–1922.* Hamburg and Berlin, 1962.

———. *Krisenjahre der Hitlerbewegung.* Preussisch Oldendorf, 1975.

Frick, Wilhelm. *Die Nationalsozialisten im Reichstag 1924–1931.* Munich, 1932.

Fricke, Dieter, ed. *Die bürgerlichen Parteien in Deutschland. Handbuch der Geschichte der bürgerlichen Parteien und anderer bürgerlichen Interessenorganisationen vom Vormärz bis zum Jahre 1945.* 2 vols. East Berlin, 1968.

Frommelt, Reinhard. *Paneuropa oder Mitteleuropa.* Stuttgart, 1977.

Funcke, Oscar. *Der Kampf in der Eisenindustrie.* Hagen: privately printed, 1934.

Gates, Robert A. "German Socialism and the Crisis of 1929–33." *Central European History* 7 (1974): 332–59.

Gatzke, Hans W. *Germany's Drive to the West.* Baltimore, Md., 1950.

Gemein, Gisbert Jörg. "Die DNVP in Düsseldorf 1918–1933." Diss., Universität Köln, 1969.

Gereke, Günther. *Ich war königlich-preussischer Landrat.* East Berlin, 1970.

Gies, Horst. "The NSDAP and Agrarian Organizations in the Final Phase of the Weimar Republic." In *Nazism and the Third Reich,* ed. by Henry Ashby Turner, Jr. New York, 1972, pp. 45–88.

Ginzberg, Lev Israelevic. "Auf dem Wege zur Hitlerdiktatur." *Zeitschrift für Geschichtswissenschaft* 17 (1969): 825–43.

———. "Die Beziehungen der reaktionären Kreise der USA und Englands zur Hitlerpartei (1930–Januar 1933)." *Sowjetwissenschaft. Gesellschaftswissenschaftliche Abteilung,* Heft 6 (1955), pp. 834–44.

Glaus, Beat. *Die Nationale Front. Eine Schweizer faschistische Bewegung.* Zurich, 1969.

Glum, Friedrich. *Zwischen Wissenschaft, Wirtschaft und Politik.* Bonn, 1964.

Goebbels, Joseph. *Das Tagebuch von Joseph Goebbels 1925/26,* edited by Helmut Heiber. Stuttgart, [1960].

———. *Vom Kaiserhof zur Reichskanzlei.* Berlin, 1934.

Görgen, Hans-Peter. *Düsseldorf und der Nationalsozialismus.* Düsseldorf, 1969.

Görlitz, Walter. *Geldgeber der Macht*. Düsseldorf, 1976.

Gordon, Harold J., Jr. *Hitler and the Beer Hall Putsch*. Princeton, N.J., 1972.

———. *The Reichswehr and the German Republic 1919–1926*. Princeton, N.J., 1957.

———. "Ritter von Epp and Berlin 1919–1923." *Wehrwissenschaftliche Rundschau* 9 (1959): 329–41.

Gossweiler, Kurt. "Fritz Thyssen. Forderung des Monopolkapitals." In *Sturz ins Dritte Reich*, ed. by Helmut Bock et al. Leipzig, 1983, pp. 58–64.

———. *Grossbanken, Industriemonopole, Staat. Ökonomie und Politik des staatsmonopolistischen Kapitalismus in Deutschland 1914–1932*. East Berlin, 1971.

———. "Hitler und das Kapital." *Blätter für deutsche und internationale Politik* 23 (1978): 842–60, 993–1009.

———. *Kapital, Reichswehr und NSDAP 1919–1924*. Cologne, 1982.

———. "Kurt von Schröder. Das Bankkapital stellt die Weichen." In *Sturz ins Dritte Reich*, ed. by Helmut Bock et al. Leipzig, 1983, pp. 65–71.

———. "Die Rolle des Monopolkapitals bei der Herbeiführung der Röhm-Affäre." Diss., Humboldt Universität, 1963.

———. "Die Vereinigten Stahlwerke und die Grossbanken." *Jahrbuch für Wirtschaftsgeschichte*, 1965, Teil 4, pp. 11–53.

Gottschalch, Wilfried. *Strukturveränderungen der Gesellschaft und politisches Handeln in der Lehre von Rudolf Hilferding*. Berlin, 1962.

Gottwald, Herbert. "Franz von Papen und die 'Germania.'" *Jahrbuch für Geschichte* 6 (1972): 539–604.

Granier, Gerhard. *Magnus von Levetzow*. Boppard, 1982.

Grill, Johnpeter Horst. *The Nazi Movement in Baden 1920–1945*. Chapel Hill, N.C., 1983.

Grotkopp, Wilhelm. *Die grosse Krise*. Düsseldorf, 1954.

Grübler, Michael. *Die Spitzenverbände der Wirtschaft und das erste Kabinett Brüning*. Düsseldorf, 1982.

Günther, Albrecht Erich, ed. *Was wir vom Nationalsozialismus erwarten*. Heilbronn, 1932.

Guratzsch, Dankwart. *Macht durch Organisation: Die Grundlegung des Hugenbergschen Presseimperiums*. Düsseldorf, 1974.

Hackett, David A. "The Nazi Party in the Reichstag Election of 1930." Diss., University of Wisconsin, 1971.

Hale, Oren J. "Adolf Hitler: Taxpayer." *American Historical Review* 60 (1955): 830–42.

———. *The Captive Press in the Third Reich*. Princeton, N.J., 1964.

———. "Gottfried Feder Calls Hitler to Order." *Journal of Modern History* 30 (1958): 358–62.

Hallgarten, George W. F. "Adolf Hitler and German Heavy Industry, 1931–1933." *Journal of Economic History* 12 (1952): 222–46.

———. *Hitler, Reichswehr und Industrie*. Frankfurt, 1955.

Hallgarten, George W. F., and Joachim Radkau. *Deutsche Industrie und Politik von Bismarck bis heute*. Frankfurt, 1974.

Halperin, S. William. *Germany Tried Democracy*. New York, 1946.

Hamilton, Richard F. *Who Voted for Hitler?* Princeton, N.J., 1982.

Hammerstein, Kunrat von. *Spähtrupp*. Stuttgart, 1963.

Hanfstaengl, Ernst. *Hitler—The Missing Years*. London, 1957.

———. *Zwischen Weissem und Braunem Haus*. Munich, 1970.

Hansen, Ernst W. *Reichswehr und Industrie*. Boppard, 1978.

———. "Zur Wahrnehmung industrieller Interessen in der Weimarer Republik. Die Geschäftsstelle für industrielle Abrüstung (GEFIA)." *Vierteljahrshefte für Zeitgeschichte* 28 (1980): 487–501.

Hardach, Karl. *Wirtschaftsgeschichte Deutschlands im 20. Jahrhundert*. Göttingen, 1976.

Hartmann, Heinz. *Authority and Organization in German Management*. Princeton, N.J., 1959.

Hartwich, Hans-Hermann. *Arbeitsmarkt, Verbände und Staat 1918–1933*. Berlin, 1967.

Hass, Gerhart, and Wolfgang Schumann, eds. *Anatomie der Aggression*. East Berlin, 1972.

Hassell, Ulrich von. *Vom anderen Deutschland*. Frankfurt and Hamburg, 1964.

Hayes, Peter. "The *Gleichschaltung* of IG Farben." Diss., Yale University, 1982.

———. "A 'Question Mark with Epaulettes'? Kurt von Schleicher and Weimar Politics." *Journal of Modern History* 52 (1980): 35–65.

Heiber, Helmut. *Die Republik von Weimar*. Munich, 1966.

Heiden, Konrad. *Adolf Hitler. Das Zeitalter der Verantwortungslosigkeit*. Zurich, 1936.

———. *Der Fuehrer*. Boston, 1944.

———. *Geburt des Dritten Reiches*. Zurich, 1934.

———. *Geschichte des Nationalsozialismus*. Berlin, 1932.

Heidenheimer, Arnold J., and Frank C. Langdon, *Business Associations and the Financing of Political Parties*. The Hague, 1968.

Heinrichsbauer, August. *Schwerindustrie und Politik*. Essen, 1948.

Helfferich, Emil. *1932–1946. Tatsachen*. Jever, 1969.

Hennig, Eike. "Industrie und Faschismus." *Neue Politische Literatur* 15 (1970): 432-49.

———. "Materialien zur Diskussion der Monopolgruppentheorie." *Neue Politische Literatur* 18 (1973): 170-93.

Hentschel, Volker. *Weimars letzte Monate*. Düsseldorf, 1978.

———. "Zum Verhältnis von Industriewirtschaft und Politik in der neuesten deutschen Geschichtsschreibung." *Jahrbuch des Instituts für Deutsche Geschichte* [Tel-Aviv] 8 (1976): 483–513.

Herle, Jacob, and Heinrich Gattineau, eds. *Carl Duisberg. Ein deutscher Industrieller*. Berlin, n.d.

Hermann, Walther. "Otto Wolff." *Rheinisch-westfälische Wirtschaftsbiographien*, vol. 8. Münster, 1962.

Hertz-Eichenrode, Dieter. *Wirtschaftskrise und Arbeitsbeschaffung. Konjunkturpolitik 1925/26 und die Grundlagen der Krisenpolitik Brünings*. Berlin, 1982.

Herwig, Holger H. "From Kaiser to Führer: The Political Road of a German Admiral, 1923–33." *Journal of Contemporary History* 9 (1974): 107–20.

Herzog, Bodo. *Kapitänleutnant Otto Steinbrinck*. Krefeld, 1963.

Heuss, Theodor. *Hitlers Weg*. 2nd ed. Tübingen, 1968.

———. *Robert Bosch*. Stuttgart, 1946.

Heyen, Franz Josef. *Nationalsozialismus im Alltag*. Boppard, 1967.

Heyl, John D. "Hitler's Economic Thought: A Reappraisal." *Central European History* 6 (1973): 83–96.

Hildebrand, Klaus. *Vom Reich zum Weltreich*. Munich, 1969.

Hitler, Adolf. *Hitler's Secret Conversations, 1941–1944, with an Introductory Essay on the Mind of Adolf Hitler by H. R. Trevor-Roper.* New York, 1953.

———. *Hitlers Tischgespräche im Führerhauptquartier 1941–42*, ed. by Henry Picker. Bonn, 1951.

———. *Hitlers Tischgespräche im Führerhauptquartier 1941–1942*, ed. by Henry Picker. Stuttgart, 1963.

———. *Mein Kampf.* 2 vols. Munich, 1933.

———. *Monologe im Führerhauptquartier 1941–1944*, ed. by *Werner Jochmann.* Hamburg, 1980.

———. "Warum musste ein 8. November kommen?" *Deutschlands Erneuerung* 8 (1924): 199–207.

———. *Hitlers zweites Buch. Ein Dokument aus dem Jahr 1928*, ed. by Gerhard L. Weinberg. Stuttgart, 1961.

Hock, Wolfgang. *Deutscher Antikapitalismus.* Frankfurt, 1960.

Hoepke, Klaus-Peter. *Die deutsche Rechte und der italienische Faschismus.* Düsseldorf, 1968.

Hörster-Philipps, Ulrike. *Grosskapital und Faschismus 1918–1945. Dokumente.* Cologne, 1981.

———. "Grosskapital, Weimarer Republik und Faschismus." In *Die Zerstörung der Weimarer Republik*, ed. by Reinhard Kühnl and Gerd Hardach. Cologne, 1977, pp. 38–141.

———. *Konservative Politik in der Endphase der Weimarer Republik.* Cologne, 1982.

Hoffmann, Heinrich. *Hitler Was My Friend.* London, 1955.

Holborn, Hajo. *A History of Modern Germany, 1840–1945.* New York, 1969.

Holdermann, Karl. *Im Banne der Chemie. Carl Bosch. Leben und Werk.* Düsseldorf, 1953.

Holtfrerich, Carl-Ludwig. *Die deutsche Inflation 1914–1923.* Berlin and New York, 1980.

Holzbach, Heidrun. *Das 'System Hugenberg': Die Organisation bürgerlicher Sammlungspolitik vor dem Aufstieg der NSDAP.* Stuttgart, 1981.

Hoover, Calvin B. *Germany Enters the Third Reich.* New York, 1933.

Horkenbach, Cuno, ed. *Das Deutsche Reich von 1918 bis heute.* Berlin, 1930, 1931, 1932, 1933.

Horn, Wolfgang. *Führerideologie und Parteiorganisation in der NSDAP (1919–1933).* Düsseldorf, 1972.

Hubatsch, Walther. *Entstehung und Entwicklung des Reichswirtschaftsministerium.* Berlin, 1978.

Hüttenberger, Peter. *Die Gauleiter.* Stuttgart, 1969.

Hughes, H. Stuart. *Contemporary Europe: A History.* 5th ed. Englewood Cliffs, N.J., 1981.

Hughes, Thomas Parke. "Technological Momentum in History: Hydrogenation in Germany 1898–1933." *Past & Present* no. 44 (1969): 106–32.

Hunt, Richard N. *German Social Democracy, 1918–1933.* New Haven, Conn., 1964.

Institut für Gesellschaftswissenschaften beim ZK der SED. *Imperialismus heute.* 5th ed. East Berlin, 1968.

Institut für Marxismus-Leninismus beim Zentralkomitee der SED. *Geschichte der deutschen Arbeiterbewegung.* 8 vols. East Berlin, 1966.

International Military Tribunal. *Trial of the Major War Criminals before the International Military Tribunal, Nuremberg, 14 November 1945–1 October 1946.* 42 vols. Nuremberg, 1947–49.

Jacobsen, Hans-Adolf. *Nationalsozialistische Aussenpolitik 1933–1938.* Frankfurt and Berlin, 1968.

Jaeger, Hans. *Unternehmer in der deutschen Politik (1890–1918).* Bonn, 1967.

James, Harold. "State, Industry and Depression in Weimar Germany." *The Historical Journal* 24 (1981): 231–41.

Jeschke, Gerhard. "Vom 'Neuen Staat' zur 'Volksgemeinschaft.' Unternehmerverbände und Reichspolitik vom Sturz Brünings bis zu den Märzwahlen 1933." *Ergebnisse. Hefte für historische Öffentlichkeit* [Hamburg] Heft 8 (Oct. 1979): 11–96.

Jochmann, Werner, ed. *Im Kampf um die Macht. Hitlers Rede vor dem Hamburger Nationalklub von 1919.* Frankfurt, 1960.

———, ed. *Nationalsozialismus und Revolution.* (Frankfurt, 1963).

John, Jürgen. "Die Faschismus-'Kritik' in der Zeitschrift 'Der Arbeitgeber,'" *Zeitschrift für Geschichtswissenschaft* 30 (1982): 1072–86.

Jonas, Erasmus. *Die Volkskonservativen 1928–1930.* Düsseldorf, 1965.

Jones, Larry Eugene. "'The Dying Middle': Weimar Germany and the Fragmentation of Bourgeois Politics." *Central European History* 5 (1972): 23–54.

———. "Inflation, Revaluation, and the Crisis of Middle-Class Politics: A Study in the Dissolution of the German Party System, 1923–1928." *Central European History* 12 (1979): 143–68.

———. "Sammlung oder Zersplitterung? Die Bestrebungen zur Bildung einer neuen Mittelpartei in der Endphase der Weimarer Republik 1930–1933." *Vierteljahrshefte für Zeitgeschichte* 25 (1977): 265–304.

Junker, Detlev. *Die Deutsche Zentrumspartei und Hitler 1932/33.* Stuttgart, 1969.

Kaelble, Hartmut. *Industrielle Interessenpolitik in der wilhelminischen Gesellschaft. Centralverband Deutscher Industrieller 1895–1914.* Berlin, 1967.

Kanter, Hugo. *Staat und berufsständischer Aufbau.* N.p., 1932.

Kater, Michael H. "Heinrich Himmler's Circle of Friends 1931–1945." *MARAB—A Review* 2 (Winter 1965–66): 74–93.

Kaun, Heinrich. *Die Geschichte der Zentralarbeitsgemeinschaft der industriellen und gewerblichen Arbeitgeber und Arbeitnehmer Deutschlands.* Jena, 1938.

Kehr, Eckart. *Der Primat der Aussenpolitik. Gesammelte Aufsätze zur preussisch-deutschen Sozialgeschichte im 19. und 20. Jahrhundert,* ed. by Hans-Ulrich Wehler. Berlin, 1965.

Kele, Max H. *Nazis and Workers.* Chapel Hill, N.C., 1972.

Kirdorf, Emil. "Erinnerungen, 1847–1930." Privately printed.

Kissenkoetter, Udo. *Gregor Strasser und die NSDAP.* Stuttgart, 1978.

Klass, Gert von. *Albert Vögler.* Tübingen, 1957.

———. *Die drei Ringe.* Tübingen, 1953.

Klein, Burton H. *Germany's Economic Preparations for War.* Cambridge, Mass., 1959.

Klein, Fritz. "Neue Dokumente zur Rolle Schachts bei der Vorbereitung der Hitlerdiktatur." *Zeitschrift für Geschichtswissenschaft* 5 (1957): 818–22.

————, "Zur Vorbereitung der faschistischen Diktatur durch die deutsche Grossbourgeoisie (1929–1932)." *Zeitschrift für Geschichtswissenschaft* 1 (1953): 872–904.

Kleinewefers, Paul. *Jahrgang 1905. Ein Bericht.* Stuttgart, 1977.

Klemperer, Klemens von. *Germany's New Conservatism.* Princeton, N.J., 1957.

Koch, Max. *Die Bergarbeiterbewegung im Ruhrgebiet zur Zeit Wilhelms II., 1889–1914.* Düsseldorf, 1954.

Kocka, Jürgen. *Klassengesellschaft im Krieg 1914–1918.* Göttingen, 1973.

————. *Unternehmensverwaltung und Angestelltenschaft am Beispiel Siemens 1847–1914.* Stuttgart, 1969.

Koebel-Tusk, Eberhard. *AEG: Energie, Profit, Verbrechen.* East Berlin 1958.

Könnemann, Erwin. "Dokumente zur Haltung der Monopolisten im Kapp-Putsch." *Beiträge zur Geschichte der Deutschen Arbeiterbewegung* 9 (1967): 1003–23.

Koszyk, Kurt. *Deutsche Presse 1914–1945.* Berlin, 1972.

————. "Jakob Stöcker und der Dortmunder 'General-Anzeiger' 1929–1933." *Publizistik. Zeitschrift für die Wissenschaft von der Presse* 8 (1963): 282–95.

————. "Paul Reusch und die 'Münchner Neuesten Nachrichten,'" *Vierteljahrshefte für Zeitgeschichte* 20 (1972): 75–103.

Krause, Werner. *Wirtschaftstheorie unter dem Hakenkreuz.* East Berlin, 1969.

Krebs, Albert. *Tendenzen und Gestalten der NSDAP. Erinnerungen an die Frühzeit der Partei.* Stuttgart, 1959.

Krogmann, Karl Vincent. *Es ging um Deutschlands Zukunft, 1932–1939.* Leoni am Starnberger See, 1976.

Krohn, Klaus-Dieter. *Stabilisierung und ökonomische Interessen. Die Finanzpolitik des Deutschen Reiches 1923–1927.* Düsseldorf, 1974.

————. *Wirtschaftstheorien als politische Interessen.* Frankfurt, 1981.

Kroll, Gerhard. *Von der Weltwirtschaftskrise zur Staatskonjunktur.* Berlin, 1958.

Kruck, Alfred. *Geschichte des Alldeutschen Verbandes, 1890–1939.* Wiesbaden, 1954.

Krumm, Paul. *Der Sozialismus der Hitlerbewegung im Lichte Spenglerscher Geschichtsforschung oder die tiefste Ursache für den Aufstieg des Nationalsozialismus in Deutschland.* Geldern, 1932.

Kuczynski, Jürgen. *Die Geschichte der Lage der Arbeiter unter dem Kapitalismus.* Vol. V. East Berlin, 1966.

————. *Klassen und Klassenkämpfe im imperialistischen Deutschland und in der BRD.* Frankfurt, 1972.

Krüger, Peter. *Deutschland und die Reparationen 1918/19.* Stuttgart, 1973.

————. "Zu Hitlers 'nationalsozialistischen Wirtschaftserkentnissen.'" *Geschichte und Gesellschaft* VI (1980): 263–82.

Kühnl, Reinhard. *Die nationalsozialistische Linke 1925–1930.* Meisenheim am Glan, 1966.

————. "Zur Programmatik der nationalsozialistischen Linken: Das Strasser-Programm von 1925/26." *Vierteljahrshefte für Zeitgeschichte* 14 (1966): 317–33.

Kühnl Reinhard, and Gerd Hardach, eds. *Die Zerstörung der Weimarer Republik.* Cologne, 1977.

Küster, Fritz. *Die Hintermänner der Nazis. Von Papen bis Deterding.* Hanover, 1946.

Kuhlo, Alfred. *Die Organisation der deutschen Industrie.* Berlin, 1928.

Kuhn, Axel. *Hitlers aussenpolitisches Programm.* Stuttgart, 1970.

———. "Die Unterredung zwischen Hitler und Papen im Hause des Baron von Schröder." *Geschichte in Wissenschaft und Unterricht* 24 (1973): 709–22.

Lammers, Clemens. *Autarkie, Planwirtschaft und berufsständischer Staat?* Berlin, 1932.

Laursen, Karsten, and Jørgen Pedersen. *The German Inflation 1918–1923.* Amsterdam, 1964.

Layton, Roland V. "The *Völkischer Beobachter,* 1920–1933: The Nazi Party Newspaper in the Weimar Era." *Central European History* 3 (1970): 353–82.

Lebovics, Herman. *Social Conservatism and the Middle Classes in Germany.* Princeton, N.J., 1969.

Leckebusch, Roswitha. *Entstehung und Wandlungen der Zielsetzungen, der Struktur und der Wirkungen von Arbeitgeberverbänden.* Berlin, 1966.

Leopold, John A. *Alfred Hugenberg.* New Haven, Conn., 1977.

Lewinsohn (Morus), Richard. *Das Geld in der Politik.* Berlin, 1930.

———. *Die Umschichtung des europäischen Vermögens.* Berlin, 1925.

Ley, Robert. *Deutschland ist schöner geworden.* Munich, 1940.

Liesebach, Ingolf. "Der Wandel der politischen Führungsschicht der deutschen Industrie von 1918 bis 1945." Diss., Universität Basel, 1957.

Link, Werner. *Die amerikanische Stabilisierungspolitik in Deutschland 1921–32.* Düsseldorf, 1970.

Lochner, Louis P. *Tycoons and Tyrant. German Industry from Hitler to Adenauer.* Chicago, 1954.

Lorenz, Ottokar. *Die Beseitigung der Arbeitslosigkeit.* Berlin, [1932].

Ludecke, Kurt G. W. *I Knew Hitler.* New York, 1937.

Ludloff, Rudolf. *Kasernen statt Wohnungen. Zur Geschichte der deutschen Zementindustrie im Imperialismus bis 1945.* East Berlin, 1963.

Ludwig, Karl-Heinz. *Technik und Ingenieure im Dritten Reich.* Düsseldorf, 1974.

Lührs, Wilhelm, ed. *Bremische Biographien 1912–1962.* Bremen, 1969.

Lüke, Rolf E. *Von der Stabilisierung zur Krise.* Zurich, 1958.

Lüthgen, Helmut. *Das Rheinisch-Westfälische Kohlensyndikat in der Vorkriegs-, Kriegs- und Nachkriegszeit und seine Hauptprobleme.* Leipzig and Erlangen, 1926.

Luther, Hans. *Vor dem Abgrund 1930–1933.* Berlin, 1964.

Lutz, Hermann. "Fälschungen zur Auslandsfinanzierung Hitlers." *Vierteljahrshefte für Zeitgeschichte* 2 (1954): 386–96.

———. *German-French Unity.* Chicago, 1957.

Mai, Gunther. "Die nationalsozialistische Betriebszellen-Organisation." *Vierteljahrshefte für Zeitgeschichte* 31 (1983): 573–613.

Maier, Charles S. *Recasting Bourgeois Europe.* Princeton N.J., 1975.

Manchester, William. *The Arms of Krupp 1587–1968.* Boston, 1968.

Marcon, Helmut. *Arbeitsbeschaffungspolitik der Regierungen Papen und Schleicher.* Frankfurt. 1974.

Marquard, Alfred. *100 Jahre Franck, 1828–1928.* N.p., [ca. 1928].

Maschke, Erich. *Es entsteht ein Konzern. Paul Reusch und die GHH.* Tübingen, 1969.

———. *Grundzüge der deutschen Kartellgeschichte bis 1914.* Dortmund, 1964.

Maser, Werner. *Die Frühgeschichte der NSDAP.* Frankfurt and Bonn, 1965.

Mason, Timothy W. *Sozialpolitik im Dritten Reich.* Opladen, 1977.

Matthias, Erich, and Rudolf Morsey, eds. *Das Ende der Parteien 1933*. Düsseldorf, 1960.

Maurer, Ilse. *Reichsfinanzen und grosse Koalition. Zur Geschichte des Reichskabinetts Müller (1928–1930)*. Frankfurt, 1973.

Maurer, Ilse, and Udo Wengst, eds. *Politik und Wirtschaft in der Krise. Quellen zur Ära Brüning*. 2 vols. Düsseldorf, 1980.

Medalen, Charles. "State Monopoly Capitalism in Germany: The Hibernia Affair." *Past & Present*, no. 78 (Feb. 1978): 82–112.

Meissner, Otto. *Staatssekretär unter Ebert—Hindenburg—Hitler*. Hamburg, 1950.

Meynen, Otto. "Dr. Paul Silverberg." *Der Volkswirt* 5 (1951): 9–11.

Michels, Rudolf K. *Cartels, Combines and Trusts in Post-War Germany*. New York, 1928.

Mielke, Siegfried. *Der Hansa-Bund für Gewerbe, Handel und Industrie 1909–1914*. Göttingen, 1976.

Minuth, Karl-Heinz, ed. *Die Kabinette Luther I und II. Akten der Reichskanzlei. Weimarer Republik*. 2 vols. Boppard, 1977.

Möller, Horst. "Parlamentarisierung und Demokratisierung im Preussen der Weimarer Republik." In *Gesellschaft, Parlament und Regierung*, ed. by Gerhard A. Ritter. Düsseldorf, 1974, pp. 367–87.

Mohler, Armin. *Die konservative Revolution in Deutschland*. Stuttgart, 1950.

Mommsen, Hans. "Heinrich Brünings Politik als Reichskanzler: Das Scheitern eines politischen Alleinganges." In *Wirtschaftskrise und liberale Demokratie*, ed. by Karl Holl. Göttingen, 1978, pp. 16–45.

———. "Der Ruhrbergbau im Spannungsfeld von Politik und Wirtschaft in der Zeit der Weimarer Republik." *Blätter für deutsche Landesgeschichte* 108 (1972): 160–75.

Mommsen, Hans, Dietmar Petzina, and Bernd Weisbrod, eds. *Industrielles System und politische Entwicklung in der Weimarer Republik*. Düsseldorf, 1974.

Mommsen, Wolfgang J. "Domestic Factors in German Foreign Policy Before 1914." *Central European History* 6 (1973): 3–43.

Morsey, Rudolf, ed. *Die Protokolle der Reichstagsfraktion und des Fraktionsvorstands der Deutschen Zentrumspartei 1926–1933*. Mainz, 1969.

———. *Der Untergang des politischen Katholizismus*. Zurich, 1977.

———. *Zur Entstehung, Authentizität und Kritik von Brünings 'Memoiren 1918–1934.'* Opladen, 1975.

Mowrer, Edgar Ansel. *Germany Puts the Clock Back*. New York, 1933.

Müller, Johannes. *Die Industrialisierung der deutschen Mittelgebirge* (Jena, 1938).

Müller, Karl Alexander von. *Im Wandel einer Welt*. Munich, 1966.

Müller, Werner, and Jürgen Stockfisch. "Borsig und die Demokratie." *Beiträge, Dokumente, Informationen des Archivs der Hauptstadt der Deutschen Demokratischen Republik* 4 (1967): 1–44.

———. "Die 'Veltenbriefe.' Eine neue Quelle über die Rolle des Monopolkapitals bei der Zerstörung der Weimarer Republik." *Zeitschrift für Geschichtswissenschaft* 17 (1969): 1565–89.

Murphy, Robert D. *Diplomat Among Warriors*. New York, 1964.

Muthesius, Volkmar. *Peter Klöckner und sein Werk*. 2nd ed. Essen, 1959.

Neebe, Reinhard. *Grossindustrie, Staat und NSDAP 1930–1933*. Göttingen, 1981.

———. "Unternehmerverbände und Gewerkschaften in den Jahren der Grossen Krise 1929–33." *Geschichte und Gesellschaft* 9 (1983): 302–30.

Neumann, Franz. *Behemoth. The Structure and Practice of National Socialism.* New York, 1942.

Nipperdey, Thomas. "Interessenverbände und Parteien in Deutschland vor dem ersten Weltkrieg." *Politische Vierteljahresschrift* 2 (1961): 262–80.

Noakes, Jeremy. *The Nazi Party in Lower Saxony, 1921–1933.* London, 1971.

Noakes, Jeremy, and Geoffrey Pridham, eds. *Documents on Nazism.* New York, 1975.

Nocken, Ulrich. "Corporatism and Pluralism in Modern German History." In *Industrielle Gesellschaft und Politisches System,* ed. by Dirk Stegmann, Bernd-Jüngen Wendt, and Peter-Christian Witt. Bonn, 1978, pp. 37–56.

———. "Inter-Industrial Conflicts and Alliances as Exemplified by the AVI-Agreement." In *Industrielles System und politische Entwicklung in der Weimarer Republik,* ed. by Hans Mommsen et al. Düsseldorf, 1974, pp. 693–704.

———. "Das Internationale Stahlkartell und die deutsch-französischen Beziehungen 1924–1932." In *Konstellationen internationaler Politik 1924–1932,* ed. by Gustav Schmidt. Bochum, 1983, pp. 165–202.

Nolte, Ernst. "Big Business and German Politics: A Comment." *American Historical Review.* 75 (1969): 47–55.

Norden, Albert. *Fälscher.* East Berlin, 1959.

———. *Lehren deutscher Geschichte. Zur politischen Rolle des Finanzkapitals und der Junker.* East Berlin, 1947.

Nuss, Karl. *Militär und Wiederaufrüstung in der Weimarer Republik.* East Berlin, 1977.

Nussbaum, Manfred. *Wirtschaft und Staat in Deutschland während der Weimarer Republik.* East Berlin, 1978.

Oehme, Walter, and Kurt Caro. *Kommt 'Das Dritte Reich'?* Berlin, 1931.

Oestreich, Paul. *Walther Funk. Ein Leben für die Wirtschaft.* Berlin, 1940.

Ogger, Günter. *Friedrich Flick der Grosse.* Bern and Munich, 1971.

Olden, Rudolf. *Hitler the Pawn.* London, 1936.

Orlow, Dietrich. *The History of the Nazi Party.* 2 vols. Pittsburgh, 1969–73.

Osthold, Paul. *Die Geschichte des Zechenverbandes 1908–1933.* Berlin, 1934.

Pätzold, Kurt, and Manfred Weissbecker. *Geschichte der NSDAP 1920–1945.* Cologne, 1981.

Papen, Franz von. *Vom Scheitern einer Demokratie, 1930–1933.* Mainz, 1968.

———. *Der Wahrheit eine Gasse.* Munich, 1952.

Patch, William Lewis. "Christian Trade Unions in the Politics of the Weimar Republic, 1918–1933." Diss., Yale University, 1981.

Petzina, Dietmar. "Elemente der Wirtschaftspolitik in der Spätphase der Weimarer Republik." *Vierteljahrshefte für Zeitgeschichte* 21 (1973): 127–33.

———. "Germany and the Great Depression." *Journal of Contemporary History* 4 (1969): 59–74.

———. "Gewerkschaften und Monopolfrage vor und während der Weimarer Republik." *Archiv für Sozialgeschichte* 20 (1980): 195–217.

———. "Hauptprobleme der deutschen Wirtschaftspolitik 1932/33." *Vierteljahrshefte für Zeitgeschichte* 15 (1967): 18–55.

Petzold, Joachim. *Die Demagogie des Hitlerfaschismus.* Frankfurt, 1983.

———. "Grossbürgerliche Initiativen für die Berufung Hitlers zum Reichskanzler." *Zeitschrift für Geschichtswissenschaft* 31 (1983): 38–54.

———. "Monopole—Mittelstand—NSDAP." *Zeitschrift für Geschichtswissenschaft* 28 (1980): 862–75.

———. "Wirtschaftsbesprechungen der NSDAP in den Jahren 1930 und 1931." *Jahrbuch für Wirtschaftsgeschichte*, 1982, Teil 2, pp. 189–223.

Pfaff, Alfred. *Der Wirtschafts-Aufbau im Dritten Reich.* Munich, 1932.

Pierenkemper, Toni. *Die westfälischen Schwerindustriellen 1852–1913.* Göttingen, 1979.

Pinner, Felix. *Deutsche Wirtschaftsführer.* Charlottenburg, 1925.

Plewnia, Margarete. *Auf dem Weg zu Hitler. Der 'völkische' Publizist Dietrich Eckart.* Bremen, 1970.

Plum, Günter. *Gesellschaftsstruktur und politisches Bewusstsein in einer katholischen Region 1928–1933.* Stuttgart, 1972.

Poensgen, Ernst. "Hitler und die Ruhrindustriellen. Ein Rückblick" (unpublished memoir, copy in NA, RG 238, Case 10, Dokumentenbuch Bülow I).

Pohl, Hans. "Die Konzentration in der deutschen Wirtschaft vom ausgehenden 19. Jahrhundert bis 1945." In *Die Konzentration in der deutschen Wirtschaft seit dem 19. Jahrhundert,* ed. by Hans Pohl and Wilhelm Treue. Wiesbaden, 1978, pp. 4–44.

Pohl, Karl Heinrich. *Weimars Wirtschaft und die Aussenpolitik der Republik 1924–1926.* Düsseldorf, 1979.

Pohl, Manfred. "Die Finanzierung der Russengeschäfte zwischen den beiden Weltkriegen." In Beiheft 9 of *Tradition. Zeitschrift für Firmengeschichte und Unternehmerbiographie.* Frankfurt, 1975.

Preller, Ludwig. *Sozialpolitik in der Weimarer Republik.* Stuttgart, 1949.

Pridham, Geoffrey. *Hitler's Rise to Power. The Nazi Movement in Bavaria, 1923–1933.* New York, 1973.

Prym, Agnes M. *Staatswirtschaft und Privatunternehmung in der Geschichte des Ruhrkohlenbergbaus.* Essen, 1950.

Pudor, Fritz. *Nekrologe aus dem rheinisch-westfälischen Industriegebiet. Jahrgang 1939–51.* Düsseldorf, 1955.

———. *Lebensbilder aus dem rheinisch-westfälischen Industriegebiet. Jahrgang 1958–1959.* Düsseldorf, 1962.

Pünder, Hermann. *Politik in der Reichskanzlei. Aufzeichnungen aus den Jahren 1929–1932,* ed. by Thilo Vogelsang. Stuttgart, 1961.

Radandt, Hans. *AEG—Ein typischer Konzern.* East Berlin, 1958.

———. "Die Betriebsarchive bieten wichtige Quellen für die Geschichtsforschung." *Zeitschrift für Geschichtswissenschaft* 5 (1957): 842–49.

———. "'Freie Wahlen' und Monopolkapital." *Zeitschrift für Geschichtswissenschaft* 9 (1961): 1321–22.

———. "'100 Jahre Deutsche Bank.' Eine typische Konzerngeschichte." *Jahrbuch für Wirtschaftsgeschichte,* 1972, Teil 3, pp. 37–62.

———. *Kriegsverbrecherkonzern Mansfeld* (East Berlin, 1958).

———, et al. *Siemens—Rüstung—Krieg—Profite.* East Berlin, n.d.

Rämisch, Raimund. "Der berufsständische Gedanke als Episode in der nationalsozialistischen Politik." *Zeitschrift für Politik,* n.F. 4 (1957): 263–72.

Rahm, Hans-Georg. "'Der Angriff' 1927–1930." Diss. Universität Berlin. 1938.

Rauschning, Hermann. *Gespräche mit Hitler.* Zurich, 1940.

———. *Makers of Destruction.* London, 1942.

———. *Men of Chaos.* New York, 1942.

Reupke, Hans. *Der Nationalsozialismus und die Wirtschaft.* Berlin, 1931.

———. *Das Wirtschaftssystem des Faschismus.* Berlin, 1930.

Ribhegge, Wilhelm. *August Winnig.* Bonn, 1973.

Riedel, Matthias. *Eisen und Kohle für das Dritte Reich. Paul Pleigers Stellung in der NS-Wirtschaft.* Göttingen, 1973.

Rieker, Karlheinz. *Das Wirtschaftsprogramm des Nationalsozialismus.* Berlin, 1933.

Rittberger, Volker, ed. *1933. Wie die Republik der Diktatur erlag.* Stuttgart, 1983.

Ritter, Gerhard. *Carl Goerdeler und die deutsche Widerstandsbewegung.* Stuttgart, 1955.

Ritter, Gerhard A., ed. *Gesellschaft, Parlament und Regierung.* Düsseldorf, 1974.

Roberts, Glyn. *The Most Powerful Man in the World.* New York, 1938.

Röseler, Klaus. "Die Stellung der deutschen Unternehmer in der Wirtschaftskrise 1929–1933." Diss., Technische Hochschule Hannover, 1966.

———. "Unternehmer in der Weimarer Republik." *Tradition. Zeitschrift für Firmengeschichte und Unternehmerbiographie* 13 (1968): 217–40.

Rohe, Karl, and Herbert Kühr, eds. *Politik und Gesellschaft im Ruhrgebiet.* Königstein/Ts., 1979.

Roloff, Ernst-August. *Bürgertum und Nationalsozialismus 1930–1933. Braunschweigs Weg ins Dritte Reich.* Hanover, 1961.

Romeyk, Horst. "Die Deutsche Volkspartei in Rheinland und Westfalen 1918–1933." *Rheinische Vierteljahrsblätter* 39 (1975): 189–236.

Roselius, Ludwig. *Briefe und Schriften zu Deutschlands Erneuerung.* Oldenburg, 1933.

Rosenberg, Alfred. *Freimauerische Weltpolitik im Lichte der kritischen Forschung.* Munich, 1929.

———. *Wesen, Grundsätze und Ziele der Nationalsozialistischen Deutschen Arbeiterpartei.* Munich, 1923.

———. *Das Wesensgefüge des Nationalsozialismus. Grundlagen der deutschen Wiedergeburt.* Munich, 1932.

Roth, Hermann. "Die nationalsozialistische Betriebszellenorganisation (NSBO) von der Gründung bis zur Röhm-Affäre (1926 bis 1934)." *Jahrbuch für Wirtschaftsgeschichte,* 1978, Teil 1, pp. 49–66.

Ruge, Wolfgang. "Die 'Deutsche Allgemeine Zeitung' und die Brüningregierung. Zur Rolle der Grossbourgeoisie bei der Vorbereitung des Faschismus." *Zeitschrift für Geschichtswissenschaft* 16 (1968): 19–53.

———. *Hindenburg.* East Berlin, 1974.

———. *Weimar—Republik auf Zeit.* East Berlin, 1969.

———. "Zur Taktik der deutschen Monopolbourgeoisie im Frühjahr und Sommer 1919." *Zeitschrift für Geschichtswissenschaft* 11 (1963): 1088–1117.

Ruge, Wolfgang, and Wolfgang Schumann, eds. *Dokumente zur deutschen Geschichte 1929–1933.* East Berlin, 1975.

Rupieper, Hermann. *The Cuno Government and Reparations, 1922–1923.* The Hague, 1979.

Ryder, A. J. *Twentieth-Century Germany.* New York, 1973.

Saage, Richard. "Zum Verhältnis von Nationalsozialismus und Industrie." *Aus Politik und Zeitgeschichte. Beilage zur Wochenzeitung das Parlament,* Mar. 10, 1975, pp. 17–39.

Salin, Edgar. "Paul Reusch," *Mitteilungen der List-Gesellschaft,* no. 8 (1957): 194–200.

Sasuly, Richard. *IG Farben*. New York, 1947.

Saul, Klaus. *Staat, Industrie, Arbeiterbewegung im Kaiserreich*. Düsseldorf, 1974.

Schacht, Hjalmar. *Grundsätze deutscher Wirtschaftspolitik*. Oldenburg, 1932.

———. *76 Jahre meines Lebens*. Bad Wörishofen, 1953.

Schäfer, Dieter. *Der Deutsche Industrie- und Handelstag als politisches Forum der Weimarer Republik*. Hamburg, 1966.

Schäfer, Wolfgang. *NSDAP. Entwicklung und Struktur der Staatspartei des Dritten Reiches* (Hanover and Frankfurt, 1956).

Schaumburg-Lippe, Friedrich Christian Prinz zu. *Zwischen Krone und Kerker*. Wiesbaden, 1952.

———. *. . . Verdammte Pflicht und Schuldigkeit . . . Weg und Erlebnis, 1914–1933*. Leoni am Starnberger See, 1966.

Schausberger, Norbert. "Österreich und die deutsche Wirtschaftsexpansion nach dem Donauraum." *Österreich in Geschichte und Literatur* 16 (1972): 196–213.

Schieck, Hans. "Der Kampf um die deutsche Wirtschaftspolitik nach dem Novemberumsturz 1918." Diss., Universität Heidelberg, 1958.

———. "Die Behandlung der Sozialisierungsfrage in den Monaten nach dem Staatsumsturz." In *Vom Kaiserreich zur Weimarer Republik*, ed. by Eberhard Kolb. Cologne, 1972, pp. 138–64.

Schieder, Theodor. *Hermann Rauschnings 'Gespräche mit Hitler' als Geschichtsquelle*. Opladen, 1972.

Schirach, Baldur von. *Ich glaubte an Hitler*. Hamburg, 1967.

Schleunes, Karl A. *The Twisted Road to Auschwitz*. Urbana, Ill., 1970.

Schmidt, Klaus Werner. "Die 'Rheinisch-Westfälische Zeitung' und ihr Verleger Reismann-Grone." *Beiträge zur Geschichte Dortmunds und der Grafschaft Mark* 69 (1974): 241–382.

———. "Rheinisch-Westfälische Zeitung (1883–1944)." In *Deutsche Zeitungen des 17. bis 20. Jahrhunderts*, ed. by Heinz-Dietrich Fischer. Pullach, 1972, pp. 365–79.

Schmidt, Ernst Wilhelm. *Männer der Deutschen Bank und der Disconto-Gesellschaft*. Düsseldorf, 1957.

Schmidt-Hannover, Otto. *Umdenken oder Anarchie*. Göttingen, 1959.

Schmidt-Pauli, Edgar von. *Die Männer um Hitler*. Berlin, 1932.

Schnabel, Thomas, ed. *Die Machtergreifung in Südwestdeutschland*. Stuttgart, 1982.

Schneider, Michael. *Das Arbeitsbeschaffungsprogramm des ADGB*. Bonn–Bad Godesberg, 1975.

———. *Auf dem Weg in die Krise*. Wentorf bei Hamburg, 1974.

———. *Die Christlichen Gewerkschaften, 1884–1933*. Bonn, 1982.

———. *Unternehmer und Demokratie. Die freien Gewerkschaften in der unternehmerischen Ideologie der Jahre 1918 bis 1933*. Bonn–Bad Godesberg, 1975.

Schneider, Werner. *Die Deutsche Demokratische Partei in der Weimarer Republik 1924–1930*. Munich, 1978.

Schön, Eberhard. *Die Entstehung des Nationalsozialismus in Hessen*. Meisenheim am Glan, 1972.

Schoenbaum, David. *Hitler's Social Revolution*. New York, 1966.

Schorr, Helmut J. *Adam Stegerwald*. Recklinghausen, 1966.

Schreiner, Albert. "Die Eingabe deutscher Finanzmagnaten, Monopolisten und Junker an Hindenburg für die Berufung Hitlers zum Reichskanzler (November 1932)." *Zeitschrift für Geschichtswissenschaft* 4 (1956): 366–69.

Schröder, Arno. *'Hitler geht auf die Dörfer.' Der Auftakt zur nationalen Revolution. Ergebnisse und Bilder von der entscheidenden Januarwahl 1933 in Lippe.* Detmold, 1938.

Schröder, Rudolf. "Die Ausschussprotokolle der IG-Farben als Quelle zur Betriebsgeschichtsforschung über die Zeit des Kapitalismus." *Jahrbuch für Wirtschaftsgeschichte.* 1967, Teil 1, pp. 250–69.

Schubert, Günter. *Anfänge nationalsozialistischer Aussenpolitik.* Cologne, 1963.

Schüler, Wilfried. *Der Bayreuther Kreis von seiner Entstehung bis zum Ausgang der wilhelminischen Ära.* Münster, 1971.

Schüren, Ulrich. *Der Volksentscheid zur Fürstenenteignung 1926.* Düsseldorf, 1978.

Schulz, Gerhard. *Aufstieg des Nationalsozialismus.* Frankfurt and Berlin, 1975.

———. "Der 'Nationale Klub von 1919' zu Berlin. Zum politischen Zerfall einer Gesellschaft." *Jahrbuch für die Geschichte Mittel- und Ostdeutschlands* 11 (1965): 207–37.

———. "Räte, Wirtschaftsstände und die Transformation des industriellen Verbandswesen am Anfang der Weimarer Republik." In *Gesellschaft, Parlament und Regierung,* ed. by Gerhard A. Ritter. Düsseldorf, 1974, pp. 355–66.

———. "Reparationen und Krisenprobleme nach dem Wahlsieg der NSDAP 1930." *Vierteljahrschrift für Sozial- und Wirtschaftsgeschichte* 67 (1980): 200–22.

———. "Über Entstehung und Formen von Interessengruppen in Deutschland seit Beginn der Industrialisierung." *Politische Vierteljahresschrift* 2 (1961): 124–34.

Schumacher, Martin. *Mittelstandsfront und Republik, 1919–1933.* Düsseldorf, 1982.

Schuman, Frederick L. *The Nazi Dictatorship.* New York, 1935.

Schumann, Hans-Gerd. *Nationalsozialismus und Gewerkschaftsbewegung.* Hanover and Frankfurt, 1958.

Schumann, Wolfgang, and Gerhard Hass. *Deutschland im zweiten Weltkrieg.* 2 vols. East Berlin, 1974–75.

Schweitzer, Arthur. *Big Business in the Third Reich.* Bloomington, Ind., 1964.

Schwerin von Krosigk, Lutz Graf. *Die grosse Zeit des Feuers. Der Weg der deutschen Industrie.* 3 vols. Tübingen, 1957–59.

———. *Staatsbankrott.* Göttingen, 1974.

Serlo, Walter. *Die Preussischen Bergassessoren.* 4th ed. Essen, 1933.

Sheehan, James J. *The Career of Lujo Brentano.* Chicago, 1966.

Shirer, William L. *The Rise and Fall of the Third Reich.* New York, 1960.

Siebarth, Werner, ed. *Hitlers Wollen.* 8th ed. Munich, 1940.

Siegrist, Hannes. "Deutsche Grossunternehmen vom späten 19. Jahrhundert bis zur Weimarer Republik." *Geschichte und Gesellschaft* 6 (1980): 60–102.

Siemens, Georg. *Geschichte des Hauses Siemens.* 3 vols. Freiburg and Munich, 1947–51.

Silverberg, Paul. *Reden und Schriften.* Cologne, 1951.

Simpson, Amos. *Hjalmar Schacht in Perspective.* The Hague, 1977.

Sörgel, Werner. *Metallindustrie und Nationalsozialismus.* Frankfurt, 1965.

Sohn-Rethel, Alfred. *Ökonomie und Klassenstruktur des deutschen Faschismus.* Frankfurt, 1973.

———. "Die soziale Rekonsolidierung des Kapitalismus (Sept. 1932)." *Kursbuch* (Sept. 1970), no.21: 23–26, 29–34.

SPD. *Parteitag der Sozialdemokratischen Partei Deutschlands vom 1. bis 5. Juni 1966 in Dortmund.* Bonn, 1966.

SPD. *Reichstagswahl 1930. Referentenmaterial.* Berlin, [1930].

SPD Landesausschuss Bayern. *Hitler und Kahr: Die Bayerischen Napoleonsgrössen von 1923.* Munich, 1928.

Speer, Albert. *Spandauer Tagebücher.* Frankfurt, 1975.

Spencer, Elaine Glovka. "Between Capital and Labor: Supervisory Personnel in Ruhr Heavy Industry before 1914." *Journal of Social History* 9 (1975): 178–92.

Spethmann, Hans. *Zwölf Jahre Ruhrbergbau.* 5 vols. Essen, 1928–1931.

Spiller, Jörg-Otto. "Reformismus nach rechts. Zur Politik des Reichsverbandes der Deutschen Industrie in den Jahren 1927–1930 am Beispiel der Reparationspolitik." In *Industrielles System und politische Entwicklung,* ed. by Hans Mommsen et al. Düsseldorf, 1974, pp. 593–602.

Stachura, Peter D. *Gregor Strasser and the Rise of Nazism* (London, 1983).

———, ed. *The Nazi Machtergreifung.* London, 1983.

———, ed. *The Shaping of the Nazi State.* London, 1978.

Stackelberg, Roderick. "Houston Stewart Chamberlain: From Monarchism to National Socialism." *The Wiener Library Bulletin* 31 (1978): 118–25.

Stadtler, Eduard. *Als Antibolshewist 1918/19.* Düsseldorf, 1935.

Statistisches Reichsamt. *Deutsche Wirtschaftskunde.* 2nd ed. Berlin, 1933.

———. *Konzerne, Interessengemeinschaften und ähnliche Zusammenschlüsse im Deutschen Reich Ende 1926.* Berlin, 1927.

Stegmann, Dirk. "Antiquierte Personalisierung oder sozialökonomische Faschismus-Analyse? Eine Antwort auf H. A. Turners Kritik an meinen Thesen zum Verhältnis von Nationalsozialismus und Grossindustrie vor 1933." *Archiv für Sozialgeschichte* 17 (1977): 275–96.

———. "Kapitalismus und Faschismus in Deutschland 1929–1934." *Gesellschaft. Beiträge zur Marxschen Theorie 6.* Frankfurt, 1976, pp. 19–91.

———. "Die Silverberg-Kontroverse 1926." In *Sozialgeschichte Heute,* ed. by Hans-Ulrich Wehler. Göttingen, 1974, pp. 594–610.

———. "Zum Verhältnis von Grossindustrie und Nationalsozialismus 1930–1933." *Archiv für Sozialgeschichte* 13 (1973): 399–482.

———. "Zwischen Repression und Manipulation." *Archiv für Sozialgeschichte* 12 (1972): 351–432.

Stegmann, Dirk, Bernd-Jürgen Wendt, and Peter-Christian Witt, eds. *Industrielle Gesellschaft und politisches System.* Bonn, 1978.

Stein, George H. *Hitler.* Englewood Cliffs, N.J., 1968.

Stein, Gustav, ed. *Unternehmer in der Politik.* Düsseldorf, 1954.

Steller, Paul. *Führende Männer des rheinisch-westfälischen Wirtschaftslebens.* Berlin, 1930.

Stocking, George, and Myron Watkins. *Cartels in Action.* New York, 1947.

Stone, Norman. *Hitler.* Boston, 1980.

Strandmann, Hartmut Pogge von. "Entwicklungsstrukturen der Grossindustrie im Ruhrgebiet." In *Politik und Gesellschaft im Ruhrgebiet*, ed. by Karl Rohe and Herbert Kühr. Königstein/Ts., 1979, pp. 142–61.

———. "Grossindustrie und Rapallopolitik." *Historische Zeitschrift* 222 (1976): 265–341.

Strasser, Otto. *Aufbau des deutschen Sozialismus*. 2nd ed. Prague, 1936.

Strauss, Willi. *Die Konzentrationsbewegung im deutschen Bankgewerbe*. Berlin and Leipzig, 1928.

Streisand, Joachim. *Deutsche Geschichte von den Anfängen bis zur Gegenwart. Eine marxistische Einführung*. Cologne. 1972.

Stürmer, Michael. *Koalition und Opposition in der Weimarer Republik 1924–1928*. Düsseldorf, 1967.

Tänzler, Fritz. *Die deutschen Arbeitgeberverbände, 1904–1929*. Darmstadt, 1929.

Tammen, Helmuth. "Die I.G. Farbenindustrie Aktiengesellschaft (1925–1933)." Diss., Freie Universität Berlin, 1978.

Taylor, A. J. P. *The Course of German History*. London, 1945.

Thyssen, Fritz. *I Paid Hitler*. New York, 1941.

Timm, Helga. *Die deutsche Sozialpolitik und der Bruch der grossen Koalition im März 1930*. Düsseldorf, 1952.

Treue, Wilhelm. "Der deutsche Unternehmer in der Weltwirtschaftskrise 1928 bis 1933." In *Die Staats- und Wirtschaftskrise des deutschen Reichs 1929/33*, ed. by Werner Conze and Hans Raupach. Stuttgart, 1967, pp. 82–125.

———. "Die Einstellung einiger deutscher Grossindustrieller zu Hitlers Aussenpolitik." *Geschichte in Wissenschaft und Unterricht* 17 (1966): 491–507.

———. "Hitlers Denkschrift zum Vierjahresplan 1936." *Vierteljahrshefte für Zeitgeschichte* 3 (1955): 196–202.

Treue, Wilhelm, and Helmut Uebbing. *Die Feuer verlöschen nie. August Thyssen-Hütte 1926–1966*. Düsseldorf and Vienna, 1966.

Treviranus, Gottfried. *Das Ende von Weimar*. Düsseldorf, 1968.

Trial of the Major War Criminals before the International Military Tribunal, Nuremberg, 14 November 1945–1 October 1946. 42 vols. Nuremberg, 1947–49.

Trials of War Criminals before the Nuernberg Military Tribunals under Control Council Law No. 10. 15 vols. Washington, D.C., 1949–53.

Trumpp, Thomas. "Zur Finanzierung der NSDAP durch die deutsche Grossindustrie. Versuch einer Bilanz." *Geschichte in Wissenschaft und Unterricht* 32 (1981): 223–41.

Turner, Henry A., Jr. "Big Business and the Rise of Hitler." *The American Historical Review* 75 (1969): 56–70.

———. "Emil Kirdorf and the Nazi Party." *Central European History* 1 (1968): 324–44.

———. *Faschismus und Kapitalismus in Deutschland*. Göttingen, 1972.

———. "Fascism and Modernization." *World Politics* 24 (1972): 547–64.

———. "Fritz Thyssen und 'I paid Hitler.'" *Vierteljahrshefte für Zeitgeschichte* 19 (1971): 225–44.

———. "Grossunternehmertum und Nationalsozialismus, 1930–33." *Historische Zeitschrift* 221 (1975): 18–68.

———. "Hitlers Einstellung zu sozial-ökonomischen Fragen vor der Machtergreifung." *Geschichte und Gesellschaft* 2 (1976): 89–117.

————. "Hitler's Secret Pamphlet for Industrialists, 1927." *The Journal of Modern History* 40 (1968): 348–72.

————. "The *Ruhrlade*, Secret Cabinet of Heavy Industry in the Weimar Republic." *Central European History* 3 (1970): 195–228.

————. *Stresemann and the Politics of the Weimar Republic.* Princeton, N.J., 1963.

————. "Das Verhältnis des Grossunternehmertums zur NSDAP." In *Industrielles System und politische Entwicklung in der Weimarer Republik*, ed. by Hans Mommsen et al. Düsseldorf, 1974, pp. 919–31.

————, ed., *Hitler aus nächster Nähe. Aufzeichnungen eines Vertrauten 1929–1932.* Berlin, 1978.

————, ed. *Nazism and the Third Reich.* New York, 1972.

————, with Horst Matzerath. "Die Selbstfinanzierung der NSDAP 1930–32." *Geschichte und Gesellschaft* 3 (1977): 59–92.

Tyrell, Albrecht, ed. *Führer befiehl . . . Selbstzeugnisse aus der 'Kampfzeit' der NSDAP.* Düsseldorf, 1969.

————. "Führergedanke und Gauleiterwechsel. Die Teilung des Gaues Rheinland der NSDAP 1931." *Vierteljahrshefte für Zeitgeschichte* 23 (1975): 341–74.

————. "Gottfried Feder and the NSDAP." In *The Shaping of the Nazi State*, ed. by Peter D. Stachura. London, 1978, pp. 48–87.

————. *Vom 'Trommler' zum 'Führer.'* Munich, 1975.

Ufermann, Paul. *Der deutsche Stahltrust.* Berlin, 1927.

————. *Könige der Inflation.* 3rd. ed. Berlin, 1924.

Uhse, Bodo. *Söldner und Soldat.* 2nd ed. East Berlin, 1956.

Ulbricht, Walter. *Der faschistische deutsche Imperialismus.* East Berlin, 1956.

Ullmann, Hans-Peter. *Der Bund der Industriellen.* Göttingen, 1976.

Verein für die bergbaulichen Interessen. *Jahrbuch für den Ruhrkohlenbezirk.* Essen, 1932.

Vietzke, Siegfried, and Heinz Wohlgemuth. *Deutschland und die deutsche Arbeiterbewegung in der Zeit der Weimarer Republik.* East Berlin, 1966.

Vogelsang, Reinhard. *Der Freundeskreis Himmler.* Göttingen, 1972.

Vogelsang, Thilo. *Reichswehr, Staat und NSDAP.* Stuttgart, 1962.

Vogt, Martin. "Zur Finanzierung der NSDAP zwischen 1924 und 1928." *Geschichte in Wissenschaft und Unterricht* 21 (1970): 234–43.

————, ed. *Das Kabinett Müller II. Akten der Reichskanzlei. Weimarer Republik.* 2 vols. Boppard, 1970.

Volkland, Gerhard. "Hintergründe und politische Auswirkungen der Gelsenkirchen-Affäre im Jahre 1932." *Zeitschrift für Geschichtswissenschaft* 11 (1963): 289–318.

Volkmann, Hans-Erich. "Das aussenwirtschaftliche Programm der NSDAP 1930–1933." *Archiv für Sozialgeschichte* 17 (1977): 251–74.

Volz, Hans. *Daten der Geschichte der NSDAP.* 9th ed. Berlin and Leipzig, 1939.

Wagenführ, Horst. *Kartelle in Deutschland.* Nuremberg, 1931.

Wandel, Eckhard. *Hans Schäffer, Steuermann in wirtschaftlichen und politischen Krisen.* Stuttgart, 1974.

Wegner, Konstanze, ed. *Linksliberalismus in der Weimarer Republik.* Düsseldorf, 1980.

Wehler, Hans-Ulrich, ed. *Sozialgeschichte Heute. Festschrift für Hans Rosenberg zum 70. Geburtstag.* Göttingen, 1974.

Weicher, Wilhelm. "Wie ich Adolf Hitler kennenlernte." *Der Türmer* 36 (1934): 90–91.

Weinberg, Gerhard L. "National Socialist Organization and Foreign Policy Aims in 1927." *Journal of Modern History* 36 (1964): 428–33.

Weisbrod, Bernd. "The Crisis of German Unemployment Insurance in 1928/1929 and Its Political Repercussions." In *The Emergence of the Welfare State in Britain and Germany* ed. by Wolfgang J. Mommsen. London, 1981.

———. "Economic power and political stability reconsidered: heavy industry in Weimar Germany." *Social History* 4 (1979): 241–63.

———. *Schwerindustrie in der Weimarer Republik.* Wuppertal, 1978.

Welter, Erich. *Der Weg der deutschen Industrie.* Frankfurt, 1943.

Wengst, Udo. "Der Reichsverband der Deutschen Industrie in den ersten Monaten des Dritten Reiches." *Vierteljahrshefte für Zeitgeschichte* 28 (1980): 94–110.

———. "Schlange-Schöningen, Ostsiedlung und die Demission der Regierung Brüning." *Geschichte in Wissenschaft und Unterricht* 30 (1979): 538–51.

———. "Unternehmerverbände und Gewerkschaften in Deutschland im Jahre 1930." *Vierteljahrshefte für Zeitgeschichte* 25 (1977): 99–119.

Wenzel, Georg. *Deutscher Wirtschaftsführer. Lebensgänge deutscher Wirtschaftspersönlichkeiten.* Hamburg, 1929.

Wernecke, Klaus. *Der Wille zur Weltgeltung.* Düsseldorf, 1970.

Wernecke, Klaus, and Peter Heller. *Der vergessene Führer. Alfred Hugenberg.* Hamburg, 1982.

Werner, Lothar. *Der Alldeutscher Verband 1890–1918.* Berlin, 1935.

Wheeler-Bennett, John W. *The Nemesis of Power.* New York, 1954.

Wickel, Helmut. *I.-G. Deutschland.* Berlin, 1932.

Widmaier, Hans-Peter and Karl B. Netzband. *Währungs- und Finanzpolitik der Ära Luther 1923–1925.* Basel and Tübingen, 1964.

Wiedenfeld Kurt, ed. *Die deutsche Wirtschaft und ihre Führer.* Gotha, 1925.

Wiel, Paul. *Wirtschaftsgeschichte des Ruhrgebietes. Tatsachen und Zahlen.* Essen, 1970.

Wiesemann, Falk. *Die Vorgeschichte der nationalsozialistischen Machtübernahme in Bayern 1932/1933.* Berlin, 1975.

Wilamowitz-Moellendorf, Fanny Gräfin von. *Carin Göring.* Berlin, 1934.

Williams, Robert C. *Culture in Exile: Russian Emigrés in Germany, 1881–1941.* Ithaca, N.Y., 1972.

Williamson, John G. *Karl Helfferich, 1872–1924.* Princeton, N.J., 1971.

Winkler, Hans-Joachim. *Preussen als Unternehmer 1923–1932.* Berlin, 1965.

Winkler, Heinrich August. *Mittelstand, Demokratie und Nationalsozialismus.* Cologne, 1972.

———. "Unternehmer und Gewerkschaften in der Weimarer Republik." *Archiv für Sozialgeschichte* 16 (1976): 574–80.

———. "Unternehmer und Wirtschaftsdemokratie in der Weimarer Republik." *Politische Vierteljahresschrift* 11 (1970): 308–22, Sonderheft 2.

———. "Unternehmerverbände zwischen Ständeideologie und Nationalsozialismus." *Vierteljahrshefte für Zeitgeschichte* 17 (1969): 341–71.

———, ed. *Organisierter Kapitalismus.* Göttingen, 1974.

Winnig, August. *Vom Proletariat zum Arbeitertum.* Hamburg, 1933.

Winschuh, Josef. *Der Verein mit dem langen Namen.* Berlin, 1932.

Wolff, Otto. *Die Geschäfte des Herrn Ouvrard.* Frankfurt, 1932.

Wolffsohn, Michael. "Grossunternehmer und Politik in Deutschland: Der Nutzen der Arbeitsbeschaffung der Jahre 1932/33 für die Schwer- und Chemieindustrie." *Zeitschrift für Unternehmungsgeschichte* 22 (1977): 109–33.

———. *Industrie und Handwerk im Konflikt mit staatlicher Wirtschaftspolitik? Studien zur Politik der Arbeitsbeschaffung in Deutschland, 1930–1934.* Berlin, 1977.

World Committee for the Victims of German Fascism. *The Brown Book of the Hitler Terror.* New York, 1933.

Wulf, Peter. "Die Auseinandersetzung um die Sozialisierung der Kohle in Deutschland 1920/1921." *Vierteljahrshefte für Zeitgeschichte* 25 (1977): 46–98.

———. *Hugo Stinnes. Wirtschaft und Politik, 1918–1924.* Stuttgart, 1979.

Zumpe, Lotte. *Wirtschaft und Staat in Deutschland 1933 bis 1945.* East Berlin, 1980.

Zunkel, Friedrich. *Industrie und Staatssozialismus. Der Kampf um die Wirtschaftsordnung in Deutschland 1914–18.* Düsseldorf, 1974.

———. *Der rheinisch-westfälische Unternehmer 1834–1879.* Cologne and Opladen, 1962.

Index